VICTIMS OF YALTA

VICTIMS OF YALTA

The Secret Betrayal of the Allies, 1944–1947

NIKOLAI TOLSTOY

PEGASUS BOOKS

NEW YORK LONDON

VICTIMS OF YALTA
Pegasus Books LLC
80 Broad Street, 5th Floor
New York, NY 10004

First Pegasus Books cloth edition 2012

Library of Congress Cataloging-in-Publication Data is available.

ISBN: 978-1-60598-362-2
10 9 8 7 6 5 4 3 2 1

Printed in the United States of America
Distributed by W. W. Norton & Company, Inc.
www.pegasusbooks.us

To the Memory of the Victims

Acknowledgments

For years I received an enormous amount of assistance in the research and writing of this book. Many friends have continued to help me over long periods of time, whilst people concerned in the events of which I write have, with very few exceptions, been prepared to spend hours recapitulating their experiences. In some cases I had to come back again and again with enquiries; never once did I experience anything except a frank willingness to help in any way possible.

I only regret that I cannot be more specific in individual cases; space forbids what would be an impossibly invidious task. Perhaps, however, I may be allowed to single out two instances where special gratitude is due. Mr. Robert Temple first suggested the writing of this book, and drew my attention to the release of the relevant British documents. Mr. Rivers Scott, of Hodder and Stoughton, spent many hours going through an exceptionally long and difficult text with me; I hope the resultant vast improvement is sufficient compensation.

I extend grateful acknowledgments to His Serene Highness the Reigning Prince of Liechtenstein; His Imperial Highness the Grand Duke Vladimir; Lieut.-General Sir Terence Airey; Mr. Edvard Alksnis; Herr Robert Allgäuer; Mr. John Antonevics; Mr. D. L. W. Ashton; the Rt. Hon. the late Earl of Avon; Mr. W. Backshall; Mr. Jack Barnett; Captain Patrick Bent; Mr. Michael H. H. Bayley; Mr. J. de Berg; the late Mr. August Bergman; Mr. Ivan Bilibin; the Dowager Lady Birdwood; Major-General Sir Alec Bishop; Mrs. Marie Halun Bloch; Mr. Ian Bogaert; *Der Bote*; Colonel K. C. Boyd; Major-General H. E. N. Bredin; Mr. Vladimir Britniev; Mrs. Humphrey Brooke; Mr. Patrick Bucknell; Mr. J. Budzich-Bunchuk; Mr. Victor Cavendish-Bentinck; the Ven. Edward Carpenter, Dean of Westminster; Major John Charters; Mrs. Anna Child; the late Mr. Ian Colvin; Miss Violet Conolly; Major-General K. C. Cooper; Major P. H. Cordle; Mr. Feodor Czernikov; Mr. N. F. Chawner; *The Daily Mail*; *The Daily Telegraph*; Professor Alexander Dallin; Colonel B. Dalton; Mrs. Elma Dangerfield; Mrs. Tatiana Danilievitch; Major W. R. Davies; the

Ministry of Defence; Colonel Gerald Draper; Major George Druzhakin; Mr. Geoffrey Dunn; Mr. Peter J. Dyck; Mrs. Violet M. Dye; *Dziennik Polski*; Mr. Frank H. Epp; Professor John Erickson; *The Evening News*; the Dowager Lady Falmouth; Baron Edward von Falz-Fein; Mrs. Joy Fawcett; the late Brigadier R. C. Firebrace; Sir Gerald Fitzmaurice; Mr. David Floyd; Lieut.-Colonel L. S. Ford; Colonel J. H. Frankau; Major J. W. French; Mr. Michael Frewer; Dr. Alexander Frick; Mr. John Frost; Mr. and Mrs. Josef Garlinski; the General Services Administration, United States of America; Princess Nicholas Galitzine; Dr. Martin Gilbert; Major-General P. B. Gillett: Mr. Anatol Goldberg: Mr. Ivan Gordienko; Mr. Tom Gorringe; Mr. Reg Gray; Mr. Joseph N. Greene, Jr.; Count S. Grocholski; Major-General Sir Colin Gubbins; Prince Azamat Guirey; Dr. John Guy; Mrs. Yvonne J. Haggett; Mrs. Jana Hale; Mr. H. Haley; Mr. W. Haluk; Mr. G. C. Hamilton; Major Claud Hanbury-Tracy-Domvile; the Rt. Hon. Lord Hankey; Mr. H. G. F. Harcombe; Field-Marshal Lord Harding; Major George Hartman; Mr. E. G. Henson; Mr. Denis Hills; Brigadier James Hills; General A. Holmston-Smyslovsky; Colonel Sir Andrew Horsbrugh-Porter, Bart.; Lieut.-Colonel Henry Howard; Mr. Peter J. Huxley-Blythe; the staff of the Imperial War Museum; Mrs. Helene Janzen; Mr. Czeslaw Jesman; Mr. Josef Josten; Mr. George Kennan; *Kleine Zeitung*; Mr. George Knupffer; Mr. Alfred Kolatov; Herr Julian Kollnitz; Mr. Boris Komaroff; Mr. V. Kozhevnikov; Dr. Erhard Kroeger; Mr. N. Lambert; the Lambeth Palace Librarian, Mr. E. G. W. Bill; Herr Hermann Langbein; Mrs. George Lawrence; Colonel Semeon Levchenko; Monsieur Claude Levy; Mr. Harry B. Lewis; Prince Alexander Lieven; Lt.-Colonel Leonid Lieven; Mrs. Austra Liepins; Angela Countess of Limerick; Mr. Gerhard Lohrenz; the staff of the London Library; Lieut.-Colonel R. B. Longe; Mr. A. C. Lord; Major-General J. D. Lunt; Mr. Marvin Lyons; Mr. Neil Macdonald; Mr. Geoffrey Macdermott; Sir Robert Mackworth-Young; Major David Macnab; Lieut.-Colonel A. D. Malcolm; Mr. L. H. Manderstam; Mr. Andreas Mayor; Mr. Bruce Marshall; Mr. Duncan Macmillan; Mr. Patrick Martin-Smith; Mr. Garry Maufe; Herr Sieghart Mertlitz; Sir Iain Moncreiffe of that Ilk; General Sir William Morgan; Mr. and Mrs. Max Morgan-Witts; Mr. David Morrissey; General Sir Horatius Murray; General Sir Geoffrey Musson; Mr. I. A. Nicholls; Professor Theodor Oberländer; *The Observer*; Mr. Brian Pearce; Mr. Jeremy Pemberton; Mr. J. Pereira; Dr. John Pinching; Mr. Jan Pirozynski; Captain K. K. Pekhovsky; the staff of the Public Record Office; Major H. A. F. Radley; Mr. Fred Ralph; the late Mr. Edward Renton; the Rev. Malcolm H. Richards; Sir Walter Roberts; Lieut.-Colonel

ACKNOWLEDGMENTS

David B. Rooke; Lieut.-Colonel Robin Rose Price; the Rt. Hon. Lord St. Oswald; Monsieur Pierre de Saint-Prix; Mr. Walter Sawatsky; Herr Norbert Schluga; Major James Scott-Hopkins, M.P.; the Rt. Hon. the Earl of Selborne; Lieut.-Colonel Laurence Shadwell; Colonel Sir Geoffrey Shakerley; Mr. Anthony Shorland Ball; Mrs. B. Skalska; the Rev. Janis Sapiets; Major-General Eric Sixsmith; Mr. Tom A. H. Slack; Mr. C. C. Smellie; Mr. Anthony Smith; Lieut.-Colonel J. R. G. Stanton; Mr. Edward Stewart; Mr. Henryk Szmuniewski; Mr. A. R. Tainsh; Lieut.-Colonel C. H. Tamplin; Mr. W. Thompson; *The Times*; Mr. Jack H. Taylor, Jr.; Mr. A. Tomas; Brigadier C. E. Tryon-Wilson; the Rev. Kenneth H. Tyson; Mr. K. Trebicki; Mr. V. Ugrechelidze; Mr. James Urry; Brigadier Clive Usher; Mr. Robert Vas; Major Peter Verney; Monsieur P. Vibert (Comité International de la Croix-Rouge); Sir Charles Villiers; Monsieur Alban Vistel; Mr. Igor Vinogradoff; Colonel Constantin Wagner; Professor Alexander Wainman; Lady Warner; Mr. John Waterfield; Mr. and Mrs. Julian Wathen; Herr Edgar M. Wenzel; Colonel Alex C. Wilkinson; Sir Geoffrey Wilson; Major-General Sir John Winterton; Mr. Mykola Wolynskyj; Lieut.-Colonel Denys Worrall; Mr. John Yeowell; Mr. G. K. Young; the late Lieut.-Colonel Count Stepan Zamoyski; Frau Albertine Zeiner; Mr. Constantine Zelenko; Mr. Sergei Zezine; Mr. Eriks Zilinksis.

Lastly, I wish to recall the fond memory of my beloved great aunts, Maroussia and Lily Pavlovna Tolstoy-Miloslavsky. Their inspiration and generosity prepared me over the years for my task; indeed, but for them, it would never have been accomplished.

Contents

Chronology

1941

22 June	Operation 'Barbarossa'—Germany invades Russia.
22 August	Kononov's 436th Infantry Regiment volunteers to join the Germans.

1942

8 November	Von Pannwitz appointed commander of Cossack formations.

1943

2 February	German army surrenders at Stalingrad.
21 April	1st Cossack Division raised at Mlawa.
September	Refugee Cossack settlement established at Novo-grudok. Cossack Corps transferred from Eastern Front to Yugoslavia.
10 October	Hitler orders all Russians in German service to be transferred to Western Europe.

1944

6 June	Allied landings in Normandy.
21 July	Lord Selborne protests at proposed forcible repatriation of captured Russians.
4 September	British Cabinet decides on forcible repatriation.
16 September	Himmler meets Vlasov.
16 October	Eden in Moscow assures Molotov that Russians will be repatriated regardless of their wishes.

31 October	First shipload of Russians leaves Britain for Murmansk.
8 November	Stettinius agrees that 'claimants' to Soviet nationality will be repatriated.
14 November	Prague Manifesto on human rights for Russians issued by Vlasov and KONR ('Russian Liberation Movement').
29 December	First shipload of returning Russians leaves United States.

1945

28 January	German Government recognises 'independence' of KONR.
11 February	Agreement at Yalta on repatriation of prisoners of war.
22 February	Allied Forces Act in Britain extended to cover Russian prisoners.
22 March	First shipload of Turcomans despatched from Italy to Odessa.
18 April	Massacre of prisoners from *Almanzora* at Odessa.
8 May	Germany surrenders.
9 May	*Kazachi Stan* and 15th Cossack Cavalry Corps surrender to British in Austria.
12 May	Soviets capture General Vlasov in Bohemia.
22 May	Halle agreement on East-West exchange of nationals in Germany.
29 May	Krasnov, Shkuro and other Cossack officers surrendered to Soviets in Austria.
1 June	Beginning of deportation of Cossack people at Peggetz to Soviets at Judenburg.
29 June	Franco-Soviet agreement on return of respective citizens.
12 July	Americans experience first serious Russian opposition to return when suicides occur at Kempten.
23 July	Churchill raises abortive opposition to forced repatriation at Potsdam Conference.
29 October	Montgomery, following Eisenhower's example in the US zone, forbids further forcible repatriation in British zone of Germany.
21 December	US issues McNarney-Clark Directive, defining restricted classes of Russians still liable to forcible repatriation.

1946

19 January	US forced repatriation at Dachau.
25 January	Sweden surrenders Baltic refugees to Soviets.
24 February	US forced repatriation at Plattling.
6 June	British Cabinet agrees to accept US McNarney-Clark definition.
29 June	Russian suicides at Fort Dix in face of US attempt to enforce repatriation.
12 August	Soviets announce execution of Vlasov and colleagues.
14 August	Operation 'Keelhaul' begins in Italy: screening of Russians liable to be returned under McNarney-Clark Directive.

1947

12 January	Soviets announce execution of Generals Krasnov, Shkuro, Domanov and von Pannwitz.
8 & 9 May	Last Russians forcibly repatriated in Italy by British and Americans in Operation 'Eastwind'.
14 November	French close Soviet Camp Beauregard outside Paris.

But since, so jump upon this bloody question,
You from the Polack wars, and you from England,
Are here arriv'd; give order, that these bodies
High on a stage be placed to the view;
And let me speak, to the yet unknowing world,
How these things came about: so shall you hear
Of carnal, bloody, and unnatural acts,
Of accidental judgments, casual slaughters;
Of deaths put on by cunning, and forc'd cause;
And in this upshot, purposes mistook
Fall'n on the inventors' heads: all this can I
Truly deliver.

HAMLET, V. 2

Preface to the 2012 Edition

Victims of Yalta was first published in Britain in 1978. Over the ensuing weeks, the scandal it provoked filled the press and resulted in numerous radio and television interviews. Among media and public alike, the reaction was one of almost universal horror and disgust at what could only be regarded as major war crimes.

Particular obloquy was directed against the British Foreign Secretary, Anthony Eden, and his underlings in the Northern Department of the Foreign Office. The generally reluctant rôle played by British troops in despatching hundreds of thousands of men, women, and children to what Harold Macmillan blithely anticipated as 'slavery, torture, and probably death' was viewed with mingled dismay and compassion.

Feeling ran so high that before long a committee was formed of members of the three principal political parties and both Houses of Parliament, to raise funds for erection of a monument to the memory of the victims.

The only opposition of note came from the Foreign Office, which expressed concern in a letter to the Appeal's secretary, the Hon. John Jolliffe, that the memorial be not erected in central London. A few years earlier, the Foreign Office had successfully arranged for a memorial to thousands of Allied Polish officers, massacred by the Soviets in 1940 at Katyn and elsewhere, to be banished to the obscurity of a West London cemetery.

This time, however, matters did not go as the mandarins desired. Jolliffe enclosed with his reply a copy of a recent letter containing a generous donation. 'I think you might be interested to see this', he wrote. It came from one Margaret Thatcher, then resident at 10, Downing Street. The Foreign Office promptly recollected that it had always sought a prominent location for the Memorial, and dropped its objection.

The Memorial was built—and rebuilt, after being mysteriously damaged one night. Today it stands in a little garden opposite the Victoria and Albert Museum, where pilgrims and passers-by regularly pause to pray or reflect. I understand it is the only monument in London named from the title of a book.

Here matters might have appeared to have come to rest. Although I appreciated that further information would inevitably come to light, the broad details of the shameful story were now in the public domain. My writing moved for a while to quite different fields.[1]

However, a particular episode in the forced repatriation continued to fascinate me. Chapters 7 to 10 of *Victims of Yalta* describe in some detail the vicissitudes of 50,000 Cossacks, who surrendered to British forces in Austria during the week following the German surrender. A combination of force and treachery was employed by the British 5 Corps to deliver them to an anticipated savage fate at the hands of the Soviets.

In Chapter 11, however, I confessed myself baffled by a uniquely sinister aspect of the operations. This was the inclusion among Cossacks betrayed to SMERSH of several thousand Russians who had emigrated during and after the Bolshevik Revolution. As non-Soviet citizens, their handover was consistently prohibited under Allied policy. Every relevant order despatched from Field-Marshal Alexander's headquarters emphasized this essential point.

Yet the evidence made it clear that the delivery of the émigrés to the Soviets resulted from no blunder or dire emergency, but arose from deliberate policy on the ground. Thus it was not only the Cossacks who were deceived, but the Allied governments and higher military command. Who could have arranged this unauthorized and totally unnecessary crime?

My attention remained focussed, but some time passed before fresh information came my way. Meanwhile, I became further intrigued by the parallel handover of tens of thousands of Yugoslav nationals, who, fleeing Communist terror in their own country, trustingly sought refuge with the British in Austria. It struck me, not only that this tragedy ought likewise to be explored, but that it might throw fresh light on the betrayal of the Cossacks.

Eventually, I assembled sufficient material to warrant publishing a new book on the subject. This was *The Minister and the Massacres*,

---

1 Here I would like to draw attention to two important books on the repatriations which appeared subsequently. The first is the skilful examination of US policy by Mark R. Elliott, *Pawns of Yalta: Soviet Refugees and America's Role in their Repatriation* (Urbana, 1982). The second, which examines events from the essential Russian perspective, is by Pavel Polyan, Жертвы Двух Диктатур: Остарбайтеры и Военнопленные в Третьем Рейхе и их Репатриация (Moscow, 1996): 'Victims of Two Dictators: *Ostarbeiter* and Prisoners of War and their Repatriation'.

which was published in Britain in 1986. About half the book described the gruesome fate of the 'Yugoslavs', including eyewitness accounts from survivors of mass graves where Tito slaughtered his victims. But what caused a major sensation was my indictment of former Prime Minster Harold Macmillan. In 1945 he was political adviser to Field-Marshal Alexander, and on 13 May he flew to Austria, where he gave General Keightley a 'verbal directive' to hand over the Cossacks, which secretly included those White Russians who were not liable for surrender.

Public reaction was again aroused, but this time outrage arose in influential quarters regarding my revelation of Macmillan's conspiratorial action. In the eyes of the British Establishment and its followers, the wily old fraudster had oddly acquired status as an archetypal statesman of the old school.

Almost at once, I discovered what I was up against. Interviews had been extensively arranged by my publishers with the BBC on wireless and television. At the last minute, all were abruptly cancelled, in consequence of a secret directive from the BBC's Director-General, Alasdair Milne. Milne was educated at Winchester College, the public school also attended by Toby Low, the 5 Corps Chief of Staff who arranged the brutal operations in Austria. Some years before, Low had been raised by Macmillan to the peerage, under the title of Lord Aldington.[2]

The story became highly controversial in the press, where my book enjoyed doughty defenders as well as assailants. However, I was no stranger to controversy, and welcome forthright public debate. What I was unprepared for were the methods by which the British Establishment treats those it regards as dangerous enemies.

A month after the book's publication I was telephoned by a Brigadier Cowgill, who expressed great interest in my book and suggested a meeting. As I frequently receive such requests, I saw no reason to object, and we met for lunch in our local pub. The Brigadier explained that he was greatly impressed by the case I had made, and had particular reason to be concerned about the dubious part played by Lord Aldington, with whom he had a business relationship.

Expressing himself satisfied that my case was a strong one, he asked to keep in touch. Before long, he informed me that he was organizing a committee, whose remit would be to re-examine the evidence, and in due course make their conclusions public. In this way, he explained,

---

2 Aldington was a member of the BBC general advisory council, and been a longstanding Deputy Chairman of the Conservative Party.

more information might be acquired, and the case against Macmillan and Aldington substantiated by support from an independent body.

My wife Georgina's suspicions were aroused—as mine should have been—when Cowgill informed me of three people he had invited to join him in forming his 'Committee'. The first was Thomas Brimelow, whose callous activities as a Foreign Office functionary in 1945 are recounted in *Victims of Yalta*.[3] The second was Brigadier Tryon-Wilson, a senior colleague of Aldington's at 5 Corps Headquarters. Finally, Cowgill selected a journalist called Christopher Booker, who knew nothing about the subject beyond what he had read in my books.

Cowgill explained that inclusion of Brimelow and Tryon-Wilson would assure the Committee's balance, since Booker's review articles echoing my books had been undeviatingly laudatory. Initially, my sole misgiving arose from the fact that none of the four was an historian, which made it hard to envisage in what way they could materially advance understanding.

In the event, as is generally the case with wives, the sagacious Georgina was proved RIGHT.

Cowgill came regularly to see me, eager to obtain copies of fresh documents I discovered. Eventually, he informed me that the case now appeared so strong against Macmillan that his 'Committee' planned to issue an 'Interim Report'.

In fact, they failed to discover fresh evidence of any moment, save what I had naïvely supplied them. While researching my two books on the subject, I had become increasingly struck by the extent to which significant documents were missing from relevant files in the Public Record Office.[4] For example, the vital AFHQ screening order of 6 March 1945 has disappeared altogether from the British archives.

After a while I discovered that the United States had retained copies of AFHQ[5] files, in consequence of its being an Anglo-American command. Under the Freedom of Information Act, I obtained microfile copies of the entire archive. They arrived at the end of 1986, sadly too late for inclusion in *The Minister and the Massacres*.

---

3 In 1945, returned home after three years' service at the Moscow embassy, Brimelow hailed Stalin's establishment of puppet states throughout Eastern Europe, which in his view assured an equitable Socialist redistribution of property (FO.371/47987).

4 It is generally not difficult to identify the absence of a signal from FO and WO files, since all signals are numbered, and these numbers are cited in related signals.

5 Allied Force Headquarters, based in Naples, whose area of command under F-M Alexander included British-occupied Austria.

However, my principal aim was to place the evidence before the public, and, rashly overriding Georgina's reservations, I telephoned Cowgill with the exciting news. He rushed to see me the next day and drove me to a photographic shop, where we had photocopies made of key documents in the microfilms. These he took away with him, murmuring effusive thanks.

Here I leave the bouncing Brigadier for a space, while I explain how I found myself venturing into further unanticipated choppy seas. At the beginning of 1985, chance contact brought me in touch with a man named Nigel Watts. Watts was involved in a private dispute with Lord Aldington, as Chairman of Sun Alliance Insurance. He had learned of Aldington's actions in Austria in 1945 and was indignant that a man of such dubious antecedents should be Warden of Winchester College, one of England's most famous public schools.

In due course, Watts declared his intention of issuing a circular to all Governors, old boys, and parents of boys at the College, alerting them to their Warden's responsibility for war crimes. He professed no expertise on the subject, and when at his request I read a draft of his proposed circular, I found so many factual errors that I wrote the piece myself. Entitled 'War Crimes and the Wardenship of Winchester College', it recapitulated in brief outline Aldington's responsibility as Chief of Staff of 5 Corps for the war crimes perpetrated in Austria.

Watts duly sent out several thousand copies, which provoked an extraordinary furore among the recipients. I understand the majority was horrified, many writing to insist that he either resign, or take legal action against Watts. The Governors brought pressure on Aldington to sue.

As my name did not appear on the leaflet, while Watts might be presumed to know little about the subject, Aldington felt little compunction in issuing a writ against him. Historically, English libel law strongly favours the rich and (as they often go together) powerful. There is no need to expatiate on the issue, it being notorious that many US states do not accept libel awards issued by English courts, since the English system violates fundamental rights guaranteed by the US Constitution.[6]

I took Watts to see my lawyers, who to my surprise enquired whether I wished to be joined to the Defence. They explained that, as the author, I could insist. Not wishing to leave Watts carrying the can, I agreed. Aldington, however, proved not at all anxious to include me,

---

6 For weighty advantages accorded a plaintiff in English libel law, *cf*. David Price, *Defamation: Law, Procedure & Practice* (London, 1997), p. 207. Price also notes procedural factors devized to assist judges desirous of swaying a jury's verdict (p. 215).

twice emphasizing that he 'has no quarrel with Count Tolstoy'. Only when he learned that my lawyers intended to take legal action compelling him, did he reluctantly issue a writ against me.

By the early autumn of 1988, Cowgill declared his project to be nearing the point of publication. Despite Georgina's warnings, I remained serenely confident that he would draw conclusions from the evidence similar to mine. So, he certainly assured me, was the case.

Some time before this, I had received an invitation to deliver lectures in Chile. When I mentioned this to Cowgill, he expressed interest in the dates of my absence. I flew to Santiago on 21 September, and that morning he kindly rang to wish me a good flight, checking casually that I was departing on schedule.

The next day, my Chilean host shewed me with some embarrasment a succession of faxed articles from the British press, claiming that the Cowgill 'Interim Report' had exposed my work as fraudulent. Macmillan and Aldington were now shewn to be innocent of wrong-doing, and the handover of Cossacks and 'Yugoslavs' represented no more than an unfortunate operational necessity. A running conclusion to several of these articles was that 'Count Tolstoy has left the country, and cannot be contacted'.[7]

Thus, it appeared that no one was responsible for any wrong-doing—except the irresponsible author of *Victims of Yalta* and *The Minister and the Massacres*.

What appeared odd to some was the purpose of an 'Interim Report'. The explanation now seems clear. The appointed time of the Aldington trial was fast approaching, and a publication so clearly designed to generate opinion hostile to me might be halted by an injunction, were it to appear too close to the hearing. Moreover, as the event shewed, it could prove effective to publish a further edition of the polemic in the wake of the trial.

Soon, it was not only my wife that was warning me against Cowgill. Early in 1988 my friend Chapman Pincher, a renowned expert on intelligence matters, advised me that he had learned from a close relative of Harold Macmillan that the Cowgill 'Committee' was in fact acting under instructions from the Government.[8]

---

7 My wife naturally had my telephone and fax numbers in Chile, but was not approached. Press attacks were led by two writers, John Keegan and Alistair Horne (Macmillan's official biographer), materially assisted by the editor of the Tory *Daily Telegraph*, Max Hastings. All three were subsequently knighted, presumably in recognition of their literary endeavours.

8 The cat was inadvertently let out of the bag, when Brimelow's close friend Tam Dalyell MP revealed in his obituary: 'Count Nikolai Tolstoy published a book, *The Minister*

A year later, in the colourful atmosphere of a Russian Imperial Ball at the Café Royal, my cousin Anne-Marie Obolensky displayed interest in the Cowgill affair, and offered to discover more. As she worked for Kroll Associates, she possessed access to useful resources. It turned out that Cowgill was no ordinary retired soldier turned businessman, as he had informed me.

1963/64 Cowgill was the No 3 in the British Services Security Organisation, itself the successor to the now defunct Control Commission. The BSSO was initially run by the Army Intelligence (in 1963 a man called Crash Adams) but it was then taken over and run by MI5 officers. The deputy in 1964 was Leonard Lancy, who was Cowgill's boss.

Later, a whistle-blower at the Ministry of Defence leaked documents revealing, not only how close was Cowgill's 'Committee' to the Government, but that its prime purpose was to pervert the course of justice at the Aldington trial. Furthermore, Aldington himself was a secret member of the 'Committee'! In a letter dated 2 November 1986, Cowgill briefed an official at the Ministry of Defence, regarding the current study

I am engaged in concerning the events in Austria in May and June 1945 which I am doing in conjunction with the two surviving senior staff officers of 5 Corps, Lord Aldington (then Brigadier Toby Low BGS) and Brigadier Tryon-Wilson (then Brigadier A/Q) . . .

Lord Brimelow (late of the Foreign Office) is also assisting us . . . I would be grateful for your help in this matter as this study is being done in the national interest. . .

At the foot of the page, a Ministry of Defence official commented sardonically:

Lord Brimelow 'indep[endent]*!*

---

and the Massacre (1986), bitterly criticising Lord Aldington and others. **A committee was set up by the Foreign Office, under the Chairmanship of Brigadier Anthony Cowgill** [bold type inserted], including the journalist Christopher Booker and Brimelow. They published a properly thought-out report on the whole horrible business, "The Repatriation from Austria in 1945"' (*The Independent*, 4 August 1995).

Officials at the Ministry of Defence, together with their counterparts at the Foreign Office, were ordered by Ministers to provide Aldington before and during the trial with evidence he required, including documents barred to public access. Still more importantly, they were instructed to remove evidence essential to the Defence from the Public Record Office. In the absence of a Freedom of Information Act in Britain, this they were at liberty to do without revealing their covert purpose.

Later, documentary evidence emerged demonstrating the extraordinary extent of this hidden intervention. A file of particular significance (FO.1020/42) was withheld during and after the trial. Challenged by my friend Lord Braine, formerly Father of the House of Commons, Foreign Secretary Douglas Hurd avowed it to be lost. However, on learning that a television company was planning a documentary film on the subject, he swiftly declared that it had been unexpectedly discovered by a cleaning woman in a broom cupboard!

On 28 May 1992, the investigative journalist Richard Norton-Taylor published an article in *The Guardian*, entitled 'MYSTERY OF A MISLAID FILE'. That evening he rang me, to report with understandable excitement that he had just been telephoned by a senior MoD official, who wished to speak to him. The official insisted on their meeting under the open sky by the Embankment, 'on the other side of the river, away from the possibility of bugging'. There he confirmed that, when Aldington issued his writs in 1987, measures were co-ordinated by the Foreign Secretary and Minister for Defence (both personal acquaintances of Lord Aldington) for the full resources of their respective Ministries to be placed at Aldington's disposal throughout the coming hearing.

This operation was authorized 'by Number 10 [Downing Street]'. Norton-Taylor's informant was the official responsible for the department seconded by the Ministry of Defence to assist Aldington (he could recite by heart many of the relevant WO file numbers). A priority of this assistance lay in concealment of evidence damaging to Aldington's case. This activity began in a fairly small way, but grew into a major operation designed to ensure a favourable verdict for Aldington. In consequence, most of the relevant files were hastily withdrawn from the Public Record Office to the respective Departments, where Aldington and his advisers were provided every facility for consulting them.

Throughout the trial, Cowgill conferred almost every morning with officials at the Ministry of Defence, and after each day's hearing repaired to the chambers of Charles Gray QC (Aldington's Counsel, since appointed a High Court judge), to advise on evidence, and discuss fresh measures. In the court-room Cowgill seated himself daily behind Aldington and Gray, whispering advice at regular intervals.

Norton-Taylor's informant added that, having become increasingly disgusted by the Government's flagrant interference with the course of justice, he now wished to get the matter off his chest. He was clearly a brave man, who risked losing his job and pension, as well as prosecution under the Official Secrets Act. He vouchsafed that many of his colleagues in the middling ranks of the service were likewise disgusted by the manner in which the Ministry manipulated the archives for covert or partisan purposes. He reiterated that 'truth will out', and intimated that more revelations would follow.[9]

There is not space here to recount the history of the libel trial, which lasted three months in the High Court at the end of 1989. The Judge, Michael Davies, who had selected himself from the list for the post, acted throughout as though he were Aldington's advocate. Among other measures, he ordered a private investigation of the jurors' circumstances, ordered the public gallery closed to spectators, repeatedly insulted Defence witnesses, and at the last moment refused the jury access to the trial transcript. Since Davies's three-day summing-up frequently misrepresented the proceedings, the precaution is understandable.

Unfortunately for Aldington, the Judge perpetrated a cardinal error in his summing-up. Having urged the jury to find for Lord Aldington, he warned them not to award 'Mickey Mouse' damages. Subsequently it transpired that he understood the expression as a homely term signifying 'excessively large'—a contingency to be avoided, lest it provoke an appeal.

Regrettably for Aldington, the jury took the expression literally, and awarded him damages of £1,500,000—almost three times larger than any other award in English legal history. The amount of the fine has entered the Guinness Book of Records. There it is likely to remain, for on 14 July 1995 the European Court of Human Rights ruled that it

> **Holds** unanimously that the award, having regard to its size taken in conjunction with the state of national law at the rel-

---

9 A detailed revelation of the British Government's involvement in perverting the course of justice was published by Tim Rayment in *The Sunday Times* on 7 April 1996, which may now be consulted on the internet: **The Massacre** and the **Ministers**. Access to this link is apparently censored by Wikipedia.

evant time was not "necessary in a democratic society" and thus constituted a violation of the applicant's rights under Article 10:

'Everyone has the right to freedom of expression'.

In the event, Judge Davies need not have worried. A High Court hearing ruled that I could only appeal if within a fortnight I paid £124,900 into Court, to cover Aldington's costs. Any extension of time—even a week—was refused. The Forced Repatriation Defence Fund, raised by subscribers (its patrons included Graham Greene and Alexander Solzhenitsyn) to enable the case to be fought, was frozen by a special injunction, despite the fact that it was known not to constitute a personal asset. Evidently the High Court feared that funding for the appeal might somehow prove forthcoming. Such unusual precautions may explain this curious exchange between Aldington's counsel and Judge Davies during the trial:

> Gray: My Lord, there is a feature of this case which I will not of course mention even in a non-reportable session, which suggest to me that any appeal on damages is likely not to take place.

> Davies: No, I follow that . . .

More than twenty years later, I feel a chill on recalling this sinister exchange, which is drawn from the official transcript.

This chicanery was exacerbated by the notorious fact that Aldington never incurred any costs, which were throughout secretly paid by the Sun Alliance. Twice in court his solicitors Allen & Overy submitted sworn affidavits that Aldington was paying his own costs, which even the judges found themselves unable to accept. Eventually, in 1994 chairman Sir Christopher Benson acknowledged that the Company had subsidized Aldington's costs to the tune of £530,000.

Throughout the 1989 trial, the Court was throughout preoccupied with the vexed question of Aldington's date of departure from Austria in 1945. That he returned to England in the latter part of May to contest the General Election was not in doubt. Nor was it at issue that he left some days before the Cossack handovers began on 29 May. Throughout the trial, concern was with the extent to which he was responsible for orders implementing the operations.

Prior to Aldington's initiation of libel proceedings, he had over a period of years supplied dates for his departure ranging from 24 to 29 May. Once it was realized that his participatory rôle would be subjected to intense scrutiny in court, it became of utmost importance to establish the earliest date possible. Shortly after issuing his writ against Watts, Aldington suddenly recalled for the first time:

> I left Austria on 22nd May 1945 before any detailed arrangements had been made about the handover of the Cossacks . . .

Any earlier date was precluded by the fact that an order issued on the afternoon of 21 May bore his signature.

An official document established that Aldington arrived in England on leave on 24 May, but throughout the trial no direct evidence was adduced establishing where he was between early on the 22nd, when he claimed to have left Austria, and the evening of the 24th, when he arrived in Blackpool to contest the parliamentary seat.

This gap he sought to plug with belatedly recalled detail. This included an early morning flight from Klagenfurt on 22 May, his seeing the sun shining on the snow of the Karavaken Mountains, and his arrival in Naples. There he recalled spending the nights of the 22nd and 23rd, apparently seeing no one and doing nothing capable of corroboration, and eventually returned to England on the 24th. To illustrate how clear was his refurbished memory of events, he added for good measure that upon his return he dined twice at the home of Foreign Secretary Anthony Eden, who overcame his modest misgivings, persuading him to stand as candidate for Blackpool North.

Facts emerged, which made the veracity of this vividly described itinerary not a little suspect. Thus, it emerged that from 20 May Allied command prohibited all military flights near the Yugoslav frontier, while rain fell throughout 22 May at Klagenfurt aerodrome. So far as his relations with Eden were concerned, every detail Aldington submitted proved false. As early as 21 March, he had written eagerly accepting the Foreign Secretary's invitation to stand for parliament, and Eden's belatedly discovered diary shewed that the two dinners at which he supposedly entertained Aldington never occurred.

In his summing-up, the Judge suppressed the crucial weather evidence, and pronounced Aldington's detailed account of his relations with Eden an interesting illustration of the fallibility of human memory. Fortunately for Aldington, the Judge's precautionary edict pre-empted any possibility of the jury's checking his version of events against the trial transcript.

If Judge Davies's undeviating protection of Aldington throughout the trial appear extraordinary to readers unacquainted with the workings of the English higher courts, a newspaper article published in the Evening Standard a few months after the trial may serve to clarify understanding.

Golf links

I thought there was nothing we had not learned about Lord Aldington, following the libel action in which a jury awarded £1.5 million against Count Nikolai Tolstoy in the presence of Mr Justice Michael Davies. But a golfing friend tells me that, although unknown to each other, both Aldington and Davies are members of the historic Rye golf club.

Coincidentally, Aldington has been a member of Rye, one of England's oldest clubs, since 1957, while Davies joined only relatively recently, in 1985. "He visits during weekends and holidays," Davies's clerk at the Royal Courts of Justice tells me. His main club is Stourbridge in the Midlands.

Lord Aldington tells me he started playing golf 65 years ago. "I've won the parliamentary golf cup four times," he says. When I pointed out that Justice Davies was a fellow member, Toby Aldington told me he seldom plays at Rye now. "I've never met him there," he says cheerfully. "I don't know what he looks like without a wig on."

Members of the Rye Golf Club have expressed incredulity that the Judge and His Lordship never met there, given that Davies's home at the small and exclusive club lay just six miles from Aldington's house. They also sardonically recalled Davies's snobbish reverence for the great and good of the British Establishment.

Aldington's alibi was vital to his case, which depended on reducing to a minimum his responsibility for the Cossacks' brutal treatment and betrayal. Of yet greater significance, as the Judge conceded, was its application to the reliability of his testimony, and his character as a witness.

Within a year, evidence establishing Aldington's true date of departure from Austria in 1945 unexpectedly came to light. The missing
signal had been discovered in the Public Record Office! Dated 7.30 pm
on 24 May 1945, it reported succinctly:

BGS left 5 Corps for England on FLIAP[10] on 23rd May.

To anyone ignorant of the modus operandi of the British Establishment, this evidence might have appeared more than sufficient to blow
Aldington's case out of the water. After all, as Judge Davies had emphasized during his summing-up:

> members of the jury, in the end a document means what it says,
> what it means in the English language. You have to put your-
> self back into 1945 and ask yourselves: what does that docu-
> ment mean? What did it convey to the person to whom it was
> addressed? What was meant by the words used? Because those
> are the basic questions about a document which have to be
> faced up to.

The message emanated from a special signals unit known as 'Phantom',
and before long I traced its senior surviving officer, Colonel John
Morgan. He explained to me in detail how the unit operated. Established in 1944, its function was to provide Eisenhower and Alexander with accurate information direct from the front line. In Austria,
the 'Phantom' unit operated its own transmitter from a lorry parked
beside Aldington's caravan. It would have been inconceivable, Morgan
explained, that the 'Phantom' officer did not know on a daily basis
who was 5 Corps Chief of Staff, whose regular briefings he obliga-
torily attended. Nor was there any realistic possibility of error, since
such rare mistakes as occurred were promptly corrected in the log, as
Colonel Morgan shewed me from occasional entries in the 'Phantom'
log-book.

When my solicitors were presented with this evidence of Aldington's
deceit, they arranged with Counsel to bring an action for perjury against
him. The Ministry of Defence whistle-blower informed Richard Norton-Taylor that, on the day the Guardian article publicly revealed its
existence, 'Aldington rang the Ministry of Defence, enquiring in a state
of some agitation after the 'Phantom' file'.

---

10 Advance leave.

Meanwhile, other pertinent documentation came to light. Early in 1992 I conducted fresh researches in the National Archives at Suitland, Maryland. It was now becoming increasingly clear how serious and relevant was the operation concerted between Eisenhower and Alexander to transfer responsibility for Cossacks settled beside the town of Lienz from the British 5 Corps to the US 3rd Army.

On 22 May American troops under Patton's command arrived at the border of 5 Corps territory, with orders to occupy the valley occupied by the Cossacks. That afternoon, the Chief of Staff (BGS) of 5 Corps sent an urgent appeal to 8 Army for all further advance by US troops to be halted:

Do NOT now consider necessary for us to be relieved up to boundary . . . as situation in Lienz well in hand and can be organized by one unit.

It was this signal that effectively consigned 25,000 Cossack men, women, and children to death, torture, and slavery in the Gulag. As the 'Phantom' signal confirmed beyond reasonable doubt, the BGS who so eagerly intervened to frustrate Eisenhower's humane design was none other than our friend Brigadier Low, afterwards Lord Aldington.

In light of this evidence, confidence brimmed high that justice would finally be done. But my legal team, experienced as they were, had yet to reckon with the full duplicity of the High Court. Before long I received ominous news. My Counsel informed me that the judge appointed to hear the perjury action, Andrew Collins QC, had ordered the hearing to be held 'in Chambers': i.e., in secret. I was astonished, having been brought up to believe that it was a proud boast of English justice that proceedings are conducted openly, so that justice be seen to be done. To my enquiry whether the decision could be challenged, I was told that it could—but in that case, Collins would indubitably pronounce the application 'an abuse of process'. The case would then be heard in secret regardless, while the judge would become yet more hostile than his decision now indicated him to be.[11]

The hearing took place at the beginning of 1994, in an underground room of the Royal Courts of Justice. Press and public were rigorously denied entry. The hearing lasted three days, on account of the extent of evidence of Aldington's perjuries. On the first day, the Judge's preju-

---

11 Collins acted as a Crown prosecutor in the 1992 Ordtech case, where he played a major rôle in suppression of evidence damaging to the Government's case. Shortly afterwards, he was appointed a judge, and I understand that the Aldington perjury case was the first he was assigned.

dice became clear, when he abruptly declared that the 'Phantom' signal 'cannot be correct'. When my Counsel enquired why not, Collins replied with a smile: 'because Lord Aldington says it is not'.

It being evident that the verdict was decided before the hearing began, my Counsel declared himself unprepared to proceed unless we were guaranteed a transcript of proceedings for submission to the Court of Appeal. This was agreed. Collins duly rejected our submissions, adding for good measure an order for my solicitors to bear costs of this and any future proceedings undertaken on my behalf. This penalty was extended to any firm which might consider representing me, so that thereafter I was effectively prohibited from undertaking legal action, even in my own defence. I had become an outlaw, like my boyhood idol Robin Hood!

Next day, my solicitor attended the court-room to receive the promised transcripts, only to be regretfully informed that on each of the trial's three days the tape-recorders had experienced successive mechanical failures. Consequently, when the Appeal Court on 23 July 1996 rejected my application for leave to appeal against Collins's judgment, their verdict was grounded on what Aldington's lawyers chose to tell them.

Space forbids further detail of the machinations that ensued on my revelation of this atrocious war crime. An ironic contrast to the British Government's concealment of evidence is afforded by the attitude of the Russian Government. President Yeltsin signed a decree, permitting me to inspect and photocopy all relevant material held by their Ministries. In January 1993 I visited Moscow, where I received full co-operation from all relevant depositories, and returned with copies of scores of significant documents never released before. This remarkable evidence has yet to be published, as has much else of comparable importance. Fresh eyewitness evidence includes that of a former Yugoslav Commissar, who on 15 May 1945 negotiated with Aldington terms for the handover of thousands of fugitives in Austria, which Aldington denied on oath ever existed.

Whatever the truth of this murky story, it is unlikely to be published in England. On 2 July 1990, Aldington's lawyers Allen & Overy issued a threatening letter to all major public and university libraries in Britain. All copies of my book *The Minister and the Massacres* were required to be withdrawn forthwith, on the grounds that it libelled their client. As Aldington had been careful not to pursue any court action against the book (which would have required a jury to read its compromising evidence), an unusual stratagem was devised. The cover of Allen & Overy's menacing document proclaimed it a 'Statement in Open Court', resolving a settlement 'Between: The Right Honourable Toby Low Baron Aldington *Plaintiff* - and - (1) Nigel Watts (2) Count Nikolai Tolstoy-Miloslavsky *Defendants*'.

It was on the day prior to circulation of this document that the High Court upheld the damages of £1,500,000 as eminently fair and appropriate, while Judge Davies's arbitrary freezing of the Forced Repatriation Defence Fund precluded further appeal. Most libraries, including such famous repositories as the Bodleian at Oxford and the London Library, scurried to obey Lord Aldington. Even in Scotland, where English libel law does not run, Edinburgh University complied as abjectly as the rest. The fact that there were some honourable exceptions, like the British Museum library, indicates that the threat was patently unenforceable. The library censorship was essentially voluntary.

No librarian saw fit to seek a response from me or my lawyers.

But for their eager haste to comply with this diktat, the librarians might have noticed that Allen & Overy's document was in fact a forgery. Since Aldington had never undertaken proceedings against me in respect of my book, no such 'Statement in Open Court' could ever have occurred. When challenged, Allen & Overy asserted that the misrepresentation resulted from 'error'—but refused to alert libraries to the fact.

Plainly, aspects of the history first unveiled in *Victims of Yalta* appear sufficiently dangerous to require such a bizarre parade of mendacity and conspiracy. Before the prohibition and destruction of copies of *The Minister and the Massacres*, it was long since a book in England was censored on political grounds. So far as I am aware, the previous instance occurred almost exactly two centuries earlier. It was in 1792 that Thomas Paine was found guilty of seditious libel for publishing *The Rights of Man*.

—Nikolai Tolstoy, April 2012

Introduction

THAT WELL OVER TWO MILLION RUSSIANS WERE HANDED OVER TO STALIN in the years 1944–7 by the Western Allies, and that the fate accorded to almost all of them was terrible, has been known to an increasingly large public for a number of years. At first the knowledge was confined largely to émigré circles directly concerned with the tragedy; more recently some well-researched studies have appeared in English.[1]

The truth is, however, that despite the existence of an array of published work, much of it scholarly and well informed, only a small part of the story has seen the light of day. For a start, much of the most crucial material remained inaccessible even to the most recent writers. Under the British thirty-year ruling, state papers are gradually released annually, with the result that before the publication of the present work no historian had been able to use documents extending from the Potsdam Conference in July 1945 to the end of 1946. These constitute the evidence for half the period in question, and are clearly essential to a full understanding of the story. Numerous surviving participants, many occupying key positions at the time, have remained until now uninterviewed; in many cases their testimony must seriously alter the accepted picture.

Perhaps the clearest way of indicating what work yet remained to be done is to explain that some three-quarters of the material of *Victims of Yalta* has never before appeared in print. The circumstances that led so many Russians to fall into the hands of the Germans; repatriation operations conducted from Norway, North Africa, France, Belgium, Holland and neutral countries; the question of British and American infraction of the Geneva Convention; the Soviet side of operations, conducted by the NKVD and SMERSH; the fate of the returned Russians; all these are for the first time described in detail.

A crucial chapter of *Victims of Yalta* examines a sinister episode, which, most astonishing of all, has been entirely overlooked by historians. Thousands of Tsarist fugitives, who had never lived in Soviet Russia, who had fled their country in 1919 as allies of the British and Americans and who were not in consequence covered by the Yalta

Agreement, were surrendered to SMERSH in Austria under an arrangement so secret that exceptional measures are still employed to suppress the evidence.

The British Government admits to having destroyed vital files and refuses to consent to the American Government's release of photocopies in its possession—despite frequent Pentagon requests to be allowed to do so.

The story of the forced repatriation is still a living issue. Lord Avon, who as Anthony Eden was responsible for initiating the whole policy, wrote frequently to the author to justify the measure, but equally persistently declined to answer specific questions on crucial issues. Only one Foreign Office official intimately concerned with the arrangements in 1944-5 agreed to speak to the author, and then only to explain that he had suffered a fit of amnesia covering exactly that period. The remainder declined to be interviewed, and the author only learned later the pretext for this silence. This was that it is the Foreign Secretary who authorises policy, and it is for the civil servants merely to carry it out. Whatever may be thought of this argument in general terms, it can have little application to the subject of this history.

Halfway through the period of forced repatriation came the British General Election of July 1945. Ernest Bevin succeeded Eden as Foreign Secretary and, with a view to considering whether the policy would continue, he asked for a full account of all measures taken so far. The resultant report stated that 'no resort has ever had to be made to violent measures' in compelling Russians to return home. It was on the basis of this falsehood that Bevin reluctantly agreed to continue operations for a further year and a half, and successfully pressed the Americans to adopt the same policy. Until now the activities of anonymous civil servants have been largely ignored, interest being almost exclusively concentrated on the politicians and their decisions. The full story reveals the power possessed by these shadowy figures, and the use they made of it.

It was no accident that the story remained unknown to the general public in the West for so long. Alexander Solzhenitsyn has suggested that, because 'public opinion did not prevent' the operations, 'did not want to take the matter up, did not ask for explanations . . . we do get the feeling that the *entire* British nation has committed a sin . . .'.[2] This is scarcely fair. In 1945 barely a few hundred Englishmen at most were aware of the implications, or even the fact, of what was being done in their name. George Orwell's was a lone voice at the time, lamenting fruitlessly that there appeared to be a voluntary conspiracy on the part of the press to suppress the whole cruel story. This, he suggested, was in part due to 'the poisonous effect of the Russian *mythos* on English intellectual life'; that is, the prevalent view of the British Left that Stalin's Russia was a truly free and just society.[3]

Orwell's strictures were undoubtedly valid. British reporters, with or without editorial prompting, were reluctant to print news unfavourable to the Soviet system, though few went as far as the 'liberal' A. J. Cummings, whose article in the *News Chronicle* (3 October 1944) declared that: 'With the exception of one man, all these Russians are . . . eager to get back to . . . their own land.'

There were other influences at work besides the widespread cult of 'Uncle Joe'. When a number of terrified Russians held in camps in Britain committed suicide, Patrick Dean of the Foreign Office noted that, if the news got out, it might 'possibly cause political trouble', urging 'that the Foreign Office should speak to the News Department with a view to doing all that is possible to avoid publicity',[4] 'which might be embarrassing'.[5]

What was referred to, of course, was the realisation that large sections of the British public would revolt against the application of brutal measures to compel the return of unwilling Russians, particularly large numbers of women and children. This was frankly admitted by another official, John Galsworthy, when it came to a question of people it was not intended to repatriate. 'I think that any publicity given to the Soviet demand . . . is a good thing. An enlightened public opinion can only strengthen our position in refusing to transfer these luckless folk to the Russians'.[6]

But such candour was exceptional—and for a purpose. The general Foreign Office view, expressed on numerous occasions in 1944–5, was that operations must be carefully concealed from the British public, lest there be a 'scandal with talk about irregular procedure, cheating people into accepting repatriation to the U.S.S.R. etc.' This had 'to be avoided at all costs'.[7]

All this contrasts strangely with what apologists for the Foreign Office decision assert today. In a House of Lords debate on the subject on 17 March, 1976, Lord Hankey claimed that the Government 'would have been subjected to an irresistible storm of criticism' had it attempted to retain Russians unwilling to return—because this would have imperilled the return of British prisoners liberated by the Red Army.[8]

This leads to the essential point: would Stalin have considered holding such liberated British and American prisoners hostage for the return of the millions of Soviet citizens held in Western Europe? This consideration will be discussed at length in *Victims of Yalta*. At this stage it will suffice to say that there exists no evidence that anyone in the Foreign Office at the time feared such a contingency. True, Stalin might have been even less co-operative than he was in implementing the provisions of the Yalta Agreement, but the worst the Foreign Office envisaged was that Britons in Red Army hands might continue for a few weeks to return home by sea from Odessa instead of overland through Germany. That Stalin contemplated retaining them as a *quid pro quo* was never considered by Eden or his advisers. Furthermore, striking evidence will be brought forward for the first time to show that, if Stalin ever did contemplate such a move, it was to reject it.

For the first time, too, it will be shown in detail how very different was United States policy on the matter. The State Department delayed acceptance of the principle of forced repatriation for months after the British had conceded it. It then reluctantly gave in, but was so revolted at the relatively minor scenes of bloodshed that ensued that it temporarily abandoned the policy. Finally, under strong British pressure, a few score Russians who had served in the German Army were sent back.

This tough attitude on the part of the Americans did not result in a delay of one day for any GI returning from Russia, nor did the Soviets ever threaten the reprisals which Foreign Office officials now claim to have feared. The British Government was fully informed of the American stance and of Soviet failure to react harshly. It was not necessary to speculate on the merits of an alternative policy; it was there to be seen.

Then again, if the return of the British prisoners was the issue at stake, why was the policy continued for nearly two years after the last prisoners had come home? More telling still is the fact that, by implementing forcible repatriation of Russians in Wehrmacht uniform, the same British prisoners for whom the supporters of forcible repatriation profess such overriding concern were exposed to a very real risk of Nazi reprisals whilst they were still in German hands. And this was a far more terrible danger, one which the Foreign Office accepted *at the time*.

The real considerations underlying British and American policy will appear as the story unfolds. So also will the tragic drama of the Russians themselves: how they came to be in German hands; why so many volunteered to join the German army to fight Stalin; and above all what took place in the repatriation operations, conducted by largely disgusted British and American troops. Lord Bethell has already provided a vivid picture of what the latter involved, but the full story of the Russian prisoners in 1941–5 will reveal the extent of a tragedy which, both in the numbers involved and the depths of suffering experienced, is fully comparable to Nazi treatment of the Jews.

The cruel irony of this Russian tragedy lay in the fact that to a large extent Russians in the Red Army and their opponents in the German-raised 'Russian Army of Liberation' were fighting for the same ideal. A former Red Army hero, Viktor Nekrassov, has recently explained his motive for fighting for Soviet power in 1941–5. 'This was the reason, namely, that when we had put an end to the slavery of Fascism, we . . . would, ourselves, be saved from tyranny. We had thought to cleanse with our own blood the infamy of the pre-war Soviet-German Pact, that the terrible past would never return, and it was with this hope that I had continued my adherence to the Communist Party'.[9] Whether this course was more honourable than that of Nekrassov's compatriots who took up arms against Soviet tyranny may be a matter for argument, but scarcely for facile judgments. Only detailed and exhaustive examination of the facts can advance the cause of truth and justice.

Before beginning this remarkable history I may perhaps be permitted to add a personal note. I was drawn to the subject by an early acquaintance with many who had evaded despatch to the death-camps of GULAG. Latterly, I came across some odd coincidences that confirmed my long-standing intention to attempt to do justice to the memory of so many of my fellow-countrymen.

In his chapter in *The Gulag Archipelago*, 'That Spring', Solzhenitsyn discusses the very topic to which this book is dedicated—that is to say, the appalling blunders, diplomatic and military, that led to the Germans capturing so many prisoners in 1941–2, and the fearful fate of those prisoners when subsequently presented to Stalin by the Western Allies. And at one point he pauses—to ask what Tolstoy is going to describe *that* Borodino for us.[10] I had already completed serious researches when those words were printed; none the less, and however diffidently, I could not but feel the spur.

I had in any case a family connection with a forced repatriation problem that demanded redemption. My illustrious though highly unscrupulous ancestor, Count Peter Tolstoy, was the minister chosen by Peter the Great to lure back to Russia his fugitive son, the Tsarevich Alexei. Unable to endure his father's capricious violence and militaristic discipline, the young Tsarevich had fled to the domains of the Holy Roman Emperor. Despite fierce demands and violent threats, the Emperor (no Roosevelt or Churchill) resolutely refused to hand over his uninvited guest to what was clearly an uncertain fate. It fell to Peter Tolstoy to hunt down the hapless youth, then living in domestic simplicity with his young wife at Naples. By a mixture of glib promises and sinister threats, he finally induced Alexei to return to his father. Despite absolute assurances of immunity and forgiveness, the young Tsarevich was savagely murdered at the Tsar's orders.

I hope I will be pardoned for noting a third such coincidence. In

October 1944 Churchill and Eden flew to Moscow to confer with Stalin. It was at this meeting that Eden, without argument or objection, hastened to promise Stalin the return of all his subjects, whether willing or not. The code name for this conference was 'Tolstoy'.

It is now time to turn to the story itself, one which is perhaps more than just a grim phantom from the past. The consequences live on, particularly in the consciousness of millions of Russians at home and abroad. As recently as 1977 a former SS officer was sentenced in Hamburg for having (in the judge's words) 'selected Jews for extermination in the full knowledge of what would happen to them', though he had not himself participated in their murder. A policy that caused the herding of millions of ordinary Russians into cattle-trucks to certain death, torture or unbearable privation was, the reader may feel, not so very different. But only by exposure of the truth can Solzhenitsyn's wholesale indictment of the British and American peoples be answered.

Indeed, of the few who were aware of what was happening, a majority strongly opposed what they regarded as unjustifiable and unnecessary inhumanity. On the British side, moving protests, extending on occasion even to ignoring unpalatable orders, came from distinguished figures such as Lord Selborne, Sir James Grigg, Field-Marshal Alexander and General Montgomery. Amongst Americans the objection was almost universal, opposition being led by diplomats such as Joseph C. Grew, Robert Murphy and Alexander Kirk, and soldiers like Eisenhower and Bedell Smith.

Victims of Yalta is a long book. I have done my utmost to leave no important document and no essential first-hand evidence uncited. It is hoped that in this way the reader will be able to assess who were responsible, and in what degree, for a policy and its implementation that caused such a horrendous catalogue of suffering.

I

Russians in the Third Reich

On the morning of Sunday, 22 June 1941, Shalva Yashvili* had planned to enjoy an extra hour in bed. A young Red Army lieutenant in the army occupying Soviet Poland, and by his own account a shy and rather gentle young man, he had three months of his two-year service to go. After that he would return to the sunny mountains of his native Georgia. It seemed unlikely at this late stage that anything would occur to impede his return to civilian life, though it is true that senior instructors visiting his artillery regiment had of late devoted time to teaching recognition of German tanks, field artillery and other items of the Wehrmacht's weaponry. This seemed odd, as relations between the Third Reich and the Soviet Union appeared as cordial as they had been since the two greatest powers of the Eurasian land mass had joined in dividing Poland between them.

The day before, Yashvili had been relieved of the boredom of mounting guard at the regimental ammunition dump, and had set off with a friend for the nearby town of Lida, in Byelorussia just across the border, on the traditional Saturday night's search for entertainment. After seeing a film they returned to the great barracks, solidly built in the days of Tsar Nicholas II, and stayed up late chatting. The friend, who came from Buryat-Mongolia, was fascinated by Yashvili's descriptions of the rugged, smiling land of Georgia, so different from the bleak and windy tundra of his own remote province. He particularly loved the luscious oranges Yashvili received in parcels from home, and could hardly be brought to believe that there existed a land where such apples of the Hesperides could be plucked freely by any wayfarer.

But neither young man was to enjoy a late lie-in. To his disgust a half-awakened Yashvili was aroused abruptly by the wholly unexpected sound of the barracks alarm. It was six in the morning, and barely light.

* 'Yashvili' is not my informant's real name (his mother still lives in the Soviet Union). Otherwise, every detail of this story is as he told it to me.

Trying to collect his thoughts, he rushed out, pulling on his uniform as he went. But even as he and his comrades emerged, bleary-eyed and disgruntled, they were met by an officer going round to say that it was a false alarm and all could go back to sleep.

Grumbling at their superiors' insensitivity, the soldiers tumbled back into bed. This time their slumbers lasted an even shorter time. Within two hours a distant thud of explosions shook the barracks windows, and the alarm rang out again. The artillerymen dressed hastily and piled out into the town square. There they found a huge crowd of officers and soldiers of units gathered from all parts of the town, shouting excitedly and asking questions.

Yashvili heard a number heatedly explaining that, ten minutes before, aeroplanes had bombed and machine-gunned certain quarters of the town. Several houses had been destroyed, and some people had apparently been killed. Others declared that there could not have been an attack; it must have been manoeuvres. Yashvili soon decided that something more than manoeuvres was happening, particularly when it appeared that the mysterious raiders had discharged a number of bombs onto the town railway station, destroying quantities of guns, tanks, ammunition and petrol stacked on sidings and by the tracks. Still, no orders came and only confusion reigned. The crowd of soldiers milled about, and it was not until ten o'clock that anyone felt impelled to start issuing instructions.

The different units had assembled and moved to open country encircling the town. Yashvili and his company stood waiting and wondering, when up came an officer to enquire whether anyone present knew how to fire a four-barrelled anti-aircraft gun. Yashvili stepped forward. He was at once ordered to take his company, with four such guns, to protect a neighbouring aerodrome from the possibility of attack by paratroopers. He was given a three-ton truck for transport and, at about six o'clock in the evening, set off on a laborious journey to the aerodrome.

Yashvili had himself as yet seen no signs of war, if war it was. But during the midday wait he learned that he had unwittingly been close to death. The ammunition dump which he had only just been relieved from guarding was sited some five miles out of town. In the half-light of early dawn dive-bombers had come spinning out of the sky, hurling down bombs which had sent the whole dump up in one blinding explosion, and killed all twenty-two of the guard company. 'Operation Barbarossa', the German invasion of Russia, had begun.

Yashvili's truck was now driving through the night, with no headlights permitted and for the most part in first gear. Two or three times they ended up in a ditch, and it was after dawn next morning when they reported to the aerodrome. There a major directed them to take up a defensive position in woods on the outskirts. Yashvili and his fellows (there were twenty-four of them, including the driver) accordingly moved off, positioned their guns, and settled down to wait.

As the day drew on and nothing occurred to disturb the tranquillity of the fields and forests in which their post nestled, the soldiers unbuttoned their military shirts and relaxed. Not far off was a building, which Yashvili and some of his comrades went over to investigate. It turned out to be the kitchen for a nearby prison camp, and a Polish girl asked if the men would like some food. They followed her to a great storehouse. It was locked, but the girl proved able to open it, and when the soldiers entered (a little gingerly), they found themselves in a veritable Abanazer's cave of comestibles; the place was stocked to the ceiling with giant hams, strings of sausages, sides of bacon, and crates of vodka. The soldiers' mouths watered, but knowledge of penalties exacted in the Soviet Union from those who laid hands on state property held them in check.

The girl reassured them, and from her and a bewildered prisoner who returned from a week-end's leave they learned the situation. The inmates of the prison-camp were driven out each day to perform forced labour on the aerodrome.[1] As soon as news of the German invasion was confirmed, the whole population, guards and captives, vanished. None knew where they had gone, but at any rate they were unlikely to reappear soon. As for the riches of the storehouse, these were the supplies kept for the mess-room of the NKVD guards. As became the foremost guardians of the Revolution, they did not stint themselves. The delighted soldiers spent the next hour cramming their truck and stomachs with good things. That evening they did not trouble to send to the aerodrome for their rations.

It had been an uneventful and leisurely day, but as night came on matters resumed their former unpredictable course. The major's orderly who should have done the rounds of the outposts failed to appear. After waiting some time, Yashvili sent a messenger to the lieutenant commanding their neighbouring company. The soldier returned, scratching his head, and reported that there was nobody there. The young officer then despatched his messenger to the major in charge. Back came the envoy: the major and everyone else had vanished too! All had melted away, leaving the lone twenty-four with their lorry.

There was nothing for it but to try to rejoin the regiment. They piled into the truck and returned to the town. All was confusion, with the streets and square packed with retreating troops. Making their way through the throng, the lost company drove first to Regimental Headquarters. Once again they drew a blank: the building was a blackened and empty shell, having received a direct hit from German bombs. Faced with this final check, the young Georgian decided he had no alternative but to join the fleeing throng pressing eastwards back to Russia.

With no plans beyond this, Yashvili and his men drove out of the town as evening was coming on, and billeted themselves on a grumbling Polish farmer. A sentry was posted by the main road to keep an eye out for units of their regiment. The men were settling down, when the sentry ran in to say that he had just stopped one of their captains on the road. Yashvili came out, and was told by the captain that his battery had been moved nearer the front to protect a road. In the meantime they were to follow him and rejoin the rest of the regiment.

They drove all that night, reaching the regimental camp in a wood next day. There they learned that Yashvili's battery officer had been killed and the entire battery destroyed. This news did not by now seem very shocking or surprising, as it was evident that chaos reigned throughout their section of the front.

At midday, Yashvili was ordered to join the regimental ammunition convoy. This consisted of sixty trucks, under the command of a captain. They were given a map-reading as their destination, but no further explanation or alternative orders. Still, at least they were part of the integrated structure of the army once again.

Bumping along the forest road, they continued for several miles until the braking of the foremost truck brought the column to a halt. Yashvili, about twentieth along the line, leaned out and saw that his captain was being harangued by two senior officers. One wore on his collar the red and black tabs of a general from the Headquarters Staff, whilst the other was a field general. After some discussion the convoy captain jumped out of his truck and got into the next one. The two generals took his place in the leading lorry and the procession trundled on, to come to a halt shortly afterwards.

The captain told the men they could have a short rest period, and then came over to Yashvili. It appeared that he had received a ferocious lambasting from the generals for being so foolish as to drive by daylight. 'Are you mad, *dourak* (blockhead), to drive by daylight? Don't you realise what will happen if the Stukas catch you in the open? Learn a little sense, if you can, and from now on keep under the trees by day and drive only by night!'

Not daring to excuse himself by quoting his previous orders, the poor subaltern jumped to obey. When darkness fell, the two martinet generals once again sat in the leading truck and directed the pace of the journey. It proved an unnerving experience for the drivers, as they were not allowed to use their headlights. In addition, the leading vehicles moved in a most erratic way, constantly stopping unexpectedly— presumably through fear of hidden obstacles. All each lorry-driver saw was the sudden flashing of the brake lights of the truck in front. During the entire night they moved by recurring stops and starts a few miles only. And, needless to say, a number of accidents took place. Russian military trucks had their radiators situated right at the front of the bonnet, so that a relatively mild collision with the rear of the preceding truck resulted almost invariably in a burst radiator and a useless lorry. The vehicles so damaged had to be nosed aside into the ditch. Of sixty trucks which had set out the night before, only twelve were still intact next morning.

However, the generals made no comment, and explained to the captain that they were now only a dozen miles from an ammunition dump. They gave him documents empowering him to collect as many shells as they were able to take back to the regiment. The generals then departed, leaving strict instructions that once again the convoy was to wait for darkness before moving off.

When night came the captain took the remains of his convoy slowly and carefully along the allotted route. Despite the shortness of the journey, it was not until morning that they reached their destination. When they did, they found that the entire ammunition store was no more. It too had been blown to pieces by an aerial attack.

The reality of their situation began to dawn on the two young officers. The two 'generals' were in fact German agents who had succeeded in depriving a Red Army artillery regiment of vital ammunition for some three days, destroying forty-eight lorries in the process. If they were achieving elsewhere even a tithe of this success, these enterprising agents alone must be spreading chaos in Soviet ranks.[2]

Two factors had greatly assisted the impostors. One was the fact that, as Yashvili stresses, 'in the Red Army no one questions an order; he just obeys.' The other was that the disguised generals spoke perfect Russian and had perfected the hectoring manner which Red Army soldiers expected from their generals. Ironically, the disguised Russian generals were almost certainly Russians, and quite possibly generals in reality as well! For the Counter-Intelligence Department of the Wehrmacht, the Abwehr, had set up special commando units for operation behind the Soviet lines. Recruited from White Russians and Russian-speaking Balts, Poles and Ukrainians, and given impecably tailored Soviet uniforms, they were able to achieve successes far beyond the ordinary in this type of warfare.[3]

The two young officers returned with their twelve trucks (the ninety-six lorryless drivers and mates came as passengers) to the regiment. When their colonel learned that he had not only not got the expected shells, but had also lost four-fifths of his precious trucks in this foolish way, he was beside himself with rage. Still, there was nothing to be done, and as German units launched an attack shortly afterwards, the ammunitionless artillery regiment was obliged to continue its retreat. Continually attacked from the air when on the highroads, they were obliged to move slowly through the woods. There the ground was too soft to take the heavy 122 mm. guns, and an order came to abandon them. The demoralised remnant of the regiment was regrouped with other units to form a somewhat ragged division of survivors. News had come that the Germans had already reached Minsk, far to the east, and so the retreat continued through the forests.

It was at this time that Lieutenant Yashvili underwent his first and brief experience of actual fighting. Sent out on patrol, he came round a bush to find himself face-to-face with a German. Both fired off a round and bolted for cover, neither having been hit. But after this slightly ludicrous incident, events took a more serious turn, and the Georgian was hit by a bullet which passed through both legs. He was treated by an attractive young woman doctor (he can still recall his acute embarrassment when she told him to take down his trousers: he was, after all, not yet twenty-one). He was then taken to the battalion casualty section, where he found a corner of a lorry in which to rest.

But there was no rest for the Red Army in the summer of 1941. The Germans began to press home another attack, and bullets came whipping through the sides of the parked lorries. Ignoring his wounds, Yashvili flung himself from the lorry and dragged himself along the ground to the safety of some bushes. But this spurt of energy proved too much for his weakened frame, and he fainted. Debilitated from pain and loss of blood, he slept all that day (2 July) where he lay. When he finally woke, the sun was already setting behind the birch trees. He raised himself up, and found he was lying in the midst of an archipelago of mortar-bomb craters. They had been crashing and splintering all around the spot on which he lay: he is understandably convinced that the hand of God was upon him that day.

Everywhere was quiet; even the leaves of the trees had stopped rustling. Yashvili picked himself up gingerly, and staggered off—whither, he was not very certain. He had no gun, no knapsack, and no idea where to find his or any other unit of the Red Army. That morning he had been one amongst fifty thousand armed men; he was now unarmed and alone, except for the corpses. The only living creatures there besides him were some army horses from the artillery train. With extreme difficulty, he crawled to one and managed to scramble into the saddle. Despite the serious nature of his wounds, the young lieutenant felt little pain, and his main concern now was to find somewhere he could receive medical attention.

His first act was to remove his military tunic and stuff it into a saddle-bag. There was now nothing to single him out as a soldier; his fear was that, with daylight failing, he might be shot by either side as he emerged from the trees. An hour's ride brought him to the edge of the forest, and there, about three miles off, he could see a village. As he approached, he became aware from the distant hum and twinkling lights that a great crowd was assembled. Drawing nearer, he came on two bedraggled officers sitting on their horses beyond the perimeter of the houses. They shouted to Yashvili to join them, suggesting they could help each other. They also asked him if he was prepared to go amongst the milling horde of undisciplined soldiers occupying the village, and beg some food. They explained that, as officers, they were afraid of being shot by the men if they went amongst them. A great many officers had been killed by their men during the first weeks of war. As there was now nothing about Yashvili's appearance to suggest his being an officer, he agreed.

He rode in amongst the cheerful, drunken mob to where a group was cutting up a cow they had just killed, and asked for a piece. A burly soldier with a knife looked up and, seeing the stained trousers and blood-filled boots of the rider, hurled across with rough good humour the throat and lungs of the slaughtered beast. The hideous slippery object nearly knocked Yashvili from his horse, but he clutched hold firmly and rode back in triumph with the prey to his waiting comrades. They were delighted, and all three rode off furtively. They boiled portions of this unappetising joint in their helmets by a woodland stream.

Yashvili's companions then planned from their map a route, avoiding dangerous centres of population, by which they could attempt to rejoin the army. But first, as no one had the least idea where the enemy was, it was decided to scout out the early part of the march. The two stranger officers decided to ride out some of the way first, and then, if all appeared well, return for the wounded Yashvili. They departed and never returned.

Once again, therefore, he set off alone. He returned to the village he had just visited and enquired whether amongst the soldiers could be found a doctor to change his dressings. Of doctors there were a number, but neither bandages nor any other medical supplies, and so he rode off disconsolately along the dusty road eastwards. Perhaps a peasant woman could provide lint; perhaps he might still find a Soviet unit not totally disorganised. He entered another village. This one was apparently deserted, and he rode slowly between the expressionless wooden houses. At the end of the street, however, he found an old woman, weeping at her garden fence. When she saw the Georgian, she called out in impassioned tones: 'Son, if you have a gun, throw it away!'

He gazed down at her in astonishment as his horse trotted steadily past and round the corner of the street. The woman stared anxiously after him. As she disappeared from sight, Yashvili looked ahead: straight into the muzzle of a rifle. Two enormous German soldiers were standing with levelled guns, one on each side. 'They were so tall, their heads were almost on a level with mine!' He looked from one to the other, and slowly raised his hands. Lieutenant Yashvili's service in the Red Army had come to an abrupt end, and he was a prisoner.

He was not exceptional in this, but he was luckier than most. He was not destined, by the chance of fate, for the horrors of Maidanek or Molodechnoe. His wounds were treated by a doctor in a Minsk pigsty, and he became cook to number 666 Transport Regiment of the Wehrmacht, working for them until, nine months later, they returned to Germany. He himself entered the Fatherland and worked in a bath-house for prisoners of war at Eisenach. There he met healthy and high-spirited English and Americans one week—and emaciated, dying skeletons—his countrymen—the next.

Then, to his horror he was sent to work in Buchenwald. His dread was that the Germans would take his aquiline Georgian nose for that of a Jew. From Buchenwald he was sent to Auschwitz, and now he really thought his time had come. He had already been informed by knowing Germans that his fellow-Georgian, Stalin, was a Jew, and here he was in a place where ethnological judgments tended towards the arbitrary. One factor, perhaps, saved him: as a Christian, he had never been circumcised.

Fortunately for him he spent only one day in Auschwitz. The next, he was whisked out and transported to Katowicz, in Poland. By one of those strange turns, common enough in wartime Germany, he had been grabbed from the abyss and placed where he would most have longed to be—among his compatriots! There was a group of friendly Georgians, gathered from camps all over the Third Reich, and amongst them, of all people, was an old school-friend. They fell weeping on each other's shoulders. It was difficult to believe their good fortune, with the friendly Georgian faces and the old familiar language all around them, and yet they were thousands of miles from home.

But it was not for their pleasure that the Germans had collected together the scattered Georgians. They were informed that they were to join a newly-formed Georgian army unit, intended to assist in the struggle against Bolshevism, and ultimately perhaps free their native mountains from the Russian yoke. Without reflection or hesitation Yashvili accepted his new role, and set off in the company of his compatriots for the Crimea, where the Georgian Division was forming. What was there to consider? In the year of young Yashvili's birth, the Georgian people had seized the opportunity offered by the chaos of the Russian Revolution to restore the independence they had lost in the previous century. In January 1920 the Allied powers had recognised Georgia's independence, and in May they were followed in this by the Soviet Government. Totally distinct from the Russians in history, language and culture, the Georgians now felt that they had (like Finland and Poland) at long last regained their nationhood. But their freedom was short-lived. On 11 February 1921, the Red Army invaded and conquered the country. Thenceforward the Soviets ruled it by force and terror (the first head of the Georgian secret police was the Soviet Himmler, L. P. Beria).

The Yashvilis had felt the effects of the foreign occupation as much as any. Shalva's father had built a small inn in the mountains. This was confiscated by the invading power, and the Yashvilis turned out to live as best they might.

That he had become a traitor by joining an anti-Soviet unit was something Yashvili would have indignantly denied. It was not just that in any case he regarded himself as a Georgian and not a Russian, a Christian and not an atheist. Nor was it that he knew, as everyone else in Russia knew, that great numbers of Russians hated Bolshevik rule, and would welcome its overthrow from whatever quarter (at least, until they began to know the nature of the Nazi beast). As much as, or more than all this was the undeniable fact that Stalin had denied all rights of citizenship and even official recognition of existence to the millions of prisoners who had fallen into German hands.

From the time of the Bolshevik *coup d'état* in 1917, the Soviet Government no longer considered itself a party to the Hague Conventions; nor did it become a signatory of the Geneva Convention of 1929, which defined more precisely the conditions to be accorded to prisoners of war. Despite this, immediately after war broke out in June 1941, the German Government approached the International Red Cross Committee with a view to regulating the conditions of prisoners on both sides. Lists of Russian prisoners were passed to the Soviet Government until September 1941. They then stopped, in the face of continued Soviet refusal to reciprocate. Over the winter the Germans made further efforts to establish relations with the Soviets with a view to introducing the provisions of the Hague and Geneva Conventions, but were rebuffed again.[4] The Red Cross Committee itself then took a hand, approaching the Soviet ambassadors in London and Sweden; these made favourable noises, but on referring the matter to Moscow reverted to an impassive refusal.[5]

Meanwhile Germany's allies, Italy, Rumania and Finland, after likewise trying in vain to come to any mutual arrangement, decided to apply the terms of the Conventions unilaterally to the Russian prisoners in their hands. This generous gesture evoked no response either.[6] The Finns in particular became very concerned about the wretched state of the 47,000 Russian prisoners they held, and gratefully accepted large-scale Red Cross aid, despite the Soviet refusal to allow similar aid to go to Finns imprisoned in Russia.[7]

Not surprisingly, the attitude of the German Government to their Russian prisoners began to harden,[8] and those sections of opinion that opposed ill-treatment lost the influence they might otherwise have had. In any case, the Germans held infinitely more Russian prisoners than the Russians did German. Nearly two-thirds of all Russian prisoners captured fell into German hands in the year 1941.

Hitler himself urged Red Cross inspection of camps. But an appeal to Stalin for prisoners' postal services received a reply that clinched the matter: 'There are no Russian prisoners of war. The Russian soldier fights on till death. If he chooses to become a prisoner, he is automatically excluded from the Russian community. We are not interested in a postal service only for Germans.'[9] Henceforward, not surprisingly, 'the principal base of Hitler's ideology of the conduct of war was the fact that the Soviet Union had not signed the Geneva Convention of 1929, and would therefore certainly not treat German prisoners of war according to its provisions.'[10]

Thus a humane German camp commander provided some small ameliorations in the harsh life of his charges, but explained to a Russian doctor that he could do no more, since Stalin had declined to enter into any agreement.[11] M. Junod, of the Swiss Red Cross, came up continually against this insuperable obstacle when he protested on behalf of the Russians during his tours of camps in Germany. He noted, for example, the striking contrast between a well-run camp for British PoWs at Doessel, where the text of the Geneva Convention was prominently displayed, and an appalling one nearby for the abandoned Russians.

The Convention was by no means a mere 'scrap of paper'.[12]

It would be a mistake to think that Hitler, with all his ruthlessness, did not have a realistic respect for the Convention, once effected. In February 1945 Goebbels, outraged by the Allies' bombing of Dresden, proposed to Hitler the renunciation of the Geneva Convention and the shooting of captured enemy air crews. Hitler approved, but a horrified aide leaked the news to the foreign press. The BBC at once broadcast sharp warnings of retaliatory measures, and the scheme was hastily dropped.[13]

It may be suggested that the Soviet Government's attitude was not a Marxist innovation, but derived from a generally backward Russian heritage. It is in that case salutary to consider for a moment the fate of Russians captured by the Germans in the 1914–18 war. As the Imperial Russian and German governments were both signatories of the Hague Conventions of 1899 and 1907, measures were taken from the beginning to alleviate the prisoners' sufferings. Lists were exchanged, postal services set up, nurses and priests permitted to travel from Russia to German camps, and Orthodox churches were established for the prisoners. The Spanish Government acted as Protecting Power for Russian prisoners, and in effect their interests were also catered for by the United States, Protecting Power for the Russians' allies—British, French and Serb— alongside whom they were generally imprisoned.[14]

A committee was set up by the Empress Alexandra to supply comforts to the prisoners. 'You know my committee will have to ask the government for big sums for our prisoners,' she wrote to the Tsar in 1915; 'we shall never have enough, & the number will be, alas, several millions.' A few weeks later she could report that '4 times a week we send off several waggon loads of things.' On hearing of alleged ill-treatment, she 'cried reading of the horrors the Germans did to our wounded & prisoners . . .'; despite this the Empress urged the Tsar to have German prisoners treated well, as 'then they will be more willing to help our prisoners too.'[15]

Statistics illustrate the comparison. In the war of 1914–17, the Central Powers took 2,417,000 Russian prisoners, with a total mortality of 70,000.[16] In 1941–45, some 5,754,000 Russians were captured by the Germans,[17] 3,700,000 of whom died.[18]

Again, it might be alleged that the catastrophic disasters of 1941 required draconian measures. But the knowledge that prisoners in German hands in 1914 were being well treated does not seem to have had any adverse effect on the loyalty of the Tsar's soldiers. Russian officers were singled out as being the most persistent escapers from German camps;[19] altogether about 260,000 Russians got away, a high proportion to serve again in their own army.[20] Despite intensive German and Bolshevik propaganda in the camps in 1917, a paltry total of 2,000 Ukrainian nationalists was induced to desert to the German Army.[21] In 1944, nearly a million Russians did so.

What Stalin's policy meant for these discarded Russians in 1941 Yashvili had seen at Eisenach. And worse than what he had seen there was what he had smelt when he was cook for the Wehrmacht at Minsk. Outside the city was a camp for Russian prisoners, soldiers and civilians. Or rather, it was not a camp. It was a great expanse of open plain surrounded by electrified wire and machine-gun towers. There lived (not for very long) 60,000 Russians. They were unhoused and virtually unfed; the winter of 1941-2 came on. Month after month in his kitchen Yashvili caught the all-pervading smell of the daily load of Russian corpses heaped onto the camp incinerators. Within a few months the 60,000 had been reduced to a more manageable 11,000.

In the eyes of Western statesmen and diplomats, Yashvili had become a traitor on that day in Katowicz when he volunteered as a recruit for the Georgian Division. But to Stalin he became one on the day he rode slowly past the weeping old woman and into the arms of the German sentries. To surrender, not to die fighting, was the act of a traitor to the Soviet Motherland, and those in this category were written off as though dead. Indeed, about the same time as Shalva Yashvili was being bundled off by the two German giants, his brother was killed in a tank battle on the Baltic frontier, and the boys' father (living in penury after the seizure of his inn) was informed of the *deaths* of both his sons. With the fierce love of their children—especially sons—common to all Caucasians, this was too much for the broken-spirited parent. He suffered a severe heart-attack and himself died shortly afterwards.

I have singled out the story of Shalva Yashvili because it seems to illustrate virtually every important link in the chain that led to so many Soviet citizens falling prisoner to the Germans. The total unexpectedness of 'Operation Barbarossa', the chaos of the opening weeks, the lack of orders, the deserted slave-camp, the fear felt by many officers for their men, the extraordinary efficiency and cunning of the Germans, the inevitable surrender, the horrors of Minsk, the cheerful volunteering for the anti-Communist legion: multiply all these a hundred-thousandfold, and you have the story of the Russian captives. Add to this the fact that Shalva ended the war in Italy, whence he was handed back to the Soviets by the British army—and the outline is complete.

★ ★ ★

By the end of the Second World War, several million Russians had fallen into German hands. The circumstances under which they had done so were very varied, but generally they fell into distinct categories.

First came the forced workers. Nearly three million (including, of course, Ukrainians) volunteered or, more frequently, were tricked or forced into working in the forced labour battalions of National Socialist Germany. By the autumn of 1941, as a result of 'Operation Barbarossa', great areas of western Russia had come under German rule, and thousands of the inhabitants, lured by promises of good pay and conditions, travelled to Germany in search of work. Their own lot was so wretched, and German propaganda so persuasive, that many were grateful for this opportunity. They were swiftly disillusioned: though nominally free labour, they were in fact regarded by many of the German authorities and people as 'niggers', to be exploited as economically as possible. This degrading attitude was epitomised by the offensive Nazi publication, *Der Untermensch*. Himmler's favourite reading, it specialised in contrasting photographs of blond, handsome Germans and hideously subhuman Slavs. As a result, this flow of voluntary labour began to dry up, and six months after permission had been granted to Russians to work in the Reich it was found that only the relatively small number of 70,000 had responded.[22]

But the Russian campaign was swallowing up resources of manpower and machinery unprecedented in history, and the need for labour on a mass scale in German farms, factories and mines had become overwhelming. It was accordingly decided to conscript Russian workers, despite the fact that such a move must militate against the Russians' acceptance of the Germans as deliverers.

The plan for using compulsion on Russian civilians was first put forward by Göring at the end of 1941. The duty for enforcing it fell on Fritz Sauckel, Reich Plenipotentiary for Labour. The ensuing operations resulted in the brutal kidnappings of thousands of men, some whisked off singly, whilst elsewhere the German-employed militia would march an entire church congregation or cinema audience to a waiting transport train. Then they could spend weeks in rickety, old and unheated railway cars, the trucks with their doors sealed and windows wired. Disease, malnutrition and suffering from exposure were rife, and the corpses frequently lay among the living (sixty to a box-car) for days, until they were unceremoniously hurled out on to the embankments. Within a few months even the German authorities had to return 100,000 of these captives as too weak to work.

Once in the Reich they had to work from hideous camps, fully comparable to those operating on an even more massive scale in the

USSR. Nazi propaganda represented the workers as cheerful if primitive artisans, putting their shoulders to the German wheel, and the excellently-produced Nazi magazine *Signal* carried photographs of laughing, well-dressed Ukrainian girls viewing the sights of Berlin. The reality was different. In the camps conditions were squalid beyond conception, with the inmates the worst-fed foreign workers in the Reich (bread made from turnips was a staple diet). During brief hours of relaxation allowed outside the camps, the *Ostarbeiter* were compelled to wear degrading badges identifying them as racially inferior, and were forbidden to enter cinemas, restaurants and other places of public entertainment. Above all, they were forbidden to associate with German women.

Far worse than all this was the fate of those grabbed by Himmler for labour in the concentration camps, in particular Auschwitz and Buchenwald, both of which Yashvili briefly visited. About a hundred thousand died of ill-treatment in such camps—perhaps the lucky ones. The secret agreement whereby Himmler arranged for these transfers with the Ministry of Justice coolly used the phrase 'working to death'. A particularly horrible aspect, in which, as in so much else, the Nazis found themselves vying with their Soviet rivals, was the enforcement of child labour. Boys and girls, from the age of 10 upwards, were conscripted for factory labour, suffering much the same conditions and mortality as their elders.

Altogether some 2,800,000 Soviet citizens were driven into forced labour, of whom about two million were still living in Germany at the end of the war.[23] These formed the greater proportion of the teeming horde of Russians liberated by the Allies in 1945.

Next in number were probably those prisoners of war who had survived the horrors of their conditions of confinement. Of about 5,754,000 Russian prisoners captured by the Germans after 1941, there were some 1,150,000 surviving by May 1945.[24] Add to them two million surviving forced workers, and it will be seen that over three million of the Russians liberated by the Allies had been drawn by force into the vortex of the Third Reich.

A third contrasting category is that of the refugees proper. The lightning speed of the initial German advances, the striking contrast between living standards in the USSR and the rest of Europe, the vengeful attitude of the Soviet Government to any of its citizens 'contaminated' by contact with foreigners—these and a variety of other considerations, political, economic and personal, led thousands to shift westwards from their homes. Many who were in disfavour with the authorities or who had reason to dread ever coming again under the shadow of the NKVD took advantage of the German occupation to remove themselves. Far more fled or were compelled to withdraw as the tide of German victory ebbed. Often, to stay put meant spending days or weeks inside the fighting line, and so, for reasons purely of survival, peasant families piled their scanty possessions in carts and wagons to trudge rutted roads leading to Poland.

The populations of whole districts trekked west after the raising of the siege of Stalingrad in 1943 had heralded the ultimate downfall of Hitlerite Germany. Ethnic and tribal groups had little choice but to escape. There were, for example, the ethnic Germans (*Volksdeutsche*). They were evacuated after 1941, at first to the Warthegau (western Poland)—the region from which their ancestors had migrated two centuries previously.[25]

Again, in the Caucasus a high percentage of the whole population attempted to escape to the Ukraine and further. Amongst the Cossacks of the Kuban and the nations and tribes of the mountains had survived the most prolonged resistance to Bolshevism. It was from there that the White Armies of Generals Kornilov and Denikin had drawn many of their best troops in 1918–20, and guerilla warfare against their Soviet conquerors had persisted endemically ever since. The German occupation forces there behaved on the whole with exemplary restraint, and received broad support from the inhabitants.[26] But when the German Army was ordered to withdraw from the Caucasus at the end of 1943, large sections of the population, Cossacks and others, set off in the depths of winter to escape a fate of which they were only too well aware. An eye-witness in a city through which the exodus passed described how, all night, 'I could hear the creaking of wagon wheels and the shouts of the drivers under my window. People rode on horseback, on bulls, on cows, or just walked, having loaded their travelling bags on someone's carts ... In some villages almost all the houses were deserted.'[27] In the freezing weather of a Russian January, terrified crowds crossed the steppe, to be ferried across the frozen straits of Kerch to the Crimea. Many died of cold and hunger; others were strafed by low-flying Red Airforce planes.[28]

It is difficult to estimate even approximately the total number of such wartime refugees. Possibly one million would be near the mark, but as great numbers later joined (or were pressed into) the Russian labour and military units formed by the Germans, it is impossible to separate them statistically from those other categories considered in this chapter. Nor would there be any great value in doing so, as the motives and circumstances which impelled them to leave their native land were so varied. Their social and intellectual backgrounds were equally heterogeneous, ranging from frightened peasant women to engineers, doctors and scholars.

From the millions of Russians who came to Germany after 1941, as refugees, prisoners, or victims of forced labour camps, we now turn to that significant section that elected to fight, or to assist the Germans to fight, the Red Army. Altogether, between 800,000 and a million volunteered to help the invaders of their country.

The first major defection of Russian soldiers to the German Army took place on 22 August 1941, when the war between Germany and Russia was exactly two months old. It was at the front, near Mogilev in Byelorussia, that Lieutenant-General Count von Schenckendorff received a Cossack emissary, offering the surrender of his unit. This was the Soviet 436th Infantry Regiment, commanded by a Major Ivan Nikitich Kononov. On receiving von Schenckendorff's assurances of safe-conduct, Kononov assembled his men and laid bare his intentions. He explained that now had at last come a chance to fight against Stalin and the hated Communist system, and ended with words similar to those of Pizarro on the Isle of Gallo: 'Those who wish to go with me, take up their position on the right, and those who wish to stay, on the left. I promise those who wish to stay that they will not suffer.' The entire regiment moved to the right, and some hours later General von Schenckendorff found himself one regiment to the good.

Kononov, born in the Don Cossack territory in 1903, had an exemplary Red Army record. But ever since the gross mismanagement of the Finnish War he had contemplated this step, and now had come his opportunity. In his ignorance of the realities of Nazi policy towards Russia, he imagined that his unit could form the nucleus of a Russian Liberation Army. Millions of his suffering compatriots would come over to join him, and Stalin would be left alone with his NKVD cronies. Count von Schenckendorff, an intelligent and honest officer, entirely shared Kononov's view. But he also knew something of Hitler and the Party chiefs' plans for the total destruction of Russia as a nation. For the moment he kept his fears to himself, and Kononov and his delighted companions found themselves reconstituted as the 102nd Cossack Regiment. As such they fought bravely against the Red Army and the partisans.[29]

In all, hundreds of thousands of Russians came forward to assist in the overthrow of Stalin, and in time a leader was found for them. General Andrei Andreievich Vlasov was one of the ablest generals in the Red Army. His forces were surrounded and cut off by the enemy in the summer of 1942, and on 13 July he became a prisoner. He came of a family of poor peasants from Nizhni-Novgorod, but was a man of exceptional charm and integrity. The Abwehr and influential quarters of the General Staff saw in him the ideal leader for the Russian Liberation Army (*Russkaya Osvoboditel'naya Armiya*: ROA) whose alliance perceptive Germans realised had become essential to victory over Bolshevism. Hauled out of his prison camp at Vinnitsa, Vlasov agreed to work towards this aim, despite insulting restrictions imposed on him, his cause and his compatriots by the Nazi leadership. After many vicissitudes and complex intrigues, Vlasov eventually found himself appointed nominal leader of an 'army' that came to total nearly a million men.

But, except for a few brief weeks at the end of the war, the ROA existed as an army only on paper, largely for propaganda purposes. Men were drafted into the Todt labour battalions, the Caucasian legions, auxiliary units (such as Kononov's regiment) of regular German detachments (*Hiwis*), or into the Cossack Corps. But General Vlasov himself could not, until 1945, give orders to a single Russian private. Hitler's ideology left no more room for a free, national Russia than it did for a Bolshevik one.

Thus General von Schenckendorff's fears proved justified, and Vlasov and those who joined him were caught between the two sides. In that front line that Stalin never quite brought himself to visit, a Red Army sergeant had been wounded, decorated twice, and was only captured by the Germans when they dug out his unconscious body from the ruins of Odessa. Later he joined Vlasov's ROA, justifying his action in this terse and bitter speech:

> You think, Captain, that we sold ourselves to the Germans for a piece of bread? Tell me, why did the Soviet Government forsake us? Why did it forsake millions of prisoners? We saw prisoners of all nationalities, and they were taken care of. Through the Red Cross they received parcels and letters from home; only the Russians received nothing. In Kassel I saw American Negro prisoners, and they shared their cakes and chocolates with us. Then why didn't the Soviet Government, which we considered our own, send us at least some plain hard tack? . . . Hadn't we fought? Hadn't we defended the Government? Hadn't we fought for our country? If Stalin refused to have anything to do with us, we didn't want to have anything to do with Stalin![30]

2

Russian Prisoners in British Captivity: The Controversy Opens

By THE SPRING OF 1944 IT WAS CLEAR THAT THE LONG-DEFERRED SECOND Front was about to be opened. The daring and dangerous venture required meticulous planning, and among the factors to be taken into account was the question of the Russian troops in German service. Following his suspicion that they were more interested in the restoration of Russia than the preservation of Germany, Hitler had had nearly all transferred from the East to the Balkans, Italy, France and Norway. Western Intelligence was therefore anxious to appraise their fighting capacity, and to consider means of eliminating them from the coming struggle.

On 21 February 1944 Military Intelligence in London submitted a 'Most Secret' report on 'Employment of Russian natives in France'. This divided the Russians into three basic categories. First came the Eastern Legions, that is, the German-officered regiments of Kalmucks, Georgians, Azerbaidjanis and other anti-Soviet minorities. These included the Cossacks in the Balkans, 'who are in a class by themselves and to whom fighting, for anyone who will hire their services, is the breath of life'. Next came former Russian prisoners of war enrolled in the more or less paper 'Vlasov' Army of Liberation. These two categories were reported as being viewed with suspicion, and officered by Germans. Lastly came the forced-labour battalions of the Todt organisation, who were employed in military construction work but came officially under the aegis of the Legions and Vlasov units.

It was estimated that a total of 200,000 such Russians had already arrived in France since the previous year, and that many more were likely to pour in. It must have been clear to them all that the end of Hitler's Germany was but a matter of time. As the MI3 report pointed out: 'They have burned their boats and have little to hope from a victory by either side. In these circumstances it is reasonable to suppose that they will fight well, so long as they do fight. But it is further reasonable to suppose that they would seize the first chance of escaping from their dilemma by deserting to the opposing forces, if any hope of rehabilitation were held out to them.'

The report ended by suggesting that the Russians in France represented a particularly fertile field for propaganda. Could not assurances be given to these people that desertion to the Allies or the Resistance would earn them the right to more lenient treatment than they would otherwise have a right to expect?[1]

Clearly there was little to lose by making the attempt. Unfortunately, there was one hurdle to be crossed before Political Warfare Executive could set to work. Could the Soviet Government be persuaded to confirm such a policy of leniency to capitulating Russians, and, if not, how far was it possible to offer or implement any promises? This would involve a political decision, and the report was passed to the Foreign Office for consideration.

The Foreign Office experts were pessimistic about the prospect, and a long ding-dong debate ensued. As Victor Cavendish-Bentinck of MI3 pointed out: 'I think that later on, perhaps after the war, it will be very difficult to defend the attitude of refraining from weakening the will to resist of 200,000 Russians in France and the Low Countries and thereby losing British and American lives for the sake of sparing Russian susceptibilities.'

Sir Robert Bruce Lockhart, for Political Warfare Executive, agreed. As the proposed recipients of propaganda appeals were of enormously diverse political opinions, the only effective bait would be the promise of good treatment. 'But before we can make such promises we would have to be sure that HMG would not agree under pressure from Moscow to hand the men over to the Soviet Government. Can we be sure of this and also that at the first breath of Russian criticism we shall not be told to stop the broadcasts?'

But to this Geoffrey Wilson, today Chairman of Oxfam but at that time in the Foreign Office's Northern Department, responded: 'I think we could ignore Russian criticism of our broadcasting to these men but I do not see how we could refuse to hand them over to the Russians after the war if we were pressed to do so by Moscow. If such an assurance is a *sine qua non* of broadcasting to them, I think we shall have to drop the matter.'

Two months had passed since the first proposals to undermine the morale of the Russians in France, and still no decision had been made. Wilson's superior, Christopher Warner, put 'the matter up for decision on high': would Russians responding to such an appeal have on demand to be handed over to the Soviets? And if so, could any effective guarantees of fair treatment be extracted? D-Day was looming nearer, and, with every nerve stretched, General Eisenhower was desperately anxious that the landings should not prove to be another Dieppe. Every possible method of weakening or confusing the Germans must be tried. From SHAEF Headquarters at Bushey Park he despatched an urgent message to the Combined Chiefs of Staff, asking them to check with the Soviets what promises could be made to Russian elements in France, and stating that whatever could 'sow some seeds of distrust in the minds of the German associates of these foreigners . . . will be a bonus to the operations in varying degree'.[2]

As a result of these pressures from the military authorities, the British Ambassador in Moscow (Sir Archibald Clark Kerr) wrote on 28 May to Molotov. He requested Soviet approval for an offer of amnesty to be made to those Russians who had been compelled (this was the tacit assumption) to serve the Germans, and who surrendered at the earliest opportunity. Known traitors, volunteers, and members of SS units were specifically excluded.[3]

The answer came three days later in the form of a telegram to the Chiefs of Staff from the Allied Military Missions in Moscow. The message was dourly abrupt: 'Word has just been received from the Soviet Foreign Office concerning amnesty of Russians forced into service with German Forces in the west. The Soviet Foreign Office stated that according to information at the disposal of the Russians, the number of such persons is insignificant and that no political interest would be served in making a special appeal to them.'[4]

As the current British estimate of the number involved now stood at 470,000, Victor Cavendish-Bentinck pointed out that this was, 'as the Soviet Government are well aware, a lie'. It was a lie the Foreign Office felt obliged to swallow.[5]

It was presumably on the same grounds that the USSR refused to enter into an arrangement with SHAEF in regard to the anticipated refugee problem that would follow the invasion.[6]

In the event neither the Foreign Office nor SHAEF felt the game worth the candle and, officially at any rate, dropped the scheme of sowing dissension among the Germans' Russian auxilaries. Time in any case was rushing on, and the discussion was overtaken by events. Within a week of the receipt of the Soviets' denial that there were any

Russians worth speaking of serving alongside the Germans, the most gigantic transmarine invasion ever launched was under way. By nightfall on 6 June well over 100,000 troops had established bridgeheads on the Normandy coast.

Within two days the War Office notified the Foreign Office that British troops had captured half a dozen Russians in their haul of prisoners. Geoffrey Wilson told his War Office opposite number that for the moment they should be treated as ordinary (i.e. German) prisoners of war. At the same time he requested that they be interrogated as to the circumstances of their joining the German forces, their views on the possibility of being returned to the USSR, and their assessment of the morale of their compatriots as yet uncaptured. The Foreign Office was thus from the beginning provided with innumerable case-histories of very humble Russian subjects of Stalin.

As the interrogation reports soon revealed,[7] the Russians had enlisted for a variety of motives. But it was clear that the majority had had little choice in the matter and felt little enthusiasm for the German cause. Even amongst the volunteers there was a marked distaste for fighting the British and Americans: they had, after all, joined to free their country from Communism. For the most part they were frightened and confused, and felt only relief at being captured by such humane enemies.

Many had suffered fearfully at the hands of the Germans. On 28 June *The Times* reporter recounted a harrowing story:

At a hospital in Bayeux today I heard a terrible story of German treatment of Russian prisoners in the Channel Islands, to which they had been transported to work on fortifications. Of one group of 2,000 only 1,000 remained alive after six months, and of these 500 were unable to stand. They had been given sacks for clothing and foot-wear, and had suffered unspeakable tortures from the rubber truncheons of their guards. Eventually the 500 dying men were brought to the mainland through Cherbourg, but the locomotive of their train was destroyed by allied aircraft, and five of them managed to crawl away into fields, where they were found starving by French people, and were handed over to the care of nuns. They had lived for months in captivity on 20 grammes of bread a day. One had a jaw broken in three places, and his body was a mass of scars. Tears ran down their faces when they heard that Cherbourg had been liberated.[8]

Of politics these pitiful people knew nothing. All their lives they had been harried hither and thither in the name of confused ideologies by commanders whose languages they frequently could not understand. A photograph in the Imperial War Museum may be taken to epitomise the predicament of these lost souls. A Turkestani prisoner is standing before two of his captors in Normandy: officers of the 51st Highland Division. His unit can be distinguished by the badge on his sleeve, the embroidered image of a mosque below an invocation to Allah. He is smiling amiably, like a good-natured and hefty child. He cannot understand what they are saying, any more than he could previously understand the German NCOs of his regiment, or before that (in all probability) the Soviet Russian rulers of his native land.[9]

George Orwell, who was reporting on events in Normandy, provided an equally pathetic and even stranger story. Amongst the 'Russians' captured in France were found two men, of oriental appearance, whose nationality at first no one could identify. Eventually, after prolonged investigation, it was discovered that they were Tibetans. They had strayed with their herds on to Soviet territory, been conscripted into a labour battalion, and captured by the Germans. Their new masters sent them to work in North Africa and subsequently to join a fighting unit in France. There they surrendered to the British. During all this time they were unable to speak to anyone but each other, as they spoke only Tibetan![10]

Confirmation of the probable accuracy of Orwell's story comes from an account by a German imprisoned in the Soviet forced-labour camp at Vorkuta from 1949 to 1954. A fellow-prisoner was a Tibetan named Babi, whose history reads remarkably like an abbreviated version of the story just related.[11]

Prisoners taken during the Normandy fighting were promptly transported to the United Kingdom, where they were placed in some of the camps recently vacated by the troops employed in 'Operation Overlord'. One month after D-Day, there were 1,200 Russian prisoners in Britain.[12] The question of what to do with them was becoming a pressing one.

Within two days of the Normandy landing, a party of Russian prisoners was being interrogated at Kempton Park. They had for the most part been captured by the Germans in 1942 and conscripted into labour battalions. Harshly treated by their German NCOs, their life had been one of brutalised drudgery. They were forbidden to write home, and, speaking only Russian, were entirely cut off from the outside world. 'When the Allies started bombarding the beach, the Russians say—they just sat and waited for things to happen. The German NCOs did not interfere and did not even try to force them to put up any resistance'. Now they were in British hands, they appeared as resigned as ever to a fate that had long ago removed any element of choice in their lives. 'Many seemed to feel, however, that after having served in the German Army, even though forcibly conscripted, they would be treated as traitors by the Russians and probably shot.'[13]

Not all the prisoners contented themselves with gloomy sentiments, and soon the authorities received their first glimpse of what it meant to be a Russian faced with the possibility of compulsory return to the world's first Marxist state. On 17 July the War Office notified the Foreign Office Prisoners of War Department of the suicides of two prisoners, named Agofanow and Melnikow. Agofanow had drowned himself, whilst Melnikow died of self-inflicted wounds. The latter was said to have been afflicted by 'acute melancholia'.[14]

The majority, however, reacted to similar fears in a different fashion. It is necessary to keep in mind a clear picture of the prisoners' peculiar situation. In some respects they were enjoying a happier life than most of them had hitherto experienced. Even a spartan and drab existence in an army camp on the edge of a bleak Yorkshire moor must have seemed a haven of security and tranquillity after a lifetime of blows and privations under Stalin and Hitler, and the Russians were pathetically grateful for the smallest comforts.

Despite this, most were aware that their predicament was uncertain and dangerous. In small, tightly-knit communities of isolated and relatively ignorant men, rumours and fears abounded. It was, as my friend Mr. Czeslaw Jesman (who knew the camps and their inmates probably better than any man) has told me, in a state of 'limbo-GULAG' that these bewildered folk found themselves suspended. Their knowledge of the political situation was minimal; they had after all lived out their lives under two political systems, one of whose principal purposes was the suppression of information inimical to their dogmas. They were, moreover, in general men of little education. Their first emotion on entering the British camps must have been one of relief.

But, starved of information as they were, they were not entirely unaware of the direction in which events were moving. Some of the early Allied propaganda directed at these men when still in German service had naïvely promised them repatriation to the USSR as a reward for desertion.[15] German propaganda had more realistically held this over them as a warning of what surrender would entail.

The fears and speculations of the prisoners were greatly heightened by the mysterious—eventually sinister—silence of the Soviet authorities. Three months passed from the arrival of the prisoners in Britain until the first appearance of Soviet officials in the camps. British officials were unable to fathom the purpose of this delay; the prisoners were utterly bewildered. Many suspected that the British themselves were preventing any contact. Fearing that their enforced silence might accentuate Soviet estimates of their guilt when their presence was discovered, they began to clamour to be allowed to see embassy or other representatives of their country. Long accustomed to propaganda representations of the English as masters of perfidy and double-dealing, many prisoners began to fear that some deep deception was being practised that could cost them dearly. A harassed Colonel Baxter wrote from the War Office to Patrick Dean at the Foreign Office: 'If anything can be done to persuade the Soviet authorities to go to the Camp at which these men are kept at Canons Park in North London the position would be greatly eased.'[16]

Fearing their anomalous position, the prisoners were desperate to enlighten the Soviet authorities as to their motives and predicament. One such appeal, signed by three subalterns, simply begged of their camp commandant: 'We, the undersigned, wish to know whether we may communicate with the Russian Representative in England to clear our position?'

Others directed their letters to the Soviet Embassy itself, recapitulating at length their terrible sufferings at the hands of the Germans, and declaring themselves to be 'animated by a burning desire to resume our fight against fascism in which all the Soviet people are taking part'. Such appeals were forwarded to the Embassy, but an ominous silence was all they elicited.[17]

The Soviet official attitude appeared still to be that there were no Russians worth speaking of serving with the German Army or captured therefrom. In early July Soviet pressure forced General Eisenhower himself to repudiate an innocuous press report allegedly made on the subject by one of his staff officers.[18] The Soviet dilemma is easy to detect. Its apparatus of dictatorship and terror rested for justification entirely on its claim to represent the will of the down-trodden millions. Other governments sustained themselves in power only by a mixture of cajolery and brutality, and their subject populations were waiting for an opportune moment to rise in revolt. Lenin, Trotsky and Stalin had in turn deluded themselves that the workers of Germany would turn on their capitalist-militarist masters rather than fight their fellow-workers' republic in Russia.

Yet the facts pointed the other way. Of all the nations in Europe, the USSR was the only one to witness nearly a million of its subjects enlisting in the enemy army. (A protracted campaign to raise a similar force from among British prisoners resulted in the recruitment of thirty drunken misfits.)[19] Lenin had boasted that the deserting Russian armies in 1917 had 'voted with their feet' against the Provisional

Government and its war policy. What then of those who had deserted Stalin, taken up arms against him, and now preferred in so many cases suicide or self-mutilation to a return to Russia? Western public opinion had been persuaded that the rule of the Communist Party in Russia rested on a popular basis: how would that opinion, so vital to Stalin's postwar expansionist aims, bear up to the spectacle of thousands of hostile Russians abroad? Russians, moreover, who were unmistakably working-class, of a material poverty unknown in the comfortable West, and who could reveal to the West the horrors of GULAG.[20]

Despite earlier Soviet denials that there were any Russians in the Wehrmacht, the Foreign Office soon felt obliged to consider raising the matter with the Soviet Government. Something had to be done soon, in view of the numbers involved.

On 17 July the War Cabinet met to consider the matter. The Foreign Secretary, Anthony Eden, opened the brief discussion by explaining that there were now about 1,500 Russian prisoners in the country. He was in favour of handing them back to the Soviets. Winston Churchill summed up the ensuing discussion by suggesting that the Soviet authorities be notified of the presence of the Russians. Their ambivalent position as former allies of the Germans should be shown in the most extenuating light, and if possible their return should be delayed.

The feeling of the Cabinet was clearly uneasy as to the reception the prisoners might experience on their return. Eden suggested a proviso: 'In order not to discourage surrender on the part of others impressed by the Germans to fight against us, we should ask that no steps should be taken to deal with these Russians until the end of hostilities.'[21]

Following the Cabinet's direction, Eden wrote three days later to the Soviet Ambassador. After explaining the circumstances and numbers in which the prisoners had come into British hands, he pointed out the difficulties of maintaining such large numbers in transit camps. He suggested therefore that the Soviet Military Mission in London contact their opposite numbers in the War Office as soon as possible with a view to coming to a satisfactory arrangement.[22]

It will be noted that this letter made no mention of the Cabinet hope that the Soviet Government would refrain from harsh treatment of the prisoners until the war was over. This possibly provocative reservation was to be held over until the Ambassador's reply was received.[23] The Foreign Secretary was obliged to wait for over a month for this, as we have seen; meanwhile the numbers continued to increase, and vexed questions in connection with the issue to be aired.

Long before the D-Day landing, Russian prisoners had been falling into the hands of the British Army. As the Allies fought their way from opposite ends of North Africa to Tunis in 1942–3, they seized many of these ubiquitous Russians. Most were, as in Normandy, members of forced-labour contingents. All these men generally spent a week in a transit camp at Alexandria, before travelling on by rail and road to Haifa, Baghdad and Teheran, and so to the Soviet frontier. Many in each party expressed terrified fear as to what would happen to them in the USSR. Others, however, assured concerned British officers in Baghdad that they were confident of receiving a hero's welcome on returning home. Some managed to escape, but the presence of NKVD commissars ensured that the majority reached home safely.[24] There they were instantly placed in a wired camp on a desert gulf of the Caspian, preparatory to being transported in cattle-trucks to the Arctic labour camp at Vorkuta.[25]

With the invasion of Italy, the number of Russians being shipped out to the transit camp in Egypt increased substantially.[26] The situation was different from that obtaining in Normandy in one respect, however. On 9 July 1944 it was reported by Lord Moyne, the Resident Minister in Cairo, 'that no Russians have actually been captured with the German formations as in France and any who may have served therein have in all cases deserted'.[27] Many were escaped prisoners of war or deserters from German units in Greece.[28]

On 15 June, at the same time as the first prisoners from Normandy were arriving in England, Lord Moyne had notified the Foreign Office that forty-one of the escapers from Greece were being repatriated via Aleppo and Teheran.[29] Heavily involved in discussions on this very theme in London, the Foreign Office did not reply for a fortnight. Conceding that it was probably too late to stop the despatch of the forty-one, the telegram, when it came, instructed Moyne not to return further Russians likely to face serious punishment which might provoke German reprisals.[30]

A Soviet mission under a General Sudakov was operating in Egypt, selecting Russians due for repatriation. As Lord Moyne pointed out in telegrams to the Foreign and War Offices, the distinction between those volunteering to return and those refusing was far from effectively answering the question. Lord Moyne's reply is significant in its own context, and also in that it exemplifies a situation that was to recur on an ever-increasing scale.

> Of party of 408 shipped as ex PW offrs 3 O[ther] R[anks] 6 have opted to remain, about 15 have expressed intention to escape en route. Others who would like to stay fear further change of British policy would result in them being handed over to the Soviet authorities before the end of the war

with the result that their fate, having opted not ... to return to the USSR, would be even more certain. The presence of three Political Commissars in this party probably prevented further applications to remain. ... Sudakov admitted that the 2,006 PW included about 15 men held under close arrest by other Russian PWs on his orders. One he specifically mentioned was alleged to have served with the German Gestapo. He indicated that the Soviet authorities had a special fate in store for these. Sudakov left a Russian Major Bolobokov to live with prison camp staff until question of final disposal of the 2,006 was decided. There can be little doubt that his control exercised through Political Commissars among the prisoners is responsible for the small number who have openly opted to remain. It is for these reasons that it is impossible to guarantee that no ... punishment will be given to repatriates with subsequent risk of reprisals against British PWs in German hands.[31]

The view of the British Foreign Office on the repatriation question passed through a succession of logical stages, affected in large part by the increasing inevitability of German collapse. These consisted, firstly, of refusing to send back any prisoners whom it was feared the Soviets might punish before the cessation of hostilities (and hence avoiding any possibility of German reprisals).[32] The only effective way of sifting such repatriates was by fulfilling the wishes of individual prisoners. The next step was to send all back, at the same time requiring an undertaking by the Soviet authorities that no public punishment of repatriates should occur until the collapse of Germany. This, however, was not forthcoming, and in any case would hardly have been 'worth the paper it is written on'. [33] Finally the never very strong hope of obtaining any Soviet undertaking was abandoned, and the policy of repatriating all, regardless of their wishes, came fully into being, without conditions.

This gradual progression in policy took place over the summer months of 1944, and it was events themselves that in large part overtook policy decision-making. Firstly, the Soviets, for reasons of their own, remained commendably discreet over the fate of their returned citizens. Secondly, the Germans evinced no desire to take up the cudgels on this question; indeed, every month that the war progressed saw the power of the German Government dwindle. Its attitude could be increasingly discounted.

By June 1944 the Foreign Office was determined that all the Russians should be returned eventually, whatever the fate in store for them. Geoffrey Wilson in March had anticipated the possibility. On 24 June, Patrick Dean (Assistant Legal Adviser at the Foreign Office) asserted: 'In due course all those with whom the Soviet authorities desire to deal must, subject to what is said below, be handed over to them, and we are not concerned with the fact that they may be shot or otherwise more harshly dealt with than they might be under English law.'

The proviso referred to was the necessity for obviating any danger of German reprisals.[34]

But the War Office attitude was different. On the same day that the Cabinet had met to consider the problem for the first time (17 July), the Foreign Office was notified that: 'The War Office is only prepared to agree to hand over to the Soviet Authorities those Russians who are willing to go and we do not agree that any pledge should be given in a contrary sense to the Soviet Government.'[35] As we saw, the Cabinet adopted a muted version of this proviso, but omitted even that from its letter to the Soviet Ambassador.[36] In the absence of any reply from M. Gousev little could be done but settle increasing numbers of Russian prisoners in camps in Britain. Their status and fate were still uncertain.

It was at this point, however, that the stranded Russians in 'limbo-GULAG' found a powerful ally. The Minister of Economic Warfare was Lord Selborne; he was also responsible for the sabotage and espionage units operating in occupied Europe under Special Operations Executive. A staunch Christian and a high-principled statesman, Lord Selborne felt a rising horror at the crime he sensed was about to take place. On 21 July he wrote in strong terms to the Foreign Secretary, Anthony Eden:

> I am profoundly moved by the decision of the Cabinet to send back to Russia all Russian subjects in the German army who fall into our hands on the battlefields of Europe. I propose to address the Prime Minister on this subject, but before doing so, would like you to know the grounds of my opposition, in the hope that we may find ourselves in agreement on the subject.
>
> As you may know, one of my officers has during the past four weeks interviewed a number of Russian prisoners, and in every case their story is substantially the same. In the first place they were subject to incredible hardship and treatment on being taken prisoner. They were marched in many cases for several days without any food. They were placed in concentration camps under appalling sanitary conditions and were starved. They became infested with vermin, they were the victims of loathsome diseases, and starvation was carried to such a point that cannibalism became prevalent. In more than one instance the Germans filmed cannibalistic meals for propaganda purposes.[37]

After several weeks of such treatment, Lord Selborne continued, the prisoners were required to volunteer for service in a German labour battalion. As those who declined were shot, it was not surprising that numbers did volunteer. Now they were in British hands, the Russians, almost without exception, expressed the greatest fear at the prospect of being returned home. Forty-five had been interviewed from three separate camps, and their stories were convincingly similar. They expected to be shot on arrival, or at least despatched to Siberia. They frequently drew attention to the well-known fact that the Soviet Government did not even acknowledge the existence of Russian prisoners in German hands. Those who had borne German uniform felt particularly compromised, and could expect short shrift. Finally, the fact that they had witnessed the immeasurably higher standard of living enjoyed by workers in Western countries would render them permanently suspect.

Lord Selborne felt these accounts carried conviction, and was deeply concerned at 'the prospect of sending back many thousands of men to die, either by execution or in Siberia . . .' Not only would this be inhumane, but also it would effectively deter Russians still uncaptured from surrendering or joining the Maquis. The Cabinet, he urged, should not enter into any commitments over the prisoners' fate at this stage.

Lord Selborne concluded this moving appeal by noting that he had been told by M. Emmanuel d'Astier, Commissioner of the Interior in the French Provisional Government, that it was likely that France would offer her traditional political asylum to Russians who offered to join Free French forces—either in the Foreign Legion, or in Madagascar or some other French colony. The Soviets had in any case not asked for the prisoners (Gousev's demand reached Eden two days later), and might well be suspicious of an unsolicited offer.

'I therefore suggest that, in the interests of humanity, we keep our hands free as to what to do with these Russian prisoners after the war. If their number is not too great there should be no difficulty in absorbing them in some of the underpopulated countries of the world.'

Lord Selborne sent a copy of this letter to Major Desmond Morton, who was then Personal Assistant to Winston Churchill. In his covering letter he stressed: 'I feel very strongly on this matter.'[38]

As he had told Eden, Lord Selborne sent the Prime Minister a brief summary of the letter quoted above. Passing it on to its destination, Major Morton informed Churchill of the recent reply received from Moscow, which demanded the return of all the prisoners, and added that, 'Lord Selborne's proposed solution would seem to come too late.' The Prime Minister studied Lord Selborne's appeal at once, writing next day to Eden: 'I think we dealt rather summarily with this at Cabinet, and the point put by the Minister of Economic Warfare should certainly be reconsidered. Even if we are somewhat compromised, all the apparatus of delay may be used. I think these men were tried beyond their strength.'[39]

Churchill clearly felt unhappy at the thought of subjecting these unfortunate people to further sufferings, but it is hard to see in what way he could regard the British position as 'somewhat compromised' on the issue. So far the Government had communicated once only with the Soviets on this subject. This was the letter of 20 July, which merely stated the British anxiety 'as soon as possible to learn the views of the Soviet Government as to disposal of these Soviet nationals'. The Cabinet decision of 17 July, which had decided on compulsory return of prisoners if demanded, had not been communicated to the Soviets. The British Government, in theory at least, was free to adopt any policy it chose.

Eden had now to consider the weighty arguments advanced by Lord Selborne against his proposed policy of forced repatriation, backed as they were by the troubled conscience of the Prime Minister. His immediate reaction was one of testy impatience. He scrawled across Selborne's letter: 'Dept. what do you say to all this? It doesn't deal with point, if these men don't go back to Russia, where are they to go? We don't want them here.' However, it would require more than this to win over the Prime Minister and Cabinet. Eden's prime difficulty in answering the Minister of Economic Warfare's charges lay in the fact that they were true; indeed, if anything they represented an under-statement of the terrible fate and dilemma of the Russian prisoners. To Lord Selborne himself Eden replied in an informal acknowledgment: 'I realise that many of them must have suffered terribly while they were in German hands, but the fact remains that their presence in the German formations is at the least helping to retard our own forces.'[40] This can hardly have satisfied Lord Selborne, the point of whose proposal was that the Russians should be induced to work for the Allies.

The officer whom Lord Selborne mentions as interrogating the prisoners was Major L. H. Manderstam. Of South African origin, he had been born in Riga and as a result was brought up as a fluent Russian-speaker. When the war broke out in 1939, an adventurous spirit led him into a series of Richard Hannay-like operations against the enemy in Africa. He was clearly ideal material for SOE, and soon became one of their most daring operatives. Soon after D-Day he was sent to France to interrogate any Russian prisoners falling into British hands. There he interviewed some of the earliest prisoners taken; later, he returned to interrogate prisoners in camps in England. He felt particularly badly about their fate, as numbers had been induced to surrender as a result of SOE leaflets promising (in good faith) that Russians surrendering would receive asylum in the West, if they wished.

The pathetic stories he heard rang true, and were confirmed by unprompted repetition. After Lord Selborne had sent his letters, based on Manderstam's reports, to Eden and Churchill, the Foreign Office set its best brains to work to test the evidence there set out. Manderstam learned of this, and himself called on Christopher Warner, then Head of the Northern Department, who dismissed Manderstam's reports as inaccurate and naïve. Manderstam, who, unlike Warner, had seen and conversed with the proposed victims, replied heatedly. Warner haughtily ordered him from his office, and sent in a damning report to SOE, which that organisation rejected.[41]

It so happened that the Foreign Office, unlike Lord Selborne, did not have to rely exclusively on Major Manderstam's testimony in order to form an accurate estimate of the prisoners' predicament. For on the very same day (21 July) that Lord Selborne sent his plea to Eden, the Foreign Office received a highly significant report from Lord Moyne in Cairo from which a passage has already been quoted. Russian prisoners shipped out from Greece and Italy confirmed at every point the history and fears related by their fellows captured in Normandy. More than this, Lord Moyne provided proof on the one point in Major Manderstam's report that rested unavoidably on conjecture. Many of the prisoners Manderstam spoke to were 'convinced that if they are sent back they will certainly be shot'; Lord Moyne heard from the Soviet repatriation General himself, Sudakov, that many of the prisoners 'are due for liquidation on their return'.[42]

The Foreign Office had in fact been long aware of the Soviet Government's callous abandonment of all its citizens who fell into German hands. In February 1942 the International Committee of the Red Cross telegraphed Molotov that the United Kingdom had given permission for the USSR to buy food for the prisoners in her African colonies, the Canadian Red Cross was offering a gift of five hundred vials of vitamins, and Germany had agreed to collective consignments of foodstuffs for PoWs. 'All these offers and communications from the ICRC to the Soviet authorities remained unanswered, either directly or indirectly', states the report of the Red Cross. And all appeals by the ICRC itself, parallel negotiations undertaken by the Protecting Powers'or by neutral or friendly Powers, met with no better response.[43]

In Britain, the Foreign Office considered appeals from various sections of public opinion anxious to help the Russians, but concluded that there was regretfully nothing that could be done. In September

1942, Anthony Eden informed Sir Stafford Cripps that 'the Soviet Government . . . have throughout displayed a remarkable indifference to the plight of their prisoners. Their consistency indeed on this subject shows clearly that there are strong motives of policy behind their attitude . . .'[44] The matter was raised again a year later, but with the same negative result.[45] In May 1942 Molotov had similarly rejected a suggestion by Roosevelt that some humanitarian arrangement be made with the German Government.[46]

It was not for the Foreign Office to intervene futher; indeed, it did not feel intervention was really called for. As one of its officials, Donald Maclean, put it: 'My own feeling is that we have already pushed the parcels business to farcical lengths by sending a *parcel a week* to our own prisoners, and that we should do well not to open the question of parcels for Russian prisoners of war who probably number about 3,000,000 unless the Russians ask our help.' A chorus of 'I agree's' followed from his superiors.[47]

(Stalin's attitude was not so harsh, oddly enough. He did not disapprove of Red Cross parcels for British prisoners; indeed, thousands of tons of food and medicine were landed at Vladivostock under the auspices of the Red Cross, and transported across Soviet territory to provide relief for British, American and Dutch prisoners of the Japanese.[48] It was only *Russian* prisoners that he wished to deny aid and comfort.)

When Eden and his Foreign Office aides set out to compile a reply to Lord Selborne's plea, they were therefore exceedingly well informed as to the realities of the situation. On 2 August Eden's brief was prepared, and he wrote at length to the Prime Minister. His reply to Lord Selborne is a document of the first importance, since it provides the fullest and most closely-reasoned argument in favour of the policy of compulsory repatriation.

His first argument scouted Lord Selborne's suggestion that measures of forced repatriation would be inhumane. 'In spite of the report to which the Minister of Economic Warfare refers there are other reports and evidence which show that a large proportion of the prisoners, whatever their reasons, are willing and even anxious to return to Russia. They were captured while serving in German military or paramilitary formations, the behaviour of which in France has often been revolting. We cannot afford to be sentimental about this.'

Since the list of prisoners sent to Patrick Dean at the Foreign Office on 26 July included civilians who had spent their entire time in France in hospital; civilians who had been in gaol as a result of refusing to help the Germans; hospital orderlies, a doctor, escapers from prisoner-of-war camps, and several children[49]—perhaps Eden could have afforded to be more sympathetic.

Also, although elements of a few units are said to have behaved badly, the vast majority had little inclination for committing atrocities. Many had been too brutally treated by their German officers and NCOs to be capable of injuring anyone. Moreover, no less than 8,000 joined the French Resistance, and the Soviets themselves claimed that these inflicted 3,500 casualties on the Germans.[50]

From the voluminous archives now available to the historian it appears that only one piece of evidence existed at the time that could have been used to suggest that Russian soldiers' conduct had been in any way reprehensible—apart from the fact that they had chosen to join the German side, and were captured in German uniforms. The incident that stood in grim contrast to this was indeed brutal, but how far it could be fairly utilised to condemn Russian prisoners in Britain may be judged from the circumstances.

Immediately after the Normandy invasion, the Resistance in the Rhône Valley responded with extreme gallantry, if over-enthusiastically, to Allied instructions broadcast over the BBC. Their members rose, and committed a whole series of daring acts of sabotage to German installations, principally in the valleys of the Rhône and Drôme.

The German revenge for these acts was sudden and horrible. The most ghastly operation took place at the ancient town of St. Donat, in the Drôme. On 15 June 1944 about two thousand 'German' troops, accompanied by armoured cars, drove into the town. As the dust settled, the frightened inhabitants saw that the newcomers bore the high cheekbones and slanted eyes of some backward oriental race; they appeared quite undisciplined, and savage to a degree. With hideous shouts this weird horde threw itself on the town in an orgy of pillage and destruction. By the time the raid was over, an estimated seven or eight million francs' worth of damage and loss had been committed in the town. But this was the least of the horrors. No fewer than fifty-three women and young girls, many of the latter no older than thirteen or fourteen, had been hideously raped and abused by the raiders. M. Chancel, the Mayor, from whose account I give this description, was the father of one of these young schoolgirls. She died a few weeks later.

Similar crimes were taking place all over the region. M. Chancel appealed to his Bishop (Monsignor Pic) who at once approached the local German commander. That officer apologised, and explained that the troops concerned were Mongols, levied from amongst the prisoners taken on the Russian front, and now serving as auxiliaries in the German Army. After two hours' argument with Monsignor Pic, the German general agreed, to preserve the reputation of the German Army, to recall the troops responsible and restore the loot removed, where possible.[51]

On this piece of 'revolting behaviour'—and revolting it was indeed—appears to have hinged the Foreign Office case for denying asylum to all Russians in the West. What this version did not disclose was that the rapine unleashed was no voluntary outburst by a typical anti-Soviet 'Vlasov' unit: it was a carefully arranged piece of Nazi policy. At St. Donat and at Crest (further south) Pierre de Saint Prix's informants saw notices stuck up by the Germans:

Frenchmen, you love the Russian Communists: here they are!

From all the millions of Russian prisoners in their hands, the Nazis had selected a few hundred of the most primitive; men who could probably not speak Russian,[52] let alone French, and who could scarcely have been expected to have known what country they were in, or whom and why they were fighting.

As M. de Saint-Prix, the Resistance leader, points out, it is clear that the Nazis had banded together this ferocious gang for the sole purpose of simultaneously terrorising the French population, and impressing on them the barbarity of their Russian allies. As soon as the Bishop of Valence's protest had compelled the German general to withdraw these odious auxiliaries, the Nazis had no further use for them. When the local German withdrawal began on 31 August, the Mongols were abandoned. It was in this way that they fell into the hands of the French, and were promptly imprisoned.

But even this little band was not amongst the prisoners in England whose fate was under discussion. They were released by a Major Ivanov, former collaborator with the Nazis, whom the Soviets had employed since September 1944 as commandant of the collecting camp for Russians at Camp Beauregard, outside Paris. From there they would have been despatched overland to the Soviet Union once hostilities had ended.[53]

In this way the logic of the Foreign Office dictated that the tortured invalids of Bayeux must be considered as tarnished by the crimes of the Mongols of Valence. And it was the innuendo based on such reasoning that served to overcome Churchill's moral misgivings at the Cabinet meeting of 4 September 1944 and the Potsdam Conference a year later.

Eden's further argument in favour of forcible repatriation was that 'a large proportion of the prisoners, whatever their reasons, are willing and even anxious to return to Russia.' As an argument it would appear to be irrelevant, since clearly Lord Selborne's plea was solely concerned with those who did not wish to return. However, it is instructive to glance at what lies behind the words 'whatever their reasons'.

Eden was relying on a report of 1 July, containing information based on interrogations of Russian prisoners held at Devizes. After noting that virtually all had been forced to join German units, and had thenceforward been treated abominably, the report goes on to claim that most of the Russians, though fearing punishment on their return, wished to go back to Russia.

Christopher Warner minuted: 'Most of these Russians want to go back, if given the chance to prove themselves.' Two days later, however, he received a letter from the troublesome Major Manderstam. Manderstam had interrogated Russian prisoners at Kempton Park, where he too reported that all expressed their desire to return to Russia. They told him they would receive a week or a fortnight's leave before rejoining the Red Army. Manderstam, however, doubted whether this curious unanimity and confidence were altogether spontaneous. Amongst the group he interviewed was an NKVD agent, and he was assured by the British Interrogating Officer 'that the attitude of the Russians interrogated by me was a most unusual one and attributed this to the presence of the NKVD man amongst them'.[54]

Though Warner hotly denied Manderstam's assertion that the prisoners were speaking under duress, elsewhere he implicitly accepted the charge. Indeed, he does not appear to have been altogether averse to the use of such pressures. At a meeting on 16 August, when it was suggested that the Americans might only send back volunteers, '*Mr Warner* [states a report] rather doubted whether this was possible and felt that in any case after the Soviet authorities had seen the men they would almost all express a wish to return to the Soviet Union.'[55]

This was the background to Eden's assertion that a large proportion of the prisoners was anxious to return. Clearly some genuinely wished to return to their homeland, falsely confident perhaps that a creditable history of resistance to the Nazis would stand them in good stead. But it was not about these that Lord Selborne was protesting.

As for the suggestion that Soviet punishment of returned prisoners might provoke German reprisals on British prisoners, Eden pointed out that for months Russians had been returned home from Egypt unconditionally and without ill effect. This assertion was in fact entirely false, as no Russian held in Egypt was compelled to return until after 15 September, i.e. a month and a half later.[56]

Moving on to Lord Selborne's suggestion that asylum should be found for those unwilling to return, Eden argued that 'We surely do not wish to be permanently saddled with a number of these men and if we do not return them we shall have to decide what to do with them both here and in the Middle East.'

Clearly the logistical problem could prove to be a serious one. It was one, moreover, likely to appear especially daunting to Eden. He had already been faced with a somewhat similar question in the previous year, when US Secretary of State Cordell Hull

> raised the question of the 60 or 70 thousand Jews that are in Bulgaria and are threatened with extermination unless we could get them out and, very urgently, pressed Eden for an answer to the problem. Eden replied that the whole problem of the Jews in Europe is very difficult and that we should move very cautiously about offering to take all Jews out of a country like Bulgaria. If we do that, then the Jews of the world will be wanting us to make similar offers in Poland and Germany. Hitler might well take us up on any such offer and there simply are not enough ships and means of transportation in the world to handle them.[57]

It is not surprising that Eden proved even less enthusiastic about diverting overstretched Allied resources to assist men whom in any case he regarded as traitors.

But the objections raised by Churchill and Selborne had rested largely on a moral basis, and so consciously or unconsciously, the Foreign Office seems to have felt it must destroy any moral claim the Russians might have had on Britain. Why this became necessary was succinctly set out by Eden in his closing paragraphs.

> (5) To refuse the Soviet Government's request for the return of their own men would lead to serious trouble with them. We have no right whatever to do this and they would not understand our humanitarian motives. They would know that we were treating them differently from the other Allied Governments on this question and this would arouse their gravest suspicions.
> (6) Finally the position of our own prisoners in Germany and Poland who are likely to be released by the Russians in the course of their advance is material to this question. It is most important that they should be well cared for and returned as soon as possible. For this we must rely to a great extent upon Soviet good will and if we make difficulty over returning to them their own nationals I feel sure it will react adversely upon their willingness to help in restoring to us as soon as possible our own prisoners whom they release . . .
> For these reasons I am convinced that, if the Soviet Government want these men back for their own forces or war effort, we should agree to send them back from both here and the Middle East, subject to the exigencies of transport and subject to obtaining from the Russians a firm undertaking covering the risk of German reprisals.[58]

These two considerations were clearly of vital importance. No British government could lightly afford to risk any real possibility of the Soviets holding up the return of British prisoners in consequence, and any act which might seriously endanger the alliance between Britain and the Soviets would clearly be dangerous to contemplate at this critical juncture of the war. The Foreign Office was convinced of the dangers of not falling in wholly with Soviet wishes, and then, as all too often occurs, tried to persuade itself and everyone else that such a policy was not only politically expedient, but also morally justified.

3

The 'Tolstoy' Conference: Eden in Moscow

IT MUST BE REMEMBERED THAT THE IMPASSIONED DEBATE BETWEEN THE British Cabinet Ministers as to the fate of the Russian prisoners had so far been conducted in ignorance of what the Soviet Government would require. The only communications on the subject had been Molotov's assertion of 31 May 1944, that 'the number of such persons in the German forces is very insignificant'; this was followed by the Foreign Office letter to the Soviet Ambassador of 20 July, pointing out that 1,114 such Russians were now in Britain with more to come, and enquiring about Soviet wishes on the matter.

For several weeks the Foreign Office had been kept waiting whilst the Kremlin considered this highly embarrassing and awkward situation. The delay itself may well be put down to Stalin's notorious habit of procrastinating when faced with awkward decisions; in such cases he tended to write on the relevant reports: '"For the archives", and "To be filed", and put them out of his mind.'[1] But a further Foreign Office request for a decision (20 August), coupled with pressures by the British Ambassador in Moscow, made a decision and reply unavoidable. The Foreign Office message pointed out that there were now over 3,000 Russian prisoners in Britain, and contained what must from the Soviet view have appeared the veiled threat that these and others coming in might have to be transferred to Canada and the United States.[2]

Three days later M. Gousev replied, demanding the return of all the prisoners 'at the earliest opportunity'. Britain was urged to supply the requisite shipping, and, in order to organise the prisoners whilst in British custody, the Soviet Military Mission would be contacting the War Office. The Ambassador also asked for a list of the prisoners and their camps.[3]

The ball was in the British court, and a final decision as to what if any provisions should be made to protect the repatriated prisoners from too public retribution had to be decided. It will be recalled that, though the Cabinet had urged that some undertaking from the Soviet Government should be required, this reservation was omitted from the ensuing notification given to the Soviet Ambassador. It had been suggested that it could be brought up once the Soviet authorities did reply, and further delays could be counted on, owing to difficulties in finding adequate shipping, before the Russians in Britain came into any danger. Moreover, as the German capacity for reprisals ebbed with every defeat, the main problem from the British point of view might solve itself. For the vital point, as Patrick Dean had stressed, was not to hinder any harsh measures the Soviets might employ against their returned compatriots, 'but merely to delay such steps being taken until all fear of reprisals against British and United States prisoners had been removed'.[4]

Now that the Soviet attitude had been made clear, the need for a definite decision on British policy became pressing. Realising that the implementation of his proposed policy was at stake, Eden began to prepare a full exposition of his views for the coming Cabinet meeting. Meanwhile a second member of the Cabinet followed Lord Selborne in speaking up for the unhappy prisoners.

This was the Secretary of State for War, Sir James Grigg, who entertained serious misgivings at the thought of the role the soldiers might be called upon to play in such a policy as that envisaged by Eden. On 24 August he wrote to Eden to express his disquiet at the prospect of handing over Russians to certain death, and his fears of possible German reprisals. It was true that, 'if the choice is between hardship to our men and death to Russians, the choice is plain' but he thought it in any case unlikely that the Soviets would co-operate helpfully in speeding the return of British prisoners. Grigg concluded by requesting a Cabinet decision on the matter, as it was the soldiers (for whom he was responsible) who would have to act 'in this very unpleasant business'.[5]

Eden replied courteously on 1 September, agreeing that it was right that the Cabinet should have a chance to re-examine the question and enclosing a draft copy of his paper for the War Cabinet.[6] The Cabinet itself met to consider the matter on 4 September, when Eden's final memorandum was circulated. This followed his earlier letter to Churchill fairly closely, the only concession to the objections of Grigg and Lord Selborne being an admission (with reservations) that in many cases the Russians had been and would be again exposed to unmerited suffering. But he followed this with the arguments already examined, repeating their urgency, and again forcefully recommending 'that the Cabinet should decide . . . to agree to the Soviet Government's request to repatriate their prisoners from the United Kingdom . . . [and] the Middle East . . . irrespective of whether the men wish to return or not'.

Immediately after this he added: 'Both these decisions would depend upon my obtaining from the Soviet Government a satisfactory assurance that they would take no action as regards bringing the men to trial and punishment during the continuation of hostilities with Germany.'[7]

The War Cabinet approved his proposals 'after a short discussion'.[8] Presumably all present were now in agreement. The two Ministers who had objected so strongly to the earlier Cabinet decision had already more or less conceded their positions in the face of Eden's reasoning. On 18 August Lord Selborne had replied to Eden's justification of his proposals, agreeing 'that the reasons you give are very weighty, and some of the points you stress cannot be gainsaid'.[9] And Grigg in any case had merely requested that he should be backed by a Cabinet decision when being obliged to implement a policy, aspects of which were 'revolting'. But Lord Selborne's conscience continued to be repelled by the unprecedented inhumanity of the tragedy he rightly sensed was impending. Four years later he joined with the Bishop of Chichester in denouncing the cruelty of enforcing the return of fugitives from tyranny.[10]

All that he or anyone else could do now was make a final attempt to use the largely anti-Nazi captured Russian prisoners to further Allied war aims. The few thousand Russians now in Allied hands represented only a tiny percentage of the six million or so still within the Greater Reich. To SOE these represented a fertile field for creating disorder, mistrust and even open revolt behind the German lines. They included several fighting units up to corps strength, and in France provided troops to keep the Maquis pinned down. Not only this, but in Germany itself thousands of them worked as agricultural labourers in virtually unprotected countryside. Militarily, of course, they could not have accomplished much against Wehrmacht and SS units, even with Germany's power shaken and crumbling. But a carefully fostered propaganda of resistance could have had an important dual effect on Germany's offensive capacity.

In France, Italy and Yugoslavia, Russian anti-partisan units would have had to be replaced from the already overstrained German forces. And in Germany itself, the prospect of a rising of the millions of Russian slaves working in fields and factories could have caused panic and distress out of all proportion to its actual military value. Both Hitler and Himmler expressed fear of such a rising of the *Ostarbeiter*, and contingency plans to combat such a revolt had been prepared so early as 1942, under the title '*Walküre*'.[11]

On 1 August SOE presented to the Chiefs of Staff Committee a memorandum, urging *Subversion of Russian Troops Operating Against the Maquis*. This advocated the recruiting of selected personnel from amongst the Russian prisoners-of-war. These would be specially trained by SOE, and then dropped into areas of Maquis resistance. There they would try to suborn members of Russian anti-partisan units. That such a plan could enjoy a strong measure of success was evidenced by the fact that the Maquis itself had already, unassisted, succeeded in detaching many of the Russians to their side.

The plans for this operation had been drawn up by SOE in consultation with the Free French and SHAEF Headquarters. 'The Foreign Office have now agreed to the plan subject to the Soviet Government being informed as soon as the Russians are sent back to France.'[12]

The Foreign Office raised no objection, but rejected any hopes of offering volunteers the alternatives of British or United States citizenship, or a guarantee of indemnity from the Soviets.[13] But the need to offer some sort of indemnity remained. It was not so much the inducement required to get men to volunteer to return to France, but that necessary to persuade those still in German service to desert. British interrogation officers had been told by the Russian prisoners in England that: 'Strong Nazi propaganda (admitted by many to have been effective) took the line that "Russians" would be instantly shot on falling into the hands of the Anglo-American captors or, later, in retaliation, by the Soviets.'[14]

The purpose of SOE was to do everything possible to bolster resistance movements and undermine morale in Axis Europe, and the project of attempting to draw over Russians from the units in France could not be discarded, despite the difficulty of finding much to offer prospective turncoats. Forty volunteers from amongst the prisoners in England, eager to help the Allied war effort, were screened by SOE officers and given special training for their dangerous task. Several of them told of contacts in Germany who were eager to set up active resistance to the Nazis who, they felt, had cheated and betrayed their cause.

Four of these volunteers were earmarked for the first 'drop', but first it was necessary, as the Foreign Office advised, to notify the Soviet authorities of the whole project. This meant the NKVD, whose emissary, Colonel Ivan Chichaev, worked in close collaboration with the Foreign Office from his residence at Flat 4, 10 Palace Gate, London W.8. In view of the NKVD's habitual delays in receiving instructions from Moscow (*i.e.* from Abakumov or Beria himself), Warner of the Foreign Office somewhat surprisingly suggested that: 'Colonel

Chichaev should be told quite frankly what was afoot and informed that, in view of the urgency of the matter, we proposed to go ahead with the scheme within about a week.' But his superior, Sir Orme Sargent (Deputy Under-Secretary of State) stated firmly that, in view of the prospective agreement to hand all Russians over to the Soviets, the explicit consent of the NKVD was obligatory.

Weeks passed by without news from Beria or Abakumov, but in the interval Colonel Chichaev explained that he was most anxious to interview the four Russian volunteers. This Major Manderstam of SOE was determined to prevent. He had already seen examples of what sort of pressure the NKVD could apply to prisoners, and balked all Colonel Chichaev's efforts to obtain access to them. The Colonel, a man of disarming charm of manner, repeatedly expressed to Manderstam his anxiety to be able to meet the four Russians, so long separated from their Motherland. At the same time he expressed his regret that no decision had yet arrived from his superiors upon the matter of sending the men to Germany.

Weeks passed, and at last Manderstam arranged a meeting with Chichaev on 16 October. He bore with him a letter, in which it was stated that SOE would be only too happy to allow Chichaev to interview the four—that is, provided authorisation for the proposed operation had arrived from Moscow.

The two men met at midday, and Chichaev at once delivered his organisation's final verdict:

> I have now received authority from Moscow to advise you officially that not only do we not agree to your organisation's using Russian prisoners of war for work in Germany, but we would also like to make it quite clear that we are not prepared to associate ourselves with your organisation in the contemplated action, and would strongly advise you to 'forget' about the Russians in Germany. Why on earth did you pick on the wretched Russians? The sooner you forget about them and leave them to us, the better it will be for our future relations.

Manderstam enquired whether Chichaev had with him a written reply on these lines, but received an indignant reply. 'Moscow is most mystified that you insist on a written answer. Surely there is no necessity for it, bearing in mind that all our previous negotiations have always been conducted orally. The whole thing is most mysterious. I am sure that in proposing this action, you must have had something at the back of your mind.'

What Colonel Chichaev had at the back of *his* mind was very likely an awareness of how awkward it would be on a future occasion to explain away a document in which the Soviet Union openly obstructed a British measure that might well have shortened the war.

Having thus brusquely disposed of SOE's plan for spreading sabotage and panic in the heart of Nazi Germany, Chichaev turned to the subject in which his seniors were really interested. He was very anxious to pay a visit to the four Russian volunteers. They were now at the SOE training school; could he not call on them?

Manderstam replied genially that, as the Soviet authorities had renounced any interest in the proposed operation, there was no further point in seeing them. In any case, they would (in view of the abandonment of the project) shortly be returned to a PoW camp. There Chichaev could doubtless arrange an interview through the normal channels. Chichaev persisted: could SOE not help in arranging an interrogation? When would the four be returned to a camp? Manderstam could give no precise answers; the NKVD had taken weeks to answer SOE's request for co-operation, and British red tape was pretty well as dilatory. He was afraid 'some patience would be needed'.

Baffled, Chichaev turned to another line of enquiry. The SOE representative in Moscow was Brigadier George Hill, whose arrival had been hailed with delight by Soviet Intelligence chiefs; he was a source of unprecedented security leaks.[15] Chichaev now asked Manderstam 'whether there was any chance of getting a catalogue of our "toys" which was apparently promised to him by Brigadier Hill during his last stay in UK, when he took Chichaev to visit one of our stations'.

The 'toys' referred to were the special explosive and other instruments of sabotage issued by SOE to its agents in Nazi-occupied Europe. They included such ingenious devices as pencil-guns, gas pistols, and a deadly poison which left no traces except those of endemic syphilis. They were stored in a gallery of the Natural History Museum, taken over by SOE for the purpose.

Manderstam, however, was not eager to oblige. 'I told him that I would enquire into the matter and would naturally expect that we should receive a similar catalogue from them. He said this was perfectly all right; there was no reason why we should not—after all, were we not Allies?!' But SMERSH did not see the 'toys', and the 'First Circle' of GULAG was obliged to deflect some of its top scientists to the fruitful task of creating its own 'toys'.

Blocked by Manderstam at every turn, Chichaev abruptly switched over to a denunciation of supposed British ill-treatment of Russian prisoners in their camps. When Manderstam pointed out that Chichaev himself had in the past often accused the British of being too soft-hearted, and referred to the tommies' reputation for good-nature,

Chichaev murmured softly: 'Yes, but you never know when the beast may come out in a man.'

Despite these exchanges, the meeting ended on a cordial note, with the two arranging to go to the Savoy theatre on the following Thursday.

This interview might well have been taken as a model of how to conduct negotiations with the Soviets. Whilst the NKVD had successfully blocked British proposals, Manderstam had conceded nothing on his side. There had been no recriminations, and indeed Chichaev went out of his way to express his friendship for Manderstam. The statesmen of Yalta and Potsdam might have learned much by pondering the implications of this exchange.[16]

But when Manderstam reported the outcome to Geoffrey Wilson of the Foreign Office, the reaction was one of dismay. Wilson thought it scarcely surprising that the Soviets had decided not to co-operate over the proposed operation. It was clear that they had been justly offended by SOE's mysterious refusal to allow the NKVD a prior interrogation of the volunteers. Wilson's minute ended with the tart comment: 'I doubt if Col. Chichaev has a very high opinion of Major Manderstam.' His colleague, Christopher Warner, added that it might be a good idea to chide Manderstam for his foolishness next time they saw him.

The Foreign Office went on to order SOE to hand over to the NKVD the forty Russians being trained to land in Germany. SOE was naturally obliged to agree; but when the forty were sent for, it was found that someone had tipped them the wink. SOE was full of apologies, but they had disappeared and could be found nowhere. There was nothing to be done.[17]

But to return to the results of the War Cabinet's decision on 4 September to accede to the demand of the USSR for the return of all its subjects. It will be remembered that only one condition had been decided upon, that the Soviet Government should undertake not to subject any prisoners so returned to treatment risking German reprisals.

On 11 September Soviet Ambassador Gousev called on Eden. He was in an aggressive frame of mind, and showered reproaches on the surprised Foreign Secretary. (Gousev had graduated to ambassadorial status from the ranks of the NKVD.[18]) His chief complaints were that the Russian prisoners in Britain (whose very existence had been ignored for weeks by the Soviet government) were being ill-treated by their British guards, and that anti-Soviet propaganda, spread by Fascist elements, was making a minority of prisoners reluctant to return to the Motherland. He declared in addition that the Russians should not be treated as prisoners of war, since the majority of them had been compelled under duress to serve in German units, and had therefore never become part of the enemy's fighting forces.[19]

The Foreign Secretary knew that these complaints were without foundation. He felt resentful, and what his colleague Orme Sargent termed 'a stormy interview' ensued. As Eden himself related, he very nearly reproached the Ambassador openly for his unreasonable accusations. But he restrained himself, and merely looked rather cold when bidding Gousev farewell.

The Cabinet decision of a week earlier had included only one reservation with regard to repatriating the Russians. Immediately afterwards the Foreign Office confirmed that they had 'interpreted the Cabinet conclusions to mean that no prisoners of war in the Middle East should be handed over to the Russians until the Soviet assurance is received'.[20] And two days later the Foreign Office submitted to the War Office a draft letter to the Soviet Ambassador, notifying him of the Cabinet decision, and laying down at length their insistence on the Soviet observance of the 'no punishments that could provoke German reprisals' proviso.[21] Despite an objection by the Adjutant-General, the War Office approved the text of this letter.[22]

But at this point Eden intervened. Possibly feeling he had been too forthright in his interview with Gousev, he decided it was foolishly provocative to stipulate any conditions at all. Sir Orme Sargent hastily telephoned Sir Frederick Bovenschen, asking for War Office approval of the Foreign Secretary's proposal. This was given, and the suggested demand for Soviet restraint in dealing with returned Russian subjects was permanently dropped.[23]

But now a new question arose. In his telephone call to Bovenschen, Sir Orme Sargent had touched on this. Urging the dropping of the Cabinet's recommended proviso, he argued 'that to ask for this assurance . . . will merely exacerbate matters and may recoil on the Russian treatment of our own prisoners of war when they fall out of German hands into Russian hands'.

British and American troops captured by the Germans tended to be placed in camps in the eastern regions of the Greater Reich, in eastern Germany, Poland or the Balkans. Over the winter of 1944–45 Allied Intelligence estimated that there were some 40,000 British and 75,000 Americans so imprisoned,[24] and it was clear that the majority were likely to be freed by the Red Army as it pressed forward into Poland and the Balkans. The speedy and safe return of their nationals after liberation was a matter of the first importance for the Allied governments. On 11 June 1944, the heads of the British and United States Military Missions in Moscow approached the Red Army General Staff, asking to be notified when camps containing Allied prisoners were liberated, and for appropriate facilities to ensure that good care was taken of the freed prisoners. Soviet authorities gave assurances that all would be satisfactorily arranged—but from then on frustrated or ignored all efforts at co-operation.[25]

Now, however, that the Soviets were pressing for the return of their own citizens captured in Western Europe, it seemed possible that they might be persuaded to be more helpful. Indeed, Major-General Vasiliev of the Soviet Military Mission in Britain gave the impression that 'the Russian Government would be just as ready to send our men back as they were to recover their own', and he himself seemed 'evidently out to help'.[26] But a week later the War Office received a disquieting telegram from the head of the British Military Mission in Moscow, General Burrows. He complained that 'everything possible' had been done to induce the Soviets to co-operate over assistance to liberated British prisoners, but that they had 'met with complete non-co-operation on part of Russians'. Faced with this impasse, Burrows suggested 'that it is important that at a suitable opportunity Vassiliev be informed that early repatriation Soviet prisoners depends on facilities afforded to ours'.[27]

This suggestion received cautious approval at the War Office, though a note of resigned pessimism was struck by Sir James Grigg, the Secretary of State. 'On the whole I agree,' he wrote, 'though I am tempted to suggest that we propose to the F.O. a tougher line straight away. But they wouldn't accept the proposal anyway!'[28]

Grigg was right in thinking the Foreign Office would jib at such blunt diplomacy. But they did go so far as to suggest that 'a strong hint' should be dropped to General Vasiliev that it would be much easier to meet Soviet requirements if they would reciprocate.

On 27 September the 'strong hint' was dropped by Brigadier Firebrace of the Russian Liaison Group. On instructions, he explained to Vasiliev that it was not the practical measures for repatriating Russians that might be delayed by Soviet intransigence, but simply the legal procedure necessary to define the Russian prisoners' status in Britain. Vyshinsky in Moscow and Gousev in London objected strongly to the British classification of the captured Russians as prisoners of war as insulting to the citizens of an Allied power, and demanded that they be treated 'as free citizens of an Allied Power'. The British had no objection to this change, but explained that a special law—the Allied Forces Act, drawn up to meet the problems of exiled governments such as the French and the Poles, who wished to maintain military units on British soil—would have to be passed in order to effect it.

Now the Foreign Office was suggesting that the passing of such an Act might be delayed until the Soviets responded. Firebrace at first experienced some difficulty in explaining the situation to his Soviet counterpart. Vasiliev could scarcely be brought to believe that even the government must abide by the law in Britain, and believed he had stumbled upon some mysterious act of British perfidy. But whether Vasiliev understood the intricacies of the British legal system or not, the British authorities resolved to delay the implementation of the Allied Forces Act until the Soviets became more amenable. General Burrows in Moscow was notified of this move.[29]

Unfortunately the force of the Foreign Office threat was lessened by the fact that the Soviets violently objected to the Allied Forces Act. Through a misunderstanding of its purpose, they continued to oppose its implementation for months, and only agreed to it in the following year. By the end of September the situation was summed up by Colonel Phillimore of the War Office:

> The situation in fact is that we are committed here to meeting the Russian demands and have gone a long way to doing so, but are holding up the conclusion of the matter and the vital questions of discipline and status until we get something out of the Russian Authorities in Moscow. . . . Meanwhile the Russians are pressing the matter hard both here and now in the States also, and you will notice the technique by which their notes start with a series of complaints . . .[30]

The most ferocious of these complaints had come in the form of a letter from Gousev to Eden on 27 September, reiterating in hectoring tones those raised in his interview with the Foreign Secretary of 11 September.[31]

It must be remembered that Gousev had received as yet no written notification of the Cabinet's decision to fall in with Soviet wishes over repatriation, and possibly did not feel fully confident of British co-operation. He also, in all probability, felt obliged to advance, in the form of sweeping accusations of external tampering with the Russians' loyalty, charges that could explain away any disturbances or protests on the part of Russians reluctant to return. By imputing to the British direct or indirect responsibility for such resistance, they might induce them to take on the distasteful responsibility of suppressing it.

Highly indignant at these accusations, the British authorities began to prepare a lengthy refutation of Gousev's charges, exposing their falsity in detail.[32] The Soviets had really gone too far on this occasion, and it was necessary to show them precisely how and where they had gone wrong. That the Soviets were well aware of the realities of the situation, and merely launched their attack for tactical reasons, never occurred to any member of the Foreign Office. Almost at once, however, came a further switch in Soviet techniques.

From Moscow General Burrows telegraphed that his new Soviet opposite number, who had just taken over, 'was most sympathetic and promised to expedite the matter' of granting the British facilities to help repatriate their liberated troops. 'He assured me that he was in a position to state that all Red Army Commanders had instructions to afford the best possible treatment to liberated allied prisoners of war. I signal you this at once as it is the first indication here that the Soviet General Staff intends to play.'[33]

Yet two days later Vyshinsky was complaining to the British Ambassador in Moscow about the injurious treatment afforded to the Russians in Britain.[34] It was all so confusing, being alternately patted on the head and kicked up the backside—almost as if Soviet officials had been instructed to treat the British as their own Ivan Pavlov had treated his dogs.

Whilst British hopes were being pulled this way and that, events suddenly took a new turn. Increasingly troubled by the apparent clash of Allied interests in Poland and the Balkans, Churchill proposed that he or Eden should travel to Moscow in an attempt to settle matters personally with Stalin. On 1 October a favourable reply was received from the Generalissimo, and it was arranged that both should fly over in a week's time.[35] Here at last was the opportunity to clear up the whole vexatious business of the liberated Russian and British prisoners.

Both Foreign Office and War Office hastily prepared extensive briefs on the subject for the Foreign Secretary. The main objectives were:

1. To persuade the Soviets to co-operate fully in arrangements needed for the care and repatriation of British prisoners freed by the Red Army.

2. To assure their hosts that the Russians in Britain, France and Egypt would be returned as soon as the practical problems of providing transport could be resolved.

3. As the Soviets were so adamant in objecting to the prisoner-of-war status of their nationals in Britain, to persuade them to accept the Allied Forces Act as the only feasible alternative.

4. To refute the unpleasant charges levelled by Gousev.[36]

Meanwhile the British Chiefs of Staff informed the Foreign Office that suitable shipping for the return of the Russians could be found, 'and it would be possible to arrange for the repatriation of 11,000 men, without affecting our other commitments, provided that the shipping employed was back in the UK by the end of November.' They went on to suggest, in view of the Soviet attitude so far, 'that the Russians might be more likely to meet our wishes if we did not make the first move'.[37] This was the last suggestion that Britain should attempt to tie the Soviets down to an agreement establishing mutual obligations in the matter of repatriating prisoners. But once again events took a dramatic new turn.

On 11 October 1944, two days after the Chiefs of Staff had made this recommendation, the two British leaders were acting as hosts to Stalin and Molotov at a dinner in the British Embassy in Moscow. It had been a beautifully sunny day, and both Prime Minister and Foreign Secretary had every reason to feel exuberant and optimistic. They had just conducted the swift and skilful negotiations whereby most of the Balkans were conceded as coming under future Soviet control.[38] Molotov had called that afternoon in unusually benign humour, and this meeting of the Allied leaders appeared to be bringing to a satisfactory conclusion many negotiations that could otherwise have dragged on indefinitely.

At nine o'clock the guests arrived, and all sat down to dine in ebullient spirits. Eden was able to talk much with Stalin, who was separated from him only by the interpreter Pavlov. The Soviet leader was in superb form, exhibiting alternately wit, humour, and gentle wisdom. He made amusing remarks at the expense of the troublesome Poles, and embarked on a lengthy joke (which Eden could not quite understand) about a consignment of Crimean wine captured from the Germans. Eden found his old admiration for Stalin welling up once more with increased fervour. Nine years before, Eden had met this extraordinary man for the first time, and at once he had been overcome by an indefinably emotional respect that transcended barriers of class, ideology and nationality. In 1935, he had found that 'Stalin impressed me from the first and my opinion of his abilities has not wavered. His personality made itself felt without effort or exaggeration. He had natural good manners, perhaps a Georgian inheritance. Though I knew the man to be without mercy, I respected the quality of his mind and even felt a sympathy which I have never been able entirely to analyse.'[39]

Suddenly Stalin became grave and, glancing sideways at Eden, broached a new topic. What followed was so gratifying and exciting for Eden that his euphoria almost bubbles through the telegram he sent the next day to Sir Orme Sargent in London.

At dinner last night my conversation with Marshal Stalin turned for a moment on the Russian troops whom we had in England. The Marshal said he would be extremely grateful if any arrangements could be made to get them back here. I said we should be glad to do anything we could to help and that I knew that though shipping difficulties were very considerable we were now re-examining the possibility both in respect of troop-ships to carry the men and the necessary escorts. The Marshal repeated that he would be deeply in our debt if we could arrange matters for him about this. I replied that he could be sure that we would do all we could to help and in return I felt sure that his Government would give all the help in their power to our prisoners in Germany as and when the Red Army reached German prison camps in which they were located. The Marshal said at once that certainly this would be done. He would make this his personal charge and he gave me his personal word that every care and attention would be given to our men.

I feel that in view of this conversation it would be most unwise to try to bargain the transport of the Russians against the care of our prisoners but that we should go ahead with the arrangements and when we definitely inform the Russians of the action we are able to take we should remind them of what Marshal Stalin has told me about Russian care of our men.[40]

So the whole problem of the prisoners had been solved in a trice! The statesmen laughed, drank and gossiped around the festive table until the early hours of the morning. When a weary but happy Eden rose from his bed next day, it was nearly lunchtime. In the evening he dashed off his exuberant telegram quoted above to Sir Orme Sargent. By chance it crossed an incoming message from Sargent himself, who had, it transpired, anticipated Eden's view, and likewise recommended that all bargaining should be set aside in favour of 'tactics of sweetening the hostile atmosphere'.[41]

The Permanent Under Secretary, Sir Alexander Cadogan, wrote that the whole awkward business had 'been cleared up by a most satis-factory assurance which my Secretary of State has received from Marshal Stalin'.[42] The Chiefs of Staff at once ordered arrangements to be put into effect for the speedy repatriation of the Russian prisoners, and within four days Cadogan was informed that two troopships would be ready for the purpose by 23 October.[43]

Eden was convinced that, in the light of Stalin's assurances, any bargaining was out of the question. He also abandoned any idea of answering the points raised in Gousev's 'rude note' as this might 're-open the controversy'.[44] The new position was summed up by Bovenschen at the War Office:

(a) repatriation goes on.
(b) No rude note to the Embassy.
(c) No order under the [Allied Forces] Act till F.O. ask us.[45]

At 4.30 p.m. on 16 October Eden conferred with Molotov at the Kremlin. He explained that arrangements were in hand for the return of the first 11,000 Soviet nationals, and that the remainder would follow as soon as possible. Molotov expressed his gratitude and passed swiftly on to a point of deep concern to the Soviet leaders:

Were His Majesty's Government of the opinion that all Soviet citizens without exception should be returned to Russia as soon as possible?

Mr. EDEN said they were, and tonnage had been made available.

M. MOLOTOV said he was interested in this question of principle. So far he had had no reply from the British Government.

Mr. EDEN replied that there was no doubt in his mind . . .

M. MOLOTOV said he would be grateful, but the question was one regarding the rights of the Soviet Government and Soviet citizens. It was not a question of shipping. Did the British Government agree that the question of the return of a Soviet citizen to Russia could not be settled merely by the wish or otherwise of the individual? Some Soviet citizens might not wish to come back because they had been helping the Germans, but the Soviet Government demanded the right of return for all their citizens.

Mr. EDEN said he had no objection. The British Government wanted all these men to be placed under Soviet administration and discipline.

M. MOLOTOV suggested that the Soviet authorities should decide about their own citizens.

Mr. EDEN agreed that . . . until they came home the Russians in England should be under Soviet authority within the limitation of British law.

Molotov closed the discussion in the customary Soviet manner, by making a wild accusation apparently at random about conditions in one of the British camps.[46] The charge was unusually half-hearted, though— almost as if even Molotov realised that Eden could not have conceded more.

Eden telegraphed home the news of this latest success,[47] and before the Moscow visit (codename 'Tolstoy') drew to a close, Churchill himself had a few jocular words with Stalin on the agreement.

THE PRIME MINISTER said . . . Talking of eating, Britain had managed to arrange for the despatch of 45,000 tons of corned beef to the Soviet Union to meet Marshal Stalin's request. We were also sending 11,000 Soviet ex-prisoners of war to eat the beef.

MARSHAL STALIN said he would not like to eat Hitler. With regard to the Soviet prisoners a great many had been made to fight for the Germans while others had done so willingly.

THE PRIME MINISTER pointed out that that was our difficulty in separating the two. As they surrendered to us we had the right to speak for them and he hoped that all would be sent back to Russia.[48]

At the same time as this bizarre exchange was taking place, the unhappy British delegation was handed a Soviet *note verbale*. It contained another ferocious attack on British treatment of Soviet prisoners, recapitulating all Gousev's previous accusations and adding a series of new ones for good measure.[49] Perhaps the British delegation had been too deferential, and the Soviets were suspicious that some deception or reservation was planned.

4

British and American Agreement at Yalta

On 6 March 1931, Winston Churchill, then in the political wilderness, addressed an important meeting in the Royal Albert Hall, in London, held 'to protest against the brutalities practised in Soviet prison camps and to demand that Russian goods produced by prison labour shall not be allowed to enter this country.' He did not mince his words. He referred to the horrible conditions prevalent in the Russian timber camps, then went on to add, according to *The Times* next day, that:

> The conditions there were tantamount to slavery. That government possessed despotic power, and used that power against their political opponents, and sent them in scores of thousands to those hideous places of confinement ... If to-day we found the Government of the day apologising for these villainies in Russia, and patting on the backs those who greased their paws (cheers)—if to-day we found that situation, and if to-day we found a certain sluggishness in our life, that was because we were for the moment—let us frankly admit it—passing under a cloud of weakness and confusion ... By voting for the resolution which had been proposed, those present would record their definite protest against a system of convict and forced labour in Russia, which, to quote a phrase of Mr. Gladstone, 'Scarcely finds its equal in the dark and melancholy catalogue of human crime.'[1]

Fourteen eventful years passed by, during which Stalin's purges and economic policies increased the population of the forced-labour camps from the two million on whose behalf Churchill had appealed at the Albert Hall, to some fifteen to twenty millions.[2] Conditions for the prisoners had deteriorated, the numbers had increased eight or tenfold, and the huge pool of slave-labour administered by the GULAG authorities had become a (perhaps *the*) major factor in the Soviet economy.

It is a bitter irony of history, therefore, that Churchill should almost have travelled to the Crimea Conference with a shipload of such future slaves. 'Marshal Stalin', explained General Sir Hastings ('Pug') Ismay, writing to the Prime Minister on 1 January 1945, 'is pressing for the repatriation of Soviet Nationals taken prisoner by us on the Western Front, and it is proposed to put one or two thousand of these into the *Franconia*, if you approve. I am assured that they can be completely segregated from our Party, and that they will be reasonably sanitary. They will, of course, be disembarked directly we get to our destination so that they will in any case not be in your way.'[3]

The suggestion was, however, not adopted, and other means had to be found of shipping out the victims. And of course the cataclysmic events of the Second World War had placed Churchill in a very different situation from that of 1931.

The outline arrangements at the 'Tolstoy' conference in Moscow left many important details unsettled. There were, on the British side, questions of the maintenance of the liberated Russians, their discipline, and their legal status in Britain. There was also the purely logistical problem of returning the thousands already collected together in camps in Western Europe and North Africa. And for the Allied prisoners in Eastern Europe, Britain and the United States wished to be able to rush liaison officers up behind the Red Army lines to contact their freed citizens, wandering dazed and half-starved after their liberation. How soon could direct overland exchange of prisoners be arranged once the Russians and Americans linked up in the heart of Germany? All these and related questions remained to be settled, and so it was that the Big Three at Yalta found themselves attempting to lay down the lines on which the massive transfers of personnel were to be conducted.

On the American side, for some time after D-Day, there was little awareness that any problems could exist. This was not because the Americans had not as many Russian prisoners in their hands as the British. After the first trickle captured during the opening days of Operation 'Overlord', thousands began to fall into American hands. And once this happened, the Soviets as usual launched into a series of virulent complaints.

One month after D-Day, for instance, a Soviet complaint was handed to the US Secretary of State (Cordell Hull), in which it was alleged that one of Eisenhower's staff officers had issued a statement in London highly defamatory of the Russian prisoners. A careful American investigation revealed that no such statement had been made, though reports similar in content to that quoted by the Soviet spokesman had been despatched home by American war correspondents. In any case it must have been difficult to see quite what it was in the Soviet-quoted report that had given so much offence. It told of the appalling privations and cruelties that led many Russians to join German units, with the greatest reluctance. It described how many took the first opportunity of deserting (in some cases shooting their German corporals), and subsequently joined local bands of anti-Nazi partisans. The report stated roundly that the Nazis had failed almost entirely to gain the hearts and minds of the enforced recruits in the East Battalions, and that the 'majority of these soldiers have preserved untouched their moral principles and political views, and they consider themselves as citizens of the USSR'.

What then did the Soviet authorities have to object to? The answer is to be found in a small parenthesis, which stated that about ten per cent of the Russians in German service 'may be considered as pro-German', and for the former Red Army officers 'this percentage should be considered as somewhat higher.'[4] The Soviet Union was reluctant to admit publicly that any of its subjects were opposed to their Marxist government, still less that the percentage so doing was the highest of any combatant nation.

At first, however, the Americans found their Russian prisoners no problem. They were for the most part in German uniform and members of German units. United States policy therefore was to treat them in the same way as all their other German prisoners. In practice this involved a different procedure in each of the three great Army Groups now embattled with the Germans in France. In the north was the 21st Army Group, commanded by Montgomery. Until September 1944, all Russian prisoners captured in that theatre were shipped to camps in Britain. In the centre was the 12th US Army Group, commanded by Omar Bradley. There the Russians were held in US-administered PoW camps in liberated France. Finally, General Devers's 6th US Army Group in southern France transported its prisoners to British adminis-tered camps in North Africa.[5] Thus only the prisoners taken by Bradley's troops remained a directly American problem, and these were in any case not distinguished from German prisoners.

As related in the previous chapter, the British were already engaged in their own approaches to the Soviet Government. At the same time as Eden was asking Molotov what he wished to be done with the prisoners, he instructed Lord Halifax, the British Ambassador in Washington, to inform the United States Government of the situation, 'since it seems desirable that the treatment of these Russian nationals should be, broadly speaking, on parallel lines'.

Any decision as to the ultimate fate of the prisoners must of course wait on the expected reply from Molotov. The Foreign Office draft of the telegram to Lord Halifax contained proposed stipulations that the Soviet Union should be required not to court German reprisals by putting any of the prisoners on trial on their return. But, as if anticipating the subsequent capitulation on this point, this provision was omitted from the telegram itself.[6]

At about the same time came a query from SHAEF Headquarters, enquiring whether it was possible to employ the captured Todt Labour Force Russians in work on Allied military installations behind the lines.[7]

The United States reply was swift and uncompromising. *All* prisoners captured in German uniform were considered as coming under the provisions of the 1929 Geneva Convention, to which Great Britain, the United States and Germany were signatories. They could not therefore be employed on work furthering the Allied war effort (this is expressly forbidden by Article 31 of the Convention), and only those who would definitely be absorbed into the Red Army should be returned. It was felt that any other course would incur the risk of German reprisals on Allied prisoners.[8]

At the same time the United States Government was quite as well aware as the British that any decision on the treatment and disposal of their Russian prisoners must in some degree be related to the situation of the American prisoners likely to be released by the Red Army. Their status was not similar, for the Americans were simply liberated prisoners of war, whereas the Russians had been captured in German uniform. Amongst the Russians, too, were many civilians, which posed another problem. But questions of the care, sustenance and ultimate return of each other's nationals were similar, and inevitably the questions became linked in negotiations.

As early as 11 June 1944, the heads of the British and American Military Missions in Moscow had approached the Soviet General Staff with a request that measures be taken to care for any Western Allied prisoners freed during the coming Red Army offensive. Later, on 30 August, United States Ambassador Harriman proposed to Molotov measures for co-operation in dealing with both sides of what was clearly destined to become a matter of ever-increasing concern.[9]

Molotov declined to answer until three months later; when he did so, his reply came in the form largely of a series of unsubstantiated complaints.

In the meantime, however, Andrei Gromyko, the Soviet Ambassador, approached the State Department and demanded that all Russians taken by the Americans should be sent back forthwith (in American ships) to the USSR. He was particularly concerned about those Russians who had been caught up amongst the thousands of German prisoners transported across the Atlantic, and who now found themselves on American soil. Permission was requested and granted that a Soviet representative might visit seventeen such prisoners at Camp Patrick Henry, Virginia. The First Secretary of the Embassy, Bazykin, accordingly called at the camp, to return with tales of ill-treatment and infiltration of anti-Soviet propaganda. Gromyko took the opportunity to issue (12 September) a stern complaint to the Under Secretary of State, Stettinius. [10] A further accusation followed almost immediately: that the United States had recruited some of the captured Russians into her armed forces. This, and a suggestion that the prisoners had received anti-Soviet propaganda, was rejected by the Americans with undisguised sarcasm.[11]

The Soviets never referred to either charge again in their dealings with the United States. But the more important demand, the request for the instant return of all captured Russians to the USSR, remained to be answered. Secretary of State Cordell Hull telegraphed on 15 September to Averell Harriman, US Ambassador in Moscow, a full résumé of the stance taken by the US on this question of the prisoners, requiring him at the same time to ascertain Soviet wishes in the matter.

Hull started by stating firmly that: 'So long as they remain in American custody they continue to have the status of German prisoners of war and to enjoy treatment in accordance with the provisions of the Geneva Prisoners of War Convention.' To this he added that any who claimed to be Soviet citizens could be returned at their own request to the USSR. But none should be returned by force, 'to avoid the risk of reprisals against American nationals in enemy hands'. This policy had been made known to the Soviets as early as 13 December 1943.

Following visits by Soviet representatives, a number of prisoners had indeed requested their repatriation, and this had taken place. What was now required was a formal approach to the Soviet Government, 'with a view to ascertaining that Government's desire regarding the disposition to be made of those persons in question who may claim to be Soviet citizens or nationals'.

Hull suggested to Harriman that he co-ordinate his approach with the British Ambassador (Sir Archibald Clark Kerr), in view of the fact that the Foreign Office had recently addressed similar enquiries to the Soviet Embassy in London.[12]

It will be noticed, however, that there was a radical difference between the British and American attitudes. Hull merely wished to make arrangements for the return of those Russians who claimed Soviet citizenship and who desired repatriation. The British, on the other hand, had asked Ambassador Gousev to inform them of Soviet wishes in regard to *all* prisoners currently or formerly holding Soviet citizenship. And in the recent Cabinet meeting of 4 September they had decided in advance to agree to repatriation of *all* Russian prisoners, if the Soviet Government so requested. This decision was secret and as yet unknown to the State Department.

It is clear throughout that, where the State Department consented to deviate from a rigid application of the principles of the Geneva Convention, it was with the greatest reluctance and only as a result of extreme political pressure. The Foreign Office attitude was wholly different, and consisted largely in attempting to meet Soviet desires even before they were expressed. The United States was now to learn for the first time of her ally's differing viewpoint.

The news came from the United States Political Adviser in Italy, Alexander C. Kirk. Kirk had been Chargé d'Affaires at the US Embassy in Moscow at the height of Stalin's terror, and was able to make a shrewd assessment of the tragic possibilities inherent in Britain's abandonment of principles that had hitherto formed a part of the national heritage.[13]

From Allied Headquarters in Caserta he telegraphed Hull:

> According to information received at AFHQ from War Office in London an agreement has now been reached with Soviet Government for repatriation of Soviet citizens now or in future held as prisoners of war in Mid East irrespective of whether the individuals desire to return to Russia or not. Statements will not be taken from Soviet nationals in future as to their willingness to return to their native country. Mid East has received instructions from London to implement this agreement and arrange as soon as possible for transfer of these persons to Tehran. Macmillan [at that time British Minister resident at Allied Forces Headquarters, Caserta] is apparently receiving instructions to this effect from the Foreign Office.

The next day Kirk continued in a further telegram: 'I assume Department is considering advisability of assuring itself of the nature of methods which may be applied in compelling those Russian prisoners of war, who under previous arrangements were given option of retaining prisoner-of-war status, to return to Russia, especially in view of fact that I understand some were taken by our forces and delivered to British under arrangement whereunder that option prevailed.'

This last allusion was to Russians surrendering to the US 6th Army Group in southern France, who had been transported for convenience to camps in Egypt, thus passing from US to British control. With the recent switch in British policy, there was now a serious danger that the

British might return American-captured Russians to the USSR. The USA would then involuntarily incur the stigma of allowing the resultant breach of the Geneva Convention, and in consequence the danger of German retaliation. In fact the Americans had handed over more than four thousand such Russians to British control.

Macmillan informed the Foreign Office of Kirk's attitude and report. British official opinion made light of the American's fears. Patrick Dean at the Foreign Office argued that there was no breach of the Convention arising out of the repatriation of the Russians, and Colonel Phillimore of the War Office declared that 'if the United States authorities won't accept this surely they must take them back.'[14]

In any case, American squeamishness was not going to hold up British operations. Lack of shipping as yet prevented the return of prisoners in Britain to Russia, but instructions had already reached the Middle East ordering the return of prisoners held there, 'irrespective of whether individuals wish to return to Russia or not'. The Commander-in-Chief in Persia and Iraq enquired how the returning Russians should be treated—whether, for example, 'as friendly allies in transit or as PW and subjected to appropriate restrictions?' General Gepp, Director of Prisoners of War, minuted (with or without intentional humour) that 'there would be no objection to treating the Russians as friendly allies, whatever that means, provided they do not escape en route.' This appeared an ideal example of British compromise, and a possible snag in the form of C-in-C Middle East's reluctance to order British troops to fire on escaping prisoners was obviated by the employment of Soviet guards afflicted with no such scruples.[15]

United States officials were frankly puzzled by the dawning realisation that Britain had apparently decided on a radically new policy. Ambassador Harriman in Moscow replied to Cordell Hull's telegram of 15 September, stating that the British Embassy could give no information as to precisely what policy was now envisaged. All Clark Kerr had seen was a copy of the telegram to the Middle East authorities that Kirk had already commented on from AFHQ in Italy. From this it was to be presumed that repatriation by force where necessary was contemplated. For the United States, Harriman concluded, the main consideration should be whether they too could envisage employing force, and if so to reflect seriously on the danger of German reprisals.

The British Cabinet decision of 4 September was still not made directly available to her great ally. Indeed, on 26 September Paul Gore-Booth (later Permanent Under-Secretary at the Foreign Office) of the Washington Embassy informed the appropriate American authority that his government had not yet made a final decision on the use of force. This was of course quite untrue, but Foreign Office motives in thus misleading the US remain obscure.[16] Lord Halifax, the British Ambassador, reported to the Foreign Office American anxiety to obtain full information as to British intentions. He related the complaints already made by Gromyko and refuted by Hull and Stettinius, but noted that the 'State Department are somewhat at a loss to know the reason for this sudden pressure . . .' 'There have been local causes for irritation,' he added, 'which are of some relevance, e.g. refusal of United States immigration authorities at Seattle recently to compel return of part of a crew who had deserted from a Soviet ship'; also the fact that the 'United States authorities had in the meantime been screening prisoners of Russian origin and out of one party of seventeen, eight had stated they did not wish to return to the Soviet Union.' But the Americans felt 'however that there might be something more important at the back of all this, and would welcome your comments'.[17]

But it was almost certainly precisely these ominous incidents that had excited Soviet wrath. The British had not yet announced their total compliance with Soviet demands, whilst the Americans were beginning to show signs of non-co-operation on that point most vital to Soviet interests: *viz.* the return of *all* fugitives. The Soviet tactic in such cases was invariably to issue a stream of strident complaints, in whose composition factual content played little part. These complaints, delivered simultaneously in London and Washington, agitated the Foreign Office and puzzled the State Department.

Kirk reported from Italy the Foreign Office minute sent to Macmillan, in which Patrick Dean had set out the viewpoint that the Russian prisoners were not entitled to the protection of the Convention. Force, therefore, was implied as justified; but a lengthy official British memorandum of 11 October gave details of the proposed Allied Forces Act (which it was hoped would fall in with Soviet wishes), without any mention of the crucial issue of force at all.[18] This memorandum was delivered on the same day as the ebullient Eden was conceding all to Stalin over dinner in the Moscow Embassy.

Puzzled by the apparent contradictions and reservations of British policy, and indignant at Soviet accusations and pressure, the United States continued to maintain the view that all prisoners captured in German uniform who claimed German citizenship in consequence would have that claim upheld. So Alexander Kapustin of the Soviet Embassy in Washington was informed on 19 October.[19]

Any Russian not wishing to return to the USSR, and aware of his rights under international law, could therefore expect to be treated as a German prisoner by the American authorities. Few seized on this

chance to save their skins—in the end only a few score out of the
thousands of Russian prisoners taken by the Americans. The majority of
Russians so captured were bewildered, harassed folk, used only to
blows, harsh treatment, and orders given without explanations. Most
were probably of low education, and quantities were even illiterate.
And even amongst the officers it is understandable that they should
have been ignorant of their rights under the all-important Geneva
Convention: they had after all been brought up in a state which had not
only refused to sign the Convention, but had also virtually abandoned
the rule of law altogether.

The majority of Russians in American camps were prepared to
return to the USSR. The camps where they were held were visited by
the Soviet Military Attaché, Colonel Saraev. As in Britain, the prescribed mixture of cajolement, lies and threats was in general fairly
effective, though there was an embarrassing incident in a camp at
Indiatown Gap, Pennsylvania, when one of the inmates greeted
Saraev with an ironical Nazi salute.[20] Probably the majority believed it
when they were told they would be returned in the end anyway, and
thought it wise to appear willing from the beginning.

Some of those politically aware enough to anticipate their real fate
refused to return. They had, however, made the mistake of owning to
being Soviet citizens. The question as to what should be done with this
intermediate category of prisoner now began to exercise the minds of
those in authority in America. As they had not claimed prisoner-of-war
status as Germans, the only remaining curbs on their return were the
traditional American policy of granting political asylum to persecuted
refugees, and the fear that Soviet punishment of the repatriates might
provoke German retaliation. On the other hand it was difficult to deny
Soviet claims on people who actually admitted to being citizens of the
USSR.

For a long time the United States hesitated over a decision.

Bernard Gufler, the State Department official concerned with
prisoner-of-war problems, enquired on 17 October whether the United
States really contemplated the introduction of a 'new policy' which
would 'result in the delivery to the Soviet authorities of persons hitherto
withheld from them because they were unwilling to return to the
Soviet Union.'[21] Gufler was plainly distressed by the proposal and
opposed to its implementation, but pressures began to mount towards a
concession to the Soviet view on this point.

A few days later Eisenhower wrote to the Combined Chiefs of
Staff from SHAEF Headquarters. He pointed out the anomaly already
noted whereby it was only the Russians taken by Bradley's 12th Army

Group who remained in US custody, and therefore subject to American rather than British procedure. He went on to urge that the United States adopt a policy in accordance with the requirements of the newly-arrived Soviet Mission to SHAEF.[22] This request was backed by the Foreign Office, who dreaded in the event of its rejection 'a further shoal of complaints addressed to us, which may be very difficult to answer'.[23] The Combined Chiefs issued a draft approval of Eisenhower's request,[24] but authorisation to implement this decision was withheld by the State Department.

Eisenhower's impatience with the delay over any decision on this matter can be understood: it was hard to explain to the Soviet Commission why one set of Russians captured by the Americans was being repatriated with no questions asked, whilst others sat kicking their heels in camps. But the decision was at last being made, though expressed somewhat ambivalently, and with an 'escape clause' in the form of the word 'claimants' which could if desired render the entire commitment nugatory. On 23 September Soviet Ambassador Gromyko had written to Secretary of State Hull, demanding the speedy return of all Soviet citizens in United States custody.[25] This request was studied by the Joint Chiefs of Staff, and on 2 November Admiral Leahy (President Roosevelt's Chief of Staff) forwarded a draft reply to the Secretary of State. In a covering letter, Leahy recommended, in view of established British policy, that 'from the military point of view... it is not advisable for the United States Government to proceed otherwise vis-à-vis the Soviet Government with respect to persons in this category.'

The draft was adopted more or less *in extenso* in a letter addressed by Acting Secretary of State Stettinius to Soviet Ambassador Gromyko six days later. In it, Stettinius declared that:

> This Government will make the necessary arrangements to segregate any claimants to Soviet citizenship at some place to be decided upon where representatives of the Soviet Embassy may have access to them for the purpose of interviewing them.
>
> *Any such personnel whose claims to Soviet citizenship are verified by the American military with your Embassy's co-operation, and whose return to Soviet control is requested by you, will be turned over to your authorities.*[26] [author's italics]

The United States, two months after the British decision, had now expressed its intention of repatriating (by force if necessary) Russian prisoners in its custody. Though the announcement was necessarily issued by the State Department, it was primarily the military authorities who had made the decision. Their considerations were doubtless similar to those influencing the British Government, and the State

Department was induced to concur with that decision. George Kennan, who was then at the Moscow Embassy, has explained recently to the author:

> I was in Moscow throughout that period. Knowing, as we did, that the entire responsibility for the handling of the repatriations, and the punishment of those repatriated, was in the hands of the NKVD, and being under no illusions as to the fate that awaited these people on arrival in the Soviet Union, I was full of horror and mortification over what the Western governments were doing. But I cannot recall that anyone at the time ever consulted any of us in Moscow about this policy, or even kept us informed officially of what was being done. In the case of the United States, the military authorities were supreme in war time; and it seldom occurred to them to consult anyone on the diplomatic side, least of all junior officers like myself, stationed in the field.[27]

Professor Kennan's estimate appears to be correct. The military authorities were naturally anxious to retrieve American prisoners being released by the Red Army as swiftly as possible. They wished to eliminate any unnecessary obstacle to co-operation with the Soviet general staff. And in addition, the US 6th Army was now coming under SHAEF command, which meant that Russian prisoners in its hands could no longer be shipped to the USSR via the Middle East route under the aegis of the British military authorities. Hitherto the Americans had managed to deal with the problem by ignoring it: this was no longer possible.[28]

Stettinius's letter of 8 November, informing Gromyko that the US was prepared to use force in returning captured Soviet citizens, was very likely the spur to a renewed Soviet press campaign urging the speedy return of her homesick sons.[29]

But at the same time it seems that Stalin had decided that the United States's proffered concession on the use of force went far enough to merit a reply to Ambassador Harriman's letter of nearly three months earlier, in which he had first broached the idea of co-operation on the mutual repatriation of liberated nationals. At last came Molotov's answer, on 25 November. The obligatory complaints were followed by agreement that such measures were necessary and acceptable to the Soviet Government. Molotov went on to stress that it was *all* Soviet citizens who were being claimed, irrespective of their circumstances or desires. He also urged that they be released from PoW status and be designated 'free nationals of an Allied power', this presumably following a report from the Washington Embassy that some prisoners were successfully claiming *German* PoW status.[30] This could not be admitted openly, and the Soviet stance was one of righteous indignation at the idea of Russians being in the same camps as Germans, 'our common enemies'.[31]

Though the State Department had accepted the recommendation of the Joint Chiefs of Staff, it displayed none of the British Foreign Office's enthusiasm for implementing the policy of forcible repatriation. It was over a month after the decision had been communicated to Gromyko, on 10 December, that Stettinius received a puzzled enquiry from Alexander Kirk at AFHQ in Italy. Pointing out that the British were now assuming that the Americans had reconciled themselves to the use of force, Kirk asked whether this was really the case. Ten days later came the reply: 'The policy adopted by the United States Government in this connection is that all claimants to Soviet nationality will be released to the Soviet Government irrespective of whether they wish to be so released.'[32]

It is to be noted that the category of those now liable to enforced repatriation was restricted to 'claimants to Soviet nationality'; those who had the wit or luck to know that their German uniforms entitled them to protection under the Geneva Convention as German prisoners were unaffected by this decision. But the fate and feelings of the 'claimants' became at once apparent.

The military authorites in the USA had recently been sifting Soviet citizens from the camps in which they were held, and collecting them at Camp Rupert, Idaho.[33] On 28 and 29 December 1,100 Russians left Rupert for a west coast port.

> The Soviet colonel at Rupert told the military authorities there yesterday just before the departure of the group that he had received word from Washington that the shipment was not to take place. About an hour later he reported that he had received new instructions from Washington that the shipment was to go forward. Among the 1,100 men sent to the ship about seventy did not want to go. These seventy men had, however, previously claimed Soviet nationality. Three of them attempted suicide, one by hanging, one by stabbing himself, and one by hitting his head against a beam in one of the barracks. In the end the three men have departed for the port.[34]

Despite apparent State Department misgivings (indicated by the temporary respite), the Russian prisoners sailed for Vladivostok the same day. By 1 February United States military authorities reported 'that approximately 2,600 of these persons who claim Soviet citizenship have departed on Soviet ships bound for Siberian ports'.[35]

Their fate on arrival we know from the account of a fellow-prisoner who met some of their number later in the Soviet slave-camp complex at Vorkuta: 'The Russians were sent across the Pacific to Vladivostok.

There they were imprisoned at first; but there was a shortage of men at the front and for the second time they found themselves soldiers of the Red Army, which was by now advancing across Poland. They took part in the capture of Berlin and were then brought up for trial. They were given twenty-five years for treason.'[36]

The winter was drawing on, and everywhere shiploads of Russian prisoners were crossing the oceans back to their homeland. On 29 December the first cargo had set out across the Pacific. Two months before, the first batches from Britain had left for Murmansk, and across the Mediterranean and the deserts of Iraq and Persia continued the convoys that had been returning Russians since the previous year.

Though the fate on return was the same, the Middle Eastern route was the most pleasant on the way. The British military authorities took great pains to entertain their charges well, and those Russians who survived the initial home screening and found themselves in Vorkuta or Magadan must often have recalled cool drinks around the swimming-pools in Baghdad, and a British band playing under the palms in the background as supper was being prepared. Amongst the repatriates were many Crimean Tartars and other Soviet Moslems, 'who prayed in all the Mosques. They were particularly appreciative as being Mohammedans, they said their own mosques had been destroyed'.[37]

This exotic interlude between imprisonment and slavery remained vividly in the minds of many of their escorts as well. In early December 1944, J. H. Frankau, an officer of the Royal Engineers, sailed from Taranto to Haifa, on the old troopship *Franconia* (the same that was to be used by Churchill and the British delegation at the Yalta Conference two months later). On board was 'a New Zealand battalion, completely Maori from the commanding officer downwards, and several hundred released Russian prisoners of war'. A Polish officer on board spoke to the prisoners, and told Frankau 'that the Russians were already firmly in the grip of their political Commissars. They would suffer no penalty on their return—they said—for having surrendered to the Germans. Many of them had been in Switzerland . . . When asked what they thought of Switzerland they said, it seems, "It's a pleasant country but, of course, the standard of living is not as high as in Russia."' Frankau's account continues:

> The Maoris and the Russians must have posed a mutual problem in communications. Nevertheless soldiers seem to have no difficulty in solving such problems, for after we had sailed over a calm and moonlit sea, a sing-song arose spontaneously on the upper deck. First the Maoris would sing one of their haunting songs . . . Then the Russians would reply antiphonally with an unfamiliar but beautiful air. Occasionally the British

would feel it necessary to offer a banal popular song but soon we desisted because we felt that we were spoiling an uniquely wonderful experience. The moonlight, the strange wordlessly appealing singing and the deep feeling of comradeship left very few of us without tears in our eyes when we went to bed; besides, for us, the war in Europe was happily over.[38]

But to return to the deliberations proceeding in London, Washington and Moscow. With the irruption of the Red Army into Poland and the Balkans, the United States was becoming increasingly concerned with the problem that had loomed so large in Eden's estimates of the situation. From June onwards General Deane of the US Military Mission in Moscow had been pressing for the Soviet Union to co-operate in drawing up arrangements for the care and speedy repatriation of liberated American prisoners. Despite repeated attempts to induce Molotov to act, no reply was received until the end of November. Even then, it was only a general concurrence on the principle of co-operation that was conceded, and the practical measures suggested by Deane and Ambassador Harriman were ignored.

In the meantime the first US prisoners in the East—about a thousand —had been not only liberated but also actually flown out by the US Air Force. This was in the beginning of September, in Rumania. But this had been through the assistance of the Rumanian Government, not yet fully under Soviet control. King Michael had personally approved the move, which had however been made with some assistance from local Red Army commanders. Secretary of State Hull tactfully thanked the Soviet Government for its help.[39]

This was an exceptional incident, though, and the US negotiators grew uneasy as Zhukov's troops approached the first camps known to contain Americans. On 5 December the US Embassy in Moscow raised the matter once more, to no avail. Harriman waited for over three weeks, then wrote again. To everyone's astonishment, a reply from Vyshinsky arrived the same day. It announced that two Soviet generals had been appointed to negotiate with Deane over the mutual repatriation of their countries' nationals. Deane first met his Soviet opposite numbers a month later; as he pointed out, 'just a little over six months after my first approach to the General Staff on the subject'.[40]

At that meeting (19 January 1945) Deane was presented with a complete Soviet draft agreement, and the next day a similar one was presented to the British Embassy. To the representatives of the two Western Allies, this proposed agreement seemed on the face of it reasonable enough, and only required a few minor amendments. It provided for the concentration and care of liberated 'citizens'; the immediate notification of the prisoners' government of their release and whereabouts; the admission of repatriation representatives 'into the concentration camps and points where citizens of their country are located'; and the 'quickest possible repatriation of these persons'. In Deane's words: 'The agreement was a good one, but, so far as the Russians were concerned, it turned out to be just another piece of paper.' However, that could not yet be known, and the easiest course appeared to be to accept the draft more or less *in toto*.

Only one serious reservation required consideration, and Deane telegraphed his comments to SHAEF Headquarters. This was the crucial question as to what constituted a Soviet citizen. Pointing out 'the possibility of reprisals by the enemy if we permit Soviet authorities to claim German prisoners of war as Soviet citizens and assist in returning them to Russia possibly to be punished', Deane suggested that an easy way out would be to make the Soviet authorities responsible for such identification.

On the diplomatic level, Deane 'suggested to the representatives that the British be included in these negotiations since their problems parallel ours. The Soviet representatives agreed to consider this but do not seem receptive to the idea. They appeared to prefer to have separate negotiations with the British.'[41]

The only British concern was to effect an agreement as swiftly as possible. They wanted to be able to set up arrangements for the protection and return of the British and Commonwealth prisoners. The negotiations appeared to have reached a stalemate, as the status of the 12,000 Russian prisoners still in Britain had not been satisfactorily arranged. It was believed that the Soviets had 'made it very clear that they regard the whole problem as one of reciprocity and do not propose to go further until they get satisfaction with regard to the status of their nationals in the United Kingdom'. Accordingly, the Foreign Office hoped that a reciprocal agreement could be speedily drawn up, which would include a satisfactory proviso on this issue. It was suggested that a suitable occasion at which to discuss and settle this vexed question would be at the forthcoming meeting of Allied leaders at Yalta, codenamed 'Argonaut'.[42]

Churchill, Roosevelt and Stalin would be present, and it should be possible to include military and diplomatic experts on the problem of the prisoners, who could tackle the issue with their United States and Soviet counterparts.

One point with which the Soviets were deeply concerned was their insistence that 'such an agreement should extend also to Soviet citizens and British subjects interned and forcibly deported by the Germans'.

As the British Embassy in Moscow commented: 'Whilst forcibly deported Soviet civilians other than prisoners of war run into many thousands, I assume that there are few if any British subjects in this category.' This striking anomaly caused some raised eyebrows, 'but in the opinion of the Foreign Office this must be accepted if we are to secure agreement about prisoners of war'.[43]

On 29 January Eden submitted a paper on the subject to the War Cabinet, urging acceptance of the Soviet terms and swift agreement, preferably 'at the impending Conference'. When the War Cabinet met two days later to consider and approve this recommendation, neither Eden nor Churchill was present.[44] They had already arrived in Malta on the first stage of the road to Yalta.

The British position was settled and clear. But, despite the Soviet preference for separate negotiations, it was unavoidable that agreement would have to be reached with the Americans 'in view of the integrated nature of the British American Commands in Western and Southern Europe'. It was also essential that it should 'be regarded by the Allied Commanders-in-Chief . . . as workable'.[45]

The trouble was that the Americans did not find the problem or its settlement nearly so straightforward. Above all, several distinguished State Department officials were unhappy about authorising their country's adhesion to anything that appeared dishonourable or in-humane. The same situation had arisen in the British Cabinet. But it was now many months since the objections of Lord Selborne and Sir James Grigg had been overruled, and the Prime Minister's qualms allayed. The Cabinet had delivered its ruling, and the matter was one for the Foreign Office to settle. At no time was a dissentient voice raised within the Foreign Office, and at no time then or since is one of its members known to have expressed a regret or reservation.

Not so the State Department. Edward R. Stettinius (who had succeeded Cordell Hull as Secretary of State on 21 November 1944) understood the nature of Soviet Communism no better than his President. But, unlike Roosevelt, he 'was a decent man of considerable innocence. All his impulses were correct. He was certainly no intriguer, no infighter, no politician.'[46] On 3 January he telegraphed Harriman in Moscow to stress his anxiety that the repatriation of released American prisoners should not be linked with the return of Soviet nationals found amongst German prisoners. He explained that a 'difficulty has arisen here in the determination of claimants to Soviet nationality whom this Government is prepared to turn over to the Soviet authorities'. He also noted that there were 'a few with Slavic names who disclaim Soviet nationality'.[47]

Such were Stettinius's reservations at the beginning of January. On 25 January he set off for the Yalta meeting. He arrived in Morocco the next day, and spent the following three days discussing the problems to be raised at the coming conference. Stettinius himself tells how there 'were many incoming telegrams from Acting Secretary of State Joseph C. Grew, in Washington'; amongst these must certainly have been a copy of the telegram Grew sent SHAEF Ambassador Murphy in London on 27 January. Grew expressed his concern that the British proposed draft agreement, of which the State Department now had a copy, was 'at considerable variance' with the proposals now being drawn up by the United States experts. Grew urged Murphy to ensure that American experts with SHAEF await further instructions based on these proposals.[48]

Meanwhile at Malta the British had learned that the Soviets would be providing an expert to discuss the problem at Yalta. It was necessary therefore for the British and Americans to co-ordinate their policy first.[49] The problem was that those policies diverged considerably. The British had long before conceded everything the Soviets desired; the Americans were apparently concerned to hold by the Geneva Convention and their view of international justice and humanity.

Grew had now forwarded United States counter proposals to the American delegation. These contained important variations on the British-Soviet draft accepted by the War Cabinet on 31 January. A lengthy preamble went out of its way to define who were liberated prisoners or citizens liable to repatriation: 'Persons . . . who shall have been liberated . . . and who themselves claim US citizenship or USSR citizenship . . . such persons being hereinafter referred to as "claimants to" US or USSR citizenship as the case may be'. And Paragraph 8 laid down clearly that: 'The contracting parties agree also that this agreement will not apply to citizens of the contracting party who are captured as members of or accompanying the enemy forces and who claim the protection of any applicable international convention, or agreement by which the custodian party has heretofore become bound.'[50] These passages would have provided the safeguard of the Geneva Convention to any prisoners laying claim to it.

In the view of the Acting Secretary of State, no other course was consonant with America's commitments in international law. Moreover, any other interpretation would result in serious risk to American prisoners on two separate counts. Firstly, the Germans might retaliate on Americans held by them for any ill-treatment accorded to 'German' prisoners who had surrendered to the Americans. And secondly, if uniform was not the final indication of citizenship, then numerous

American servicemen of German, Italian or Japanese origin might find themselves likewise denied the protection of their uniform.

On 1 February Grew pointed out these considerations in a stern note to the Soviet Chargé d'Affaires, Nikolai Novikov. Novikov had demanded the return of those Russians at Camp Rupert who had evaded repatriation by claiming German citizenship, and this Grew resolutely refused.[51]

Before flying on to the Crimea, the British and American parties conferred at Malta (codeword 'Cricket') to see how far they could settle the preliminary aspects of topics likely to arise at the conference. On 1 February Eden and Stettinius met on board the British warship *Sirius*. Conversation covered a range of subjects, including the prisoner-of-war agreement. Stettinius later described this as 'brief and inconclusive', but soon afterwards discussions began between British and American experts. News had come through of the liberation of the first party of American servicemen in Poland,[52] and United States officials seemingly began to be affected by the British viewpoint. At least, Eden reported to the Foreign Office that their 'present view seems to be to approve the provisional draft single text drawn up before I left London and not to attach too much importance to the comments of State Department . . . which appear to them and us to be rather out of date in present circumstances when camps are being overrun rapidly by advancing Soviet Armies'.[53]

Colonel Phillimore reported to the War Office that Charles Bohlen fully concurred in preferring the British draft, 'and thought little of the objections made by Washington . . . Bohlen is, I think, convinced that if we are to get a quick agreement we must stick to the main points and cut out any frills, and we are going ahead on those lines.'[54]

Matters of greater importance than the agreement on prisoners were up for discussion by the Big Three, but already on 4 and 5 February Eden was urging Churchill to raise the matter personally with Stalin.[55] Meanwhile Stettinius and his advisers were swiftly coming round to Eden's viewpoint. Messages from Eisenhower had stressed the urgency of coming to a decision over the 21,000 Russians now in US custody. 'Our experience shows that about five per cent of prisoners captured from the Germans are Russian citizens. Also, approximately four per cent of these Russians require hospital treatment. We shall, therefore, have a continuing accession of Russians as operations proceed. The only complete solution to this problem from all points of view is the early repatriation of these Russians.'[56] Eden took this up in a letter to Stettinius, urging in consequence speedy acceptance of the British draft, and on the same day the US Admiral Land assured the Secretary of

State that shipping could be found for this purpose.[57] Eden also wrote to Molotov, accepting in principle the Russian draft, and expressing a strong desire that the agreement should be ratified before the Conference broke up.[58]

Stettinius and his advisers had been completely won round to the Foreign Office viewpoint. An anguished telegram from Grew in Washington provided the swan song of those who had hoped for a firmer attitude. He had learned that the British text was on the point of being accepted, and urged Stettinius to ensure that certain vital points be covered. These included:

> Protection of Geneva Convention which we have informed Soviet Government we will accord to Soviet citizens captured in German uniform who demand such protection ... Soviet citizens in the United States not prisoners of war whose cases the Attorney General feels should be dealt with on basis of traditional American policy of asylum ... Persons claimed as citizens by the Soviet authorities who were not Soviet citizens prior to outbreak of war and who do not now claim Soviet citizenship.

But Stettinius dismissed the necessity for the incorporation of these points into the final agreement. He wrote on 9 February:

> The consensus here is that it would be unwise to include questions relative to the protection of the Geneva Convention and to Soviet citizens in the US in an agreement which deals primarily with the exchange of prisoners liberated by the Allied armies as they march into Germany. With respect to 'claimants', notwithstanding the danger of German retaliation, we believe there will be serious delays in the release of our prisoners of war unless we reach prompt agreement on this question.[59]

The Combined Chiefs of Staff had approved a draft text which contained no mention of the protection of the Convention; at the same time the shipping requested by Eisenhower was ordered to be provided.[60]

Short of any final hitch, the agreement remained only to be signed. Churchill's approval was required for the British, and at the same time Eden again urged him to raise the matter personally with Stalin. He provided the Prime Minister with a brief résumé of points that might be brought up, stressed the urgent need to conclude the agreement 'before the Conference breaks up', and provided a list of seven German camps overrun by the Red Army, which were estimated to hold some 50,000 British Commonwealth prisoners.[61] The opportunity came on the afternoon of 10 February, when Stalin and Molotov received Churchill and Eden at the former palace of Prince Yusupov.

After a discussion on the fate of Poland, Churchill spoke of the embarrassment caused by the large number of Russian prisoners held in the West. Some had already been returned, whilst others were on their way. But what did the Marshal want done with the rest?

MARSHAL STALIN hoped they could be sent to Russia as quickly as possible. He asked that they should not be ill-treated and that they should be segregated from the Germans. The Soviet Government looked upon all of them as Soviet citizens. He asked that there should be no attempt to induce any of them to refuse repatriation. Those who had agreed to fight for the Germans could be dealt with on their return to Russia.

THE PRIME MINISTER explained that we were anxious that these prisoners should be repatriated, and the only difficulty arose from the lack of shipping space ...

Neither of the leaders brought up the question of forcible repatriation in the case of those unwilling to return, but question and answer are implicit in this terse dialogue. Again, without acknowledging to each other the reason, the two leaders agreed that only the fact of the agreement, and not its text, should be published. Why risk inquisitive analyses?[62]

Now it merely remained to sign the completed text. A British diplomat, Pierson Dixon, has left this description of the scene:

It was decided that the agreement on Prisoners of War should be announced separately, so as soon as the meeting broke up I went into the 'Sun Room' [of the American delegation's headquarters in the Livadia Palace] and drafted the announcement, also a letter to Molotov, covering all our outstanding points. I then went up and had lunch with the Americans in their mess ... After lunch I was called into the President's dining room. The President and his party were just leaving and, shortly after, Stalin said goodbye, stepping out of his path to extend a large paw with a broad grin to me, saying 'au revoir'. The PM then drove back to Vorontsov, and the Foreign Secretaries re-entered the room for their final meeting. The atmosphere was very friendly and informal. In the middle of the meeting A.E. and Molotov broke off to sign the Prisoners of War Agreement, which had been concluded only a few minutes before.[63]

The next day the War Cabinet in London read and approved the arrangements telegraphed from the Crimea. In the absence of Churchill and Eden at the Conference, the leading figures at the session were Attlee and Bevin. [64] In five months' time the responsibility for implementing the agreement just concluded would fall on them.

The selection of the Crimea as the scene of the ratification of the agreement on prisoners of war was tragically appropriate. But Churchill, who loved to reflect on precedents from the past when considering current issues, could not know that in the very peninsula on which they were gathered there had recently taken place such an operation as that which he was now in the process of arranging. Only eight months earlier, the NKVD had, after preliminary massacres, deported the entire Crimean Tartar population to Siberia.[65] Transport vehicles for the operation were supplied by British and American forces in Persia, and Soviet officials believed they were aware of the purpose for which the trucks were required.[66] However, Stalin had in turn been anticipated, though abortively, in this project by his predecessor's government in the Crimea. Hitler had also planned to deport the entire population, and replace them with Germans from the Tyrol—a project frustrated on Himmler's orders.[67]

The massive Soviet transfer of the Crimean population was not merely a forerunner of the agreement Eden and Churchill were now offering Stalin. The Agreement itself in turn helped to complete the operation. Some Tartars had managed to escape westwards before the Red Army retook the Crimea in May 1944. Thousands were murdered by the SS, who took them for Jews (as Moslems, they were circumcised).[68] But some 250 survived, to fall into the hands of the British Army in Germany. They pleaded to be allowed to emigrate to Turkey, but in June 1945 the 21st Army Group received firm instructions from Patrick Dean of the Foreign Office that, under the Yalta Agreement, the Crimean Tartars were to be handed back to Stalin.[69] As is well known, the survivors of the Crimean Tartar nation are still not permitted to return to their homeland.

The Yalta Agreement on Prisoners of War contained no provisions regarding the return of unwilling citizens to the USSR. Though urged by Acting Secretary of State Grew to insert clauses protecting such people, Stettinius and his advisers had finally come over to the British view. This was that it was essential above all to reach an agreement whilst the Big Three were assembled in the Crimea, and that precise interpretations could be worked out in due course.[70] Charles Bohlen was one of those who argued (against Grew) that provisos and reservations on this issue should be excluded in the interests of concluding the agreement speedily. But equally it was he who wrote later: 'There was nothing in this agreement that required the forcible repatriation of unwilling Soviet citizens to the Soviet Union.'[71]

Therefore, as matters stood immediately after the Yalta Agreement, the options of the United States on this point remained open. The British felt themselves bound by Eden's prior pledge at the 'Tolstoy' Conference in Moscow in the previous October, but no such commitment tied the Americans. Roosevelt himself 'never saw the document' signed at Yalta; it was General Deane and the military who were largely responsible for the text, and their sole concern was with the safe return of American prisoners of war.[72] The Soviets did not raise the issue of force, and Deane had no reason to anticipate it. State Department participation was largely bypassed by President Roosevelt's concept of 'personal diplomacy', and it seems clear that those who guided State Department policy were largely taken by surprise when the problem burst upon them after the German surrender.[73]

On 1 February 1945 Grew had informed the Soviet Chargé d'Affaires that the United States would continue to uphold a strict interpretation of its obligations under the Geneva Convention, and this remained American policy for some months after the Yalta Agreement.[74] On 23 March, however, Ambassador Gromyko challenged Grew's arguments concerning the correct application of the Geneva Convention, and Grew replied, restating the State Department's position. The interpretation was given as before, ending with a brief résumé of what the United States would or would not do. 'This Government will continue to return to Soviet control all Soviet citizens captured as members of German formations in German uniform other than those who demand to be treated as German prisoners under the Prisoner of War Convention. With respect to those who make such demand, this Government must retain them for the time being in its custody.' So far so good, but the next and final sentence bore an ominous ring. 'However, the Soviet Government may be assured that their disposition will be taken up again between the two Governments when organised resistance in Germany shall have ceased.'[75]

On 3 May, when that resistance virtually had ceased, Grew went further. 'This Government has no intention of retaining these persons permanently and will be glad to take up their disposition again when there are no longer any American prisoners of war in the custody of the German armed forces.'[76]

Four days later Germany surrendered, and any threat of German retaliation on prisoners of war vanished overnight. As John Galsworthy of the Foreign Office was to write a few days later: 'The basis of the American interpretation was the desire to ensure that persons wearing American uniform, who were not, however, American citizens, were treated as American PoWs by the Germans. Since the surrender of Germany this consideration has lost its force, and it remains to be seen whether the Americans will continue to stick by their principle for its own sake.'[77]

In ignorance of the moves being initiated in governing circles, American troops in the field were continuing to act in accordance with what they took to be United States policy.

In May 1945, [wrote George Orwell] I visited a large prisoner-of-war camp not far from Munich. Prisoners were passing through it from day to day, but at a given moment the number there was about 100,000. According to the American officer in charge, the prisoners were on average 10 per cent non-German, mostly Russians and Hungarians. The Russians were being sorted by asking the simple question, *'Do you want to go back to Russia or not?'* A respectable proportion—of course, I have no exact figures—answered 'not', and these were regarded as Germans and kept in the camp, while the others were released. I saw numbers of them: some were from the TODT organisation, others from the Wehrmacht.[78]

But from the moment that, on 25 April, Russian and American troops met at Torgau on the Elbe, mass exchanges of liberated Allied prisoners became a subject of urgent discussion.[79] George Kennan at the Moscow Embassy warned the State Department that a final decision on the use of force could be postponed no longer.[80]

5

The Allied Forces Act:
The Foreign Office
versus The Law

ON THE DAY THAT ANTHONY EDEN SIGNED THE AGREEMENT ON prisoners of war at Yalta, he and Molotov also subscribed a subsidiary agreement on the status of those Russian prisoners who were held in camps in Britain. Despite the dull and routine appearance of the text, there lies behind it an intriguing (in both senses) history. So far the story of the forced repatriation of Russians had taken place in far-off places: Egypt, the south of France, the Crimea. But much of the drama was unfolded in such prosaic spots as Worthing and Guildford, and it is to events in Britain that we must now turn.

In an earlier chapter it was shown how the Russians captured after the D-Day landings in June 1944 were, for reasons purely logistical, shipped back to England and placed in camps recently vacated by the troops employed in the invasion. When Eden first notified the Soviet Ambassador of their presence on 20 July, there were some 1,600 in British hands. By October there were ten times this number.[1]

Once in Britain the Russian prisoners were gradually segregated from the Germans, and placed in separate camps, but they were still technically prisoners. Pending a decision on their future, it was in any case necessary to keep them under control in camps, for purposes of administration and discipline.

General Vasiliev, head of the Soviet Military Mission, proposed that the captured Russians 'should be released from prisoner-of-war status and should enjoy the status of Soviet citizens temporarily on Allied territory'. He also 'suggested that all those who had been members of the Red Army should be organised under their own officers and NCOs in their present or similar accommodation . . .' This proposition was quite acceptable to the British, and all apparently that remained was to place this change of status on a proper legal basis. A special procedure for such a contingency already existed in the form of the Allied Forces Act (1940). This, as already explained, made it legal for Allied governments in exile to maintain military units in Britain. It was only necessary for the Soviets to fulfil certain formalities with regard to the proposed Soviet-organised bodies of prisoners, and for an Order under the Act to be issued in the name of the King.[2] It seemed simple enough; nevertheless there were difficulties.

But why were the Soviets so anxious to release their nationals from prisoner-of-war status? First, and obviously, came national prestige. The fact that the Russians continued to be regarded as enemy prisoners was a constant reminder of the fact that the USSR alone of all the Allies had provided the enemy with thousands of recruits.

Secondly came the necessity of gaining effective control over the prisoners, so that any actions likely to impede or embarrass the smooth running of repatriation operations could be prevented.[3]

Thirdly, the Soviet Government may well have been concerned about the possibility of the prisoners invoking the protection of the Geneva Convention. It is probable that it was not until about this time that the Soviets understood that the Russians' enlistment into the Wehrmacht entitled them to claim to be treated as Germans. This was then the view of the American State Department, which was conveyed to the Soviet Embassy as early as 27 September 1944.[4] The British did not share this view, but the Soviets were not to know this, nor that they might not change their minds. So long as the Russians continued to be regarded as prisoners of war, so long could they have the chance of claiming German citizenship under the Convention, in this way evading repatriation.

Discussions opened between the War Office and the Home Office concerning details of the application of the Allied Forces Act to the Russians. Theobald Mathew of the Home Office set out the measures requisite to make the Act effective. Chief amongst these was a precise definition of what would constitute a member of an Allied Force, under the Act:

> In view of the statutory definition in Sec. 5(1) of the Allies Powers (War Service) Act, 1942, of a member of an Allied Force, it is essential that the Russians should be able to prove that any particular individual has *served* in their forces since August 22nd, 1940. Mere enrolment may not be enough unless accompanied by some act of service such as receiving pay, attending a parade or putting on uniform. This should not present any difficulty in

practice, but it may be important if our courts have to deal with an alleged deserter or absentee.

In other words, it would be necessary to transfer the Russians from prisoner-of-war status into genuine organised military units. It was also stressed that it would not be acceptable for death sentences or corporal punishment to be inflicted by Soviet officers while the newly-formed units remained on British soil.[5]

Eden telegraphed a despatch to the British Ambassador in Moscow, Sir Archibald Clark Kerr, explaining that 'we are prepared to meet requirements of Soviet Military Mission in full and to do our best to complete as soon as possible necessary formal arrangements.'

A draft agreement was meanwhile drawn up, which, if the Soviets agreed to it, would provide the basis for the effecting of the Act. Experts noted, however, that the Act could only relate 'to "members of the Soviet forces" and does not cover Soviet nationals who are not serving in those forces. (There is no provision for the Soviet Union to conscript their nationals in the U.K.)'[6]

At a meeting with the Russian Military Mission, General Gepp (Director of Prisoners of War) attempted to make the British position clear, but to no avail.[7] British officialdom was distraught. What was to be done? From all sides came flurried demands that the matter be settled as soon as possible. On 3 October, Herbert Morrison, the Home Secretary, wrote to Eden: 'I agree with you that it is desirable to repatriate these Russians as soon as possible. Apart from other consider-ations, if they remain on our soil as members of the Soviet Armed Forces ... there is at least a risk that we shall have a considerable number of complaints about ill-treatment by the Soviet officers of the men ... while others may be reluctant to recognise their Soviet citizenship.'[8] From the Foreign Office, Sir Orme Sargent stressed the same worrying aspect.[9]

Eden and other supporters of the policy of forcible repatriation have repeatedly stressed that it was justified by the necessity of obtaining satisfactory guarantees that the USSR would co-operate in the return of the liberated British prisoners. On a more general basis, the Foreign Office hoped too that obliging the Soviets in this instance would generate overall goodwill in relations between the two countries.[10] It is important to note that there was a third motive: the fear lest the situation of the Russian prisoners should erupt into an open scandal in Britain. Herbert Morrison and Orme Sargent had voiced this fear; now Eden's Under-Secretary at the Foreign Office indicated the nature of the danger. On 15 October, when Eden was in Moscow, Sir Alexander Cadogan expressed his anxious desire that Russian *civilians* (who could not legally be incorporated into the proposed Allied Force) should be repatriated as soon as possible.[11]

Two days after this, Eden, who was with Churchill in Moscow for the 'Tolstoy' visit, held his meeting with Molotov at which he agreed that all Soviet citizens should be returned, 'without reference to the wishes of the individuals concerned'. He at the same time took the opportunity of handing Molotov a copy of the draft agreement needed to sustain the Act.[12]

But matters were not so satisfactory as might appear. No sooner had Eden returned to England, than Clark Kerr in Moscow notified him 'that the People's Commissariat for Foreign Affairs did not like the draft agreement which you handed to M. Molotov . . . as it would have the effect of organising these people into an armed Allied unit in the United Kingdom which did not conform to the wishes of the Soviet Government'. It was pointed out to M. Novikov of the People's Commissariat that this 'was the only practicable method of enabling the people to be regarded as free citizens of an Allied power pending their repatriation'. After some discussion, Novikov appeared to concur with a face-saving arrangement whereby Soviet officers could have free access to the prisoners' camps, though 'the Soviet citizens concerned would remain technically prisoners of war until they were repatriated'.

These ponderous exchanges, which resembled a game of poker played by blindfolded antagonists, suddenly aroused the Jovian wrath of the Prime Minister himself. Unfairly, he blamed the Foreign Office for the delays, whereas, as has been seen, they were desperately anxious to conclude an agreement. On the Foreign Office desk descended one of those celebrated Personal Minutes: 'Are we not making unnecessary difficulties? It seems to me we work up fights about matters already conceded in principle, and in this detail the lower grades of Soviet officials obtain an undue prominence. I thought we had arranged to send all the Russians back to Russia.'

Sir Alexander Cadogan replied at length, explaining the Foreign Office desire to fall in with Soviet wishes, and the frustrating and inexplicable reluctance of the Soviets to accept what was 'not only the best but the only practicable solution . . .' Churchill testily scrawled a note at the foot of Cadogan's letter: 'We ought to get rid of them *all* as soon as possible. This was your promise to Molotov as I understood it.'[13]

Why did the Soviet authorities object so strongly to a measure that had been devised solely for their benefit? They were as anxious to regain all the prisoners as the Foreign Office was to be rid of them; why then did they for so many months obstruct negotiations in this apparently obtuse way? This no one in the Foreign Office could answer; experts could express only bewilderment and continue negotiations in the dark.

Though no one in the Foreign Office appears to have registered the fact, the Soviets had quite clearly stated their reason for objecting to the procedure following the Allied Forces Act. Both in London and Moscow Soviet officials had, as we have seen, rejected the Act, 'as it would have the effect of organising these people into an armed Allied unit in the United Kingdom which did not conform to the wishes of the Soviet Government'. Clearly this was no improvised pretext; but it emanated from a central authority.

Had Foreign Office experts reflected on this, they might well have noted that the Soviet Union had an almost obsessive fear of its subjects abroad bearing arms. In strong contrast to Nazi Germany and Fascist Italy, the Soviet Union had not dared to send military units to fight in Spain in 1936.[14] We have already described how SOE's project for employing liberated Russian prisoners to work with the French *Maquis* or to organise resistance amongst slave-workers in Germany had been quashed by the NKVD. M. Gousev had alleged that the British military authorities in Egypt 'are enlisting Soviet prisoners of war'—a charge which, after a painstaking investigation, had recently been reported by Lord Moyne as being 'baseless', as had 'previous allegations of this nature . . .'[15] In November SHAEF was asked 'to investigate a report that 850 Russians were shipped from Marseilles to North Africa to be conscripted into the French Foreign Legion, but before the enquiries could be started the Soviet Embassy informed us that they had evidence that the report was untrue . . .';[16] despite this wild-goose chase, NKVD agents travelled as far as Indo-China in an unsuccessful effort to track down Russian recruits in the Legion.[17] In the United States Gromyko accused the Americans of similar conduct, but received a sarcastic rebuff from Secretary of State Hull.[18]

These allegations reflected very real fears held by Stalin and the Soviet leadership. Despite the most appalling brutalities inflicted on the Russians, Hitler had succeeded in raising nearly a million anti-Communist legionaries from amongst the prisoners in German hands. What success might not the humane democracies have if they tried the same game? Every Russian who caught even a glimpse of life outside the USSR was suspected of being infected with unsound views, and if he returned had to be isolated in a labour camp. Units of the Red Army that had merely been temporarily encircled by the German Army were at once suspect; how could Stalin then feel safe with a disciplined force of 20,000 on British soil, far from his control? It was no good sending over tried Red Army officers to command them, for who knew that they might not follow the example of that brilliant young officer, General Andrei Vlasov?

Meanwhile the British Embassy in Moscow was urged to make another effort to convince the Soviets of the necessity of accepting the Allied Forces Act. It could be pointed out that there would be no need to arm the units so formed, if that was what was objected to. The matter was becoming ever more urgent, since 'sooner or later also public interest may be aroused in this question of status which might be embarrassing'.[19] Patrick Dean expressed fear lest this might be debated in Parliament, recommending that all mention of the Act be suppressed in the House of Commons.[20]

The Soviets reiterated their demands for the ending of prisoner-of-war status, and the British patiently submitted to them a new draft agreement, substituting the word 'formations' in lieu of the apparently objectionable 'forces'. On 1 December the new draft was handed to Novikov in Moscow. It was carefully explained that the use of some such term was unavoidable, in that

> The existing British legal and constitutional position does not permit the liberty of citizens of a friendly foreign power to be restricted whilst they are in the United Kingdom unless the authorities of that power in the United Kingdom are prepared, if a case ever comes to court, to prove that the citizens over whom they are exercising jurisdiction are in fact serving in units or contingents of their forces. The domestic law of the United Kingdom in this respect could not be altered excepting by Act of Parliament.[21]

As officials confessed privately, 'a Bill for this purpose would cause undesirable publicity, delay, and possibly controversy'.[22]

Both Novikov in Moscow and Sobolev at the London Embassy appeared at last to grasp the point. But they seemed powerless to go further, and a lengthy red herring had to be dealt with, in the form of an entirely false assertion by General Vasiliev that Eden had months ago agreed with Gousev that the prisoners could become 'free citizens', as opposed to prisoners of war.[23]

When the new year opened, consequently, matters were scarcely more advanced than in the previous August. On 4 January, Patrick Dean noted that 'in spite of all our efforts, therefore, we are making no progress'; the Russians in Britain were still classed as prisoners of war, and the latest Soviet note (27 December) was once again demanding that they 'be regarded by all British authorities not as prisoners of war but as the free citizens of an Allied Power'. Dean now put forward a bold suggestion, which could well force the Soviets' hand.

In order to try and settle the matter once and for all what we should like now to do is to tell the Soviet Embassy in writing that if they want these persons to be 'free Soviet citizens' we are fully prepared to agree, but that means that they will be let out of the Soviet camps and allowed such freedom and facilities as are normally permitted to Allied nationals in the United Kingdom, subject always to considerations of security. In particular if this course is followed we cannot in any way guarantee that these persons will be sent back to the Soviet Union, since we have not powers to do so, and within the ordinary limitations they will be free to go about the country and take any employment which is offered to them.

The Soviets would not of course accept this, 'since above all they want to keep these people together under military discipline in order to repatriate them', but the threat might bring them to reason.[24]

The threat was a potent one, as the British had a long and honourable tradition of granting asylum to political refugees. In 1943, for instance, two Russian sailors had deserted from their ship in a British port. A Soviet demand for their return had been firmly refused.[25]

However, the intriguing possibility that the Soviets might through this misunderstanding have accidentally freed all the Russian prisoners in Britain came to nothing. It was decided that the whole matter could best be settled at the forthcoming Crimean Conference.[26] In addition, the grey fog of Soviet perception seems to have been partially penetrated by a belated awareness that the Foreign Office was desperately trying to assist them rather than the prisoners. Novikov in Moscow drew up a counter draft in reply to the one handed to him by the British on 1 December. In this he accepted the subtle compromise use of the word 'formations' instead of 'forces', though the persisting fear of the prisoners being formed into regular units was evinced by the omission of the word 'military' where reference was made to the prisoners being 'subject to Soviet military law'.

Mr. Balfour of the British Embassy

therefore asked Novikov whether I was correct in assuming that notwithstanding omission of word 'military' from Soviet re-draft, the Soviet authorities in the United Kingdom would be prepared, if a case ever came to court, to prove that citizens over whom they will be exercising jurisdiction are, in fact, serving in units or contingents of their forces. To this enquiry he laconically replied 'that will be all right'. Although this is apt to be a stock phrase with Novikov, I feel satisfied, in the light of very precise explanation of point which I have previously supplied to him [the point made by Dean, see above], that he understands and meant what he said.[27]

Patrick Dean felt that this compromise could be made workable and should be accepted.[28]

Dean and Phillimore travelled to Yalta as experts on the prisoner-of-war problem for the Foreign Office and War Office respectively. Both sides were more or less content with the compromise wording now settled, and the final Agreement was signed on 11 February. The Soviet objection to the words 'military' and 'forces' was sustained, and the neutral terms 'Soviet law' and 'formations and groups' were employed instead.[29] All that remained was for the Order under the Allied Forces Act to be officially promulgated; it appeared on 22 February.[30]

Officially, from that date onwards, the Russians in Britain were no longer prisoners of war but members of an Allied military force stationed on British soil. But this was merely a form of words, and the Soviet Repatriation Commission bore strict instructions that nothing was to be done that might organise the prisoners into an actual force. This led to some awkward situations.

In April General Ratov, who had arrived in Britain to organise the repatriation, requested of Brigadier Firebrace that he should provide British guards and prison facilities for some of the men. Ratov had placed ten under arrest: 'They are all cases of men who have stated that they refuse to return to the Soviet Union. Some of them are desperate and have openly threatened suicide in preference to returning home.' Firebrace arranged temporarily for the offenders' detention, but 'told General Ratov that I expected him to make arrangements to guard his own men at the Soviet Camp at Newlands Corner. He told me that he did not think that he could do this as his men were not armed and he did not think that the Soviet Government would give permission for them to be armed.'

In a letter (25 April) Firebrace pointed out to Ratov that the Agreement specifically laid down that the Soviet authorities were obliged to maintain their own discipline. Somewhat reluctantly Firebrace agreed to arrange for a limited number to be detained in a British military prison, but in general he remained unsympathetic and unco-operative.[31]

The organisation of the Russian prisoners did not in reality constitute an Allied Force under the meaning of the Act. This was unlikely to come into the open under normal conditions. British and Soviet officials were determined to sustain the pious fraud, and none of the prisoners was likely to become aware of the precarious legality of the Act—at least not so long as they remained obedient and in camp. But what of those who deserted? This was a highly awkward situation. The Foreign Office was concerned that such men should be returned promptly with no publicity; above all they must not appear in court. But as Sir Frank Newsam of the Home Office explained to Patrick

Dean: 'It is clear, however, that the police would be acting in a manner directly contrary to the law if they were to hand over to a military escort an absentee from the Soviet Forces who had not expressed his willingness to be so handed over, and I am afraid there can be no question of the Home Secretary instructing or advising the police, either orally or by circular, to take such action.' Despite this, Newsam continued with the remarkable proposal that the police should temporarily detain a suspected deserter at their station for questioning. At the same time they would telephone the local Command HQ, notifying the time and place that the suspect would be released. The Army could then have a military escort lying in wait, who would 'arrest the man *on their own responsibility* soon after his release from custody. It is essential, however, that such an arrest should not take place immediately outside the police station or in circumstances which would be tantamount to the police handing the man over direct to the military escort.' With this letter Newsam enclosed a draft circular to chief constables, urging them to follow this unusual procedure.

On 13 April Dean replied optimistically: 'We concur in the suggested procedure which, though it inevitably involves some risk of trouble, will probably, we feel, work out all right in practice.'

The whole scheme came to nothing, however, as the War Office declined to take on the role of kidnapper: 'We are unable to accept the procedure suggested in the letter of 5th April. We cannot see any justification for concluding that the military authorities can properly arrest on their own responsibility members of an Allied Force when the appropriate procedure has not been followed, a proceeding which in our view would be no less directly contrary to the law than that which you, for your part, decline to accept.'[32]

However, fortune favoured the Foreign Office officials. Few Russians tried to escape, and fewer succeeded. The victims were well aware of what was likely to be their fate if they displayed any aversion to returning, and their only hope seemed to be to put a brave face on the matter and pray that they might be amongst the tiny percentage that survived the camps of GULAG.

Matters did not always proceed smoothly, however. As soon as it proved feasible, the shipment of Russian prisoners to Britain had been halted.[33] British law had proved the stumbling-block we have noted, whereas in camps on the Continent 'it is possible to meet the wishes of the USSR fully in practice whilst notionally retaining Prisoner of War status'.[34] But the refusal of the Soviets to provide shipping for the return of their nationals in Britain had meant that the transportation in British ships of the thousands held here had dragged on until the summer of 1945. By the autumn virtually all had gone (apart from a group whose nationality was still under dispute), except eight who were reported 'escaped and not recaptured'.[35] They had fled from camps in Yorkshire, Durham, Surrey and Sussex at various dates in the spring and summer. Their names, of course, were known, and in the case of at least two so were their present whereabouts. Both had found refuge with English people who pitied their desperate situation.

Ivan Faschenko, for example, was a boy of sixteen who had been befriended by a family named Rockley, in Nottingham. Colonel Hammer of the War Office was able to report that very likely he could be traced without difficulty. Why then was he not arrested at once and handed over to SMERSH? Sir Samuel Hoare of the Home Office (a future Member of the Human Rights Commission of the United Nations) explained the predicament to Major Wallis, who had taken over Firebrace's position:

> As it appears unlikely that we have any means of compelling this young man to return to the camp, and it is undesirable for that reason to bring him before a court, it is equally undesirable that the police should make enquiries about him because his friends in this country will immediately protest, and there is in fact no effective action that the police would be in a position to take. We can only suggest that you should again, as you did before, endeavour to use your good offices to persuade him to return for repatriation.

What was particularly awkward was the fact that Faschenko was a *civilian*, and so (even apart from his tender age) could not possibly be held to be a member of the illusory 'Allied Force' to which the prisoners were supposed to belong for the purposes of the Act.

Thomas Brimelow of the Foreign Office (later Permanent Under-Secretary) confirmed Hoare's fears.

> We entirely agree with your views about FASCHENKO. Having become a 'deserter', he is most unlikely to surrender himself voluntarily to the Soviet authorities, and there would be serious trouble with the latter if they heard that we had been in touch with him but failed to arrest him. On the other hand, any attempt to arrest him would almost certainly give rise to the kind of publicity which we are most anxious to avoid . . . and it would be most undesirable for him to be brought before a magistrate. This latter objection applies equally to the other civilian deserter,[36] LAURENCHUK.
>
> As regards the remaining six runners, who are said to have been serving members of the Red Army, we would again counsel caution, though we recognise that the problem is primarily one for the Home Office. As you are aware, there never has been an organised 'Soviet Force' in the UK . . . , and the application of the Allied Forces Act procedure to the inmates of the

camps for liberated Soviet citizens in this country, while being the only method by which we could implement the Yalta Agreement . . . , has always implied a risk, which has caused us to hope that the arrangement would never be subjected to scrutiny in a court of law.

As John Galsworthy (then at the Northern Department of the Foreign Office in London, now British Ambassador to Mexico) confided to Colonel Hammer:

> The whole arrangement was thus rather specious . . . We have always hoped that no such case would arise in connexion with any of the Soviet citizens in this country. Many of them, while regarded by us as members of the Soviet 'Forces' for purposes of administrative convenience, were, in fact, civilians who had never served in the Red Army, and if any such person had come before a magistrate, there might well have been embarrassing consequences. [Any attempt to order the arrest of the escapers] would be likely to provoke the kind of trouble (and publicity) which we have avoided so far, and I suggest we should advise against it.[37]

The retrieval of another of the eight 'deserters' was demanded by an NKVD officer, Colonel Kleshkanov. The resulting Foreign Office discussion served to bring out just what was the nature of the publicity feared. It was Thomas Brimelow again who minuted:

> The snag . . . is that Krokhin might well refuse to come quietly; in which case there would . . . be a scandal . . . A scandal with talk about irregular procedure, cheating people into accepting repatriation to the USSR etc. is to be avoided at all costs . . . If, after arrest, Krokhin denies that he is liable to such arrest and handing over to Soviet military authorities, he will have to come before a magistrate. Having been at large since April, he may have friends who will tell him to engage a solicitor; and if the solicitor knows his job, he will get into touch with one or other of the lawyers who know all the ins and outs of the Allied Forces Act . . . and in that case we may expect a strong defence.

The possibility of avoiding the use of the dubious Allied Forces Act by means of a deportation order by the Home Secretary, naming Krokhin as an undesirable alien, was considered. But the snag was 'that it might be embarrassing if we were asked why we had decided to deport this man instead of dealing with him under the Allied Forces procedure as a deserter. There is a further complication: a deportation order wd not permit of his being handed over to the Russians in this country, but I said that we cd almost certainly arrive at some understanding with the Russians on this score.'

But this theme was not elaborated further and Galsworthy concluded: 'An enquiry could easily reveal just how thin is the ice on which we have been skating ever since the Allied Forces Act ... Anti-Soviet sections of the press might easily make embarrassing use of such a disclosure.'[38]

6

From Paradise to Purgatory

FOR SEVERAL MONTHS AFTER THE DECISION TO REPATRIATE THEM HAD
been taken, the Russian prisoners in Britain lived in the 'limbo-
GULAG', under conditions that to them appeared ideal beyond anything they had conceived possible. Everyone who came in contact with
them appears to have been agreed on this. The relatively free and
comfortable life they led, in a countryside untouched by war or
tyranny, must have appeared in retrospect like an unreal dream. Their
subsequent fate may perhaps have been all the more terrible as a
result.

Within two days of the Normandy landings a few Russian prisoners
had been carried to Britain in returning tank-carriers and placed in a
camp at Kempton Park in Surrey.[1] They were members of one of the
forced-labour battalions conscripted to work on the Atlantic Wall
defences. Most had been captured in 1942. They had been given no
military training worthy of the name, and 'When the Allies started
bombing the beach,' the Russians said, 'they "just sat and waited for
things to happen".' They appeared to be men of low education and had
been quite cut off from communication with the outside world for
two years, as they spoke only Russian. Despite this, 'when asked if they
would like to go back to Russia, most of them were just indifferent or
even said "No".'[2]

But a group of about a thousand interrogated three weeks later at a
transit camp at Devizes were said for the most part to wish to return to
Russia 'provided that the opportunity to prove their devotion to their
own country should be given them ... They fear swift punishment
upon returning to the Soviet Union, yet evidence a will to return on a
real assurance that they will be given a chance to redeem themselves.'
This assumption of 'automatic punishment' was held despite the fact
that they all had been compelled to serve the Germans as a result of
force and 'starvation and terrible living conditions in PW camps'.[3]

Before this two prisoners in other camps had already expressed their fears by committing suicide.[4]

Whatever their motives, numbers of Russians were clearly desperately anxious to be allowed to lay their case before the Soviet authorities before any misunderstanding ensued. They were eager that the unbearable pressures which had led to their working for the Germans should be fully appreciated. 'Minor mutinies and hunger strikes' took place; these were generally staged by prisoners who imagined that it was the British who were obstructing their desire to explain their predicament to the Soviet Embassy, or who were trying in ostentatious fashion to dissociate themselves from fellow-prisoners who for one reason or another might be regarded as tainted out of the ordinary in their co-operation with the Germans. The Foreign Office accordingly became anxious to persuade Soviet representatives to meet the prisoners, so that these misunderstandings could be cleared up.[5]

The first serious trouble on this score arose at Butterwick Camp, near Malton in Yorkshire. There were held several hundred 'Russians', transferred from transit camps in the south. They spoke a multiplicity of tongues, for amongst them were men of races as diverse as Georgian, Turkestani and Tartar; there were even bemused Tajik tribesmen from the Pamirs. They had no idea what fate was intended for them, and their nervous frame of mind was apparent the moment they arrived at Butterwick. When their trucks drew up at the camp entrance the prisoners refused to alight. The camp duty officer and interpreter, Czeslaw Jesman, asked what was the matter and was able to put their minds at rest. A group of curious British staff officers, who had driven over to witness the Russians' arrival, had been taken for officers of the NKVD sent to supervise a massacre of the prisoners. About twenty of the prisoners were children, and a sizable group had been freed from the German prisoner-of-war camp on Alderney shortly before the D-Day landings.

A group of prisoners began soon after their arrival to agitate that they be allowed to return to Russia and join in the fight against Nazism. Petitions urging this were sent to the British military authorities, and also to the Soviet Embassy and Military Mission. The camp commandant, basing his findings on reports from a Russian-speaking officer, Captain Narishkin, commented: 'The agitation for return to Russia may be due more to fear of what might happen to them if they do not by agitation proclaim their position than for any other reason.'[6] Patrick Dean at the Foreign Office urged that the prisoners be informed that the delay came from the Soviet authorities and not the British, but this of course served only to increase the prisoners' agitation.[7]

Frightened by the silence of their country's representatives, and aware of the compromising nature of their situation, a group of about 550 of the Butterwick inmates became increasingly restive. A petition of 30 August complained that they had been 'issued with PW uniforms which we considered insulting'. These were men who had been captured in civilian clothes, and who were desperate not to be lumped with those who were probably compromised irrevocably by being captured in German uniform. In their fear they resorted to strike action, and refused to wear the PoW clothing with which they had been issued. When they persisted in this action, the Camp Commandant attempted to put pressure on them to conform by striking the rebels' tents and placing them on a bread-and-water ration. But despite the fact that some in consequence fell ill, and a heavy rain fell during a day and night, 'they show no sign of weakening, except that some of them have put on their clothes again.' As a report to the War Office pointed out, 'they have however become so inured to hard treatment in Concentration Camps on the continent, that it is considered very doubtful whether they will weaken to this treatment ... No improvement in the present position is anticipated until they have received either a visit, or a reassuring communication, from the Soviet Embassy.'

Noting that the prisoners had relented a little ('They have put on their trousers again'), the War Office strongly recommended 'that these Russian prisoners of war should be visited as soon as possible by one of the Soviet mission so that their position can be made clear to them.'[8]

It will be remembered that for some weeks the attitude of the Soviet Military Mission had been that the Russian prisoners simply did not exist ('I can show them to you,' Brigadier Firebrace had murmured in reply to Admiral Kharlanov). But now, in September 1944, the Soviet representatives had finally received instructions from Moscow as to what attitude to take. It was announced that Major-General Vasiliev of the Soviet Military Mission was to visit the camps for Russians in Yorkshire.[9]

Before this could take place, however, it was necessary for the Soviet representatives to go through a ritual that was a prerequisite of any Soviet negotiation. Captain Soldatenkov, an émigré Russian acting as a British Intelligence Officer, submitted a report from the reception camp at Kempton Park, in which he set out details of a massive conspiracy organised by White Russian émigrés to corrupt the Soviet prisoners from their instinctive loyalty to the Bolshevik state and Party. Established originally at a council of Orthodox Church dignitaries at Karlovtsy in Serbia, the tentacles of this latter-day Black Hand had stretched hideously across to London, and were even now extending to the camps in northern England. The subordinate chiefs of the group in England were listed as General Galfter (formerly Commander of the Moscow Guards Regiment), George Knupffer (leader of the *Mladorus* émigré party in England), and a Princess Mestchersky. The capacities for intrigue of such a group would appear to have been limited. The General and the Princess were prevented by age from any activity at all, and the *Mladorus* party had been dissolved some years previously. Mr. Knupffer informs me that the nearest attempt at subversion was some showings in towns near the camps of an early newsreel of the coronation of Nicholas II.[10]

Anyone might have been expected to realise the true purpose of Captain Soldatenkov's report. With contacts between the Soviet authorities and the prisoners in the camps about to open, it was necessary as insurance to provide a prior explanation of the widespread hatred and fear expressed by many for the Soviet Union.[11]

A more legitimate objection was to the visit of a Russian Orthodox priest to one of the Yorkshire camps. In accordance with the dictates of humanity (or possibly Article 16 of the 1929 Geneva Convention), the commandant of a camp at Catterick had given permission for a priest of the Orthodox Church in London to visit the prisoners and minister to their spiritual needs. Father Michael Polsky travelled to Yorkshire, where he was surprised to find many of the Soviet citizens familiar with the liturgy. A service was held in a large barracks hall, which was completely packed by devout prisoners. Even the forty or so Soviet-inspired officers of the 'inner ring' watched curiously from the rear. About seventy of the inmates were confessed and received Holy Communion. Afterwards, Father Michael chatted on general subjects with the prisoners, and presented them with musical instruments and literary works in Russian of a non-political nature collected amongst his congregation. He noted the excellence of the food supplied, and was told by British officers that it was hoped the Russians would carry home with them a favourable impression of British goodwill. Following Soldatenkov's complaint, however, all further such visits were forbidden.[12]

The camp was about to have a very different visitor. On 8 September, when most of them had been prisoners for three months, the Russians met their first Soviet representative. Major-General Vasiliev, who was about to take over as head of the Soviet Military Mission, travelled to Yorkshire with a party of Soviet and British officers. The British hoped that this belated attention might calm the situation in the Russian camps.

On the first two days of the tour General Vasiliev visited Butterwick camp. There were nearly 3,000 Russian prisoners, 450 of whom were still on strike. Those who had served in the German Army were formed up into a hollow square and addressed by the General. He told them that they had not been forgotten by the Soviet Government and that eventually they would return home, though transport difficulties were causing delays. Vasiliev then left the parade ground, pausing only to speak with a group who called out to him as he passed.

'What are you going to do with us when we return to Russia?'

'You don't need to worry about that,' replied the General. 'There is enough room in the Soviet Fatherland for everyone.'

'The dog knows what happens to him when he steals bacon,' interjected a gloomy voice.

'You need not worry, because you were forced to serve against us.'

To which another replied defiantly: 'We were not forced. After all, we carried rifles against you!'

To which the General replied benignly: 'Well, don't worry—the Soviets never treat people in bulk—we shall find out who amongst you are guilty and who not. And this' (here he fingered a German uniform on one of the soldiers) 'we shall burn in a crematorium.'

A voice: 'We know—and us inside them too!'

That day, as the Soviet officers moved about the camp, the Russian prisoners were on the whole surly and defiant. Some still proudly sported ROA badges, and when a Soviet colonel came near them declined to salute, or did so in an offensive manner. When he reproved them, one swore loudly and the group lounged off. In discussions, the ROA men accused the Red Army generals of having deserted them in 1941–42.

But during that night it appears that means were found of making the prisoners aware of the realities of their situation. For next day their behaviour had altered radically; ROA badges had been torn off, and the men appeared crestfallen and apprehensive. The Soviet officers again addressed them in small groups, and went to some lengths to search out evidence that British officers had been conducting anti-Soviet propaganda. They had small success, until they finally induced a couple to say that Captain Narishkin, a White Russian interpreter, had told them Stalin was no longer interested in them.

'Ah, Narishkin,' ruminated Colonel Grodetski, '... isn't he a White Guard?' The Soviet delegation put in a strong complaint about Narishkin's alleged remarks, and it was agreed he should be removed from any contact with the prisoners.

All in all, the prisoners were left in a confused state of mind. Some began to cheer up and suggest optimistically that there might be something in Vasiliev's bland promises, but others declared emphatically their intention of committing suicide rather than return.

To his British colleagues, Vasiliev made a little speech, complaining that Britain was treating his unfortunate compatriots unkindly. After all, they had been forced by the Germans to work for them, and had surrendered at the first opportunity. It was essential they should be treated with humanity. Were not several ill in hospital? Could the working parties not be paid? And what about cigarettes, baths, extra blankets? The War Office did not swallow this, and a report referred sarcastically to 'the Soviet Government having now decided to pose as the Benevolent Fatherland . . .'

On the third and final day of the tour, General Vasiliev and his party called at Stadium Camp, Catterick. There things passed off smoothly, until the Commandant proudly showed off for inspection his collection of Russian literature provided for the prisoners' recreation. These were the books provided by Father Michael Polsky on his visit. Vasiliev was aghast, and offending editions of Turgenev, Aksakov, and Lermontov were hastily packed off back to Russian Church House in London.

Back in the capital, Vasiliev expressed himself as being in general content with British administration of the camps. He pointed out again that these men could not be regarded as traitors, particularly the very young, the very old, and the infirm. He urged that more be done to make the men's living conditions as congenial as possible. He also condemned the unnecessarily harsh measures meted out to the strikers, 'but stated that all this was past history and he merely wished it to be put on record to prevent any recurrence'.[13]

In view of the supposed embarrassing allegations made by Captain Narishkin, British military authorities instituted strict measures to ensure that no one holding suspected anti-Soviet views, and in particular no member of the White Russian community, should be permitted to have contact with the prisoners. No Russian books other than those supplied by the Soviet Military Mission were to be retained, and Father Michael Polsky was not to be allowed another visit. Above all it was vital, if internal discipline was to be maintained in the camps, to scotch rumours 'that the Soviet Government is no longer interested in them and that they have nothing to hope for from their Government. Such allegations are entirely without foundation; a serious view will be taken of any anti-Soviet propaganda of this nature.'[14]

The time was drawing near when the first batch of Russian prisoners was to be returned to their homeland. From the British point of view it was felt that a certain category should have priority in this respect. The majority of Russians captured in Normandy had been members of units which at least in theory belonged to the German Army, and were in consequence treated as prisoners of war. A smaller proportion had been members of the Todt labour battalions. They were not soldiers in the normal sense of the word, but as they had worn a uniform and worked on military installations the War Office decided to categorize them likewise as prisoners.[15] It was a party of 500 of these who had been sent by the Home Office to Butterwick, thus sparking off the trouble described above.

There were, however, some civilians still held by the Home Office. These had not been in the Todt or any other organisation, and so could by no interpretation be classed as prisoners of war; they were therefore held under Home Office jurisdiction at a reception centre in London. Under British law they could not come even under the liberal interpretation of the Allied Forces Act noted in the last chapter. Strictly speaking, they faced only two alternatives: to be permitted to remain as resident aliens, or to be deported (but not repatriated against their will).

The problem exercised Patrick Dean. In a letter to the Home Office of 15 October, headed 'MOST IMMEDIATE. SECRET,' the Foreign Office legal expert urged:

> It seems to us that the obvious course is to ensure that all the Russian nationals at present at the London Reception Centre are sent home among the first batch, since this will relieve you of the responsibility and will avoid the legal and political difficulties which are likely to arise if these people are detained as civilians much longer in the U.K. . . . It is rather a nuisance that some of these Russians are women, since I understand that they require more accommodation, but fortunately their number is comparatively few, and we very much hope that it will be possible to get them home as soon as possible.[16]

In a month's time, the Secretary to the Chiefs of Staff Committee notified the Foreign Office that: 'The shipping situation has altered . . . and the Chiefs of Staff have instructed me to state that shipping can now be made available to lift 11,000 personnel, provided that the move takes place in time to ensure the return of the ships by the end of November, 1944.'[17]

This extra shipping had unexpectedly become available as a result of the postponement in the Far East of a planned assault on Rangoon.[18] The Admiralty's proviso that the ships employed must be back in regular use by the end of November lent weight to Eden's arguments for the need for haste. He had continually before him the 'urgent desirability of getting as many as possible of Soviet prisoners of war out of this country lest trouble issues [ensues?]'.[19] By this of course he indicated the fear that a public outcry could at any time erupt.

As soon as shipping was made available, and the War Cabinet had given its assent, the War Office set about organising the embarkation of the Russian prisoners scattered in camps across Yorkshire. This was by no means a minor task, as the thousands of destitute prisoners would need personal equipment suitable for the harsh climatic conditions likely to be awaiting them on their journey through northern seas and on their arrival in Russia, with the winter coming on. Anxious that the wanderers should receive the very best of treatment after their terrible experiences at the hands of the Nazis, the Army Director of Clothing and Stores (M. D. Sieff) arranged for thousands of woollen vests, long drawers, socks, great-coats, boots, hairbrushes, soap tablets, etc. to be prepared for issue before the voyage.[20] With generous concern for the men's comfort, the authorities went so far as to stipulate 'that all Russians for repatriation are being equipped with new rpt new khaki-battledresses and great-coats and that all German uniform or dyed and patched or part worn khaki outer clothing in possession is being withdrawn'.[21] It will be shown later what was the fate of all this expensive clothing and personal equipment.

On 20 October the Directorate of Prisoners of War (headed by Major-General E. C. Gepp) held a meeting at Curzon Street House in London, to discuss last-minute arrangements. General Gepp explained that 10,220 Soviet Nationals were to be repatriated in this first party. Clothing and kit had already been issued, and the men would leave the camps on 29 October. General Vasiliev, the Soviet representative, after assenting to arrangements being made for the prisoners who would be left behind, enquired solicitously about the condition of the clothing being issued to the men. He was reassured about this, and those present at the meeting dispersed for lunch.[22]

General Vasiliev, it must be stated, was not altogether a credit to the formidable organisation he represented. Two people who knew him have described him as bearing a marked resemblance to a rat.[23] In addition he apparently gave off an odious smell, and was a most pronounced snob. On one occasion he strutted proudly for a moment, and reflected aloud: 'Just think: I, once a Corporal in a Tsarist dragoon regiment, can be received as an equal in the Cavalry Club in London!'[24]

At an early stage of the preparations for the Russian prisoners' return, the British authorities enquired of Vasiliev: 'What steps are to be taken in respect of Soviet nationals who do not wish to be repatriated?'[25] Brigadier Firebrace was not keen for British troops to become involved in this unpleasant business, and suggested that Vasiliev provide Soviet officers to guard the transport. But Vasiliev insisted at once that *British* troops be detailed to check that no prisoners escaped *en route* to the docks. As Vasiliev would be backed in all his demands by the Foreign Office, Firebrace had no option but to accede.

The same day there went out to camp commandants a careful order: 'Possibility exists certain Russian subjects will not wish leave England and may attempt to escape . . . provide armed guards for trains to port but guards will not repeat not use arms except in self defence . . . retain sufficient train escorts at port until sailing of ships to prevent escapes at port. This should be done as inconspicuously as possible.'[26]

On 31 October[27] the ships left Liverpool for Murmansk. The total of Russian male prisoners was 10,139. Also shepherded on board under the eyes of the discreetly 'inconspicuously' armed British guards were thirty women and forty-four boys.[28] They would arrive in northern Russia just in time to celebrate the anniversary of the Revolution.

The Soviet news agency Tass broadcast on 14 November an emotional account of the arrival of the two transports, and the landing of the liberated prisoners.

They were warmly welcomed by Plenipotentiary representatives of the Council of People's Commissars for Matters Concerning Repatriation of Soviet Citizens from Germany and Countries Occupied by Her, as well as representatives of local State organs and of the Soviet public.

It was an exciting picture when the Soviet citizens returning from Fascist captivity met the working people of Murmansk. A spontaneous meeting started. On an improvised platform Soviet citizens, who had been forcibly torn from their Motherland by the Fascist scoundrels, rose one after the other to express their deep gratitude to the Soviet Government and to Comrade Stalin for their solicitude . . . The local State organs display great solicitude for the repatriated people. They are provided with food and lodgings. The Soviet people who have regained their Motherland show tremendous interest in the happy events of the war fronts and life in the Soviet Union. On November 6th they heard Stalin's speech. They are being sent in groups to their native places. The orphan children are going into children's homes.[29]

An independent eye-witness account has preserved a rather less rosy picture.

On November 7th, in Murmansk, I was in a car returning from the Naval Mission Headquarters to the War Port. En route, we were passed by a long column of Russian repatriated Nationals, who were being marched from their transport, the *Scythia*, under armed guard to the camp just outside the town. It appeared that they were being treated as having the status of nothing more than enemy prisoners of war. The guards were armed with rifles and were probably allotted at the rate of one per 10/15 Nationals. There was no sign of a welcome reception being arranged for these repatriates, whose demeanour was added proof of their unfortunate status. They were all dressed in British battledress, carrying a small parcel of personal belongings in most cases, and at that stage they had not been provided with any Russian equipment, insignia or 'comforts'.

2nd December 1944   (signed) S. J. Cregeen,
                                                           Major.

This report was sent to Brigadier Firebrace, who forwarded copies to General Gepp and C. F. A. Warner of the Foreign Office, adding: 'In view of the insistence on the privileged treatment and comfort of the "liberated Soviet citizens", the attached eye-witness account of their arrival in Murmansk may be of interest.'

After marking the passage in Major Cregeen's report stating that the prisoners lacked Russian equipment, Geoffrey Wilson, on Warner's behalf, noted: 'Hardly surprising as they had only just disembarked from a British transport. Nor is the armed guard in the least surprising. I shd. like to know a good deal more about Major Cregeen...'[30] Cregeen's report had struck a distastefully jarring note amidst the general satisfaction.

General Vasiliev was certainly pleased, and thanked General Gepp warmly at the next meeting.[31] Sir Alexander Cadogan, Permanent Under-Secretary to the Foreign Office, also had reason to feel satisfied. On 2 November he replied to Winston Churchill, who had sent a minute asking why delays were occurring in achieving total repatriation.[32] In answer, Cadogan stated: 'As you say, we have arranged to send them back to Russia and some 10,200 have just embarked on ships provided by us. All but 12 of these went quite willingly and most of the recalcitrants were put on board by force. About 9,500 are still left in the United Kingdom and we shall send these back as soon as an opportunity occurs.'[33]

Some months were to pass, however, before such shipping could be made available, and those Russians still in Britain settled down to make the most of their stay. It was indeed an odd and slightly unreal existence in the camps, for prisoners and guards alike.

Mr. Harry Lewis, for example, recalls with lively amusement his days as Accounts Clerk at Bramham No. 2 Camp in Yorkshire, where five hundred prisoners were housed. They were drawn from an assortment of races, being for the most part powerfully built, with immense heads and feet. For their heads they were issued with the largest British forage caps obtainable, but even these perched on their heads 'like a pimple on a haystack'. Boots large enough were found, and these the Russians wore stuffed with paper, explaining that such had been their practice in the Red Army.

Their major pursuits were threefold, being, in the words of the old Russian song, 'wine, women and cards'. Every week they were given five shillings pocket money, in the form of two half-crowns. By the same evening, after a frenzied bout of gambling, virtually all this money had passed into the hands of a lucky few.[34] Those who had money then rushed to the camp canteen with a heterogeneous collection of receptacles to buy beer. When asked how much, they replied as they had learned in Germany: '*Alles*'. They would travel by bus into Leeds, the conductress giving up the vain linguistic struggle by demanding no fare. There in the lowest pubs were passed happy hours, purged as often as not by violent vomiting in the returning late-night bus. A fortunate few managed to earn extra money on these occasions by sleeping with soldiers' wives in the city, and returning with a grubby pound note as reward.

During the day the prisoners were marched out to work on neighbouring farms. They were not guarded (there were only thirteen unarmed British soldiers in the camp) and seemed to have enjoyed their work. Their tastes, as indicated, were simple. They often sang— beautifully—the songs of their native lands, and were goodnatured, humorous and loyal. It was a hard winter in 1944-5, and the prisoners insisted on having their barracks stoves burning twenty-four hours a day, with the result that they had soon burned not only their ration of coal, but also most of the camp furniture. On the other hand, a popular pastime was to emerge into the frosty Yorkshire air and drench each other with ice-cold water from stirrup-pumps.

The British staff also conducted their lives on musical-comedy lines. One of the senior officers was in private life connected with the clothing trade, and conducted a great deal of business from the camp HQ, which was filled with specimen skeins of wool. Another was an Irishman who scarcely appeared, being busy with a girl in Thorner, and the remainder of the staff got up to all the usual camp dodges, such as plundering the stores and making threepence a pint on the beer by selling the Russians short measure. Nobody minded and everybody enjoyed himself.

Harry Lewis became interested in the men, and learned from them the familiar tales of indescribable hardships in the Red Army and the Wehrmacht, coupled with an extreme and universal aversion to returning to Russia. As accounts clerk, he had occasion to observe that an overwhelming majority of the prisoners were illiterate, being obliged to record the receipt of their pay with a mark. This chance survey may throw some light on the critical faculties of Western experts, who had swallowed the Soviet Union's pre-war claim to have reduced illiteracy to a mere 2 per cent.[35] All in all, Harry Lewis retains very affectionate memories of his bear-like Russian charges. 'They were great gamblers, they were great drinkers, they were great womanisers, they were rotten with V.D. . . . but they were very likeable!' was his verdict.

The national *penchant* for strong drink was not indulged in all camps, however. Mrs. Violet M. Dye was living in the spring of 1945 at Worthing, where Warne's Hotel had been commandeered for the use of the Russians.

> They were not allowed in the public houses, and it was surprising how many hobbled into chemists' shops, complaining, in signs, of sore and stiff knees. Until the chemists realised that the methylated spirits they let them have was drunk, in lieu of alcohol otherwise unobtainable, they dispensed it freely. Then a circular went out to all of them warning them to be more discreet. One day when I was walking out with the pram, a really charming little man attempted to sell me his spare uniform.

As in other camps, the inmates continually expressed dread at the thought of their return.

It would, however, be wrong to believe that the Russians were an indistinguishable bunch of child-like peasants, inured to privation and suffering, to whom freedom and comfort meant less than to Englishmen. Occasionally there came in contact with them an officer who had reason to understand the Russian temperament. One such was Czeslaw Jesman. Another was an old friend of the author's, Prince Leonid Lieven. Born in Courland, he had come to Britain and enlisted in the Royal Fusiliers. The shortage of Russian speakers in Britain at that time meant that a number of émigrés of British nationality had to be employed as duty officers in the camps. The anguish suffered by many of these Russians at being placed in the terrible position of actually arranging for their fellow-countrymen to return to a fate, the nature of which they well knew, has become a memory from which few have fully recovered.

It was not just that they were compatriots in whose misery they were actively assisting. As fellow-Russians they conversed freely in the camps, and knew the prisoners as individuals, and not as a mere mob of prisoners who, in the words of Churchill, Eden and Morrison, we must 'get rid of' as quickly as possible.

Prince Lieven, who had on account of his Russian been seconded to Brigadier Firebrace's Russian Liaison Group, was sent first to a camp at Oakley, near Leeds, and in October 1944 found himself in another at Thirsk. Two things struck him on arrival. First was the sight of genuine

Russian peasants, bearded, simple and melancholy. Secondly was their oft-expressed amazement at the epaulettes worn by visiting Soviet officers from the Military Mission. Since most of the prisoners had been captured in 1941–2, before Stalin had restored this insignia of rank,[36] they could only conjecture that these must be Tsarist officers, come to organise them for a final reckoning with the Soviets!

However, not all were men of the people. Prince Lieven got to know well a Russian doctor, a man of considerable intelligence and integrity. He explained that he had fought with the White Army under Denikin, and then after the fall of Wrangel had decided to accept the amnesty offered by the Soviets, and stay on in Russia to help his people. After falling into the hands of the Germans, he agreed on the same principle to work with them in order to alleviate the sufferings of his fellow-prisoners. He knew enough about the nature of the Soviet state to guess what his fate would be if he were returned. He was nevertheless prepared up to a point to face that if it were really inevitable. But, as he confessed one day to Lieven, 'I do not fear death, but I am afraid of torture.'

Aghast, Lieven tried to persuade the Camp Commandant to arrange for the unfortunate man to be withheld from repatriation. Poles from another camp had offered to help, perhaps by certifying him as a Ukrainian from west of the Curzon Line. The Commandant, well aware that he was powerless in the matter, angrily told Lieven not to raise the matter again. 'You are a White Guardist, Lieven,' he snapped. 'If you persist in this hopeless folly, you will find yourself under arrest.' Notwithstanding this, Lieven managed to interest the Adjutant in the case, but before anything could be done Lieven had to leave suddenly to embark on the *Duchess of Bedford* at Liverpool, and the doctor went to his fate.

Other prisoners were simple men of that child-like innocence and goodness still found in Mother Russia. One soldier stood for three hours before the great front of York Minster, unable to move and mesmerised by its soaring beauty. Another told the Prince of a meeting with God held in a Ukrainian forest. Shortly before the German invasion, the Almighty (habited, like Wotan, in the guise of an old man) stood unexpectedly before him. 'Hide yourself, my son, for evil times are coming,' the devout peasant was told. He did so, and escaped death. The freedom, luxury and ease of English life never ceased to amaze him. 'Why, it's like heaven!' he repeated time and again.

The Foreign Office had already marked him down for a very different locale.

In a camp at Thirsk was a turbulent character named Sharavatov. He was recognised as camp leader until he became involved in a riot led by a Tartar against the Communist Party members who, it was claimed, stole all the camp meat. The Tartar was sent to a camp for Italian Fascists, a new camp leader was appointed, and Sharavatov joined his fellows in labouring on nearby farms. Like them, he was more than content with the easy, friendly life. Until one day in a muddy lane near Thirsk he stood aside to watch the young daughter of the local squire riding by on a sleek and splendid thoroughbred. Amongst the brown leaves, rising mists and damp smells of an English autumn passed this vision of youth and comeliness. Not in all the length and breadth of Soviet Russia could the emotional Sharavatov have seen such a sight. More members of the hunt splattered and jingled by, but Sharavatov stumbled on his way, unconscious of all but the one aching passion. In pub after pub in Thirsk he consumed drinks worthy in quantity of his love. At last he blundered through the moonlight towards Upsall Castle. Perhaps a light in an upper storey was the one! Unable to leave the spot, he groped his way to a barn, where next day a military patrol found his recumbent body. A gentle smile warmed his broad features, whilst empty bottles festooned the straw around.

Did Sharavatov think of the snug hedgerows and villages around Thirsk, as his manhood froze and shrank amid the icy swamps of Kolyma, or festered in a dank cell in the Lubianka? Did he remember Miss Turton, her confident poise in the saddle, her air of self-possession and youthful enthusiasm? How often was the pleasing dream shattered by the strident clattering of the iron triangle that sent the cowed *zeks* crawling from their louse-infested bunks?

It seems unlikely that the dream reached so far. For Sharavatov was a marked man, who had troubled the Party leadership in Thirsk Camp. His name would have appeared on a special list kept by General Ratov, and passed on board the ship taking Sharavatov and thousands like him to Odessa. More probably his last sight on earth was a grinning NKVD man in an Odessa warehouse, slowly raising a submachine gun and pointing it at his stomach.

On the Channel sea-coast was a camp at Bexhill. Many inhabitants of the little resort had left during the war, but among those who remained were Mr. and Mrs. William Backshall, who came to know well four of the prisoners from No. 631 Working Company, based at a nearby school run by the Canadian Army. The little group of men often came to the Backshalls' house. There they loved to sit by the fire drinking tea and chatting, or playing billiards with Bill Backshall. The life led by British tommies was a never-failing source of wonder to them.

'Why, every weekend they polish their boots, smarten themselves

up, and go home to their families!' declared Alex Koorkin in astonishment. 'In the Red Army we were lucky if we saw our families once in
six months. It wasn't as bad in the German Army, but here in England
is the place to live. Nobody is bullied or starved, the people are kind and
friendly, and everyone has the right to live his own life. Who would
have thought that such a country existed?'

Alex could speak quite good English. His parents had been peasants
who had been liquidated by the Communists in the 1920s. Their small-
holding had been confiscated, and he had joined that army of orphans
(*bezprizorni*) that was so familiar a feature of inter-war Soviet Russia.
His friend Feodor Chernyshuk was a young man of twenty-six.
Both frequently expressed dread at the thought of what would happen
to them if the British compelled them to return to Russia. 'All *kaput*!'
Feodor would mutter. Mr. Backshall, after long conversations with his
new friends, began to realise that these fears were not idly expressed.
In the atmosphere of the wartime alliance it was often difficult to
realise that in Russia existed a government that had seized power by
force and had made virtual war on its fellow-citizens ever since. But in
getting to know so well these four visitors, of humble origins and no
political persuasion, he had become impressed by the consistency and
patent honesty of their accounts.

The Russians spent Christmas Day 1944 with their new friends, and
asked whether the Backshalls could not somehow arrange for them to
be allowed to stay in England. Clearly Mr. Backshall could do little, but
he told them he would write to the Home Office to see if permission
could be granted for the young men to stay. On New Year's Day he
wrote to enquire 'as to the procedure whereby these Russian nationals
may become British'.

No reply came for a while, but unknown to him he had set the
pigeons fluttering in the dovecot. Patrick Dean sent a copy of the letter
to Henry Phillimore, asking him to enquire into the matter. If, as he
suspected, the men were Soviet citizens, then 'they will have to be
repatriated whether they like it or not.' But it was necessary to check
the matter and clear it up if possible, since 'the legal position of these
men is somewhat dubious and it is as the result of private enquiries like
this that trouble is ultimately to be expected.'

Five days later Dean received a further report from a War Office
official:

> As arranged on the telephone, I am enclosing herewith a translation of a
> petition signed by 42 Soviet Nationals of No. 631 Working Company
> asking for the protection of the British Government against their repatria-
> tion to Russia. A copy of a report by an officer of L.M.4 is also attached.

As these men are admittedly Soviet Nationals, we presume that they will be repatriated to Russia whether they like it or not.

Meanwhile the only course appears to be to keep them as a separate party in the above Working Company as is being done at present.

Not content with relying on Mr. Backshall's efforts, Alex, Feodor and forty of their fellows had taken this precautionary measure. And some days later Mr. Backshall, prompted further, wrote another and longer letter to the Home Office. In this he enlarged on the pathetic hopes and fears of the two Russians and suggested that, in view of their skill at making toys, they could, in the event of being granted permission to stay, make a home in his house until they were established.

But all this was of course a vain endeavour. On 8 February John Galsworthy wrote from the Foreign Office to Major James of the War Office:

Thank you for your letter ... of the 25th January last, addressed to Dean, concerning the group of 42 Soviet nationals of No. 631 Working Company, who have asked to be taken under the protection of the British Government.

As Soviet nationals, these men must, of course, be repatriated to the USSR when opportunity arises, irrespective of their wishes. Moreover, they admit to having gone over to the enemy to fight against the Allies and we have presumably no proof that their statement that they gave themselves up voluntarily is true. They seem to us to deserve no sympathy and we think our principal aim where they are concerned should be to ensure that they cause no trouble between us and the Soviet authorities over here.

If there is any danger of such trouble or of the prison camp authorities showing them any sympathy we think the prison camp authorities should be instructed accordingly.

At the same time Mr. Backshall received a brief reply from the Home Office, informing him that his request could not be granted, as the Russians were under Soviet jurisdiction and so outside British control.[37]

On 5 February the Backshalls were expecting to see their Russian friends at home, and as usual their teenage son, Roland, bicycled over to the camp to accompany them home. They were not to be seen, and when he enquired of the Canadian sentry at the gate, he was laconically handed a note. In halting English, it read: 'Mr. Bill. We today 12 Klok to ride in another kamp 50 miles. Excuse us whate no to go ... Very little time, Feodor Alex.' That was the last the Backshalls were to hear of Feodor and Alex, until thirty years later.

As a result of the petition, the Soviet Military Mission had been asked whether they wished 'the traitors ... at 631 Working Company' to be included in the next repatriation voyage now being planned. (The 'traitors' were, of course, the forty-one signatories to the camp petition, who were henceforward segregated from their fellows.) On receiving an affirmative reply, the War Office issued a directive to the effect that: 'The 41 Soviet Nationals in 631 Working Coy. who have refused to return to the USSR will *not* be informed of the impending repatriation but will be transferred immediately to No. 9 P.W. Reception Camp.' This precaution was necessary because, as John Galsworthy explained on a parallel occasion, 'if they suspect repatriation several may attempt escape or suicide.'[38]

On 16 February, Alex, Feodor and their fellows who had signed the fatal petition travelled under armed guard north to Liverpool ('The train guards will carry out their duties as unobtrusively as possible . . .'). On a dark wet February evening they assembled with hundreds of others on Canada Dock, preparatory to boarding the *Duchess of Bedford* and two sister transports.

There also were the prisoners from Prince Lieven's and Harry Lewis's camps, as well as many others. As soon as rumours of the impending repatriation had begun to circulate, panic had spread amongst the prisoners. Harry Lewis had to assist in recapturing an escaped Russian officer, and heard on reliable evidence that at the larger Bramham No. 1 Camp there had been five to eight suicides. At Thirsk, many prisoners fled into the Pennines, only to be driven back by the bitter cold. Only one managed to evade return; his body was found in the camp after the party had left.

As for young Feodor and his comrades, even as they were preparing to go on board a ghastly incident took place on the quayside. I give it as it was described to me by Harry Lewis, from whose camp the prisoner in question had come.

> Pals of mine with whom I was very friendly had a most unhappy experience. When they got to Liverpool, one of the chaps (Russians) in one of the coaches (and this I got absolutely first hand) saw a boat, realised he had been tricked—realised that they were all being shipped back to Russia —grabbed a rusty knife out of his pocket and started sawing away at his throat. He didn't succeed in cutting his jugular vein, so he then hooked his finger round his windpipe and did his best to break that, and they managed to restrain him. He was taken on the boat as a horribly bloody mess, treated completely unsympathetically by the Russian troops who were on board; and was carted below with a couple of these pals of mine and put onto a bed in the sick-bay. One of the Russians said, 'let the dog die.' They had no sympathy whatsoever for these men. Now that I can vouch for second-hand from men whom I can utterly trust and who came back looking very sick about it.

Mr. Lewis added, incidentally, that the only reason that the English soldiers accompanied the mutilated Russian down to the sick-bay was that the Soviet officers simply left him where he lay on the deck.[39]

But Feodor, Alex and their forty companions had little time to reflect on what they had seen. They had refused to dress properly when they began to have suspicions as to their destination, but when British officers apologised for this and offered to replace the missing clothing, they found Soviet officers 'not particularly interested'. A British report noted that:

> The 42 had caused no trouble during the journey and were embarked at 2200 hours without mishap. The five ringleaders were put into the cells and the remainder placed in a small troop-deck with a Soviet guard. Before embarkation they were harangued by General Ratoff, who is reported to have expressed sorrow at their unfortunate behaviour, told them that their fears were without foundation and that on their return home all would be forgiven.[40]

Leonid Lieven sailed on the *Duchess of Bedford* and can remember the details of the voyage vividly. One of the five ringleaders, seemingly unconvinced by General Ratov's gentle words, razored open his stomach after an appendix operation. We cannot tell now whether this was Alex or Feodor, but in any case there is not much more to be said concerning them.

The convoy reached Odessa in the first week of March 1945. No sooner had the ships been docked than NKVD squads came swiftly up the gangways. Handed lists of names and reports by the Russian officers on board, they acted with speed and efficiency. From the special lists names were called out; prisoners stepped forward, deathly white. A speedy interrogation followed, and the selected groups were marched off the ship, across the quay and out of sight. NKVD men with tommy-guns flanked the stumbling and bewildered little columns. Then they were gone, and the more laborious business of disembarking the mass of prisoners began.

English sailors watched indifferently from the deck. Every port they visited was swarming with soldiers and military installations. Bodies of troops and civilians came and went, and Odessa appeared different from Naples or Costanza only in that its buildings had suffered more terribly at the hands of the Nazis. Ships' sirens hooted, men shouted, and gulls circled above.

Suddenly a deep roar filled the air, as two bombers appeared in the sky and circled slowly round and round the harbour. The sailors ducked instinctively, then straightened up as they saw the red stars of the Soviet Air Force on the wings. All the same, the manoeuvrings of the planes seemed strange. For a quarter of an hour or more they droned in circles above the harbour. And no sooner had the curious watchers become accustomed to the noise, then another harsher, more tearing and strident mechanical shrieking opened up in competition. A mobile sawing-mill, drawn up on the quayside, was being put to work. All other sounds and thoughts were drowned by the raucous hum of the aeroplanes and the high-pitched howling of the saws. Those present grimaced and thrust their fingers in their ears. The inferno continued without abatement for about twenty minutes, and the purposeless circling of the aircraft and screeching of the mechanical saws seemed to reverberate the ether around.

Filled with horror, young Lieutenant Lieven ran to the British colonel who had come to supervise the return of former British prisoners of war on the same ship. Colonel Dashwood looked up, to see a white, distraught figure before him.

'What is it, my boy?'

'*Sir, sir, they are murdering the prisoners!*' stammered Lieven, consumed with agitation.

'No, no, that's impossible!' shouted Colonel Dashwood confidently above the all-pervading cacophony.

Lieven insisted he was right but, realising the futility of protest under such conditions (what could Colonel Dashwood do?) made his way below, sick and horrified.

Minutes later the terrible noise ceased, and the dockside resumed its normal medley of mechanical and human sounds. The bombers disappeared behind the roof-tops, and the saw, having apparently ripped through enough logs for a morning's work, was likewise still. The disembarkation proceeded without further incident, and only Lieven was left reflecting on what other sounds—staccato, screaming or moaning—might have gone unheard in the din.

Prince Lieven's guess was within the mark. A Finnish prisoner in Lefortovo tells how, next to the gaol, 'there must have been a workshop for repairing aeroplane engines, as day and night our eardrums were shattered by the roar of engines being tried out . . . Often in the evenings, and during the night, we could hear, even above the din of the engines, shrieks coming from the interrogation department, though this was some distance away.'[41] And Solzhenitsyn, speaking of the task of the Soviet executioner, describes how: 'While a motor roars its accompaniment, he fires his pistol bullets, unheard, into the back of a head . . .'[42] The methods inculcated at the NKVD training school at Babushkin[43] were thorough. A short report of this repatriation voyage in *The Times* of London summed up the tragedy better than its author knew. It noted: 'there were moving scenes when the Russians set foot again on the soil of their homeland.'[44]

So ends the story, so far as it can be known, of the four homeless and friendless Russians who, a few weeks before, had sat down to the Backshalls' Christmas dinner. Their fate overtook them for one reason only: the British authorities had taken upon themselves to inform General Ratov of the petition drawn up in the Bexhill camp. As John Galsworthy had written a month previously: 'They seem to us to deserve no sympathy . . .'

The other prisoners disembarked at Odessa and not massacred on the quayside were subjected to an efficiently executed formality before being marched off 'to an unknown destination'.

It will be remembered that the British Government had been very concerned that the returning Russians should be fully equipped with new winter clothing. This was a matter close to the heart of the head of the Soviet Mission, General Vasiliev, and one in which he took a solicitous and pertinacious interest.

At a meeting of the Directorate of Prisoners of War held on 20 October 1944, we find him complaining to General Gepp (Director of Prisoners of War) 'that some of the uniforms issued had been new and some part worn'. General Gepp promised to check on this.[45] He was as good as his word, and the very next day issued the directive quoted earlier. The Soviet authorities nevertheless continued to be exacting and tireless in their demands on behalf of 'Soviet prisoners of war and citizens of the USSR, deported by the German invaders to Fascist slave labour and freed by the Allied troops'.[46] On 21 December 1944, SHAEF Headquarters reported that

> Russian representatives in this theatre have indicated verbally that they expect all their personnel . . . to be reclothed by the Allies . . . Following scale of clothing is requested:
> *Clothing*. One each blouses B.D., cap comforter, greatcoat, jersey pullover, boots prs, gloves knitted prs, trousers B.D. Two each drawers woollen prs, shirts silver grey, vests, socks.
> *Equipment*. One each blanket, brushes shaving, combs hair, haversacks, razor, tins mess, soap, bottles water, brushes tooth, forks, knives, spoons, towels.[47]

Shortly before the voyage described above, Vasiliev wrote to check that the standard of equipment was fully up to scratch.[48] Two days later, on 9 February 1945, he wrote testily to General Gepp to complain that 'the scale of underwear which must be issued to Nationals being repatriated has been established as one pair . . . The Soviet Military Mission asks to take into consideration the climatic peculiarities of the

Soviet Union during the winter months and the distances to be traversed. It therefore considers it quite normal that in addition to the other articles of clothing at least two suits of underwear be issued.'[49]

Thus the clothing, so peremptorily requested and obligingly supplied by the British authorities, accompanied the prisoners on the long sea-journey to Odessa. It accompanied them no further.

Five separate eyewitnesses have recorded an interesting ceremony which took place at each disembarkation of Russians in their homeland. Mr. G. C. Hamilton was one of those British prisoners liberated by the Red Army, who made the hazardous journey across Poland and the Ukraine to Odessa, where they were to return on the British vessels then depositing Russians. He writes:

> I had the misfortune of falling into the hands of the Soviets in 1945 and saw at first hand the plight of some of the Soviet citizens who were being re-patriated from East Germany. I was able to make my way to Odessa and reached there on 8 March 1945 together with a small number of British ex-prisoners of war. We obtained passage on the *Highland Princess* which had called at Odessa with a large number of Russian ex-prisoners of war who had been liberated in France. According to the crew of the *Highland Princess* these prisoners had been given a complete change of clothing and had been landed in British battledress. We had seen from a barracks in Odessa a squad of these prisoners being marched to the railway station for transport no doubt to the East and they were clothed in rags and wore very inadequate footwear . . . having just read the book *Gulag Archipelago* by Alexander Solzhenitsyn, I find that he describes at various places exactly what we saw happening to the Russian prisoners who landed at Odessa. I say 'saw happening' to them but the actual stripping of the British uniforms and underclothing, boots, socks, etc. took place in a warehouse. They went in very well clad and came out dressed in rags including the foot cloths so graphically described by Solzhenitsyn . . .[50]

An exactly similar account was given to me by an English girl who saw the same occurrence on a different occasion (she too had made the perilous journey to Odessa after being liberated from Nazi occupation).[51] And three British liaison officers who made the return journey accompanying repatriates also saw the same cruel and degrading incident on more than one occasion.[52]

What was the motive for what amounted virtually to a crude confidence trick on the part of the Soviet Government? Obviously the clothes were in themselves useful and indeed valuable; there was an appalling shortage of clothing in the USSR.[53] But the slightly absurd insistence on details such as extra pairs of underpants, coupled with the total lack of any attempt to conceal the ultimate confiscation, seems odd.

On the one hand, many English people had ample opportunity to observe what was happening and report back to the authorities in the United Kingdom. On the other, the Soviet authorities were capable of going to extreme—one might say extraordinary—lengths to hide from foreign observers what they did not wish seen. To give but one example: when Roosevelt's Vice-President Henry Wallace went on his USSR tour of 1944, he visited the vast forced-labour complex in Kolyma. To impress their simple-minded visitor, the NKVD in a single night razed scores of wooden watchtowers lining the roads to the slave-built city of Magadan. Thousands of prisoners were confined to their barrack rooms for three days; a model farm was spruced up for inspection (the girls who minded the pigs were in fact senior NKVD officers' 'secretaries'); a play was staged at the Magadan Theatre, whose actors were slave-labourers whipped into trucks and away immediately after the performance; and the shops were temporarily crammed with goods that no Russian not a Tchekist had seen for a generation.[54]

In the light of this and a great deal of other circumstantial evidence, it seems probable that the Soviet authorities were successfully engaged in rubbing the Allies' noses in the dirt. After all, who could have believed that the British would so meekly have rushed to send back the emigrants in their thousands? That as they did so they would have accepted an endless stream of public and private Soviet abuse about the way in which they were doing it? So why not make these arrogant English jump to it and dress the sacrificial victims at maximum expense? And if they found out later they had been hoaxed, why, then, how much the more foolish they would look! Stalin himself had declared that 'Churchill is the kind of man who will pick your pocket of a kopeck if you don't watch him.'[55] Did he and Beria laugh together in that little room in the Kremlin where the light burned all night, as they reflected how cleverly they had drawn the kopecks from Mr. Churchill's pockets?

Throughout the first half of 1945 regular convoys steamed from Britain to the USSR. On one of them in particular occurred some bizarre incidents described to me by Czeslaw Jesman. He sailed from Glasgow on board H.M.T. *Almanzora*, on 27 March 1945, bound for Odessa, with the inmates of the camps in Yorkshire.

Also on board was quite a different body of men; this was the remnants of the Czech government-in-exile, who were being shipped out to resume control of their country on its liberation (Dr. Benes had already flown out).

The *Almanzora* passed through the Mediterranean and on to the Dardanelles. At Constantinople were picked up three or four Russians who had jumped overboard from the previous repatriation convoy.

They were handed over by the Soviet Consul General to the NKVD officer on the *Almanzora*, Major Shershun, who in turn presented them to his superiors at Odessa.

At Costanza, on the Black Sea, the Czech ministers were to be disembarked. But before they were, a reception was held in their honour by the Soviet officers on board. Speeches were made and toasts drunk, and a Czech minister rose to thank his hosts. He told the Russians of the warmth and strength of friendship he and his colleagues felt for them, and ended by extending an invitation to them to come to Prague in the near future. Lieutenant Jesman clearly heard the Soviet officer sitting next to him murmur sardonically: 'Well, you don't need to invite us— we'll be there anyway.'

At last, on 18 April 1945, the *Almanzora* berthed at Odessa. What happened next was described by Lieutenant Jesman in a report submitted to Brigadier Firebrace, who in turn passed it on to the Head of the Northern Department of the Foreign Office.

> While the Soviet Nationals were disembarking on the Odessa pier, there were two salvoes of sub-machine pistols heard from behind the large shack on the pier. Later on, the NKVD guard told me that two men were executed on the spot. The guard told me furthermore that both the executed were 'bad men' and 'sold to the capitalists'. The guard was an Usbek or a Turkman and became very friendly when I spoke to him a few words in Usbeki, and later accepted gratefully a packet of cigarettes. I reported the incident at the time of its occurrence to the O.C. Troops on *Almanzora*, Colonel Boyle, and to the ship's master, Captain Bannister.[56]

Later, when he was being driven in a jeep through the semi-ruined city, Jesman came on an execution squad in the process of shooting down a dozen prisoners. His Soviet companion informed him laconically that they were 'traitors'. Elsewhere bodies littered the streets.

What of those who survived? 'Major Shershun admitted frankly that they will be sent to what he termed as "educational labour camps" and only very few of them will be allowed to join the armed forces.'[57]

A problem that began to exercise the Foreign Office was that of potential repatriates who claimed a nationality other than Soviet. The Yalta Agreement had referred specifically to the return of 'Soviet citizens', and the deliberate return of those who had never been such was not contemplated by the Foreign Office.

At first the problem had been solved by allowing the Soviets themselves to decide who was or was not a Soviet citizen.[58] But as early as October 1944 the War Office received reports that amongst the prisoners listed by Vasiliev for repatriation was a group claiming Polish, Latvian, German or Nansen passports.[59] The sort of complication that might arise if care were not taken was instanced in the case of Antonas Valizkas, who claimed United States nationality. As Patrick Dean pointed out: 'It would be disastrous if, on top of all our other troubles, we laid ourselves open to a complaint from the United States Government that we had sent back one of their nationals to the Soviet Union, particularly if he was to be shot on arrival.'[60]

The dangers were clearly so great that the Foreign Office resolved to be firm, at any rate for the moment. The Soviet Ambassador was accordingly informed that claimants to non-Soviet nationality would have to have their claims investigated. If these were substantiated, they would not be sent to Russia.[61] A definition was issued that 'Soviet citizens are *prima facie* all persons coming from places within the boundaries of the Soviet Union as constituted before the outbreak of the present war.'[62]

Of course a spate of Soviet complaints descended on the harassed Foreign Office. The gist of them was that 'the British military authorities have arbitrarily and without cause removed Soviet citizens from certain camps . . .', the point at issue being that the British had not yet decided whether these people were Soviet citizens in British eyes.

Other grumbles were added. To counter the growing realisation amongst British personnel concerned that great numbers of Russians were terrified of returning, it was alleged that a certain British officer had told camp inmates that half the 10,000 prisoners already returned to Russia had been shot.

Other complaints were more frivolous. An Englishwoman, secretary of the Normanton 'Friends of the Soviet Union', visited the camp at which Harry Lewis was accounts clerk, and was said to have stated to a Russian prisoner that: 'We here in England have developed a partisan movement and are striking at landlords and capitalists. You Russians are great specialists in partisan movements—help us and tell us what should be the tactics of partisan warfare.' Why the Soviets should have objected to this we are not told.

There were other subversive females around, but with a more human set of interests. General Vasiliev alleged that a number had penetrated the camps, disseminating 'with entire freedom anti-Soviet propaganda of a manifestly hostile character . . .' On which the British general refuting these charges commented: 'The Commandant had reasons to suspect that local women were occasionally smuggled in by Soviet citizens in contravention of the Camp rules. It is assumed they were there for other purposes than that of propaganda.'

At Hutton Gate Camp a Major Fletcher was alleged to have directed the following remarks to the Russian prisoners: 'Russian officer—no good, Russian officer—children, Russian officer—"wet", Russian officer—like pig.' The War Office was amused by this supposedly literal rendering.[63]

To return to the problem of cases of disputed nationality: if the persons concerned could prove their non-Soviet nationality they were not despatched to the Soviet Union. But if they failed to do so, they were repatriated without exception. At least, there was only one known exception, whose case was described to me by Brigadier Firebrace:

> I played the game, except with one man, who was extraordinarily brave. He spoke excellent Russian, but I said he was a Pole. He stood up in front of us and he said, 'Go back to that country? No, you murdered my father, you raped my sister—I'd sooner die!' He stood to attention in front of me and said, 'I ask the British General to shoot me here and now rather than send me back.' God help me, I said he was a Pole. General Ratov was furious, but I knew that once I'd got the man on the Disputed List he was all right.

This was after the British Government had taken measures to screen prospective repatriates. Before that there was little to prevent Vasiliev or Ratov from including non-Soviet citizens in the batches of prisoners destined for the USSR.

Brigadier Firebrace had raised the whole business with the Foreign Office: 'So far the Soviet Military Mission has had practically a free hand in determining the nationality of people in Soviet camps, and unless a man makes a strong protest, he is claimed by them as a Soviet national whether he is one or not. I have seen a copy of the forms filled up by each man and it is interesting to note that there is no column for citizenship, only one for nationality' (31 March 1945). In this way the cryptic entry 'Russian' could mean that the signatory was equally an escaped Soviet citizen, or a stateless Russian émigré holder of a stateless person's League of Nations' Nansen Certificate.

That spring and summer brought many unpleasant and irritating headaches for Patrick Dean, Geoffrey Wilson and the rest of the hard-pressed Foreign Office team. On 28 March, Dean wrote of the suicides mentioned earlier that

> Brigadier Firebrace and Colonel Tamplin are doing their best to prevent any publicity, and have asked that the Foreign Office should speak to the News Department with a view to doing all that is possible to prevent publicity, either about the incidents themselves or about the proceedings which will have to take place in coroners' courts. Perhaps Northern Department would look into this and do all they can ... these suicides (of which there have now been four or five instances at least) might possibly

cause political trouble, and Sir O. Sargent may wish to know what is happening.

Dean's colleague Geoffrey Wilson, got in touch with Sir J. Cameron of the News Department to see what could be done. After conceding that it would be impossible to ask 'that the inquests should be held *in camera* or that the press should be excluded', Cameron had the clever idea of suggesting 'that the way in which the cases should be presented in the coroners' courts was to indicate that the men were frightened about the consequences of their having collaborated with the Germans. This is in fact probably true . . . and if this is the way in which the stories come out, it should avoid any real difficulties.'

An ingenious solution, but Dean and Wilson's superior, Sir Orme Sargent, considered it over-subtle, and dangerously near to risking public comprehension of the whole policy: 'I wish it had been possible to hush this up under 18B or some other war-time regulation.' Higher up still, Sir Alexander Cadogan, Permanent Under-Secretary, added: 'Failing that, the above line [Wilson's and Cameron's] is the right one to take.'

Wilson was then able to allay his superiors' fears by informing them 'that the military are being instructed to suggest to the Coroners that they should advise the press that it would be better not to report these cases. This has worked successfully before.' The correspondence closed with a general explanation by Dean of the extreme difficulty of hushing up the proceedings of British courts.[64]

In the event the Foreign Office need not have worried. There was no public outcry, and the suicides continued. The quay at Liverpool seemed to exert a strange attraction on sufferers from 'acute melancholia', as one case was labelled.[65]

When Czeslaw Jesman, on board the *Almanzora*, was still four days' sail from the scenes of tragedy at Odessa, Brigadier Firebrace was dealing with the first cases of disputed persons coming before the newly-formed board presided over by General Ratov and himself. On 14 April 1945 he wrote to Christopher Warner to report on progress so far.

On Thursday I had my first meeting with General Ratov to examine the cases of alleged Soviet nationals on the disputed list. As the result of eight hours' strenuous work, we dealt with fifty. I will not give you details now as I will report in full when I have finished the job. General Ratov was accompanied by four other Soviet officers, the Soviet Consul Krotov and a shorthand writer who took down every word said by the men concerned.

The majority of the men seen were either Balts or Eastern Poles and there was one Bessarabian. The remainder admitted Soviet citizenship, and with these there was no difficulty, although many strenuously protested against being sent back to the Soviet Union. They were, however, all handed over to the Soviet authorities and will be sent to the Soviet camp, with the exception of 10 whom I am temporarily keeping under arrest at the request of General Ratov. Of those claiming Polish nationality, the vast majority maintained their claim and were kept on the disputed list. Two however were clearly lying and were transferred to the Soviet list. I had no doubt about the correctness of the Soviet claim to them . . .

You have given me a most unpleasant task as, with few exceptions, the men, whether claiming Polish or Soviet nationality, protest violently at being sent back to the Soviet Union or even to their homes in Poland. A large number insisted on giving reasons for their not wishing to go back and related with a wealth of detail their experiences in the Soviet Union or in Poland after the entry of the Red Army. It was one long story of shootings, arrest, ill treatment and deportation of families. They stated that they did not want to return to a land where these things were allowed and where a man had no rights. There were cases of kulaks' sons who had been chased from pillar to post and one young man stated that he had been in prison from the age of twelve until released to join the Red Army. Most of them said they preferred death to returning to the Soviet Union and some even invited the British to shoot them in preference to handing them over. I have never in my life seen such human misery or such despair. Throughout all these outbursts, which bore every mark of being true, General Ratov was extremely uncomfortable but did not attempt to stop them. He obviously did not enjoy their revelations as to Soviet methods being made in the presence of British officers. I enclose in greater detail three of the cases as recorded by the officer who was with me. I can only hope that some way will be found to prevent subjects of the disputed areas being sent back to the Soviet Union, as the ones I interviewed, whose every word was recorded, will be going back to their death.[66]

The three case-histories were as follows:

535118 KATCHEN, W.—Soviet (under arrest)
Katchen's story is short, starting when he was 10 years old. His father was put to death and his mother gaoled by the NKVD; he was taken with her. After a few years in the prison, where they were together with women who had babies as young as a few months with them, his mother died but he was not released in spite of his age. He managed to escape from prison during an air raid, (on hearing this, General Ratov said, 'Nonsense, people do not escape from NKVD prisons,'[67]) and found his way to the German lines.

5709 BATSCHAROW, A.—Soviet (under arrest)
Batscharow, a man in his late thirties, was nervous at first, then lost his nervousness and when the General asked why he did not wish to go back, he answered he would be ashamed to consider himself a Soviet.

His father had been a priest and in 1929 was found out and his tongue cut out so that he would not preach any more; later he was shot, and his mother died of the shock. He (Batscharow) ran away and was in hiding until caught and was thrown into prison. After a number of years in prison, he escaped and lived in the woods like a hunted animal until war broke out. He went freely to the Germans to fight the Communists but was finally sent to the western front and captured.

B 50797 BOJKO, Leonid—Disputed

Bojko was not anxious to go home if his part of the country were in Soviet hands. He had had enough of Soviet power when after 1918 part of his family was in Soviet hands. His parents and brother were all shot and for a long time he had been in hiding. In 1939 he was working away from home and learned that there was trouble there. He went back but it was too late: his wife and child were gone and neighbours told him that they were taken by the NKVD. He went into hiding and eventually was taken by the Germans.

Bojko's story was a little mixed as he was obviously under a heavy strain in the presence of General Ratov.[68]

On 23 May yet another shipload of Russians set out on the *Empire Pride* for Odessa. They included the three men whose brief lives we have just read; also 'some Russians who had not seen Russia since the Czar's days.'[69] The journey and its outcome were described by the accompanying Canadian liaison officer from the RLG, Captain You-matoff: 'No. 2 Lower Deck has been prepared by wiring off with barbed wire. In this hold were four cells constructed to hold two persons per cell. On arrival, the Russians promptly put all their 51 arrestees into these 4 cells and refused to consider using the remainder of the deck for their prisoners.' Some days later, this overcrowding was alleviated at the Captain's insistence. He also ordered that the prolonged screams coming from the cells be stopped forthwith.[69] On 30 May, after rounding Gibraltar, a prisoner named Dacenko threw himself overboard and was not recovered. Another man attempted suicide in the Bosphorus, but was rescued.

Finally came the arrival at Odessa:

The disembarkation started at 1830 hrs. and continued for 4½ hrs. The Soviet authorities refused to accept any of the stretcher cases as such and even the patients who were dying were made to walk off the ship carrying their own baggage. Two people only were carried off, one man with his right leg amputated and left one broken, and the other unconscious. The prisoner who had attempted suicide was very roughly handled and his wound opened up and allowed to bleed. He was taken off the ship and marched behind a packing case on the docks; a shot was then heard, but nothing more was seen. The other 32 prisoners were marched or dragged into a warehouse 50 yards from the ship and after a lapse of 15 minutes, automatic fire was heard coming from the warehouse; twenty minutes later a covered lorry drove out of the warehouse and headed towards the town. Later I had a chance to glance into the warehouse when no one was around and found the cobbled floor stained dark in several places around the sides and the walls badly chipped for about five feet up.[70]

These were not the only victims. Altogether about 150 Russians were separated from the rest and marched behind sheds on the quayside. There they were massacred by executioners, many of whom appeared to be youths aged between 14 and 16. Mr. Ted Henson, Second Steward on the *Empire Pride*, saw their departure and later spoke to a shipmate (Sergeant-Major Watson, of the military escort), who had ventured near and seen the corpses being laden into bullock-carts under the youths' direction. The whole scene appalled him and his fellows. A small group of half-clothed children, aged between 3 and 5, were running up and down the quay. They were begging for food and clothing, which members of the *Empire Pride*'s crew threw down to them. All at once Soviet policemen appeared and began chasing the urchins. 'One child,' Ted Henson recalls with disgust, 'about three years old, was caught, picked up in the policeman's arms, and the policeman smashed his fist right into the child's face, then threw him to the ground.'

Some may find it strange that the Soviet authorities apparently made no attempt to conceal these scenes of gratuitous cruelty. The explanation seems to be that at first (as at Murmansk in the previous November) they did indeed take elaborate precautions. The repatriates were received with welcoming banners, etc., and permitted to retain their British clothing until well out of sight of the port. But as time went on and no reproach emanated from the British Government, who clearly must have had some idea of what was happening, they became increasingly open. Eventually they became quite indifferent to British reactions, and committed their atrocities when and where they chose.

Brigadier Firebrace, enclosing Youmatoff's report, despatched a full account to the Foreign Office and the Directorate of Prisoners of War. He has expressed to the present writer his horror at the task imposed upon him, and indeed his indignation comes out in every line:

From Report A, you will be interested to note the summary justice meted out to the arrested men, whose crime was not that they had served in the German Army, as had 99 per cent of the remainder, but that they had either refused to return to the Soviet Union or in addition had attempted to evade returning by trying to enlist in the Polish Army.

An analysis of the list of men whom I feel certain have been shot shows that of the 33, 20 were Russians who had denied their nationality and had attempted to join the Polish Army in the UK; one was arrested on board ship for an unknown reason, jumped overboard in the Dardanelles and attempted suicide on board by slashing his arteries with a razor blade; 6 were Volga Germans who had stated they were not willing to return to the USSR; 5 were Russians who refused to return, some of them reviling the Soviet Union in the presence of General Ratov and myself. The thirty-third was the guard who inadvertently supplied the attempted suicide with the razor blade. He was immediately stripped, put in the cells and landed with the remainder of the arrested men, presumably sharing their fate. Thus, as far as I know, all the men in this party who had refused to return to the Soviet Union were shot.

I must admit that this report has impressed upon me the necessity for the most thorough screening of all doubtful cases, and I can only hope that no man on the Disputed List will ever be sent back to the Soviet Union as they have all refused to go back and therefore be considered as probable candidates for the fate that has overtaken the above-mentioned Soviet citizens. It must be remembered that in the eyes of the Soviet authorities, the 'disputed' are equally Soviet citizens. Several men on the disputed list, in the presence of Soviet officers and myself, spoke against the Soviet Union and gave detailed descriptions of atrocities and rough handling by the Red Army when they went into Poland in 1939. Such men will be shot on arrival without the slightest doubt.

In Report D there is an interesting admission by Major Shershun that the bulk of these men will be sent to 'educational labour camps'. Whenever these men are addressed by a Soviet officer, they are invariably promised, sometimes on the honour of a Soviet officer, that they will on arrival in the USSR be sent immediately to their homes.[71]

Firebrace's report was read by Christopher Warner, Patrick Dean, Thomas Brimelow and others at the Foreign Office. 'The trouble is that under the Crimea Agreement we are bound to send back all undoubted Soviet citizens,' noted Dean.[72] Yet it was he who, only four months later, was to admit that the phraseology of the Crimea Agreement contained 'no definite obligation upon HMG to repatriate to the Soviet Union Soviet citizens who do *not* want to go ...'[73]

It would be salutary, when reflecting on the hundreds of thousands of Russians sent back to Stalin, to read and re-read the case-histories of Katschen, Batscharow and Bojko, all three slaughtered in the incident described by Youmatoff.

Another case was that of Sophia Poleschuk. Her parents were deported to Siberia in 1930-1, leaving her to be brought up by a local doctor. Under his guidance she qualified as an Army nurse. She served in the Finnish and Polish campaigns, and was taken prisoner by the Germans in August 1941. During her military service she had married the Regimental MO, Captain Guseinov. He was captured too, but they were separated almost at once. After a year in a prison camp, Sophia escaped, but was recaptured in 1943 and sent to work in Germany. There she asked the German authorities for permission to join her husband, who had become MO to a Russian PoW camp at Neuhammer in Silesia.

She worked at a local laundry and her husband was given regular leave from the camp to visit her. In May 1944 he escaped, telling Sophia he was aiming for Yugoslavia, but that whatever happened he would never return to Russia. Later, she received a message that he was alive and well; but she never saw him again.

Once more she was alone—except for her baby, born a month after her husband's escape. Eight months passed by, and the Red Army overran Neuhammer. Sophia and the other liberated Russians were told to make their way on foot eastwards. Behind the Red Army lines the scene was one of anarchy, murder, torture and pillage.[74] Despite the tiny child in her arms, Sophia was menaced with rape by roving bands of soldiers.

But fortunately for her, she fell in with a small group of liberated British soldiers making their way eastwards to Odessa. One of them was a Private Jones, who had been a prisoner of war for a lengthy period. Sent out to work on German farms, he had learned to speak German and in this way could talk with Sophia Guseinova. During the long trudge eastwards she told him her tragic story. He still remembers vividly the lonely figure clasping her baby, and when I spoke to him he at once recalled long conversations held on dusty roads in Poland and the Ukraine.

With some of his companions, also freed from German camps, he took Sophia under his protection. Together they travelled the hundreds of miles to Odessa, Jones assiduously protecting mother and baby under the pretence of being her husband. There he managed to persuade the British Consul to allow his 'wife' and 'child' to travel on the returning transports to England.

Somehow, amidst all the chaos, she had heard news of her husband. He had joined an anti-Communist partisan unit, but had eventually fallen into the hands of the Western Allies. For this reason Sophia hoped to be reunited with him—in a prison-camp once again if need be. But of course she would never see her husband again, nor her baby its father. Once Captain Guseinov fell into Allied hands, the 'provisions of the Crimean Agreement' must be upheld, for 'we cannot afford to be sentimental', as Eden had written.

When her ship arrived at Glasgow on 5 May 1945, Sophia was

interrogated by the immigration authorities. In the words of the Immigration Officer:

> Alien does not now wish to return to Russia. She states that the least that would happen to her would be arrest as a 'political' prisoner, but she also undoubtedly has in her mind the possibility of more serious trouble in view of her husband's service in an anti-Soviet unit under the Germans. There is also the fact that she deliberately evaded the Soviet controls before and after reaching Odessa. She states she has no particular concern in her own life, but was hoping to give her baby a chance of living in a decent and free country.
>
> The whereabouts of her husband are not so far known, but if he did reach the UK as a prisoner of war, he is undoubtedly now in Soviet hands ... There is no doubt Guseinova was anti-Communist long before this war started, and although one feels a certain reluctance to commit a woman, who is enmeshed in the web of circumstances through (it is thought) little fault or cause of her own seeking, to what may mean either death or Siberia, it would seem there is no other course to follow ... Instructions as to alien's disposal are requested.

Foreign Office instructions came swiftly back and the Home Office were able to inform them that 'the woman and her child left the Patriotic Schools for Liverpool this morning and I hope that their departure concludes the last chapter.' It did: Sophia and her baby 'commenced her return journey on 22 May.' A Foreign Office official summed it all up succinctly. 'A sad story, but there was nothing else to be done.'[75]

The final destination of Sophia Guseinova and her child cannot be traced. But one place where many such girls ended up at that time was the gold-mining region of Kolyma in the Soviet Arctic.

A German-Jewish girl condemned to forced labour in the Kolyma camp complex has described the arrival there of hundreds of young girls—those who, like Sophia Guseinova, worked for the Germans or who were held in some other way to have betrayed the Soviet state. 'They came as adolescents and were instantly transformed by Kolyma into fully-fledged prostitutes.' Some were Ukrainian nationalists. 'But why had Soviet officers, interrogating seventeen-year-old girls, broken the girls' collar-bones and kicked in their ribs with heavy military boots, so that they lay spitting blood in the prison hospitals of Kolyma?' The life of women in Kolyma was wretched but not long; tuberculosis, syphilis, malnutrition and suicide saw to that.[76]

And what of the baby? Sophia could not leave it behind, as a Foreign Office official had suggested in the case of another child.[77] That mother had told the Foreign Office: 'My little boy is five months old, they will take him away from me—I know that only too well.'[78] She was right.

As the Poles dragged to the camps in 1941 discovered, 'Children born in *lagier* remain a few months with their mothers and are then removed to special institutions.' For the first two years the mothers could visit their children; after that they were sent away to orphanages.[79] But even this two years' grace could not be relied on. When one such baby became seriously ill, the mother was refused permission to visit her and was also prevented by the camp guard from attending her burial ('No!' he replied, 'you'll only think of something else next').[80] In Magadan Elinor Lipper visited a children's combine. There the babies were held *a week after birth*. The mothers were allowed a month's respite, and then returned to convict labour (felling timber in the summer and clearing snowdrifts in the winter). Several times a day they were marched to the children's combine to suckle their infants, and then returned to labour at bayonet point.

Criminals were appointed to care for the children. But even those who were well-intentioned had no time to do more than give the infants' shaven heads a wipe with a towel and push some unpalatable food before them.

> These children rarely have toys; they rarely smile. They learn to talk late and they never experience affection. The smaller children forget their mothers from one visiting day to the next. Just when they are beginning to thaw out a little, a guard comes along and calls to the mothers, 'Come on now, get going, it's time.' Out in the yard they still hear the children crying. Children are always crying in the combine, and it always seems to each mother that the one crying is her own. The larger children put their noses to the window and watch knowingly as their convict mothers are marched off in rows of five—behind them the soldier with the fixed bayonet.[81]

In spite of its belief that it 'could not afford to be sentimental' the Foreign Office did occasionally make exceptions to its general policy. Amongst the Soviet citizens who fell into British hands in the same month as Sophia Guseinova was a professor, a scholar with an international reputation. I cannot publish his name nor any indication of his identity, as he has relatives still living in the USSR. His son wrote to me recently in response to my enquiry: 'Apart from a few minor incidents immediately after the German collapse, my family was never exposed to a real danger of repatriation. In fact, the British informed my father that the Soviets were looking for him, and offered protection. They did this because Cambridge University was interested in my father as an expert on . . ., and also to keep him away from the Americans, who wanted him for the same reason.' The professor was not repatriated.

In tragic and sinister contrast is the case of Alexander Romanoff, a boy from a camp for Russian prisoners at Newcastle. He had been taken as a child by the Germans in 1941, and later compelled to work in the Todt organisation in France. He was captured by American troops after the landings, and thenceforward became one of those thousands of prisoners in Britain whose story we have been describing. In the camp he heard rumours of the appalling fate that awaited those being returned and, being very young, became extremely frightened. Twice he ran away from the camp, but each time he was captured and returned. This now marked him down for certain death if he were repatriated.

Perhaps aware of this, a friendly British officer at the camp, acting as interpreter, warned Alexander of the danger facing him and advised him to escape again. Knowing of the failure of his two previous attempts, he advised him to go to the representative of the White Russian community in London. There, if anywhere, he could find sympathy and help. Alexander managed to raise enough money for his fare and eventually found himself in Brechin Place, off the Gloucester Road. There, at number 5, was the Russian House, home of Monsieur Sabline, representative of the anti-Communist White Russian émigrés in London. After waiting agonising minutes when he had rung the bell, Alexander heard footsteps within and was ushered over the threshold and into a large room on the right. As he waited he gazed with some awe at an enormous full-length oil painting of his illustrious namesake, the Tsar Alexander I, flanked by one of his successor, Nicholas I. Everywhere were ikons, engravings of old Russia, and photographs of the martyred Nicholas II. What followed is drawn from a subsequent Foreign Office report.

Suddenly there was a soft footfall in the doorway, and Alexander turned with a start to see an elegant, rather dandified gentleman standing there.

'Sabline,' the newcomer introduced himself. He waved Alexander to a chair and drew up another. 'Now, how can I help you, my boy?'

Alexander burst into an excited account of his fears, his two escapes, the kindly advice given him by the British officer, and his hopes that he could now be hidden away by the White Russian community. Sabline listened attentively, asked him one or two questions about the British officer, and then requested him to wait a moment whilst he made a telephone call. Romanoff nodded eagerly, and M. Sabline left the room.

Once outside he made straight for his office and put through two calls. They were to the Home Office and the War Office.

At this point the narrative must read more like an episode from the adventures of Richard Hannay than sober history. For M. Sabline, 'Representative of the Russian Refugees Community in the United

Kingdom (Former Imperial Chargé d'Affaires for Russia in Great Britain)'—as his writing-paper proclaimed him—had gone over to the Soviets.[82]

Within an hour or so of Sabline's telephone calls, the doorbell at 5 Brechin Place rang again and in hurried Captain Soldatenkov, who is described in a War Office report as 'acting in some liaison capacity between the War Department and the Soviet authorities'.[83] He asked young Romanoff a number of searching questions. He then departed to make his reports.

Meanwhile, Sabline was in an awkward predicament. As a Home Office report explained: 'He does not wish to keep the boy on the premises, nor does he wish to turn him loose.' If he turned him loose, the boy might really escape, or meet with someone who would have enough knowledge to persuade him to challenge the jurisdiction of the Allied Forces Act. As he had never been a member of the Red Army, a solicitor would have no difficulty in proving before a magistrate that Romanoff could not in law be a member of the illusory Russian force on British soil.

Sabline could continue to offer Romanoff 'asylum' in the Russian House, 'but he feels that this might be extremely embarrassing to him, having regard to the friendly relations which he has established with the Soviet authorities.' As in the cases of Faschenko and Krokhin, the Home Office was in the embarrassing situation of not being in a position to arrest the 'deserter', nor would Sabline's 'cover' as a leader of the White Russian community have perhaps survived such an arrest in the Russian House itself. All the Home Office, in desperation, could suggest was that Sabline should find somewhere for Romanoff to live and continue spying on his movements until the Home Office was in a position to effect his arrest.

None of this was very satisfactory to Sabline, who saw himself in danger either of being exposed to the émigrés for what he was, or of arousing the suspicions of the ever-mistrustful Soviet Embassy. He could see only one satisfactory course, and resolved to take it.

Apologising for the interruptions, Sabline invited the young fugitive to have lunch with him. Comforted by the sympathy displayed by this elegant gentleman, as also by the charming Soldatenkov, Alexander Romanoff began to feel a new confidence growing inside him. The gentleman was so understanding, appeared to know so much about the situation and, moreover, plied him with wine. The boy felt his cares slipping away. Gradually Sabline began to explain gently that there was really no alternative to returning to the camp at Newcastle. On the one hand, the authorities could not fail to recapture him in the end, and then he really would be in trouble. On the other, if he returned voluntarily and said he wished to fight for the Red Army, then there was no doubt that he would be fairly treated on his return home. He, Sabline, was of course an émigré, and as such by tradition opposed to the Soviet régime. But he had wide contacts, and had come—reluctantly, perhaps —to realise that Stalin had changed much in the last few years. With the destruction of the German invaders a new era of prosperity and justice was dawning in Russia. Who knew? Perhaps he might himself return one day.

Sabline glanced at his watch. Look, if you leave shortly, you can be back in Newcastle by this evening. There would be no reason for anyone to know you had planned to escape. Now, here's some money— no, take it, you can use anything left over to treat your friends when you return. Not at all, my dear boy, not at all. If we Russians don't help each other, no one else will. By the way, I suppose you can't recall the name of that British officer who advised you to escape? He was tall and wore glasses, I think you said. No? A pity, I should have liked to thank him, even though I fear his advice was not good.

It was all too easy. Murmuring confused thanks, Alexander made his departure. Sabline saw him on his way: the escape was over, as is the story of Alexander Romanoff. Patrick Dean wrote the obituary: 'This is the 3rd time Romanov has escaped & he is in for a rough time if he gets back to the Soviet Union.'[84] In December John Galsworthy referred more plainly to 'a man who has earned a certain death sentence by his desertion . . .'[85]

As it was on 9 March that this episode took place, Romanoff will almost certainly have sailed with the next delivery of prisoners on the *Almanzora* from Glasgow to Odessa on 27 March. And, in the light of all our evidence, it is scarcely possible to doubt that he was amongst those whom Czeslaw Jesman reported as having been shot on arrival. For, as Brigadier Firebrace had discovered, it was those who had unsuccessfully attempted to evade repatriation who were marked down for death.

More fortunate were three Latvians, who on 1 May 1945 escaped from the camp at Newlands Corner, Guildford. Suspecting the fate accorded to unsuccessful claimants to the 'disputed' list, they had asserted their Latvian nationality before Brigadier Firebrace and General Ratov. But near the camp lived a Latvian lady married to an Englishman, Mrs. Anna Child, who spoke to them and warned them of the situation. She advised them to escape and go to the Latvian Legation in Eaton Place. This they did, only to find themselves amongst officials almost as terrified as themselves. As Mrs. Child told me, 'to my understanding they appeared too scared to talk, or do anything to aid in the cause'. Mr. Zarine and his staff were in a state of the most lively fear lest the British Government, in their efforts to placate Stalin, should find it expedient to repatriate them too. However, all was well, as the Foreign Office, in the words of Geoffrey Wilson, felt obliged 'to act quickly in order to avoid the risk of a serious public scandal'. Provided with assurances that they would as Latvians not be repatriated against their will, they spent a few days in the Legation. They were then transferred to a PoW camp for non-Soviet citizens and ultimately released.[86]

By the middle of 1945 most of the Russians in camps in Britain had been returned. It was no longer necessary to make arrangements for long voyages, as with the collapse of Germany the prisoners could be returned overland. The last major consignment—the eighth—to make the journey was a party of 335 Russians, who travelled in the middle of August from the camp at Newlands Corner to the Soviet Zone of Germany, via Dover and Ostend. Captain Crichton of the Russian Liaison Group, who accompanied them, was alternately amused and disgusted at the conduct of the three Soviet officers in charge. Clearly the Soviets were as frightened as the Foreign Office of the possibility that the British public might find out what was happening. 'Major Gruzdiev . . . accused Lieut. Col. Ludford of having purposely stopped the lorry containing the arrested men so that they had to be marched in full view of the general public.' Captain Crichton was also subjected to a tirade from Gruzdiev when he incautiously suggested that the officers might travel alongside the men; he was later intrigued to find the same officers arrested by the orders of the Soviets on their arrival at Luneburg.

One Russian slipped away at Dover, and in Holland another pulled the communication cord and made a run for it across some fields. He was captured and brought back, but in the early hours of the morning Major Gruzdiev had to report another absconder. Next evening occurred a tragedy.

> As the train was passing over a bridge, leaving Celle at 1900 hrs. I saw a man fall off and crash to the ground, about 30 ft. below. The train was stopped by communication cord and while Russians were collecting him I rang up the RTO at Celle and asked him to send first-aid kit and an ambulance, straight away. On return to the train I found the Russians about to load the man on to the train to the great disgust of a party of British troops who were also travelling. I informed the Major of what I had done, he told me he was taking the man on, I informed him that I considered it inhuman and that I wished to see the man loaded on the ambulance, in this I was supported by the other British officer present and this was done. Subsequently, I heard that the man (H. Funk) died in hospital.

Altogether eight men were lost on the way, though six were later recaptured. At a barracks in Luneburg, which was the collecting point for returning Russians, the Soviet authorities ordered 140 to be placed under close arrest.[87]

Operations in Britain were drawing to a close. On 12 November 1945, the War Office instituted a 'final search' in PoW camps for prisoners of Soviet nationality.[88] Sixty-six were found, who were sent off via Ostend on 12 December. But a Soviet attempt to include a further sixty Polish Ukrainians in the party was frustrated, the letter of the Yalta Agreement being now much more rigidly adhered to.[89]

Despite this 'final search', prisoners in Britain could not feel safe for a while yet. Over a year later, in December 1946, a party of fourteen Russians was transferred under armed guard via Dover and Calais to the Soviet camp outside Paris.[90]

All in all, some 32,295 Russian prisoners were held in Britain and despatched to the USSR between 1944 and 1946.[91] For the most part they were the men of the *Ostlegionen* and Todt labour battalions, captured in Normandy and brought to England until September 1944.[92] Many could be regarded as traitors from their attitude and activities, had they been citizens of a normal civilised state. Many could not be so regarded under any circumstances, particularly the large number of women and children.[93]

Solzhenitsyn has criticised the British people for allowing the crime of forced repatriation to take place without effective protest. But the remarkable fact is that this enormous operation, involving as it did kidnappings, suicides and widespread infractions of British law on a scale involving thousands, was known only to a very few. Had even a small section of the public become aware of what was taking place in their midst, and had they engaged in vociferous protest, it is possible that the whole policy, on British soil at least, would have ground to a halt. But the vigilance of the Foreign Office, coupled with the isolation of the prisoners in their 'limbo-GULAG' preserved the shaky edifice of the Allied Forces Act. Let us hope that such scenes are never repeated in Britain, with SMERSH ranging freely in search of its prey. For next time it is unlikely that the victims will be Russians.

7

The Cossacks
and the Conference

OVER THE WINTER OF 1944–5, ALLIED INTELLIGENCE IN ITALY BEGAN TO receive reports of a large Cossack settlement in the extreme north of the country. Though this was the first appearance of that formidable fighting people in the Alps since Suvorov's celebrated campaign of 1799, the presence of Russians as such was not a cause for great surprise. From the time of the Anzio offensive to the breakthrough on the Gothic Line, British and American forces had continually received a trickle of Russian prisoners, mostly workers in forced-labour battalions.[1]

None the less, the situation of the Cossacks was remarkable. In 1942 the German Army arrived in the Kuban region, north of the Caucasus, to find themselves welcomed by most of the population as deliverers from Bolshevik oppression.

The Cossacks of the Don, Kuban and Terek were descended from heroic freebooters who, in the sixteenth and seventeenth centuries, moved southwards to escape the constraints of their Russian and Polish rulers. They fought bravely against the Turks and Tartars, and were rewarded with military and social privileges when in due course the Tsar's authority was extended over them. Their history was checkered and violent. Earlier they had risen in rebellion against the Tsars; later they were employed by them to suppress revolutionary agitation. In 1914–17 they covered themselves with glory fighting on the Eastern Front; after that the majority opposed the Bolshevik Revolution. They still recalled with pride the traditions and privileges they had enjoyed under the Tsars, and the bravery with which they had opposed the Bolshevik seizure of power just over twenty years before. Revolt had simmered endemically ever since the Soviet conquest of the Kuban in 1920, and it can scarcely have occurred to any of its inhabitants that it was treason to resume the struggle now that deliverance appeared to be at hand.[2]

German military rule in the Kuban was largely benevolent, avoiding the savageries perpetrated elsewhere by the invasion forces. Stolen property was returned to its owners, and the Cossacks lived quietly and contentedly in their restored *stanitsas*. Many of the men joined volunteer units helping the Germans, and when at the end of 1942 Soviet partisans attempted to infiltrate the country they were strongly resisted. But after Stalingrad it became clear that it was only a matter of time before the Wehrmacht would have to withdraw westwards. The German military authorities informed the inhabitants, and a general exodus of all who feared Soviet retribution took place.

Thousands of Cossacks withdrew westwards. Despite German aid, the journey was one of great hardship, as families made their way across the steppe, bringing with them their possessions in horse-drawn carts. The Germans had assigned to them as a place of settlement the district around the town of Novogrudok, about 100 versts west of Minsk in Byelorussia.[3] There, hopeful that the tide of war might turn again, the Cossacks settled down to cultivate the land, pasture out their cattle, and attempt to continue life free from the attentions of the Commissar or the Tchekist. In accordance with Cossack tradition, they elected as their leader, or Field Ataman, an officer of engineers named Pavlov. Pavlov was a man of exceptional organisational ability, and is remembered still by all Cossacks as an inspiration to their 'nation'. Under his direction a church was built at Novogrudok, and hospitals and schools were constructed. It had been largely thanks to his leadership that the Cossacks had achieved the arduous journey from the shores of the Black Sea to the frontier of Poland.

However, on 17 June 1944, Ataman Pavlov was killed on the outskirts of the town. A minor mystery remains as to the cause of his death, but it seems probable that he was shot either by Red partisans, or by one of his own sentries on failing to give the correct password. Under the supervision of the resident German liaison officer, Major Müller, a new Field Ataman (*Pokhodny Ataman*) was 'elected'. He was Timophey Ivanovich Domanov, a former major in the Red Army. Though well-intentioned and conscientious, he had none of Pavlov's charisma. Many Cossacks now hold that, had Pavlov survived, he might somehow have saved them from their ultimate fate.

The Cossack settlement (*Kazachy Stan*) at Novogrudok was run on traditional Cossack lines. It was primarily a haven of refuge for the dispossessed Cossacks from the Kuban, Don and Terek. Thither also came émigré Cossacks from western Europe, eager to return from the frustrations of exile to work once again for the liberation of their country. Amongst these were distinguished figures from the first struggle against Bolshevism in 1918–21, such as General Peter Krasnov (in 1918 Ataman of the Don Cossacks) and General Vyacheslav Naumenko, former Ataman of the Kuban Cossacks. The Cossack traditional *cherkeska* began to be worn again, and occasionally a uniform could be seen that had been last used by its owner when serving the Tsar and Autocrat Nicholas II. Old ways, old songs and old decorations came back into widespread usage. It was a brief and pathetic resurgence of a way of life that was soon to be destroyed for ever.

The uniforms were not purely ornamental. The forests around Novogrudok were permeated by Soviet partisans, against whom the hard-pressed Wehrmacht was powerless to operate. This did not worry Ataman Pavlov, who (and Domanov after him) organised the male Cossacks into military units. Armed partly with a scanty supply of small-arms provided by the Germans, and afterwards with captured Soviet *matériel*, the Cossacks were more than able to hold their own. The partisans kept at a respectable distance. But for all the traditional regimental names and ranks employed, the Cossack levies at Novogrudok were never more than a para-military defence corps.

In spite of the hardship of their life, surviving Cossacks look back on this time with nostalgia. Murder, torture and slavery appeared to be things of the past; the children received a civilised education; men and women were free to enjoy the fruits of their own labours in the fields; and in the evening the bells of the church summoned the Orthodox faithful to prayer. But it was not to last.

In September 1944, the German authorities allocated the Cossacks a new asylum. This was in northern Italy, a region chosen because it was far removed from the Soviet line of advance, and was one of the few non-German territories still lying within the power of the dwindling Reich.

Across Poland, Germany and Austria moved the little Cossack 'nation', still with its train of wagons, cattle, horses and dromedaries. In Italy they were settled first at Gemona in Friuli, soon afterwards at Tolmezzo in the Carnia. Before the Cossacks' arrival, land and houses had been appropriated for their use, which naturally aroused considerable resentment amongst the inhabitants. With the ever-nearing advance of the Allied armies up the peninsula, Italian partisans were becoming increasingly active. Once again the Cossacks established a vignette of life in a Don *stanitsa*, remaining as before rather a settlement than a military force, although once again their 'regiments' fought against Communists. Such was the situation in the spring of 1945, as the war drew to its close.[4]

Near the Cossacks at Tolmezzo was a settlement of several thousand Caucasians: Georgians, Armenians, Azerbaidjanis, Ossetians and others. Their history and reasons for being in North Italy were similar in many ways to the circumstances of the Cossacks. They represented, largely, detached units or survivors of the national legions formed by the Germans with the ostensible purpose of liberating their homelands. When this became no longer feasible, some of the more martial units were employed on the western front in France and the Low Countries, whilst many of the Azerbaidjanis found themselves serving on the Italian front in the 162nd Turcoman Division, a front-line unit with a reputation for tough fighting. Like the Cossacks, the scattered Caucasians were instructed by the Germans to settle in the Carnia. Their headquarters was at Paluzza, in the mountains some miles north of the Cossack settlement at Tolmezzo. Their discipline and organisation were much inferior to that of the Cossacks, possibly on account of the difficulty of imposing uniform order on a series of tribes speaking (it is said) seventeen separate languages, and ranging in religious belief from the Orthodox Christians of Georgia to the Shiite Moslems of Azerbaidjan. Like the Cossacks, during their peregrinations they had attracted numerous compatriots wandering individually or in groups through the chaos of central Europe.[5] It would seem likely, though it is difficult to be certain, that it was the Caucasians who were largely responsible for a series of depredations and atrocities committed in the region against the inhabitants. As in France, the local Resistance forces learned that it was German policy to create in this way a general hostility to all things Russian.[6]

It was in the early spring of 1945 that AFHQ at Caserta first paid serious attention to the Cossacks at Tolmezzo. Plans were being drawn up for the overrunning of the Gothic Line and the seizure of Bologna—preludes to bursting into the open valley of the Po. Operating in the Carnian Alps in a roving SOE unit was Mr. Patrick Martin-Smith. He was informed by the local non-Communist partisans (*Osoppo*) that the Cossacks had established contact with them, with a view to trying to 'reinsure' with the Allies, whose victory seemed increasingly certain. Martin-Smith at once became excited by the possibility of persuading the Cossacks to cut the Villach-Udine railway line, one of the two main German lines of communication into Italy. If this could be made to coincide with the coming offensive, the effect on the enemy's capacity to resist could have been devastating. He contacted Caserta, but received only non-committal replies. As he realised, a serious snag would be the security danger involved in informing (even by implication) the Cossacks of the date of the forthcoming offensive. And then events caught up with the whole romantic plan. The Germans launched a massive 'clean-up' of the partisans in the Carnia, and by the second week of April, Alexander's armies had surged irresistibly forwards, seizing Imola and Bologna. By the end of the month the Allies themselves were in a position to pounce on Tolmezzo.

It was the 8th Argyll and Sutherland Highlanders who, on the night of 6 May, received orders to operate against the Cossack Division. Advancing from the east along the mountainous valley of the Taglia-mento, they left camp at dawn in full fighting order. But it soon became apparent that no resistance was likely to be offered, and the battalion pushed on at greater speed. By noon they were in Tolmezzo, to find the birds had flown—'probably back into Austria'. All they found of the departed legions were a few dispirited Turcomans. The men were not displeased to find their entry so easy, and just after teatime came 'the best news of the war', as the Brigade War Diarist put it. 'The un-conditional surrender of all German forces in the field had been con-firmed. Unfortunately the Bn was not in a suitable position to celebrate but an extra beer issue was authorised. The evening passed very quietly.'[7]

Further north, a Georgian unit surrendered, many of whose officers were princes,[8] and whose commanding officer was a beautiful Georgian princess named Mariana. These noble Georgians lived in a romantic dream-world, soon to be destroyed for ever. Only ten days before, Prince Irakly Bagration had knocked on the door of the British Embassy in Madrid, offering to arrange the surrender of 100,000 Georgians serving in the German Army, provided guarantees could be given that they would not be sent to the Soviet Union. The Foreign Office instructed the Embassy not to reply.[9]

Meanwhile, where were the main bodies of Cossacks and Caucasians, who had apparently melted away from Tolmezzo? With the impending collapse of German power, arguments had swayed this way and that as to the best course to be taken in the circumstances. *Obergruppenführer* Globocnik, the local Nazi commander, ordered them to stay put, but the Cossacks were little affected by his impotent threats.[10] And the German officers commanding the Caucasian Division disappeared one night, leaving a Georgian émigré, Sultan Kelech Ghirey, in command.[11] The exiles were free to decide their fate, but their choice seemed distinctly limited. Eventually it was virtually made for them.

Now that the destruction of Nazi power was clearly only a matter of days, Italian partisans began to appear increasingly openly, and in larger and better-equipped units. A formidable Communist band, led by a Catholic priest, appeared particularly threatening, and one day the

Cossack military hospital was burned to the ground with many wounded Cossacks inside.[12] Finally, on 27 April, three Italian officers came to Domanov's headquarters in Tolmezzo, demanding that the Cossacks surrender all their arms and withdraw from Italian soil. Little inclined to place himself so totally at the mercy of such enemies, Domanov agreed to lead his Cossacks from Italy, but declined to give up their arms. The Italians agreed, and on 28 April virtually the whole of the Cossack group and a large detachment of Caucasians struck camp and began the arduous march northwards.

They set off at midnight, bearing with them everything that could be borne in the wagons or on their backs. The mounted units came first, led by Domanov's staff: first came the Don Regiment, then the Kuban, and after them the Terek. Trailing behind these wound a seemingly endless column of wagons, bearing their supplies and personal possessions and as many of the old, sick or very young as the horses could draw. Near the head of the column drove a Fiat car carrying the aged General Peter Krasnov. Domanov himself waited with his bodyguard regiment for a detached unit from Udine to catch up with the main column. A rear-guard of several hundred Don and Kuban Cossacks was placed south of Tolmezzo to check the partisans from launching an attack on the unwieldy column as it set off northwards.

The march of the Cossacks into Austria was a journey of appalling hardship and danger. In the early stages they had to fend off attacks by the Italian partisans. Then, as they ascended the heights to where the road winds perilously round the precipitous chasms of the Plöckenpass, the weather also turned against them. Torrential rain fell upon the struggling column, to be followed higher up by a prolonged snowstorm. There were numerous deaths, first from the partisans' bullets, and later from cold or from the precipitous, snow-covered trackway where a missed foothold could be fatal. In the midst of the driving storm the Cossacks crossed the Austrian frontier and descended from the rocky fastnesses of the towering Hohe Warte, round the wooded and boulder-strewn crags until they reached the shelter of the Gailtal. Late in the evening of 3 May, advance units of Domanov's staff arrived in the first village in Austria, Mauthen-Kötschach.[13] General Krasnov's Fiat had broken down, and was being towed by a transport bus. The trumpets of the bedraggled Don Regiment blared out defiantly from behind as two officers from the staff went forward to see what reception they would receive. After all, the Reich still stood, if shakily, and the Cossacks had been strictly forbidden to leave Italy.

Herr Julian Kollnitz was then *Kreisleiter* of the local region, and remembers the arrival of the Cossacks. A Cossack general in full-dress uniform came up to negotiate their entry into Austria. Through his adjutant, a German-speaking émigré from Berlin, he asked where the fighting was going on and where they should report. Kollnitz had received orders from Headquarters in Klagenfurt that the Cossacks were to be let through without hindrance. He informed the general that his men could continue their march, but that the war was virtually over and all fighting at an end. The Cossack seemed disappointed at this news, and was only convinced of its truth when his adjutant spoke on the telephone to Deputy Gauleiter Timmel at Klagenfurt.

It was arranged that the Cossacks (Herr Kollnitz was told there were 32,000 of them) should move on to the north. Their destination, soon to be the scene of such dramatic and tragic events, was chosen quite by chance. The commander of the local *Volkssturm* detachment defending the Plöckenpass was *Kreisstabsführer* Norbert Schluga. He was a native of the Gailtal, the valley on to which the Cossacks intended to advance. Herr Schluga tells me that he regarded this prospect with great misgiving; the Cossacks might or might not plunder his own and his neighbours' villages, but their thousands of horses would certainly eat every blade of grass in the valley. By agreement with *Kreisleiter* Kollnitz, Schluga persuaded the Cossacks that the road through the Gailtal was far too broken and treacherous for their horses, and that they would do better to move north to the Drautal.

The Cossacks accepted the new direction, and for three days and two nights their squadrons passed through to the north. At the crossroads in Mauthen, Schluga set up a detachment of *Volkssturm* to prevent any Cossacks from wandering down to the Gailtal. He himself stayed up the whole time, and frequently had to come forward to explain to doubting Cossacks that their route really had been changed.

In Mauthen the railway hotel was placed at the disposal of the Cossack generals and staff. General Krasnov took up quarters there, and from his window saw with melancholy resignation scenes that portrayed the end of all his hopes. The Cossacks, destitute of fodder for their beloved horses, were straggling on northwards, camping at night on the roadside wherever they happened to find themselves. Amongst them moved scattered groups of German soldiers, betraying by their shattered appearance a consciousness that their country was wholly defeated. At one point the old General was troubled at witnessing a degrading scene: a group of Cossacks in their frustration turned upon passing Germans and began to plunder them. This shameful breach of discipline, perpetrated as it was on the troops of a beaten ally, seemed to portend also the end of the Cossacks. However, no serious violence took place during the stay, so Herr Kollnitz informs me: certainly not the 'pitched battle' reported in *The Times* on 8 May.[14]

On 4 May, Domanov brought up the Cossack rearguard and joined Krasnov in the Mauthen Hotel Bahnhof. There they conferred together as to what should be their next move. Meanwhile, the cavalcade of thousands of Cossacks with their baggage-train (it was a movement of a people rather than an army) streamed on northwards to the valley of the Drau. Crossing the Gailbergsattel, they moved slowly up the valley. A few miles upriver the land broadens out below the mountains, where the sleepy Carinthian town of Lienz stands amongst carefully-cultivated fields. Here at least was a place where there was room to set up tents and pasture the thousands of horses.[15] It was Easter, a day of hope, and the priests conducted services in the fields. 'Christ is risen!' cried the Cossacks, kissing each other in the meadows as they met.

The two Cossack leaders, Domanov and Krasnov, discussed long and urgently what should be done next. The choice was small, being virtually limited to the question of whether to surrender to the Americans or to the British. Krasnov, who as an émigré had by far the greater knowledge of European affairs, urged that the British would view their case with the greater sympathy and understanding. It was they, after all, who had been the most ardent supporters of the White cause in the struggle against the Bolsheviks, and it had been Churchill, then Secretary for War, who had been the most vociferous supporter of British military intervention on the anti-Communist side. The years had passed and times had changed, but surely English chivalry would come to the aid of a former ally in distress? Krasnov looked, too, to the influence of the Allied Commander-in-Chief in Italy, Field-Marshal Alexander. For at the time that Churchill had been despatching men and munitions to assist Denikin's armies, Alexander had been actually fighting against the Bolsheviks in Courland. He still bore proudly a Russian Imperial order, bestowed on him by the White General Yudenitch (just as Krasnov bore the British Military Cross, awarded for services in the same cause), and must appreciate the Cossacks' predicament. Amongst the rank-and-file Cossacks had even grown up a romantic legend (still current) that the Field-Marshal had, in his admiration for all things Russian, wooed and won a beautiful Russian bride.[16]

Against this Domanov, who had been a simple major in the Red Army, was hardly able to argue, and he acquiesced. It was decided to send a delegation back across the Plöckenpass to parley with the nearest British force. The party was headed by a General Vasiliev, who was accompanied by young Lieutenant Nikolai Krasnov, grandson of the General, and an English-speaking Cossack woman, Olga Rotova. The two latter have both left first-hand accounts of these negotiations.

Hastily pinning a piece of white sheeting as a flag of truce to their car, the party set off southwards. As Olga Rotova thought, 'what was awaiting us ahead, God only knew.' But even as they began to leave the village, they were unexpectedly halted by a British armoured car. On explaining their mission, they were sent on to Regimental Headquarters at Paluzza. There the Colonel in turn passed them on to Brigade Head-quarters in Tolmezzo. It was somewhat disconcerting to find themselves back where they had started a week before, particularly as their uniforms were recognised by Italians who shook their fists and howled 'Cossack barbarians!' And the building where General Domanov had held his headquarters a week before was now that of Major-General Robert Arbuthnott, commanding the 78th Infantry Division.

Inside, General Arbuthnott greeted the envoys politely. General Vasiliev asked whether he could speak privately with him, and Arbuthnott ushered the Russians into his office. He offered them seats, but Vasiliev, a former officer of the Emperor in the Cossacks of the Guard and a man of impressive personality and appearance, insisted on standing whilst he explained his purpose. But the two generals were speaking sadly at cross purposes.

Vasiliev explained that the Cossacks had no quarrel with the Western Allies, and only wished to continue their struggle against Bolshevism. In order to prosecute this aim, he requested that they be permitted to join General Vlasov. 'Who is this General Vlasov?' asked Arbuthnott. Vasiliev explained about the ROA, its hopes and plans. The Englishman replied: 'You must first hand over all your arms.'

Vasiliev enquired whether that meant that they were to become prisoners of war. No, replied Arbuthnott, that term applied only to soldiers captured in battle; the Cossacks would be regarded merely as having voluntarily given themselves up. This enigmatic distinction was taken by the Cossacks as at least implying a status less subject to arbitrary treatment than that of ordinary prisoner of war.

But before the important question of status could be discussed further, Brigadier Geoffrey Musson of the 36th Infantry Brigade (now General Sir Geoffrey Musson) entered the room. At Arbuthnott's request, Vasiliev again explained the Cossacks' position. Musson waited until the General had finished, and then repeated that it was essential for the Cossacks to be disarmed as quickly as possible. Vasiliev explained that he could not answer in this for General Domanov, and so, after a brief consultation, the two British generals declared that the following morning they would come to Domanov's headquarters at Kötschach and settle terms.

Knowing that Domanov and Krasnov would be impatiently awaiting their return, Vasiliev and his party were anxious to return across the pass as soon as possible. But Arbuthnott and Musson would hear nothing of this, and insisted that they stay for tea. In this more relaxed atmosphere, Arbuthnott asked young Lieutenant Krasnov some friendly questions about himself. Nikolai explained that he had left Russia as a baby with his parents, and thereafter lived in Yugoslavia. When war broke out he had served in King Peter's army against the Germans. He was taken prisoner, and was later offered and accepted the chance of joining an anti-Soviet Cossack unit. But he had refused to serve in Africa when ordered, as that would have involved serving against Russia's allies of the previous war.

Though in thus showing interest in his young guest's history, Arbuthnott's motive was undoubtedly simple curiosity coupled with good manners, it is of the highest importance to remember that from his very first dealings with the Cossacks he was made aware that large numbers were not Soviet citizens.

Before their departure, Musson pressed on Olga Rotova, the interpreter, a large packet of tea, sugar and chocolate. He brushed aside her thanks, and, together with Arbuthnott, came into the street to see the party off. This demonstration of British goodwill greatly impressed the volatile Italian crowd: cries of 'Viva!' rent the air, and a girl, overcome with emotion, thrust a bouquet of lilies into Olga's arms. Escorted by British armoured cars, General Vasiliev and his party drove back to Kötschach, arriving at 9.30 p.m. at Domanov's Headquarters, where they reported to Generals Domanov and Krasnov on their mission. In the Cossack Headquarters that night all stayed up late, vainly trying to prise deeper implications from the largely non-committal replies of Arbuthnott and Musson.[17]

Next morning, half an hour earlier than expected, Brigadier Musson and his staff arrived at the Cossack Headquarters. The meeting was held in the dining-room of the hotel occupied by Domanov.[18] After handshakes all round, the discussion proceeded on a cordial note. The Cossacks, eagerly pinning extravagant hopes to any demonstration of British goodwill, noted that they did not appear to be treated as enemies or prisoners, but as colleagues in an administrative operation. Brigadier Musson's opening words seemed encouraging also: he told the Cossacks they were to keep their arms whilst *en route* to their concentration area. A map was then spread out on the table, and Musson explained that all Russian forces must set up camp in the Drau Valley— the Cossacks upriver between Lienz and Oberdrauburg, and the Caucasians downstream between Oberdrauburg and Dellach.

This was all that was discussed concerning conditions of the Cossack surrender. The Cossacks felt relief that the British appeared so understanding, and Brigadier Musson likewise felt that what might have been an awkward business had passed off very smoothly. As the 36th Brigade War Diary explained, the Cossacks 'would have been still a force to be reckoned with if they had refused to capitulate and until that capitulation was complete we could not feel secure'. The serious business over, both sides took breakfast, drinking wine and chatting in friendly fashion.

Later in the day newspaper correspondents from *The Times* and the *Daily Mail* came to interview the Cossack leaders. They wanted to know how and why the Cossacks had left Russia and come all these hundreds of miles to Austria. Speaking through the interpreter, Olga Rotova, General Domanov explained with the aid of a map how the Bolshevik régime had waged virtual war on the Cossack lands, how they had made the arduous journey from the Kuban and Don to Tolmezzo, not knowing where they were going nor what would happen to them, and determined only on one thing: that they should never again fall into the hands of Stalin.[19] General Vasiliev had been similarly interviewed the day before,[20] presumably by the same reporters, but neither of these fascinating interviews, nor the photographs said to have been taken at the same time, was published.

That evening the first formations of the 36th Infantry Brigade descended into Austria. The two foremost battalions, the 8th Argyll and Sutherland Highlanders and the 5th Buffs, were assigned the tasks of controlling the Cossacks and Causasians respectively. As the Russians moved into their allotted areas, the British never ceased to be intrigued by their picturesque appearance.

> As an army they presented an amazing sight. Their basic uniform was German, but with their fur Cossack caps, their mournful dundreary whiskers, their knee-high riding boots, and their roughly-made horse-drawn carts bearing all their worldly goods and chattels, including wife and family, there could be no mistaking them for anything but Russians. They were a tableau from the Russia of 1812. Cossacks are famed as horsemen and these lived up to their reputation. Squadrons of horses galloped hither and thither on the road impeding our progress as much as the horse-drawn carts. It was useless to give them orders; few spoke German or English and no one who understood seemed inclined to obey. Despite this apparent chaos it was remarkable how swiftly and completely they carried out their orders to concentrate . . . by next morning they were all in position—men, women, children, baggage, horses, carts, cows and—camels![21]

The administrative problem facing the 36th Brigade was an enormous one. As General Musson wrote to me recently:

Commanders and staffs had a multitude of problems. Conditions were chaotic with the ending of hostilities, after a very rough winter, and the occupation of Austria. The Austrians were 'lost' and did not know where they stood. There were masses of people wandering about, some friendly and some hostile, all homeless and all with their own problems. Distances were great and road conditions bad. (We had no helicopters in those days!) Our headquarters were on a wartime basis and we were working in tents or billets.

So that even without the problem of the Cossacks and Caucasians the Brigade's hands were full, and it must be remembered throughout (as all concerned have stressed to me) that those faced with this problem were working under great strain.

The numbers alone were formidable. No census was taken in the Cossack camp by the British authorities, but according to an estimate based on the Cossacks' ration claims, there were 23,800 Cossacks in all; this figure included several thousand women and children. Of Caucasians there were thought to be 4,800, but for both these figures it was reckoned that a 10 per cent deduction could be allowed,[22] although the Cossacks' own estimates were considerably higher. Their reckonings varied from totals of 30,000 to 35,000, but as there had been so many desertions and accessions latterly it is impossible to say exactly how many were present in the Drau Valley in May 1945.[23] However, the figure for the Caucasians would appear to be about right, as one of their officers provides the figure of 5,000 as having been at Tolmezzo just before their removal to Austria.[24]

By the second week of May the Cossacks were concentrated in the valley between Lienz and Oberdrauburg.[25] Through the encampments ran the turbulent river Drau, and a main road and railway line. In Lienz itself both Domanov and Colonel Alec Malcolm of the Argylls set up their respective headquarters. The Caucasians were moved to Grofelhof, further down the valley, while the Buffs' headquarters were nearby at Dellach.[26]

The Caucasian leader, Sultan Kelech Ghirey, had surrendered on behalf of his motley band of followers at the same time as Domanov. Like Krasnov, Ghirey was an old émigré who had co-operated with the British forces of General Holman in the Civil War, and had remained with Baron Wrangel until the failure of the last abortive raid launched from the Crimea in 1920.[27] Like Krasnov with the Cossacks, Ghirey enjoyed great moral prestige amongst the peoples of the Caucasus. Soon after he and his followers were installed at Grofelhof, he assembled them, 'and made a speech to the effect that those who were able should try to leave as soon as posssible—especially the young—and forget about the dream of freeing the Caucasus and the nations therein. He however was too old to continue and would honour his surrender and wait to see what was to happen'.[28]

A number so exhorted did take the opportunity of disappearing, which serves to illustrate the important fact that, though the Cossacks and Caucasians were technically prisoners, the British were quite unable to prevent large-scale desertions. The camps were not wired, and were largely self-policed. Despite this, however, there were for the moment few absconders from the Cossack camp. The steep snow-topped mountains walling in the valley formed a serious obstacle, as did the knowledge that they were in an alien country of whose language and people they knew little. But a far greater consideration than this was the fact that the Cossacks were banded together by a strong hope that they would be allowed to hold together as a community and be permitted to find asylum somewhere in the free world.

Though this hope may seem unreal now, it is important to realise that many intelligent Cossacks genuinely believed Britain and the United States would adopt at least a hostile attitude to the Soviet Union once fighting had ceased and the temporary bond of unity had dissolved. It should perhaps be kept in mind how relatively recent were the events of the Russian Civil War. In 1945 the British intervention against the Bolsheviks was almost as recent as the Korean War is now. The vast cataclysm of the Second World War produced a watershed sharply dividing the worlds before and after it. To us today, the Russian Revolution may seem a remote event, but in 1945, to the Cossacks especially, it was a story familiar and readily recalled.

Even on the British side there were still many distinguished figures who had played an active part in the intervention. Winston Churchill had then been Secretary for War, and the most ardent advocate of support for the White Armies; Lord Killearn (Ambassador to Egypt, the staging-post for so many Russians being shipped back in 1943–5) had been Acting High Commissioner in Siberia with Admiral Kolchak; Lieutenant-General Burrows (Head of the Military Mission in Moscow from March 1944) and Major-General Colin Gubbins (Head of SOE) had been with General Ironside at Archangel in 1919; and Field-Marshal Alexander, whose army now held the Cossacks, had fought with the Baltic Landeswehr against the Bolsheviks. Thus whilst more pressing events had long occupied their minds to the exclusion of a cause now dead, there were many in British political, diplomatic and military circles to whom the history of the Cossacks was far from unfamiliar.

These considerations will make some of the Cossacks' wilder

requests appear less unreasonable, at least from their limited standpoint. For instance, on 13 May, Battalion Headquarters in Lienz was approached by a Captain Kantemir, who was in charge of a group trained by the Germans in North Italy 'in the organisation of Partisans, sabotage, and espionage, behind the Soviet lines': services which the Captain offered to conduct on behalf of the Eighth Army. Alarmed at the suggestion, Brigade HQ sent a request to General Arbuthnott for instructions. The message concluded: 'If no instrs by 0900 hrs 15 May they will be sent to sabotage div HQ!' No sooner was this problem disposed of than the entire Cossack Division requested permission to drill; this was refused likewise.[29] Despite this, some irrepressible 'Cossacks volunteered to fight against Japan rather than go back to Russia. Offer not accepted.'[30]

Sophisticated men like General Krasnov did not imagine that the British would authorise an immediate onslaught on the Red Army lines in Styria. But he did hope and expect that something might be done, not only to provide the Cossacks with asylum in the West, but also to enable them to keep together and so preserve their unique heritage.

Soon after the transfer of the Cossack Headquarters from Kötschach to Lienz, Krasnov wrote to Field-Marshal Alexander, recalling their mutual experiences fighting for the White cause in the Civil War, explaining the situation of the Cossacks, and urging him to use his influence to assist them. He received no reply, and was unable to tell whether the letter had been delivered.[31]

Krasnov was indeed a remarkable figure. Born in 1869 of an old Don Cossack family, he had behind him in 1945 a long and varied career. He shared many characteristics with his younger contemporary, Winston Churchill; in particular a deep knowledge and romantic love for the stirring history of his own people. Like Churchill in his younger days he had satisfied a thirst for adventure by combining the professions of cavalry officer and war correspondent. He travelled with a military mission to Ethiopia in the 1890s, and covered the Russo-Japanese War in 1904 for the journal *Russki Invalid*. He distinguished himself in command of a cavalry corps during the Great War, and received the highest award obtainable, the Order of St. George the Victor. When the March Revolution took place and the Tsar abdicated, Krasnov immediately placed himself amongst the ranks of those who were prepared to use force if necessary to restore order in the crumbling state. He not only supported the old order from instincts of class and upbringing, but he also felt deeply that all the glorious traditions of the old Russia to which he was so attached were in danger of being swept away.

After the final victory of the Bolsheviks, Krasnov joined the millions of his compatriots driven into exile. Living in France and Germany, he devoted his time chiefly to literary pursuits. He wrote a series of novels, the most famous of which was the partly autobiographical *From Double Eagle to Red Flag*. When in 1941 Germany attacked Russia, he saw once again the opportunity of striking at his enemies. In 1918 he had, with Churchill's expressed approval, worked with the invading Germans to inflict defeats on the Bolsheviks. Then the Germans had been obliged to withdraw, following the Allied victory in the West, and Krasnov was able to continue the struggle with the aid of the Entente powers and the United States. He saw nothing dishonourable in raising forces from patriotic Russians who had deserted or been made prisoner; again, this had happened in 1918 with the strong approval of Churchill and other Western statesmen.[32]

By the years of the Second World War, however, Krasnov was an old man. (He was seventy-six when he surrendered to the British.) He was accordingly only able to work for the cause by lending the prestige of his name to the Cossack movement, by visiting the soldiers' camps, and by writing effective propaganda appeals in émigré Russian publications. He never stayed for any length of time in the Cossack encampments and only joined Domanov's command a month or so before the surrender.[33]

Such was the man to whom the Cossacks looked for advice and inspiration to guide them out of their present troubles. Domanov was leader in name, but it was the passing of Krasnov's car that brought the Cossacks flocking from their tents. Now their camp was to be joined by another figure from the heroic past—one almost equally celebrated, though of very different character.

On 10 May armoured cars of the 56th Recce Regiment moving up the Lieser valley north of Spittal came to the village of Rennweg. There 'the surrender of a Cossack Rft. Regt. was accepted, including the personal surrender of an old Cossack Gen. Shkuro, who had fought under Denikin'.[34] A week later Shkuro and 1,400 men of his training unit were transferred to Domanov's camp at Lienz.[35]

If Krasnov represented the splendour of the Russian Imperial Army, Andrei Grigorievich Shkuro personified the wild and daring Cossacks of the time of Bogdan Khmelnitsky and Stenka Razin, and he could have been depicted without incongruity in *Taras Bulba* or Repin's *Reply of the Cossacks to Sultan Mahmoud IV*. A Kuban Cossack, he was a full colonel at thirty-one when the Great War ended in 1918. He had signalised himself in a series of dare-devil exploits with a band of partisan Cossacks, who harassed the rear of the German lines. When the

Cossacks rose against the Bolsheviks, he put his special talents to work in the new cause.

A British officer, Brigadier Williamson, serving with the Russians has left a vivid description of his picturesque appearance:

Short, weatherbeaten and sporting a long yellow moustache, Skouro was one of the characters of the Civil War. Never without his wolfskin cap and the red, blue and white ribbon of the Volunteer Army on his sleeve, he was a Caucasian from one of the mountain tribes, savage and cruel as the best of them, and his regiment of three to four hundred cavalrymen all wore wolf-skin caps instead of astrakhan wool. They had their headquarters in their own special collection of railway trucks, on which were painted a pack of wolves in pursuit of prey, and they were a particularly fierce and relentless collection of mountaineers, carrying the usual armoury of a *kinjal* or dagger at their waist, a sword slung over the shoulder, a revolver whenever possible, and rows of cartridge cases for rifles across each side of their chests. Skouro was undoubtedly a great cavalry leader but, as we'd been told, he was also a bit of a brigand and, on one occasion, accompanied by three or four of his officers, he entered the ballroom of a big hotel in Rostov where dancing was in progress and invited all the guests to contribute in jewellery or cash towards the maintenance of his Wolves. Confronted by glittering eyes beneath the shaggy wolf's hair and remembering the Wolves' reputation for ruthless pillage and lack of mercy, no one argued. He made a very successful haul.[36]

Shkuro left Russia in 1920 to join the emigration. At one time he took to performing dare-devil feats on horseback in a circus, though generally he was to be found drinking with his old comrades in the bars of Belgrade or Munich. When Germany attacked the USSR, Shkuro came forward to volunteer his services. Lacking the moral stature of Krasnov, Shkuro all the same had a name to conjure with. A hundred tales of his bravery and cunning were circulated wherever Cossacks gathered in their camps or *stanitsas*, and he maintained what may roughly be described as a roving commission, visiting Cossack units everywhere. Nominally in charge of a training regiment for the 15th Cossack Corps,[37] in fact he did much as he pleased. This generally consisted in visiting the camps and appearing in the centre of any company when a vodka bottle was being opened. His soldier's repertoire of bawdy jokes and songs was apparently limitless. Colonel Constantin Wagner told me he would not allow Shkuro to approach his 1st Cossack Cavalry Division, as all his stories related to 'between here, and here'—indicating the waist and knees. He felt that such language from a general was unbecoming and bad for discipline; but to many simple Cossacks the visits of *batka* Shkuro were a source of delight.

> In his red shirt, curly-haired and ruddy-cheeked,
> He came out into the street, merry and tipsy;
> Caught hold of a pretty girl in the ring,
> Snatched out his jingling money-purse . . .

sang Shkuro, as dusk fell on the square at Lienz. Austrian waiters
bustled out to his pavement table, outside the *Zum goldenen Fisch* Hotel,
with glasses and bottles of schnapps. At the sound of the jolly *batka's*
voice, young Cossacks came flocking round, laughing and calling to
wives and girl-friends to join them. Balalaikas and accordions took up
the tune, whilst stolid Austrian townsmen and Scottish soldiers on the
edge of the crowd felt their hearts jump at the infectious rhythm.

Lights began to twinkle in the little town and beyond, in the tented
camp and barracks of Peggetz. All around was the steep, dark forest
and the noise of the turbulent river Drau hurrying past. High above,
the last rays of the dying sun rested on snowy peaks above Dölsach
before giving way to the dark. Down in the square of Lienz a favourite
chorus rang out, stirring and melancholy . . .

> Oh, the clouds, the clouds are hanging low,
> And fog has settled on the plain;
> Tell us of what you're thinking,
> Tell us, our Ataman!

A British officer who well remembers Shkuro, Krasnov, Domanov
and the other Cossacks was Major 'Rusty' Davies, a lone young Welshman serving in the Argylls. Soon after Colonel Alec Malcolm had set
up his headquarters in Lienz, he gave Davies the massive duty of supervising the Cossacks. As there were over twenty thousand of them camping in an area twelve or fourteen miles across, it was a daunting task.
But, as Davies told me, he looked on it as both intriguing and challenging. Of course, there was no question of his policing and organising the
entire body of Cossacks. This was done by the Cossacks themselves,
Davies merely transmitting his requirements to General Domanov. As
Davies could speak no Russian, he appointed a young émigré, Lieutenant Butlerov, as his interpreter and liaison officer. Butlerov, General
Musson recalls today, had an English grandmother.

Rusty Davies still finds it difficult to believe that he was with the
Cossacks for a bare three weeks, so well did he get to know them, and
so vivid even now is his recollection of them. He became extremely
friendly with Butlerov, who tried to teach him to ride and wandered
about the camp with him on duty. The discipline of the Cossacks was
excellent, but Davies was not satisfied with certain aspects of camp
organisation, in particular sanitation. He encouraged them to follow

more efficient British military practice, and felt he was achieving some success in this line.

But such tasks, though arduous, were not what made the lasting imprint on his memory. For above all it was the camaraderie, the cheerful openness and the colourfully picturesque appearance of the Cossacks that impressed him. Though he could only communicate with them through Butlerov or Olga Rotova, he soon felt himself entering into their life. As he moved on his daily rides through the camp, Cossack families came to the entrances of barracks, huts and tents to wave and call out greetings. Naturally warm-hearted, they wished also to display their gratitude to the English, who fed and supplied them, and treated them in friendly and easy style—better far than their allies the Germans had done. Cossack children, swarming everywhere, ran after the 'Gospodin Major', laughing and calling out for chocolate. The good-natured Davies kept a supply in his pockets for regular distribution. The prevalence of women and children was due to the fact, explained earlier, that the Cossacks were a Division virtually in name only; in reality they represented a cross-section of the population south of the Don, who had managed to escape before the Red Army advance.

What the future held for them worried a few Cossacks, though most found the camp conditions so idyllic after all they had been through that they were content to take life as it came. Amongst the senior officers there was much speculation, but as both Krasnov and Shkuro had written to the British High Command and received no reply, there was for the moment nothing they could do but talk.

When Davies asked the Cossacks what they would choose if they had the option, there were various suggestions. But on one question they were united: they could under no circumstances return to the Soviet Union. It was not just that it was a state which had abandoned all the legal and moral standards so painfully built up in Europe over the centuries, and which had indeed introduced barbarities unknown to the ancient world. It was that, having worn German uniforms, they would be branded as traitors. For those whom Stalin regarded as traitors there was reserved the single alternative: death, or the horrors of the slave camps. And on top of these was the dreadful prospect of torture.

Davies tended to discount the Cossacks' fear of returning to Russia; he imagined it to be an exaggerated prejudice, rather (as he explained, half-humorously, to me) as if he, a Welshman, should be ordered to live in England. But his equanimity was seriously disturbed when an old lady explained to him the cause of her fears. 'That's what they did to me,' she explained calmly, holding up her outstretched hands. The fingernails had been torn out at the roots.[38]

Davies reassured the Cossacks. He did not believe that his government was capable of taking any action that was genuinely inhumane. He had no interest in or knowledge of Russian affairs, but everything about his upbringing and experience told him that decent men like Field-Marshal Alexander could not give orders that would result in cruelties such as the Cossacks described. After all, Britain had entered the war to defend the rights of small nations and defenceless peoples, and in the moment of victory was hardly likely to go back on ideals so nobly and long sustained.

Most Cossacks were reassured by Davies's words. A few, however, began to have nagging fears, particularly those who were Soviet citizens. No one in Lienz, British or Russian, knew of the secret agreement signed on the last day at Yalta. But news had filtered through of the surrender to the Soviets of many of Vlasov's men earlier in the month. Others again must have known of the shiploads of victims returned from British ports since the previous October. But these fears were largely stilled by the reflection that the Cossacks, as former allies of the British, were in a special position; that Field-Marshal Alexander, with his known humanity and experiences as a former combatant with the White Army, would look with sympathy upon their plight; and that, as the majority of officers and many of the men were old émigrés, they could not be 'returned' to Soviet authority, under which they had never lived. These views were shared by the wisest and most respected leader amongst them, General Krasnov, and he had already written to Alexander setting out the whole position. True, no reply had come as yet, but the Field-Marshal was no doubt still consulting his political superiors.

The attitude of the British with whom they came in contact seemed also to convey a sense of security. Major Davies had been given an exciting and challenging job, and was determined to do it well. He regarded with approval and encouraged the Cossacks' administration of their schools, church services and choirs. And on 20 May he gathered together all the journalists in the camp to suggest they start a Cossack newspaper, working in premises provided by him in Lienz.[39] Filled with gratitude, the Cossacks provided for Davies the fantastic displays of horsemanship (*dzhigit*) for which they are so famous. On Sundays they gathered in the open for services conducted by their priests, and the chanting of the Orthodox liturgy mingled distantly in the warm May air with the bells of parish churches sounding through the Drau Valley.

On 15 May the Red Cross arrived to assist in administering camp food and supplies.[40] An air almost of permanency began to descend on the camp. Towards the middle of the month British soldiers took away some of the Cossacks' beloved horses. The Cossacks were upset, but soon afterwards had an opportunity to make their complaint to Major-General Arbuthnott, under whose command the Cossacks and Caucasians in the Drau Valley came, and who, on 18 May, paid a visit of inspection to Lienz and its camp.[41]

General Arbuthnott toured the camp and the barracks at Peggetz, where the women and children lived. He appeared pleased with all he saw, joked and laughed, and showed especial interest in the cadets' school. He spoke a few words to the boys about his hopes for Russia in the future, tried their food, and ordered their rations to be increased. He met the senior officers, and congratulated them on the discipline maintained in the camp. General Domanov responded politely, and then brought up the matter of the abducted Cossack horses. Arbuthnott's tone changed abruptly, and he replied with asperity: 'There are no Cossack horses here. They belong now to His Majesty the King of England, whose prisoners the Cossacks are.'[42] This was the first occasion on which the Cossacks had heard themselves referred to as prisoners of war, and to many it seemed as if an unpleasant change in their status had occurred.

In fact there was nothing intrinsically sinister in the use of this phraseology. As prisoners of war the Cossacks, under international law, had important guarantees relating to their treatment in captivity and ultimate release.

But ignorant as he was of the implications, Domanov turned as usual to his mentor, Krasnov. The old General agreed that this development was disturbing, and at once decided to write a second appeal to Field-Marshal Alexander. In it he again evoked the memory of the days when both were fighting for the White Army against the Bolsheviks, drew attention to the Cossacks' unhappy situation, and begged the Field-Marshal to save them. To this letter too there came no reply.[43]

It was with some disquiet, therefore, that the Cossacks next received an unexpected order that seemed to confirm that the easy relationship they had enjoyed with the British was altering. Early on the morning of 27 May, Rusty Davies informed the Cossack staff that all arms in the possession of their troops were to be handed in by midday. It should be explained here that under the original surrender terms of 8 May, Brigadier Musson had agreed that the Cossacks should retain their arms for self-defence against Germans or Italian partisans. Once settled in their camp, the main body of arms that were no longer required in their new situation was placed under British supervision in dumps. But for guard duties and camp policing, Domanov's staff was empowered to issue rifles where necessary. In addition, the officers retained their revolvers and sabres. (The Caucasians to the east had been much more completely disarmed on 15 May[44]—perhaps an indication that the British held them responsible for the rapine committed earlier in the Carnia.)

This order naturally aroused apprehensive speculations. According to Cossack sources, these were then quieted when they were told that they were to be issued with uniform British arms in exchange for their own heterogeneous collection.[45] For, as the Germans never regarded Domanov's force as a regular combatant unit, his men had received a mixed bag of German, Italian, French and other arms and ammunition. Much of this had been captured or 'borrowed' by the Cossacks themselves. At any rate, whatever the reason, the Cossacks obeyed promptly and by midday all arms except a few secreted by their owners had been surrendered. Reassured by Davies, and satisfied by the explanation given, the Cossacks' confidence returned. After all, if it were true that the arms were to be exchanged in the manner promised, then it was a mark of increased British goodwill, rather than mistrust.

But the Cossacks had not heard an ominous message which had been read out to the supervising British troops on parade that morning. It was from Brigadier Musson, to explain that all surrendered troops were to be disarmed during the day. As a general guide to conduct whilst undertaking this operation the Brigadier added: 'After 1400 hrs any surrendered tps found in possession of arms or ammunition will be arrested immediately and will be liable to the death penalty . . .

'I realise that we are dealing with people of many nationalities whose languages we cannot talk and that there are many women and children amongst them . . . If it is necessary to open fire you will do so and you must regard this duty as an operation of war.'

The message concluded with a vigorous reiteration of the need to shoot to kill if at any point a situation appeared to be getting out of control.[46]

To the soldiers of the 8th Argylls this must have seemed a strange prelude for an operation to which the Cossacks submitted with perfect equanimity.[47] And what had the women and children to do with it? But after the relative inactivity of the past fortnight, events were beginning to move fast.

That evening Major Davies appeared at Domanov's Headquarters in Lienz.[48] With him was the officer acting as interpreter, Lieutenant Butlerov. Davies handed Domanov a written order, whilst at the same time explaining its contents through Butlerov. In it Domanov was told that all Cossack officers were to travel the next day to a conference to be held somewhere east of Oberdrauburg. It was explained that Field-Marshal Alexander himself wished to address the officers there, and inform them of an important decision taken regarding their future disposal. Davies then saluted and departed with Butlerov.

Butlerov, to whom the announcement was as unexpected as it was to Domanov, took an early opportunity of getting Davies on one side. This there was no difficulty in doing, as in the three weeks of their common duties in the camp a bond of friendship had grown up between them. Butlerov asked, was there really to be a conference, or did some deceit lie behind the order? Davies reassured him: it was all perfectly straightforward.

'But it all sounds so improbable,' persisted Butlerov. 'Why should the Field-Marshal put you to the trouble of organising trucks and cars to take about two thousand of us down the valley, when he could come up here to visit us in his staff-car? It seems quite unbelievable; what's the point?'

Davies shrugged his shoulders. 'I don't know. There is the order: it is not for me to explain it, and obviously I can't say what was in the Field-Marshal's mind. Perhaps there is a cinema or other public building suitable for such a meeting. There are no facilities in this camp.'

But Butlerov was not convinced, and appeared very distressed. 'Look,' he said, 'you're a soldier and must obey orders. But I hope you are also a friend. As you know, I have a wife and child in Peggetz Camp. Will you give me your word as an officer and a gentleman that we will all be back in the camp by this evening?'

'Of course I do,' rejoined Davies. Butlerov still looked uneasy, but in face of this assurance could press his friend no further.

Meanwhile General Domanov telephoned his scattered field officers, informing them of the plan and instructing a number of the more senior to attend a conference at his Headquarters at 11 a.m. Domanov read out Davies's order, which stated that all officers must parade by 1 p.m. in the barrack square at Peggetz, where they had the previous day surrendered their arms. He spoke in calm and measured tones, and seemed undisturbed by the import of his words. A brief silence followed as the officers digested what they had been told. Then came a flurry of questions, as the startled men blurted out whatever came first to their minds:

'Do we take our belongings with us?'

'No, you will be back by the evening!'

'What should those officers do who don't believe the order, and who decide to escape to the mountains?'

'You are the commander of a regiment. You understood me.'

Domanov's calm contrasted oddly with the agitation and surprise that seized his senior officers. They dispersed to give their orders, speculating volubly with everyone they met as to what it could mean.[49] Conjecture ran rife, but despite the strange necessity of apparently calling the mountain to Mohammed, the majority opinion was that the conference was real, and that a decision favourable to their future settlement was likely to be announced there. Some thought they would be offered the chance of settling in an underpopulated British colony.[50] A Don Cossack who instinctively mistrusted the plan, and who subsequently escaped to the mountains, found that most people he accosted in the camp were confident that all was above board.[51] In Peggetz Camp, Olga Rotova had started her daily English lesson to the cadets in the school, when she was called away to be asked by an old general what she made of it all. Clearly he hoped that Olga in her role as part-time interpreter might have picked up some clue. But she knew nothing, and after some fruitless discussion, she departed, having first at the General's request bestowed the sign of the Cross upon him.[52]

Despite such misgivings, most felt confident that, whatever the purpose of the conference, they would be back in camp that evening. After all, all that seemed at all suspect was the suddenness of the order, and the seemingly unnecessary project of transporting hundreds of officers to meet one Field-Marshal. But against this militated the high regard all Cossacks, particularly those who remembered the intervention in the Civil War, felt for the honour and trustworthiness of British officers. Major Davies had given his word to Butlerov that the officers would be back in Lienz that evening, and other British officers, when accosted, gave the same categorical promises. 'On the honour of a British officer,' specified one lieutenant. And when some weeping wives asked Olga Rotova to find out what would happen, a lieutenant of the Argylls whom she knew told her to comfort them.

'They'll all be back this evening. The officers are only going to a conference. The women are crying about nothing!'[53]

Apart from their trust in British honour, many Cossacks were impressed by General Domanov's calm acceptance of the order. The Field Ataman saw nothing to fear in the events of the past two days. The disarmament, he believed, was effected in order to restore order amongst the Caucasians beyond Oberdrauburg, who had latterly caused trouble again. And as for the conference, he had a particular reason for feeling confident that at last the British were about to take measures to give the Cossacks a permanent refuge. For, to himself and General Krasnov, it must have seemed that the order had come in direct response to Krasnov's letter of two or three days earlier, in which he had appealed to his old comrade-in-arms Alexander to act on behalf of the Cossacks. Domanov and Krasnov had not made the sending of this letter generally known, as its occasioning had been General Arbuthnott's sharp reply over the removed horses, and it was felt that knowledge of the reference to 'prisoners' might have disturbed the camp.[54]

Krasnov's wife Lydia has recounted how one of Domanov's adjutants arrived to request the General's presence at the conference. Lydia Krasnov was disturbed and frightened at the prospect, but Peter Nikolaevich appeared calm and confident. He embraced and kissed his wife, and told her there was nothing to worry about.

'I'll be back between 6 and 8 this evening?' he added cheerfully. And, leaning on his stick, the old gentleman descended to the street to find his car. If only he could meet Alexander again face-to-face, he was certain all would be well. For the Field-Marshal was a gentleman of honour, and who could better explain the Cossacks' case than their old Ataman, soldier and writer at the same time?

Lydia Krasnov remained tearful and praying in her room. Hours passed, and the evening drew on. When seven o'clock struck, and then eight, her apprehension grew. Peter Nikolaevich was a wise and great man, and understood politics infinitely better than she did. But he had promised to be back by eight, and in forty-five years of marriage she had never known him fail to keep such a promise . . .[55]

Before Domanov, Krasnov and other senior officers set off separately in cars from the Headquarters in Lienz,[56] the rest of the officers gathered as instructed in the barracks square at Peggetz. There were 1,475 in all (about fifty were left behind with their units as duty officers),[57] and they presented an unusually smart and picturesque appearance. In view of the impending meeting with the Field-Marshal, the Cossacks realised the importance of presenting themselves with soldierly appearance. Those who had them wore their best uniforms, and wives had been put hastily to work pressing and mending. The men were formed up in three columns, the names 'Don', 'Kuban' and 'Terek' embroidered on their shoulder-straps. At the head of each column marched the *ataman*; all wore their decorations, many of them awarded by the Tsar for services in the Great War. Many veterans in the Kuban and Terek regiments wore the Cossack national uniform, the *cherkess*, and a bystander was particularly struck by the ensign of the Terek Cossacks, a tall and noble-looking old man with a broad white beard flowing down his chest. Gazing proudly ahead, he bore on high the old tricolour of Imperial Russia.[58]

It was midday of a lovely May morning that these, the cream of the

Cossack 'nation', paraded in the barrack square at Peggetz. All around were gathered their families, many of the women weeping fearfully. Outside the gates were drawn up sixty three-ton trucks and, at a signal from Major Davies, the columns swung out of the gates and, breaking up into pre-arranged groups, clambered aboard. The operation was completed in silence; this was suddenly broken by the shrieks of a little girl, who broke away from her mother and ran crying towards one of the lorries. She had seen her father climb in, and imagined she would never see him again.[59]

The long column roared along the dusty road eastwards between the open fields. On either side were the tents and wagons of the Cossack units. Crowds of men and women were standing amongst them, watching the departure of their leaders. Soon their own camp was left behind, but shortly afterwards they came to a temporary halt on the edge of the forest skirting the mountains. Several of the senior generals were there in cars, but there was no sign of Domanov. All around stood British troops and, at orders given, a couple of soldiers armed with Sten-guns were detailed to accompany each truck. The column set off again, but this time in three successive groups. And as it did so, from the forest shadows emerged armoured cars and armed motor-cyclists, who wheeled into line as the lorries moved on.

This new development alarmed some of the Cossack officers who had been dubious about the reality of the conference, but others pointed out that this was probably a precaution against attacks by partisans. Alexander Shparengo was a Kuban Cossack who had had a long and agitated discussion with a group of his fellows that morning. A general of his unit had reproved Shparengo for his sceptical attitude, but a younger officer shared his doubts.

'No, you can't trust the English,' he reflected philosophically.

'But if you don't believe them, why are you going?' Shparengo had asked in surprise.

'Well, does HQ's command apply to me any less than you? But I still don't trust them; look how cheerfully they entered into the alliance with Stalin . . .'

As his truck tore along the road by the Drau, arguments raced through Shparengo's head. Could one trust the British? How could one make sense of this conference? That some senior officers should be consulted or informed of an important decision was understandable, but to strip every regiment of its last subaltern? It didn't make sense . . . but then, what did he know of the matter? Perhaps they were to be asked to vote in some way on an issue that would materially affect the fate of all. No, that seemed too improbable.

Suddenly an overwhelming sense of impending danger seized him, and he resolved to escape. But how? Would not the guards shoot him him if he jumped from the lorry? No, he reflected shrewdly, that was unlikely. For if the conference were genuine, the soldiers would be hardly likely to attempt to kill someone refusing to attend. And if it were a blind for something more sinister, then to shoot an escaper would give the game away. No, there was little risk in that direction. He gazed down at the surface of the road that flew away below the tailboard of their truck. Glancing about, he recognised on their left the railway station of Nikolsdorf: they must be nearing Oberdrauburg! His mind was made up in a flash.

'Well, gentlemen,' he cried, 'do what you like, but I'm going no further. I don't trust them!'

'The *Sotnik* has fallen out!' someone shouted. But Shparengo rolled hurtling down the slope at the edge of the road, sprang lightly to his feet and dashed into the surrounding forest. Glancing back, he saw the column trundling on; after every five or six trucks came an armoured car of the escort. From what he took to be his lorry he glimpsed waving hands, but a moment later all was borne out of sight. *Sotnik* Shparengo removed his tell-tale uniform jacket, and made his way back along the now deserted road to the camp.[60]

Almost at that very moment Ataman Domanov himself was drawing up in his car at the Headquarters of the 36th Infantry Brigade, three-quarters of a mile east of Oberdrauburg. On Major Davies's instructions, he had set out from the Golden Fish Hotel half an hour earlier than the main column accompanied by Lieutenant Butlerov. The pause was momentary, but long enough. The Brigade Commander, Brigadier Geoffrey Musson, appeared and informed Domanov politely but brusquely that he had a special announcement to pass on to him, as General Officer commanding the Cossack Division.

'I have to inform you, sir,' he declared, pausing as Butlerov hastily translated, 'that I have received strict orders to hand over the whole of the Cossack Division to the Soviet authorities. I regret to have to tell you this, but the order is categorical. Good day.'

Neither Domanov nor Butlerov made any reply, but turned, ashen-faced, to their car. With an English officer accompanying them as guard, they drove towards the East.[61]

8

From Lienz to the Lubianka: The Cossack Officers Return Home

Two days before his announcement to General Domanov that all Cossacks were to be handed over to the Soviets, Brigadier Musson had summoned his battalion commanders to a conference at Brigade Headquarters at Oberdrauburg. It was then, on the morning of 26 May, that they learned for the first time what was to be the fate of those they had been guarding for the past three weeks. Musson explained that the policy had been decided upon at the highest level, and though aspects of it might appear distasteful, there was no option for all concerned but to obey. Because of the large numbers involved, careful precautions would have to be taken to prevent mass attempts at escape. A detailed plan would be issued shortly, but in brief it had been decided that the most effective method would be to start by separating the officers from the men. Without their officers, it would be unlikely that the men would be capable of staging any effectively organised resistance.

But the separation of the officers was not a straightforward matter. The majority were scattered throughout the camp in their units, and any attempt to arrest them would of course precipitate the very opposition it was essential to avoid. It had therefore been decided by those from whom the orders emanated that a tactic of deception would be employed. The Cossack officers were to be informed that they would attend a conference with Field-Marshal Alexander, where it would be announced what was to happen to their Division. It would also of course be necessary to disarm the camp and this would be done as a preliminary step the next day.

Once this move had been successfully accomplished the rest should be easy. The officers would be gathered for the night at a specially prepared cage at Spittal, further down the valley, and on the following day turned over under heavy guard to the Soviet authorities at Judenburg. After that would begin the shifting of the leaderless other ranks and families. As any further attempt at deception would clearly be ineffective, force would have to be applied to whatever degree was necessary to complete the operation successfully. The main body of Cossacks would be despatched by train on successive days.

Most officers present at this meeting, including Brigadier Musson, felt dislike in varying degrees for what might prove a very unpleasant operation. Nor did they feel very comfortable about the role they were being called upon to play in connection with the 'deception'. But, as Musson stressed, the orders he had received left no alternative and must be obeyed.

Lieutenant-Colonel Alec Malcolm of the 8th Argylls returned in his staff-car to Lienz. As he went he passed the length of the Cossack camp. It was not a very military scene: men were riding about exercising the horses, wives were hanging out washing, and children were everywhere playing in the grass. Back in Lienz, Malcolm assembled his company commanders and informed them of the coming operation. Rusty Davies, who was of course the most nearly affected, was horrified. It was not so much the prospect of returning the Cossacks to Russia to which he objected, for he had little knowledge of what that involved. It was the immediate realisation of the entirely false position in which he would be put in helping to implement the 'deception'. For the Cossacks knew and trusted him, and for him to turn now and abuse that confidence was unthinkable.

He explained his position to Malcolm, requesting at the same time that he might be relieved from his posting as liaison officer to the Cossacks. Malcolm listened patiently, and then absolutely declined to allow this. As he made clear, the operation was likely to be a very tricky one in all events, and it was only by successfully extricating the officers first that one could ensure that things would run smoothly. The alternative was very serious: the possibility of mass break-outs, considerable bloodshed, or very likely both together. But if Davies were at this stage to step aside, would this not arouse the gravest suspicions in the Cossack officers' minds? And equally, if Davies, the one British officer they knew intimately and trusted, were to be the one to inform them of the 'conference', would this not then make the success of the ruse much more likely?

Faced by this argument and the firm order of his commanding officer, Davies reluctantly agreed to continue working with the

Cossacks. It was a decision that has caused him considerable anguish ever since. By it he was led into lying and deceiving his friend Butlerov and all the other Cossacks amongst whom he was so popular. But he felt then, and still feels, an immense respect for the abilities and wisdom of Alec Malcolm, and was not prepared to go to the lengths of disobeying an order. Alec Malcolm in turn, and Musson above him, knew that the decision had been taken at the very highest level, by Field-Marshal Alexander himself—and beyond him by the towering figure of Winston Churchill. No successful army can be run by officers who make a practice of questioning orders, and in this case both Musson and Malcolm realised that their superiors had access to a whole range of facts denied to those operating in the field. In what position then were they to form judgments?[1]

But to the Cossacks it was the lying that was perhaps the most repulsive aspect of the whole grim business now unfolding. It was not just that British officers found themselves capable of lying on so deep and persistent a scale that disgusted them; it was also that Russian officers, brought up in the honourable traditions of the Imperial Army, were pathetically easily deceived.[2]

Recently Nicholas Bethell, in his book *The Last Secret*, has attempted to defend the measure: 'Of course deceit and lying are part of modern warfare and there is no reason to suppose that the Cossacks did not do their share of it, for they fought the war more fiercely than most.'[3]

Most officers, British and Russian, of the present author's acquaintance would however make a very large distinction between stratagems employed to deceive an enemy in the heat of battle, and the use of lies designed to lure helpless prisoners to their deaths in peacetime. Moreover, far from having 'fought the war more furiously than most', Domanov's 'Division' had never actually fought as a unit at all. Though individual members may have engaged in battle elsewhere as soldiers of other units, the *Kazachi Stan* was what its name proclaimed it to be; a Cossack settlement. As they were at all times accompanied by their families, the case could not have been otherwise.

As for the Caucasians, 'They were even less of a military body than the Cossacks and were composed entirely of voluntary refugees from the Caucasus during the German retreat from Stalingrad.'[4]

Quite apart from this, the fact that the *Kazachi Stan* provided a collecting-point and a refuge for dispossessed Cossacks meant that a sizable number of its inmates had gathered there during the last weeks before withdrawing from Tolmezzo to Austria. There were, for example, a number of old émigrés who had been compelled to leave Yugoslavia at the end of 1944, who had nowhere else to go, and who joined their compatriots in Italy.[5] General Krasnov himself had been only twelve weeks with Domanov's force before their surrender to the British.[6] And even those of the original group that had made the hazardous journey from Novogrudok to Tolmezzo included a large number of people who can only be regarded as civilian refugees. Typical of these was a Byelorussian couple of Polish nationality; they lived near Novogrudok, and joined the Cossacks in their migration southwards. Had they stayed, they would probably have been massacred by Red partisans.[7] None of these people could possibly be regarded as having worked, still less fought, against the British, whose arrival they naïvely awaited as a future ally against Bolshevism.

In fact, the British military authorities themselves do not appear to have felt altogether happy about this particular 'part of modern warfare'. The day after the 'deception' had been successfully practised, the 78th Division Headquarters issued the following directive:

1. Many offrs and OR in the Army are aware that the Allies have made extensive use of cover and deception plans in sp of factual ops.

2. It is of the highest importance that no unauthorised disclosure of Allied practice on this and kindred subjects should be made in any form whatever, even now that hostilities have ceased. This applies equally to methods used in specific ops as to gen policy. Any knowledge of the subject will continue to be treated as TOP SECRET.

3. Fmns and units will therefore ensure that this order is brought to the notice of all who are concerned. As it is obviously undesirable to arouse undue comment, its circulation should be strictly limited to those who have had knowledge of deception methods. The actual method of publication is left to the discretion of fmn/unit comds.[8]

At ten o'clock on the morning of 28 May Colonel Bryar of the 1st Kensingtons held a conference of his officers at Battalion HQ in Spittal. After explaining the Divisional Order providing for the return of the Cossacks, he went through the elaborate security measures necessary to ensure that all ran smoothly. There was no real reason why it should not, if everyone did as he was told, but in case of serious trouble a grim provision was appended to the instructions:

'Orders for Gds will incorporate the following:—

i Any attempt whatsoever at resistance will be dealt with firmly by shooting to kill.

ii Any attempts by the officers to commit suicide will be prevented if there is no danger whatever to our tps. If there is the slightest danger to our tps the suicide will be allowed to proceed.'

The officers took up their posts and awaited the arrivals with curiosity. The first Cossack officer to appear, at about 2.30, was General Domanov in his staff-car. He had come straight from the briefing delivered by Brigadier Musson at Oberdrauburg, and was now taken with Butlerov to a barrack room in the enclosure and held under guard.[9]

Half an hour afterwards arrived the first convoy. This consisted of the Caucasian officers, 125 in number, who arrived in two lorries preceded by Sultan Kelech Ghirey in an open car. Their treatment had been identical to that of the Cossacks: told that they were being summoned to a conference at Dellach that day, Ghirey was required to appear first. Colonel Odling-Smee of the 5th Buffs told him of the decision taken, and then he and his fellow-officers were despatched onwards to Spittal. Dignified and resigned, Ghirey presented a striking sight to the men of the Kensingtons as his car swung through the gates: he was wearing the full-dress uniform of an officer of the Tsar.[10]

After the arrival of the Caucasians, a steady stream of trucks appeared, depositing Domanov's officers at the camp entrance. One of the first to arrive was old General Krasnov, who had to be helped down from his car by his son, General Semeon Krasnov.[11] As each lorry-load passed in, the men were searched for weapons, and the 36th Brigade Intelligence Officer checked each name against a roll brought with him. This slowed up proceedings considerably, and Colonel Bryar of the 1st Kensingtons, who was anxious to have everyone safely inside before darkness fell, took it on himself to cut the procedure short. He then went to General Domanov's hut and explained to him what was required. The Cossacks and Caucasians were to spend the night in the camp before moving on next morning. Domanov was to continue holding responsibility for maintaining discipline amongst his officers, and between 7.30 and 8.30 would address them in groups of 500 to explain the programme.

Domanov 'said he would do his best to carry out these instructions', a reply which Bethell suggests 'lends weight to the theory that Domanov was privy to the British plans and assisting them in the repatriation, perhaps hoping thereby to save his own skin when he found himself in Soviet custody.'[12] This is an allusion to a legend that grew up amongst one section of émigré Cossacks to the effect that Domanov was in league with the British to betray the Cossacks to the Soviets.[13] That such a story should flourish under such circumstances is understandable. When a cause is lost, people search for a scapegoat. But for a writer to repeat the smear today does cruel injustice to the memory of General Domanov. The British went to extraordinary lengths to conceal their fate from the Cossacks: this we know well. What possible benefit could have justified the risk of informing Domanov of their plans? But we do not need to speculate: if Domanov had even offered his services in the way suggested, it would have been either to Major Davies or Colonel Malcolm. Needless to say, neither of these officers has any memory of such a transaction, nor does their superior, Brigadier Musson.

Domanov left Bryar and went to break the terrible news to his fellow-officers. In a few broken words he passed on the message given him by Musson and Bryar: a message that most regarded as a death-sentence. Domanov himself appeared shattered, and uttered little beyond his instructions. The ridiculous story of his being secretly in league with the British may owe something to this dramatic moment. For after the meeting in Lienz that morning, at which he had passed on the news and orders concerning the 'conference', none of the Cossacks had seen him again until this terrible moment. We may imagine what wild fancies may have gripped minds faced with a doom as ghastly as theirs.

Seized with panic, many began throwing down their officers' insignia, tearing off tell-tale jackets and *cherkesses*, and flinging away documents that could reveal their ranks to the vengeful NKVD. For it was on the officers that the most ferocious treatment would fall, as they well knew. The British knew it well also; the most careful precautions had been taken to prevent even one from escaping, and a roll was taken to check this. No roll was taken of the rank-and-file.[14] Fierce arguments broke out as the stunned and amazed Cossacks began to hurl out accusations. That treachery had taken place was self-evident, but who was responsible? So great had been their trust and respect for the British that many could only imagine that it was from amongst their own ranks that the poison had arisen.[15]

The wrangling was stilled by General Krasnov. He pointed out calmly that if it were true that they were to be handed over to death at the hands of the Bolsheviks, they could at least face it with dignity. His only reproach to Domanov was to remark that he might have tried to check the purpose of the British order.

General Krasnov called for pen and paper and sat down to draw up a petition. He wrote in French, and though the text itself has vanished under mysterious circumstances (to be examined later in this book), eye-witnesses have supplied the gist of it. Krasnov declared that he and the other leaders were prepared to accept their fate *if* the British were able to prove them guilty of war crimes, but he pleaded passionately for mercy to be shown to the mass of ordinary Cossacks and their families, who could not possibly fall under such an accusation. The petition was signed by most of the officers in the camp, and copies were addressed to

King George VI, Field-Marshal Alexander, the Pope, the Headquarters of the International Red Cross, and King Peter of Yugoslavia (whose subjects several of the old émigrés were).[16]

Meanwhile another famous Cossack general was also learning of the fate in store. A Russian doctor, Professor Verbitsky, who had arrived amongst the officers, was asked to attend on a general who had suffered a heart attack. Accompanying the British soldier who made the request, Verbitsky went to a drab-looking building in the street outside. Upstairs he was shown into a room where he saw to his surprise, lying on a bed, his old acquaintance General Shkuro. As soon as Verbitsky approached, he realised that the wily old general had nothing the matter with him. Glancing at the English soldiers in the doorway, Shkuro murmured in Russian: 'Who have arrived, and where are they being sent?' When Verbitsky in the same tones explained that it was the whole body of Cossack officers from Lienz, and General Krasnov in particular, Shkuro turned pale and made a despairing gesture. He remained silently thinking for some time; and then, before they could say more, a British soldier came forward and indicated that it was time to leave. Verbitsky descended the staircase and returned to the camp with a heavy heart and strong sense of foreboding.[17] Not long after this, Colonel Bryar visited Shkuro and informed him that he was to be handed over to the Soviets the next day. Shkuro demanded to be shot at once, but Bryar informed him curtly that that was impossible and returned to his quarters.[18]

Shkuro had already been held at Spittal for thirty-six hours when Domanov's main party arrived. On the morning of 26 May, Olga Rotova had watched him driving in joyful triumph through the camp at Peggetz. As he made his circuit, he was surrounded by a jubilant crowd of Cossacks, men, women and children, all laughing, jostling and shouting, 'Hurrah for *batka* Shkuro!' Shkuro saw Olga watching and waved cheerily to her. He shouted that he had just heard from her husband Misha; he was in Salzburg and she could join him shortly. She laughed and watched as his car crawled slowly back on the road to Lienz, impeded by the enthusiastic crowd.

That evening Shkuro had dined with General Domanov in his Headquarters. There he 'jested, quaffed and swore' until a late hour, when with winding gait he sought his bed. Not long after, just before 3 a.m., came a knock at the door. It was the hour favoured by the NKVD in Russia. Looking out, Shkuro saw a British officer standing in the shadows. He was told he was under arrest and being taken to a destination as yet unrevealed. At dawn a lone jeep left Lienz for Spittal. Already Shkuro was convinced that the British intended to betray him to the Soviets, so that it was with little surprise that he received Bryar's intimation.[19]

At nine o'clock the Cossacks were obliged to retire to their huts for the night. Few slept, least of all the wretched General Domanov. Faced with imminent death, preceded very likely by prolonged torture, he was aware that many of his comrades now mistrusted him. Two officers who had come to their barracks door at two in the morning for a quiet talk saw him coming up to them.

'If only I had known what the English intended two days earlier, all would have been different,' he groaned.

But the officers remained silent; they were convinced he *had* known of the preparations.[20]

Next morning at five o'clock breakfast was served. Soon afterwards, one of the priests in the party asked Colonel Bryar if they might conduct a service—presumably the last any present would ever attend. Bryar agreed, and as he himself wrote: 'The service they held was a most impressive affair and the singing quite magnificent.' But there was scant time for Christian reflection, and at 6.30 the first truck was backed up to the gate. An officer approached the hut occupied by General Domanov and his staff, and told them to climb aboard. Domanov refused, adding that he no longer had any authority over the other officers.[21] Colonel Bryar said he could have ten minutes in which to change his mind, after which if he still refused 'methods would be employed to ensure that he and all his officers got on to the transport'.

The ten minutes passed, and as neither Domanov nor any of the other officers evinced any signs of obeying, a platoon of soldiers was sent in. Some were armed with rifles and bayonets, others with pickaxe helves. But it proved by no means an easy task to extricate the prisoners, even by ones and twos. They sat on the ground and linked arms, resisting passively. But then a British sergeant-major, who was attempting to drag an officer by main force from his comrades, was bitten in the hand. This gave the guards the excuse that had been looked for, and a ferocious attack was launched on the unarmed men. Amongst them were old men such as General Tikhotsky (who was in such poor health he could only crawl on hands and knees).[22] For several minutes the British soldiers were free to lash out indiscriminately with rifle-butts and helves, until many Cossacks were battered unconscious. Others of the attackers did not scruple to stab the recumbent Cossacks with their bayonets.

As Colonel Bryar wrote, the 'display had the right effect', and thereafter the Cossack officers reluctantly clambered on board.

General Krasnov had not been in the open square during this time, but had sat at an open window in his hut watching. Some English soldiers saw him suddenly, and ran to seize him. But this the Cossacks would not stomach; a group of young officers rushed to the window, gently lifted out the 76-year-old General, and bore him to a lorry. He was permitted to sit in the front seat with the driver. As he took his seat, his grandson saw him cross himself and murmur: 'Lord, shorten our sufferings!'[23]

General Krasnov travelled in the first lorry of the departing column. The rear was brought up by another containing Shkuro and his staff. Altogether about 1,600 Cossacks and Caucasians passed through Spittal on the night of 28–29 May. A few went no further. The official British report noted that 'three attempts of suicide were made, two of which were successful.'[24] But the British officer who actually had the task of loading the officers and searching the camp afterwards recalled a number of eight to twelve. Three at least had hanged themselves with electric-light cords, and the others had slashed their throats or wrists with broken glass.[25]

Apart from this dozen or so who finished their journey at Spittal, there were other officers who were determined not to answer to the register at Judenburg. Three concealed themselves during the embussment, and then managed to crawl out of the wired perimeter.[26]

Meanwhile the hundreds of Cossack officers less fortunate than these were driving at speed towards the Soviet zonal frontier at Judenburg. A Cossack who flung himself from a moving lorry was recaptured; shots were fired at others. Lieutenant J. T. Petrie, of the 2nd Lancashire Fusiliers (who were entrusted with the task of providing guards for the convoys) remembered these incidents, as also a shower of 'belts, spurs and badges of rank thrown out of trucks all the way between Spittal and Klagenfurt.'[27] In the trucks the Cossacks were also anxious to discard anything the NKVD might wish to seize as loot. The Lancashire Fusiliers plied a roaring trade, using cigarettes as currency. Frequently a single cigarette purchased a gold watch.[28]

After several hours' journey, the head of the column sighted Judenburg before them in the steeply wooded valley of the Mur. The river itself was the demarcation line between the two armies. The lorries drove slowly up to the bridge, the approach road being lined with British armoured cars and machine-guns. The whole convoy then drew up to one side, whilst one truck at a time set out across the bridge to deposit its inmates on the Soviet side and return. Above hung limply on a pole the blood-red flag of Soviet Russia.

The Cossacks peered out from their trucks as they waited. One asked permission to make water in the urinal bucket that had been placed by the bridgehead for the purpose. The Fusilier escort nodded (there was no chance of escape now), and the man sprang down and walked over to the drum. Without a word he suddenly ran forward and sprang over the edge of the cliff. It was nearly a hundred foot drop to the jutting rocks below, and British soldiers rushing to the edge could see the tiny sprawled body far beneath. It seemed as if the escort would have the embarrassment of having to explain that the complement was one man short, but by great good fortune the deficiency was remedied. As Major Goode of the armoured car escort reported later, the officer was with some difficulty 'recovered and handed over mangled and dying to the Soviet forces'.

Major Goode strolled across the bridge to see what was happening on the other side. He was watching the reception of the Cossacks by the Soviet force, when a Cossack officer near him suddenly whipped out a razor, drew it sharply across his own throat and fell dying at his feet.

The disgusted Major Goode enquired of a Soviet woman officer what would happen to the surrendered Cossacks. She assured him 'that the Senr Offrs would be re-educated, and that the junior ones would be set to work on reconstruction work in destroyed Soviet towns'. But shortly afterwards he received a different version. In reply to the same question, a Red Army captain grinned delightedly and drew his hand across his throat in a meaning gesture.[29]

Not all the officers from Lienz had been handed over, and two days later another eighty-three arrived. These were the duty officers who had been left behind, together with some stragglers. Heading the escort in a jeep was Lieutenant Dennis Hemming of the 1st Kensingtons. As they approached the bridge, Hemming noted that 'between the town and the barrier a distance of approx one mile were British soldiers at 100-yard intervals handling tommy guns in a most business-like manner'.

The Cossack officers were handed over to the care of a Soviet colonel, who provided a receipt for the delivery. Hemming's report concluded: 'I was not allowed to venture further than the barrier but as far as I could see the streets appeared void of civil population who no doubt preferred to stay in their homes.'[30].

The absence of the citizens of Judenburg was not due to indifference. As Major Claud Hanbury-Tracy-Domvile, then Military Government Officer for Judenburg, wrote recently to me: 'I do of course remember the horror expressed by the Austrians in the town and the frank disbelief that it would really be undertaken by the British, who they evidently looked upon as just and humane . . . I also remember finding roadside graves near Judenburg signifying failures of desperate attempts to escape. The whole operation shocked the local Austrians.'

The scenes witnessed by Major Goode and Lieutenant Hemming were the last that any British soldiers saw of the Cossack officers. But one or two heard sounds that gave them a disturbing vision of what might be happening on the other side of the Mur. Edward Stewart was a corporal despatch rider in the Royal Corps of Signals. He was at Judenburg, and sent me this account of his memories:

> I was called out one day, to guard the British end of a bridge in Judenburg whilst a convoy consisting of Russian Cossacks were handed over to the Russians, who were at the other end of the bridge. We were never officially told the reason for the handing over of these unfortunate people but we all understood they had been fighting with the Germans against us. [This of course was quite untrue. N.T.] We also understood they were going to their deaths. Of this, there was never any doubt whatsoever.
>
> Close to the bridge was a urinal bucket, and many Cossacks used it before the crossing, but not for Nature's needs. They filled it full of German reichmarks, watches and other trinkets. It might seem extraordinary that a bucket was even placed there, as all troops had been using the countryside as a vast midden ever since hostilities began. I did not see any violence towards the Cossacks at that time, but I did not ride with the Convoy, but merely stationed myself at the point of no return . . .
>
> It was that night and the following day that we started to count the small-arms fire coming from the Russian sector to the accompaniment of the finest male voice choir I have ever heard. The voices echoed round and round the countryside. Then the gunfire would be followed by a huge cheer.[31]

The Cossacks knew how to die well. Perhaps they sang to face death with the words of the liturgy on their lips, perhaps too to let the British know how they were dying.

The British troops present at the time could only guess at the fate of the Cossacks. But, by what was almost a miracle, a young officer at the centre of the Cossack command ventured into the pit of hell, and actually succeeded in returning from it ten years later. This was young Nikolai Krasnov, grandson of the old General. He was one of the first of Domanov's Cossacks to whom General Arbuthnott had spoken, and who at Tolmezzo had in response to the General's question recounted his brief history. He had left Russia with his family when only four months old, and had ever since lived in Yugoslavia. Now, following the order transmitted by General Arbuthnott, he was condemned without trial to ten years' slave labour in the harshest camps in Siberia. Only a tiny percentage survived, but one of that percentage was a greatly changed Nikolai Krasnov. Unusual in surviving to the end of his sentence, he was still more unusual in being then permitted, on the grounds of his Yugoslav citizenship, to leave the Soviet Union.

In December 1955 he was allowed to travel to Sweden. There he sat down at once to write all he could remember, from the promises of the British at Lienz to the hell of Karaganda. His grandfather and others had urged him to write such a memoir if ever he escaped, so that the world might know the treachery of the British and the savagery of the Soviets. He wrote and wrote lest a single vital fact escape him, and then when he could raise the money he travelled to the Argentine where now lived his adored wife Lili. (She had managed to escape capture by hiding in the mountains.) Nikolai's book was published in Russian and English in the United States. It was read by few and has never been republished. Its author in any case died shortly after its appearance; he was almost certainly poisoned by Soviet killers whose chiefs *had* read the book.[32]

The events that Nikolai Krasnov related bore a dream-like quality. Generals Krasnov, Shkuro, Domanov and others of the senior officers were separated from their fellow officers and held apart. All were held in a large steel foundry, then disused, and the generals were confined in what had been the plant office. Nikolai accompanied his grandfather; two other Krasnovs, his father and uncle, were also in the party. At first they were politely treated, their guards being regular Red Army men. Throughout it was clear that the seizure of the famous White generals was to the Soviets the key aspect of the whole business. The commander-in-chief of the local Red Army units invited Krasnov and Shkuro to his headquarters. He turned out to be a veteran of the Civil War himself, and spent some time discussing old campaigns with his former adversaries. There was no talk of politics, and his attitude was one of respectful courtesy.

Other officers and men were frequent visitors to their prison chamber, and spent much time discussing the great days of 1918, when Red cavalry and White Cossacks clashed in the Don lands and the Ukraine. To Krasnov they listened with respectful interest, but it was the racy accounts of the legendary Shkuro, liberally interspersed with picturesque oaths and bawdy metaphors, that aroused delighted enthusiasm. Subalterns, too young to remember the earlier struggle, roared with laughter at the good-humoured exchanges of the older men. Every Soviet child had heard tales of this most reckless and turbulent of cavalry leaders; it was hard to believe that, after a quarter of a century, they were present with him in the flesh. His inimitable camp-fire humour was as instant a success with the Red Army men as it had been with von Pannwitz's Cossacks. 'What a man!' they roared joyously, as Shkuro confessed, with graphic phraseology, that the Red cavalry had on occasion 'burned holes in the seats of our breeches!'

The Cossack leaders put a brave face on matters. But from time to time came reminders that, whatever the camaraderie amongst serving soldiers, their fate rested with a very different set of functionaries. 'We were also called on by silent visitors, officers of the Soviet counter-intelligence, SMERSH, and of the NKVD. They came in, looked around as if counting noses, and left, closing the door firmly behind them.' Amongst the Red Army soldiers there seemed to be an odd but uniform attitude to their prisoners. The White officers they looked upon with some respect as consistent enemies who had never ceased to wage open struggle against the Bolsheviks. But the former Red Army men, such as Domanov, were regarded with contempt, or otherwise altogether ignored.

After two days in the Judenburg steel-mill, the four Krasnovs, Domanov, Shkuro, Kelech Guirey, Vasiliev and other senior officers were taken away in trucks. Before they got in they were ordered to pause and witness a little Soviet ceremony. One of von Pannwitz's German lieutenants from the 15th Cossack Corps was led up to a fence and shot. The execution was clumsily performed, and had to be completed by an NKVD officer, who kicked and spat on the still-moving body.

This unfortunate German was not the only prisoner delivered by the British, who went no further than Judenburg. For several days and nights the firing squads were at work in the steel mill, the continual volleys half-muffled by engines started up for the purpose.[33]

After this warning, the small party was driven under guard to Graz. After a night in a SMERSH prison, they were taken on to another gaol at Baden bei Wien, where SMERSH officers subjected them to a close and hostile interrogation. As others who have passed through the hands of this curious organisation have found, many of the questions were so puerile as to be seemingly the product of deranged minds or a deranged system. But one thing both SMERSH and the Red Army had in common was a fascinated interest in the famous personalities now in their hands. One morning official SMERSH photographers appeared and took a group photograph of the Krasnov family.

This interest, official and unofficial, followed the party throughout its journey. On 4 June they were taken to a nearby airfield. A former SMERSH officer, who defected soon after to the Americans, recalled the occasion.

'On one occasion, in the late spring of 1945, when we were already in Baden, my boss the lieutenant-colonel invited me to accompany him, so that I should, as he put it, "glimpse a piece of history".'

They set off for the aerodrome where the Krasnov party was gathered.

An aeroplane was standing on the airfield, ready for take-off, when we arrived. Beside it stood a truck with a tarpaulin cover, and a group of Smersh officers, whom we joined. My lieutenant-colonel was the senior officer amongst those present.

'Well, then,' said a major from the Operational Branch, addressing the lieutenant-colonel, 'shall we start?'

The latter nodded. An old man climbed slowly down from the cab of the lorry, where he had been sitting next to the driver. He was wearing German uniform, but his shoulder boards were the broad shoulder boards of a Russian general. He also wore a Tsarist decoration in the form of a white cross. 'It's Krasnov,' said the lieutenant-colonel, nudging me . . .

'That one is Shkuro,' the lieutenant-colonel said. He was a small man of good bearing, also wearing general's uniform. In the Civil War he had been one of the main opponents that Budyonny's cavalry had to deal with and into the bargain they had clashed right in my home town. I looked at them both with an interest that I, like the rest of our Chekist officers, was unable to conceal.

'They're a grand lot, the English', laughed the lieutenant-colonel. 'They give Shkuro their decoration, called after some saints, Michael and George, I think it was. Now, if you please, they're quite happy to deliver him to our door.' All our chaps who were standing near began to laugh.

A further group of officers in the same uniforms emerged from the back of the lorry. They disappeared into the aeroplane, followed by a soldier of NKVD troops, armed with a sub-machine gun, and a major of ours from Smersh Operational Branch. The aeroplane picked up speed and soared up into the sky, heading for Moscow and the scaffold.[34]

The plane flew to Moscow, and the next stage of the journey was undertaken in one of those Soviet prison vans labelled 'Bread', that so impressed Western correspondents describing Soviet prosperity.[35] Before long the van drew up close to the entrance of a building. The White officers were ushered inside, led along corridors, and locked into isolation cells. Nikolai Krasnov recalled the horror of that moment.

The lock clicked. I looked around. There was nothing to see. I was in an empty cubicle like a telephone booth, with a low curving top. I had to stoop, or I could sit on the floor with my knees doubled up. It was so brightly lighted my eyes hurt. The silence was absolute, and it was hot and stuffy . . . the deathly silence was broken now and then by heart-rending screams or animal-like howls of someone either dying or being tortured.

They were in the Lubianka Gaol.

Nikolai Krasnov was not long in his cell. He was taken by silent guards to the basement of Lubianka, where he was searched.

The examination was nearing its end when the door opened and an MVD colonel came in. 'Looked him all over?' he asked in a half whisper. Evidently everyone in Lubyanka had acquired the habit of speaking in low voices.

'Everywhere!'

'. . . there too?'

The supervisor struck his forehead with the palm of his hand, as if to say, Idiot, I quite forgot! 'Lean over,' he ordered. I leaned over and then exclaimed with surprise, pain and revulsion. The colonel of the MVD himself, without any gloves, did me the honour of poking his fingers into my anus, quite unceremoniously trying to find what I might have concealed there.

'Shut up!' he bellowed. 'No yelling!'

The examination was over.

'Put your clothes on,' ordered the colonel, as he wiped his fingers on his own handkerchief. Then turning to the supervisor he added: 'For the time being let him keep everything, even his buttons, shoulder straps, and belt. And take Krasnov directly to *him*.'

Who the mysterious *him* was, Nikolai was to discover shortly. But first he was led to an antechamber, where to his delight he once again met his father. They were able to exchange a few whispered greetings before being led through to a spacious reception hall.

At the extreme end of the room there was a gleaming broadtopped desk, on either side of which were tables covered with cloth. On the wall hung a portrait of the 'Leader' in his uniform as Generalissimo. It was a full-length picture, about nine feet high. On the opposite wall there was a portrait of Beria. Along the walls between the windows, which were hung with dark red velvet, there were portraits of the members of the Central Committee of the All Union Communist Party.

The entire floor was covered with valuable Bokhara rugs. Facing the desk and at a distance of about thirty feet there was a small table and two chairs.

There was the usual complete silence, as though we were outside of time and space, as though all Moscow had ceased to drill, to make a noise, to move.

A general in the uniform of the MVD sat motionless behind the desk. 'That's Merkulov,' whispered the officer behind us.

Though the name would probably have conveyed nothing to Anthony Eden or the Foreign Office, Merkulov was in effect the third most powerful man in the Soviet Union. It was he who, as Beria's deputy, had played a key role in the organisation of the slaughter of 15,000 Poles at Katyn and elsewhere early in 1940. Neither Stalin nor Beria's views on British concessions are known, though they may be guessed. But Merkulov addressed Nikolai Krasnov openly on the subject, and Nikolai Krasnov was the only repatriated man to hear such a speech from such a man, and live. How miraculous was his survival can only be appreciated by those who have read his book in full. That the young man who stood before him, pale and visibly perspiring, should, after eleven years in the slave-camps, make his way to the West and publish his account of their meeting would have seemed at the time incredible to Merkulov, or indeed to Nikolai himself.

'The General remained silent and we did not stir. Then he slowly raised his massive head and quite coolly, without embarrassment, looked us over much as you would examine wax figures in a show.' Merkulov ordered tea and cakes to be brought in, and then the three men were left alone together. At first the NKVD Minister made a few polite, if sinister, remarks. Then his mood began to change.

There was a pause. The General paced back and forth behind his desk, lightly swinging his hips and turning neatly on his heels. 'What kind of a trip did you have? Were you airsick in the plane? . . . Did anyone disturb you? Are there any complaints?' And then, without waiting for any answers—he obviously showed no interest in them—he turned directly to father: 'Why aren't you smoking, Krasnov, or taking your tea? You're not very chatty or friendly. I think you are silent in order to cover up your anxiety . . . your terror . . . and yet, on the whole, there is nothing to be upset about. At least not in this office. Now when they take you to the examiner I advise you to speak only the truth and answer all questions; if not, we . . . know how to string you up.' Merkulov gave a low laugh. 'At first it's done very gently, easily, it doesn't even really hurt, but then . . . By the way, didn't Ataman Krasnov describe this sort of examination in his books?'

My fingers turned to ice. My temples throbbed madly. My heart beat so loudly Merkulov must surely have heard it, even though he was standing thirty feet away. My father did not speak. His face was pale but intensely composed. How I envied him.

'Do not have any hope of going free,' continued the General. 'However, if you are not obstinate you will get through the formalities easily; you will sign something; you'll spend a couple of years in the Correctional Labour Camps, and there you'll get used to our way of life . . . you'll learn its good sides . . . Then, perhaps, we'll let you out. You will live!'

There was another pause.

'You see, Colonel Krasnov, you have a choice. Will you take truth and life or denial and death? Don't think I am trying to frighten you. On the contrary. Your father, your brother Semyon, and you are our old acquaintances! In 1920 you managed to slip through our fingers, but now . . . all the cards are on the table. You won't get away!' He took a few more turns, holding his hands behind his back. He wiggled his fingers and one could not fail to notice the flashing ring on one of them.

'Well, Colonel, are we agreed?'

'There is nothing for me to agree with you about,' said my father in an abrupt tone.

'What do you mean "nothing"?' said the Police General with a low laugh. 'Agreement is worth more than money, Krasnov. We are not interested in your past. We know all about you. Still . . . there are certain small details about your recent activities that it would do no harm to hear from your own lips.'

'I have nothing to tell you! I don't understand all this delay. Get it over with. A bullet in the back of the head . . .'

'Oh no, Mr. Krasnov,' said Merkulov with a crooked smile as he sat down in his armchair. 'Things aren't done as simply as that. What do you think? A bullet in the back of the head and that's all? Nonsense, Your Honour! You have to work for it! There's time enough for you to get in your coffin. Plenty of time to turn into fertiliser. But first you will do something for the good of your fatherland. A stretch of lumber felling, a bit in the mines with the water up to your middle. You will spend some time up on the 70th parallel. It's so interesting, you know. That will be the life, as we say. You don't know how to talk *our* language. You are quite ignorant of all the labour camp lingo that has sprung up in the region of the Arctic Circle. You'll hear it! You'll get skinny and hollow. You'll get the "macaroni leg gait".' With that the General roared with laughter. 'But you'll work! Hunger will see to that.'

We sat in silence. There was a racket in my head, and my hands were sweating from impotent rage.

'We've got to build, Colonel Krasnov. And where will we get the labour? There's no great profit in the gallows. Times have changed. Death by shooting—that's used only in rare instances. We need hands to do work, hands we don't have to pay for. For twenty-five years we have waited for this happy meeting with you. You've been long enough pulling the wool over the eyes of young people among the émigrés abroad.'

Merkulov was a little out of breath from his monologue. A heavy vein stood out on his forehead, and his eyes filled with stinging hatred.

'Well, are you frightened now? What of? Does the work frighten you? . . . But what are we talking about? You don't believe a single word I say and I don't believe you. For me you are a White and a bandit, and for you I am a Red cad. However, we Reds are top dog. As in 1920, the power is on our side. We do not flatter ourselves with the hope that we will succeed in re-educating Krasnov and making an obedient sheep out of him; you will never love us, but we will be able to make you work for communism, build it up, and from this we will derive the greatest moral satisfaction.'

Merkulov stopped and glared expectantly at my father. 'Why all this long preface?' Father replied in a tired voice. 'I understand everything even without explanations, General. The hopelessness of our situation is quite clear to me. My son and I are soldiers. We have both looked death in the face, and we shall die whatever the parallel, be it the 70th or the 100th, when the Reaper cuts us down. I reproach myself with just one thing; why did I trust the English? However, since I am about to lose my head anyway ...'

'Oh, if it were only death!' sneered Merkulov. 'You might as well stop talking about "a soldier's death". That's old-fashioned rot. Death passed you by without even noticing you. But the fact that you did trust the English—that was genuine stupidity. They are famous shopkeepers. They will sell anyone and anything and never bat an eye. . . . We don't trust them, Colonel. That's why we took the reins into our own hands. They don't know that we have them checkmated and that we have made them dance to our tune like pawns. Sooner or later there will be a clash between the Communist Bear and the Western Bulldog. There will be no mercy for our sugar-coated, honey-dripping, wheedling, grovelling allies! We'll blow them to blazes with all their kings, with all their traditions, lords, castles, heralds, Orders of the Bath and Garter, and their white wigs. When the Bear's paw strikes, no one will remain to nurse the hope that their gold can rule the world. Our healthy, socially strong young idea, the idea of Lenin and Stalin, will be the victor! That's how it will be, Colonel!'

Merkulov paused, and then switched his attack to young Nikolai.

'What kind of muscles do you have, king's officer? I'll send you to a place where you'll sing a different tune! You will make good what those Fascist swine ruined. It's too bad that we hauled in so few of you young counter-revolutionaries. Too many of you got off the hook and are hiding under the petticoats of the West. Never mind. We'll get them later on. We'll dredge them up from the bottom of the sea!

'You will not get a bullet in your forehead. Not in your forehead and not in the back of your head. We will make you live. Live and work! The time will come when your life will be given for the sake of socialist construction.'

'I think this conversation is not leading anywhere,' my father broke in sharply. 'Whaaat?' roared the General of the MGB. 'Do you realise where you are and with whom you are speaking? In Lubianka! With Merkulov! I am boss here. I say what I please. Did you get anything out of your petition that your dear Ataman drew up in French and sent from Spittal? Do you think we didn't know about that? No one will help you, not your Churchills or your Trumans, not kings or diplomats. When we roar they sit tight on their tails! I am told that there were Tsars who watered their horses in the Oder. Well, the time will come when we will water Soviet horses in the Thames!'

After this outburst, Merkulov pressed a bell and dismissed the two Krasnovs, father and son.

That same day, in the Lubianka baths, Nikolai saw his grandfather for the last time. Ataman Peter Krasnov, general and novelist, impressed upon Nikolai that it was his sacred duty one day to tell the story to the world of the Cossacks' betrayal. The young man adored and admired his grandfather, and was deeply affected by his parting words of advice. General Krasnov began by expressing a firm premonition that the boy would survive the trials that lay ahead.

If you do survive, [he went on] 'then you must carry out my testament: Describe everything that you experience or hear, the people you meet. Describe things as they are. Do not exaggerate the bad. Don't lay on extra colours. Do not depreciate what is good. Tell no lies! . . . Keep your eyes wide open. Here, under these circumstances, you will have no chance to write. Not even brief notes. So use your mind as a notebook, as a camera. This is important. This is gravely important. From Lienz to the end of your sufferings, remember everything. The world must know the truth about what has happened, what is happening, and what is yet to happen, from the betrayal and treachery on to the end.

Nikolai Krasnov never forgot this advice, and when, nearly eleven years later, he found himself free in Sweden, he sat down then and there and in exactly one month had completed the written account of his sufferings. All the evidence available serves to confirm the reliability of his story; and of the interview with Merkulov he himself said: 'Despite the fact that eleven years have elapsed, this meeting with Merkulov and everything he said made such an indelible impression on my memory that I believe I have reproduced it exactly as it happened. I may have omitted some things, but I have added nothing.'[36]

This is important because Merkulov's speech is likely to be as authentic a representation of Bolshevik motives and reactions as we could hope to obtain. Much of the phraseology and many of the ideas are recorded by a reliable independent source to have been expressed by Merkulov's close colleague Abakumov and other MGB officers.[37] Merkulov's menaces may read a little like those of master villains in old-fashioned schoolboy detective literature, but it is one of the basic facets of Soviet Communism that it has translated into fact the clichés of crime writers. The Polish Underground leader, Stypulkowski, who was also interrogated in the Lubianka Gaol in 1945, listened to similar boasts and threats from his interrogator, Major Tichonov. Like Merkulov, 'Tichonov said it was easy enough to part with one's life, but not so easy to face life-long internment in the Siberian *lagry* (camps),' and later expressed similar contempt for British cowardice and duplicity.[38] Doubtless these concepts percolated downwards from the NKVD leadership.

That Merkulov should have taken the apparently unprecedented step of himself interviewing the returned Cossack leaders is a strong indication of the importance Soviet leaders placed on their recapture. How much this was due to a real fear that the émigrés might, under more favourable circumstances, have toppled the régime, and how much they attached symbolic significance to this unexpected triumph over their oldest and most inveterate enemies, we can only surmise. But that Merkulov spoke what he really believed is very probable. He could not possibly have foreseen that the conversation might one day be published to the world. The two Krasnovs were about to depart for the northern camps, whence no one is recorded to have escaped (at least between the end of the war and Stalin's death) and which few survived. Nikolai Krasnov's father was in fact placed in an unmarked grave a few months later.[39]

But what People's Commissar V. N. Merkulov could not have foreseen was that, following Stalin's death eight years later, both his master Beria and himself would be liquidated by the emergent rival gang headed by Khrushchev. Bolshevism continued triumphant, but tended, in moments of stress, like an adder or a rat, to devour some of its own children. Nor could Merkulov have looked still further into the future, to a day when Khrushchev should seek to strengthen his power base by closing many of the slave camps. To Merkulov and his contemporaries, slavery must have appeared a permanent institution of the Marxist state. But in 1955 its economic contribution was seen to be small when balanced against social and political disadvantages. Slavery was abandoned as a major sector of the economy, being retained henceforward only as a penal measure. And then, perhaps most miraculous of all, Khrushchev decided to allow some of the foreign citizens released from the camps to return to their country of origin. Nikolai Krasnov found himself in this category, for he was a Yugoslav citizen—a fact that General Arbuthnott and Brigadier Musson had learned the first day they met him. Just after Christmas (Western style) 1955, he was freed in West Berlin, bearing with him the memory of his grandfather's injunction and a mental record of every detail of his ten and a half years' suffering.

But for his uncle, grandfather, and other senior Cossack leaders a special fate was reserved. On 17 January 1947, a brief notice in *Pravda* announced that Krasnov, Shkuro, Domanov and von Pannwitz and other senior Cossack generals had been executed for their crimes.[40]

A few details were garnered by Nikolai Krasnov in his far-off camp:

... later on I met a man who told me he had been in the same cell as my grandfather for over a year in Lefortovo Prison. He said that all the condemned bore themselves with composure and dignity. Even the decision of the court and the prospect of death had failed to break their calm.

They were executed in the courtyard of Lefortovo Prison.

During the time of the examination Grandfather was affected, but only physically. His legs swelled. He was twice removed to the prison infirmary. The food was very bad, and only once did they give him port wine to stimulate his heart. He wore prison garb all of this time, for his uniform had been taken away, cleaned, pressed, and preserved in the prison arsenal. But this man told me that, according to rumour, when General Krasnov appeared in court he was dressed in his uniform. According to the same information the MVD museum preserved the uniforms of all those who were hanged, including, of course, that of the German General von Pannwitz.[41]

It may still puzzle some that the government of the USSR should, in its moment of victory, have been so very anxious to lay hands on aged generals who had last fought them in an age of cavalry squadrons and biplanes. Clearly only NKVD men could gaze on the relics; therefore the aim in this instance cannot have been the usual one of impressing the Russian public with the irresistible nature of Soviet power. But NKVD men then (and presumably KGB men now) could be shown the splendid uniforms and arms of their inveterate adversaries, the first to offer fierce opposition to the Bolsheviks. They had escaped. But even after a quarter of a century the long arm of Soviet power had stretched out and hauled them back. 'We actually ordered their old allies, the British, to give them up,' seems the moral intended. 'No threats—we just snapped our fingers and they jumped to obey: that's the sort of people they are!'

The NKVD hoped in addition to spread terror amongst Russian émigrés everywhere and to destroy any faith they might have in the power of the democracies to help them.[42] Stories of harsh treatment of repatriates were circulated in the USSR as a warning by the Soviet authorities; on occasion a victim was 'beaten to a pulp' and exhibited to Red Army units as a warning.[43] It may appear unlikely that the rulers of the USSR should genuinely fear the scattered bands of exiles, but they could have reason. As a Soviet leader confessed: 'That's the way we got our start!'[44] To Vishinsky there was only one safe place for an exiled Russian: underground.[45]

Further clues to Soviet thinking can be found in the brief announcement of the Generals' execution. This contains a number of serious inaccuracies, or rather falsehoods. It was stated that Domanov was a general of the White Army during the Civil War. He had of course been no such thing: he had been a major in the Red Army until his capture by the Germans, who had subsequently raised him to the rank of Major-General. Neither General von Pannwitz nor the 15th Cossack Corps had belonged to the SS, as was also alleged.[46] The majority of Domanov's and von Pannwitz's Cossacks were not 'White Guardists' but fugitive Soviet citizens. Finally, neither of the two formations had been directed by German Intelligence, nor were they employed in 'spying, diversionist and terroristic activity against the USSR', or any other country. The Cossack Corps was a regular Wehrmacht unit, and Domanov's *Kazachi Stan* was a mixture of refugee centre and local militia. The intention was to convey to the Soviet public the impression of small, ruthless bands of saboteurs, recruited from amongst reactionary émigré elements, and directed by the Abwehr and the SS.[47]

9

The End of the Cossack Nation

SUCH WAS THE FATE OF THE COSSACK LEADERS. 'HAVE OUR SUPPER ready: we'll be back this evening!' some of the generals had shouted cheerfully to a Cossack who attended them as they left for the Spittal 'conference'.[1] But the evening drew on, and no officers appeared. Lydia Krasnov in her hotel room watched the hours passing—six o'clock, seven, eight—it was now past the latest time Peter Nikolaevitch had named for his return. Feeling increasingly agitated, she went below, where she found Major Davies and the Battalion chaplain, the Rev. Kenneth Tyson.

'Are the officers not coming back?' she asked anxiously.

'Well, not here, at any rate,' Davies admitted.

'But shall we see our husbands again soon? Where are we to meet them?'

Davies replied awkwardly that he did not know. Lydia turned pleadingly to Kenneth Tyson and implored his assistance. But the Chaplain could only utter calming platitudes: he himself did not yet know what was the fate in store for the Cossacks. Lydia Krasnov felt a sinister premonition that she would not see her husband again.

In the camp at Peggetz, Olga Rotova was also waiting fearfully for news. At eight o'clock she was told that her services were again required as interpreter. She was taken to two British officers, whom she recognised as having accompanied the convoy that afternoon. By them stood one of the lorries, ominously empty. Olga turned pale.

'Where are our officers?' she asked.

'They're not coming back here.'

'But where are they?'

'I don't know.'

'But you told me four times that they were returning,' she protested; 'then you were deceiving me?'

Unable to meet her gaze, the British officer replied in embarrassed tones: 'We are only British soldiers and are obeying the orders of our superiors.'

They wished to see the Cossack duty officers, and soon afterwards it was announced that Major Davies wanted to see at his office in the camp at Peggetz all the senior non-commissioned officers. The meeting was to be that evening at nine o'clock, and they were to bring with them lists of the various regiments and *stanitsas*, with the names and ranks written in English. This was done, and the men assembled at the time designated. But hours passed, until by midnight they were obliged to assume that Davies was not appearing. Even so commonplace a mischance seemed to strike a chill amongst the men assembled there in the gloom. They concluded that the meeting must have been deferred until the following morning, and that all should return to their quarters. Before doing so, however, they decided to elect one of their number as representative and leader, in place of the mysteriously absent Ataman. Their choice fell upon a certain Kuzma Polunin, a senior sergeant much respected by the men.

Olga herself stayed on, when the electric light suddenly failed. Settling down in the darkness, she tried to doze a little. But she stayed awake, like most people in the camp that night. At 2.30 a torch flashed around and Olga sat up to find Major Davies before her. He wanted the list of camp inmates, and when she told him that all had dispersed for the night he told her the meeting would now take place at 8.30 next morning.

At 8.30 all were assembled outside Davies's office. No one appeared, and the suspense grew. Then, at nine o'clock, a British lieutenant appeared. Accompanying him was an interpreter, but it was to Olga Rotova that he turned.

'Read this out!' he ordered abruptly, handing her a sheet of paper.

The document contained an order set out in Russian, and the assembled Cossacks listened in silence as Olga recited its contents:

'1. Cossacks! Your officers have betrayed you and led you on a false path. They have been arrested and will not return. You can now, no longer fearing or guided by their influence or pressure, discuss their lies and speak out about your wishes and beliefs.

2. It has been decided that all Cossacks must return to their homeland.'

There then followed general instructions to the Cossacks to continue to preserve their internal organisation and obey the commands of the British military authorities.

Olga's clear voice died away, to be followed by a deathly silence. By now there must have been few in Peggetz who did not fear the worst, but to hear this order read out, so calmly consigning them to death, torture or the icy hell north of the seventieth parallel . . . At last a loud voice rang out in protest, declaring that the words slandering their officers were lies, that all Cossacks loved and respected their officers, and that if only they would be returned to them they would follow them anywhere in the world.

The British lieutenant listened in silence to this speech, tersely informed the Cossacks that he was now handing them over to Major Davies, and departed.[2]

Meanwhile Davies himself was in Lienz. He had been allocated what was perhaps the most appalling rôle a British officer has ever been compelled to undertake. His job was to break the news to the officers' wives, now gathered in the hotel that had been Domanov's Head-quarters. He had been obliged the night before to mislead Lydia Krasnov, but now the truth had to come out. Not only had all their husbands been despatched to an unspeakable fate, but also the hundreds of women there assembled were to follow them.

Davies made his announcement in as sympathetic a fashion as he could, assuring his audience that there was no reason necessarily to suppose that the worst had happened to their husbands, and that arrange-ments were in any case being made for the wives to join them. Before the torrent of protest and agony that his words unleashed, Davies could only reply that, as a soldier, he had no choice but to obey his orders. But what orders! Extricating himself from the crowd of despairing women, he drove in his jeep to the camp at Peggetz.

There the news had been broken an hour before, but Davies still had the daunting task of facing those with whom he had been on terms of close friendship, to tell them that he had lied repeatedly in assuring the officers of the reality of the 'conference', and that now all must return willy-nilly to the Soviet Union. At the same time he was frankly puzzled at the extremity of their despair and determination not to return. He was a young man, and all he had heard for the past three years was praise for the heroic Red Army and its gifted leader, Marshal Stalin. After appalling losses and sufferings, it was they who had hurled back the apparently invincible Nazi hordes, had stormed into Berlin, and were now fraternising in much-publicised incidents with British and American troops where the three armies had met in the heart of Germany.

Speaking through Olga Rotova, he explained that 31 May, two days hence, was fixed for the date of their repatriation. The regiments would be entrained in the order Don, Kuban, Terek, the main intention being to keep families together. Everything would be done to enable them to keep their possessions with them, to preserve the *stanitsa* groups and in general to make the journey as comfortable as possible. Special arrangements would be made for those incapacitated by age or infirmities from travelling in the general crowd.

Davies was doing his best, but those present could see he was deeply disturbed. He thought their fears were largely unfounded, but that they feared greatly was patent. Shouts arose that they would never go willingly; many of the women were weeping, whilst a large number stood stunned. Major Davies's anguished reassurances about the conditions of the journey appeared a cruel mockery. Were the British vicious as well as treacherous, or so naïve as to surpass belief? Opinions were divided—and have remained so.

Davies departed, declaring before he left that he would be back again in the afternoon. Soon afterwards two lorries arrived, in which it was announced that the luggage of the officers should be placed for transmission to its owners. (They had been told to bring nothing to the 'conference', as they would be back the same evening.) The weeping wives took the opportunity of sending off numbers of letters and parcels, but what happened to them is not known. For, unknown to anyone, British or Russian, at Lienz, the officers were already in the hands of SMERSH. Many at that moment were lying in twisted heaps on the bloodstained floor of the Judenburg steel-mill. This cruel but unintentional hoax led many wives to believe that they might yet see their husbands.

After this the Cossacks of Peggetz gathered together with improvised black flags and placards. The latter bore pleas scrawled in faulty English: 'Better death here than our sending into the SSSR.!!'

When trucks arrived with their midday meal, the Cossacks declared they would refuse to eat. The soldiers shrugged their shoulders, dumped the food in piles, and drove off. At four o'clock Davies reappeared. He seemed momentarily unnerved by the black flags, placards and milling crowd calling out reproaches and pleas.

He explained that he had received orders, decided upon at the highest level, that all Russians must go back to the Soviet Union. He had no choice but to obey. When this had been interpreted to the crowd a number pushed their way forward, thrusting before Davies passports and Nansen certificates. 'We are not Soviet citizens,' they explained forcefully. In law they were, as the documents proved, French, Italians, Yugoslavs, or registered stateless.

'How can you do this?' cried one. 'In 1920 the British sent ships to the

Dardanelles to rescue us from the Bolsheviks, and now you are handing us back again!'

Davies was aghast, and for the first time realised that something was seriously wrong. But the orders given to him and Colonel Malcolm were unmistakable: *all* Cossacks in the Drau Valley must be handed over. Davies would have been very much more perplexed had he known that, a mere ten miles away in Brigade Headquarters at Oberdrauburg, there lay in Brigadier Musson's files the two written Corps Orders authorising the handovers. These contained a precise definition of what constituted a Soviet citizen, and stated that *only* Soviet citizens should be surrendered to the Soviets. Why these instructions never reached Colonel Malcolm or Major Davies will be discussed in a later chapter.

That people who were not Soviet citizens should be delivered by force to a régime under which they had never lived seemed inconceivable, and Olga Rotova, dropping her role of interpreter and speaking in her own person, asked:

'Will the Vlasov troops have to go?'

'Yes,' Davies replied.

'And the old emigrants?'

'The old emigrants as well.'

'Then I must go too?' For Olga had lived for the past quarter-century in Yugoslavia, and learned her English working for the Standard Oil Company.

'Yes, you too. All Russians without exception.'

'But look, Major: the men are weeping.'[3]

Once again few slept that night. The improvised churches were filled with congregations confessing and receiving communion. Next morning was 30 May, and it was at dawn on the following day that the Cossacks were to be delivered over into the hands of their enemies. Under the leadership of Kuzma Polunin, meetings were held to decide what to do should the British resort to the use of force. A few still refused to believe that the British were capable of fulfilling such threats; others thought that it was all a terrible misunderstanding. A petition was drawn up and handed to Colonel Malcolm. It declared that: '*WE PREFER DEATH* than to be returned to the Soviet Russia, where we are condemned to a long and systematic annihilation. We, husbands, mothers, brothers, sisters, and children *PRAY FOR OUR SALVATION!!!*'[4]

Other petitions, to King George VI, the Archbishop of Canterbury and Winston Churchill, were handed to Major Davies.[5] It was afterwards alleged that Davies threw them into the wastepaper basket,[6] but, as he now attests, this is untrue. The petition from which an extract is quoted in the previous paragraph certainly reached Brigade Headquarters, but the ultimate fate of all these documents is unknown.

Throughout 30 May the valley of the Drau presented a grim spectacle. On the barrack huts and tents, and even along the main Lienz–Oberdrauburg road, black flags were hung out. A hunger strike was declared, and the food brought to the camp by the British authorities was left piled up and untouched. Into each heap was thrust a pole supporting a black flag. Continuous services were conducted by the priests, and agitated groups of Cossacks gathered under the leadership of Polunin and his aides to consider what desperate action they might take. Weeping mothers clutched their children, well aware that by the following evening they would very likely be separated from them for ever. Bitter words were spoken against the sanctimonious advocates of the Four Freedoms and Democracy.[7]

As the day drew on, there came a temporary reprieve. Major Davies reappeared in the camp to announce that the operation had had to be postponed for twenty-four hours, as the following day was the Catholic Feast of Corpus Christi. The Cossacks began to feel a glimmer of hope, and wondered whether some last-minute intervention might not yet save them.[8] The real reason for the delay was, however, less consoling. The Soviet authorities had declared they could receive only 2,000 prisoners on the first day, and so two trains had been cancelled.[9]

Only one trainload could leave on 31 May, and it was decided that the first batch should come from the Caucasians east of Oberdrauburg. It has been necessary to ignore them temporarily whilst relating the plight of the Cossacks. But it must be remembered that several thousand of the mountain 'tribes' were also held under guard. As was described in the previous chapter, they had, like the Cossacks, been deprived of their officers. The first the men and their families knew of their fate was when a British officer and interpreter entered the camp to announce that their officers had been delivered to the Soviets, and that their turn must now follow. This was at five o'clock on 28 May, and the officer was Colonel Odling-Smee, commander of the 5th Buffs. Though prepared for a hostile reaction, he was visibly taken aback by the outbursts of weeping, shrieks and protest that greeted his announcement.

Colonel Odling-Smee placed strong guards on the camp that night and ordered constant bren-gun carrier patrols. Despite this, some two hundred Caucasians succeeded in escaping to the forests. Of these, half left in a single body, led by a determined Karachaev tribesman. Some old men and children got away with them. Amongst them was an Ossetian under-officer, Tuaev, who set off with a close friend. He heard the English shooting at the unarmed fugitives, but with his companion succeeded in crossing the mountains to Italy.[10]

Next day a petition was presented to Odling-Smee. Setting out the history of their sufferings, it begged the British to provide them with a refuge from persecution.[11] The British C.O. replied enigmatically 'that the USSR was our ally and promised that when they returned they would be sent to depopulated areas of the USSR'. Both statements were true, but appeared to offer the mountaineers small comfort.

On the afternoon of 30 May the first men of the Kabardinar tribe were detailed for entrainment at Dellach station. D Company of the 5th Buffs arrived at 2 p.m., to find that the prisoners had made little arrangement for their departure, whilst others were preparing a stubborn passive resistance. Major McGrath, commanding the Company, reported on his difficulties afterwards:

> Next to the track leading to the road a party of men, women and children approximately 200 strong, had formed themselves into a circle. It appeared that they had no intention of moving, for they had put up a black flag, and were chanting hymns and wailing.
>
> I ordered four 3-tonners to back up to them and with about 20 men tried to get them into the vehicles. The wailing increased and a number indicated that they wished to be shot by us rather than [be] sent to the USSR. With great difficulty a few were forcibly put on one of the trucks, but it was impossible to prevent them from jumping off, which they all did. It appeared that certain men were the ringleaders of this sit-down strike and as an example I ordered four men to forcibly put one of these ringleaders on a vehicle. However he created such a disturbance that I was compelled to hit him on the head with an entrenching tool handle (a number of my men were armed with these) and blood was drawn. This appeared to have a sobering effect on the crowd, for from then onwards they dispersed to their carts and belongings. About half an hour later they had all dispersed and were eventually directed onto the road with the rest of the tribe as my men rounded them up.

These people stayed in a guarded pen at the railway station all night; they were entrained with a further batch of prisoners without difficulty. With the Kabardinars were also despatched 169 Caucasians who had actually petitioned to return to their homeland.[12]

The Kabardinar families had good reason for their reluctance to return to Russia. They had fled after the Germans had occupied their homeland in 1942, but behind them they left a scene of horror.

In the tiny Kabardino-Balkar Soviet 'autonomous republic' in the Caucasus, near the city of Nalchik, there were a molybdenum *combinat* of the NKVD operated with convict labor. When the Red Army retreated from this area, several hundred prisoners, for technical transport reasons, could not be evacuated in time. The director of the *combinat*, by order of the Commissar of the Kabardino-Balkar NKVD, Comrade Anokhov, machine-gunned the unfortunates to the last man and woman. After the area was liberated from the Germans, Anokhov received his reward, becoming President of its Council of People's Commissars, the highest office in the autonomous region.[13]

So that if any Kabardinar were fortunate enough to be sent home instead of to the coalmines of Vorkuta, he could be sure of a welcome from Commissar Anokhov.

Altogether, on the two days 31 May and 1 June, 3,161 Caucasian men, women and children were sent off in three trainloads to Judenburg. The men were bolted in, thirty-six to a wagon, whilst the women and children were loaded on afterwards with the baggage.[14] So they pass out of our story.

Meanwhile, the Cossack families had just another twenty-four hours in which to make their farewells to each other—a necessary ritual since it was an invariable rule with the Soviet authorities to break up family groups when despatching them to the labour camps.[15]

Many a son gazed with sadness at aged grandparents who had travelled on his wagon the hundreds of *versts* leading from the Kuban to Poland, and from Poland to Italy and Austria. How long would they survive in Karaganda or Pechora? Ten days? A fortnight? And the wives, the children . . . Everybody knew what was the fate of a woman in GULAG, particularly if she were young and pretty. But 'we cannot afford to be sentimental,' as Eden wrote.

Another separation was, to many, almost as agonising. During that Thursday, Cossacks everywhere could be seen talking fondly to their horses, stroking their manes and muzzles, and spoiling them with lumps of sugar. Weeping openly, they comforted their intelligent beasts, companions of their travels and hardships. Sometimes a Cossack, shamefaced and heart-broken, led his friend under the trees, where a revolver-shot put an end to any possibility of neglect after his master's departure. Professor Verbitsky witnessed a scene where an ill-favoured old Cossack was offering his equally plain but much-loved grey cow to an Austrian family. The family was as delighted with the gift as the old man was with the thought that at least his cow had a good home.[16]

The night of 31 May passed by (it was the third since the departure of the officers), and the first dawn of the new month saw the haggard Cossacks preparing for their ordeal. At six o'clock the previous evening they had been told to prepare themselves with their luggage for the journey, and Rusty Davies told Olga Rotova to meet him at the gates at 7 a.m.[17] As soon as this was known, the Don Cossack priest Father Vasily Grigoriev told his fellow clergy to assemble all the Cossacks in their *stanitsas* for a service in the camp square. This was to take place an hour before the arrival of Major Davies.[18] It was only to God they could now look for aid. A Cossack told the Austrian family with whom he was staying: 'No bread this morning, my sister. This morning we are to die.'[19]

But one thing the Cossacks were resolved to show the world. Major Davies had begged them to co-operate in the arrangements made for the morrow. But they knew that if they did so, it could afterwards be said that they had voluntarily returned to Russia. The British would have to compel them to go. Never should the British escape the moral consequences of their actions.

We have already seen that where repatriated Russians did *not* resist, as in the camps in Britain, officials could claim, after suppressing the rest of the evidence, that they had gone willingly. The Cossacks knew nothing of this, but their instinct was right. Though their 30,000 people were a drop in the ocean of wretched victims returned to Stalin by the Allies at that time, it was the terrible events of 1 June at Lienz that will most vividly illuminate the tragedy of the Russian prisoners as the truth emerges.

Before an improvised altar in the camp square the Cossack priests, dressed in their full vestments and carrying ikons, began to intone the liturgy. The vast congregation of thousands took up the familiar chant. It was their holy Orthodox faith that had enabled their ancestors to emerge intact from the dark time of the Tartar conquest; and who knew whether, whatever the outcome of this day's events, God might not yet intend the salvation of His faithful children?

Olga Rotova was in the congregation, supporting the sick wife (already possibly the widow) of a colonel who had attended the Spittal 'conference'. Joining in the comforting responses, she could not help listening for another sound that must come soon. Then suddenly she heard the hum of a vehicle entering the gates, and saw Major Davies being driven into the camp in a jeep. Beside him was the under-officer Kuzma Polunin, whom Davies vainly hoped might assist him in enforcing compliance with his orders.

It was 7.15 a.m. Rusty Davies estimated that there were about four thousand people assembled in the barrack square, and it was abundantly clear that they had no intention of co-operating in any way. Having formed up his Company, who had jumped out of their trucks behind him, he waited some minutes to see if the service was ending.

Then he ordered his interpreter, a young officer sent from Divisional Headquarters, to give an order through a loudspeaker that he was giving them ten minutes in which to finish the service. The ten minutes passed, after which he gave them a final five minutes. Numerous pale faces were turned in his direction, but the singing and praying continued.

Meanwhile, Colonel Malcolm had appeared, and he instructed Davies to move in and start loading the Cossacks onto the waiting trucks. A platoon was ordered forward, but immediately the Cossacks reacted in a clearly concerted fashion. As the vast crowd shifted and surged away from the advancing soldiers, it could be seen that there was an outer ring of the younger and fitter men, whilst beyond them were gathered the women, children and aged. As the British troops approached, the mass of Cossacks nearest them knelt or crouched on the ground, interlocking their arms and making it impossible to draw out individuals. Faced with this passive resistance, the troops returned to Davies.

Davies realised that moves against the main mass of people were likely to be fruitless, or, if pressed to the limit, to cause bloodshed. His prime responsibility was to his own men, but he was also desperately anxious to complete the task without injuring the Cossacks. He and the other men of the Argylls had never liked the task assigned them, but now that they were face to face with an unarmed crowd, which included large numbers of women and children, the toughest amongst them began to feel very distressed. As the Battalion Chaplain, Kenneth Tyson, has emphasised to me: 'They could not believe that this was what they had been fighting the war for. They were repelled by the whole business.'

Rusty Davies had a job to do, and though he would make every effort to accomplish it with the minimum of violence, he was determined to fulfil his orders. Following the regular procedure for crowd control, he now sent forward a platoon to move in and cut off one of the corners of the crowd. Armed with rifles and pick-helves, the platoon was formed into a wedge and successfully forced their way through a section at the edge. About two hundred Cossacks were thus unwillingly detached, though still huddling together in a small body. As the gap opened between them and the remainder, Davies ordered in his two remaining platoons to ensure that the two parties remained separate.

Now the first platoon advanced upon the sundered group in order to start loading them on to the waiting trucks. What followed was described by Davies in his report made shortly after:

As soon as the platoon approached to commence loading, the people formed themselves into a solid mass, kneeling and crouching with their arms locked around each others' bodies. As individuals on the outskirts of the group were pulled away, the remainder compressed themselves into a still tighter body, and as panic gripped them started clambering over each other in frantic efforts to get away from the soldiers. The result was a pyramid of hysterical, screaming human beings, under which a number of people were trapped. The soldiers made frantic efforts to split this mass in order to try to save the lives of these persons pinned underneath, and pick helves and rifle butts were used on arms and legs to force individuals to loosen their hold. When we eventually cleared this group, we discovered that one man and one woman [had] suffocated. Every person of this group had to be forcibly carried onto the trucks.[20]

As each truck received its complement of prisoners, it tore out of the camp gates and drew up a few hundred yards to the north where a train was waiting. This consisted of fifty cattle-trucks, their windows strongly barred. In the middle was an open freight-car, on which sat a couple of shirt-sleeved soldiers of the Lancashire Fusiliers with a machine-gun. As each wagon received its complement of thirty-six Cossacks, it was strongly bolted down; all that could be seen was an occasional hand thrust through the grille, waving an imploring handkerchief to powerless friends.[21]

In Peggetz camp Major Davies had now to hive off a second group. After a vain appeal to Father Grigoriev to end the resistance, he ordered his men in once again. With weapons advanced menacingly, the soldiers made towards the huddled mass of Cossacks, seeking once again to break their way through and split off another section. But the crowd had watched with increasing horror the brutal treatment meted out to those already taken. They now realised, what they could not quite bring themselves to believe hitherto, that British soldiers acting under orders would employ any methods, however violent, to shift them.

As the first soldiers began smashing their way through the densely-packed throng, a wild fear gripped the people.

A young mother later recalled:

There was a great crush; I found myself standing on someone's body, and could only struggle not to tread on his face. The soldiers grabbed people one by one and hurried them to the lorries, which now set off half-full. From all sides in the crowd could be heard cries: 'Avaunt thee, Satan! Christ is risen! Lord have mercy upon us!'
Those that they caught struggled desperately and were battered. I saw how an English soldier snatched a child from its mother and wanted to

throw him into a lorry. The mother caught hold of the child's leg, and they each pulled in opposite directions. Afterwards I saw that the mother was no longer holding the child and that the child had been dashed against the side of a lorry. What happened then I don't know. The altar was knocked over, the vestments of the clergy were torn . . . we were so crushed in the crowd that mother (who wore on her chest an ikon of Our Lady of Kazan) began to look livid and gasped for breath.

'Oh Lord,' I prayed, 'why did I have a child in such a time? Lord! What shall I do? St. Theodosius of Chernigov, save my daughter! If I can only preserve her just through this terrible Friday, I promise to fast rigidly every Friday so as never to forget this one!'

And so it was that a miracle took place: that very crowd which had just been on the point of crushing us now began gradually pushing us out, releasing us. And how they shoved . . . not towards the chain of soldiers, but in the opposite direction in such a way that now there opened before us a way leading to the bridge, across the river and into the forest.

This was a little bridge across the river Drau, which bounded the south side of the camp. Even in summer the Drau flows with incredible swiftness, and as the equally hard-pressed flood of fugitives poured over the bridge, the girl whose account we have followed saw another mother clasp her child and deliberately hurl herself into the fiercely rushing waters. The writer and her family got away safely to the mountains after several more hazardous moments; she kept her vow and from that day onwards confined her diet on Fridays to bread and water.[22]

To the Cossacks the men of the Argylls seemed to have gone berserk. Lashing out with their heavy weapons, they inflicted fearful blows which rained down indiscriminately on male and female, young and old alike. The priests and their assistants were dashed to the ground and dragged away, their vestments and ikons being trampled in the dust. A middle-aged Kuban Cossack, who was bearing an ikon of the Virgin during the service, had been so badly beaten that blood was splashed over his neck, face, hands, shirt—and even on the ikon itself.

Eight years later another Kuban Cossack wrote: 'On my memory is impressed the following scene. [A British] soldier was escorting with his gun a young Cossack wife with a year-old baby in her arms. The hand of the baby was slightly wounded or scratched. The soldier, stopping ten metres from the edge of the crowd, bound a field bandage round the baby's hand, gave him water to drink from his flask; and then, in spite of the mother's pleas, took him off to the lorry.'[23]

It was about this time that the Battalion Medical Officer, John Pinching, arrived on the scene. Summoned the moment it was apparent that people were getting seriously hurt, he remembers treating a dozen or so middle-aged casualties, mostly for head-wounds. In some he inserted stitches on the spot; two or three semi-concussed victims had to be sent to hospital in Lienz. It was whilst he was tending these people on a nearby grassy bank that Olga Rotova came upon him. 'The doctor expressed to me his indignation over the use of arms against our people. "It's inhuman," he said, weeping openly.'[24]

A priest, Timofey Soine, describes how his wife was separated from him in the press and knocked to the ground. Fortunately, just as she felt she was about to go under, she was helped to her feet. As the crowd was swept this way and that, she saw on the ground a mother and child—crushed to death. Everywhere children were screaming for their parents, and parents, immovable in the throng, were gazing around for their offspring. Where possible the men of the Argylls grabbed children first and thrust them into the lorries. This was partly to save them from danger, and also because it frequently happened that the agonised parents then rushed out and could be seized likewise. But both the despairing, instinctive efforts of parents and the more detached desire of Rusty Davies to keep families united were generally of little avail.

As panic swept across the crowd, the whole mass began to move. Whilst elements broke from the main body and made for the little bridge across the Drau, the rest huddled together and began to move in a blind struggling mass away from the British, who were engaged in slicing off another group for loading. Above the infernal noise Cossack leaders could be heard shouting to all to keep together. This was in accordance with the agreed plan that only by doing so could they hope to avoid being picked up in detached groups by the soldiers. Now borne along by its own momentum, the crowd of terrified and shrieking Cossacks was herded against a strong fence of planks that bounded the camp to the east. The pressure built up unbearably until it seemed that hundreds would there be crushed to death, when a portion of the stockade collapsed and the people gushed out into a field beyond. Eventually the majority of the crowd of thousands had moved into this open field. Whilst Cossacks moved around shouting for friends and relatives, the priests began again their interrupted service. Gasping from heat and exhaustion, the people began to recover a little. Huddled together in a forlorn and frightened group, those nearest the gap in the fence glanced fearfully back, expecting to see the British soldiers springing through. But though a cordon of troops was hastily thrown round the field, no one molested them.[25]

There were in fact enough stragglers left in the camp for Davies's needs at that moment, and as he noted in his report: 'Quite a number left the crowd voluntarily now in order to search for, or join lost relatives and children. This gradual trickle of "volunteers" provided sufficient numbers to complete our first train load.'

In fact there were not enough, but Colonel Malcolm feared the situation was getting out of hand and decided for the present to call it a day. As his report stated, he ordered Major Davies 'to stop collecting people forcibly and to start clearing the huts of those who had by then returned to them. By this means 1,252 persons were loaded on to the train by 1130 hrs. The full complement should have been 1,750, but I decided not to continue the forcible methods in view of the inevitable injuries inflicted.'[26]

The casualty list was indeed heavy. Apart from the large number who had been wounded by the soldiers or crushed in the press, there was a considerable number of deaths arising directly or indirectly from the morning's work. Colonel Malcolm stated that, when the Cossacks clung to each other,

> it was necessary to hit the men hard to make them let go, and then many had to be dragged by three or four soldiers to the trucks. Many minor struggles and scuffles developed in the course of which a number of Cossack men got hurt and cut. My troops were using axe helves and the butts of their rifles, but bayonets had been fixed and some wounds were caused accidentally, none deliberately, by them . . . four people apparently got knocked down in the crowd and were killed: or it is possible that they had previously been suffocated under the heaps of people who had thrown themselves down in many cases several deep.

And Rusty Davies wrote that, during the second assault, 'one of the crowd clutched at one of the soldiers' rifles and deliberately pulled the trigger in an effort to shoot himself. The bullet killed a youth standing alongside. During this stampede a man was trampled to death.'

In the Argylls' War Diary the total enemy casualty list after the battle was given as '5 Killed; 3 Evacuated with gunshot wounds; 7 head injuries; collapsed 2; Women and children 2.'[27]

But it seems that this refers to deaths in the camp area itself. There appear to have been many more in the countryside around. Even before the handovers began, two officers who held somewhat cynical views on the value of British assurances had shot themselves in the woods. During the operation itself soldiers were firing constantly at the continuing trickle of escapers, particularly those who succeeded in dashing across the footbridge over the Drau. A surviving Kuban Cossack, Daniel Kolomeic, recalls how he escaped into the mountains, but his companion was shot down as they fled.[28] A Cossack woman, hiding in the undergrowth, was given away by the barking of her dog and killed in a burst of automatic fire.

Many, perhaps twenty or thirty, were drowned in the waters of the Drau. A woman doctor, Praskovia Voskoboinikova, deliberately hurled herself in, accompanied by her whole family: children, mother and sister.[29] Numerous similar cases were witnessed, many likewise involving the sacrifice of children whom mothers sought in their despair to save from the torments of a labour camp upbringing.[30] An eye-witness saw a Cossack strap himself to his saddle and spring with his horse into the whirling current of the Drau.[31] In a hospital in Lienz itself, a sick Cossack threw himself from a window to his death when the troops came for him.[32]

British officers were horrified by those instances of total despair. Kenneth Tyson recalls seeing a corpse suspended from a branch in the trees near Dölsach station, and Rusty Davies remembers seeing 'several' such during the day. The worst case of all was perhaps that which the latter came across whilst walking about the site after the morning's proceedings. In a woodland glade lay five bodies. Four were those of a mother and her three children, the youngest of whom was a baby girl just one year old. They had each been shot once in the back. Some way off sprawled a man's corpse; beside him lay a revolver, with which he had shot himself through the head. It was this scene which brought home to Davies more than anything else the fear which had gripped the Cossacks at the thought of returning to the Soviet Union. For there could be only one interpretation of the tragedy: the father, in what frame of mind we can only surmise, had killed all his family one by one. He had then walked a little way off and put an end to his own sufferings.[33]

That evening the scene at the camp at Peggetz and its surroundings resembled the aftermath of a battle. Bloodied figures wandered about, seeking for lost relatives. Masterless horses cantered here and there, their plaintive whinnying accompanied at times by the harsh cries of the Cossacks' camels. Small groups of people made off furtively for the mountains, whilst others returned from skulking in the woods to take up quarters once again in the quietened camp.[34] And everywhere the wounded and the dead lay around.

How many people died on that day, either by their own hands or killed by British troops? British sources suggest only about a dozen, but this appears to be far too low. The normally accurate Olga Rotova estimates 700 victims, including people crushed to death, shot, drowned and self-immolated.[35] This figure must be too high, though in the forests around there were undoubtedly casualties of which the British knew nothing. An Austrian living at nearby Nikolsdorf, Bartholomäus Plautz, still suffers from nightmares as he recalls the scenes around his home on 1 June 1945. With a friend, he set off with a horse-drawn wagon to collect and bury the dead Cossacks. He remembers all too vividly finding women clutching their dead babies, lying in the fields with their throats cut. Few, he says, could be identified.[36]

By the site of the camp at Peggetz is a little cemetery where some of the victims lie buried. Every year Russians come from all over the world to hold commemorative services and to pray for the souls of the departed. There is also in Lienz a charming little Orthodox church; both of these are zealously supervised by a small, one-eyed old Cossack named Ivan Gordienko. He is himself a survivor of the events described above, and conducted the author over the scenes of thirty years earlier.[37]

It was not only in the camp at Peggetz that scenes of violence and tragedy occurred that day. Further to the east, at Oberdrauburg, men of the 6th Royal West Kents and the 56th Recce Regiment were faced with a similar task in rounding up and despatching to Judenburg thousands of followers of the *Kazachi Stan*. As at Peggetz, on the two previous days black flags were hung out and petitions against return submitted. A few Cossacks there expressed a desire to return to the USSR and were placed for their own protection in a detention barracks east of Lienz.[38]

On 1 June arrangements were made for entraining similar to those at Peggetz. And again the Cossacks made a concerted and desperate effort to resist. Lieutenant E. B. Hetherington, of the 6th Royal West Kents, remembered the opening of the operation.

> On entering the camp it was very evident that the vast majority of Cossacks had no intention of being evacuated. This was borne out by the fact that they bunched together at the end of the camp, the outer ring linking arms to prevent any infiltration by our troops. I ordered the men of 11 Pl to fix bayonets in an attempt to rouse the Cossacks into surrender, but it was without success. They replied by taking off their shirts and asking the British soldiers to stab them. The interpreter was then called for and he spoke to them telling them it was foolish to act the way they were acting and that if they did not come quietly now they would be taken by force. Loud cheers greeted this statement.

The leader of the Cossacks had already been seized and placed in the waiting train, and it was decided to employ as forceful methods as were necessary to accomplish the task laid down.

So determined was the passive resistance of the prisoners, however, that the West Kents were obliged to call for assistance. They were joined by forty-five men of the Lancashire Fusiliers, who had been detailed for escort duties on the train. After a prolonged beating and the use of firearms, 1,749 Cossacks (including 102 women and 4 children) were loaded into the cattle trucks. Lieutenant R. Shields of the Inniskillings, watching the operation, wrote: 'I was witness to many amazing incidents of fanatical fear and dread of the future they thought was in store for them. Men outstretched on the ground baring their chests to be shot where they lay. There were many women in a state of frenzy amongst the Cossacks also.'

Eight hundred of the Cossacks on this train came from another camp a little further up the line. Lieutenant Shields now travelled on to this camp,[39] where a Company of his regiment had arrived to supervise the entraining.

By this time [runs Shields's eye-witness account] Capt Campbell had arrived with the main body of A Coy. Then the trouble started again. The minute we moved to remove them to the train they immediately sat down where they were with arms inter-laced, refused to move, and demanded that we 'shot them where they lay.' Capt Campbell decided that this was no time to be gentle and try and coax them to move—it was a case of move them by force. The troops fixed their bayonets, and started breaking the body into small groups. This proved no easy job. After 10 mins of beating with sticks, rifles, and even to the extent of bayonets points being used, and not too gently either.

The men were by this time very much aroused, and it was then that someone opened up with an automatic. This gave the troops the thing they had waited for. Weapons were fired above the heads of the Cossacks, and into the ground in front of them. Scenes were pretty wild by this time, and the big worry was that we might shoot up our own people, fortunately that did not happen. By this time quite a number had moved to the trucks to embus for the train, but the main body still would not move an inch despite the really rough handling they had received. One man in particular, I thought he must have been the ringleader because he seemed to have all the control over them. He by the time he had been dragged to the trucks was bleeding from the blows he had received and the leather coat (which was a very good one too before the fight started) was in shreds, likewise the jacket and shirt underneath.

With his removal plus the additional firing which was becoming more erratic as the men's tempers became aroused, they started moving towards the trucks with the exception of about 200 who tried to make their escape through the woods.

They of course were met by the Bren fire, out to stop any such attempt. This stopped most of them but not before there were casualties.[40] The few that did manage to escape were eventually rounded up by the RWKs in the adjoining camp.

From then on the job was easy. We cleared the camp, collected the wounded and killed which amounted to 3 killed and 4 wounded, two of them serious who were sent to hospital.

All told it took the Coy 2 hrs to clear one camp which totalled some 800 Cossacks.

All this bloodshed and brutality was employed to drive 800 people onto trucks. Yet at the same time, a few miles to the west, Major Davies with exactly the same number of men managed to deal with a crowd of about four thousand with considerably less harshness. It is relevant to note that whilst the men of the Argylls had been living for three weeks in close association with the Cossacks, the Inniskillings had newly arrived from Villach to assist in the operation. Curiously, however, not a single Cossack memoir appears even to mention the Inniskillings, whilst Rusty Davies and the Argylls are held up to near-universal execration. After their prolonged dealings with them at Lienz, the names of Major Davies and the Argyll and Sutherland Highlanders have passed into Cossack history. Cossack writers seem unaware that other units were called in to assist in the entraining; certainly they would hardly have retained the names of formations encountered so briefly. It may well be, therefore, that events at Oberdrauburg became conflated in some Cossacks' memory with those at Peggetz, and that could account for the introduction into Cossack memoirs of events on 1 June at Peggetz of circumstances which in reality occurred further east.[41]

The first and most terrible day of the repatriation operation was over.[42] For thousands of people it had been one of horror or remorse. Obviously the Cossacks now being received by the NKVD at Judenburg were the real sufferers. But there were others on whom the day's events would leave a lasting and agonising impression. The ordinary soldiers of 'Y' Company of the 8th Argylls were seen by many to be weeping as they conducted their incomprehensible and much disliked job.

The Revd. Kenneth Tyson remembers how many came to him afterwards, asking in bewilderment and obvious distress what they should do. He could only answer that they must continue to obey their orders; but he himself did not feel satisfied. His duties had not permitted him in the preceding weeks to see as much of the Cossacks as others, but the whole grim business seemed to him quite contrary to everything that Christ's teachings enjoin. He had arrived halfway through the morning's proceedings, when the main crowd of Cossacks had broken through the camp fence and reassembled in the neighbouring field. He had seen no violence, only troops inexorably pushing unresisting Cossacks towards the trucks. But the sight preyed on his mind, and on

3 June, which was a Sunday, he preached on the text: 'And Jesus, when he came out, saw much people, and was moved with compassion toward them, because they were as sheep not having a shepherd: and he began to teach them many things.' (Mark 6, 34)

The soldiers gathered in the Lienz cinema, which was used as an improvised chapel, heard Tyson preach movingly and with obvious feeling on the necessity for compassion in war.

'I didn't criticise the commanding officer at all,' he recalls, 'and I wouldn't dream of doing so, as I had no responsibilities. But I left no doubts in anyone's mind what *my* thoughts about the whole thing were: that it was wrong, that it was completely contrary to our Christian tradition and what we'd fought for.'

He remembers that his congregation was still profoundly agitated by what they had experienced. 'They were perplexed, stunned, at what they had been asked to do.'

The two men who had borne the prime immediate responsibility, Colonel Malcolm and Major Davies, also disliked what they had been obliged to do, though in differing degree.

Colonel Malcolm thought then and still thinks that the Cossacks were traitors to their country, and deserved to be sent back to whatever punishment lay in store for them. Many of his regiment had been captured before Dunkirk, and, as he now asks, 'what fate would they have deserved had they volunteered to fight for the Germans?' But whatever may be thought of this argument, it does not cover those thousands of unfortunates despatched to the USSR who were women and children and who were not Soviet citizens.

Colonel Malcolm also feels that the force employed in loading the Cossacks was no more than was necessary. And of course it is very clear that if his orders were to be fulfilled, then some degree of force or violence was unavoidable in view of the Cossack refusal to co-operate. Nevertheless, Malcolm felt repelled by the bloodshed and panic his orders were causing and, as we have seen, ordered the loading to cease prematurely despite the fact that the train should have included a further 500.

Shortly after giving this order, Colonel Malcolm walked from the camp to the railway line where he found Brigadier Musson, who had driven over from Oberdrauburg. Malcolm took the opportunity of telling Musson that he would not be prepared to employ the same degree of force in continuing the operation the next day, to which Musson replied only with a grunt. That evening Malcolm spoke to Musson on the telephone again on the subject, stating further that he would not issue the troops with live ammunition.

For his part, Rusty Davies is unhesitating in expressing sympathy and affection for his unfortunate charges, and condemns outright the policy he was obliged to implement. Moreover, he considers his superiors' argument, that any screening of non-Soviet citizens was impractical, to be unjustified. He was disgusted at the dishonourable rôle foisted upon him in having to deceive people who looked upon him as their friend; finally, he feels that the violence found necessary for the entraining on 1 June should in itself have been enough to have the measure cancelled.

Amongst the Cossacks the name of Major Davies is one still mentioned with contempt and opprobrium. All they knew was that he had lied to them and deceived them, and that he had supervised the brutal events of 1 June. But what could he have done? Two alternatives to obeying his orders existed: to disobey them, or to resign his commission. Neither of these courses was to be contemplated by any soldier at that time without the greatest misgiving. Corporate loyalty had been built up in the battalion over the past years of hard fighting in Africa and Italy. Davies had the highest respect for his CO's judgment, was not a regular soldier, and was moreover a youthful twenty-six years old. Perhaps we may epitomise his position in the words used by Winston Churchill of the French General Barré: he was 'baffled by a problem the like of which, gentle reader, you have not yet been asked to solve . . .'

A moving testimony to the anguish of Major Davies is supplied by Olga Rotova, a witness little likely to whitewash British actions or individuals. She remembered standing in the crowd watching the first onslaughts by the Argylls. Suddenly she was summoned out of the crowd to appear before Major Davies.

'At last I've found you! Why didn't you meet me at the entrance?'

'My place is with my own Russian people,' she replied.

Davies passed on to explain hurriedly that he was anxious to find Domanov's wife, so that she might be properly treated, away from the milling crowd.

'I'm not sure that I believe you, Major,' replied Olga dubiously.

After a vain search for the General's wife, Davies, 'pale and upset', made a new request.

'Tell them not to resist,' he said, indicating the frenzied crowd.

'Major! Produce a great stove with a fire in it and give orders to jump in. Would you jump?'

'I don't know.'

'You know very well, Major, that you would not. To return to the Soviets is worse than the fire of a stove!'

'But I, a British officer, cannot watch longer the beating of unarmed people . . . women, children. I can't authorise any more violence, I can't any more, I can't!'

He was weeping copiously.

'I can't go on, I can't!'[43]

Davies in addition went to some lengths to sift out a few of the more obvious old emigrants; they included the wives of Generals Kraznov and Domanov. These were placed in an improvised guard hut during the confusion, and thus evaded repatriation. In subsequent years he used to receive Christmas cards from several of these people, who were living in Genoa and other cities in the West. Another remarkable case was that of Domanov's Intelligence Officer. He had been decorated with the MC by King George V, and had until recently been an officer of the British Crown, serving in the Hong Kong Police. To hand such a man over to the Soviets for execution was more than the Argylls could stand. He was provided with civilian clothes and allowed to escape.[44] Those accounts which have laid the major blame on Major Davies or Colonel Malcolm are committting a real injustice.

One other officer's reaction to the day's events will be mentioned, as it draws attention to a much wider issue—one so far-reaching that it unfortunately cannot be covered within this book. Dr. John Pinching, medical officer of the 8th Argylls, felt then and still feels considerable bitterness over the part he and his comrades were called upon to play. Like Kenneth Tyson, he could not condemn the officers who issued the orders. For Colonel Malcolm as a soldier he had nothing but respect, and he in any case was but obeying orders in his turn. The ultimate responsibility, Dr. Pinching thinks, lay quite outside the whole chain of command, military and political.

He and his fellow-officers had not questioned their orders, because they genuinely believed the Cossacks' fears to be illusory. For three years British wartime propaganda had represented the USSR 'as a kind of utopian socialist state. One rather believed this . . . this echoed the Stephen Spender, Bernard Shaw kind of intellectual Left with which I was associated in Oxford, and which I swallowed hook, line and sinker . . . Really, I think I was brainwashed by the Psychological Warfare Branch into thinking that Russia was a socialist state, and that they would behave compassionately towards these people whom we were deputed to send back.'

By the end of a fortnight a total of 22,502 Cossacks and Caucasians was despatched by the 36th Infantry Brigade from the Drau Valley to the Soviet-occupied zone of Austria. Colonel Malcolm's threat to refuse further use of extreme violence was never put to the test, as subsequent entrainments passed off much more peacably. There were further individual tragedies,[45] and on 2 June the Royal West Kents had once again to resort to beatings when loading a party of 1,750 Cossacks at Nikolsdorf Station. But in general the prisoners seemed to have been cowed into resigned submission by the terrible events at Peggetz and Oberdrauburg on 1 June.

With such large numbers living in unwired camps it will come as no surprise to learn that many escaped, both before and after the tragic events described. British sources estimated that 'those that had managed to escape evacuation amounted to well over a thousand, probably considerably more',[46] and throughout General Naumenko's edited collection of Cossack letters and memoirs are numerous references to successful escapes by groups and individuals. Perhaps the outstanding case was that of Kuzma Polunin, the young NCO whom the Cossacks had chosen as their leader after the departure of the officers on 29 May. He had actually entered Peggetz camp on the fatal morning of 1 June in Major Davies's jeep. How he got away is not known, but Olga Rotova met him in the camp (to which he had returned) two months later.[47] On 26 May, the 36th Infantry Brigade HQ issued elaborate instructions to all units concerned, detailing various posts and passes to be guarded and patrolled.[48] But despite this and the formidable natural obstacles facing anyone wishing to leave the Drau Valley, large numbers made their way into the forests of the foothills and attempted the dangerous journey across the snow-covered heights beyond.[49] Determined efforts were made to comb the mountains and recover the scattered groups. A report made by the 56th Recce Regiment noted that:

> In the early days parties of Cossacks and Caucasians were large and reluctant to expend energy in evading patrols. As time went on they were seldom found in parties of more than 12 and sat high up on the snow line during the day with sentries out who gave the alarm by shouting. By night they often occupied summer farms or bivvied in the woods on the lower slopes. The regular Cossacks and Caucasians requested to be shot rather than handed over, but having been taken they made no determined efforts to escape and readily obeyed British orders.[50]

Kenneth Tyson described to the author such a search party which he accompanied on 3 or 4 June, and remembers also the Cossacks' resigned acceptance of their fate. The patrol he was with went up a pass leading below the Spitzkofel Mountain south of Lienz. After ascending two or three thousand feet they came upon a group of fifty or sixty men, women and children. Without resistance these turned round and were escorted back to the camp. On other occasions, however, patrols fired on and even killed would-be escapers. Frequently the Soviet authorities were permitted to send in SMERSH officers to participate in such operations.[51]

During the period 7 to 30 June 1,356 Cossacks and Caucasians were recaptured in the mountains. On 15 June 934 of these were taken by trucks to Judenburg; the Soviet authorities requested that they be taken on to Graz, where they arrived the following morning. It was the impression of several of the British troops guarding this convoy that all or part of the prisoners delivered were massacred by the Soviets soon after their arrival.[52] It will be noticed that 422 still remained in British hands. What happened to them must be reserved for a later chapter; curiously, infinitely more controversial negotiations and discussions arose over the fate of this little group than were ever spent on the 50,000 already surrendered.

During the first week of June thousands of Russians travelled on the one-way journey from the Drau Valley to Judenburg. For nine hours they were packed together in sealed cattle-wagons.

At the other end of the hundred and thirty mile journey a young British soldier watched the daily procession of trains arriving at Judenburg. Towards the end of May 1945, 25-year old Sapper Reg Gray of the 192nd Railway Operating Company, Royal Engineers, found himself near Klagenfurt. There he was detailed to act as driver to an Engineer officer, Lieutenant Sykes. One night he drove the Lieutenant to an officers' mess outside the town. As Reg Gray sat in his jeep waiting in the road, he could hear from some distance off the sound of great crowds of men singing. Occasionally this was punctuated by bursts of rifle fire, and a red glow burned in the darkness from where the sounds emanated. At that moment another jeep drew up alongside, and Gray asked the driver what was going on. The other explained that there were forty thousand Russians gathered there who were being sent back to Russia.

Just then Lieutenant Sykes reappeared and gave Gray instructions to pick him up next morning at four o'clock. 'It was perishing cold' when they set off, he recalls. However, there was little time for reflection, as Sykes now told him they were to drive north to Judenburg. As they sped up the valley, the officer explained that he had been detailed to act as liaison officer at the handover point where the returning Russians were to pass under Soviet control.

As they approached their destination they were waved to a halt. A column of lorries was coming down the highway and made for the bridge over the Mur. In the trucks were seated Cossack officers in German uniforms. As the convoy streamed slowly over the bridge there was a brief halt, and in a flurry of excitement word was passed back to those waiting that a Cossack had hurled himself over the parapet to his death. Eventually the road was cleared, and Reg Gray's jeep drove over the high-arched bridge to the Soviet-occupied side of the town. The first thing that struck him was an extraordinary change in the atmosphere. On the British side all was cheerful noise and bustle. On the other, the very houses seemed to become abruptly drab, and the people around looked frightened. An eerie feeling of fear permeated the atmosphere.

At the railway station half a dozen Red Army soldiers sat playing cards on the deserted platform. After some time there was a trembling of the lines, and a train came slowly steaming in. As it drew up, Gray could see that the windows of the trucks were sealed with barbed wire. Between the strands of wire fluttered hands dangling watches and other valuables. There were no guards in sight, only the engine personnel. At once two Soviet soldiers jumped into the seats of a nearby 37 mm. light anti-aircraft gun and swung the barrel round menacingly to cover the train. A Soviet officer began walking the length of the wagons, banging each one in turn with a length of twisted steel cable. After a while the doors were unlocked and the prisoners descended, blinking in the sunlight.

They were lined up in a great queue, men, women and children intermingled. They were not allowed to bring a single article of luggage with them and all portable personal possessions were left piled in the trucks. A Jew acting as interpreter to the British officer was standing nearby, and Reg Gray asked him if he knew what was going to happen to the Cossacks. The interpreter went off, to return with the reply that all the officers would be shot and the rest sent to Siberia. To Gray, young and apolitical, this meant little at the time, and he admits now that his first thought was for the pickings to be had from the empty train.

Inside he found pathetic little bundles of cherished possessions— tattered suitcases, clothes, blankets, watches. Everywhere were festooned pieces of German insignia torn from uniforms, and welcoming heaps of Italian *lire* and Austrian *schillings*. There was a Singer sewing-machine, which an old woman was pleading in vain to be allowed to take with her. In another was a pair of abandoned gold wedding-rings which Reg Gray still possesses. What did strike him with disgust at the time was the discovery that each wagon-load of forty people had been supplied for the needs of nature with half a forty-gallon oil drum. As men, women and children had been intermingled during the day-long journey, the squalor could be imagined. At least one of the returning victims had decided he would escape the fate for which he had been destined. In the corridor of a Pullman car lay the blanket-covered body of a Cossack suicide. Moving hastily past this macabre sight, Gray completed his search of the train. His pockets were bulging with Austrian and Italian notes, which were of course useless to the Russians. Perhaps the oddest item he encountered was a box of fifty tins of Players cigarettes in the guard's van of this and every subsequent train. They had evidently been placed there for the use of the prisoners, but were at the same time completely inaccessible! The gesture, however, may have looked good in some report.

Up and down the platform outside walked three important Soviet officers in resplendent uniforms. No matter how many times they did so, every time they passed before a Red Army soldier the latter would spring to attention and salute. Thus struck Gray as excessive, certainly by British standards, but then he did not realise to what dreadful organisation the officers belonged.

For the first fortnight of June Gray drove Lieutenant Sykes every day from their billets on the British side of the river to meet the trains shuffling into Judenburg station. Each arrival was the same: the train drew up, hissing. There were no guards on board, only the personnel to drive the engine—and they were never permitted to descend. Soviet soldiers unlocked the wagons and shepherded away the prisoners. What happened to them Reg Gray never saw; he had only the report of the interpreter to go by.

What he did witness was the fate of the prisoners' belongings. As each train was unloaded, every Cossack was stripped of all his possessions. These were dumped nearby in an ever-growing heap, which by the end of the fortnight had assumed massive proportions; it was 'as big as a gasometer'. And when the last train had left, Soviet guards poured kerosene on to the base of the pile and watched it go up in a column of black smoke.

His duty over, Reg Gray returned to his unit. In the other direction endless columns of bowed figures set off on the long journey eastwards. Their ordeal had begun.[53]

10

The Fifteenth
Cossack Cavalry Corps

When Brigadier Musson arrived at Kötschach on 8 May to accept the surrender of General Domanov's Cossacks, he came on the rearguard of what appeared to be a whole people on the march rather than a military detachment. For fifteen to twenty miles ahead, over the pass into the next valley, straggled thousands of men, women and children, dragging their possessions on waggons and camping in groups where they stopped. Amongst them moved bodies of disciplined cavalry, but the majority were dispirited and suffering from the effects of the hazardous climb over the Plöckenpass.

At the same time, several miles to the east, officers and men of the British 6th Armoured Division were witnessing a spectacle similarly picturesque, but very different in quality. By the village of Griffen, between Völkermarkt and Wolfsberg, the men of the 15th Cossack Cavalry Corps were parading for the last time. The commander, General Helmuth von Pannwitz, sat his horse at the head of a mounted escort. With drawn sabres glittering in the fresh spring air, his veterans gazed stiffly ahead. Many had fought in the army of the Tsar, and bore themselves as they had once when reviewed by their Orthodox Emperor. Then the Trumpeter-Corps of the 1st Cossack Cavalry Division mounted on white horses, raised their instruments and struck out into the stirring 'Prinz Eugen Marsch'.

At once the 1st Don Cavalry Regiment broke forward in perfect parade order, and passed at full gallop, squadron after squadron, before their General. They were followed by the 2nd Siberian Cavalry, dressed in white furred caps with rifles slung across their backs. Officers and men were armed with curved swords, and all wore the traditional skirted *cherkess* borne by their ancestors in battle for centuries. The senior officers were almost exclusively Germans, drawn from the noblest families of Germany and Austria. The whole scene, with its setting of snow-capped mountains and sunshine, seemed a last triumphant reminder of the pageantry of warfare before the advent of mechanisation. It was on this note that the last fighting units of national Russia had come to end their existence. To British officers watching, many of whom were themselves cavalrymen, the sight of so many splendid horsemen executing perfect drill was supremely stirring.[1]

But decorative and picturesque as they undoubtedly were, the Cossacks of the 15th Cavalry Corps, unlike those commanded by General Domanov, were also a formidable fighting force. In early 1943 Red Army advances had compelled the inhabitants of the Cossack steppes to withdraw westwards behind the shield of the retreating German Army. Many, as has been related, gathered at Novogrudok with their families to establish the *Kazachi Stan* under the leadership of Ataman Pavlov. This settlement was in reality a refugee centre, with a defence militia organised from the able-bodied men. But German commanders were well aware of the Cossacks' value as troops in the field, and it was decided to set about forming regular units for use against the Soviets. Such units, scattered amongst the Wehrmacht command in the East, had already proved their potential value, and in March 1943 General von Kleist ordered all Cossacks of military age to assemble at Kherson on the Dnieper.

Eager to serve against the Bolshevik enemy, thousands of Cossacks flocked to the colours to be enlisted in three newly-formed regiments: two from the Kuban and one from the Don. The man appointed to command them, with the rank of Major-General, was Helmuth von Pannwitz. Now in his forties, von Pannwitz came of a family settled for generations in Upper Silesia. He had served as a cavalry lieutenant in the Great War, and afterwards in a *Freikorps* detachment in the east. He spoke Polish fluently, but little Russian, though in time he improved sufficiently to be able to conduct conversations in the latter tongue.[2] Everyone who came in contact with General von Pannwitz—Cossacks, Germans and British—is agreed that he was an exceptionally good soldier, honourable and conscientious. The Cossacks universally adored him.

In the month after the inception of the new Cossack levies, their base was withdrawn further west to Mlawa, north-west of Warsaw. There von Pannwitz set about drilling and disciplining the Cossacks for the type of warfare to which they were used. German cavalry officers were brought in to command the different units; these were generally of very high calibre, partly on account of von Pannwitz's selectiveness, partly because the posting attracted those cavalrymen who welcomed the chance of continuing to work with horses. The General endeared himself to his men by adopting Cossack uniform and encouraging the use of traditional ranks, uniforms and arms. Religious services conducted by Orthodox priests were attended by all, a prominent member of the congregation being the (Protestant) General himself.

Realising how much their glorious history could sustain their fighting spirit, von Pannwitz went to great lengths to stress the links between the newly-recruited units and their predecessors who had served Russia and her Tsars for so many centuries. Emigré officers living in Western Europe were welcomed as officers or interpreters, and legendary figures from the Civil War, such as Generals Krasnov, Naumenko and Shkuro, visited the camp from time to time. Great ceremony was accorded these visits; Cossack bands would play the old national anthem, 'God protect the Tsar', and other majestic tunes from the past, and Cossack choirs sang as visiting generals reviewed the proud new levies.

Von Pannwitz's Cossacks never fought on the Eastern Front, as they had always hoped they would. In September 1943 they were transported to Yugoslavia to fight Tito's Communist partisans. Hitler had recently developed an obsession that the Russian volunteers were unreliable and likely to go over to the Red Army. The Führer's information, or his interpretation of it, was faulty, but as a result he ordered that all the thousands of anti-Communist volunteers should be turned into slave labour for the coalmines. This drastic and disastrous project was avoided by the High Command only by arranging to transfer all the volunteers to the West. On 10 October Hitler ordered that all of the six or eight hundred thousand anti-Communist Russians in German service should be removed from the eastern theatre of war.[3]

To ensure the preservation of a crack unit, von Pannwitz's Cossacks had already been transferred to Yugoslavia in the previous month. The men were bitterly disappointed that they were not to fight the Bolsheviks after all. But an *esprit de corps* had grown up that would see them through anything, and as von Pannwitz explained that they would still be fighting Reds, they became reconciled. And in the mountains of Bosnia and Serbia they soon found fighting after their own hearts. Utterly fearless and loyal, they used their horses to move swiftly through regions where no mechanised vehicle could go. They soon created havoc amongst Tito's levies, who had become accustomed to the heavy-handed methods of Wehrmacht reserve units. Guarding communications, supply dumps and settlements friendly to the Germans, the Cossacks settled down to a regular routine. They became expert at flushing out Titoist partisan detachments in the mountains, and reconciled themselves to the idea (for the present at least) of fighting Yugoslav Communists instead of their own native variety.

On their first arrival in Yugoslavia, in the winter of 1943–4, the Cossacks' discipline and morale had been poor. Not infrequently there were cases of rape and rough handling of the local inhabitants, and, very disturbingly, numbers of Cossacks were found to be deserting to Tito's partisans. General von Pannwitz was determined to halt this. More émigré officers were encouraged to join, as they could act as interpreters and counsellors between the German officers and the Cossacks. One such, George Nikolaevich Druzhakin, is a close friend of the present author. He had lived in Paris since the Civil War, and was in Brest when the Wehrmacht sent for him. After a brief period of instruction in a heavily-bombed Berlin, he arrived at the Headquarters of Colonel Constantin Wagner, commander of the 1st Cossack Cavalry Division. Fluent in French, German and Russian, it was through him that Wagner hoped to develop more satisfactory relations with his men. Druzhakin recalls how Colonel Wagner at once gave him *carte blanche* to investigate the causes of the Cossacks' discontent, and report to him in person, no matter who was implicated in his accounts.

Druzhakin, who had served in General Krasnov's Don Army in 1918, had no difficulty in establishing friendly relations with his fellow Don Cossacks, and it was not long before he found what was wrong. Many of the German non-commissioned officers were boorish martinets who imagined they were dealing with a species of native levies. Of course this was only in part due to the loutish ignorance of these functionaries; daily they read happily in their newspapers of the innate racial superiority of their own people over the subhuman Russians.

Every Cossack had a tale of crude bullying at the hands of these men, and when Druzhakin was told by a weeping Cossack how he had been punched down a flight of stairs, he went straight to his Colonel. Wagner did not hesitate; to every NCO who acted unjustly he had one word: do it again, and you will be posted to the Eastern Front. The Cossacks were assured of firm but fair treatment, and Druzhakin (who was eventually promoted to Major) sat at courts-martial to ensure that the views of the Cossacks were fully understood. Within a very short time the grumbling ceased, and not long after that desertions ended. Better still, the flow was reversed and Cossacks who had formerly absconded returned to serve faithfully to the end.

Unfortunately no history of the campaigns of the 15th Cossack Corps exists in English, though there are good accounts in German and Russian. All we can say here is that, after a shaky start, the Corps soon established a well-deserved reputation for bravery, skill and good discipline. As the frontiers of the Reich contracted in 1944-5, the Cossacks found themselves progressing from fighting partisans to taking part in regular front-line combat against Yugoslav and Bulgarian divisions. And on Christmas Day (Western style) 1944, the Corps engaged for the first time in battle with a unit of the Red Army itself. At Pitomacha on the River Drava they fought a ferocious engagement against infantry and artillery of the 133rd Soviet Infantry Division, which satisfyingly bore the sobriquet 'Stalin'. After fierce fighting, much of it hand to hand, the 15th Cossacks repulsed the enemy with heavy losses. Many of the Red Army prisoners voluntarily joined the Cossack Corps.[4]

This was what really amounted to the last engagement of the Russian Civil War, for with the new year the German South-Eastern Front was being rapidly driven back on to the frontiers of Austria. By the first days of May the Commander-in-Chief, General von Löhr, had announced to all units the capitulation of the German Army. The two divisions of the Cossack Corps crossed the Drava into Austria at Lavamünd, the rear units conducting a fighting retreat against Bulgarian forces pressing behind.[5] All that was left now for General von Pannwitz was to arrange honourable surrender terms with the British. Only from them could fair treatment be expected.

Whilst the Cossacks were withdrawing into Austria from the east, the British were driving up as fast as they could from the south. The intention was to gain as much ground as possible before meeting the Red Army. The day after VE Day found the 8th Army commander, General Sir Richard McCreery, on the Italo-Austrian frontier. From the north he received continual reports of fighting between the Cossacks and Yugoslav partisans. Anxious to restore order without bloodshed, the General sent for an SOE officer, well known to the Yugoslavs. This was Major Charles Villiers, who had had a long and warm association with Tito's partisans in Yugoslavia. Disabled by typhoid, he had set off on a 200-mile trek through the mountains to the sea, accompanied by Tito's son, who had lost an arm. A British plane had flown in to rescue them and brought them safely to Italy. McCreery felt he had just the man to appeal to the Yugoslavs, and gave him the brief order: 'Your Jugs won't stop fighting; go and see about it.'

As it happened, Villiers never spoke to the 'Jugs' on this occasion. He tied a white sheet over his jeep and set out westwards from Klagenfurt, looking for signs of trouble. It was the Cossacks he came upon first, in open country between Völkermarkt and Wolfsberg. At their first vedettes he enquired for the *Herr General*, and was directed onwards until he came to a farmhouse which formed a temporary HQ. There he was ushered in, to find General von Pannwitz and some of his senior officers gathered round a table. Charles Villiers, in General McCreery's name, demanded their surrender. Von Pannwitz explained that he was agreeable to this, but asked for certain stipulations to be included in the terms. The principal of these was that they should not on any account be surrendered to the Bolsheviks. Major Villiers curtly replied that he had received explicit instructions to offer no conditions: the Cossack Corps was simply to surrender to the British 8th Army. Faced by *force majeure*, the General agreed, it being arranged that he should bring his troops in to the nearest British formation and surrender their arms.

The whole scene was reminiscent of a more picturesque age of warfare. From outside came a jingle of bridle-chains, as the Cossack sentry's horse stamped its hoof on the flagstones. Through the low windows mounted squadrons could be seen trotting past, whilst inside German and Russian officers in furred *shapkas* argued with the impassive English Guards officer. The conversation moved on to a more social key as General von Pannwitz suddenly recalled that he and Charles Villiers had met last at a house-party on the Bismarcks' East Prussian estate. He pressed the Englishman to dine at their mess; Villiers declined politely and left, having agreed that the Cossacks should ride into the British lines next day.

General von Pannwitz was clearly disturbed by this encounter. Though Major Villiers was a gentleman like himself, his attitude had been formal and unbending, and his reported instructions that no surrender terms were to be offered aroused a feeling of unease. Did the British fully appreciate the position adopted by the Cossacks? He resolved to make another attempt to clarify the situation, and sent off an emissary to establish further contact. This was his Chief of Staff, Colonel von Renteln. Von Renteln, a former officer of the Russian Imperial Guards, had served in General Yudenitch's White Army during the advance on Petrograd in 1919. It was in that campaign that he had come to know the then Major Harold Alexander, commanding the anti-Bolshevik Baltic Landeswehr. He had maintained these friendly relations, meeting Alexander at his club in London between the wars. If von Renteln could meet Alexander, he could ensure that the British did not make any unfortunate mistake through ignorance of the Cossack predicament.[6]

North of the Cossack encampment, armoured cars of the most advanced units of the British 6th Armoured Division had raced ahead in an attempt to beat the Red Army into Graz. Colonel Andrew Horsbrugh-Porter, of the 27th Lancers, had set up his headquarters at Wolfsberg, where the mountain road winds upwards over the Pack

Sattel to Köflach and Graz. It was there that he witnessed the arrival of von Renteln and his escort.

One day, a cavalcade headed by the most wonderful, tall, good-looking aristocratic gentleman with an enormous white Cossack hat came, and in perfect English said that he surrendered. He had an escort of Cossack troops. I instantly formed a tremendous liking for this old-fashioned, cosmopolitan gentleman. He said he understood that Alexander was Commander-in-Chief, and that 'if I can see Alex, everything will be all right', or words to that effect.

The two cavalrymen chatted further, and the Russian was then sent back to Divisional Headquarters in a staff car.[7]

General von Pannwitz had no time to await the outcome of this mission if he were to fulfil the agreement made with Major Villiers. Next day (10 May) he rode towards the British lines, encountering their outpost just east of Völkermarkt. He was taken before the commanding officer, Major Henry Howard of the 1st King's Royal Rifle Corps. Howard was anxious to have the Cossacks disarmed and safely out of the way as soon as possible. Yugoslav partisans were setting up posts ominously far inside the Austrian frontier, and in addition he wanted the roads cleared for the British advance on Graz. The Yugoslavs were demanding that the Cossacks should be surrendered to them, but were not anxious to come too near whilst the Cossacks were still armed. What if the British were to disarm them, and *then* hand them over? Henry Howard realised that unless the Cossacks were quickly moved out of the picture, his battalion might well find itself not only prevented from continuing its march but also involved in a nasty three-sided battle. He told von Pannwitz to bring in his corps next morning. Captain Julian Wathen remembers driving back to the Cossack camp with the General in an open staff car. He was entertained in the mess, where the German officer expressed concern for their horses. It was all very gentlemanly.

Next morning the first Cossack unit rode in and began piling their arms in an open field just outside Völkermarkt. General von Pannwitz, with Charles Villiers at his side, watched impassively. As each regiment completed the task it resumed the march westwards to sites detailed by British Corps Command.[8]

But the trouble was not over yet. Tito's partisans recovered their courage when they learned that the Cossacks were disarmed, and began sniping at them from a distance, and stealing their horses. In Major Howard's laconic phraseology: 'It was necessary to use carriers to herd the now stampeding Cossacks back through the Tito troops and to threaten the latter with tanks if they continued to behave like children.'

The disarmed Cossacks rode on in their regiments through Völker-markt, their route being westwards through St. Veit.[9] In case of molestation by the irrepressible 'Jugs', Major Howard stationed armoured-car patrols at intervals to protect the column. For three days a seemingly endless stream of horsemen passed by. Lieutenant Garry Maufe was a subaltern detailed to man one of the posts. He and his men were stationed by a large pond, where squadron after squadron paused to water their horses. Maufe told the riflemen with him that they were witnessing a sight which it was unlikely the world would ever see again. A faint haze of dust hung over the green May meadows, as nearly twenty thousand horses and riders came up the hill and moved on. In fact they were to meet the Cossacks again in a bare three weeks, though under different circumstances.[10]

Beyond St. Veit the Cossack Corps was directed to two separate areas to set up camp. General von Pannwitz and his staff moved north to an area around Althofen. With him went the 3rd (Kuban), 4th (Kuban), 5th (Don), 6th (Terek) and 8th (dismounted) Regiments, all except the 4th Kuban belonging to the 2nd Division. The main part of the 1st Division, comprising the 1st (Don) and 2nd (Siberian) Regiments, under Colonel Constantin Wagner, pushed on westwards and bivou-acked in the fields about Feldkirchen. The whole area was under the command of the British 6th Armoured Division.[11] Colonel James Hills of the Essex Yeomanry took control of Wagner's force, and both men got on well together. Colonel Hills used to pay frequent visits to the camp and to the small castle on the edge of the forest where Colonel Wagner lived. He was greatly impressed by their discipline and cheerful spirits.[12]

At Althofen, General von Pannwitz continued to chafe nervously over the predicament of his men. To his fellow German officers and Cossacks he appeared calm and confident. He told Colonel Wagner he thought the British would ship the Corps off to serve in Persia. But it seems clear from his actions and from British accounts that he was in reality far from confident about the situation. Von Renteln's mission had failed; he had never reached Alexander, and he rejoined the Corps at Althofen. Jeremy Pemberton, then attached to 61st Brigade HQ within the 6th Armoured Division, spent a day in May in a staff car with von Pannwitz and von Renteln inspecting the Cossack camps. Pemberton and von Renteln talked together in French, and soon dis-covered they had a friend in common: Count Benckendorff, a neigh-bour of the Pembertons' in Suffolk. Amidst this friendly talk, however, von Renteln made it clear he was under no illusions as to what the Cossacks' fate was likely to be.[13]

Privately, General von Pannwitz continued to make further efforts to save the Corps from destruction. Edward Renton was second-in-command of Charles Villiers's SOE unit, and was present at a meeting with the General and his staff at a house just north of 5th Corps Headquarters at Klagenfurt. Von Pannwitz expatiated eloquently on the fighting qualities of the Cossacks, banging his fist excitedly on the table. He implored the British to take the Corps into their service, or to pass them on to the Americans. Renton left the room to telephone Corps HQ for instructions. At the centre of all these operations was the Brigadier General Staff, Toby Low (now Lord Aldington). Low explained at length that no promises of any sort could be made, and the Cossacks must just sit tight in their valley until a decision was arrived at. Von Pannwitz cannot have returned to Althofen very heartened by this exchange, nor can it have added to his comfort when he received strong hints via Austrian contacts from the same source (Major Villiers's unit), to the effect that the German officers would do well to slip away and lie low in their homes.[14] Disguising his feelings from all around, General von Pannwitz continued attempts to contact the British authorities and put the Cossack case before them. Several times he asked Major Villiers to approach General McCreery, and on another occasion he sent one of his staff officers on a vain mission to 5th Corps HQ at Klagenfurt.[15]

These moves must have resulted from a feeling of increasing desperation. For it was only a few days after the Corps had settled down in its new cantonments that its most senior officers received an authoritative hint that what they feared might well come about. The commander of the British 6th Armoured Division, under whose control the Cossacks came, was Major-General Horatius 'Nap' Murray. A remarkable and much-loved officer, he had little time for commanders who believed their duty to consist merely in transmitting orders. 'Under such circumstances why have generals at all?' he was to comment later.

About the middle of May, Murray summoned the senior officers of the Corps to his headquarters outside Klagenfurt. Speaking in German, he told them he had reason to believe that they might be going to be sent to Russia, and advised them to consider their position seriously. He had not as yet received any orders, but the indications were there for those who chose to read them. With these emphatic words he closed the interview. Von Pannwitz and his officers left in haste, their faces pale and set.

Von Pannwitz's feelings can only be guessed at. On the one hand, there was little point in spreading despondency and panic. Any rumour authorised by himself could clearly have disastrous effects on discipline.

Nor were General Murray's words in any way final. The Cossacks clung pathetically to a belief that if they could impress the British by their order and good behaviour, this might weigh with those pondering their fate. If the camps were to break up in disorder, on the other hand, this would provide the British with every justification for adopting harsh measures. General Murray and others of his senior officers had shown clear sympathy for their prisoners, and there would be much to gain by behaving in a manner that would continue to earn them this good opinion. Unsatisfactory though it was, the only reasonable course would seem to be to keep the Corps together, whilst continuing to put out appeals to the authorities. There was a further consideration. During his two years' service with the Cossack Corps, a powerful mutual bond of loyalty had grown up between von Pannwitz and his faithful Cossacks. He felt a deep responsibility for them. Until the Corps could find asylum somewhere in the West, it was the General's duty to stay with them and look after their interests.

But he also had a separate responsibility towards his German officers, all of whom were volunteers and soldiers of exceptional quality. Despite all his appeals, the British might decide to hand over the Cossack Corps to their Soviet Allies. The Cossacks could be regarded as 'traitors', if all the circumstances were to be ignored. The German officers, however, could not by any conception be termed traitors; moreover, the Geneva Convention expressly stipulates that prisoners at the close of hostilities must be returned as speedily as possible *to their own country*. But was there not a danger that the British might include the Germans, scattered amongst their different regiments, as an integral part of the Corps—and surrender them to the Soviets too? It seems to have been considerations of this sort that prompted von Pannwitz to initiate measures to replace the Germans with native Cossack officers, and form all the supernumerary Germans into 'an all-German Regiment or Battalion'. This he proposed to the British on 25 May. Meanwhile, elements of the Cossacks were themselves demanding that their German officers should be replaced by Cossacks: some units even mutinied. Here, one can only speculate on their motives. Perhaps the continued suspense was playing on their nerves. It is possible they may have felt the British would be more understanding of the motives of an all-Russian anti-Soviet force than of one apparently composed of mercenaries under German command. They would then hope to appear more in the light of a 'third force' than as mere German auxiliaries.

However, all these desperate plans bore little substance in reality. The only result of the difference between Cossacks and Germans was to enable the British to obtain separate nominal rolls of the two groups without exciting suspicion.[16] Moreover, events were moving forward with ever-increasing momentum. The day before, Soviet and British officers had met at Wolfsberg to concert plans for the delivery of the entire Cossack Corps into Soviet hands.[17] Divisional commanders had received the final order and all that remained was to draw up logistical details necessary for the orderly transfer of so large a body of men. By the end of the month von Pannwitz's men were held by three separate commands within the 5th Corps area: 6th Armoured Division, 46th Infantry Division, and 7th Armoured Brigade. The majority had been transferred from the 6th Armoured Division responsibility to ease congestion in that region.[18]

The 46th Infantry Division, under whose control General von Pannwitz, his staff, and the majority of his Corps now lay, had already been handing over Russian former prisoners of war and slave-workers at Judenburg since 16 May,[19] and now preparations were undertaken for the sudden and swift transfer of the 15th Cossack Cavalry Corps to Soviet hands. Secrecy was essential, for 'if they had known of this plan there would have been wholesale attempts at desertion and suicide'.[20] Arrangements for their reception by the Soviet authorities were completed by 25 May, and it was stressed that (what must have been known to be untrue, or at least unsubstantiated) 'the German increment of the Cossack Corps will also be handed back, many being required for war crimes.'[21]

As a preparatory move, General von Pannwitz was informed on 26 May that he was deprived of his command of the Corps. He, 144 fellow German officers and 690 other ranks were placed under arrest, many however seizing the opportunity of escaping.[22] Von Pannwitz himself was moved from his Headquarters at Althofen, north to the little village of Mühlen. This was the first stage of the journey to Judenburg. According to Cossack sources British officers offered him the chance of being released, or of conniving in his escape. He refused, declaring that he had been with the Cossacks in good times, and would not desert them in bad.[23] This is confirmed by the senior surviving officer of the Cossack Corps, Colonel Wagner. He informed me that, immediately after receiving such a warning himself, he telephoned the General, suggesting he escape and join the Yugoslav Royalists, the Chetniks. Von Pannwitz replied that all his officers were at liberty to make an individual choice in this matter, but that he would not now desert his Cossacks. The bonds of loyalty had been greatly strengthened by his election on 24 May as Field Ataman of the Cossacks (*Pokhodny Ataman*) —a dignity never before conferred on a foreigner. Senior British officers had attended the ceremony, though probably without being aware of its significance.[24]

On 28 May General von Pannwitz with a number of his fellow German officers was handed over to the NKVD at Judenburg.[25] There in the notorious steel-mill he met his fellow-victims, Generals Krasnov, Shkuro and Domanov. He accompanied them as far as Baden-bei-Wien, but remained behind when the Krasnovs were flown to Moscow. What trials he underwent at the hands of the NKVD in the Lubianka Gaol and elsewhere are unknown. He was, as mentioned in a previous chapter, hanged in 1947 along with Krasnov and Shkuro.[26] In this way the British Government had in essence sentenced to death without trial German officers who had been received by them as prisoners of war.

For the main body of Cossacks similar plans had been laid to those employed by the 78th Division against Domanov's Cossacks. By 25 May arrangements were completed.[27] Captain Michael Frewer was at that time Intelligence Officer with HQRA at 46th Divisional Head-quarters, and remembers well the great care with which plans were drawn up. A vast fleet of three-ton trucks was assembled, each one containing a driver, co-driver and two guards armed with loaded rifles. The route chosen was barred to all other traffic and guarded at frequent intervals by troops. Five artillery regiments were detailed to provide the men and equipment. An ingenious deception plan was worked out and applied with perfect efficiency. The Cossacks were informed the night before that they were being transferred to new camps in Italy: news that was bound to cheer them, since it meant they were being moved away from any proximity to the Soviet zone. Thus they were persuaded to enter the lorries without difficulty.

For ten miles or so the trucks rumbled southwards, the Cossacks becoming ever more light at heart at the thought that they were putting an increasing distance between themselves and their enemies. But suddenly the head of the convoy swung round and began to drive furi-ously for the north. At forty to fifty m.p.h. the trucks flew past barely glimpsed groups of heavily-armed British soldiers. Panic broke out, and a rain of watches, rings, cameras—even gold teeth—and other valuables poured on to the road. Despite the precautions, one or two Cossacks were reported to have flung themselves to their deaths. And when the column finally drew up at Judenburg, there were numerous cases of Cossacks springing from the lorries, somersaulting as they did so in attempts to break their necks on falling. All this was reported back to headquarters.[28]

Another such operation for which the 46th Infantry Division was responsible was the return of a dissident Cossack regiment, which had separated itself on surrender from the rest of the Corps. The 5th Don Cossack had been the only regiment in the 15th Cavalry Corps to be commanded by a Russian. This was the well-known Colonel Ivan Kononov, who had been the first Red Army officer to come over voluntarily with his unit to the Germans. He was something of a latter-day Shkuro, being not over-scrupulous in his methods of waging war or maintaining discipline. He had amongst his staff his personal executioner, a ferocious fellow with gold earrings, half Cossack and half Greek. At a nod from Kononov this unsavoury henchman was prepared to put a 9mm bullet into anyone who displeased his colonel. At the time of the Corps's surrender to the British, however, it happened that Kononov was not with his regiment. He had been despatched as Cossack liaison officer to General Vlasov, during negotiations intended to unite the various anti-Soviet Russian units operating within or alongside the German Army. As a result Kononov escaped the fate of the other Cossacks. He went first to Munich, in the American-occupied zone, and subsequently migrated to Australia.[29]

Left in charge of the regiment was a Rittmeister Borisov, promoted to Lieutenant-Colonel. For reasons still unclear, the 'Kononov Brigade' (as the British termed it) declined to obey General von Pannwitz and his German officers, successfully insisting that they should be administered separately by the British. They camped around Klein St. Paul, and were distinguished above all the other regiments by their efficiency. Perhaps they hoped to persuade the British to exclude them from whatever fate they had in store for the remaining German-officered regiments.[30] On the evening of 27 May, Colonel Borisov was informed by a British officer that he and his officers were to assemble at 8 a.m. next morning. They were to be taken in trucks to a special camp in North Italy, where arrangements would be effected for their migration to Canada. Their suspicions lulled by repeated assurances that British honour would never permit their surrender to the Communists ... they were placed in trucks and driven under guard to Judenburg. There a list of their names was handed to an NKVD officer, and they found themselves in the infamous steel-mill. They included numerous White Russian émigrés such as Captain Anatol Petrovsky, who had left Russia in 1920, where he had fought in the army of Britain's ally, General Wrangel. He later returned to the West after eleven terrible years in the slave-camps, his health totally ruined.[31]

On 30 May the rest of the regiment, unaware of their officers' fate, rode down from their camps in the hills to a wired camp at Brückl. Colonel Denys Worrall, commanding a battalion of the Durham Light Infantry responsible for setting up and guarding the cage, clearly recalls the groups of thirty or so ('fine-looking chaps') riding jauntily into camp. That night two powerful searchlights were trained on the barbed-wire and tents within. Exultant at their coming journey to a free life, the Cossacks stayed up all night, singing and dancing. They had an excellent band, and the catchy tunes were soon being taken up and whistled by British guards outside. Next day all departed northwards, except for the band, which was retained to entertain further batches passing through during the next few days. From officers who accompanied the convoys to Judenburg, Colonel Worrall heard the usual depressing stories of officers and men (including a brigade commander) committing suicide *en route* or on arrival.[32]

Altogether, in the week following 28 May, 17,702 Cossacks (including German officers) were handed over by the 46th Infantry Division to the NKVD at Judenburg. These included 47 women, 5 children and 7 priests (at least one of the latter died in the Soviet Belsen at Karaganda).[33] A similar operation, with no recorded untoward incidents, took place to the north, in the region occupied by the independent 7th Armoured Brigade. Brigadier K. C. 'George' Cooper found himself in charge of a large and well-disciplined body of Cossacks. Their camp was organised entirely by themselves, and included a school, hospital, orchestra, etc. After a fortnight, Brigadier Cooper received the Corps Order to hand over all these men to the Soviets. He was present at the discussion where the use of deception was decided upon. In his case the Russians were told they were going to a new camp in Italy. They were completely hoodwinked, and an elaborate charade ensured that they did not discover the truth until the last moment. They were driven southwards, and then swung round in a long detour northwards to Judenburg. It was not until the prisoners detected the first faint light of dawn appearing over the mountains on their right that they realised that something was amiss. It was too late: the trucks tore on towards Judenburg. Apparently resigned and hopeless, the Cossacks debussed at their destination and walked slowly in file across the bridge.

There was a great deal of ill-feeling amongst the men of the 7th Armoured Brigade over this operation. It was not just that there had been women and children amongst the victims. All ranks had had particular opportunity to learn something of the nature of Communism. The Brigade had fought alongside the 2nd Polish Corps in Italy, and officers and men had received too many first-hand accounts of Soviet savagery to be able to discount them in the manner of a Sartre or an O'Casey. More recently they had themselves taken over an area occupied by Soviet troops. There they had seen evidence of the barbaric nature of Red Army troops in action. No objects of beauty or aids to a civilised life had escaped vandalisation. What could not be smashed to pieces or put to the flames was covered with excreta. A favourite occupation of these new barbarians was to take priceless chandeliers found in old houses and castles, and drop them from the uppermost windows. Wooden lavatory seats had been wrenched off their hinges and despatched by officers to the Motherland—to be used as picture-frames.[34]

Some sources claim that not all Cossacks were handed over to the NKVD at Judenburg. An officer, apparently from the 15th Cossack Cavalry Corps, later described to a fellow-inmate of the camp of GULAG at Vorkuta how he and others who had volunteered to fight for the Allies in the East had been despatched *in an aeroplane* to Soviet territory. This occurred just before the main handovers.[35] Whilst there seems no reason to doubt the story, it is hard to see what lay behind this special treatment. No record of such an operation is preserved in available British documents.

It remains only to describe the transfer of the Cossacks held in the Sixth Armoured Divisional area. As will be recalled, on 22 May the majority of Cossacks from the 6th Armoured Division were transferred to the control of the 46th Infantry Division, but the 6th Armoured retained control of part of the 1st Division, commanded by Colonel Constantin Wagner.

At 9 a.m. on 26 May Major-General Horatius Murray, the officer commanding the 6th Armoured, held a conference to establish procedure for the handover of this body. This conference took place at Schloss Osterwitz, the home of Count Khevenhüller-Metsch and at that time also the Headquarters of Murray's Artillery Commander, Brigadier Clive Usher, who had been placed in charge of the Cossacks. Up to now, General Murray had made it abundantly clear to all concerned that, if Cossacks succeeded in escaping, he would not be overmuch concerned. Like his near-namesake Horatio Nelson, he knew when to turn a blind eye. Now, however, explicit orders had been received, and he could do no less than see them obeyed. He explained to the unit commanders present what was planned, and outlined the proposed measures of caging and transport.

At once it became clear that the officers of the 6th Armoured Division would not react in the generally pliant manner of those in the 78th Division. General Murray's whole demeanour was expressive of considerable distaste, and many officers present were clearly dismayed and affronted at the instructions issued. Colonel Robin Rose Price, of the 3rd Welsh Guards, openly remonstrated with the General for some time, and it was only after a prolonged and at times heated discussion that Rose Price acquiesced. General Murray was as disgusted as he was, but was not prepared to flout the order openly. Moreover, he felt that any Cossacks with a strong desire to escape could have done so, following his hint to the German officers. Until late in the afternoon those present at the conference travelled over the ground, planning the proposed moves in detail. It would be a tricky operation, and preparation and implementation would have to be meticulous. It was not until six o'clock that Colonel Rose Price returned to his Battalion Headquarters at Rosegg—to order his men 'to carry out the most ignoble task which I could ever given them'.[36]

He was not the only officer present who was dismayed at the task lying ahead. At the same time that Colonel Rose Price was glumly issuing his instructions, Brigadier Usher rode out on his horse from the Schloss Osterwitz to visit Colonel Wagner at Sirnitz. There he informed the Cossack officer that he was to prepare his men for transfer to wired camps at Weitensfeld. When asked how long this would take, Colonel Wagner said he would need from 5 a.m. to 8 p.m. The roads were narrow and winding in the mountains, and 10,000 men with horses could not be moved swiftly under these conditions. Usher nodded, mounted his horse, and rode off. Wagner issued preliminary orders, and two hours later Usher returned to see how matters were progressing. Wagner gave him a report and then, gazing at him frankly, asked a pointed question:

'Herr General, the first step is the march into wired camps, I take it? The second is our surrender to the Soviets, and the third is our transportation to Siberia?' To which Brigadier Usher replied enigmatically:

'We are both soldiers—true?'

'Jawohl, Herr General!'

'Then you know we must obey our political superiors.'

About this time Wagner also received a visit from the sympathetic Colonel Hills. 'I remember him asking me if they were being handed over to the Russians. I could only say that I was not at liberty to say, but of course it might be so—but anyhow he had obviously guessed what was happening. I gave him a couple of trout which I had caught in the Gurk that afternoon and departed.'[37]

Colonel Wagner now telephoned General von Pannwitz, telling him the disastrous news and urging an escape to join the Yugoslav Chetniks. Von Pannwitz said that he would remain with his Cossacks, but added that all Germans with the Corps were now absolved of their oath of allegiance and could decide for themselves what course to take. Wagner's own mind was already made up. Once in Soviet hands, he was certain that the Germans would at once be separated from the

Cossacks and sent to different camps. In any case, what help could the German officers afford their Cossacks in captivity? Colonel Wagner was resolved on escape.

The senior Russian in his regiment was a Major Vladimir Ostrovsky, and to him Wagner explained what was happening. Visibly agitated, he declared his own intention of escaping and urged Ostrovsky and his fellows to do likewise. He then summoned his Tartar servant and, bidding an emotional farewell to Ostrovsky, rode off into the mountains. Recalling memories of the Red Indian tales of Karl May he had read in his youth, he and his follower rode along stone-filled streambeds and through the darkest recesses of the forests to throw off any British pursuit. After a long and adventurous journey, they succeeded in crossing over to Bavaria and the safety of the American-occupied zone.

That night many soldiers, German, Cossack and British, were the prey of gathering doubts and fears. Attached to Colonel Hills's Headquarters as liaison officer from Colonel Wagner was a young German, Count von Stohlberg. On the night of 27 May, Hills

> was working fairly late in my office with the adjutant when he announced that young Stohlberg wanted to see me. I said show him in and Count von Stohlberg came in with his saddle over his arm and said 'Colonel, I understand we are being handed over to the Russians tomorrow. They will cut our throats, but I should like you to have my saddle because I know how keen you are on horses and riding'—and he saluted and went out.

Despite this, Hills was glad to discover later that Stohlberg escaped after all.[38]

Amongst the rank-and-file Cossacks, who were as yet unaware of what lay in store for them, there still reigned that atmosphere of carefree happiness they had known since their reception by the British early in the month. Lieutenant Garry Maufe of the 1st King's Royal Rifle Corps was detailed to take his squadron of bren-gun carriers to a Cossack encampment and prepare them for the next day's march. That night no one slept: liquor appeared from somewhere, and a party started up that lasted all night. Garry Maufe found himself at first light with an aching head and limbs. The drink had extorted its toll and further inspired the young Englishman to try his luck on a Cossack steed. All around galloped the Cossacks, singing, shouting and performing fantastic feats of agility in their saddles. Occasionally there was a burst of laughter as a Cockney rifleman was abruptly dislodged by a mutinous horse. At dawn the party ended as a somewhat pallid and fragile Lieutenant Maufe formed the Cossacks up in line. Escorted by his carriers, they moved down the road until they were handed over to a relief unit.[39]

The route was heavily guarded by infantry, bren-gun carriers and scout cars. Scout cars of the Derbyshire Yeomanry picketed the route, and even despatched a squadron some fifty miles into the hills to recapture a group of escaped Cossacks.[40] Their destination was a large wired camp prepared by the Welsh Guards at Weitensfeld. As all German officers seemed to have disappeared, Major Ostrovsky now found himself the senior Cossack officer present. At the cage he reported to the British CO, Colonel Rose Price. A remarkably polyglot conversation ensued, conducted in a mixture of French and German, and aided by an American-born Croat officer standing by. Colonel Rose Price explained that Cossack officers must move into a small cage, whilst their men passed under guard into a larger one. When Ostrovsky asked what was to happen to them all, Rose Price replied that he did not know; but the Croat interposed hurriedly in his native tongue (which Ostrovsky understood) that he was certain they were all to be betrayed to the Soviets. Ostrovsky requested and received permission to return some way along the route in order to pass on the Colonel's directions to the Cossacks. Rose Price assented, and the Major drove back in his staff car alongside the mounted regiments. To different officers he passed on the dread news, urging them to escape with as many of their men as possible. He was rewarded by seeing individuals and groups slipping away into the trees. But in general the route was so heavily guarded and the column so far advanced that it was impossible to halt the flood. Ostrovsky returned to the cage designated for the officers, and with a heavy heart watched the densely-packed column disgorge itself into the camp area, as the troops dismounted and moved into their cages.

That night in the officers' cage all were in a terrible state of despair. The news had spread, though not yet officially confirmed by the British. Few slept, though all stayed within their tents to evade the brilliant glare of searchlights trained on them all night long. Some officers talked of escape but, apart from the obvious difficulties, all eventually agreed that it was not possible to desert the Cossack other ranks in the neighbouring cage. At 6 a.m. a British sergeant appeared, swinging an ominous-looking bludgeon, and ordered the officers to get up. They at once refused, declaring they would not obey until they were told what was to happen to them. The sergeant declared his ignorance, and fetched his major, who likewise said he had no idea where they were to go. Eventually Major Bruce Goff sought higher authority, and returned to announce that their worst fears were confirmed: they were to return to the Soviet Union.

This was in accordance with the declared policy of General Murray, who flatly refused to have anything to do with what General Keightley termed 'use of deception'. Thus, what in plain terms would be called lying occurred in the 78th and 46th Divisional areas, but not in the 6th Armoured.

At Major Goff's words a furious outcry arose, the Cossack officers indignantly pointing out that they were prisoners of the British, and not of the Bolsheviks. They explained to the apparently uncomprehending Englishman that they would certainly be murdered by the Soviets, and probably tortured beforehand into the bargain. Finally they demanded that the British shoot them then and there rather than let the Soviets kill them later in more brutal fashion.

Appalled by this unexpected outburst, Major Goff backed away from the shouting crowd of Cossacks, and, like his sergeant, left the cage for further instruction. When he returned, it was with a group of high-ranking British officers. At their head was Colonel Rose Price; Major Ostrovsky in addition recognised Colonel James Hills, who gave him a sympathetic look. Outside the barbed wire a fleet of lorries was standing by. Colonel Rose Price explained that he had received strict orders to return all the Cossacks to Russia: orders he was obliged to carry out. At the same time he pointed out that Marshal Stalin had reportedly granted an amnesty to all who had supported the German cause, and suggested they would be wise to go peaceably and take advantage of the offer.

At this cries of ridicule arose from amongst the Cossacks. Many had lived in Soviet Russia and knew well how much worth to attach to the word of a Communist. Again came demands for the British to shoot them forthwith, or at least to give them each a revolver and a single cartridge. The Colonel rejected these demands and, addressing Major Ostrovsky, requested him to issue the order to his fellow-officers to board the lorries. Ostrovsky refused outright and, turning to his companions, told them he would not on any account obey the order, and that they were at liberty to act as they decided.

Sizing up the situation, Colonel Rose Price issued a new order. Those Cossacks who were prepared to obey should move in a body to the right, and those who insisted on taking the consequences of disobedience should move to the left. Faced with the appalling choice of being killed on the spot, or being permitted to defer their deaths to a later and very likely more painful time, many Cossacks became understandably distraught. A girl present, the widow of a regimental medical officer, began to shriek hysterically that they were cursed: wherever they went death and persecution awaited them. Flinging about her luggage, she clambered into the nearest lorry and crouched there sobbing. Others, a majority of those present, followed their Divisional priests into the trucks. A group of about fifty, led by Major Ostrovsky, stood fast. A certain *Essaul* (Captain) Busch ran back to the group remaining, shouting: 'Gentlemen! Let's go: it is better to die by a Russian bullet than an English one; besides, we shall show the Bolsheviks that Cossack officers are not afraid!' But he was repulsed by his disgusted friends, who were determined to brave matters out on the spot.

Those who had voluntarily entered the lorries were driven off about half a mile, where they drew up and waited. About half a dozen lorries remained in readiness by the cage, but Ostrovsky's men stood fast in a rank. They bade each other farewell and were blessed by a priest amongst them. They then followed the latter's suggestion that they should all sit on the ground. A 'firing-squad' of Welsh Guardsmen had drawn up before them, and as the priest, Father Feodor Vlasenko, pointed out, death was more likely to be instantaneous if they were hit in a crouching position. Minutes passed; it was a moment of blind terror. As one of the Cossacks present related later:

> The sten-guns were levelled at us; one more minute, and good-bye to life! Feelings connected with the approach of violent death were not new to me, because back in 1918 I had been led out by the Cheka [Lenin's secret police] seven times to a firing-squad. You might think that one becomes accustomed to such a situation, but in fact that is far from being the case. Each time had as immediate an impact as the last, each time the whole of one's life flashes before one's mind in an instant, each time one loses all contact with reality, which appears as a dream, quite unreal.

The Cossacks stood pale and unyielding; Major Ostrovsky bore a half-contemptuous smile on his face. A priest comforted his seventeen-year-old daughter, Jenia.

Colonel Rose Price waited until it was clear that it would take more than this charade to break the Cossacks' nerves. Sending a messenger across to tell the officer in charge of the 'firing squad' to order his men to ground their arms, he came forward and reiterated his command to the Cossacks to enter the trucks. At the same time an armoured vehicle moved into position outside the wired fence, a score or so yards from the Cossacks. Before they could realise what was happening, a gigantic billowing jet of oily flame shot from a barrel in the machine's turret. For several seconds it enveloped a section of the wheat field before it, everything inflammable in its path being ignited and devoured in a moment. The intense heat glowed on the Cossacks; then the jet died back, leaving a long scorched and blackened track before it. The Cossacks had witnessed a demonstration of a 'Wasp' flame-thrower. So fierce had been the first leap forward of the blazing squirt that two

Welsh Guardsmen standing on guard nearby were nearly hit by it. No more hideous sight could be imagined than the sudden flare of this monstrous destructive instrument and even the bravest Cossacks were gripped with terror; the two girls with them were completely overcome. Lieutenant Popov, an emigrant Russian from Yugoslavia, lost his nerve and collapsed to the ground with a terrible scream. He appeared to be having some sort of fit, and was removed at once and placed in one of the lorries.

At this psychological moment, Colonel Rose Price told the Cossacks that he had changed his mind: they would not be shot, but would instead be bound—by force, if necessary—and placed on the trucks whether they liked it or not. A file of soldiers was marched up, each one bearing a bludgeon in one hand and coils of rope and electric cable in the other.

Despite his fear, Major Ostrovsky could not restrain his indignation. The British had just received incontrovertible proof that Cossacks would face death rather than return to Soviet Russia, and yet they were still prepared to continue with their act of betrayal. He got up off the ground and strode over to the Colonel. With the Croat officer providing a stumbling interpretation, he cursed the British in a mixture of five or six languages. He castigated their childish ignorance of the nature of Marxism, their mercenary shopkeeper's values, the despicable nature of the betrayal they were now effecting, and the national hypocrisy which prated so much of democracy, honour and decency—and yet crawled to offer up human sacrifice to the Marxist Moloch.

Just as he was in the midst of relieving his overwrought feelings in this way, Ostrovsky heard one of the Cossacks behind him shout out that it might after all be better to go voluntarily and unbound, if they were in any case to have no choice in the matter. Ostrovsky stopped in mid-flow: there was sense in that cry. For unbound they might yet escape en route, or at worst commit suicide. Saluting the Colonel, he abruptly announced that they would now obey the command and enter the trucks. Turning to his officers, he issued the new order, pointing out his reasons at the same time. They obeyed, clambering onto the waiting lorries. Major Goff saluted Ostrovsky, said a few words and then escorted him out of the camp.

Where their CO was being taken, the Cossack officers did not know; at least one was convinced he had been removed to be shot for his insolence to the English Colonel. But their minds were racing feverishly in consideration of their own predicament. They were at long last in the trucks; in a moment they would set off, and the next stop an hour or so later would be at the handover point. The hangmen and torturers of the NKVD would already have been apprised of their coming and be setting about preparations. A Cossack officer began to conduct a halting conversation in German with the young British tommies on guard in his lorry. After giving them cigarettes, he broached the subject of Stalin's despotism in Russia. At the mention of the Generalissimo's name, the Guardsmen grinned and cried 'Stalin *gut*'. But when the Cossack interposed that, on the contrary, he was a bandit they smiled and nodded in agreement again. After one or two further exchanges on this subject, the Cossack (his name was Sukalo) boldly asked how he and his companions in the lorry could avoid their fate. Without any hesitation, the British soldiers at once suggested escape. Pointing out that a few miles ahead the convoy would have to ascend a very steep hill at a crawling pace, they recommended that the officers should spring out at that point and run off under the trees.

'Of course, we shall fire at you—but comfortably over your heads.'

It seems that all ranks in the 6th Armoured Division regarded the whole business with distaste and contempt.

Fortified by a resolve to profit by this chivalrous advice, Sukalo sustained reviving hopes as the column began to jolt on its way. But, soon after its start, the column abruptly came to an unexplained halt. What on earth was happening? Thirty minutes ticked by. From under the tarpaulin awning Sukalo could see only the next lorry, with a glimpse of open meadows and the wired camp beyond. The British soldiers smoked their cigarettes and chatted indifferently. Such halts and starts were nothing to them; to the Cossacks every unexplained development brought fresh hopes and fears. In the night they had drawn up a petition protesting at their proposed betrayal. Could this have unexpectedly have borne fruit? Could Field-Marshal Alexander, 'with his Russian wife', have relented or intervened? But perhaps they were awaiting escorting troops who would make the proposed escape impossible. Suddenly there was the sound of voices raised in excited discussion approaching from the rear. Lorry doors slammed, and the voices drew nearer. Finally, a group of British officers came up to Sukalo's truck and peered in. With a sudden surge of hope, the Cossack saw that amongst the new arrivals stood a smiling Major Ostrovsky.

Major Goff had explained earlier that, as Ostrovsky was now pre-pared to co-operate with the British authorities, they would permit him to travel to the Soviet lines in his own staff-car. Accompanied by his Cossack chauffeur, servant, and faithful terrier 'Karl Ivanovich', Ostrovsky jumped into the Volkswagen. As no British soldier present could speak Russian, the Cossack Major could speak freely with his companions. After a brief discussion, it was determined to seize the first opportunity offered, and drive their vehicle over a precipice or into a river. Better suicide now than a lingering death later. With hearts beating but unshaken in their resolve, they began to start up the motor. But it would not start, even with the cheerful assistance of a few hefty Welsh Guardsmen. Major Goff and Colonel Rose Price, who were standing nearby, now came forward: the Cossack soldiers were ordered to be taken to join the main column of prisoners, whilst Major Goff took Ostrovsky aboard his own jeep.

The unforeseen delay had raised his spirits a little, but now as they sped along the highway, Ostrovsky thought of his mother in Germany and commended his soul to the Almighty. But even as depressing thoughts began to seize hold of his imagination, he and those with him heard from around the bend of the road behind them the sound of a motor-hooter insistently blaring. Puzzled, Major Goff ordered his driver to pull in to the side and wait. As they drew up, a British officer in shirt-sleeves on a motor-cycle roared up alongside, sprang off and ran over to the jeep. Panting with exertion, he blurted out some message, evidently urgent, to the Major. Goff listened, gave an order to his driver, and then the jeep, accompanied by the motor-cycle, swung round and tore back the way it had come. What on earth was happening? Ostrovsky was entirely bewildered, as they raced, minutes later, back into the camp at Weitensfeld. A crowd of British officers and men were shouting and gesticulating in evident agitation. Ostrovsky's jeep was parked under the shade of a tree, where an officer approached him with tea, biscuits and cigarettes, indicating as he left that these were to help the Cossack steady his nerves. Once again on that extraordinary day (29 May) Ostrovsky felt his last moment had come: they must be about to shoot him. The same British officer who had stopped and brought back the jeep then came up with a document, requesting that Ostrovsky put his signature to it. He guessed this must be a final formality before his execution. Something in his manner must have expressed this conviction, for the British officer smilingly assured Ostrovsky that he evidently misunderstood the nature of what was happening.

'You are saved, and must fill in all your particulars on this form!'

Utterly bewildered, Ostrovsky asked what was to happen to his friends, now sitting in the waiting convoy of lorries. Once again arose an excited outcry from the British, and a senior officer stepped forward to explain.

'You are all our friends, White Russians who left the Soviet Union before 1938 and so not liable to extradition. So now come and write down the names of all your friends.'

Now Ostrovsky understood that he really was saved. He sprang joyfully out of the jeep and strode with the party of British officers out on to the highway. There stood the long column of waiting trucks. As they approached the rear, Ostrovsky called out in meaning tones to the expectant faces peering out: 'Friends! You all came out of Russia at the same time as me!'

To each of the six rear lorries the party came in turn. At each one the same questions were asked, and copies of the same form produced for signature. Major Ostrovsky continued to convey by various hints and gestures what was the answer to give: viz., that they were émigrés who had fled abroad before the war, and so could not be regarded as traitors to Soviet Russia. The British officer in charge of this screening procedure clearly understood Russian and warned the Major to desist—at the same time making it very clear that he would continue to turn a blind eye to the evasion. From the second lorry emerged the pale and tortured face of poor Popov, the officer who had been driven demented by the horror of the flame-thrower. An old officer of the Tsar who had, after the Revolution, served in the French Foreign Legion, he found the strain too much. Shrieking incoherently, he was borne off to an ambulance.

The 'screening' that followed was quite perfunctory, Ostrovsky bestowing his hints freely, and the British officers conducting the enquiry evidently content not to probe very far. Major George Druzhakin can remember today the whole exchange verbatim. The interrogating officer came up to him and asked him where he lived before the war. When told 'France', he asked Druzhakin a series of questions in French about the geography of the streets around the Place d'Italie, where the Cossack had lived. Able to answer these satisfactorily (his story was of course true), Druzhakin was asked further where all his fellows came from.

'They are all old émigrés, like me.'

'But what about these youngsters, some of whom cannot have been born at the time of the Revolution?'

Many were in fact youths who had fled from the USSR in the war, but Major Druzhakin explained that they were the younger generation of émigrés, born abroad in Yugoslavia. Fortunately the young men had picked up enough words of Serbo-Croat during their campaigning to be able to convince the not unsympathetic interrogator. In the end only three, apparently through obtuseness, admitted to being Soviet citizens. They were transferred to a truck in the further section of the convoy, which contained all those who had, under pressure, entered the trucks 'voluntarily'.

The interrogating officer blew a piercing blast on a whistle (George Druzhakin can still hear it shrieking in his ears), and the engines of the forward lorries began to roar. As they moved off, some Cossack officers in the rear trucks raised a pitiful cry that they too were old émigrés. But the officer in charge yelled back that they had volunteered by entering the trucks, and must go back. The agonised faces were glimpsed for a moment, and then hidden by a turn in the road. Many were indeed old émigrés. They were now bound for the SMERSH interrogation centre at Graz, and the death-camps of Kemerovskaya Oblast, near Tomsk in Siberia.

The party of fifty officers thus released returned to Weitensfeld camp with a mixture of emotions: jubilation at their inexplicable last-minute reprieve, lamentation for their departed comrades, and deep suspicion that they might yet not be safe. But back in the cage they received firm assurances that nothing could now be done to compel their surrender to the Soviets. That night, when George Druzhakin came to remove his cap, he found that the extraordinary stress he had been under had caused all his hair to fall out. Next day they were taken south and brought to a camp where, to the astonishment of many, they found thousands of Russians of the old emigration. The commanding officer, Colonel Rogozhin, explained that he had extracted from the British assurances that all in this camp at Klein St. Veit were safe from return. They were not returned, and were all freed at a later date to find work and homes in the West.[41]

There remained the four thousand or so Cossack other ranks in their cage. The Revd T. M. H. Richards, then Chaplain of the Welsh Guards, remembers vividly his visits to comfort them in their adversity. To the enthusiastic gatherings of little children he distributed chocolates. Many of their elders were men of remarkable dignity and physical presence; to some (presumably old émigrés) Richards could speak in English. Next day they were loaded 'without incident' on to trucks and entrained at Gurk railway station further down the valley. By three o'clock in the afternoon of 30 May all, save some grooms left to look after the horses, had departed for Judenburg.[42] The prisoners were escorted as far as that town by British armoured cars. Major Warre of the 27th Lancers visited the Soviet control point at Judenburg, where he was told by a Red Army (or NKVD) officer that all the Cossack officers would be shot and that the men, if they worked, might receive some food.[43]

As already indicated, the oblique hints and warnings given to the Cossacks in the 6th Armoured Divisional area had resulted in the disappearance of all the German officers and other ranks held in the area, together with a large number of Cossacks. In addition there was the party headed by Major Ostrovsky who had been reprieved at Weitensfeld. Finally, Brigadier Usher had declined, unlike Brigadier Musson at Lienz, to order the forcible return of women; a party of these was released.[44] At Judenburg the NKVD was beside itself with fury when it found how far below the expected total the day's haul had fallen, and sent an outraged complaint to General Murray. General Murray held a conference that evening to discuss the matter. The 1st Battalion of the Rifle Corps was ordered to conduct a search of the area for Cossack fugitives. As Major Howard had only 700 men under his command with which to search a vast area of trackless mountain and forest, he demurred.

'How many men would you need, then?' asked the General.

'About 20,000,' replied Major Howard. General Murray's eyes twinkled.

'Well, do the best you can,' he murmured.

Major Howard's men eventually roped in about a dozen from the missing thousands. No reproach came either from the Soviets or from General Murray. The latter was in fact far from displeased, and when Colonel Hills reported the losses to Brigadier Usher, he was surprised to be informed that Usher 'was really delighted that a number had got away and not to worry'.[45]

This narrative has dwelt at length on the fate of the relatively small number of Cossacks held by the 6th Armoured Division, and some readers may find that the reprieve of a mere 50 Cossacks out of 50,000 Russians handed over to the NKVD from Austria was nothing very great. However, the incident bears a significance far beyond the numbers involved, for it shows that an alternative course might well have been feasible. Had such a course been adopted, at least some, and probably all, of the old émigrés so unjustly handed over might have been saved as were Ostrovsky and his friends.

I I

Interlude:
An Unsolved Mystery

On 26 May, two days before the Cossack officers were lured to Spittal, a Foreign Office official had confirmed the policy of handing over to the Soviets 'all of them who are Soviet citizens'. The wording of the text was precise and significant: '. . . all persons who are Soviet citizens under British law must be repatriated and . . . any person who is not (repeat not) a Soviet citizen under British law must not (repeat not) be sent back to the Soviet Union unless he expressly desires to be so.'[1]

The definition of a 'Soviet citizen' was: 'a person born or resident within the pre 1 Sep 39 boundaries of Russia (who had not acquired another nationality—or a NANSSEN passport, which would render the subject Stateless) . . .'[2]

This definition correctly excluded from Soviet citizenship the millions of Russians who had left Russia at the time of the Revolution and Civil War, who had never lived under the Soviet Government and clearly could not be regarded as its subjects. These were termed 'old émigrés', to distinguish them from the 'new émigrés', i.e. persons who had been Soviet citizens and escaped subsequently from the USSR. Without exception, the 'old émigrés' were either stateless or had foreign citizenship. No one claimed that such people, though wholly Russian, could be regarded as Soviet citizens. General Vasiliev, of the Soviet Repatriation Commission, defined Soviet citizens as: 'All those who before capture or transportation were citizens of one of the Soviet Republics', declaring at the same time that only such were in consequence liable for repatriation.[3] No old émigré could of himself assert Soviet citizenship; as a Soviet official explained: 'The general policy of the Soviet Government is clear. Any Russian can present a formal request for Soviet citizenship. This is no simple matter. Soviet citizenship is not granted lightly.'[4]

The British Government made clear this distinction from the first. Within a few days of the first Russian prisoners being brought back from the Normandy beach-heads, the Foreign Office laid down that repatriation 'arrangements would not apply to persons of Soviet [*i.e.* Russian] nationality who are not Soviet citizens', defining this as implying persons who held 'other than Soviet passports or [held] Nansen certificates . . .'[5] Such was the advice of Patrick Dean, and this was the definition supplied by the Foreign Office to the United States State Department.[6] Christopher Warner minuted that 'we must not include in our figures émigré Russians such as would have Nansen passports',[7] and the Foreign Office standpoint was clearly established: 'Since . . . Soviet Government have only asked for and are only entitled to the return of Soviet citizens we cannot ignore any case which is brought directly to our knowledge that any person awaiting repatriation is not a Soviet citizen.'[8]

Thus, in pursuance of this policy, émigré Russians in Rome were reassured of their immunity from repatriation.[9] In March 1945 General Ratov attempted to smuggle a White Russian on board an Odessa-bound vessel. This was prevented by the British authorities, and the man turned out to be stateless, having fought under Baron Wrangel in the Civil War and lived in France for twenty-two years. General Ratov at once renounced any claim on him, declaring the whole affair to be an error. Even Patrick Dean felt so indignant that he urged that 'we ought to protest to the Soviet Government very firmly about this case' —though he did add the Foreign Office rider, 'as soon as it is convenient to do so . . .'[10]

Yet Nikolai Krasnov and other White Russian Cossacks held in Austria *were* forcibly repatriated. Even the Soviet authorities who received them were astonished that the British should have included these people in the consignment. At Judenburg the Red Army General Dolmatov asked in surprise why the old émigrés had been handed over:[11] to his knowledge the Soviet authorities had never demanded them. NKVD interrogators were frankly incredulous. On learning that the Cossack officer before him had lived before the war in the Balkans, one exclaimed: 'Then you are an old émigré? You aren't liable to repatriation; Comrade Stalin did not claim the old émigrés. Why are you here?'[12]

A SMERSH lieutenant-colonel burst out laughing at the apparent hypocrisy of the British in thus betraying their friends.[13]

There would appear to be only two possible explanations for this remarkable divergence from normal British practice. Either a tragic blunder had taken place, or the concession resulted from a deliberate act of policy. Surprisingly little discussion has been devoted to this question. Cossack writers, it is true, frequently allude to what they naturally consider yet another act of British appeasement and treachery, but this takes us no further in deciding why it took place.

Lord Hankey, a former senior Foreign Office official, has expressed his 'very deep regret that in the heat and utter turmoil of the summer of 1945 . . . it was impossible . . . to weed out all individual cases'. There were 'some mistakes'.[14] Another suggestion is that General Domanov advised the British to include the old émigrés.[15] But the only British officers whom he could have approached know nothing of this, nor is it probable that General Keightley would have indulged Domanov's whim in this way. No other suggestions appear to have been advanced.

Whether this episode was a tragic mistake or deliberately engineered, several thousand people died or suffered terrible cruelties as a result of it, apparently unnecessarily, and it is reasonable to wish to know whose was the decision that resulted in all this misery.

The first thing to note is that, if the decision was a blunder, it was a blunder of massive proportions. The White émigrés were not a small and obscure band amongst the thousands of Cossacks held by the 78th Division. Of all the distinguished Cossack generals handed over at Judenburg, only one (Domanov) was by the British and Soviet definition a Soviet citizen. Of the remainder, Peter and Semeon Krasnov, Shkuro, Solamakhin, Kelich Ghirey, Vasiliev and many others were famous émigrés from the time of the Civil War. From statistics based on the field returns of the *Kazachi Stan*, it was later estimated that no less than sixty-eight per cent of Domanov's officers were old émigrés: that is to say, some 1,430 men.[16] Amongst other ranks, and women and children, the proportion would have been much smaller, but it would certainly be erring on the cautious side if one suggested that at least 3,000 of the Cossacks in the Drau Valley were old émigrés not liable to extradition.

Nor were they inconspicuous. Sultan Ghirey arrived at Spittal Camp in the full-dress uniform of an officer of the Tsar,[17] whilst General Kuchuk Ulagai was brandishing an Albanian passport.[18] In Peggetz Camp Major Davies was horrified at being surrounded by men and women who thrust under his nose Nansen Certificates and passports of different Western European nations.[19]

To the commanders of the 36th Infantry Brigade and the 78th Infantry Division it might well have appeared that old émigrés ran the show altogether. Virtually all the Cossack spokesmen with whom General Arbuthnott and Brigadier Musson came in contact—General Vasiliev, Nikolai Krasnov, Olga Rotova, Captain Butlerov—were unmistakable old émigrés. The presence of 'Tzarist exiles' amongst the Vlasov levies encountered was noted in Musson's Brigade War Diary.[20]

Nor were these ordinary Tsarist exiles. Most of the older ones had fought as allies of the British in the First World War. Amongst the White generals, few had been regarded by the British with as much favour as Andrei Shkuro. The legendary courage and daring of his Wolves were regarded with as much admiration by British troops as by Russians of Denikin's Army. On 2 June 1919 he was honoured with the Companionship of the Order of the Bath[21] for his gallant actions performed alongside British troops in the Intervention.[22]

Of course the world had changed since 1919. The Cossacks were no longer allies of the British. Shkuro had played a part, albeit a largely nominal one,[23] in aiding the German war effort. But the plain fact is that the texts of all British orders relating to the handover of the Cossacks emphasised time and again that those who were not Soviet citizens were to be retained. On 21 May Brigadier Musson received the first such order from General Keightley at 5th Corps Headquarters. The text is crucial. It runs:

SUBJECT: *Definition of RUSSIAN NATIONALS*
Ref conference am 21 May at MAIN 5 CORPS on transfer SOVIET NATIONALS.
1. Various cases have recently been referred to this HQ in which doubt has been raised as to whether certain fmns and groups should be treated as SOVIET NATIONALS in so far as their return to the SOVIET UNION direct from 5 CORPS is concerned. Rulings in these cases are given below.
  RUSSIAN SCHUTZKORPS (incl RUMANIANS in this fmn) will NOT be treated as SOVIET NATIONALS until further orders.
  Following will be treated as SOVIET NATIONALS:—
  ATAMAN Group
  15 COSSACK CAV CORPS (incl COSSACKS and CALMUCKS)
  Res units of Lt-Gen CHKOURO
  CAUCASIANS (incl MUSSULMEN)
2. Individual cases will NOT be considered unless particularly pressed. In these cases and in the case of appeals by further units or fmns, the following directive will apply:—
(a) Any individual now in our hands who, at the time of joining the GERMAN Forces or joining a fmn fighting with the GERMAN forces, was living within the 1938 bdy of USSR, will be treated as a SOVIET NATIONAL for the purposes of transfer.
(b) Any individual although of RUSSIAN blood who, prior to joining the GERMAN Forces, had not been in USSR since 1930, will NOT until further orders be treated as a SOVIET NATIONAL.
(c) In all cases of doubt, the invididual will be treated as a SOVIET NATIONAL.[24]

This document clearly provides that, with some exceptions, screening *should* take place where non-Soviet citizens under the definition provided drew attention to their status. This proviso gave a commanding officer some leeway in interpretation, but he was clearly not empowered to hand over persons claiming non-Soviet status, and able to produce evidence (such as a foreign passport or Nansen certificate) to support their claim. True, there were ambiguities, but these could well have been utilised by humane commanders (however literal-minded) to save many lives.

In his book, *The Last Secret*, Lord Bethell refers to this 'Definition' issued by General Keightley, and goes on to write that it 'was contradicted by his order of May 24, in which it was made clear that all officers without exception were to be sent back. It was this May 24 order which was the valid one.'[25]

A crucial paragraph in the latter runs: 'It is of the utmost importance that all the offrs and particularly senior comds are rounded up and that none are allowed to escape. The SOVIET forces consider this as being of the highest importance and will probably regard the safe delivery of the offrs as a test of BRITISH good faith.'

From this Lord Bethell argues that the return of the White émigrés was directly ordered by General Keightley, and that subordinate officers were simply obeying his clear, if unjust, instructions. But let us look at the order further. Its opening paragraph runs:

1. *Definition*
    Throughout this letter the term 'COSSACK' is taken to mean those tps of SOVIET nationality incl their Camp followers and German cadre who have fought with or cooperated with the enemy.
    For definition of SOVIET nationals see this HQ letter 405/G dated 21 May.'[26]

In other words, the 'Definition' of 21 May which excluded Cossacks authentically claiming non-Soviet citizenship from return, was not only *not* superseded: it was actually confirmed. It is hard to see how this could have been overlooked, since it was repeated in the 78th Division's operational instructions of 28 May:

1. In accordance with the terms of the YALTA agreement all SOVIET nationals in the hands of other allies are to be returned to the SOVIET UNION.
2. Throughout this order the term 'SOVIET nationals' is taken to mean those tps of SOVIET nationality incl their camp followers who have fought with or co-operated with the enemy. A definition is given in 5 CORPS letter 405/G dated 21 May handed to 36 Bde only.[27]

All these orders were seen by Brigadier Musson and his staff, but were not passed down in this form to battalion commanders. Colonel Malcolm was told by Musson that 'all must go'; at no time did he receive even a hint that many were not included in these orders.[28] Brigadier Musson's lengthy report on the whole operation, drawn up on 3 July, states, in Paragraph 4:

YALTA conference agreement
(a) It was agreed at the YALTA conference that all SOVIET nationals found in territories occupied by the ALLIES should be returned to the USSR. This fact was made known to Commander 36 Inf Bde about 20 May 45.
(b) 5 Corps letter 405/G dated 21 May 45, of which a copy is attached at Appx 'B', provided a guide as to which formations and units were to be treated as SOVIET Nationals. It is to be noted that although this directive stated that individual cases were not to be considered unless particularly pressed, such measures as were possible under the conditions prevailing at the time, were taken within 36 Inf Bde to ensure that non-SOVIET nationals were not included amongst those evacuated to the USSR authorities . . .

This last sentence is puzzling, for if it was meant to imply that screening had in fact taken place, it is obviously inaccurate. Colonel Malcolm had received no authority to screen until after the main hand-overs. It is true that Major Davies quietly excluded a few people from evacuation to Judenburg. But this was an act of individual charity, conducted without the knowledge or authority of Brigade Head-quarters. Colonel Malcolm's orders were clear: all without distinction must go back.

The point is, however, not that the 36th Brigade report of 3 July is inaccurate, but that it contains a categorical statement that Brigade Headquarters regarded the 'Definition' of 21 May as being still wholly valid, and indeed as supplying the guide to be followed in disputed cases. In the face of this, it is clearly impossible to maintain with Lord Bethell that the Order of 24 May superseded or countermanded the 'Definition' of 21 May.

If, as has been shown, Brigadier Musson's orders were so explicit in defining only Soviet citizens as liable to return, how did it come about that 3,000 or so unwilling old émigrés were also tricked or forced into travelling to the Soviet reception-point at Judenburg? Brigadier (now General) Musson has since explained to the author that he received *oral* orders from his superiors which compelled him to return all the Cossacks under his control, irrespective of nationality. These oral orders he accepted as overriding any possibility of retaining non-Soviet

Cossacks, as his written orders repeatedly stipulated. General Musson explains that 'we had all been working together for some time in active operations[29] and were used to acting on verbal orders, more often than not without written confirmation. We never thought of using written orders with a view to vindicating someone's action! I had no doubt as to what the Commanders, and their senior staff officers, were communicating to me.'

These oral instructions were clear beyond controversy:

> The overriding impression that I had then, and still have, is that all the officers had to be sent to the East. All discussions that I had with superior commanders and their staffs confirmed this and I was told on more than one occasion that the order had come from Field Marshal Alexander's headquarters and was H.M. Government policy . . . I repeat that it was made abundantly clear to me that all officers had to go . . . and that no individual screening was practical before the initial handover, certainly not in my area.

Such, General Musson now states, was the reason given to him for ignoring all the stipulations laid down for excluding non-Soviet citizens from return. He himself accepted this explanation as valid. The practical objections to conducting an official screening operation were strong. The principal difficulties were, firstly, the establishing from scanty resources the actual mechanism of screening; secondly, the conducting of such screening in a way that would not betray to the Cossacks the impending handover, and result in widespread escapes. The difficulty was greatly aggravated by the speed with which it was necessary to make preparations.

These were real considerations. Other officers concerned with these operations have, however, expressed to the author their opinion that the problem was by no means insoluble. Generals Murray and Bredin, and Major Davies, whose tasks ranged from planning the operations to implementing them on the ground, are convinced that screening at Peggetz would have been perfectly feasible. Many of the émigrés, after all, possessed foreign passports and Nansen Certificates.

More weighty than the beliefs of even the most experienced officers is the fact that screening elsewhere was regarded as a matter of course, whether on a small or large scale. Throughout all the area (excepting that in the case under review) controlled by Allied armies in Italy and Austria, measures were taken to see that only those liberated or captured Russians covered by the Yalta Agreement were returned. Allied Force Headquarters issued on 6 May a precise definition as to what constituted a Soviet citizen. On 22 May, Fifth Corps Headquarters itself made enquiries further up the line, in order to confirm British policy, and

on this day AFHQ sent down a telegram explaining clearly that:
1. all who are Soviet citizens and who can be handed over to Russians without use of force should be returned direct by Eighth Army.
2. any others should be evacuated to 12 Army Group.
3. definition of Soviet citizen is given in AFHQ letter of ... of 6 May ... ref your A 4073 of 21 May asking for policy re Cossacks.[30]

In general the actual screening process was quite rough-and-ready and tended to favour the prisoners' claim to non-Soviet citizenship.[31] But it may be felt that such methods were impractical when applied to very large bodies of men, such as the Cossacks at Lienz. If so, let us consider two formations not yet mentioned.

In the region around St. Veit and Spittal, British forces accepted the surrender of a disciplined unit, comprising some 10,000 Ukrainians. This Division had been formed by the Germans in Galicia in 1943. Its original name was *Waffen SS Panzer Grenadier Division Galizien*, but early in 1945 it became the Ukrainian No. 1 Division, with the Ukrainian General Pavlo Shandruk as its nominal commander. This was in accord with the belated Nazi policy of attempting to raise a 'third force' of anti-Bolshevik Slavs. But in fact the Division remained under the command of SS General Freitag, who with his fellow German officers sensibly disappeared immediately before the surrender.

As the Division awaited the arrival of Eighth Army troops, Shandruk (like von Pannwitz at the same time) sent messages to the British, explaining the predicament of his men and requesting that they should not be handed over to the Soviets. An emissary was also sent to the commander of the Polish 2nd Corps, General Anders, asking him to intervene on the Ukrainians' behalf with the British. On 8 May a further envoy was sent to the British, and the Division surrendered. Shandruk subsequently sent memoranda to the British High Command, setting out the national position of the Ukrainians and asserting that they should not be regarded as Soviet citizens.[32]

Shandruk himself fled to American-occupied Bavaria, whilst the 10,000 men of the Ukrainian Division were held by the British 5th Corps around Spittal an der Drau—the ill-omened town where Domanov and his officers of the *Kazachi Stan* spent the night of 28/29 May on their way to Judenburg. Shandruk's officers and men were more fortunate; instead of being delivered to the Soviets, they were transferred in May to a camp at Bellaria, near Rimini on the Adriatic coast of Italy. Then, in October, they were transferred to another camp nearby at Cesenatico, where they remained until May 1947.

Soviet Intelligence was aware of the existence of this disciplined body of anti-Communist soldiers, who were of mixed Polish and Soviet citizenship. At Potsdam in July, Stalin himself demanded their return to the USSR, and Churchill promised to look into the matter thoroughly. At meetings with Field-Marshal Alexander on 18 August and subsequently, the Soviet Repatriation Delegate General Basilov insisted that these '10,000 Soviet citizens' be repatriated in accordance with the Yalta Agreement. The British military authorities, however, conducted a rigid screening process, and by November a Foreign Office official wrote that 'all except 112 of the Ukrainian division are Disputed persons and *not* Soviet citizens'. To cut a long story short, all the Ukrainians except a few score who volunteered for repatriation were permitted to stay in the West. Despite fears of TUC objections, the majority came to Britain in the summer of 1947, filling a labour gap made by the return of German prisoners held in British camps.[33]

The Ukrainian Division was one large fish that got away. The other was the White Russian *Schutzkorps* from Serbia. This Corps had a unique history, as it was in reality the sole surviving unit of the old Russian Imperial Army. When Wrangel's armies were evacuated from the Crimea in 1921, many of his officers and men found refuge in Yugoslavia. King Alexander welcomed them, gave them material assistance, and permitted them to maintain a skeleton military establishment. A military college trained cadets to officer a future anti-Bolshevik army, and it was to these young men that the White émigrés looked for a continued renewal of the White idea.[34]

After the German occupation of Yugoslavia in 1941, Tito began his ambitious plans to seize power in the country. Amongst other such activities, his partisans launched an increasing series of attacks on the Russian émigrés. In self-defence, these banded themselves together into a military force comprising five regiments, under the command of General Steifon. The Germans subsequently recognised this unit, and supplied it with arms and German uniforms. This was in 1942, and in that year Steifon was succeeded by Colonel Anatol Rogozhin, a former officer of the Imperial Bodyguard and a combatant in the Civil War.

When the German south-eastern front began to cave in at the beginning of 1945, the *Schutzkorps* made a fighting retreat northwards, emerging into Austria about the same time as von Pannwitz's 15th Cossack Corps. Rogozhin likewise managed to arrange the surrender of his men to the 3rd Battalion of the Grenadier Guards on 12 May 1945. They were interned at Klein St. Veit, in the same area as that occupied by von Pannwitz's men after their surrender, until their release. They appear to have numbered about 4,500, and were freed a year later to settle where they chose in the West.[35]

Both General Shandruk's Ukrainian Division and Colonel Rogozhin's

Schutzkorps were largely composed of persons originating from Russia, but the British decided that the provisions of the Yalta Agreement did not apply to them as corporate bodies. They were sheltered from Soviet demands, being later disbanded and permitted to seek homes in the free world. Yet why were Shandruk and Rogozhin not despatched to Judenburg along with Domanov and von Pannwitz? There were, on the face of it, as valid reasons for returning those who did not go as those who did.

To consider the case of the Ukrainians first: the Soviets were as persistent and strident in demanding their return as they were in any other case. In fact, the Ukrainian Division was the only such unit to be singled out by Stalin himself at a conference of the Big Three. Unlike the Cossacks at Lienz, Shandruk's men had, until shortly before their surrender, been engaged in fierce fighting against the Red Army. According to the terms of the German surrender, all Axis military formations were obliged to stay put and surrender to the Allied army opposing them. Strictly speaking, Shandruk should have surrendered to Marshal Tolbukhin. Again, the Ukrainian Division, unlike the Cossacks, officially formed part of the *Waffen SS*—a fact which might have made the Soviets more anxious to lay hands on them, and the British less inclined to baulk at any such request.

It seems equally odd that the *Schutzkorps* remained immune from the threat of forcible repatriation. When Colonel Rogozhin learned of the despatch of his fellow White Russians from Lienz to Judenburg, he feared, as well he might, that his turn could not be far off.[36] His men had fought in precisely the same campaign as von Pannwitz's; it is true that the major part of his Corps comprised old émigrés—but that status had not saved General Krasnov and hundreds like him.

No screening of either unit had been undertaken at the time of the Cossack handovers, and the relative proportions of Soviet citizens and Disputed Persons could not have been known with any degree of accuracy. In fact, a high proportion of the Ukrainians were Soviet citizens as specified in the Yalta Agreement. Mykola Wolynskyj, who was one of their number, gives a rough estimate of twenty per cent; Denis Hills, the Russian-speaking British officer who had the task of screening them, puts it much higher—well over fifty per cent. Colonel Rogozhin's men were overwhelmingly of old (White) émigré origins, but by no means all were such. Numbers were Soviet citizens: the *Schutzkorps* had maintained a recruiting-office in Rumanian-occupied Odessa.[37]

So it happened that, just before the handover of the Cossacks, the ten thousand men of the Ukrainian Division were whisked out of Austria to the safety of Italy. At the same time, Colonel Rogozhin's *Schutzkorps* became a city of refuge for Russian émigrés. Singled out in the 5th Corps Order of 21 May as not being eligible for repatriation, the camp at Klein St. Veit provided a haven for any old émigré lucky enough to make his way there. At Lienz and the camps of the 15th Cavalry Corps, a fortunate few learned of the incomprehensible distinction made by the British. Colonel Wagner recommended to the old émigré Major Ostrovsky that he should seek asylum there; he decided otherwise, but several others made their way thither through the mountains from Lienz, so evading their comrades' fate.[38] They were saved, but had no idea why the British had apparently arbitrarily selected one set of White Russians for return and allowed another to remain.

The reasons for the 5th Corps selectivity in choosing 'Russian' units for repatriation remain obscure. A choice was clearly made, and made in a hurry. Within a fortnight the two Cossack bodies were surrendered, whilst the Ukrainians were spirited away and Rogozhin's men granted immunity. In the case of the Ukrainians it seems likely that Shandruk's appeal to General Anders may have swayed the British decision. For those of the Ukrainians who were not Soviet citizens were Poles; it could not be expected that Britain's Polish ally would sit quietly by and watch thousands of their fellow-countrymen returned to slavery. And what would be the response of the Vatican to such a sacrifice of several thousand faithful Catholics? Whether reactions from that quarter could have reached AFHQ or 5th Corps HQ as early as May is doubtful, but General Shandruk did indeed appeal to the Pontiff, who as early as 5 July issued an appeal to the Allies against the forcible repatriation of Ukrainians.[39]

But what of Rogozhin's White Russians at Klein St. Veit? They had no influential friends, yet Rogozhin escaped the fate of Krasnov. Astonishing though it may be, the *Schutzkorps* appears to have been saved by the actions of a single Englishman. Colonel Rogozhin, who could have told the full story, is dead, but one of his men has described to the author their first contact with the British. A British officer, retired and working with the Red Cross, came upon the Corps where it had halted in Austria. A few enquiries told him who these men were and what were their antecedents. He explained that he himself had served with the Military Mission to the White Armies in south Russia in 1919, and that he too saw their recent struggle against Tito's partisans as but a continuation of the war against Bolshevism. A man of determined energy, he set off for the British Field Headquarters to move heaven and earth in favour of his old associates. What methods and arguments he employed are not known, but the result was that he returned to

Rogozhin with the welcome news that he had succeeded in having the entire corps registered as White Russians, and so not liable for repatriation.[40]

No documentary material has been made available that can throw a light on how and at what level this decision was made. All we know is that, as early as 21 May, Rogozhin's *Schutzkorps* had definitely been excluded from extradition. That the protests of a single officer, if delivered forcefully enough, could accomplish wonders in this context is suggested by numerous examples. The novelist, Bruce Marshall, was at that time a lieutenant-colonel, acting under Colonel Logan Gray of the DP Division in Austria.

> Once, during Colonel Gray's absence, I was ordered to inform White Russian émigrés in our camps that they were to be moved to other Russian camps, pack them, men, women and children, into lorries and have them driven into the Russian zone and handed over to the Soviets. I protested most strongly and pointed out that such an action would be inhumane and un-British. I do not know if my protest had any effect (I could see that the very senior officer who gave me the order liked it as little as I did . . .) but within 48 hours the order was cancelled . . .[41]

It seems that 5th Corps Headquarters knew itself to be walking on a tightrope, and that whenever the policy of handing over non-Soviet citizens was openly challenged, it backed down hastily.

The cases of the Ukrainian Division and the *Schutzkorps* illustrate two vital points. Firstly, screening of large bodies of men to establish Soviet citizenship was not just possible: *it actually took place*. The *Schutzkorps* was classified as non-Soviet in its entirety, whilst the Ukrainian Division was removed to a wired camp where detailed screening could be carried out. And no untoward diplomatic incident resulted from the British firm stand. We do not need to speculate, therefore: both bodies of Cossacks could have been screened so that only Soviet citizens were sent back, as the Yalta Agreement provided.

Generally speaking, whenever subordinate officers sent up enquiries concerning the position of non-Soviet citizens in their charge, instructions were hastily given to institute screening procedure forthwith. Examples have already been cited, but a much more remarkable one will now be described. It concerns members of a formation all of whose members had by an arbitrary classification been named in orders as Soviet citizens.

At the close of the last chapter, we described how Major Ostrovsky and his friends were saved at the very last moment from being sent north to the NKVD at Judenburg. As old émigrés they were not liable for return, but they were actually in the trucks on the road when the news came that the British had altered their decision. What was not explained earlier was how this dramatic change was brought about.

On 28 May the Cossacks had moved from their camp at Flattnitz down to the cages guarded by the Welsh Guards at Weitensfeld. The 1st King's Royal Rifle Corps had responsibility for the move, but once the Cossacks had passed into the cage their duty was over. However, the acting CO of the Battalion, Major Henry Howard, had had a disquieting exchange with a Cossack officer, George Druzhakin. Before the move, Druzhakin had asked him whether they were to be delivered to the Soviets. He had replied, truthfully, that he did not think so. Later he had visited the Cossack officers' cage at Weitensfeld. Druzhakin came up to him again, saluted, and reproached Howard for misleading them. Major Howard replied curtly that he was a soldier, and obliged to obey orders. George Druzhakin acknowledged this, but went on to ask him to bear a message to Field-Marshal Alexander. Somewhat surprised and intrigued, Howard asked him what it was.

'Ask him whether your orders say that we old émigrés, who have fought Bolshevism since the Revolution, are to go back. I understand that the Soviet citizens must be returned, but do your orders really include us old officers of the Tsar?'

Here was a new and disturbing factor. Major Howard thought deeply about it that night, and confided his doubts to other officers. Next day he attended a conference conducted by Brigadier Usher.

The Brigadier himself had been anxiously trying to discover whether any category of officer could be excused from forcible repatriation, and listened attentively as Howard raised a point. When Howard's Battalion had first entered Austria and received the surrender of the Cossacks, he had written to his father 'a pretty harrowing account of things there'. His father, Brigadier Sir Charles Howard, was then Sergeant-at-Arms to the House of Commons. Sir Charles wrote to his son, pointing out that no agreement made by the Government could possibly contemplate the forcible return of Russians who had fled abroad before the present war. To Clive Usher this statement seemed to offer just the loophole he was seeking. Referring back to his papers, he turned up the written orders issued to the 6th Armoured Division. Puzzlingly, these classified the whole 15th Cossack Cavalry Corps (to which Ostrovsky and his men belonged) as Soviet citizens. Yet in a following paragraph a Soviet citizen was defined as someone who had lived in Russia since the outbreak of the present war—and this applied to none of the men under discussion.

Another Battalion Commander present at the Brigadier's conference noted in his War Diary what Brigadier Musson had failed to take up:

'Since our order stated definitely that only Soviet Citizens were to be sent back to Russia, but at the same time specifically classed our particular concentration as Soviet Citizens, these two orders were completely at variance since the 50 Cossacks concerned had not been in the Soviet Union since 1920.'

It was about this time that Major Ostrovsky and his fifty officers had reluctantly embussed for Judenburg. They had actually set off and joined the rear of the main convoy, when Major Howard's jeep drove up to the camp at breakneck speed. Springing out, he dashed up to Colonel Rose Price and explained the new discovery. Colonel Rose Price, who had been more disgusted than most with the sordid task accorded his battalion, leapt into action.

'There was at once a mad rush for telephones, the transport was held; interrogators were rushed to the scene and then the answer came back that a reprieve was possible. Interrogation produced the answer expected, namely that the party of 50 were in the non-Soviet Citizen category and amidst, it must be admitted, a general rejoicing they were returned to their cage.'[42]

This incident throws new light from many angles not only onto parallel events in the 78th Division area, but also onto the nature of the main 5th Corps decision and intentions. Clearly the oral orders to which Brigadier Musson attached overriding importance never reached Brigadier Usher, who held exactly parallel responsibility. Usher was able to save émigré lives by a strict interpretation of the written orders. In this context it is worth noting that the prime concern of officers in the 6th Armoured Division lay, not with questions of Red or White Russians, but purely with the humanitarian business of saving lives.[43]

Fifth Corps orders had specified that the unit to which Ostrovsky and his comrades belonged 'should be treated as SOVIET NATIONALS'. *Despite this*, Corps Headquarters was prepared to accept without hesitation that individual non-Soviet citizens in its ranks should be screened.

A most remarkable contrast is presented with events in the 78th Infantry Division area. A chronology of the events will make the position clear.

20 May. On or just before this date Brigadier Musson was informed that, in accordance with the Yalta Agreement, 'all SOVIET nationals ... should be returned to the USSR.'

21 May. Brigadier Musson received a precise definition as to what constituted a Soviet citizen. *This definition appears to have been issued in response to his own request.* For the text states that it is being issued as a result of several specific cases being forwarded on to Corps Headquarters. And elsewhere we learn that '5 CORPS letter 405/G dated 21 May [was] handed to 36 Bde only.'[44] It must then have been Brigadier Musson's 36th Brigade that asked for clarification in the first place, in response to the 'frequent petitions' from Cossacks, mentioned in his own report. Yet on 29 May, eight days after Brigadier Musson received his requested definition, his Headquarters at Oberdrauburg received the following message from the 8th Argylls Headquarters in Lienz:

> GERMAGEN RODIONOFF was evacuated yesterday with the Cossack officers. He is not a Russian subject and has been living in PARIS for 15 years. Apparently, he is a teacher. His family is in France, and it would appear that he has been put in the Cossack camp by mistake. May we have your advice. It seems highly probable that there are a large number of persons at present in the Cossack camp who are not of RUSSIAN origin. What is the position regarding these people.[45]

Brigadier Musson had known for over a week what was 'the position regarding these people', but had not passed on the information. The query over Rodionoff was despatched at 4 p.m. on 29 May; by that time the French schoolmaster was in the hands of SMERSH at Judenburg. It was the superseding oral orders received by Musson in the interval that had effectively sentenced him to this fate.

The only reason provided was that screening would have been impractical. Yet it would be hard to think of an easier body of men to screen than the Cossack officers, the majority of whom were old émigrés, once they were isolated in the cage at Spittal on 29/30 May.[46]

Another mystery arises. Today, General Musson frankly admits that no screening took place within his Brigade area. It was impractical, he holds, and besides he had received oral orders that could not be questioned. Yet shortly after the handovers, on 3 July, his Brigade Headquarters drew up a lengthy summary of the handover operation in which it is stated that

> such measures as were possible under the conditions prevailing at the time, were taken within 36 Inf Bde to ensure that non-SOVIET nationals were not included amongst those evacuated to the USSR authorities.
> Included in these figures [of numbers of Cossacks] were an unknown quantity of displaced persons of nationalities other than SOVIET . . . Lack of documents and the speed and secrecy with which the evacuations had to be carried out made a complete check impossible. Steps were taken, however, at the time of the evacuations, to segregate persons who were obviously of these categories.[47]

Nothing of the sort had taken place. It was not until the morning of 4 June that the Argylls began screening. For the first time Colonel

Malcolm learned that only Soviet citizens could be handed over. An office was opened in Peggetz camp, at which old emigrants could register themselves by producing documents (genuine or forged) proving non-Soviet nationality.[48] Henceforth there were two camps: one for registered old émigrés at Peggetz, and another, heavily guarded, for new émigrés was established further down the valley at Dölsach.[49] Brigade Headquarters had delayed this measure until the main body of Cossacks had been safely delivered.

All in all, one receives a distinct impression that, so far as 5th Corps Headquarters was concerned, the Cossacks in the Drau Valley fell into a special category. They were the least military of the Russian formations held in Austria; they were the only ones not to have fought on the Eastern Front; and they were known to include an exceptionally high proportion of non-Soviet citizens. Yet they were returned *en bloc.* Within the 78th Division, officers at battalion level were not informed of the distinction laid down between old and new émigrés. Senior officers who did know were given orders that left them no choice but to obey.

The commander of the 78th Infantry Division was Major-General Robert Arbuthnott. There is strong evidence that he regarded his task with extreme distaste. Lieutenant-Colonel H. E. N. Bredin was at that time AQ on the Divisional Staff, in the Headquarters at Velden. As such he bore responsibility for assessing factors likely to affect Divisional morale. It was in this capacity that he became the recipient of complaints from all sides (including his own battalion, the 2nd London Irish Rifles) concerning the proposed repatriation of the Cossacks, and in turn he approached Arbuthnott to let him know the state of feeling within the Division.

'I think this is going to be a very difficult one, sir, and I don't know if the troops are going to like doing it if there is any resistance.'

'I see exactly what you mean,' replied Arbuthnott. 'We'll simply have to see. I don't like the sound of it either; but of course it may all go off quite easily, and we may be worrying about nothing at all.'

At the time Colonel Bredin received no further impression of the General's views, but later he learned that he had in fact gone direct to the Corps Commander, Lieutenant-General Keightley, and objected strongly to the task being allotted to his Division. Brigadier C. E. Tryon-Wilson was then serving on the 5th Corps Headquarters Staff. He remembers Arbuthnott's calling two or three times to protest; indeed, his objections were so strong that General Keightley was finally obliged to give him a flat order to obey. Arbuthnott acceded and returned to Velden, resolved that at least the operation should be conducted smoothly, with the minimum of disorder or bloodshed.[50]

Measures taken after the main handovers of 1 and 2 June were as exceptional and extraordinary as the preparations leading up to them. Hundreds of Cossacks had escaped, and steps were taken to round up as many as possible. Patrols were sent into the hills. The degree of rigour with which these operations were conducted depended much on the individual attitudes of subalterns conducting patrols. Some made merely a token search, rounding up those Cossacks who could not get out of the way, whilst others went to the lengths of shooting to kill or maim those whom they had difficulty in taking prisoner. Altogether 1,356 Cossacks and Caucasians, out of an estimated 4,100, were recaptured during the latter part of June.[51]

As an additional precaution, Brigade Headquarters took the remarkable course of allowing in Soviet officials, presumably from SMERSH, to check that all was being conducted properly. The Revd Kenneth Tyson, Chaplain of the Argylls, remembers one of them accompanying a search party.

'He wore khaki uniform but as far as I remember he carried no badges of rank. He was there ostensibly to act as interpreter, but his English was rather halting and indeed meagre. He was not obtrusive but the general feeling among the soldiers was that he was there to see to it that they conscientiously discharged their task.'

Mr. Tyson stresses that he appeared to be an *official*, and not an officer. These 'officials' carried guns and assisted British troops in firing on fleeing Cossacks. It was perhaps on this occasion alone that British soldiers were ordered to co-operate in the field with SMERSH operatives in hunting and killing Russian refugees.[52]

By contrast, in the 6th Armoured Division Major-General Horatius Murray had already warned the German officers of von Pannwitz's Corps of the possible fate in store for them, with the expected result that many vanished soon afterwards. When the orders came through, he says 'I made no attempt to establish exactly how my orders were to be carried out. In fact, the looser and more nebulous they were, it seemed to me possibly to be the better.' Escapes were continually connived at. 'All I know is that we lost a hell of a lot of Russians . . . Security didn't exist.' To a Soviet request for the admission of what in fact were SMERSH operatives to assist operations, as they had done for the 78th Division, he returned a flat refusal.[53]

Precisely how many lives were saved as a result of this policy cannot be known. Without any doubt the figure must run to several thousands, almost certainly a sizable majority of those held by the Division.[54]

What is noteworthy about this striking difference of approach is not so much what actually occurred. Professional attitudes vary, and the same problem may be tackled in different ways. General Arbuthnott protested against his orders, and obeyed; General Murray made no protest, but saw to it that the effect of those orders was greatly mitigated. The significance surely lies in the reactions—or lack of reactions—at 5th Corps Headquarters. Extraordinary precautions were taken before, during and after the main operations, to ensure that the Cossacks held by General Arbuthnott's 78th Infantry Division were returned. In the 6th Armoured Division area, by contrast, the evasion of orders was blatant and widespread. Yet no reproof of any sort reached General Murray or Brigadier Usher. They had never received the equivalent of Brigadier Musson's oral order, which set aside all provisions for screening. On the contrary, when old émigrés were uncovered at Weitensfeld, the 5th Corps instantly authorised full screening facilities.

The contrast appears greater still when we consider the respective attitudes to important Cossack commanders. Colonel Wagner, the second most senior officer in the Cossack Cavalry Corps, made an unhindered escape. General von Pannwitz himself, the evidence suggests, could have escaped had he chosen. Nor was it only Germans in the Corps who were permitted to evade delivery to the Soviets. Major Ostrovsky, on whom the command of the 1st Division devolved after Colonel Wagner's departure, was screened and released the instant he was discovered to be an old émigré. All this was accepted without comment or was actually authorised by 5th Corps HQ.

Within the 78th Division, by contrast, extraordinary precautions seem to have been taken to ensure that the senior commanders did not escape. In particular, Generals Krasnov and Shkuro appear to have been singled out for special treatment. Take Krasnov first. Twice he had addressed letters to Alexander, his old comrade-in-arms of 1919. In them he explained at length the Cossacks' and his own predicament. We know of these letters from Cossack sources, cited earlier, though all trace of them has vanished from Army records. Senior officers assure me, however, that there can be no question but that they would have reached their destination.

A few days after General Krasnov's second appeal, the Cossack officers received the news that they were to attend a special conference with Field-Marshal Alexander. Many were suspicious, as has already been explained. But Krasnov himself welcomed the news. Only he and Domanov knew of his recent appeal to the Field-Marshal, and Major Davies's announcement must have appeared a direct response—one arriving more swiftly than they could have expected. Krasnov's cheerful acceptance of the invitation served to allay the suspicions of many of the officers. If the British General Staff wished to entrap the senior Cossack officers, they could not have dealt a luckier card. And, certainly, they were extremely anxious that Krasnov should be at the 'conference'. On the evening preceding it, Major Davies broke the news to General Domanov. Captain Butlerov, who interpreted, remembers that he added: 'And . . . do not neglect to notify General Krasnov. The Commander is particularly interested in meeting him.'[55]

According to another Cossack eye-witness, this peculiar request was specially repeated the next morning. About midday, 'there appeared at General Domanov's hotel a tall English general, who again repeated Major Davies's order, adding: "Please do not forget to convey my request to old Krasnov. I beg this of you most urgently".'[56]

The only tall British general in the vicinity was Brigadier Musson, but he states emphatically: 'I certainly did not visit Domanov's Headquarters and I have no idea who it can have been who is alleged to have been there on 28 May. We all wore battle dress, shirts and/or jerseys with the minimum of insignia and foreigners could easily have been mistaken over ranks.' Could the 'general' in question have been a staff or intelligence officer from Divisional or Corps Headquarters?[57]

General Peter Krasnov seems to have been the object of particularly solicitous attentions throughout the delicate operation. He was placed in the first car to leave Lienz for Spittal. On arrival in the cage at Spittal, a British officer checked the leading Cossack generals and their staff against a list, taking noticeable care to ascertain that General Krasnov was amongst the party.[58] He was in any case an unmistakable figure; his age, his decorations, and the respect paid him by all the Cossack officers marked him out from the rest. To Colonel Bryar was handed a last petition for reprieve; it was drawn up and written in French by General Krasnov. Copies were requested to be forwarded to King George VI, the Archbishop of Canterbury and the Headquarters of the International Red Cross. Colonel Bryar agreed to forward the petition, and there can be no doubt that he would have done so. But once again all trace of it has vanished from the files; it certainly never reached its intended destination.[59]

British solicitude that General Krasnov should accomplish his journey without mishap was shared by Soviet colleagues. The Cossack officers were handed over at Judenburg. Before they could even descend from their lorry they were hailed by a Colonel of the NKVD, who asked eagerly: 'Is General Peter Krasnov in your group?'[60] Thereafter the old General was the object of special attention until he was done to death two years later. Senior Red Army and NKVD officers crowded to meet this most redoubtable of opponents of Bolshevism. He was flown specially to Moscow, senior officers of SMERSH travelling miles merely to see him board his aeroplane. In Moscow he was interrogated, imprisoned and killed; at the age of 78 the Soviets had finally avenged his victories over their troops in 1918.

Second only in celebrity to Krasnov amongst the Cossack officers was the formidable Lieutenant-General Andrei Shkuro. Once again, very special precautions were taken in delivering him. Two nights before the Cossack officers travelled to the 'conference', Shkuro had burst into General Solamakhin's bedroom. In a confused voice and weeping with rage, he declared that the British were about to arrest him and hand him over to the Soviets. At early dawn British soldiers came for him and drove him in a jeep to Spittal, where he was held under strict guard in a building near the barracks. When Cossack officers arrived the next day he did not join them in their cage, but remained under separate guard. Only when the column was leaving for Judenburg on 29 May was he brought down and driven off with the rest. At Judenburg he received as delighted a welcome from SMERSH officers as had General Krasnov.

What was the reason for this special treatment? Official British records state briefly: 'General SHKURO (of the Cossack Reserve Regiment) had been sent to SPITTAL two days earlier, as the move of his Regiment was then complete. The Regiment passed under direct command of General DOMANOV.'

This was an allusion to the move of his regiment from Tamsweg to Lienz, a move completed on 20 May.[61] But the explanation seems thin indeed. Why should the Reserve Regiment alone, of all regiments in the camp, no longer require a Commanding Officer once it had arrived? Why should General Domanov, already saddled with the command of some 25,000 souls, be deprived of a regimental commander? And in any case, why was it necessary to remove Shkuro surreptitiously and place him under close arrest some miles off? Why wait a week to do it? So secretive was his arrest that none of the Cossacks realised at the time that it had happened.[62]

It is difficult to avoid the conclusion that he was taken prematurely into protective custody lest in some way he evade arrest. Never one to guard his tongue, he may have betrayed his intention of escaping, resisting, or creating some open scandal that would obstruct the planned operation.

We should very likely have some idea of the true facts behind this mysterious abduction if two essential documents had not as mysteriously disappeared. A brief and tantalising item in the 36th Brigade War Diary provides a clue:

'Note: for description of the Cossack forces in general, and of General SHKURO's part in the organisation in particular, see the two letters written by him to Commander 36 Inf Bde and forwarded to 78 Div under 36 Inf Bde letters 129/G dated 23 and 24 May.'[63]

But these letters are no longer included in the War Diaries of the 36th Brigade or the 78th Division, and cannot be traced. General Musson remembers receiving the appeal but cannot bring to mind any details.

From the brief description we gather that Shkuro explained at some length the situation of the Cossacks and the nature of their struggle. He also gave autobiographical details, which presumably included his services as a British ally in 1918–19, his Companionship of the Bath conferred by George V in 1919, and his residence abroad ever since the Communist victory in 1919. All this was certainly laid before General Arbuthnott, and very likely before General Keightley as well. The preservation of these two letters would have provided proof that the British High Command in Austria was well aware that it had singled out for handover to the Soviets a man whose surrender was morally and politically wrong. General Keightley declared shortly afterwards that no White Russians had been knowingly handed over; this statement might have contrasted strangely with the presence of General Shkuro's letters in his files. The mere existence of the letters was clearly awkward. They may in addition have intimated that he was preparing more open and possibly embarrassing protests.

It seems, then, that Shkuro's fate had been decided upon at the 5th Corps Headquarters conference held on the morning of 21 May, for he is the only Cossack named in the Order of that day as being liable for return. Thereafter he became a marked man whom it was vital to guard closely. In Spittal camp a Caucasian officer, who had actually been Shkuro's commander in the Civil War, produced a passport proving his Albanian citizenship.[64] Colonel Bryar freed him without asking for instructions; a similar appeal from Shkuro he turned down flatly.

All in all, there seem to be many indications that the handover of Krasnov and Shkuro in particular, and the officers at Lienz in general, was no blunder committed by some hard-pressed staff officer in a moment of stress, but a carefully planned operation.

Another significant fact should be recorded. On 28 May a Cossack at Spittal saw an English soldier carrying a handsome sword and dagger, which he recognised as belonging to Shkuro.[65] An odd reference to these weapons appears in 78 Divisional Headquarters instructions:

'Ref Gen. Shkuro's sword.

This is NOT to be handed over to Russians yet. 78 Div. will hold and ask for further instrs from 5 Corps. Other offrs swords to be handed over as previously arranged.'[66]

The sword's intended destination was presumably that MVD museum which housed General Krasnov's uniform. This curious little transaction throws light on the considerable symbolic significance the capture of Shkuro meant for the Soviets, as well as on the careful plans for his handover made by Fifth Corps Headquarters.

If this be so, the motive presumably was to co-operate with Soviet forces in Austria. The 24 May Corps Order stated clearly that: 'It is of the utmost importance that all the offrs and *particularly senior comds* are rounded up and that none are allowed to escape. The SOVIET forces consider this as being of the highest importance . . .' On the evidence already set out, it would seem that it was the senior commanders at Lienz that this order envisaged. And as Shkuro himself was the only such officer specified in orders, it is possible that the Soviets had named names when setting out their demands. Certainly a carefully drawn-up list accompanied Shkuro and the others; it was handed on arrival to an NKVD Colonel at Judenburg.[67] The Soviet motive in wishing to lay hands on Krasnov and Shkuro in particular we know from the mouth of NKVD General Merkulov himself.

The balance of probabilities suggests a plan, not a blunder. But if there was a plan, whose was the decision? Unfortunately this is not an easy question to answer. The higher up the chain of command we move, the scantier becomes the evidence. It is clear, though, that the decision issued from 5 Corps HQ, which was in full possession of the salient facts. It has already been noted that Shkuro's appeals were received at 78th Division Headquarters; whether they were transmitted on to the 5th Corps is not known, nor under what circumstances they vanished from the files. It was on the 5th Corps Order of 21 May that Shkuro's name appeared, apparently as liable for extradition. It was the 5th Corps which decided that the appeals of Rogozhin and Shandruk should be upheld, and the *Schutzkorps* and Ukrainian Division not be handed over to the Soviets. It can only be assumed that they received and rejected the parallel appeals of Krasnov and Shkuro.

The commander of the 5th Corps, General Sir Charles Keightley, shortly afterwards provided his own version of events. In July grave reports reached British Red Cross officials heading their Spearhead organisation in Austria. The British Army was said to have been using force to return refugees against their will, many of whom were believed to have been killed by the Soviets on their return. Worst of all, it was said that émigré White Russian Cossacks, formerly living in Western Europe, had been included in these consignments. All this was so flagrantly incompatible with Red Cross principles that a senior representative had announced to the military 'that he was recommending the withdrawal' of Red Cross personnel. This was highly alarming. The Red Cross was playing a vital role in a difficult situation, and now came the suggestion of open scandal on a subject very unsuitable for public airing. General Keightley himself arranged to meet Lady Limerick, Deputy Chairman of the War Organisation of the British Red Cross. Lady Limerick

> asked him what the position was of all the displaced Russians . . . and he told me that there were two incidents which gave rise to the story. In the first incident, several thousand Cossacks were taken prisoner, but had been for the last 3½ years fighting in the German ranks; they were dressed in German uniform and were taken prisoners of war. With them were some 1,500 or so Russian men, wives and families; they were an armed body moving round in regiments. According to the policy laid down it was decided to return these people to Russia; there was evidently some protest, as he said they only had to 'shoot twice' and in neither case hit anybody. They were then interviewed and agreed to return to Soviet Territory together with their wives and children. The men went back without any more pressure; the women protested at first under the instigation of their priest, but subsequently followed him into the train, and they all went back together. A British Officer accompanied them into Russian territory and heard the officer in charge of the Soviet forces explaining that they must now be re-educated as Soviet citizens and that they must be prepared to work hard, but that they would in no way be penalised. There was no evidence at all that they had been shot.
>
> I asked whether he knew the Cossacks in question had been from districts overrun by the Germans in their invasion of Russia, or whether they had been living in Central Europe before the War, and were in fact, supporters of the old regime. He said that he did not know and it was impossible to find out—he thought some might be, but that the only evidence they had, was that they had been fighting in the German Army, and none to prove that they were White Russians.

Lady Limerick reported favourably on the basis of this account to the Red Cross and the matter was dropped.[68] General Keightley's became the official version of events thereafter. On 14 May 1952 Lieutenant-Colonel Oswald Stein wrote to *The Times* to refute charges brought by another lady of rank, the Duchess of Atholl. Colonel Stein had held an important post with the Allied Commission for Austria in 1945,[69] and claimed that: 'In the British zone of Austria the only Russians forcibly repatriated against their will . . . were citizens of the USSR. . . .' This assertion he repeated in an authoritative article written on the subject two years later.[70]

Did Keightley of his own authority order the operation to take place, or had he in turn received instructions from above? And if so, how far were those who gave him his orders aware of the presence of the White generals at Lienz? On 14 May General Keightley wrote to Field-Marshal Alexander:

On advice Macmillan have today suggested to Soviet General on Tolbukhin's HQ that Cossacks should be returned to SOVIETS at once. Explained that I had no power to do this without your authority but would be glad to know Tolbukhin's views and that if they coincided with mine I would ask you officially. Cannot see any point in keeping this large number Soviet nationals who are clearly great source contention between Soviets and ourselves.[71]

Alexander did not grant the requested authority, and three days later (17 May) he telegraphed the Combined Chiefs of Staff to request directions as to what he should do with the surrendered Cossacks.

'To assist us in clearing congestion in Southern Austria we urgently require direction regarding final disposal... Approximately 50,000 Cossacks including 11,000 women, children and old men. These have been part of German armed forces and fighting against Allies... to return them to their countries of origin immediately might be fatal to their health. Request decision as early as possible as to final disposal.'[72]

Clearly Alexander was disturbed; why else should he request a ruling on a matter that had been apparently settled by the Cabinet decision of the previous September?[73]

The urgency expressed by Alexander arose in large part from the necessity to solve the problem of how and where the Cossacks were to be housed and fed. Their presence immediately behind the lines could also prove an embarrassment if the feared conflict between British and Yugoslav forces broke out, and preparations were made for their transfer to the control of the United States 12th Army in southern Germany.[74] But even as such schemes were being contemplated and abandoned, the Joint Staff Mission in Washington was pressing for a top-level decision on the matter, noting at the same time that it 'seems to us that Cossacks are covered by Yalta agreement on repatriation of Soviet Nationals who fall into our hands'.[75]

On 18 May the Combined Chiefs of Staff discussed Alexander's request for directions as to what to do with the Cossacks. But despite this, the Chiefs of Staff were still debating the matter at the end of the month.[76] On 29 May the Chief of the Imperial General Staff, Field-Marshal Alan Brooke, confirmed that the Combined Chiefs were in favour of returning the Cossacks. Nevertheless, it was declared two days later that 'there is as yet no agreed policy that collaborationists and members of para-military organisations of Allied Nationality should be handed over to their respective authorities.' It was not until 20 June that the Combined Chiefs of Staff gave their approval to the suggested policy. But by that time the operations had already been completed.[77]

The discussion had in fact been outstripped by events. In mid-May an agreement had been concluded with Soviet representatives at Graz for the handover of the Cossacks, and Alexander notified the War Office that: 'Handover of respective nationals to Russians and Jugoslavs agreed.'[78] Arrangements for the surrender of the Cossacks could now be put into effect. On 23 May, 5th Corps Headquarters opened negotiations with the Soviets, and on 24 May at Wolfsberg routes and reception-points were planned.[79]

What had happened to make Alexander suddenly anticipate the decision he himself had requested of the Combined Chiefs of Staff? On 17 May he had asked them for a decision, and received no answer until over a month later. But it was within a few days of his placing the request that he had authorised the 5th Corps to proceed with delivering the Cossacks to the Soviets. Had he suddenly decided to proceed without seeking instruction for his actions, feeling that the Yalta Agreement and previous practice provided sufficient authority?[80] It seems on the face of it unlikely. What was the point in that case of requesting a decision in the first place?

Documents central to this affair remain classified, but available evidence suggests very strongly that Alexander would have postponed ordering the operation until he received an absolutely incontrovertible command to do so. Two months later he was to express great concern over the fate of a few hundred Cossacks who had been recaptured after the main Lienz handover. They were few in number, were all adult males, had been screened as undoubted Soviet citizens, and were presumably covered by whatever order authorised the return of the majority already sent back. Their case was weak indeed compared with that of the main body of Cossacks whose fate was being decided in May.

Despite all this, Alexander wrote privately to Sir Alan Brooke that 'So far I have refused to use force to repatriate Soviet citizens, although I suppose I am not strictly entitled to adopt this attitude—nevertheless, I shall continue with this policy unless I am orderd to do otherwise.

'I have already asked for a ruling on this matter, but have not yet got a reply. I hope you agree with my whole attitude but if you don't I hope you will let me know.'

At the same time (23 August) he wrote to the War Office, urging 'some modification of the Agreement which would allow these people to be treated as stateless people for the time being. The matter is urgent.'[81]

In August the Field-Marshal stuck to these delaying tactics so effectively that the Cossacks in question were not handed over so long as he was Supreme Allied Commander. And in May he had attempted to save Cossacks who included a multitude of women and children, as well as thousands of old émigrés whom it required no 'modification of the Yalta agreement' to save. It seems on the face of it inconceivable that he would not, without very good reason, have failed to apply his delaying tactic throughout.

As late as 22 May his Headquarters was still issuing orders that envisaged the return only of 'Soviet citizens . . . who can be handed over to Russians without use of force', accompanying this with an explicit reference to the accepted definition of what constituted Soviet citizenship.[82] As has been mentioned earlier, he understood and was strongly sympathetic to the cause of the White Armies whose generals were now his prisoners. He had fought on the same side as General Krasnov in 1919, when he had commanded the anti-Bolshevik Baltic *Landeswehr*. From the White Russian General Yudenitch he received in 1920 the Imperial Order of St. Anne with Swords, a decoration of which he was extremely proud.[83] About the end of May he was sent a moving appeal by General Krasnov, referring to their common struggle in 1920. His appeal of 17 May to the Combined Chiefs of Staff showed he felt he had not yet received such orders.

It seems probable, therefore, that after that he did receive instructions which anticipated the Chiefs of Staff's decision. On 20 May Winston Churchill began to show an interest in the matter. To the Deputy Secretary of the War Cabinet, General Ismay, he wrote:

> What is known about the number of Russians taken prisoner by the Germans and liberated by us? Can you discriminate between those who were merely workers and those who actually fought against us?
>
> Could I have a further report on the 45,000 Cossacks, of whom General Eisenhower speaks in his SCAF. 399. How did they come into their present plight? Did they fight against us?[84]

Clearly something had disquieted the Prime Minister in connection with the captured Cossacks and the degree of guilt to be attributed to Russians accused of having served the Germans. He was to express similar misgivings with greater force at Potsdam ten weeks later.

The information requested by Churchill took some time to prepare, and Ismay's reply did not arrive until 5 June, by which time most of the Cossacks had been disposed of. It was as a result largely irrelevant, and was in addition very inaccurate, whether intentionally or otherwise. The 45,000 Cossacks were described as 'primitive tribesmen' from the

Caucasus, belonging to the 15th Cavalry Corps, who had committed dreadful atrocities in Yugoslavia. In fact, well over half this number had been with Domanov in Italy, with whom also were all the Caucasians. No attempt was made to substantiate charges of 'murdering and pillaging'.[85] But this is of small account, as the reply came too late to influence any decision Churchill might have made.

The indications are that he had made a decision. On 26 May, Geoffrey McDermott of the Foreign Office wrote to Colonel C. R. Price, Military Assistant Secretary at the War Cabinet Offices:

> The Chiefs of Staff have invited the Foreign Office in consultation with the War Office to examine NAF 975 as a matter of urgency and to advise on the reply to be sent to Field Marshal Alexander ... Our views on the three categories whose presence in Southern Austria is an embarrassment to Field Marshal Alexander are as follows: (a) *Cossacks.* We agree with the JSM [Joint Staff Mission] that the Cossacks are covered by the Yalta agreement on the reciprocal repatriation of Soviet citizens and accordingly consider it essential that all of them who are Soviet citizens should be handed over to the Soviet authorities in pursuance of our general policy. If we did not do so in the case of these particular people it would be a breach of the agreement and might look like a change of policy in this matter to which the Soviet Government attach great importance and would be assumed by the Russians to indicate hostile intentions towards them. It might also have very unfortunate reactions upon the Russian treatment of our prisoners of war uncovered by them. We suggest that Field Marshal Alexander should make arrangements with Marshal Tolbukhin for the handing over of the Cossacks across the temporary occupational demarcation line.

As the proposed arrangements had already been effected a few days earlier, this suggestion may appear a trifle tardy. But two days later still, on 28 May, Colonel Phillimore of the War Office wrote to agree that:

> *Cossacks.* There can be no dispute that these should be dealt with in accordance with the Yalta agreement ... The telegrams from 15 Army Group showing that 5th Corps are in fact exchanging their Cossacks somewhat alters the position with regard to their transfer to SHAEF. We consider Sacmed [Alexander] should be told that the action of 5th Corps is approved and that all should be exchanged under the Yalta agreement, but that Marshal Tolbukhin should be pressed to exchange the British and Americans at the same time.[86]

At first sight these statements seem oddly irrelevant: the measures advocated had already been decided upon and were about to take place. They tell us, it is true, that neither the Foreign Office nor the

War Office had sent Alexander orders to act. But what was the point of the Foreign Office's presenting arguments for the adoption of a policy that was already in full process of being effected? I put this question to Geoffrey McDermott himself, who wrote back:

I was pretty junior at the time: a recently promoted First Secretary. I worked in the department, called Southern, which dealt with Austria among other countries, but not directly with the USSR.

My best guess is that F-M Alexander had been told, orally perhaps, by someone very important, such as Winston, to make the necessary arrangements for the repatriation . . . and in due course to go ahead. Then the conscientious Cabinet Offices asked for something on paper from the FO: you know how Whitehall works. Even a letter from a junior official, such as myself, would suffice for their records.

It is difficult to see what other explanation there could be. Why else should the Cabinet Offices require this Foreign Office confirmation? Neither the Foreign Office, the War Office nor the Combined Chiefs of Staff had sent Alexander any ruling. There remained only the Prime Minister. Faced with this problem at an earlier stage, Churchill had scrawled impatiently, 'We ought to get rid of them *all* as soon as possible . . .'[87] Was this his attitude now? This was after all the policy decided upon in the previous year, and it must have been hard to see just why Alexander was being so obstructive. There is no evidence that Churchill was informed of the presence of the White émigrés in Austria. It seems improbable that he would have consented to the unnecessary return of people whose cause he had once so warmly espoused. After all, it had been he who, back in 1921, had ruled firmly that 'No loyal [White] Russian can be sent back to Russia agst his will.'[88] It did not alter the matter if, in the misfortunes of exile, the émigrés took up new political attitudes. Churchill agreed to a request from a Russian General that his son, who was being threatened with repatriation to Vladivostock, should instead be allowed to settle in Britain. When a British official objected that the son was 'thoroughly unreliable and very anti-British', back came a telegram: 'We have given our promise and cannot go back upon it WSC.'[89]

What could have induced Churchill to intervene one cannot say. Harold Macmillan was British Minister-Resident in the Mediterranean Theatre. He was in direct and continual touch with the Prime Minister, with the principal duty of reporting on the political situation.[90] On 13 May he flew into Klagenfurt to confer with General Keightley and appraise the situation there. It was he who, as was shown earlier, urged on Keightley the speedy transfer of the Cossacks to the Soviets.

In his memoirs, Harold Macmillan refers briefly to the question of the Cossacks, which he had to consider during his visit to Keightley at Klagenfurt.

> Among the surrendering Germans there were about 40,000 Cossacks *and White Russians* [author's italics], with their wives and children. These were naturally claimed by the Russian commander, and we had no alternative but to surrender them. Nor indeed had we any means of dealing with them had we refused to do so. But it was a great grief to me that there was no other course open. At least we obtained in exchange some 2,000 British prisoners and wounded who were in the area and had been in German hands.[91]

Does the reference to 'White Russians' mean, as it seems it must, that Macmillan was well aware of the presence of the old émigrés amongst the Cossacks? He had certainly been long acquainted with the crucial distinction between old and new émigrés.[92]

The remarks in his memoirs are tantalisingly brief, but Mr. Macmillan has consistently declined to enlarge on them. To the historian it is frustrating to know that there are men living who must at one time have known the answers to the questions posed in this chapter. For example Toby Low (now Lord Aldington), who was Brigadier General Staff to the 5th Corps, was present at the Conference of 21 May, and issued the crucial Order of the same day. But he has informed the author that he can remember nothing of the extradition of the Cossacks. Whether we shall ever know the full story is questionable. Perhaps the mysterious File 383.7–14.1, discussed in the Postscript on p. 431, could throw some light on the problem.

12

The End of General Vlasov

On 28 January 1945 it was officially announced in Berlin that the Russian army commanded by General Vlasov was no longer part of the Wehrmacht, but an independent force under the orders of the KONR Government.[1] Hitherto, as was briefly outlined in Chapter One, the Vlasov 'Army' was a force existing on paper only, its 'General' a virtual prisoner. Although hundreds of thousands of Russians (as well as Ukrainian, Baltic, Caucasian, Tartar and other 'national' legions) were serving in the German army, it was as scattered units officered almost exclusively by Germans. General Vlasov could not issue an order to one platoon of an estimated 800,000 such Russians. The jealous refusal of Hitler and Himmler to accept Vlasov's assertion that 'only a Russian can beat a Russian' led them to look on Vlasov and his 'army' merely as a propaganda fiction useful for inducing Red Army desertions. To Rosenberg, Vlasov's unshakable determination to restore a united national Russia, purged of Bolshevism, was in direct opposition to his cherished policy of fragmenting Russia into its component parts. Of the Nazi leaders, only Goebbels was intelligent enough to realise (29 April 1943) that if 'we were pursuing or had pursued a somewhat cleverer policy in the East, we would certainly be further along there than we are.'[2]

Perhaps the most inveterate enemy of Vlasov was the Reichsführer SS, Heinrich Himmler. To Himmler, the idea that Germany should owe anything to, or require anything from, a subhuman Slav was totally repugnant. He made his feelings clear in public at a speech on 14 October 1943 at Bad Schachen:

> Herr Vlasov has begun to hold forth with the over-weening pride that is common to the Russian and the Slav. He has declared that Germany cannot conquer Russia, Russia can only be conquered by Russians. Observe, gentlemen, that this sentence is mortally dangerous . . .
>
> The morning, midday and evening prayer of the German Army ought

to be this. We have overcome the enemy, we, the German infantry have overcome every enemy in the world. If then some Russian comes along, some deserter who was perhaps, the day before yesterday a butcher's boy and yesterday a general, created by Stalin, who now delivers lectures with the insolence of the Slav and inserts a sentence that Russia will only be conquered by Russians; if then all this occurs, I must tell you something. The man shows what sort of swine he is by this sentence alone.

Such were Himmler's views in 1943. Less than a year later the same Himmler was to arrange a meeting with 'Herr General' Vlasov, at which he had to listen politely to sarcastic enquiries about the present position of the 'subhumans', and to a reminder that he, Vlasov, had commanded before his capture a Russian army which had inflicted serious defeats on the Germans in 1941. The meeting ended with Himmler's promising to assist Vlasov in taking command of a genuinely independent Russian army. The cause of this *volte-face* in Himmler's attitude is not far to seek. The eleven months' interval had seen the dramatic advances of the Allies in the West to eastern France and northern Italy, and in the East the Russians had entirely liberated their own country and were pressing irresistibly forwards into Poland and Rumania. Even so devoted a proponent of the idea of German racial superiority had to acknowledge that things were not quite what they had been. An outright military defeat of the Allies was an increasingly distant or—did he allow himself to think?—unattainable goal. There remained, it is true, the much advertised hope that the Western and Eastern Allies would fall out among themselves. But they showed no signs yet of doing so. The *Ostpolitiker* alone, whose views *Reichsheini* could safely deride in 1943, offered what appeared a realistic hope of upsetting at a stroke the balance of power. If Vlasov and his fellow-Russians were to appear in the field as an independent Russian army allied to Germany, then the war in the East could turn into a Russian civil war. This would be 1917 over again, with Vlasov playing the catspaw of the German General Staff, as Lenin had done for Ludendorff. A German-backed *coup* had forced Russia out of the war then, and it might do so again. Of course, the Russia that Vlasov aimed to restore might well be as great a menace to German ambitions as that of Stalin. But the Führer was a man of infinite genius, and on a Russia torn apart by internecine struggle he could impose a settlement that would make Brest-Litovsk seem magnanimous.

For many months factions in Himmler's entourage had been trying to interest him in different aspects of *Ostpolitik*. The Reichsführer saw nothing inconsistent with his detestation of Vlasov and his movement in using any people or methods to persuade Red Army soldiers to desert. But it was events in June and July of 1944—the Allied landings in

Normandy and the Red Army breakthrough in Poland following the
offensive launched on 20 June—that must have made Himmler think
again about the insolent 'butcher's boy'.

Amongst the more intelligent of his followers was a young SS
Standartenführer, Gunther d'Alquen. D'Alquen was editor of the SS
weekly journal, *Das Schwarze Korps*. He was also in charge of SS propaganda on the Eastern Front, and as such had come increasingly to
appreciate the importance of putting to advantage the hatred felt by so
many Russians for their barbarous régime. In the spring of 1944 d'Alquen
met Wilfried Strik-Strikfeldt, a Balt serving in the German Army who
was very close to Vlasov. Strikfeldt urged d'Alquen to employ Russian
Liberation Movement propaganda in his appeals to Soviet soldiers.
D'Alquen was impressed by Strikfeldt's arguments, and agreed to
launch such a propaganda assault on the southern front. Operation
'Skorpion' proved an unqualified success, and the flow of Red Army
deserters increased tenfold. D'Alquen became convinced of the truth of
Strikfeldt's reasoning, and agreed to sound out the SS leadership.
D'Alquen's eloquence, coupled with the catastrophic turn in the military
situation, bore fruit, and Himmler agreed to meet the man whom, nine
months before, he had reviled as a 'swine' and 'butcher-boy'.[3]

The meeting was arranged for the evening of 20 July.[4] But it was on
that day that Count Stauffenberg's bomb narrowly missed destroying
Hitler in the Wolf's Lair, and the generals' attempt to overthrow the
demented Führer was savagely crushed. It was not a day for meetings,
and Himmler had Vlasov informed that a postponement must take
place. The next day Dr. Erhard Kroeger, an SS Oberführer, held a
rendezvous with SS General Berger to discuss matters concerning the
Danish *Waffen SS*. At the end of their discussion, Berger divulged that
Himmler had deputed him (Berger) to sound out Vlasov in a preliminary conversation. Berger confessed he had little idea what Himmler
expected of him, and asked Kroeger, who was a Russian-speaking Balt,
to come along to advise and assist.

The meeting was held a couple of days later, and Berger (who had
already sounded out Vlasov once before)[5] was favourably impressed
with the Russian. He telephoned Himmler, recommending that Vlasov
be given facilities for putting his programme into action, and that Dr.
Kroeger be accorded the role of liaison officer between the Vlasov movement and the SS high command. Himmler agreed, and from now until
a few days before the end, Kroeger remained close to Vlasov, providing
the sole official link between the German authorities and the Vlasov
leadership.

Not long afterwards, Himmler announced that he was ready to meet

Vlasov in person. On 16 September Vlasov came to the Reichsführer SS's field headquarters at Rastenburg in East Prussia. Gunther d'Alquen and General Berger were present, also Dr. Kroeger, who interpreted, and who supplied the author with this account. Himmler was scrupulously polite, apologised for the delays in arranging the meeting, and listened with evident respect to the tall and impressive 'Russian de Gaulle'. So fascinated was Himmler by Vlasov's explanations of what he could accomplish if given a free hand, that he allowed the meeting to continue for six hours. By the end, Vlasov emerged to announce triumphantly to Strik-Strikfeldt that at long last they were on the road to attaining their goal. The Reichsführer SS had declared himself in favour of according the Russian Liberation Committee the status of an independent government, with the power to raise a real army from amongst the millions of Russians now in the Greater Reich.[6]

But high though the Russians' hopes appeared, realities were less happy. Given the unshakable alliance between the Western Allies and Stalin, the brilliant successes of the Red Army, and the corresponding decline in the fortune of German arms, it is questionable whether Vlasov's plans in their entirety could have come to fruition in 1944. But such was Nazi fanaticism that, even with Germany's enemies converging on her frontiers from east and west, her leaders still refused to accept in full the idea that their country could survive only with the help of a full-blown Russian ally.

Himmler's enthusiasm for Vlasov's projects was real enough. Dr. Kroeger, who spoke with both men frequently on the subject, stresses that the SS leader was intelligent enough to realise that only some new policy could save Germany from disaster. It could no longer be believed that the Wehrmacht unaided could overthrow Bolshevism, and if Vlasov could accomplish what he promised, then it was necessary to turn to him.

Goebbels, too, saw in support for Vlasov a realistic policy for Germany. But powerful interests were opposed to the proposed new strategy. Rosenberg saw in it a direct challenge to his cherished policy of splitting Russia amongst its component 'nationalities', and summoned Dr. Kroeger to demand an explanation. 'You must ask my chief, not me,' replied the Oberführer sardonically. 'Who is that?' asked Rosenberg. When Kroeger mentioned diffidently the dreaded name of Himmler, the Minister for Eastern Territories hastily dropped the subject.

Not to be fobbed off in this way, however, was the still omnipotent Führer. Though grudgingly prepared to allow the hard-pressed Wehrmacht to be supplemented at last by a few thousand Russian mercenaries, Hitler would never contemplate the creation of a real army. Such a newcomer would, he was convinced, prove a cuckoo in the nest. Consequently, Himmler's intentions were, from the outset, hamstrung by active or potential hostility from Hitler and his immediate advisers, and in a telegram to Vlasov he made reference to the raising of a force strictly limited to three divisions, where Vlasov had hoped for ten. He referred to a Russian Liberation Committee, with the inference that such a body would not necessarily speak for all the Russian 'nationalities'.

Still, it was a time to be grateful for small mercies. Backed by his supporters in the SS and Wehrmacht, Vlasov set about the task of establishing his new 'government' and levying his 'army'. To many influential Germans, use of the 'Vlasov card' appeared to offer greater and more realistic hopes than the much-vaunted secret weapons. Himmler, Goebbels, Göring and Ribbentrop all sought him out. The various 'national committees', fostered by Rosenberg, representing the Balts, Ukrainians, Georgians and other minority peoples of Russia, were urged to unite now under the new leadership: the charismatic figure of Vlasov himself; Sergei Buniachenko, an independent-minded and temperamental Ukrainian; Malyshkin and Trukhin, former Red Army officers, and before that subalterns of the Tsar; Vladimir Boyarsky, who had commanded a Soviet Guards Division. The most intriguing character of them all was Georgi Zhilenkov. One of that army of homeless children (*bezprizorni*) orphaned after the Bolshevik *Putsch*, he had brought himself up in the slums of Moscow. He had joined the Communists and risen to high rank as a *politruk* in the Party at Moscow. Captured by the Germans, he became in turn an ardent supporter of the cause of Russian liberation. His supple mind soon bringing him to the fore, he acted as unofficial 'propaganda minister' to the Vlasov movement.[7]

The intricate manoeuvres necessary to advance the cause came to a tragic end. The leaders were by no means naïvely optimistic; as the winter drew on and the cause of the Allies was clearly waxing, Vlasov, Buniachenko and others of the movement sought increasing solace in the bottle.

At last, on 14 November 1944, the moment arrived for what was hoped to be the inauguration of the new Russian national movement, the KONR (the Committee for the Liberation of the Peoples of Russia). Five hundred delegates, representing the minority races as well as the Great Russians, assembled in Prague. At 3 o'clock in the afternooon, in the Spanish Hall of the Hradschin Palace, amidst scenes of enthusiastic rejoicing, the Manifesto of the KONR was proclaimed. This significant document set out proposals for the overthrow of the Bolshevik dictatorship, and the 'setting up of a new, free democratic order'.

On the subject of their relations with Germany, the KONR welcomed 'aid from Germany, always provided that such aid is consistent with the honour and independence of our Homeland. This aid, at the moment, provides the only practical possibility of armed struggle against the Stalinist clique.' National Socialism, its doctrines and leader, were not even mentioned, and obnoxious tenets such as anti-semitism or aggression based on supposed racial superiority, were in no way endorsed. The document was a call to freedom.

Not only in Germany and Russia were Russians moved by news of the Prague Manifesto. Within an hour of the centre of Paris lay Camp Beauregard, where many thousands of the Russians liberated in France were gathered. One of the inmates, a young man whose father had been 'taken away' and who himself had been forced to subsist as a child scavenger in Stalin's Russia, recalled how his fellows received the news of the Manifesto. Crowded round a portable radio, they listened with rising hope and enthusiasm to phrases like 'abolition of forced labour', 'abolition of collective farms', 'inviolability of private property accruing from work'—*spoken in Russian*.[8] Whatever their hopes, the inhabitants of Camp Beauregard were shortly to be shipped back to the Soviet Union. But even in the camps of GULAG, in Vorkuta and Kamyshlag, the former Vlasov soldiers continued to refer with pride to the ideals expressed in the Prague Manifesto. They 'naturally looked upon themselves as a kind of élite among political prisoners', were proud of their unsuccessful struggle for freedom, and regarded with contempt their fellows who had espoused the (to them) slavish doctrines of Marx.[9]

But the Manifesto of 14 November was promulgated in a dark hour, and by the end of 1944, the possibility of any overthrow of the Soviet régime from without was highly improbable. One cannot picture a mutiny in the Red Army on a sufficient scale to overthrow the Party oligarchy. The intoxication of military success, the widespread delusion that victory would bring about far-reaching mitigation of Bolshevik harshness—these considerations are unlikely to have been outweighed by the promise of freedom deriving from such a source as that of the Vlasov movement—if indeed the ordinary Russian ever heard of it. On the contrary, the crimes committed by the Germans during the Occupation had left an indelible mark on Russian consciousness, and any stream emanating from such a fount must be irrevocably suspect and tainted.

In any case, the question of what could have been accomplished by an unfettered Russian freedom movement must remain academic. For even at this late hour the German authorities could not be persuaded to play the Vlasov card without disastrous second thoughts. Twenty-four hours before the Prague meeting, permission was suddenly withdrawn by Berlin for the proposed attendance of Ministers of the Reich and

members of the Diplomatic Corps. On 27 January following, at a Headquarters conference, Hitler delivered himself of a virulent diatribe
against Vlasov, which went on to embrace von Pannwitz's Cossacks as
well. But already the ailing leader was living in a world of fantasy, and
seems to have been unaware of much of what was happening. The very
next day came the declaration of the sovereignty of the KONR
'government'.

The most urgent requirement of the KONR was not an illusory
independence, nor yet the power to issue proclamations or propaganda.
What was needed was a separate power base: the authority to raise
troops. And despite all the crippling reservations imposed by the German
High Command, the winter of 1944-5 saw (for the first time since 1921)
the emergence of fully-fledged Russian military units taking the field
against the Red Army. In addition, there existed for a few short months
a miniature free Russian state. With the increasing devastation of Berlin,
the KONR 'Government' was moved from Dahlem to Karlsbad in
Bohemia, whilst Vlasov's 'general staff' removed to Heuberg. The propaganda and training school for officers was transferred from Dabendorf
to Schloss Gieshübel in the Sudetenland. Negotiations were entered into
with other Russian units already operative, and by the end of the war
von Pannwitz's and Domanov's Cossacks, and Rogozhin's Serbian
Defence Corps, had entered into formal adhesion to the KONR. Vlasov
was less fortunate with the Ukrainians, however. Whilst representatives
of some elements were present at the Prague meeting, the important
Galician Division under General Shandruk retained its independence.[10]

All this, of course, was merely the shadow of power, and it was the
raising of a real KONR army that was foremost amongst Vlasov's aims.
At Münsingen in Württemberg, Buniachenko was placed in charge of
the first of the three divisions authorised by the cautious Himmler. The
nucleus was formed from 5,000 men formerly commanded by the
villainous Bronislav Kaminsky in Poland, and a second grouping late of
a *Waffen SS* White Russian Division ('Ruthenia'). To these were added
men recruited from prisoners of war and *Ostarbeiter* in Germany. A 2nd
Division was undergoing recruitment and training under General Zverev
at nearby Heuberg. Finally, an air corps (as yet without aircraft) was
being raised under the command of Vladimir Maltsev, and under the
general supervision of General Aschenbrenner, former German Air
Attaché in Moscow.[11]

The nebulous character of all these preparations struck Dr. Kroeger
when he accompanied Maltsev and Aschenbrenner on a visit to Göring
at Karinhall. The purpose of their mission was to receive from the
Reischsmarschal Maltsev's commission as General. (Despite the 'sove-

reignty' of the KONR, Vlasov could not award promotions above the rank of colonel without German confirmation.) During conversation following the brief ceremony, Göring confessed that, though he felt he had a fair appreciation of the English, French and Americans, neither he nor his colleagues had ever really understood the true nature of Russia and the Russians. That the man who for so long had been second in the Reich should admit as much at this late hour struck Dr. Kroeger as rather macabre. Still more so was an occasional faint tremor that shook the furniture and rattled the windows, forming an accompaniment to the discussion. It was the sound of Zhukov's artillery, already on the west bank of the Oder.

But even these restricted measures were limited further by fears of provoking Hitler into repeating his savage repression of 1943. Though Buniachenko and Zverev were proceeding with the raising of their Divisions, arms and equipment were not forthcoming, and there was no indication of their early entry into the field. At last General Köstring, who as Inspector of Eastern Troops held ultimate responsibility for the federate Russians, decided that the only way to convince the High Command and Himmler of their efficacy was to attempt a trial venture in combat.

Buniachenko declined to allow any unit of his to take part until training and equipment were completed. Instead, a select group of volunteers was drawn from Russians stationed at Stettin. Commanded by two White émigrés, Colonel Sakharov and Count Lamsdorff, they distinguished themselves in an attack on a fortified bridgehead at Neulowin on the Oder. Still more impressive in Köstring's, and subsequently Himmler's, view was the crossing over of 100 Red Army deserters. What might not be the effect if this experiment were to be repeated on a larger scale? Of course, it was three years too late for such hopes to be realised. But it is still a fact of considerable significance that, even when Germany's survival could only be a matter of weeks, in Pomerania and Yugoslavia anti-Communist Russian units could still attract sizable bodies of deserters.[12]

Himmler was greatly impressed by this achievement, and sent a telegram to Vlasov to say so. The principal German officer concerned with raising the Russian units, Heinz Herre, visited Himmler's headquarters on 23 February, and obtained the Reichsführer SS's consent to the employment of KONR troops on the Eastern Front. Herre returned triumphing, but the sturdy Buniachenko, whose Division was chosen for the task, refused as a Russian general officer to take such an order from any but his own commander-in-chief. Dr. Kroeger remembers Buniachenko as a brave and able soldier, but one whom the Germans found difficult to manage. His experiences since his capture in 1942 (he had been before that on Timoshenko's staff) had made him justifiably cynical, and the apparent downfall of the KONR's ally, Germany, understandably brought moments of despair in which he sought consolation in drink.

Vlasov's authority having been granted, the 1st Division KONR set off as planned. The Wehrmacht could supply it with no motorised transport, and Allied bombing had put the railway line between Ulm and Nuremberg out of action. For the first 120 miles of its journey the Division marched on foot with all its equipment. On the way they were joined at intervals by groups of Russian *Ostarbeiter* and prisoners of war. In this way they had increased their number by some 3,000 by the time they reached Nuremberg on 19 March.[13]

Whilst the operation of entrainment was in process, Buniachenko established his headquarters at the nearby village of Herzogen-Aurach. It was there that an unfortunate incident took place. General Vlasov, accompanied as usual by Dr. Kroeger, arrived to see the troops off to the front. It was eight o'clock in the morning, and the General and the Oberführer presented themselves unannounced. A clearly embarrassed adjutant explained that Buniachenko could not be seen, as he was suffering from a raging toothache. When they persisted, he seemed prepared to obstruct their path physically, but the giant Vlasov (he was six foot five inches in height) thrust him to one side and strode into the room. There sat General Buniachenko and his Chief of Staff, hopelessly drunk and lolling in their chairs before a table covered with vodka bottles and half-filled glasses. Their only companions were two junior officers and a couple of half-dressed girls of unmilitary appearance. As Buniachenko was supposed at that moment to be directing the entrainment of the Division, Vlasov was understandably angry. He probably feared also that Dr. Kroeger would report this example of Russian disorderliness to Berger or Himmler. From that day forward, Kroeger received the impression that he was regarded with the greatest dislike by Buniachenko.

However, the troops set off as planned, and by 26 March the last units had arrived at the training camp at Lieberose, north of Cottbus. The arrival of this unexpected reinforcement was received with some surprise by the German commander of the Vistula Army Group, General Heinrici, and at first he could think of no suitable task for their employment. But eventually it was decided to blood them in an attack on a Red Army bridgehead at Erlenhof, south of Frankfurt-on-Oder. An abortive attack had already been launched on the position, which was known to have been heavily fortified in consequence. The task was formidable, but Buniachenko agreed to the attempt provided sufficient artillery support were supplied. The onslaught itself was delivered at five in the morning on 14 April. The result was a disaster. Lacking the stipulated effective bombardment, still more air support, the KONR men hurled themselves in waves on to the heavily entrenched and wired Soviet position. Raked by murderous flanking fire, Buniachenko's men fought bitterly for four hours, until their commander foresaw the destruction of his entire Division to no purpose, and ordered a withdrawal.

Back at Lieberose, the 1st Division licked its wounds whilst Buniachenko and his staff considered what next to do. The collapse of their German allies was imminent, and fighting under the conditions accorded them was clearly purposeless from any viewpoint. Vlasov and his senior officers had for some time considered this exigency, which indeed stared them in the face. One thing was clear: to remain in Germany itself was to invite certain disaster. Within days the junction of the American and Russian armies must take place, and even if the anticipated rupture between the Allies occurred, it would be too late for KONR units, crushed between colliding boulders. Only in the south-east did there seem to lie any prospect of hope. The Russians had still to advance up the Danube and into Bohemia. Nationalist movements in Czechoslovakia, Hungary and Yugoslavia were bitterly opposed to, and in some cases still fighting, Soviet domination of their countries, whilst in Greece British troops had crushed a Communist attempt to take over the country. There was much talk in KONR circles of the creation of a 'Third Force' from amongst these disparate but unshakably anti-Communist bodies.

And, of course, there were the Cossacks. Von Pannwitz, Domanov and Krasnov had accepted the incorporation of their units into the KONR. Dr. Kroeger attended a grand dinner at the Hotel Kaiserhof in Berlin, at which representatives of the Cossacks and the KONR were present. Despite the unfavourable situation, he recalls that all were buoyed up by a revived feeling of enthusiasm and hope.

In any case any prospect of survival, however remote, lay in the south. Buniachenko, displaying—however belatedly—the brilliant side of his highly erratic character, now began his extraordinary march, which has fairly been compared with that of Xenophon. For 300 miles the 1st Division KONR marched southwards. On their left flank lay the advancing Red Army; in addition they had to frustrate the urgent efforts of the German Central Army Group to force them back to the Front. At one point the brutal Field Marshal Schörner demanded the surrender of the disobedient Buniachenko for immediate execution. The Russian at once drew up his force in a defensive 'hedgehog' position, ready to fight to the last man. But even Schörner had to face the realities of the situation (a few days later he was a prisoner of the Americans), and Buniachenko

continued his march unmolested. Passing east of Dresden by Hoyers-
werda and Radeberg, the Russians entered Czechoslovakia south of Bad
Schandau. On 29 April the 1st Division KONR Headquarters was at
Kosojedy, north of Prague. Safe for the moment behind the Erzgebirger
Mountains, Buniachenko and his 25,000 men could pause and consider
their next move.

There were now two Russian units operating in Bohemia. On 19
April the KONR training camps at Münsingen and Heuberg had had to
be evacuated in face of the advancing US 7th Army. Zverev's 2nd
KONR Division, together with Maltsev's Air Corps and other reserve
units (a body of some 22,000 men) marched to Fürstenfeldbruck, west of
Munich. There they entrained for Linz, and from there moved north,
converging on Prague from the south. By 4 May Zverev's troops were
strung out on the Prague road between Budweis and Straknitz. The
nearest enemy troops were not the Red Army, still far to the east in
Slovenia, but General Patton's US 3rd Army, which was already on the
frontiers of Bohemia. Unaware that in a secret agreement the Western
Allies had already conceded the whole of Czechoslovakia to the Soviets,
the KONR general staff imagined that Bohemia might pass under
American control.

Now the three divisions and staff of the KONR were beginning to
fragment into their separate entities. The bubble plans for a junction
with the Cossacks or anti-Communist Yugoslavs were collapsing in face
of the swiftly deteriorating military situation, and the different units of
KONR realised they must make what terms they could individually,
whilst any freedom of decision remained. It began to be realised that all
that was left was to attempt negotiations for surrender to the Americans;
with, it was hoped, suitable guarantees.

The first such attempt was made by General Aschenbrenner, the Luftwaffe attaché to Maltsev's Air Corps. At the end of March, in Prague,
Aschenbrenner had struck up an acquaintanceship with an enterprising
academic, Theodor Oberländer. Oberländer had a unique knowledge
of Russian affairs. In the late 1920s and early 1930s he had visited Russia in
his capacity as Professor of Agriculture at Königsberg. There he had
conferred with Bukharin (whose capacities he admired) at Karl Radek's
villa outside Moscow. As he could not take the roubles so earned out of
the country, he had spent them on two successive trips to Georgia. Later,
when Operation 'Barbarossa' was being planned, the intimate knowledge he had gained drew him to the attention of the Abwehr. He
started the invasion attached to a German-officered Ukrainian battalion,
Nachtigall; and then, when in 1942 the Germans reached the Caucasus,
his earlier visits to Georgia earned him the command of an anti-Soviet

mountaineer unit. This body of some 1,100 men, initially recruited from captured Caucasians in PoW camps, was swelled by a further 1,600 desertions from Red Army units opposed to them. But on 22 June 1943, exactly two years after the invasion, Oberländer circulated widely in military circles a memorandum on German policy in Russia. Horrified by the blindness of the authorities in antagonising by pointless cruelties people who had initially welcomed the Germans as deliverers, he urged in ten well-argued propositions (aptly entitled *Alliance or Exploitation*) the adoption before it was too late of a more humane and intelligent policy. This bold move aroused fury in high places: Keitel had him dismissed from his command, whilst Himmler made efforts to have him placed in a concentration camp. From this fate he was only saved by the intervention of Staatsminister Frank in Prague. Finally, he was brought out of this semi-retirement to act as the last commandant of the KONR officers' training establishment, when it was evacuated from Dabendorf to the Sudetenland.[14]

Oberländer was in Prague when Aschenbrenner sought him out and brought him to Marienbad. There he met Maltsev and other officers of the KONR Air Corps, who were clearly extremely worried about their situation. During the discussion which followed, Oberländer agreed with those who urged the policy of surrender to the Americans. He was convinced that the only alternative was to fall into the hands of the Soviets, which was unthinkable. Aschenbrenner turned to him and asked if he could speak English. When he said yes, the General ventured the question: would he go as emissary to the Americans to open negotiations for the surrender of the Air Corps? Oberländer agreed, and set off next day with a letter from Aschenbrenner concealed in his shoe. The whole proceeding had to be kept a profound secret, for there was not only the fear that Dr. Kroeger might report the transaction to his SS superiors, but also that front-line SS units might stop Oberländer and visit summary judgment on the 'traitor'.

Armed only with a pistol, he crossed through the front line and came to where the Duke of Coburg was in residence at his castle. Here Oberländer waited three days until American tanks came nosing their way eastwards on either side of the village. He sought out an American officer, Major Stein, and gave himself up, explaining that he wished to see the general officer commanding. Stein passed him up the line of command, and the next day (24 April) he was taken to a conference room. On the walls operational maps had been hastily covered over, and Oberländer found himself being interrogated by General Kennedy and six colonels. On being asked what was the purpose of his mission, he explained that he wished to negotiate the surrender of Maltsev's Air

Corps. The only condition, he replied to an enquiry, was that they should not be handed over to the Soviets. In some puzzlement, the General asked whether these Russians were the allies of Germany or of the United States. Oberländer explained that they formed a section of Vlasov's anti-Communist army. They had never fought against the Americans, but if attacked they would naturally resist and a number of Americans would inevitably die unnecessarily. The General declared that he would certainly like if possible to avoid that contingency, but to settle anything he would have to meet the Russians' commanding officer.

Oberländer agreed, and was guided to the most advanced American post. From there he made his way through Furth im Wald back to the ROA Air Corps Headquarters. Before reaching Aschenbrenner and Maltsev at Spitzberg he was stopped by SS units, but managed to bluff his way through. Explaining the success so far of his mission, he led Aschenbrenner back to General Kennedy's headquarters at Bodenwöhr. The staff car with a white flag in which they travelled made its perilous journey by night along roads broken up by anti-tank obstructions. At Bodenwöhr Aschenbrenner conferred long and earnestly with General Kennedy. The Luftwaffe General was a man of impressive mien, one who at once inspired confidence. With his dignified yet sympathetic personality he clearly established a *rapport* with Kennedy, who displayed remarkable interest in the KONR. Nor was he ill-informed himself, as Oberländer discovered to his surprise. As proof of the envoy's identity he had demanded of the Professor a specimen signature. This was then verified by comparison with a copy of Oberländer's signed memorandum of 22 June 1943! As this had been widely circulated amongst senior Wehrmacht commanders, the US 3rd Army had doubtless acquired a copy amongst captured documents in France or Germany. That the Army staff was extremely interested in what the former Red Air Force Colonel Maltsev would have to reveal about conditions in the USSR was evidenced by an order seen by Oberländer, which was signed by General Patton himself.

At last Kennedy declared himself satisfied with the proposition. Giving his word that surrendered personnel would not be handed over to the Soviets, he arranged for Maltsev's Air Corps to come in under white flags and be disarmed. At Oberländer's suggestion, they were then to march to their old depôt at Münsingen, being fed and guarded *en route* by the American authorities. That night Aschenbrenner spent anguished hours wondering whether the measure now agreed on was wise and honourable. But Oberländer, convinced there was no alternative, reassured him, and next day the General returned to Spitzberg and informed Maltsev of what was planned.

In this way, as Professor Oberländer today points out, 8,000 men were saved in four days. For there is evidence that Kennedy honoured his agreement, presumably under the powerful protection of General Patton, and that most if not all of Maltsev's men found a refuge in the West. Confirmation of this was provided in rather a remarkable way. Ten years later Oberländer paid an official visit to Washington in his capacity of Federal Minister for Refugees. There he and his wife received an unexpected invitation to a hotel reception, where they found awaiting them a party of former officers of the KONR Air Corps. During the course of the resultant reunion, they informed him that the Americans had indeed honoured their word, and Maltsev's men had eventually been freed. Again, in 1974 Oberländer was staying at the Washington Hilton on another visit, when he was approached by a man who invited him to dine. This man, a Georgian, had also been one of Maltsev's men, and assured Oberländer that by his action in 1945 he had saved all their lives.

All, that is, save one. Maltsev himself was separated from his followers and taken first to Belgium, then to the United States. A year later, in May 1946, he was handed over to the Soviet authorities. His execution by hanging was announced shortly afterwards by the Military Collegium of the Supreme Soviet.[15] Regrettable though it is that such an exception was allowed, it seems fair to concur with Professor Oberländer in bestowing honour on the memory of General Kennedy for the exceptional stance he adopted. It has been suggested that the real heroes of the tragedy of the repatriation operations were a lady who saved one Russian and an officer who declined to form a judgment on the actions of former Vlasov men,[16] but surely something must be said for an American general who saved eight thousand people.

Whilst Theodor Oberländer was waiting at Bodenwöhr for his interview with General Kennedy, General Aschenbrenner had accompanied Vlasov and other members of the KONR staff on a visit to the home of a German sympathiser on the Austrian border. The mood was one of pessimism; all the hopes for a free Russia cherished for so long were slipping away with the speed of the last sands in an hour-glass. All were now agreed that a surrender to the Western Allies had become imperative. But how to make contact? Vlasov had already sent a member of the KONR Committee, Yuri Zherebkov, on an unsuccessful attempt to negotiate through the International Red Cross in Geneva.[17] Aschenbrenner had as yet no news of Oberländer. Would another attempt prove successful? There were few alternatives, and a new mission was determined on.

This time it was General Vasily Malyshkin who was chosen. A gentle, cultured man, he had been arrested and tortured by the NKVD at the time of the Tukhachevsky purge. He was hastily returned to the Red Army when the Germans invaded and the Bolshevik régime splintered and nearly cracked. Then he had been captured by the Germans, imprisoned under terrible conditions in a PoW camp, and finally, in 1942, succumbed to the charm and inspiration of Vlasov and joined his movement. Accompanied by the faithful Strik-Strikfeldt, he was to seek out the nearest American commander. Dr. Kroeger provided them with passes to protect them from interference by front-line SS units.

Strik-Strikfeldt (as he has written in his memoirs) bade a painful farewell to the leader he admired and loved. Vlasov was nearly at the end of his tether. But whilst he lamented the destruction of all their brave hopes, he declared resolutely that despite this perhaps inevitable end no other course would have been consistent with honour. He pointed out that, if he was a traitor for seeking foreign aid to rid his country of oppression, then so in their day were George Washington and Benjamin Franklin.

'I lost,' he continued, 'so I remain a traitor until such time as in Russia freedom comes before bogus Soviet patriotism. As I told you, I do not believe in help from the Americans. We have nothing to offer. We are not a power factor; but to have trodden on our Russian hopes for freedom and for human worth, out of ignorance and opportunism, is something that Americans, Englishmen, Frenchmen, and perhaps Germans too, will one day bitterly regret.'

At Nesselwang on the Austrian border Malyshkin and Strik-Strikfeldt encountered troops of the US 7th Army. On explaining the nature of their mission, they were blindfolded and taken in jeeps to the Headquarters of the GOC, General Patch. Patch, like Kennedy, was greatly intrigued by the KONR representative's story; he listened attentively to a long and impassioned speech by Malyshkin (an interpreter was present). In it the latter explained movingly the story of the Bolshevik usurpation of power in 1917, the subsequent cruelties perpetrated under the successive tyrants Lenin and Stalin, and finally the struggle from 1941 onwards to overthrow the power of the barbarians. Of course Hitler was an unpalatable and treacherous ally, but what choice had they? In 1919 they had been happy to accept assistance from the British and Americans. But they had made peace with the Bolsheviks and could no longer offer anything to millions in Russia struggling for freedom and justice. Hitler was probably the last ally they would have chosen freely; but where, in 1941, was their freedom of choice?

General Patch, impressed and moved, heard Malyshkin out. In answer to the Russian's appeal for asylum for all ranks of the KONR, he replied: 'Unfortunately what you ask is right outside my competence as army commander; but I promise to pass your request to General Eisenhower. I will willingly do my best.'

Next day at a further interview Patch declared that he would accept the surrender of the Russian divisions.

'Does this mean, General, that the Russians will be treated according to the provisions of the Geneva Convention?' interposed Strik-Strikfeldt. General Patch did not give a direct reply to this, only emphasising 'that they will be treated in strict accordance with the regulations in force regarding German prisoners of war'. He concluded the interview on a more cordial note. 'As general of the American Army I regret that this is all I can tell you. Speaking personally I must express my very great regret at having to do so. I understand your point of view and I want to assure you of my personal respect. You will understand that I am a soldier.'

As members of a delegation, Malyshkin and Strik-Strikfeldt should have been permitted to return across the lines. But whether intentionally or otherwise they were detained for further days until, on 8 May, they were informed of the German surrender and that in consequence they were no longer delegates but prisoners of war.[18]

In the absence of any reply from the emissaries, Vlasov and his generals continued to chase a succession of schemes during the last despairing convulsions of the KONR. In early May, Vlasov's Headquarters was at the village of Kosojedi, north of Prague. There Dr. Kroeger noticed that for the first time a number of the Russians were beginning to look askance at their German colleagues. That something was in the air was clear, though whether it amounted to more than frictions natural to men in such a predicament remained to be seen.

About 4 May Vlasov was faced with evidence of a widening crack in the Russo-German alliance. With Dr. Kroeger, he had travelled to the Panzer General Fritz Hoth's Headquarters in the Erzgebirger Mountains, on an abortive expedition to see if further armed resistance were possible. On the way they had passed a German outpost commanded by a young lieutenant. Returning, they found that the post had been attacked by mutinous Russian troops, and the officer was dead. General Vlasov, like Krasnov at Mauthen a day or so later, was horrified at this treacherous attack on the troops of a country that was still their ally. He declared that if his troops could tarnish their honour in this way, he might as well shoot himself.

Back at Headquarters, Vlasov received a visit from General Buniachenko. The details of the conference that followed Dr. Kroeger had later from some of Buniachenko's aides; he himself knew nothing of it at the time. Buniachenko told Vlasov that he had opened negotiations with Czech Nationalists. He had become convinced that their sole hope now lay in severing their fatal connection with the defeated Germans. If they were to strike a blow before it was too late to help the Czechs re-establish their state, then perhaps the new Czech Government would grant asylum to their fellow-Slavs of the KONR. To this argument Vlasov replied vigorously that he regarded it as wholly dishonourable and impracticable. Whatever the blunders and cruelties of Nazi policy in the past, German soldiers had acted as faithful allies, and it would be an act of despicable treachery to attack them at this of all moments. In any case, the Red Army would shortly be in Prague, when the whole exercise would have been in vain. Buniachenko listened unconvinced; the Germans had consistently hindered or exploited Russian efforts to free their country; their policy had been based entirely on opportunism, and the KONR commanders' prime duty was to take any actions likely to preserve the lives of their men. The two separated, neither having altered his opinion.

At the same time, on 5 or 6 May, Dr. Kroeger left Kosojedi to visit Reichstadthalter Frank in Prague to discuss the situation. He never saw Vlasov again. A day or so after his arrival, Kroeger and Frank found themselves virtual prisoners in the Hradschin Palace. Resistance groups had taken to the streets, proclaiming the restoration of the Czech state. In the virtual absence of any German garrison, they were able to claim control of almost the entire city. But this temporary success only revealed the impotence of the brave but ill-armed Czechs. Determined not to incur the reproaches poured by Hitler on their defeated predecessors of 1918, SS units stormed into the city. Germany might be beaten, but it was the duty of the SS to fight to the last man. Greatly alarmed by this setback, the Czech leaders appealed to Buniachenko to honour the commitments he had made.[19]

Buniachenko was delighted at the opportunity afforded to display his repudiation of the German cause, whilst earning the gratitude (as he hoped) of the Czechs. The 1st Division KONR was quartered around Beroun, a few miles out of Prague on the Pilsen road. Buniachenko at once gave instructions to march on the capital; at the same time orders were despatched to General Zverev to bring up the 2nd Division from the south. Without waiting for news of Zverev's reaction, the 25,000 well-armed men of the 1st Division battered their way into Prague. After fierce fighting they seized the aerodrome, radio-station and other strong-points, and by the evening the Russians and Czechs controlled the city. Two Red Army Divisions were approaching from the east, but, perhaps recalling the Soviet betrayal of Warsaw in the previous year, the inhabitants displayed fervent gratitude to their immediate deliverers.

Alternate broadcasts in Russian and Czech proclaimed the creation of a pan-Slavic state, in which both peoples would find a home.

Meanwhile, in the beleaguered Hradschin Palace, Frank and Kroeger learned from surviving German posts on the outskirts of the city that armed bodies of Communist Czechs were beginning to appear in the streets with red flags. Their triumph was near, and the exhilaration of the deliverance of Prague was followed for Buniachenko by a speedy realisation of the grim realities ahead as the Red Army approached.

Now came the news of the unconditional surrender of Germany; Buniachenko requested and received authority from the provisional (patriotic) Czech Government for his Division to evacuate the city westwards. Fearful of losing such choice victims, the Communists attempted to encircle Prague and prevent their egress. In this confused state of affairs the KONR men found themselves once again allied with Germans similarly trying to avoid capture by the Red Army, and with the aid of two companies of SS *Panzerjager* troops they smashed their way through the cordon. On 9 May the 1st Division was back at Beroun. Inadvertently, by preventing a clash between the SS and the Red Army, they had saved the city of Prague from becoming a battlefield.[20]

Meanwhile, what of Vlasov himself and Zverev's 2nd KONR Division? In the latter days of April, Zverev had marched his men north from Linz towards Prague. With him was Feodor Trukhin, Vlasov's Chief of Staff. Neither knew of Buniachenko's plan to aid the Czechs, and on 5 May they had opened negotiations for surrender to the Americans. They were given thirty-six hours in which to come over and lay down their arms. On receiving this news, Trukhin sent General Boyarsky to inform Vlasov and Buniachenko of their proposed capitulation, and to urge them to do the same before it was too late. Trukhin waited; no reply came, and the Americans' deadline was drawing nearer. Trukhin decided to go north himself. Accompanied by another general and his adjutant, Romashkin, he reached the little town of Przibram. They had not troubled to take defensive precautions, as the Czechs had always been amicable towards the Russians. But they had walked into a trap.

A Red Army captain had set up a partisan unit in Przibram, which seized the KONR generals one by one as they thought to pass through. Trukhin learned that Boyarsky had been similarly captured, and hanged on the spot. Trukhin himself was despatched to Moscow, whilst the general accompanying him was shot out of hand. Into the same neat snare fell yet another general, who had been sent to discover the whereabouts of Trukhin. All this was discovered by a captain of the 2nd Division, who arrived with his unit in Przibram and by chance found Trukhin's adjutant imprisoned there.

Not only had this succession of officers disappeared, but also the commander himself could not be contacted. General Zverev and his advance units were far off at Kaplitz, and had sunk into a despairing lassitude which is so often the refuge of Russians overwhelmed by Fate. The senior remaining commander, General Meandrov, felt he dared not exceed the time limit set by the Americans, and marched all available units of the 2nd Division across the line to be interned. Zverev remained in a state of melancholy inertia. His mistress committed suicide, and he refused to leave her body. Eventually he and those with him were seized by the Soviets, and he was sent to join Trukhin in Moscow. Only one of the regiments with him managed to escape: on the initiative of its officers, it marched westwards in time to join Meandrov.

Meanwhile General Vlasov and a party of his followers had set off towards Pilsen, with the intention likewise of surrendering to the Americans. One of these followers was Ivan Kononov, colonel of one of von Pannwitz's regiments. He had been conducting negotiations for a junction of the Cossack and KONR units. But now came the news of the German surrender, and he bade farewell, declaring he must rejoin his men in the south. Later that evening Vlasov and his party reached the nearest American outposts. A friendly major escorted them into Pilsen, where a cordial welcome was extended by the Colonel commanding. He imagined he was receiving a delegation from the Red Army, being sublimely unaware that a Russian freedom army was in existence. The misunderstanding was soon cleared up; next morning Vlasov was brought before a general, who explained that he had not the authority to provide any guarantee that they would not be handed over to the Soviets. If he and Buniachenko's Division were prepared to surrender unconditionally, then the Americans could receive them: but not otherwise.

Whilst Vlasov was pondering what course to take, another American officer appeared, who informed him that Buniachenko's Division had arrived not far off, at Schlüsselburg. He suggested that Vlasov should join them. He also enquired whether the General had enough petrol for his car. There were indications that he was hinting that an escape could be connived at. This was not the only time that a chivalrous American officer was to show compassion in this way, but on Vlasov had descended an apathetic despair. The cause of Russian freedom was now lost for who knew how long? A generation, two? His personal fate could be of no further consequence. He agreed to go to Schlüsselburg.

The Americans conducted him and his party back to the trucks. When they appeared in the street, an enthusiastic crowd of Czechs began to gather, pressing flowers and congratulations on the saviour of their beloved Prague. His face expressionless and his gaze staring straight ahead, Vlasov took his seat in a truck and waited. The column set off, arriving at nightfall in Schlüsselburg. The American garrison was quartered in a castle on the edge of the town, and there the little cavalcade drew up. On the warm evening air were borne the sounds of shouts and singing: Buniachenko's forces were camped in nearby fields.

Vlasov and his companions were kept waiting in the lorries a little while, and were then asked inside. There, in one of the main rooms of the castle, they were brought before the Town Major, a Captain Donaghue. Donaghue gazed with interest at his guest, and then asked him how he had come to fight against his own country. When his interpreter put the question to him, Vlasov replied in a dull voice that he could see no point in replying. Donaghue, whose features bore evident marks of sympathetic interest, pressed further: his question implied no criticism; he had been told that Vlasov was opposed to Stalin, and was interested to learn his reasons. The other glanced up, remarked the American's candid expression, and suddenly burst into a torrent of speech. Now he could show an Allied soldier the true picture. The nature of Marxist terror; the quarter-century war conducted against millions of simple good-natured people on the one hand, and against the highest ideals of civilisation and culture on the other; the maintenance of slavery and torture as basic institutions of the state; the betrayal by incompetence of the Russian armies in 1941: all these points Vlasov recapitulated with rising emotion. He spoke long and excitedly. When he had finished, Donaghue looked at him with open admiration.

'I thank you, General,' he replied. 'What I can do for you, I will.'

Next day, 11 May, Vlasov learned that his 1st Division was camped four miles north of the town. At American command they had laid down their arms, but still maintained excellent discipline. Donaghue explained that the following evening the American Army was due to evacuate the region and fall back on the demarcation line agreed by Eisenhower and Zhukov. He had no instructions to bring surrendered Russians back, and offered a suggestion that Vlasov should make his way independently to the British, and attempt negotiations with them. Neither knew that this would be leaping from the frying-pan into the fire, and Vlasov felt a strong inclination to accept the idea. Soviet officers and Czech partisan leaders were beginning to appear in Schlüsselburg. Recalling the fate of Boyarski and Trukhin, he felt it would be dangerous to tarry longer. Driving over to Buniachenko's quarters, he explained the situation, and recommended that the troops of the 1st Division should break up into small parties and move back with the retiring Americans. Their appearance in a larger body might result in the Americans refusing them entry to their zone. Returning to the castle, Vlasov was greeted by Donaghue with the news that he had received enquiries from General Headquarters as to whether Vlasov was in the town.

'Are you here?' asked the friendly American with a meaning look. Vlasov took the generous hint, but replied in resigned tones: 'I am here.'

At seven o'clock that evening Soviet tanks could be heard pushing their way through the snapping undergrowth, and Buniachenko issued hasty orders for his Division to evacuate the village of Chwoshdian in which they were quartered, and take refuge in the surrounding woods. A Soviet tank brigade had halted within two miles of the American lines, and immediate action was vital. Buniachenko drove off in his staff car as fast as he was able, negotiating at dangerous speed roads broken up by American tank blocks. At Schlüsselburg he requested permission to withdraw his Division along with the retiring Americans. Captain Donaghue, who, like almost every other Allied commander faced by a similar exigency, was quite unsure of what attitude to take, had to consult his superiors. Buniachenko was asked to return at ten o'clock next morning to learn the decision.

Buniachenko rejoined his staff at Chwoshdian in a state of high anxiety. What if the Soviet tank commander decided to advance at dawn right up to the American lines? Since Stalingrad the anti-Soviet Russians had been uneasily aware of nemesis slowly closing in from east and west. Like the prison walls in *The Pit and the Pendulum*, the barriers had rolled inexorably inwards, and Buniachenko's thousands were now cramped into a space barely two miles wide. If the Americans protracted negotiations an hour or two longer, or the Red Army took up its advance a similar time earlier, they were doomed. Minutes stood between massacre on the one hand and honourable captivity and possible escape on the other.

A remarkable incident now took place, which decided their fate. The same evening a Colonel Artiemiev, commander of the 2nd Regiment, set off to learn from Buniachenko what was the next move intended. On his way through the forest he came suddenly upon a Red Army officer. The game appeared to be up, as the other at once recognised the KONR officer's insignia. But Artiemiev was a man of resource: without hesitation, he expressed pleasure at the unexpected meeting, and explained that he had been deputed to find the local Red Army commander and negotiate the surrender of the KONR 1st Division. Delighted at being the first to be able to report this welcome news, the Soviet officer led him to his commander, a Colonel Mishchenko.

Mishchenko, as soon as he learned the identity of his guest, extended to him the most effusive welcome. Of course they must surrender to him! Terms? Why, as soon as they had laid down their arms, they would be received back as an erring son is by his father. How soon could they come over? Artiemiev explained that he must consult Buniachenko. Mishchenko agreed, and with many expressions of goodwill saw the KONR officer on his way. Returning to Divisional Headquarters, Artiemiev told an alarmed Buniachenko of the Soviet officer's hospitable invitation. As the General's rendezvous with the American commander was not until 10 a.m. next day, it was vital to prevent any advance by Mishchenko before that time. He told the Colonel to return to Chwoshdian with the proposal that the surrender should take place at 11 a.m.

Artiemiev returned to Chwoshdian in the night with the message. To add conviction, he included a request for a written guarantee of safety for the Division. Mishchenko jovially agreed, signed the guarantee on a scrap of paper, and invited Artiemiev to dine at his mess. Strong liquor flowed at this meal and, flushed with vodka, the Soviet Colonel expatiated in slurred tones on the blissful glories of life in Stalin's Russia. Squinting cunningly at the other, he suggested that he should not wait for Buniachenko, but should bring over his own regiment that night. He indicated that not only would he not suffer, but that he would be allowed to retain his rank on transferring to the Red Army. Artiemiev made polite excuses, and took his leave at an early hour of the morning. Mishchenko had promised that he would make no move before 11 a.m., which gave Buniachenko precisely an hour's grace from the moment of his consultation with the Americans.

Fortunately, Donaghue received a radio message from High Command during the night, which announced that the 1st KONR Division could pass into American-occupied territory. He suggested that, despite this permission, it might be wiser to stick to the plan of passing through in small groups. When Buniachenko arrived for his ten o'clock meeting, he found Vlasov, who transmitted the message. Buniachenko tore back to Chwoshdian, to issue his last commands to the Division. When he announced that all were to retreat southwards as hurriedly as possible, and that they were now released from their military oath, something like panic broke out. With nervous haste, men destroyed papers, insignia and any other evidences of military service. They crowded round their former officers, asking whither they should go. To the south! was the reply—but soon doubts made themselves felt. Would not the Americans betray them to the Soviets? Mentally and physically exhausted by the harassment of past months, a large number of the men decided it might be better, despite all the obvious risks, to surrender at once to the Soviets. Some, after all, would survive their sentences in the forced-labour camps. Such a course would at least put an end to further harrowing suspense. About 10,000 made this choice; for weeks afterwards, fugitives amongst them were hunted through the forests by Red Army units and Czech partisans in Soviet service. Scarcely one escaped death or transportation to the Arctic Circle. The remainder crossed indeed into the American Zone, but of these the majority were shortly afterwards handed over to the Soviets. Such was the end of the surviving KONR Division.

There remained now only Vlasov, Buniachenko and a few companions. At two o'clock that afternoon (12 May), a small motor cavalcade set out from the castle at Schlüsselburg. Donaghue gave Vlasov a warm farewell, regretting openly that he had not seized the proffered chance to escape. There were eight trucks in the column, escorted by an American scout car. They had driven no more than a mile, when a camouflaged vehicle moved out from amongst the trees, bringing the lorries to a halt. Peering out to see the cause of the hold-up, the Russians saw the sinister truck halted by the head of the column. On its side was the red star. Two men sprang out: the first was a battalion commissar of the Red Army, named Iakushev, the second a former captain of the KONR Army, Kuchinsky. Kuchinsky had agreed under menaces to identify his former colleagues when captured.

The two men came up to the first truck and looked in. Inside sat the redoubtable Buniachenko. Iakushev ordered him to step out; the other abruptly refused, asserting in a loud voice that he was a prisoner of the Americans, on his way to their High Command. Aware of the watching eye of the American escort officer, Iakushev grunted and moved on. By a chance of fate, Kuchinsky had not recognised the former commander of the 1st KONR Division. The two men passed along the line, peering into each lorry in turn. In the last one was General Vlasov. Iakushev ordered him out; he did not need the renegade Kuchinsky to identify the giant Russian leader. Lacking even their side-arms, the KONR leaders were powerless to resist. But Vlasov, accompanied by a Lieutenant Ressler, strode past the two men until he had come up to the American officer's car. Ressler could speak a little English, and through him Vlasov demanded, as an American prisoner, to be taken on his way unhindered. The American stared back impassively and made no reply. Either he could not understand, or he affected not to do so.

Sizing up the situation, Commissar Iakushev drew an automatic. Vlasov at once threw open his coat and invited the other to shoot him. Iakushev replied: 'Not I, but Comrade Stalin will try you!' At that moment, one of the American lorries started up its engine, swung round abruptly, and made off at speed along the road in the direction from which it had come. Years later Ressler recalled the surge of hope that welled up in him: what if the lorry were to reach Schlüsselburg in time to bring Captain Donaghue to the rescue? But hopes were ebbing for many in May 1945, and Iakushev was able unhindered to force Vlasov and Ressler into his truck. Leaving behind their comrades, they were driven at speed past Schlüsselburg. In the fields around, Soviet and American soldiers were greeting each other in a new spirit of international fraternity. Soon afterwards, Vlasov's truck drew up at a Red Army Corps Headquarters. There Americans and Russians were gathered at a festive board, celebrating the Allied victory over Nazism.

Vlasov stood by the entrance, watching. Iakushev returned, accompanied by a beaming Soviet Colonel. He demanded that the General sign a formal instrument of surrender on behalf of the KONR. Vlasov declined, explaining that the KONR no longer existed. An apathy of utter despair had descended upon him.

What happened next to the man on whom so many Russians had pinned their hopes remained for long a mystery. When Captain Donaghue learned of his abduction in the forest, he frantically despatched search parties in all directions, but in vain.[21] A month later SHAEF authorities could still report that 'Whereabouts of Vlasov and Schilenkow themselves are unknown';[22] whilst Acting US Secretary of State Grew declared that they should be handed over if caught.[23] It was over a year later that the United States Army announced publicly that Vlasov had been handed over to the Red Army. But even this account, knowingly or unknowingly, was entirely inaccurate, since it stated that he had 'been turned over to the Russians by Czechoslovak authorities after he was taken prisoner at Prague on May 5 1945.'[24]

It was subsequently established that, following his arrest, Vlasov was despatched to SMERSH Front Headquarters near Dresden, and after interrogation there he was flown to Moscow.[25] On 12 August 1946 Moscow Radio broadcast a communiqué which included the first public mention of Vlasov in the USSR since his capture.

Within the last few days the Military Collegium of the Supreme Court of the USSR have been considering charges against Andrei Andreievich Vlasov, Malyshkin, Zhilenkov, Trukhin, Zakutny, Blagoveshchenski, Maltsev, Buniachenko, Zverev, Korbukov and Shatov. They were accused of treason and espionage and of terrorist activities against the USSR as agents of the German espionage service—that is to say, crimes under Section 58, paragraphs 1, 8, 9 and 10 of the Criminal Code of the USSR. All the accused admitted their guilt and were condemned to death under Point 1 of the Order of the Supreme Soviet of 19 April 1943. The sentences have been carried out.

All but Trukhin, Zverev, Blagoveshchenski and Vlasov had been handed over to Stalin by United States military authorities. The circumstances surrounding certain of these hand-overs remains a mystery. In particular, it may be wondered why, in several prominent cases, it was found necessary to delay repatriation for over a year.[26] In the case of Maltsev, Professor Oberländer confirms that he was taken first to Belgium, then to the United States, before being handed over to the Soviet authorities in May 1946. In view of the order signed by General Patton, stating American interest in Maltsev's knowledge of Red Air Force secrets, could United States Intelligence have spent months interrogating these men, who possessed unique knowledge of the subject, about the military potential of a prospective enemy state, and then have handed them over? It is still impossible to say. But a Russian general who was not subsequently returned, and who still lives, has described to the author a visit he received after his internment in neutral Liechtenstein. The visitor was a highly inquisitive Allen Dulles, wartime head of OSS in Switzerland.[27]

For twenty-seven years after Vlasov's execution, no more was known inside or outside the USSR of the circumstances than the bare statement of fact appearing in the communiqué just quoted. Then, at the beginning of 1973, there appeared an article in a Soviet legal magazine which gave for the first time an account of his trial. The reason for the release of these details after so long may not be unconnected with the KGB's discovery in that year of Solzhenitsyn's *Gulag Archipelago*: a book which treats of the predicament of Vlasov and his supporters with sympathy.[28]

The tone of the article is strongly polemical, and its main purpose is 'to convince the Soviet reader that Vlasov was without doubt a traitor and enemy of the Soviet peoples'.[29] It begins by asserting that Vlasov threw away valid chances to save his 2nd Shock Army on the Volkhov Front in June 1942, and that he deliberately seized the opportunity to surrender to the Germans. There is not room here to refute this charge in detail; all competent authorities unite in extolling the valour and tenacity of Vlasov's defence. His encirclement was almost entirely due to Stalin's blunders in handling the Kharkov Offensive, and Vlasov could certainly not have brought his Army out intact under prevailing conditions.[30]

A major part of the 1973 article consists of ferocious diatribes against the KONR and its leadership, all of whom were, it is claimed, inspired only by the basest motives. But, admits the writer,

In the course of preliminary investigations and the trial, Vlasov stubbornly denied and rejected any responsibility for the organisation of espionage, diversion and terror acts in the ranks of the Soviet Army, as he also denied his direct participation in the confrontations with anti-fascists in the prisoner-of-war camps and in the ROA departments. Here, it was necessary to use statements by other defendants, witnesses, counter-statements and evidence to convict him.

Such glimpses of the court's proceedings are of undoubted interest. Another passage reads:

> Reporting about his talks with Kroeger and Radetsky, Vlasov adopted the posture of a 'top politician': 'Sure, I conducted armed warfare against the Soviet state and appealed among the ranks of the Soviet Army for rebellious activity. I wanted to take advantage of the SS and the SD to train the organisers of armed warfare against the Soviets on USSR territory. I had nothing to do with the training of spies and diversionaries for the Hitlerites.' I don't know [Vlasov said], maybe my subordinates did something in this direction, but without my knowledge.[31]

Finally, if we remove as 'editing' the characteristically intemperate slurs on the KONR membership, this piece from Vlasov's closing words may also represent part of a real speech: 'Speaking of his guilt *vis-à-vis* the fatherland, Vlasov further said: "I was able to get together all the remains, all the dregs, I put them together in the Committee, formed an army for the struggle against the Soviet state. I fought against the Red Army. Surely I conducted the most active struggle against the Soviets and bear the full responsibility for this." '

At any rate the last sentence is one on which all Russians, Red or White, would agree. Since Lenin's triumph in 1921, Andrei Vlasov has to date been the only Russian to have led an open political and military campaign on Russian soil against the Soviet régime. Future generations' estimate of the character and worth of the KONR movement will inevitably be swayed by the future of Russia herself.

Mass Repatriations in Italy, Germany and Norway

DESPITE RUMOURS FOSTERED CONSCIOUSLY OR UNCONSCIOUSLY AT THE time, and repeated since, none of the Cossacks had ever fought against the British or Americans. But there was one 'Russian' unit that had battled long and hard in Italy in the armies of Kesselring and von Vietinghoff. This was the 162nd Turcoman Division, formed from men of the Caucasus and Turkic lands further east. The recruits had either been released from PW camps or fled westwards after Stalingrad. Trained at Neuhammer in Silesia, the resultant Division had been despatched to the Italian front in the summer of 1944. After initial set-backs, they proved themselves tough fighters in that curious war, where Kalmucks from the steppes of Central Asia are said to have found themselves fighting Japanese Americans.[1]

As the campaign moved slowly up Italy, numbers of these men fell willingly or unwillingly into Allied hands. During 1944 most such prisoners were shipped to Egypt and afterwards despatched to Russia via the Middle Eastern route. By the spring of 1945, however, it was possible to employ the more direct voyage by sea through the Dardanelles and the Black Sea, and on 22 March a party of 1,657 former Turkoman troops was embarked from Taranto for Odessa. At Taranto there was a large camp for captured or liberated Soviet citizens; it was administered by officers of General Sudakov's repatriation mission. On arrival the men were given British battledress, supplied with tents and food, and otherwise left more or less to look after themselves. They improvised a theatre, where it was possible to view excellently performed Kirghiz traditional plays, Svanidzian dancing or Ossetian choral music. But now the major part of the inhabitants were clambering up swinging gangways on to the British ship *Arawa*. Watching them from the deckside were Major Gramasov of the Soviet Repatriation Commission, and Captain Denis Hills, officer in charge of the British escort. Hills recalls that they came on board willingly enough,[2] though at one point there was a scuffle: he was informed a man was drunk. Soon all were on board and the *Arawa* set sail. It was not until they had crossed the Aegean and passed through the Dardanelles that anyone displayed any misgivings, and even then only of a subdued nature. Several men approached the Russian-speaking Captain Hills with an air of distress, asking what was happening. They seemed anxious about the reception awaiting them, and protested in many cases that they had fought alongside anti-Nazi partisans. But these protests were muted, if disconsolate. Most of the men seemed prepared with oriental fatalism to accept whatever lay in store for them. A high proportion were in any case of low education or even illiterate. Hills himself dismissed their fears with incredulity: everything he had read or heard in the past four years led him to picture Soviet Russia as governed by men devoted to overthrowing tyranny and establishing the Four Freedoms.

Indeed, as they neared Odessa, Hills began picturing the welcome awaiting them. But at that sinister quayside—for so many the far bank of the Styx—he found only silence and indifference. For two days, in fact, no one stirred off the ship. The Soviet reception committee consisted only of the gun-boat escorting them into harbour. Then, on the third day, the party disembarked. Major Gramasov checked off each man as he descended; on the quay they were formed up and marched away. Bored with life on board the *Arawa*, Denis Hills obtained a pass and strolled into the devastated port.

In a square he came upon his late charges, formed up into a body beneath gigantic pictures of Stalin, and listening to the welcoming rantings of a Party orator. Then they were marched away. From bystanders, hovering near in the hope of obtaining tobacco, Hills learned that the Turkomans were heading for a special concentration camp just outside the city. He was to see a great deal more of Russians in the West, but this visit had opened his eyes.

The *Arawa* returned westwards with a contingent of liberated French citizens aboard. It sailed almost the length of the Mediterranean, taking the French home to Marseilles. There a party of 1,950 Russians from the nearby camp[3] was taken on board and the *Arawa* set out eastwards again. But Denis Hills was returned to Taranto *en route*, and did not see Odessa again. He had found the whole episode novel and disturbing. A White Russian interpreter who had accompanied the party had been kidnapped by the Soviet authorities in Odessa, and was never seen again; he had lived in Italy since his childhood.

The main body of the Turkoman Division surrendered near Padua after the capitulation of the German army in Italy in May. Resentment has occasionally been expressed by Allied officers that these non-German soldiers of the Reich continued fighting hard to the end, and this was even used as justification for their subsequent harsh treatment.[4] Some, in fact, had deserted earlier, but that so many fought on in desperation is scarcely surprising, for they knew well what was their fate if they did surrender. One of their number, an Azerbaidjani, had some months previously been taken prisoner by the Americans. He was one of those prisoners sent back to the USSR via the Middle Eastern route and there placed in a Siberian forced-labour camp. Soon afterwards, however, he was taken out and despatched to serve in a penal battalion at the front. The prime function of these units was the clearing of minefields, which was done by driving the men forward in waves under the threat of machine-gun fire until the area of potential danger was cleared. The prisoner referred to, a man of resource, managed to elude his guards, and cross over the lines. After interrogation he was released to rejoin his old unit in Italy. The story he told did not provide his comrades with great incentive to desert to the Allies.[5] And even had they done so, their fate would have been the same.

The 162nd Division Turkomans were sent by rail to the camp at Taranto, and some weeks later sailed on the same route to Odessa as the *Arawa*. The voyage was not so lacking in incident as that witnessed by Denis Hills, however. Before their departure, there was a terrifying incident where a *mullah* burned himself alive in protest at the repatriation, and scores drowned themselves in the Black Sea rather than endure the rigours of a Soviet labour camp.[6]

Many were prevented from evading their fate in this way, and one such, an Azerbaidjani doctor, found himself in the Arctic camp of Vorkuta.[7] But the majority were sent to work on what was perhaps the most dangerous and harsh task of all: the clearing of the flooded Donets coalmines. This Denis Hills learned in 1948–9 from returning German prisoners whom it was his duty to interrogate. All the Turkomans had received a twenty-year sentence.

Still others, though repatriated, never reached Vorkuta or the Donets Basin. In autumn 1945 Hills was instructed to accompany a party of Turkomans and other Russians being sent back from a military hospital at Udine in North Italy. The hospital was 'a very sad place', most of the inmates having suffered dreadful wounds from stepping on mines or being similarly mutilated. Most had limbs amputated, and the many sufferers from TB and cancer gave off an unpleasant smell. Arrangements were made with the Soviet Mission for the repatriation of these people. The Soviets had demanded that the entire contents of the hospital be handed over at the same time, but the British stood firm and they only received what clearly they regarded very much as second best—the patients themselves.

The Turkomans were given the option of returning or not; presumably feeling they would be best cared for at home, they agreed to go. They travelled in a hospital train to the Soviet zone of Austria. Evading the customary Soviet attempt to steal the engine at Semmering, Hills and his charges finally arrived at the Hungarian frontier. There they were kept waiting for twenty-four hours, the wretched patients groaning in their box-cars.

Finally some Soviet officials arrived to announce that they would not unload until Captain Hills signed a document confessing to gross ill-treatment of the returned sufferers on the part of the British. Hills laughed in their faces, pointing out that any inhumanity involved was that caused by the present delay. He then surprised them. Openly contemptuous of the representatives of an ideology that called for such deceits, at once cruel and puerile, he cheerfully signed the incriminating declaration. The men, many of them helpless trunks lacking limbs and delirious with pain, were bundled out into carts drawn by horses. The last Hills saw of these wretched people, victims of the vicious struggle between the parallel ideologies of National Socialism and Socialism in One Country, was their heaped bodies, piled three or four deep, being trundled away up the hill.

But not all Caucasian soldiers in Italy were repatriated as planned. At Aversa near Naples there was a camp whose inmates included 800 Chechens, Ingushes and other Soviet Moslems. The commandant was a Colonel Charles Finley, of the Royal Artillery, but now acting for the DP Sub-Commission. Soon after VE Day orders were received to transport these Soviet citizens to Leghorn for shipment home by the Soviet Repatriation Commission. The train set off. Accompanying the party were one American and one British officer. The British officer, who supplied this account, was in fact (as so often happened then) a White Russian. His name was George Hartman. Colonel Finley, a man both physically and in moral character larger than ordinary, regarded the task set him with the utmost distaste. He accordingly managed to arrange it in a way not envisaged by the War Office, and still less by the Foreign Office. The train dutifully appeared at Leghorn . . . and then as efficiently steamed all the way back again. At Naples the prisoners were hastily placed on board a ship. From the port they sailed to Egypt, where they were put under the protection of King Farouk.

King Farouk, the Mufti of Jerusalem, the secretariat of the Arab League, and other Moslem leaders were much concerned to help their persecuted co-religionists. It was arranged that different Arab countries should agree to accept a quota each of Soviet Moslems. Denis Hills learned years afterwards that a party of 100 Kabardines whom he had saved in screening from repatriation in the 'Eastwind' Operation of May 1947 had moved to Damascus, where some are still living. How many were so saved in all may never be known, but it was estimated in 1946 that there were some 80,000 still stranded in the West and unlikely to be forcibly repatriated.[8]

However, that is to glance ahead. We must now return to the end of the war in Europe, and to the major repatriations which followed the German surrender in May 1945. Up to that time, all repatriation operations had to be conducted by sea, like those just described, on long and occasionally dangerous voyages across the Mediterranean, the Norwegian Sea or the Pacific. Though thousands travelled in this way, the numbers so transported were relatively small. Wartime shipping shortages delayed movements of prisoners for months on end, and in any case the really massive numbers of Russians in German captivity were yet to be liberated. They were in Germany itself, in prisoner-of-war camps, working as *Hiwis* (volunteers) in Wehrmacht units, or as slave labour (*Ostarbeiter*) in factories or on farms. With the unconditional surrender of Germany on 8 May, not only were these teeming millions suddenly freed, but, with the junction of the Allied armies in the heart of Germany, it would now be possible to arrange direct repatriation overland.

Already at the beginning of May it had been agreed 'to accept in principle proposal made by Vyshinski for future overland transfers', and for representatives of the Soviet High Command on the one hand, and representatives of SHAEF (Germany) and AFHQ (Italy) on the other, to meet and discuss concrete arrangements.[9]

The SHAEF meeting took place at Halle, and on 22 May a plan was signed which specified: 'All former prisoners of war and citizens of the USSR liberated by the Allied Forces and all former prisoners of war and citizens of Allied Nations liberated by the Red Army will be delivered through the Army lines to the corresponding Army Command of each side.' Reception-delivery points were listed, and no time was to be wasted in implementing the colossal project; 'The delivery and reception will be initiated twenty-four hours after the date of signature of this Plan . . .'

Already, from the first moments of Allied contact with the Red Army, informal exchanges of respective nationals had resulted in some 20,000 Russians being handed over.[10] A Russian captain, who was probably the only inmate to escape, recalled the American transfer of 3,000 of his fellow-countrymen from a camp at Plaven to the Red Army across the

Elbe. On 14 May a 'tremendous fleet of Studebakers' arrived to move the prisoners. There does not seem to have been any opposition or organised protest, as the camp was firmly in the grip of 'a Party committee'.[11]

Now, with the signing of the Halle Agreement, the process was speeded up immensely. By 4 July, no less than 1½ million Russians had been transferred to the Soviet zone of Germany.[12] What proportion were willing and what unwilling, and how far Allied officers were aware of the Russians' views can of course never be assessed with any degree of exactitude. But from the testimony of those involved in the task, a consistent picture emerges. Like men coming out into glaring sunlight after confinement in a subterranean cave, the Russians were for the most part dazed and content to go wherever they were led. There was not time for reflection, nor yet for stories of the fate awaiting them to filter back.

In mid-April 1945 Major-General Bevil Wilson, working for UNRRA, took over from the US Army a camp for Russian DPs at Verdun Barracks, Giessen. His memories of the inmates' life are on the whole unmarred by tales of fear or brutality. There were nearly 5,000 people in the barracks, and almost all were engaged in a cheerful daily round of pillaging the countryside, working the black market, dancing, drinking and other sports.

'We found that 4,439 grown-up people had only 1,798 beds. Of course beds designed for one person always held two, especially after lunch when the whole of the barracks seemed to be given over to what the French call l'amour. Those who were not paired off slept on overturned cupboards or on tables jammed together or just on the floor.'

At Giessen, as almost everywhere else where Russians were gathered, drink afforded an even more desirable pastime than fornication. It was not so easy to obtain, however.

'Until the beer canteen got going, alcohol of any kind was unobtainable. During the first few days of our arrival twelve DPs died in one night from drinking chloroform in mistake for schnaps and were buried in the camp precincts.'

Other amusements were less dangerous to the participants. A 'Caledonian market' was set up by the DPs, and one day 'the market was visited by two Russians disguised as a bear and a bear leader. The bear was most agile and realistic and quick to hug all the women it could lay paws on. The small children were rather scared at first. Soon they watched the boisterous huggings with shrieks of merriment and followed the bear wherever it went.'

At last came the moment to return to Russia. The DPs were taken in

American ten-ton trucks to a railway siding in the woods, where their long journey began. Virtually all seemed cheerful and accepted their repatriation with equanimity. By 6 June the last contingent had left. Though General Wilson himself had a shrewd idea as to what was to be their fate, it seems clear that few of the DPs anticipated anything so terrible as that which awaited them.[13]

A few weeks after VE Day, the zonal boundaries in Germany and Austria between the Eastern and Western occupying forces were re-adjusted by agreement. On 29 June the American General Clay met Marshal Zhukov at his HQ to discuss details of the arrangement.

'Marshal Zhukov raised the question of Soviet citizens—former prisoners—displaced persons . . . [He] requested that camps be kept intact so that Russian military authorities can take them over . . . Russians suggest that Americans take over and remove displaced persons, but not Russians. General Clay said the Americans will allow those who desire not to go, to remain, but will take no Russians except by mistake which will be corrected later.' [14]

This was a convenient way of disposing of a fair proportion of the Russians without utilising already overstrained transport facilities. Captain N. F. Chawner of the Royal Artillery was in charge of one such camp in the region due to change hands. It was at Hagenow in Mecklenburg, and included 2,000 Russians amongst its inhabitants. Like General Wilson, Chawner found them simple, happy-go-lucky souls. But in his case he saw also something of what the Soviet Government was preparing for them. Before the date of the Soviet move westwards, a number of trainloads of Russians was sent off. One of Captain Chawner's colleagues accompanied them. He reported that, shortly before the train's arrival at the Red Army lines, it was halted by Soviet guards. The prisoners (almost all of whom had been slave labourers abducted by the Nazis) were marched out into the surrounding forest. Sounds of protracted shooting shattered the hot, pine-scented air, and the column, diminished in numbers, was shepherded back. At the border itself were displayed welcoming banners, whilst a band played cheerful music.

Soon afterwards came news that the Red Army would move forward on 4 July to occupy the region. A few days before that, a number of plain-clothes emissaries (doubtless from SMERSH) arrived in the camp and began to take charge. Characteristically, almost the first person to suffer from their displeasure was the self-elected camp commissar. Though he had consistently extolled the Soviet régime and attempted to ensure the safe return of all in the camp, he was packed off to the Soviet lines under a cloud. He spent his first night amongst his compatriots in a ditch; what happened to him next is unknown.

Amongst the mass of largely ignorant DPs was an educated man, a Russian engineer who with his wife had been captured by the Germans. Conscious of the fact that they would on being repatriated become at once liable to separation and despatch to Arctic camps, he begged to be allowed to join the non-Russian party moving back with the British. Chawner's orders allowed no possibility of making such a concession, strong though his inclination was to do so. The fate of this intelligent and likeable man he never knew. However, one of the last sights in Hagenow camp witnessed by one of Captain Chawner's fellow-officers, was that of an enormous gallows being erected, under instruction of the newly-arrived commissars. This appropriate symbol of Marxist power was not likely to be idle for long. However, in accordance with policy laid down, citizens of the three Baltic states, whose countries had been occupied by the USSR, were not liable to be handed over. Captain Chawner took especial care to see that they were removed in good time.[15]

To SHAEF authorities the main bodies of Russians, huge in number, were a real embarrassment. There was not only the question of feeding and housing them. Almost everyone with memories of those early days after the war has a consistent tale to tell of widespread drunkenness, rape and pillage committed by newly-released Russians on the countryside around. A terrible incident near the Russian slave-workers' village of Vorhalle in the Ruhr, when a farmer's daughter was raped, and afterwards had her breasts cut off, was not the only atrocity of its kind.[16]

To British and American soldiers entrusted with the task, repatriation seemed to be the only logical course for these undisciplined hordes. What was the alternative? Not a few understood that life in Soviet Russia was harsh, even cruel. But it was difficult to avoid the conclusion that such people needed a somewhat harsh régime to keep them in order. Then again, few made any very strong protest at being returned. Whatever suspicions they may have had as to the fate awaiting them, they were far too accustomed to being driven hither and thither with plenty of blows and no explanation to imagine that protesting could do much good. Frequently the very circumstances of their departure appeared to confirm these Russians' irredeemable brutishness. General Wilson and other eyewitnesses remembered how it was their 'usual practice on leaving a camp . . . to smash it up . . . the DPs positively enjoyed smashing up furniture, electric light fittings, motor cars, windows and anything else which could be damaged easily and noisily.' Wilson put this down to a hatred of anything German. A more likely explanation is that indicated by a Pole who spent a long period confined in a cell of the Lubianka with a solitary Soviet companion. The Pole was struck by the way 'this man was entirely free from an instinct for property, and had no respect for anything that was not for immediate use or consumption. Here we can find the reason why the Soviet Army destroys everything in its way, or which is an obstacle. Its soldiers do not realise that the objects they destroy have been accumulated through generations and that they are doing incalculable harm to civilisation in destroying them. This barbarous outlook gives them a great advantage in war.'[17] The description might have been taken from an account by Herodotus of some backward Hyperborean tribe.

Whether it was barbarians that produced the system, or the system that produced the barbarians, most British and American officers were relieved to see the backs of their wayward charges, even if their fate was liable to be rough. It was only when the numbers were greatly reduced after the first hurried operations of May and June that any moral problem seriously arose. Opposition to return began to manifest itself; perhaps it had not done so earlier because news of the certain fate of all those repatriated had not yet filtered back. Again, it may be that those more actively determined to remain in the West had initially evaded transportation. Colonel Vernon E. McGuckin, who had been appointed staff officer to the United States 94th Infantry Division in May 1945 and was responsible for, *inter alia*, some 55,000 Russian DPs, recalls that most went back voluntarily, and in May and June remembers no case of his Division having to apply force.[18]

The agreement made by Clay and Zhukov on 29 June had stipulated that Soviet citizens in the area to be incorporated in the Soviet-occupied zone should stand fast. In addition, the opportunity was not lost of moving others from further west into the region. Geoffrey Dunn was a British artillery officer, detailed at the time to supervise the movement of Russians from a DP camp near Salzgitten, adjacent to the Hermann Göring steel works, where they had worked. His 'task was to load army lorries with 750 Russians per convoy and send them to Magdeburg, then in the British zone, where they were deposited in a camp to await the take over of this area by Russians when the final adjustment of zones was to take place . . .'[19]

Altogether SHAEF forces shifted some 165,000 such Soviet nationals into the area which Red Army forces began to occupy on 4 July. Ten days later the Soviet maw had digested these and was ready to continue regular transfers. In all, 1,584,000 were now recorded as having been returned by SHAEF, and the daily rate began to show signs of reduction.[20] At the same time Allied officers started to note the existence of an element that was reluctant to return. Lieutenant Michael Bayley was in Princess Louise's Kensington Regiment when it took over occupation duties from the Americans in the area of Hagen-Haspe in the Ruhr. He recalls how

we had to go round the farms to collect the Russians who had been working as labourers on the farms—mostly old men and women, and were amazed and somewhat perplexed to have people who had literally been slaves on German farms, falling on their knees in front of you and begging to be allowed to stay, and crying bitterly—not with joy—when they were told they were being sent back to Russia . . . We could not understand this, but when talking about it to Poles—presumably from their armoured Division—we were told that of course the Russian peasants were better off in Germany—why couldn't we let well alone.[21]

British officers were provided with disturbing evidence of the official Soviet attitude by the ruthless conduct of its representatives in the Allied zone itself. Major W. Thompson was ideally placed to obtain a wide picture of repatriation operations during the summer of 1945. An Engineer officer, it was his task to maintain liaison with the German railway staff supplying rolling stock to evacuate the thousands of Russian slave-labourers working in the Ruhr. These were entrained in a goods yard at Wuppertal, their destination being Magdeburg, now in the Russian zone.

The Russian authorities had many of the wagons decorated with garlands, streamers and photos of Stalin. They also provided an orchestra to play patriotic airs. Every train was late in departing due to reported difficulty in getting the folk loaded to lorries and again on entrainment as they wandered off to hide underneath wagons or any other suitable hiding place. Many were most reluctant to entrain and on every train two or three wagons were reserved for reputed dangerous characters—these two or three wagons were securely bolted on the outside to prevent any escape . . . Reports reached me on the running of every train and these indicated that every train had a number of suicides and of murder. German railway people also reported that shots were fired from the trains at anyone standing on platforms as the trains passed through and as a result the Germans telegraphed to stations ahead of approaching trains so that platforms would be cleared of people.[22]

Major Thompson's reports of the shootings of would-be escapers in the Allied zones of occupation are confirmed by many soldiers serving in Germany at that time. Captain J. Pereira, of the Coldstream Guards, commanded a detachment guarding a camp near Cologne. Of the inmates' past history and future prospects he knew little. 'I only know that due to internal rows in the camp the Russian liaison officer gave us a list of about 100 people whom they wanted returned to Russia. Due to rail chaos this was not very simple and when it was put into action I heard that a large number were shot trying to escape from the train, though some got away and some ended up in Russia.'[23]

It is true, of course, that many expressed a wish to return. A Polish lady has written to me of her visit to a camp containing 1,000 Russians at Mittlerer Landweg, near Bergdorf. She 'saw the people being put on military trucks with their belongings, and they seemed quite cheerful to go back to their country, praising the idea of going back, starting life anew, relieved that the war was over.' Even more remarkable in this context was the experience of Mr. N. Lambert. Serving in the RAF at Delmenhorst near Bremen, he met in 1944 'two Russians who were returning after having lived in Paris since the 1917 Revolution. They were anxious to re-build a new Russia they told me.' It would be surprising if no one had preferred returning home to remaining indefinitely in a DP camp, and if none had succumbed to the rumoured promise of a total amnesty. Indeed, in the one case where Russians had an absolutely free choice whether to stay or return, quite a large percentage opted for return. This was in Liechtenstein: their General informed me that the motives of those so returning appeared to be overwhelming nostalgia for their own country, dislike for the prospect of an exile's lonely life, and faith in the proffered amnesty. This example probably provides a rough but fair impression of the proportion favouring return and their reasons for so doing.[24]

But, whatever their hopes and desires whilst in the West, their treatment on passing into the hands of their own people was more or less uniform. This was largely hidden from those in the West at the time, but duties allotted to some soldiers gave them a momentary glimpse of what was going on immediately behind the curtain. Captain Anthony Smith was, in the winter of 1945–6, seconded from his artillery regiment to 'what appeared (by the manner of its formation) to be a virtually un-official unit, comprising equal numbers (rank for rank) British and Russian troops . . . totalling some 30 bodies . . . We were to render the Russians assistance in repatriating their civilian nationals, out of the British Zone through to the Russian Zone.' The area of operations was around Winsen, south-east of Hamburg.

At first Captain Smith took this novel course of duty to be a welcome diversion from the tedious round of duties in occupied Germany. But very soon he found himself inextricably implicated in scenes which sickened him for life, and which to this day he can with difficulty be brought to describe. The Russians they were hunting had practically all been imported slave-labour.

It very quickly became apparent that 99% of these people did not wish to return to the Motherland, because (a) they feared the Communist Party and the life they had lived in Soviet Russia and (b) life as slave-labourers in Nazi Germany had been better than life in Russia.

Every possible lie and deception was used to persuade these people to go back to Russia, to which we had to lend our support. But once back under Soviet jurisdiction the attitude changed from sweetness to vindictive cruelty.

Captain Smith and his men became swiftly revolted at witnessing conduct and attitudes they had hitherto only suspected of being employed by the worst elements of the SS.

The incident which ruled our whole subsequent attitude to this matter was only witnessed by the Sergeant-Major and the Drivers of our transport who took a party of returning refugees to the Collecting Point in the Eastern Zone. Their report to me was of such a nature that had we willingly co-operated thereafter we should have had a mutiny on our hands; but naturally no British soldier would have co-operated from that point on . . . The report ran along the following lines: the Displaced Persons were loaded into our wagons, together with the personal possessions in cloth-bound bundles and old suitcases, etc. They had been informed that they might keep these possessions, which were mainly clothes and small items of general use. When the transport arrived at the collecting point all persons and possessions were unloaded, the bundles and suitcases, etc. being heaped indiscriminately in a centre pile, preparatory to burning. This led to scenes of distress from the DPs, which soon became worse as families were broken up, the people being divided into groups of young children, able-bodied males, young females, and old people. The Sergeant-Major said that the Russians more or less forced him and the transport to leave at gun-point, but not before this and some more had been witnessed. Before the Sergeant-Major left, he saw groups of old people being led off and heard shooting—and saw some girls being raped.

The old people were disposed of as being useless in what was in this sense most literally a Workers' State.

From then onwards Captain Smith (on his Sergeant-Major's sugges-tion) initiated a system which largely frustrated the intentions of their Soviet colleagues. 'When we knew which area we were visiting the next day, we sent someone the night before (unknown to the Russians and indeed to my own Colonel) to warn the men to be absent, as technically they had to answer for their women and children. So we made many abortive visits, to the anger of the Russian officer.'[25]

These few illustrations must suffice, however unsatisfactory, in pro-viding a picture of what the vast repatriation operations in Germany involved in human terms. By 30 September, when the flow came virtually to a halt, some 2,035,000 expatriate Russians had been handed over from the Western Allied Zones in Germany and Austria. In territory occupied by the Red Army, the Soviets owned to retrieving a further 2,946,000 by the same date.[26] What proportion of these people returned willingly and what unwillingly can never be determined. From the accounts cited in this and other works, it is clear that a large number did dread return. A British reporter learned from a Soviet source that 40% wished to remain in the West.[27] What the evidence does tell us emphatically, is that they had good reason to do so.

Whilst this great shift of population was taking place in Germany, another large-scale operation was being conducted in Norway. VE Day had found the German occupation forces still in complete control of the country, and a few days elapsed before representative SHAEF forces could be rushed in to take over. Meanwhile the Germans were ordered to stand fast at their posts. In particular, they were to continue admini-stration and guard duties at prisoner-of-war and forced-labour camps. This they did with a meticulous efficiency that was the admiration of arriving British officers—until they began to uncover evidence of German crimes against the wretched prisoners, and admiration turned to disgust.

At SHAEF Headquarters it was learned that some 76,000 Russians were amongst the prisoners, and measures were at once placed on foot for their early repatriation. There were two possible routes:

'a. By sea direct from Norwegian ports to Russia.

b. Overland to Swedish ports, then by sea to Russia.'

SHAEF ordered that shipping be provided, and that negotiations be opened with the neutral Swedish Government to allow passage across its territory.[28] The latter contingency afforded no problem, as the Swedes proved as obliging in proffering transport to assist the Soviet authorities as they had been in aiding the Nazi conquest of Norway in 1940. By 20 May the Swedish offer had been noted,[29] and early in June a conference attended by Soviet, Swedish and SHAEF representatives met at Oslo to agree on arrangements.[30] A British officer, flown out to escort Russians returning by sea, learned a few days later that 'Sweden had offered 3rd class [railway travel for Other Ranks], 2nd class for officers, but the Russians refused and said "cattle trucks" as that would be all they would get in Russia.'

On 19 June the same officer, Major Ian Nicholls, passed one of these trainloads just inside the Swedish frontier. 'As soon as they realised we were British a tremendous cheer went up; they rushed out and got round our carriage shouting Viva and Up England. We gave them what cigarettes we had. They were mad with delight, were all very fit and looked happy and their morale was tremendous. All very well disci-plined.'[31] No such descriptions appeared in the Western press, however, as facilities for Swedish journalists to cover the operation were suddenly cancelled on 11 June at the request of the inter-Allied commission at Oslo. 'According to a well-informed source both the Russians and the Western allies, although for different reasons, objected to publicity.'[32]

The majority of Russians found in Norway were despatched home in this secretive manner, whilst a lesser number from camps in the north were transported by sea round the North Cape.[33] The first convoy sailed from Tromsö on 23 June. On board the Norwegian passenger ship *Kong Dag* was Major Nicholls. The *Kong Dag* took on 600 Russians; 'the Colonel in Charge told me that they had had a terrible time with the Germans and had been treated like animals. They were used as slave labour and beaten on the least provocation. British officers (PWX) who had been supervising them on shore were keen to see them safely on their way, as Soviet representatives had begun shooting numbers all morning, 'one who had fought for the Germans and some who did not want to go back.' Apart from these, however, most appeared highly delighted at the thought of at last returning home after all the hardships they had undergone. The next day, after setting sail, great amusement was caused by the sight of several whales blowing in the sea nearby. A detour eighty miles out from the coast proved necessary to avoid minefields, and the Russians spent the day on deck, singing and laughing in the warm sunshine.

In the middle of the next day land was sighted . . . Russian soil! The men rushed to make their tattered clothes as smart as possible, and Soviet flags were flown jauntily from the masts. At the approaches to the Kola Inlet a Soviet warship, the *Archangel*, was anchored in the roads. Hundreds of sailors could be seen lining the deck. At the sight of their compatriots from whom they had been separated so long, the Russians on the *Kong Dag* went wild, shouting and waving in enthusiasm. But from the *Archangel* came an ominously chill response. Not a man moved or spoke; all stood as before, staring in silence as the *Kong Dag* slid past. From wild elation, the mood of the returning Russians turned in a moment to depression and apprehension. Nor did their reception at Murmansk do anything to allay their fears. After waiting a night whilst a companion ship discharged its complement, they moved in to the dock.

The moment the gangway was let down, one of the Russians sprang out of the crowd on the deck and ran down to the quay, where an official car was awaiting him. Subsequent events showed that he was a hidden SMERSH man, who had doubtless been preparing the usual lists. On shore there was no longer the pretence of welcome which earlier convoys had found. Troops and police were much in evidence; the atmosphere was chill. The whole embarkation area was enclosed by barbed wire. After a prolonged delay, during which no Soviet official approached the ship, permission was given to disembark. All personal goods were ordered to be thrown in a pile on the quayside. After a brief medical inspection the men were left standing in groups in the wired enclosure. About twenty were singled out and placed under guard in a waiting lorry. A considerable delay ensued; then all in the cage were marched off under armed guard—to a penal camp, as his interpreters informed Major Nicholls. That was the last he saw of his charges. Returning up the inlet they passed a Soviet naval base. A glimpse of the Soviet view of the great wartime alliance was afforded by the appearance of a Red Air Force plane, which laid a 'highly dangerous' smoke-screen on each side of the river for several miles.

In the middle of the next month another such convoy sailed from Tromsö. The reception witnessed was no warmer than that in June. A young British officer on board one of the ships recorded on his return home his horror at the astonishing inhumanity shown the wretches, who had suffered so terribly at the hands of the Germans in Norway. No help was afforded the men landing, and even cripples were left to fend for themselves. The attitude of 'some young girls in uniform who I was told were nurses with the rank of sergeant' appeared particularly callous. The officer who wrote this was frankly puzzled by the inhumanity displayed by the Soviet Government to its suffering citizens. He noted that the ordinary British soldiers witnessing these scenes 'have felt it—more perhaps than some of the officers—and they have drawn some rather hasty conclusions'.[34]

The same convoy included a hospital ship, *Aba*, which had earlier sailed from Hull to Trondheim with a number of sick Russians on board. A British Lieutenant from the Russian Liaison Group accompanied that earlier trip. Russian by origin, Vladimir Britniev remembers the pitiable state of his charges. 'I should say they were all pretty well terminal cases, and I think basically they knew it. They were either mutilated or dying of consumption. With each one of them I used to help do this: one would stick a needle into their lungs, straight through, and fill up a bottle with pus. That one did every day, or twice a day.'

At Trondheim Britniev left the ship to take up duties with PWX in Norway, and his place was taken by Czeslaw Jesman, whose testimony in connection with the screening of prisoners for the RLG at camps in Britain was quoted earlier in this book. Jesman spoke fluent Russian and knew the tale of the sufferings of these people under German occupation from conversations with hundreds of prisoners over the past year. With additional sick Russians taken on at Trondheim, the *Aba* carried 399 patients when she set out northwards to Murmansk. The reception there was as cold as that accorded to the other ships. Soviet authorities provided some broken stretchers for those who could not walk, but no blankets. The *Aba* was in Murmansk for four days. As it steamed away, those on board could see the wretched men still lying where they had been dumped on the first day. A number were dead; of these several had succumbed to their infirmities, but others had literally died of thirst on the quayside. British sailors and nurses from the ship had, unasked, done what they could, but facilities were scant. The hard-faced young Soviet women in uniform, whom previous observers had described, occasionally came to watch. Jesman learned that they were officers' mistresses, who held a recognised position in the Red Army. Only one showed even a momentary concern with what was happening. When an English sailor went along the line, ladling out precious water to the groaning sufferers, this young lady expressed fastidious disgust at the 'uncultured' failure to wash the spoon between patients.

In other respects the Soviet authorities were not idle. We have seen that it was normal practice for the officers in returning batches of prisoners to be shot. But amongst these pathetic relics of humanity there were no officers. What could be done? Such a problem was not beyond solution, however. NKVD men took the two doctors and a medical orderly to a shed about forty yards away and killed them. Leninist norms had been preserved. Jesman heard cries of pain and curses and saw the bodies later; many of the ship's company also heard the muffled volley.

Their mission over, the *Aba* and companion vessels set sail once more for Norwegian waters. When a report of the Soviet reception of their sick was passed on to the Foreign Office, Thomas Brimelow referred to it as 'disgusting and depressing', but thought it would be useful in providing ammunition (for internal Departmental use only) to counter General Golikov's claims that returning Russians were treated with loving care.[35] Nothing so tactless as an overt reproach was issued by the Foreign Office, however; that remained for someone in a much more exposed situation than the snug recesses of Whitehall.

During his duties with the RLG in Britain, Czeslaw Jesman had come to know well one of his opposite numbers in the Soviet Military Mission. This was a Major Shershun, of SMERSH. A Byelorussian who claimed to know connections of Jesman's at his former home, Shershun is described by the Pole variously as 'an honest robber' and a 'very pleasant peasant'. He was a thug, and Jesman would not have relished being in his hands for interrogation; but he had considerable charm. Now he found himself sharing a cabin with this character on the round trip to Murmansk. To Britniev on the journey from Hull Shershun had been distant and suspicious, but with Jesman he unbent considerably. There must be few men who can boast of having witnessed the acute embarrassment of a SMERSH officer at having to reveal his official issue eggshell blue overall pyjamas. All in all, Jesman felt quite an affection for this complex character.

As the *Aba* slipped away up river under the reproachful gaze of the mutilated and dying on the quayside, Shershun displayed an unexpected side of his nature. As the report handed in later described it:

> It was noticed that, on the return journey, Major Shershun did not appear at all in the Wardroom. He remained in his cabin except for meals. He did not mix with the Officers as heretofore. Enquiries were made to the Interpreter and it transpired that, after the British left the Russian Colonel's party at the hospital in Murmansk, Major Shershun told the Colonel that he thought the reception given to us British 'after all we had done for the Russian sick' was very poor and that something better should have been arranged.

Czeslaw Jesman remembers finding him seated on his bunk with his head in his hands.

'I'm so ashamed,' he groaned several times.

Unfortunately his earlier remarks had been overheard by watchful Soviet colleagues.

'He was immediately accused of having been "contaminated" by the British. He was told that he was to return from Norway to Russia in three weeks to be "eliminated".' To the indignation of the British officer in charge, two NKVD officers boarded the *Aba* in Tromsö harbour on 25 July and abducted Shershun.

It appears that this resourceful character was not 'eliminated' on his return. Whether he had friends in high places, or whether he employed his considerable charm to good effect, we shall probably never know. But he turned up again. Jesman met him later in Egypt and Constantinople.[36]

Immediately after this the Combined Chiefs of Staff were able to report that: 'The repatriation of approximately 81,000 Russians was completed by 22 July 1945; of these, 65,000 were moved by rail from Norway to Sweden and then by sea from Sweden on Russian and Finnish vessels. The remaining 16,000 were moved entirely by sea. There remained approximately 3,000 Russians in Norway whom it was expected to evacuate by the end of July 1945.'[37] The latter, hospital cases again, were landed at Murmansk on 29 July. An accompanying British officer reported on their reception: 'Everything exactly the same as on previous visit.'[38]

So ended this forgotten chapter of the repatriation operation. The

Soviet news agency Tass had had the effrontery to announce that the British had ill-treated the Russians whilst still in Norway,[39] and at the Potsdam Conference Molotov on 30 July claimed that numbers of Russians were still being held there against their will.[40] These turned out to be Balts, Poles and others whom the British did not recognise to be Soviet citizens. They were not handed over, and were transferred to Germany before the British military evacuation of Norway. The agents of General Ratov (who had arrived from Britain to supervise operations) were caught on frequent occasions in the act of abducting or murdering these people during August and September.[41] General Ratov's mission was not solely concerned with the restitution of 'Soviet citizens'; as elsewhere, the presence of the Soviet Repatriation Mission (and the insistence of the Foreign Office that it be allowed to stay as long as possible) provided excellent cover for the maintenance of espionage units in the West. And had it been decided, after the British withdrawal in October, to move Soviet occupation forces in Kirkenes southwards and instal a Socialist régime in Oslo, then the presence of Ratov and his 167 officers might have proved very useful.[42]

Thus, in three summer months of 1945, men, women and children nearly equivalent in number to the population of Norway itself, were taken by the victorious Western powers and handed over to SMERSH representatives on the interzonal frontiers or at the ports of Odessa and Murmansk.[43]

14

The Soldiers Resist

ONCE THE MAIN MASS OF SOVIET NATIONALS—TWO OR MORE MILLIONS—
had been restored to Stalin, matters took on a new aspect. Allied
prisoners liberated in the East by the Red Army had also virtually all
come home, thus removing what had originally been the prime factor in
adopting the policy of forcible repatriation. Europe was settling down
to post-war realities, and problems could be isolated and viewed in context now that the overriding demands of total war were safely left
behind. Furthermore, the nature of Soviet designs on neighbouring
countries was becoming apparent for all who wished to understand: in
Poland, in Bulgaria, in Rumania. The few thousand Soviet nationals
remaining in the West no longer in themselves represented a serious
administrative problem; they were thousands, amongst the millions
UNRRA had to house, clothe and feed. Finally, evidence of the un-
justifiably savage treatment meted out by Soviet authorities on those
returned had been widely disseminated in Western military and governing circles. Statesmen, diplomats and soldiers could afford to weigh
judgments and consider moral and political implications at more leisure.
Differing interests and strong emotions were aroused. Could Britain go
back on Eden's solemn undertaking and her interpretation of the commitment undertaken at Yalta? Would the United States continue to
uphold the principle that military uniform determines citizenship, and
hence that Russians in the Wehrmacht could claim to be treated as
Germans? In short, should all, some or none of the remaining Soviet
citizens be returned, regardless of their wishes? It was now that attitudes
began to crystallise, and a controversy raged secretly, on whose outcome
depended the fate of unwitting thousands.

The United States had never been an enthusiastic advocate of a policy
of using force to repatriate anyone. Millions of Americans were themselves fugitives from oppression, or the heirs of those who had fled
oppression. Reluctantly, it was conceded that 'US policy is to re-

patriate to Soviet Union all claimants of Soviet citizenship whose claims are accepted by Soviet authorities. In practice this means . . . that Soviet citizens originating within 1939 boundaries of Soviet Union are repatriated irrespective of individual wishes.'[1] A special SHAEF directive to this end was issued.[2] Despite the faintly apologetic tone ('in practice . . .') of the note just quoted, the resultant measures in the field were unavoidably harsh. Precisely what the practice entailed is explained in a letter written by a former American officer.

In the summer of 1945 I was one of several artillery officers in the 102nd Infantry Division who was detailed to lead a convoy of all the trucks in my battalion on the mission of picking up Russian PoWs from German internment camps and delivering them to the Russian officials at Chemnitz. For about two weeks day and night I led about seventeen trucks on shuttle service all over Germany and France on this mission. There were thousands of other trucks doing the same. We soon found out that many Russians didn't want to be repatriated and we soon found out why. They believed that any officer PoW would face execution upon return and any non-com PoW would face a term in Siberia. As a result we stood over them with guns and our orders were to shoot to kill if they tried to escape from our convoy. Needless to say many of them did risk death to effect their escape.[3]

The misgivings of soldiers obliged to implement the harsh policy were in part shared by the State Department. In response to an enquiry by Secretary of State Stettinius, Ambassador Harriman in Moscow provided on 11 June a report on Soviet treatment of returning prisoners.

While Embassy has no evidence to support reports of stern treatment of Soviet citizens repatriated from Allied occupied areas, [wrote Harriman] it would be unwise to discount the general basis for these reports. Soviet Govt and military authorities have never been at pains to disguise their scornful attitude toward Soviet troops taken prisoner. Soviet Govt is not signatory of Geneva Convention and during entire course of war refused all overtures from enemy powers for agreement regarding treatment of prisoners which might have improved lot of Soviet prisoners in Germany . . . Although repatriation of liberated Soviet citizens has now been proceeding for months, Embassy knows of only a single instance in which a repatriated prisoner has returned to his home and family in Moscow and resumed his prewar pursuits. This man was suffering from tuberculosis and was released after being held under guard in a camp near Moscow for four months.

It is known that repatriates are met at ports of entry by police guard and marched off to unknown destinations. Trainloads of repatriates are passing through Moscow and continuing east, the passengers being held incommunicado while trains stand in Moscow yards. Although little info is available, it is believed that repatriates are first subjected to an intense screening by police ... It is quite possible that persons considered guilty of deliberate desertion or anti-state activity are being shot, while some few with good war records who have been captured when severely wounded or under similar circumstances and have refused service with Germans may be released to return home. Great bulk of repatriates, however, are probably being placed in forced labor battalions and used in construction projects in Urals, Central Asia, Siberia or Far North under police supervision.

The impression derived from this estimate, which was clearly set out in good faith, was that of a crude, rough-and-ready justice. The State Department lacked the harrowing accounts of massacres and ill-treatment at Odessa and Murmansk which the British Foreign Office possessed in its files. None the less, the Moscow Embassy of the United States was approached again for further information on 11 August, this time to enquire 'whether any decrees were issued by the Soviet Government during the war divesting Soviet nationals of their citizenship because they were captured by the enemy ...' Clearly the possibility of a legal loophole justifying evasions of the policy of forcible repatriation was being sought; but on 16 August the Embassy replied, saying that it possessed no evidence of such decrees.[4]

In view of these assurances, Stettinius appears to have felt there was little option but to continue to comply with Soviet requests. No American had reported crimes such as had occurred at Odessa on 18 April and 10 June before British witnesses, nor had American troops yet been compelled to take part in demoralising scenes such as those at Lienz on 1 June. Americans were not proud of their policy, but felt they lacked sufficient justification to deny the Soviets' claims.

The British Foreign Office was still (14 July) under the impression that 'Americans always ask liberated Soviet citizens captured in German uniform whether they are willing to return to the USSR. If these people claim the protection of the Geneva Convention they are allowed to remain as German prisoners of war.'[5] But United States policy in this respect had already undergone a revolutionary change, and this reversal of the former punctiliously honourable policy was announced by the man who, more than any other, had spoken up for the maintenance of principle over expediency, Joseph C. Grew. The Acting Secretary of State had long and forthrightly argued that the United States' adhesion to the 1929 Geneva Convention obliged her to accord all prisoners captured in German uniform the status of German soldiers. The United States had successfully claimed similar protection for her own soldiers and could, Grew had pointed out to Novikov, be no less punctilious than the German Government in honouring her commitments under international law. Now came a sudden shift.

Over the winter of 1944-5 the USSR had been pressing for the return of a small group of Russians who had expressed strong opposition to being repatriated, and who had been knowledgeable and intelligent enough to claim that their German uniforms (they had all served in Vlasov units) entitled them to treatment as German prisoners of war. Almost as soon as former Soviet citizens began to be uncovered amongst German prisoners shipped to the United States after D-Day, a percentage was found so objecting.[6] The majority let their cause go by default, and about 4,300 had already been shipped to Vladivostock. One hundred and eighteen claimed the protection of the Convention,[7] and as recently as 5 May Grew had informed Novikov that the United States would facilitate the return of any Soviet citizens except these.[8]

Three days later the war ended, and four days after that Grew wrote to Forrestal, Secretary of the Navy. After recapitulating the history of the 118 Russians falling in this special category and the consistent refusal by the State Department to allow their surrender to Soviet authorities, he continued:

> I assume, now that Germany has unconditionally surrendered, that all American prisoners of war held by the German armed forces have been liberated and that therefore there no longer exists any danger that the German authorities will take reprisals against American prisoners of war. I therefore believe that it would be advisable to turn over these 118 persons to the Soviet authorities for repatriation to the Soviet Union, as well as any other persons of similar status who may be found in United States custody in the future.

What further discussion took place is not known, but on 18 May the State-War-Navy Co-ordinating Committee approved the suggestion, informing the Secretary of State on 23 May.[9]

In this almost casual way the United States was now declared ready to commit what Grew himself had earlier stated to be 'a violation of what appears to be the intent of the Convention'—which is that 'prisoners of war are entitled to be treated on the basis of the uniform worn at the time of capture and that the detaining Power shall not without their consent look behind the uniforms to determine questions of citizenship or nationality.'[10] Particularly depressing is the reason given for this volte-face: that the United States was no longer benefiting from the provisions of the Convention, and it could now afford to deny soldiers of Germany those benefits.

Following the Secretary of State's authorisation, the original 118 claimants to German nationality, together with 36 further claimants, were collected together in a wired compound at Fort Dix, New Jersey.[11] There they were informed that they were to be embarked on a ship on the afternoon of 29 June, their ultimate destination being the USSR. The prisoners had previously been suspicious and 'sullen', doubtless guessing the purpose for which they had been gathered, but on receiving this news they prepared to resort to desperate measures. The announcement of their embarkation had been made early in the morning by Lieutenant-Colonel G. M. Treisch, camp commandant. At once the Russians barricaded themselves inside their barracks, refusing to come out or allow anyone in. Colonel Treisch was informed, and came into the compound to find out what was happening. Several of the Russians had held commissions in the German Army, and he called for the three most senior to come out and discuss the matter. There was no response from within, and shortly afterwards smoke was seen to be pouring from a window.

Colonel Treisch at once ordered tear-gas grenades to be fired into the building. Immediately the whole scene erupted. A door at the rear of the barracks flew open, and the desperate men came surging out. They were brandishing improvised weapons, knives with five-inch blades taken from their mess-kits and the legs of tables and chairs. Though the place was surrounded by troops, the Americans were taken by surprise. Three soldiers who had advanced ahead of their fellows were caught up in the rush, and wounded as they tried to grapple with the prisoners. Behind these stood a rank of combat troops, armed with carbines and submachine guns. As the Russians bore down on them, they received a hasty command. There was a burst of small-arms fire, and seven Russians were brought to the ground. After a struggle lasting half an hour the remainder were overpowered, but not before two others had suffered grievous lacerations incurred whilst trying to scramble through the barbed wire fence.

The GIs now entered the building, which was still permeated with the stench of tear-gas. They must have presented a fearsome sight in their hideous gas-masks, but now they in their turn came upon a spectacle far more sinister. Three bodies were swinging from the rafters, whilst alongside dangled a further fifteen preparatory nooses. When the surviving prisoners came to be examined afterwards, they explained that only Colonel Treisch's prompt use of tear-gas had prevented the entire group of 154 men from committing suicide. The unwilling survivors were marched off under heavy guard and transported to their port of embarkation. The whole incident received widespread publicity in the press.[12]

The men were taken from Fort Dix to Camp Shanks in New York State, and then to Pier 51 at Jane Street, in New York's North River. Those who were fit were transported in trucks, each of which contained four Russians and five armed guards. The injured arrived in guarded ambulances. The pier entrance was blocked by eighty military police armed with submachine guns. Anchored in the dock was a former Italian luxury liner, the *Conte Grande*, now the US Navy transport *Monticello*. The party arrived in the early afternoon. They had scarcely been drawn up for a quarter of an hour, when Colonel John Landis, commander of the escort, suddenly received a new order. The embarkation was not to take place after all, and the men were to return to quarters. It was 3.30 p.m. on 30 June, and the 150 Russians with their 200 guards drove back to Fort Dix. No explanation was given for the change in plan, but it was understood that the War Department was reconsidering the case. Back in camp, extraordinary precautions were taken to prevent further attempts at suicide. 'On their return to Fort Dix the men were taken to the prisoner-of-war compound and quartered in barracks stripped of furniture with only mattresses to sleep on. They were also divested of all clothing that might be used in a suicide attempt.'[13]

The whole incident was highly embarrassing to both governments involved. The armed guards at Pier 51 had to keep away a crowd of curious New Yorkers, and the newspapers had reported widely this first public evidence that Russians preferred death to repatriation. Nor was the Soviet Government happy. It authorised General Golubev to issue a statement on 3 July. In it, he accused the United States of using force to prevent the return of men desperately anxious to rejoin their comrades at home. Nor was he abashed when the Americans pointed out that the Soviet Military Mission had been permitted to visit the men, and that consequent threats and cajolements produced one volunteer for return, out of 154. Besides, as Golubev pointed out, what could one not expect from the American authorities, who had spitefully and for pure love of mischief tried to poison some of the defenceless prisoners? The Americans realised on reflection that this was a reference to an episode in which some of the miserable Russians 'had broken into a store-house and drunk large quantities of methylated spirits'.[14]

The 151 survivors awaited a State Department decision. On 11 July Grew wrote that 'consideration is being given to sending this group to Germany where they will be divested of their prisoner-of-war status and turned over to the Soviet authorities.'[15] By this subterfuge it was doubtless hoped to evade any charge of betraying previous commitments. Once discharged from their prisoner-of-war status in Germany, they could no longer claim the protection of service in an Army no longer existing. They would revert to their previous Soviet status, and be able to be handed over.

But Grew continued to fear the renewed unfavourable publicity that hasty measures might provoke. Above all, it must be established beyond doubt that all the 151 men really were Soviet citizens. Further elaborate screening was ordered.[16] Meanwhile on 7 August Kirk in Italy notified Secretary of State James F. Byrnes (he had succeeded Stettinius on 3 July) that the original 118 Russian prisoners had in the 'name of humanity' addressed petitions for asylum to General Marshall and the International Red Cross. Disturbed by any evidence of United States abandonment of its traditional humanitarian role in international affairs, Kirk 'requested that action be withheld pending report to Dept and receipt of its views'. The plea was unavailing; Byrnes replied, stating that 'in conformity with commitments taken at Yalta' all of the Fort Dix group who were proved to be Soviet citizens were to be returned.[17] Eventually, on 31 August, the doomed group was shipped to Germany and presented to SMERSH under conditions of the greatest secrecy. So the final chapter of a tragic business passed without public notice. But the prisoners' resolute action of 29 June had shaken the State Department, and undoubtedly continued to influence policy decisions on the repatriation question during the summer of 1945.[18]

The British actions at Lienz and Oberdrauburg on 30 May and 1 June had passed without public comment. That this had been possible was due to the secrecy and speed of the operation. But there was one group of people who were fully aware, both of the existence of forcible repatriation and its implications. These were the soldiers to whom was allocated the distasteful task of implementing it. The brutal treachery of Lienz had horrified most of the participants, and it is questionable whether many of the troops involved could have been brought to engage in such tasks again. One of those on whom perhaps the heaviest responsibility lay was the Commander-in-Chief in the Mediterranean area, Field-Marshal Alexander. As his then Chief of Staff, General Sir William Morgan, explained to the author, Alexander was appalled when he learned of the tragedy of 1 June, and was resolved that, if it lay in his power, such scenes should not occur again under his command.

Just over a fortnight later, he despatched a cipher telegram to the War Office:

One. 55 Soviet citizens including 16 women 11 children majority of whom state they are political refugees screened in accordance with terms of Yalta agreement are refusing to return willingly to Soviet Union.
Two. Soviet Mission have requested their transfer. This would require use of force including handcuffs and travel under escort in locked box-cars.
Three. We believe that the handing over of these individuals would almost certainly involve their death.
Four. There are likely to be many more such cases.
Five. Request your ruling earliest possible as to how these personnel should

be disposed of as local Soviet Mission will certainly press for them to be handed over.

The first Foreign Office reaction was one of mild surprise that the question had been raised at all, but officials went on to explain that the way was clear, provided the Americans were in agreement. Thomas Brimelow thought that the Soviet Mission could be asked to supply an armed guard to 'apply any necessary measures of constraint'. If any of the babies was so young as actually to have been born outside the USSR a problem of nationality might arise, but in all else 'the Yalta agreement is binding, and I do not think we can do anything to save them from their fate.' Patrick Dean concurred, thinking that 'we need not bother' about the problem of the babies, and that the only possible reservation lay in the danger of American objections. He thought it possible they might be 'tender as regards Soviet women and children who are not strictly P/W.' But it seemed unlikely that arrangements would be permanently obstructed. Brimelow summed up the matter by stating that force should be employed if necessary, and American agreement secured if required.[19]

At the same time the War Office asked for details of these Russians. Where were they found? Alexander replied that they had been in German forced-labour camps in South Germany and Austria; they were now held in the transit camp at Rome (Cinecittà). In a further telegram he stressed that it was unlikely many more Soviet citizens would turn up. Alexander's misgivings were echoed at the War Office. General Gepp, Director of Prisoners of War, thought it improbable that the Americans would consent to such measures. (News of the last-minute suspension of the sailing of the *Monticello* had been reported that day in *The Times* (2/7/45).) He noted also that AFHQ in Italy felt it would be hard to persuade British soldiers to force people on to trains 'who did not want to go back to their country and who might be "done in" when they got there.'[20]

It must be explained, in parenthesis, that these fifty-five Russians were the surviving Soviet inmates of a long-standing transit camp for refugees and DPs, situated in former film studios outside Rome. Security at this camp had never been very strict. An incident in the previous November had aroused the wrath of the Soviet Military Mission: forty-seven Russians due to be transferred to a Soviet camp at Resina refused to enter the lorries and made off. That night they stole back into the camp to collect their kit. Just before dawn they piled into a seven-ton lorry parked inside and drove off in fine style, smashing down the main gate of the camp on their way.[21] Denis Hills, the Russian-speaking British officer, arrived at the camp in May 1945, to find about 100 DPs still living there. The Area Commander made it clear he would be quite happy to see this remainder 'disappear', and no restrictions were placed on their coming and going from the camp. The Ukrainian Catholic community in Rome (*Russikom*) provided a refuge for many. Hills offered no obstruction to their exodus, and indeed called at the *Russikom* centre, 'where I saw my old friends walking about in the sun'. About half chose to remain, however; the lax régime probably led them to believe they would not be handed back to the Soviets (neither Hills nor his Colonel had any idea that such a danger menaced them), and British rations were superior to food provided by the hard-pressed *Russikom* priests. It was the fifty-five so stranded who formed the subject of Alexander's telegram.

Now came another problem. After the handover of Domanov's Cossacks in early June, British units stationed in the Drau Valley had been sent out to comb the mountains and bring in any fugitives who had sought refuge in the snows. Though many escaped in spite of this, a number were brought back and held at Peggetz Camp. The 36th Infantry Brigade War Diary explained why these had not been turned over to the Soviets: 'In the normal course of events these Cossacks would have been evacuated to the Russian zone of occupation, but the Soviet maw had evidently been sated since they now requested that no more Cossacks should be surrendered to them. This meant that we had, and still have, on our hands, several hundred disgruntled Cossacks.'[22]

At Peggetz, Major Rusty Davies was now given the task of screening new from old émigrés. He detested the job, and allowed numbers to escape or register as non-Soviet citizens under false papers. But many were undoubtedly post-1939 fugitives, and in the isolated conditions of the camp there was much informing and double-crossing. The camp leader was a Russian from Belgrade named Shelikhov. Neither the Cossacks nor Davies trusted him, and he was dismissed at the end of 1945, being replaced by a much finer man, Lakich, a Yugoslav. All undoubted Soviet citizens were transferred to a special camp a little further down the valley at Dölsach. Captain Duncan Macmillan was in charge of the Company guarding this camp, and remembers that it was well wired and constantly patrolled. It was here that some 500 'screened' Soviet citizens were held.[23] On 8 July, Field Marshal Alexander telegraphed the War Office: 'We now hold 500 Cossacks rounded up in Austria. These escaped during period when Cossacks were being handed over to Russians and are not willing to be restored to them. Russians are pressing for return of these personnel and it is probable that this will involve use of force by us. Request instructions as to how these personnel should be disposed of.'

The Foreign Office was consulted on this new development. John Galsworthy did not 'think this latest telegram alters the situation', and he, Brimelow and Patrick Dean felt the best thing was for the military to clear the repatriation with the Combined Chiefs of Staff. Finally, Brimelow drafted a letter for his chief, Christopher Warner. In this, the War Office was urged to try to persuade the Soviet Military Mission to supply the armed force necessary to remove the dissident groups. In order to ensure American compliance the Combined Chiefs could be consulted, 'but this ruling, when received, will not apply to all the 55 people at Rome, since the women and children are presumably not prisoners of war, but will apply to the Cossacks in Austria, who are prisoners of war. If this is correct, there is an additional reason for dealing with the small group at Rome first and the Cossacks later.' The differing viewpoints of the soldiers and the Foreign Office came out in a meeting of their representatives held on 31 July. Thomas Brimelow explained that, despite the fact 'that this policy is an embarrassment in view of its variance with H.M.G.'s long-established policy in regard to political refugees', the Foreign Office believed that PWs and DPs 'are to be treated alike, and handed over to the Russian authorities whether they are willing to return or not'. To which Major-General A. V. Anderson replied 'that he felt that the Yalta Agreement was designed to arrive at a working arrangement for the repatriation of liberated Soviet nationals, not that it was intended to ensure the forcible repatriation of political refugees, who are guiltless of pro-Axis activities, and who do not wish to return to Russia'. Brimelow made no reply.[24]

But despite Foreign Office insistence, increasingly formidable obstacles to their policy appeared. American consent, vital where the Russians were held in an area of unified command, appeared problematical. News of the staying of the *Monticello* had come through; it was not yet known that this was merely a tactical delay on the part of the State Department. There were also disturbing and mystifying reports of obstructive measures taken by the United States military. On 29 July a worried Foreign Office learned that General Paul Paren, of the US 26th Infantry Division, 'acted on instructions from higher military authority when he did not hand over military forces in German uniform taken as prisoners of war'—these were 'several thousand' ex-Wehrmacht Russian soldiers.[25]

Worse was to follow. At Yalta the leaders of the three great Allied powers had met to plan the strategy of the final overthrow of Nazi Germany. Now, six months later, that task was completed and on 17

July, Truman, Churchill and Stalin met to confer at the Cecilienhof
Palace at Potsdam. The frontiers of what Churchill had once termed
'Bolshevik baboonery' had advanced seven hundred miles into the heart
of Europe, from the foggy swamps of Pripet to the swift-flowing Elbe.
Now it remained to see how the statesmen of the West would face the
new Europe arising on the ruins of the old.

Chickens released at Yalta were coming home to roost, and an inevitable item on the agenda was the question of Russian refugees in the
West. By far the greater proportion had already been returned, but
those who remained provided in many ways a more disturbing problem
than ever. Consciences that had accepted the barbarities of mass repatriation now became uneasy. The unanticipated scenes of horror at
Lienz, Odessa and elsewhere had aroused revulsion or fear of adverse
publicity. What if the true facts of forcible repatriation were to reach
public notice? Today, none of those concerned with arranging and
implementing the decision to co-operate with SMERSH is willing to
speak about the matter. What if they had been called upon in 1945 to
justify their decisions?

At the plenary session of the Potsdam Conference held on 22 July,
Molotov claimed that the British were holding in a camp at Cesenatico
near Ravenna a large body of Soviet citizens. What was particularly
sinister was that these men were still organised in an entire Division,
comprising twelve regiments. The officers had been appointed by the
Germans, and the total number of men was no less than 10,000. Churchill
replied that he would have this report investigated at once, and a telegram was despatched by Field-Marshal Alexander to General Morgan
at AFHQ, demanding details.

Morgan's reply was soon forthcoming, but the incident had clearly
disturbed the Prime Minister. Next day his private secretary, Leslie
Rowan, wrote to Eden's aide, Pierson Dixon: 'The Prime Minister . . .
has expressed the view that some change should be made in our present
policy regarding the return of Soviet Nationals who are in our hands.
The proposal he made was that we should take the line that we do not
require the return of any British subjects in Soviet hands against their
will. They should be quite free to choose whether they return or not to
this country. It would follow from this that Soviet Nationals in our
hands would be treated in the same way, i.e. they would not be forced
to return to the USSR against their will.'

This note was passed at once for comment to the Foreign Office legal
expert, Patrick Dean. Dean noted that there were 'serious objections' to
the Prime Minister's view. It was true that a British officer (Youmatoff)
had seen thirty-five Russians 'executed' on the quay at Odessa. But there

were 'very strong' reasons for objecting to the proposed change in policy, though possibly efforts could be made to retain one or two clearly innocent people.

If, as seems possible, [he concluded] the Prime Minister has been moved to make this proposal because of the complaint made by M. Molotov the other day at the plenary session about the 10,000 Ukrainians in Italy, it must be remembered that many of those were Poles who will not have to go back in any case, and that apparently they represent a formed unit which was operating under German command, so that we need not go out of our way to be too sympathetic to them.[26]

Sir Alexander Cadogan, the Permanent Under-Secretary, accordingly drafted a minute for Dixon, in which the Prime Minister was urged in strong terms to abandon his proposed stand. All the familiar arguments were restated: the pledges offered by Eden in Moscow and Yalta, the need to ensure the speedy return of freed British prisoners, the impossibility of effective screening, and the necessity for obliging the Soviets. The Russians in question had practically all 'collaborated more or less with the Germans', and 'many of them are extremely undesirable characters.' Above all, 'we do not see how we can go back on it without a serious row with the Soviet Government.'

No reply came from the Prime Minister for several days. Meanwhile, General Morgan telegraphed from Italy to say that the 10,000 'Soviet citizens' claimed by Molotov were in fact Ukrainians, predominantly of Polish nationality, who were in any case in the process of being screened by the Soviet Military Mission. On receipt of this at Potsdam, Alexander expressed extreme displeasure at the way Molotov had launched so ill-founded a complaint without prior communication with AFHQ. At the same time the Foreign Office supplied Churchill with a brief which in miniature encapsulates Foreign Office thinking on how to deal with the Soviets. General Morgan's testimony could be used to score a splendid point over Molotov and Golikov, who had clearly been detected making a diplomatic blunder. But one should not press triumph too far: 'it would be very dangerous to suggest to the Soviet Government that we claimed the right to keep undoubted Soviet citizens if they do not wish to be repatriated.'

Soon afterwards Rowan replied to Dixon, on behalf of Mr. Churchill: 'Many thanks for your minute dated 27th July about the return of Soviet citizens to the Soviet Union. I agree that there is no need to take any further action in this matter.'[27]

What caused Churchill to change his mind? We now know that British officers guarding the Cesenatico Ukrainians had, on learning of events in Austria, 'made the strongest possible representations to the authorities that the Ukrainians should not be given a similar fate'.[28] The officer in charge of administering their camp, Captain Tom Gorringe, sent in an even fiercer protest. Both he and the Ukrainians were under the firm impression that their repatriation had already been decided upon. Amongst the latter there were in consequence an estimated one or two suicides a day. Captain Gorringe was so furious at the prospect that 'in a wild moment' he put in this request: 'If order carried out, please send burial party.' He heard later that his report had been passed on to the Foreign Office, presumably by a sympathetic AFHQ.[29]

There were many indications that it might be difficult this time to conduct such an operation in secrecy. Influential parties had displayed interest—General Anders, commander of the 2nd Polish Corps, had complained that the Soviet Mission in Italy was attempting to kidnap Polish citizens[30]—and it was likely that many of those wanted by the Soviets would claim Polish citizenship. On 5 July the Vatican had passed on to the Foreign Office and State Department a plea that thousands of Ukrainians in the West should not be sent back. To this the Americans replied, explaining that only those who were Soviet citizens in 1939 were returned. For the Foreign Office, John Galsworthy minuted: 'We do not wish to attract attention to this aspect of the Agreement which is, of course, in opposition to our traditional attitude towards political refugees, and I submit that it wd be preferable to return no reply to the communication . . .'[31]

It seems most probable, therefore, that Churchill had feared a bloody and public repetition of the June events at Lienz. When he was reassured on this point, he withdrew his objection.[32] Though the question was raised on several occasions at the Conference,[33] the Soviet delegation clearly attaching considerable importance to it, Allied policy regarding forcible repatriation remained largely unaltered.[34]

Soviet attempts to reclaim, as their own, citizens of countries they had conquered after 1939 were never seriously considered. Both Americans and British made it clear they would not hand over Poles or Balts to Soviet vengeance: from the very beginning the terms 'Soviet citizen' (undefined in the Yalta Agreement) had been interpreted to apply only to persons living within the 1939 borders of Russia.[35] Thousands or possibly millions of people from Estonia, Latvia, Lithuania, eastern Poland and Bessarabia came under the heading of 'disputed persons', i.e. claimed as Soviet citizens by the Soviets but not recognised as such by the Western powers. For months and even years these people lived in fear that they too would be deported by force to the USSR. But in fact the Allies never contemplated their return, so far as is known; the international outcry and repercussions would have been too great. That the

Soviets grumbled but accepted this limitation suggests perhaps that they are unlikely to have contemplated drastic action had the Allies retained others whom they in fact returned. Soviet spokesmen never distinguished between pre- and post-1939 Soviet citizens when making their strident claims, but in the case of 'disputed persons' they were clearly following their usual tactics of demanding all but being privately content with what they got.

One body of men who thought they had reason to fear an Allied deal at their expense were the soldiers of the Latvian Legion of the *Waffen SS*. Of its two Divisions, the 19th ended the war trapped in the Courland pocket. But the other, the 15th, had had the good luck, following ferocious fighting on the Eastern Front, to be ordered back into Germany for re-equipment in April 1945. When the collapse drew near, they marched westwards and surrendered to the Americans near Schwerin. From there they were transferred to a camp at Ludwigslust, where they were interned along with other SS units. When the Americans were arranging the planned withdrawal of July, which extended the Soviet zone westwards, the other units were moved by train to a camp near Hamburg. Mr. Ian Bogaert, who was then serving in the Flemish Langemarck Division of the *Waffen SS*, remembers that the Latvians in Ludwigslust 'were extremely well disciplined and paraded for roll call and lowering the flag when they invariably sang their national anthem under their own officers'. Their Divisional mascot was a 'little boy of 5 or 6 years of age dressed in a miniature *Waffen SS* uniform'. Mr. Bogaert and his companions understood that the Latvians 'were to be handed over to the Russians *en bloc*, probably when this area was handed over to the Russians'.[36]

The Latvians themselves feared the worst; but their fears were dispelled, at least for the moment, as they found themselves travelling westwards also. They were interned in East Friesland, on the frontier of Holland. John Antonevics was a soldier of the 15th Division at that time, and remembers well the tense period that followed. For months they remained in camp, as well cared for as British resources allowed, and cheerful in the circumstances. But what was to happen to them? General Dragun of the Soviet Mission in Paris undoubtedly knew where they were, and must be using every pressure to bring the British to surrender these hardened anti-Soviet troops.[37] How firm a stand would the British take on their behalf, in view of the fact that the Division had fought hard against the Soviets and, moreover, formed (through no choice of its own) a unit of the *Waffen SS*—an association that was liable to certain misunderstandings?

Rumours and speculations abounded, but British troops and UNRRA teams who issued their supplies could tell them nothing. Then, suddenly, their commanding officer, Colonel Osis, returned from one of his regular visits to the British HQ. He was in a high state of excitement, and soon word spread through the camp that the 15th Latvian Division must 'disappear'. 'It is every man for himself,' explained Colonel Osis, 'otherwise we'll be repatriated.' At once the camp was in a ferment of activity. Assisted by their compatriots in DP camps, the soldiers acquired civilian clothes and papers—the latter, according to the idiom of the refugees, having 'fallen from the linden-trees'. John Antonevics himself left on New Year's Eve, and with the opening of the year 1946 the entire Division had melted away, the majority of its men taking refuge in the comparative safety of the DP camps.[38]

Evidently the British command, possibly forewarned of Soviet claims, had taken this practical method of solving a potentially embarrassing problem. These Latvians were saved, but other Balts were not so fortunate. During the latter part of 1945, Anthony Shorland Ball, a captain in the Leicestershire Regiment, was seconded to Military Government duties at Greven, near Münster. In Greven was a Russian 'village', supervised by Soviet troops. Shorland Ball's duty was to arrange transport to take groups of these Russians home when a batch was ready. Usually he would provide about ten lorries, and then, when all was prepared, he would attend their departure. Just before that took place, his task was to check that all the passengers were in fact Soviet citizens. The check took place in the following manner, strictly fulfilling instructions laid down.

The prisoners, of all ages and sexes, would be brought under guard to the assembly point, where they were placed in the trucks. Shorland Ball then approached each lorry in turn. He had with him a copy of the Yalta Agreement[39] and a map depicting clearly the 1939 frontiers of the USSR. Holding up this map, he would explain (through an interpreter) that no one then living *west* of those frontiers could be compelled to return, and announced that any such person unwilling to go could step down. Captain Shorland Ball regularly performed this duty from August to December, each batch of departing Russians consisting of about 250 people. On no occasion did any refugee respond to the announcement; indeed, they never spoke at all. Their reticence is scarcely surprising, since the convoy was surrounded by Soviet troops armed with submachine guns. The officers stood even more menacingly, their hands resting on the butts of their pistols. Shorland Ball remembers very clearly that 'They didn't dare say anything, and were absolutely terrified of the troops . . . they just sat there, glum and silent.' Even his Latvian girl interpreter was visibly in a state of terror, never leaving the British officer's side.[40] It is difficult not to conclude that numbers of Balts and Poles were removed in this way by the Soviet Military Mission.

During the late summer of 1945 the issues relating to forcible repatriation seemed clear in theory but confused in practice, or, perhaps one should say, in application. The British favoured the use of force without reservation, and the Americans had come hesitantly to take up the same position. Amongst the soldiers of both nations there existed widespread opposition to the policy. But whereas a British general like Alexander could turn a blind eye to explicit instructions, American political and military figures in the field appeared still genuinely mystified as to their Government's policy. This was no doubt a reflection of the State Department's lingering doubts and fears concerning a measure they had been led to adopt with extreme reluctance.

As long ago as the previous December, Alexander Kirk, as United States Political Adviser in Italy, had received a categorical statement from Stettinius, laying down that it was United States policy to return all Soviet citizens 'irrespective of whether they wish to be so released'.[41] Yet on 7 August 1945 he wrote to request a ruling on precisely the same point. The new Secretary of State, Byrnes, replied at once, confirming that this was still United States policy.[42] Kirk's obtuseness may not have been without purpose. He knew the discomfort the State Department felt on the same score, and presumably felt there was no harm in forcing them to state in black-and-white what was being done in their name on the other side of the Atlantic. But, unknown to Kirk, an operation was already in motion that would in a few days give American soldiers a taste of what the British had undertaken in Austria. Sheepishness and evasion could not alter the stark fact that the State Department *had* given its consent to the use of bayonets to return people to slavery, torture and death. That they were reluctant where the Foreign Office was eager did not alter the nature of the tragedy in the field.

At Kempten in Bavaria several hundred Cossacks and Russians of the Vlasov Army were held in captivity. Despite resistance, the American authorities were able after a time to draw up fairly accurate lists, distinguishing the new from the old émigrés. (At no time did the Americans, unlike the British in Austria, even consider the idea of handing over refugees of twenty years' standing to the Soviets). Then, on 22 June, an order was received for the new émigrés to move to a camp nearer Munich. Fearful of the implications, they protested strongly and the local military authorities rescinded the order. An uneasy peace descended on the camp, though alarm was felt again when an account of the British handovers in Austria reached the prisoners. This account had taken a month and a half to arrive: on 16 July a Kuban Cossack appeared with the sensational news.[43] But for some time nothing happened, until on 11 August the camp inmates were informed that the next day the Soviet citizens would be returned to the USSR. The same considerations that had, after so long, sealed the fate of the Fort Dix prisoners applied also to the men at Kempten.

Four hundred and ten men were on the list of those repatriable, careful screening having taken place. A number escaped in the night, the American guards being apparently fairly lax in their duties. The remainder prepared to resist, and scenes ensued reminiscent of those encountered by British officers in the Drau Valley ten weeks before. Early on the morning of 12 July, the camp church (a converted gymnasium) was packed with the Russians, numbers of whom were old émigrés not liable to return but naturally imbued with a strong sense of solidarity with their compatriots in distress.

When the American troops entered the building to remove the Soviet citizens, they found the whole congregation huddled together, weeping and imploring clemency. The American major saw the prospect of something for which his military training had not prepared him, and ordered his men out again. Neither he nor the soldiers was ready to employ the force required, and his superiors now ordered in a body of Military Police led by a Colonel Lambert. After once again fruitlessly requesting that those designated leave the building and enter the waiting trucks, the soldiers advanced on the terrified congregation, which backed away until brought up against a wall. The Military Police flung themselves into the resisting mass, grabbing individuals and ejecting them by brute force. The scene was particularly objectionable and appalling to all present, since it took place in a church. Men were beaten and knocked senseless with rifle-butts; the altar was knocked over, ikons were smashed and religious vestments ripped. Outside, amused NKVD officers watched the Americans' energetic efforts to oblige.

Eventually everyone had been dragged from the building, leaving inside only the wreckage of sacred objects, together with bloodstains and torn clothing. Outside, the Russians were again divided into two groups. The Soviet citizens were placed in trucks, and the old émigrés in a nearby school building in the Salzmannstrasse. But those in this school were by no means safe, and one trying to escape from a window was fired at by American troops.[44] The men in the lorries were driven to the railway station and placed in a goods train. This did not depart for the Soviet zone until the next morning, by which time more men had escaped. At this stage the American guards showed little enthusiasm for preventing their flight, and the party that finally reached the Soviet border consisted only of some two score prisoners. Some even of these might have escaped, but for the officious vigilance of Communist sympathisers in the camp UNRRA team. Particularly vicious in this respect is said to have been a Russian woman, married to a French Communist.

To watching Soviet officers the wrecking of a church and kidnapping of its congregation were a familiar enough sight, just as they had been to Lenin's Kalmuck ancestors during the period of the Tartar conquests. Such scenes had, after all, been regular occurrences in Russia over the past quarter-century. But to others present it all seemed unjustified and horrifying. Shamefaced Americans saw their distinguished Negro compatriot, Dr. Washington, leaning against the church wall and weeping like a child.[45]

The incident inspired widespread revulsion among American soldiers. On 4 September Eisenhower himself urgently demanded a reconsideration of the entire policy,[46] and the United States Political Adviser in Germany, Robert Murphy, was also deeply disturbed. A fortnight later he telegraphed the Secretary of State, and asked: 'Did we at Yalta assume the specific obligation to return these Russians by force if necessary?'

Two days later came the reply. It was written under Secretary of State Byrnes's name, by the Director of the Office of European Affairs, H. Freeman Matthews. 'Doc' Matthews had been an influential member of Roosevelt's entourage at Yalta, and at Potsdam Byrnes 'relied upon him heavily'.[47] Matthews explained in somewhat periphrastic style that American policy had indeed involved close co-operation with the Soviets in this business. There had been resistance and use of force in the United States itself. He ended on a note familiar from an earlier stage of these negotiations: 'For your confidential information, Department has been anxious in handling these cases to avoid giving Soviet authorities any pretext for delaying return of American PW's of Japanese now in Soviet occupied zone, particularly in Manchuria.'[48]

This reply was by no means a categorical definition of a policy of continued use of force. The United States was prepared to go to certain lengths to conciliate the Soviets. But how far and for how long remained obscure. It was a pragmatic and empirical approach. With the British Foreign Office the position was very different. The possibility that the Soviet might uncover a few hundred British prisoners in Manchuria was with them, as with the State Department, a consideration.[49] But the prime point was that the promise made by Eden in October 1944 must continue to be honoured until the last repatriable Russian was safely handed over. Despite War Office objections expressed by General Anderson at the meeting of 31 July, it was emphasised that this position must not be abandoned.

It might have been thought that the advent to power of the Labour Government at the end of July would have produced a review of Eden's policy in this respect. But the new Foreign Secretary, Ernest Bevin, continued to maintain the policy so forcefully advocated by his senior civil servants.[50] General Anderson had asked for a ministerial ruling on the fifty-five civilians at Rome whose return was in question, but after a discussion with Sir Alexander Cadogan, Bevin scrawled across the Minute the brief sentence: 'Let them go.'[51]

A fortnight later, in a long conversation, he assured Soviet Ambassador Gousev that there would be no change in British policy.[52] Armed with his Minister's ruling, Christopher Warner informed General Anderson that the decision was taken, and ended confidently: 'In view of this ministerial ruling, we presume that you will not be referring the matter to the Combined Chiefs of Staff, and that you will now be able to proceed with the transfer of these people.'[53]

All appeared to be settled; the Foreign Office had ruled and the soldiers must obey. The 500 prisoners at Dölsach and the 55 at Cinecittà would be turned over to the NKVD; in return the Soviets would doubtless oblige with reciprocal concessions. But the soldiers were an obstinate lot, not the least obstructive being Field-Marshal Sir Harold Alexander. While Warner was writing to Anderson, Alexander in Italy was attending a meeting with the Soviet Special Delegate on Repatriation Matters, Major-General Y. D. Basilov, who had just arrived from Moscow 'on a special mission'. Without any preamble, Basilov demanded the instant repatriation of the 10,000 'Soviet nationals' held at Cesenatico Camp. Alexander explained that his orders definitely precluded the surrender of persons living outside the 1939 frontiers of the USSR. He went further, stating that he 'was not . . . at present empowered to make people return to Russia against their will'. When Basilov challenged this, Alexander added 'that if ordered to do so, he would use force to effect repatriation'. He would apply at once to his superiors for instruction on this point. Basilov nodded, going on coolly to demand the return of 'thirty thousand Soviet citizens in the Polish Corps'—presumably those Poles whose homes lay in areas now annexed by the Soviet Union. Alexander's reply came in the form of a very blunt refusal. 'It must be clearly understood that the Poles were Allies'. He was 'most surprised' at Basilov's demands.[54]

Immediately after this meeting, Alexander wrote a personal letter to the Chief of the Imperial Staff, Sir Alan Brooke, explaining that he was determined to give the Soviets nothing to which they were not strictly entitled. In particular, he would refuse to use force to repatriate Soviet citizens until he received a definite order to do so.[55] To the War Office he despatched a request for instructions, together with a lengthy and moving appeal that his soldiers should not be compelled to repatriate unwilling people at bayonet point.[56]

In August 1945 none of the interested parties was satisfied. The Soviets blasted off as usual with accusations that the British Army in Germany was allowing Soviet citizens, eager to return home, to be intimidated and prevented from doing so.[57] The Foreign Office was angry that its instructions, unchanged since Yalta, were being unaccountably frustrated. And now came in thick and fast complaints from those most nearly concerned: the men who had to implement the policy in the field.

In Italy, officers guarding the 10,000 Ukrainians at Cesenatico had made 'the strongest possible representations' against returning their charges forcibly.[58]

In Austria the protest was even more forthright. In July the Military Government of the province of Styria had been taken over by Colonel Alec Wilkinson. Colonel Wilkinson was married to a Russian, and so had the best of reasons for appreciating that Russians are also human beings. He did not favour the delicate approach of Foreign Office diplomacy; it is only in his own words that one can fully measure the attitude he adopted, and I accordingly give here the account he kindly wrote for me.

> We had several DP (Displaced Persons) camps in Steiermark, and we had to look after them. There was one not very far from Brück an der Mur, with about 1,500 inmates.
>
> It was not long before a couple of NKVD officers from Vienna called on me in Graz, called my attention to the Yalta Agreement, and told me that I was to put them in a train and send them to Vienna. The Yalta Agreement made no appeal to me, and I told the Russians that I would do as they said, but *only* if the DPs were *willing* to go. These two bastards then rang Vienna, and within an hour or so told me I was to put the DPs on the train. To which I gave the same answer.
>
> They then said they would like to go and talk to them, to which I agreed. I then notified the DPs what was on and told them that the meeting was at 1000 hrs next day. So off went the NKVD bastards to do their stuff. The meeting took place at 1000 hrs, but only 15 of the DPs attended it. The Russians returned to Graz and were not very amiable, blaming me for it. All they got out of me was that *if* the 15 who turned up at the meeting *wanted* to go back to Russia, I would see what could be done. In fact, I heard nothing more of it.[59]

In Germany too the protests poured in. Colonel R. B. Longe was in charge of that section of the Staff of the 21st Army Group responsible for drawing up and issuing instructions for implementation of the Yalta Agreement. He had to hear continually of cases of Russians committing suicide, throwing themselves before lorries, begging not to be sent back to their own country. Officers were frequently on the telephone to him, complaining bitterly of the task allotted them; there were frequent cases of troops refusing to employ the violence necessary to force unwilling women and children onto lorries.[60]

One such officer was Colonel Laurence Shadwell, officer commanding the 506th Military Government Relief Detachment of BAOR at Kiel. As such he was responsible for a number of large DP camps in the region. A convinced Christian, Colonel Shadwell made it known that he would not become involved in repatriation measures involving the use of force. As generally happened in such cases, he was not required to do so. Most of his time was taken up with countering persistent outrages committed by the local Soviet liaison officers: intimidation of Poles and other non-Soviet citizens, kidnappings and, in one case, murder. Enlightened by a friendly Canadian-Ukrainian also serving in Military Government, Shadwell took measures to register large numbers of Ukrainians as Polish, whether they were or not. No forced repatriation took place in areas under his command, but in early August three Ukrainians arrived in his camp from nearby Flensburg. They had a terrible story to relate: a camp of 500 men at Flensburg had been surrounded by British troops and accompanying Soviet officers. After savage scenes of violence the prisoners had been forced on to lorries preparatory to repatriation. During the melée a prisoner was killed by an NKVD man 'whilst trying to escape'. The Soviet officers rendering aid were not delicate in their methods: in the same week an NKVD Lieutenant Okorokov at Flensburg was expelled by Military Government for the brutal murder of a Galician Pole. This bloody scene at Flensburg took place within a day or so of the parallel American operation at Kempten.[61]

It seems likely that all or part of the 500 Russians handed over were members of a Cossack regiment captured near Flensburg in early May by the Shropshire Light Infantry. A former corporal of the regiment remembers the colonel coming in to surrender. 'Asking if I spoke German, he said "I am the Colonel of a Cossack Regiment and have come here to make a formal surrender of my troops to you."' He explained that his men were fugitives from Communism, and had been formed into a regiment attached to the Wehrmacht: 'Their main task was to supply horses for the Germans and they were at present camped in a forest about two miles away.' A few nights later Corporal Fred Ralph accompanied his two Company officers to the Cossacks' camp, where their hosts provided them with an unforgettable evening of vodka, 'a sumptuous repast', and singing by a Cossack choir. There were many women and children to be seen in the camp.[62]

The Ukrainians in Colonel Shadwell's camps stayed up all that night in an understandable state of terror that was not abated in the days that followed. A few days later, Shadwell had access to reports dealing with the scenes of violence at Flensburg. Though they had occurred outside his area of responsibility, he felt that something must be done. His Canadian friend was visiting London and, armed with Colonel Shadwell's evidence, began remonstrating in high quarters. One of President Truman's aides in London was notified, as were the Duchess of Atholl and the Foreign Office.[63]

What appears to have happened is this. The great mass of Russians repatriated in May, June and July had been that overwhelming majority who, cowed and stunned by a relentlessly hostile fate, returned more or less voluntarily. At any rate, no large-scale application of force had proved necessary. By August the numbers had been greatly reduced, but those remaining included precisely those who had taken the most determined steps to avoid repatriation. Either because the whittling down of the numbers now brought these resisters into line, or because Anglo-American Military Government had concerted moves to grasp this nettle, the employment of large-scale violence in returning unwilling parties came to the fore in August.

At any rate, it is not until August that we find in Germany operations taking place that so fiercely aroused the despair of the prisoners and the indignation of many British and Americans involved. John Gray, a Quaker working with a civilian relief team amongst DPs around Salzgitter, directed an urgent appeal on 4 August to the Foreign Secretary. Noting that on 3 August the military authorities had received an order requiring the immediate handover of all Soviet citizens (it must have been the same order that set off the brutal incident at Flensburg), Gray protested in the strongest terms against the inhumanity involved. Pointing out that many of those threatened were vowing to commit suicide rather than go, he asserted that 'it is contrary to the liberal English tradition towards refugees to forcibly transfer these people.' UNRRA and Red Cross leaders were horrified, and Gray appealed to Bevin 'to have this matter investigated and a more humane and Christian solution found to the problem of these homeless people.'

Though Gray had made it clear he was alluding only to the danger threatening undoubted Soviet citizens from east of the Curzon Line, the Foreign Office's reply (issued seven weeks later) affected to assume that he had referred to disputed persons from *west* of the Line. It was accordingly possible to deny that such people were to be repatriated, and to refer to the whole incident as having been 'based on a misunderstanding'. Meanwhile the Political Adviser in Germany was ordered to instruct the military that forced repatriation should continue as before.[64] All that could be done by BAOR was to issue an order on 30 August, laying down more elaborate precautions to prevent the return of any Russians not clearly Soviet nationals by the British interpretation.[65] However, the gangster-like tactics of the Soviet Repatriation officers had produced increasing revulsion amongst British officers and men, who began to obstruct and ignore their Government's policy on frequent occasions. All in all, the strong reaction against the use of force which arose in August resulted in considerable amelioration of the harsher aspects of Foreign Office policy, even though that policy remained unchanged.[66]

In Italy a Soviet Mission under General Basilov was applying pressure for the return of Soviet citizens in general, and of the Ukrainian Division in particular. Only a tiny minority of the Ukrainians had volunteered for return, and all Basilov's attempts to prise out the rest were brusquely forestalled by Field Marshal Alexander. When Basilov became particularly insistent over a group of 400 children, the Allied Commander stated sharply that he would tolerate no such bullying. He declared himself willing to return voluntary repatriates, but still 'he was not allowed to use force to effect this repatriation'.[67] Meanwhile (28 August 1945) Alexander's Chief of Staff, General Morgan, despatched his own moving plea to the War Office. After pointing out that the 'use of force would probably entail driving them into railway coaches at the point of the bayonet and thereafter locking them in, and possibly also handcuffing a number of them', he continued by stating that 'such treatment, coupled with the knowledge that these unfortunate individuals are being sent to an almost certain death, is quite out of keeping with traditions of democracy and justice as we know them. Furthermore it is most unlikely that the British soldier, knowing the fate to which these people are being committed will be a willing participant in measures required to compel their departure.'

A copy of this message was forwarded to the Foreign Office. There, officials, imagining that Bevin's ruling had settled the matter, were understandably disconcerted and irritated. It had been thought that Bevin's confirmation that force must indeed be used had been forwarded to AFHQ. Instead, it had become held up in the War Office, where officials were still discussing its implications.[68] A Foreign Office telegram arrived at Caserta on 1 September, patiently confirming that the policy was settled and unalterable. Frank Roberts at the Moscow Embassy pointed out that the Soviets would never agree to any relaxation of the policy, and it was impossible at this stage to consider any alternative.[69] The matter seemed settled at last, and General Blomfield at the War Office agreed. 'In view of the Foreign Office ruling, I feel there is nothing that can be done except to hand these unfortunates over to the Russians using the minimum of force. I do not like it but I can see no alternative.'[70]

Despite these resigned words, obstructions on the part of the military were not yet ended. As Winston Churchill had noted on a similar occasion, there is always the 'apparatus of delay'. Once again it was Field-Marshal Alexander who fired the first broadside of the encounter. He 'trusted' that the provisions laid down would not apply to Italy (they were directed specifically at Italy!), and objected yet again to the use of force, particularly against women and children. He was not only disgusted with the savage implications of his orders, but was also becoming increasingly irritated by the high-handed activities of General Basilov in Italy.[71] But if Alexander found Basilov troublesome, the Foreign Office looked upon the Field-Marshal as a serious nuisance. Acknowledging that troops could be mealy-mouthed about using bayonets on women and children, John Galsworthy felt it nevertheless 'intolerable' that the Foreign Secretary's clear mandate should have been held up for over a month at the War Office. The Foreign Office had assured the Soviet Ambassador that all was in order, and this unanticipated delay now put them in danger of looking foolish. Worse still, the Soviet delegation at the forthcoming Council of Foreign Ministers might raise the matter to score a successful diplomatic point.

Alexander's prestige was such that his protest could well prolong War Office obstruction. This worried Galsworthy: could not the Soviets provide 'guards' to do the dirty work? The fact was that to alter Foreign Office policy at this late date would 'cause much trouble'. 'In any case, we made up our minds long ago that we could not try to save Russians from their Government, however much we might wish to do so on purely humanitarian grounds.'[72]

One drawback to applying effective pressure on Alexander was the failure of the Americans to combine in enforcing the policy. He was, after all, Supreme *Allied* Commander, and strictly speaking any new move in the Italian theatre required the combined authority of both powers. Alexander had received explicit orders, but the Foreign Office was taking no chances. A two-pronged attack was launched. Firstly, pressures were applied on the American State Department, culminating in a note from Bevin to Byrnes (both were present in London at the Foreign Ministers' conference).[73] Secondly, the British Joint Staff

Mission in Washington was urged to persuade the Combined Chiefs of Staff to issue unequivocal instructions. The JSM reported that the Americans might not agree over what constituted a Soviet citizen,[74] but otherwise all at long last seemed plain sailing. Lord Halifax reported from Washington that the Americans appeared to be dropping their former objections to forced repatriation, and John Galsworthy noted gratefully that 'it seems that F/M Alexander will at last receive instructions . . .'[75]

Matters were moving on, but were by no means settled yet. On receipt of Bevin's note, Byrnes replied that he was consulting the State Department on the matter. Meanwhile, he had telegraphed the Acting Secretary of State, Dean Acheson, in Washington. He noted that Bevin was particularly anxious to return the 500 recaptured Cossacks, adding: 'Bevin indicates that repatriation of this particular group might involve the use of force. I would of course hesitate about the use of force.' Acheson replied with a full summary of the situation, pointing out that the whole matter had now been laid before the State-War-Navy Co-ordinating Committee for consideration. In his view it was likely that the Yalta Agreement would be interpreted as *not* envisaging the application of force. On the other hand, it *was* 'envisaged that this interpretation of the agreement would not apply to Soviet citizens who joined the forces of the enemy and are therefore considered to be traitors of an ally of the US who should be returned to their native land as traitors, using force if necessary. Other categories of Soviet citizens would not be repatriated against their will.' The 500 Cossacks would come under the category of 'traitors', and hence should go back—particularly in view of recent American action regarding the Fort Dix prisoners.[76]

Bevin was disappointed at the prospect of delay; he had hoped to be in a position to give Molotov a satisfactory reply. The British Embassy in Washington was urged to press for a speedy decision, but Lord Halifax could only continue to answer that no decision had been arrived at yet. Probably the Americans would agree over the 500 'traitors', but they were unlikely to stomach the use of force against the fifty-five civilians. Such a decision would be, in Foreign Office eyes, disastrous; after all, 'amongst the civilians there may be many whose conduct has been no less reprehensible' than that of the Cossacks. A presumption of guilt seemed only reasonable in the circumstances. The American view was likely to rest on diametrically opposite principles. The State Department anticipated 'strong criticism from the public and in Congress here on grounds of humanity and of traditional American views of asylum if United States Government uses force to return . . . [civilians] against their will.'[77] The War Office delay in passing on instructions to Alexander had been the sole cause of all the procrastination, and the Foreign Office thought that the military had 'behaved shabbily, to say the least'. However, that was all past history, and now there was no alternative but to wait and hope.[78]

Meanwhile, there was nothing to prevent the handing over of anyone to the Soviets in the purely British-administered zones of Austria and Germany. There at least no American consent was required. But even this pious hope the Foreign Office found unexpectedly frustrated. The bombshell had burst on 5 October, when John Galsworthy opened his morning's copy of *The Times*. A small article, headed 'Men Who Refuse to Return to Russia' held his attention. The opening sentence conveyed news: 'The use of force to compel Russian citizens to return to Soviet territory from the American zone of occupation in Germany has been discontinued, at General Eisenhower's command, until the United States Government rules specifically that American troops must be used for that purpose.'

An estimated 26,400 Soviet citizens in DP camps would earn at least a temporary respite from this ruling, the report continued.

'Questioned about reports of troops firing over the heads of Russian citizens, or into the ground near their feet, to compel them to board trains bound for Russia, one officer said: "It is possible that for a time some of them were pushed on to trains without our asking many questions, but that is all stopped now." '[79]

Like Alexander, Eisenhower had long viewed his unsoldierly task with distaste. On 4 September he had asked for a definite ruling on the issue from the Joint Chiefs of Staff; soon afterwards he placed a temporary freeze on operations. In this way he and Alexander threw the onus for continuing the obnoxious policy on to the Joint Chiefs of Staff and, ultimately, their respective governments.

At a meeting in Berlin on 29 October, representatives of British military government 'noted that the Commander-in-Chief was not now prepared to use force for the repatriation of Soviet Nationals; no publicity will be given to this decision'.[80] Field-Marshal Montgomery has frequently been represented as ruthless and cold-hearted, but in the matter of the Russian refugees he was no less determined to ignore inhumane orders than were his fellow-generals Eisenhower and Alexander. Doubtless he was influenced by Eisenhower's prior action in the American Zone, but it is clear that he felt it to be no part of a soldier's business to wage war on prisoners of war, civilians, or women and children. At least where his writ ran such things should take place no longer.

In the Foreign Office Montgomery's high-handed action aroused angry responses. *No* change in policy had been authorised by the Foreign

Office or the War Office, and it was not for servants of the Crown, however distinguished, to take such decisions on themselves. A stream of minutes poured from the desks of Brimelow and Galsworthy: they were 'both mystified and alarmed by this statement which is, of course, quite contrary to HMG's policy'; 'the decision is extremely disturbing. HMG's policy is to repatriate *all* Soviet citizens ... regardless of their wishes and with the use of force, if necessary.' Perhaps the most worrying aspect was that a complaint by the Soviet General Sokolovsky, that refugees were being withheld by the British, clearly had substance. A tough note was sent off to the War Office, instructing them to investigate the matter and ensure that the correct policy was restored forthwith.[81]

The plain fact was that almost no soldier, British or American, approved of forcible repatriation. The tribunal at Nuremberg was at this very time about to try German generals for crimes against humanity. A key ruling at that court was 'that the fact that a defendant had acted pursuant to orders of his government or superior did not free him from responsibility and that the true test was not the existence of the order, but whether moral choice was in fact possible.' Without such a ruling there was clearly no basis for the findings of the War Crimes Commission. Such a concept was not of course a new discovery. That soldiers should not maltreat prisoners of war, nor harm women and children, had been a maxim of warriors since the Middle Ages. A century before the first Hague Convention, the gallant Admiral Sir Sydney Smith could refer emphatically to 'correct and established rights—the sacred rights of prisoners of war'.[82]

Major-General Sir Alec Bishop was present at the Conference of 29 October which ended forcible repatriation in the British Zone of Germany. He well recalls the differing views of soldiers and diplomats at that time:

> What I do remember is the tension which developed between the Army and the Members of Military Government (who were, at that time, largely army officers) on one side, and the civilian F.O. representatives on the other over the whole question of forcible repatriation. The Army intensely disliked being made to repatriate Russian soldiers, or people of any other nationality, against their will, and by force, and greatly resented being required to take such action. The F.O. representatives, who did not, of course, have to take part in the distasteful operation themselves, felt that the policy must, for political reasons, be implemented.[83]

Sir Alec's memory is undeniably correct. Eisenhower and Montgomery simply declined to apply the policy, whilst Alexander raised tactical obstructions. American Generals Bedell Smith and Patch took a similarly vigorous line to that of Eisenhower,[84] and no record appears to exist of any Allied soldier of any rank advocating the use of force.

Even Red Army officers, if a single example may serve, could on occasion agree with the traditional policy of asylum. General Bishop, as Deputy Chief of Staff in the British Zone of Germany, was responsible in 1947 for winding up repatriation arrangements with the Soviets. His opposite number was a Soviet general whose name cannot be given, for reasons that will transpire. About 250,000 'Russians', most of them Disputed Persons, were estimated to be still held in British camps. The Soviets were pressing for the return of these people, but it was no longer British policy to comply. General Bishop suggested a compromise: the Soviets could have all the facilities they needed to visit DP camps and persuade the inmates to return home. All those who wished would go, but the remainder would have to stay. The Soviet general was a friendly and uncomplicated soul; he had risen through the ranks of the Red Army and frankly admitted his bewilderment at being thrust into his present diplomatic post. He felt happier, like a true peasant, in helping his orderly look after the chickens he kept behind his official residence. Faced with Bishop's suggestion, he cheerfully agreed that nothing could be more reasonable.

For once, East-West negotiations seemed to be running harmoniously. But a couple of days later it was a terrified Red Army general who arrived at General Bishop's Headquarters. In his innocence the Russian had thought the suggested compromise a happy one. The moment he mentioned it to his colleagues, however, he realised that he had committed the most unspeakable blunder. A message shortly afterwards came through from Moscow ordering him to return home at once, he explained. What that implied was left unspoken, but he was trembling and yellow with fright. A sympathetic General Bishop tried to save him from his fate by withholding the pass necessary for his departure from the British Zone. But inevitably a sharp note arrived from Berlin ordering him to grant the pass at once. The poor peasant general departed in a state of visible terror.

Dislike for Foreign Office policy was not, as General Bishop correctly indicates, confined to officers of the rank of general. By October 1945 the flow of transfers to the East had nearly ceased,[85] but there remained a continuing trickle. Colonel David Rooke was at that time commanding the 7th Battalion of the Royal Hampshire Regiment, stationed at Soltau, south of Hamburg. A battalion responsibility was to assist a Soviet liaison group in collecting and sifting liberated Russian slave labourers in a huge DP camp at Munster Lager. Finally, Colonel Rooke received orders to place all the Russians so gathered on trucks for transport to the

Soviet Zone. The war having ended six months previously, Colonel
Rooke's men thought of nothing but returning home and he imagined
that these Russians must be feeling similarly overjoyed at the same
prospect.

He was accordingly surprised and horrified to find the whole group,
consisting of above a thousand men, women and children, in an obvious
state of total despair and fear. Many were pleading for mercy. The
worst moment came when a woman flung herself in the snow before the
British officer, clutching his ankles and imploring him not to send her
back. Greatly disconcerted, Colonel Rooke managed somehow to get
all the wretched refugees onto the lorries. Though desperate, they were
cowed and submissive, and no undue physical force was necessary.

The soldiers of the Royal Hampshires were greatly disturbed at
having this unpleasant task thrust upon them. Colonel Rooke too felt
disgusted, and reported to his Brigadier, Aubrey Coad. Politely but
firmly, he expressed a hope that never again would he be asked to do
such a job. If he were, he would have to risk ending what (in all modesty)
seemed a promising military career by refusing to obey an order.
Brigadier Coad said little, but his expression indicated sympathy with
Rooke's view. Rooke did not again have to undergo such an ordeal, but
the memory never left him. Immediately after the operation he had
asked the SMERSH liaison officer what would happen to these people.
They had worked for the Germans, replied the Russian; the women and
children would be sent to Siberia, and the men most probably shot.
Colonel Rooke had fought a hard war from North Africa onwards, and
had led his battalion in ferocious fighting from Normandy to Northern
Germany, but of all those terrible years two events in particular are
burned into his memory. The first was a visit to Belsen soon after its
capture, and the second was the return of the Russian hostages.[86]

Apart from military reluctance, political pressures were building up.
Questions concerning the policy of forced repatriation in general and its
possible application to Ukrainians were asked by a Conservative and
Labour M.P. respectively.[87] With such dangers looming, the only course
for the Foreign Office was to try to ship back as many Russians as
possible before real trouble started. In particular, the 55 civilians and
500 Cossacks under AFHQ control must be handed over swiftly. If
only the Americans could be persuaded to speed their decision! But,
from information received, the State Department was evidently proceeding with extreme caution. The persecution of refugees was unlikely
to go down well with large and influential sectors of American opinion.
Republican Congresswoman Clare Booth Luce publicly protested on 17
November against the proposed deportation of three Russian youths

held on Ellis Island, who had expressed strong aversion to returning to 'imprisonment and probable execution'.[88]

It came as a pleasant surprise, therefore, when the Foreign Office learned that British military authorities in Italy had unexpectedly repatriated the fifty-five civilians formerly at Rome. Evidently someone had succumbed to persistent pressure, and this *fait accompli* might speed an American decision. For it was at the return of the fifty-five civilians they had jibbed; now they were gone there would surely be no trouble over the 500 'traitor' Cossacks.[89]

Meanwhile, the commanders-in-chief of the British zones in Germany and Austria should be instructed to resume forcible repatriation. They came directly under the authority of the British Government, making American co-operation necessary only in Italy, where combined command continued. The War Office, under pressure, informed Field-Marshal Montgomery that the Yalta policy could *not* be abrogated in Germany.[90] At the same time General McCreery in Austria was instructed to hand over forthwith the 1,300 or so Soviet citizens held in Austria, together with some 1,500 or 1,800 believed to be at large in the countryside. There had been no handovers from Austria since the major surrender of the Cossacks in the summer. The delay had been possible, as Austria had formed part of AFHQ command, and so came under Alexander's ban of 31 August on forcible repatriation. But now Austria was divided into separate zones of occupation, and McCreery could act independently of AFHQ.

McCreery at once raised the strongest objections. Like Alexander, he disliked allowing SMERSH troops to operate behind British lines, and he disliked using British troops to bully women and children. Moreover, he claimed that he had not enough troops to round up those Soviet citizens still at large, and believed that attempts to enforce repatriation could only add to the number deserting and being obliged to subsist by banditry. Quite recently a group of some 400 had fled to the hills in this way after a visit by the Soviet Repatriation Mission. To John Galsworthy these arguments seemed 'disingenuous and muddled'. The Foreign Office was very anxious to be able to state that their policy was being rigorously implemented in Austria, as Bevin was in Moscow for a conference, and might have to answer to Molotov on the subject. Three copies of the Yalta text were flown to Vienna, together with a letter from Thomas Brimelow explaining why an agreement which nowhere mentions force nonetheless implies it.[91]

15

The Final Operations

MARSHAL ZHUKOV, IN HIS MEMOIRS, PROVIDES A BRIEF SOVIET VIEW OF the repatriation operations described in this book. He explains how the Western Allies succeeded in brainwashing loyal Soviet citizens with such effect that many bewildered Russians declined to return home. Zhukov himself complained to Generals Eisenhower and Clay, who protested spurious humanitarian motives. Eventually, however, they succumbed to Soviet pressures, belatedly allowing the by now desperately homesick Russians to go back.[1] There was, indeed, a final *volte face* in American policy, and it must now be considered.

In the autumn of 1945 Eisenhower, revolted by reports of the bloody repatriation operation at Kempten, had of his own accord forbidden the use of force in repatriating Soviet citizens anywhere in the areas under his command. He received whole-hearted support from Montgomery in the British Zone, and from his own Generals Clay, Bedell Smith, Patch and other distinguished commanders for his new policy, whilst Political Advisers Murphy in Germany and Kirk in Italy were no less anxious to see an end put to measures that were contrary to every principle for which the United States had fought so hard. For weeks Eisenhower's bold decision was allowed to stand without interference from Washington, and when General Bedell Smith flew home from Germany in January 1946 he quite reasonably thought that incidents like that at Kempten were a thing of the past.[2]

In fact, however, the United States had at last come to a governmental decision on the repatriation question which was to launch a new wave of bloody operations. It had been a matter of urgent consideration ever since September, when Secretary of State Byrnes had jibbed at Bevin's pressures to induce him to accept British policy in the matter. On 21 December 1945, at long last, the State-War-Navy Co-ordinating Committee in Washington promulgated a declaration of policy. After pointing out that over 2,034,000 Soviet citizens had been repatriated from Western Germany, it noted that an estimated 20,000 remained. Of these, certain precise categories would be liable for return 'without regard to their wishes and by force if necessary':

a Those captured in German uniforms.
b Those who were members of the Soviet armed forces on or after 22 June 1941, and who were not subsequently discharged therefrom.
c Those who are charged by the Soviet Union with having voluntarily rendered aid and comfort to the enemy . . . provided reasonable proof of such aid was proffered by the Soviet authorities.

This document was transmitted to the United States commanders in Germany and Austria, Generals Joseph T. McNarney and Mark W. Clark, and hence became generally known as the 'McNarney-Clark Directive'.[3]

The aim was to ensure that traitors according to the accepted conception returned home to receive their deserts, whilst other less compromised refugees would be treated in accordance with traditional American policy. It seemed a reasonable compromise, but it satisfied neither the Soviets[4] nor the British. The United States directive 'is a step in the right direction', but 'we consider that all Soviet citizens should be repatriated, forcibly if necessary', wrote Thomas Brimelow on Christmas Day 1945. The American ruling would leave loopholes wide open for the retention of all sorts of undesirables. A particularly flagrant case lay before him; as the church bells all over London chimed out for the birth of Jesus he pondered a crudely written letter:

64 General Hospital,
Milan, Italy,
December 1, 1945

From Valentin Kalkany
Dear Sir,
Will you please kindly help me in my difficulty, Mr. Prime Minister, as I am now under your rule, i.e. in territory occupied by you in Italy, and am now in hospital (British) with my right hand and right leg ripped as I rode on a motor-cycle. Will you please not take exception, Mr. Prime Minister, if, when I am fit again, I am able to find a home; for I am a Russian, but do not want to return to Russia, for I am not in agreement with the Communist system, but desire, for example, the system in Britain and America. If it is possible to find me some sort of corner, for I am still young, only 20 years of age—if it is possible to accept me in the ranks of your army, I will serve as I would my own father. If this is not possible, then please write and tell me. I beg you this, as I would my own father. With this I will say goodbye.
Mr. Clement Attlee, Prime Minister.

Brimelow raised his pen, and minuted that the petitioner '*must* go back to the USSR'.[5]

But despite this, there were frustrations. The State Department resisted an appeal by the British Embassy to include all Soviet citizens, regardless of age, sex or history amongst those to whom force could be applied.[6] This meant that *still* no agreed policy could be employed where joint Allied control existed in Italy. Both there and in the British Zone of Austria, British commanders appeared to be still wilfully ignoring or disobeying Foreign Office behests. On 4 February a rather plaintive directive was issued, which pointed out that British policy could be applied in the British zone of Austria regardless of American rulings. In Italy a united policy was still being sought.[7]

Nor was it just senior commanders like McCreery who were uncooperative. In Styria (Steiermark) Colonel Alec Wilkinson was similarly holding out:

> I was instructed by our HQ in Vienna to attend a meeting at Bruck to arrange for another lot of DPs to be sent home . . . I was *instructed* to arrange for trains to take the DPs home. I gave the same answer: *only if they were willing to go*. It was then suggested to me that they should be collected and put into the trains whether they liked it or not. I then asked how they were to be put into the trains? And I was told that a few machine guns might make them change their minds. To which I replied 'That will *not* happen while I am here.'
>
> I then made a compromise as follows. I will agree to the DPs being put into trains on the one condition that the trains go west *NOT EAST*, and I added once they are out of Steiermark they are no longer my responsibility. Within a fortnight of that meeting I was relieved of my command and sent back to England with a report that 'I lacked drive' . . . I don't believe any DPs were sent back 'home' from Steiermark, certainly not while I was there . . . You know our slogan '*Steiermark über alles*'.

Paradoxically, it was the long-delayed American McNarney-Clark directive, with its rigorous categorisation of those due for return, that was now to initiate scenes of bloodshed far more spectacular than that at Kempten which had induced Eisenhower to impose his original unilateral ban in October. For, even if it was only certain Soviet citizens who could now be compelled to return, those falling under the classification laid down could enjoy no further respite. United States military authorities in Germany recommenced preparations for large-scale handovers.

At Dachau Camp, near Munich, scene of terrible crimes under Nazi rule, a number of Russian prisoners from Vlasov's ROA were being held. It was from amongst these that the Americans decided to select the first batch for repatriation under the new McNarney-Clark directive. Rumours of what was impending spread amongst the Russians, and when they were paraded for entrainment on 17 January they adamantly refused to enter the trucks. American troops threatened them with fire-arms, upon which they begged to be shot on the spot—anything rather than deliverance into the hands of the NKVD. Baffled, the guards returned them to their barracks.

It was realised that the only way to effect the operation would be by means of a massive deployment of force. Two days later a shock force of 500 American and Polish guards arrived outside the camp. What followed was vividly described in a report submitted to Robert Murphy:

> Conforming to agreements with the Soviets, an attempt was made to en-train 399 former Russian soldiers who had been captured in German uniform, from the assembly center at Dachau on Saturday, January 19.
>
> All of these men refused to entrain. They begged to be shot. They re-sisted entrainment by taking off their clothing and refusing to leave their quarters. It was necessary to use tear-gas and some force to drive them out. Tear-gas forced them out of the building into the snow where those who had cut and stabbed themselves fell exhausted and bleeding in the snow. Nine men hanged themselves and one had stabbed himself to death and one other who had stabbed himself subsequently died; while 20 others are still in the hospital from self-inflicted wounds. The entrainment was finally effected of 368 men who were sent off accompanied by a Russian liaison officer on a train carrying American guards. Six men escaped en route. A number of men in the group claimed they were not Russians. This, after preliminary investigation by the local military authorities, was brought to the attention of the Russian liaison officer, as a result of which eleven men were returned by the Russians as not of Soviet nationality.

After recapitulating the dreadful sufferings and virtual absence of choice that had led these men to don German uniform, the report ended: 'The incident was shocking. There is considerable dissatisfaction on the part of the American officers and men that they are being required by the American Government to repatriate these Russians . . .'

No better example could be found illustrative of the contrast in pre-vailing attitudes between British Foreign Office officials and those of the State Department. Murphy despatched the report, together with an indignant covering note, to the Secretary of State. In particular he drew attention to that aspect which his British counterpart in Italy, Harold Macmillan, had apparently accepted with such equanimity in the case of the Cossacks: the surrender of non-Soviet citizens to the Soviet authori-ties.[8] Protests from distinguished non-Americans were also aroused by press accounts of the Dachau incident. The man whose armies had very nearly destroyed Bolshevism at birth, General Denikin, addressed a moving appeal to his fellow-soldier, Eisenhower. Three weeks later Pope Pius XII issued a strong condemnation of the (still) secret agreement made at Yalta, protesting against the 'repatriation of men against their will and the refusal of the right of asylum'.[9]

But already events were moving swiftly forward under their own momentum. It will be recalled from Chapter Twelve how General Vlasov's 2nd Division KONR disintegrated before the Soviet advance in Czechoslovakia. General Zverev, its commanding officer, was captured, but several regiments under General Meandrov succeeded in making their way behind the American lines. There they were interned under a deceptively lax régime at Landau. But in September 1945 they were transferred to a wired and guarded camp a few miles to the east at Plattling, near Regensburg. Now they were next on the list for repatriation. There were about 3,000 of them held at Plattling, of whom just over half were held, after screening, to be liable for forced return.

The operation followed the pattern of that experienced at Dachau, though drastic steps were taken this time to reduce the number of suicides. Once again, though, there was a preliminary mutiny, when Meandrov's men, guessing their destination, refused to board the trucks, and barricaded themselves in their barracks. Anxious to avoid another minor bloodbath, the American commandant managed to lull the prisoners' fears by assuring them they were due to be moved shortly to a fresh camp further from the Soviet Zone. The unfortunate Russians, whose suspicions, it seems, were in general only too easy to allay, relaxed and resumed normal camp routine.

In the early hours of the morning of 24 February one of the prisoners was awakened by a faint clanking noise coming from outside the barbed wire. Slipping out of his hut, the Russian saw to his horror that a column of American tanks was approaching the camp. Keeping well in the shadows, he watched a large body of guards move with ghost-like silence up to the gates. They were wearing rubber-soled shoes; at the gateway there was a whispered pause whilst they were issued with special reinforced long riot clubs. This was enough for the solitary witness, who took to his heels and scrambled under the barbed wire to the next enclosure, housing non-Russian prisoners.

Meanwhile the American soldiers divided into separate companies and moved stealthily through the shadows to each dormitory hut. Inside, dark figures crept silently about, gesticulating in dumb show. Light shone through the windows from perimeter searchlights, causing the crouching silhouettes within to vanish and reappear as the lamps swayed in the bitter night wind. At last all was still. A Russian stirred in his sleep, muttering incoherently. A floorboard creaked; otherwise the only sound was the regular breathing of the sleepers. Beside each bed stood two motionless figures.

Abruptly the stillness of the camp was broken by the shrieking blast of a whistle. Startled, Meandrov's men woke and looked about them. At once a ghastly cacophony of yells burst from all around. Without any warning, and with accompanying shrieks and curses, the Americans began to lash with the bludgeons at each recumbent figure. '*Mak snell! Mak snell!*' they shouted in pidgin German, driving the bewildered figures out of their beds, through the doorways and across to the camp gates. Anyone slow in scrambling from his bed was beaten ferociously until he too fled in his underclothes out into the night. At the gates stood a row of trucks, their engines humming, into which the prisoners were driven by their screaming guards. Off along darkened roads the speeding convoy clattered and swayed. There followed a hasty transfer to a train, and the journey was continued some hours later. The train rattled on towards the east, where already a pale cold light was failing in the darkening sky.[10] Near the Czech frontier, beyond Zwiesel, the train halted in the dripping stillness of the Bavarian forest. Blue-capped troops were waiting; officers exchanged brief words through an interpreter, and the bruised and terrified men of Meandrov's Division were shepherded down beside the railway track. Dazed, they stood in little groups amongst the puddles. The American guards, silent and awkward, jumped back into their carriages and prepared to make off. There was a brief hissing and clanking of pistons, and then the blank gaze of the Vlasov men watched swaying lights disappear back along the line.

The Americans returned to Plattling visibly shamefaced. Before their departure from the rendezvous in the forest, many had seen rows of bodies already hanging from the branches of nearby trees. On their return, even the SS men in a neighbouring compound lined the wire fence and railed at them for their behaviour. The Americans were too ashamed to reply.

The tactics employed had proved successful, however. The violence and speed of the operation had ensured that, unlike the similar incident at Dachau, suicides in the camp itself had been prevented. US 3rd Army Headquarters was able to announce that the transfer had taken place 'without incident'. But in the darkness of the railway trucks there had in fact been five successful and numerous attempted suicides. Two prisoners only had succeeded in wounding themselves in Plattling itself; one of them was photographed for the American service paper *Stars and Stripes*. Events at Plattling were briefly filmed by a unit of the Army Signal Corps, presumably as a guide to the conduct of any future operations. This is apparently the only recorded film material extant picturing an Allied forced repatriation operation, but it remains classified and closed to inspection by historians.[11]

Three months later a further party of 243 Russians was despatched eastwards from Plattling,[12] and it was not until the following year that General McNarney declared that *all* Soviet citizens living in the American Zone of Germany were safe from compulsory return.[13] But in fact the departure of the main body from Plattling marked the virtual end of such operations in Germany. American soldiers of all ranks were appalled at what had been done by them or in their name. The State Department had issued the McNarney-Clark Directive in the hope that it would form a reasonable mean between entirely refusing Soviet requests and adopting the British policy of returning everyone remotely liable to repatriation. But even this compromise aroused disgust, outrage and near-universal protest. Once again it is instructive to recall that the Americans had only employed force on a few hundred former soldiers of the Wehrmacht; never at any time did they contemplate turning their bayonets on women and children.

The grounds on which the American objections were based are revealing, and form a most interesting contrast with British official views. On 19 April General McNarney wrote for clarification of the McNarney-Clark Directive, pointing out that 'Repatriation boards, having had recourse only to American Law and procedures in absence of any other, decided against repatriation of several hundred cases on basis the individuals were not citizens, having been denied one or more of such rights of citizenship as the right to vote, to bear arms, etc., or having been members of persecuted groups, etc.' A week later McNarney wrote again, detailing the persecuted groups and noting incidentally that 'had we acted on a strictly American interpretation of Citizenship all subject Soviets would have been released.'

But the Joint Chiefs of Staff replied coldly that 'Since the political system in force in the Soviet Union is basically different from that applying in the United States, and the questions of what rights a Soviet citizen has are matters which concern the Soviet Government solely, the question does not arise ... American rules of citizenship do not apply to Soviet citizens ...'[14] This is a concept that, had it been conceded, could have proved very useful to defence counsel at the War Crimes trials then taking place at Nuremberg. But despite the apparently implacable ruling, it seems that local military and political objections caused the policy to be suspended and then abandoned in Germany soon after the second delivery of Vlasov men from Plattling in May.[15]

It was in this way that forcible repatriation of Russians was ended in the Allied occupied Zones of Germany and Austria. But there remained an area exempt from the McNarney-Clark Directive, and it was to this problem that British as opposed to American policy now directed itself. It will be remembered from the two previous chapters that all efforts to enforce the return of Soviet citizens from Italy had so far failed. The United States had declined to comply with the British Government in enjoining the wholesale return of all Soviet refugees, and the British command could not act independently, since Italy remained controlled by unified Allied command at AFHQ.

It might have been thought that the issuing of the McNarney-Clark Directive in December 1945 would have enabled the British to insist at least on compelling the return home from Italy of those categories held liable under the Directive. But here it was the British who at first hung back. Under 'McNarney-Clark' many scores of civilians would escape being sent back. Accordingly, whilst there remained any chance of persuading the United States to accept the British view, Britain was reluctant to plump for the compromise inherent in American policy.[16]

But the spring of 1946 passed by, and eventually the Foreign Office was obliged to reconcile itself to reality. There was no possible chance of the State Department's altering its opinion: American objections had been too strong. The new Labour Chancellor of the Duchy of Lancaster, Mr. J. Hynd, was raising objections, on moral grounds, and had initiated, in January, a temporary 'freeze' on the use of force; his view was supported by the newly-arrived Head of the Northern Department, Robert (now Lord) Hankey, who felt that acceptance of the American policy would save the civilians, and satisfy British military objections.[17] The Foreign Office accordingly recommended British adhesion to the McNarney-Clark Directive.

Bevin's decision to accept the McNarney-Clark ruling and the consequent forcible return of Russians held by the British resulted from pressures applied by the professional diplomats. How these pressures were brought to bear has only recently come to light. Soon after the temporary 'freeze' on forcible repatriation in the British-occupied zones of Germany and Austria at the end of 1945, Bevin had called for a full report on what such operations had so far involved. On 18 January, 1946, the Head of the Northern Department, Christopher Warner, informed the Foreign Secretary: 'So far as is known, no resort has ever had to be made to violent measures. It has been sufficient to have British troops present when recalcitrants were being moved.' This remarkable falsehood was echoed by Thomas Brimelow, who also noted that 'in the past it has been possible to avoid violence.' Brimelow went on to note, in all probability correctly, that the Americans had only agreed to hand over Russians covered by the McNarney-Clark Directive 'under British pressure to secure the repatriation of the 500 Cossacks from Italy'.

It seems likely that Bevin was on the point of abandoning the policy altogether: a possibly awkward enquiry into the case of some Georgians who had fought bravely against the Germans on Texel Island had been instituted, but was now dropped.[18] As the Americans were, as Brimelow pointed out, largely acting under British pressure, it appears probable that it was the permanent officials' intervention that prolonged forcible repatriation for a further year and a half. If Bevin believed—and there was no reason why he should not—that no force had ever been necessary to return Russians, then one can understand that he saw little justification for abandoning the measure in face of Soviet protests.

This episode provides a remarkable illustration of the truth of Sir Herbert Butterfield's dictum: 'The importance of the higher permanent officials of the Foreign Office is now accepted as a matter of common knowledge; and it has often been noted to what a degree a Foreign Secretary is in their hands. It has even been said that if the permanent officials cannot force their policy on a Foreign Secretary, at any rate they are strong enough to prevent him from carrying out any other policy of his own.'[19]

At a Cabinet meeting held on 6 June, Foreign Secretary Ernest Bevin's proposal, that Britain come into line with the United States, was accepted. The War Office welcomed the decision, as it was believed that 'it means that soldiers will not be required to use force against people with whose reluctance to return to the USSR they may well sympathise.'[20]

The War Office, initially at any rate, does not seem to have appreciated the purpose of the new move. It was not designed to protect unwilling Russians from being despatched to the USSR, but to deliver the remaining few who could not otherwise be handed over. Its initial effects were, none the less, beneficial. All 'Disputed Persons' could be released to settle where they wished or were able, and it was indicated that the Ukrainians at Bellaria would be accepted as non-Soviet citizens.[21] Those whom the McNarney-Clark Directive was designed to exclude were henceforward safe.

But the hunt was now on for the remainder. Instructions were issued to the High Command in Italy that all Russians held in camps there who came under the categories listed in the McNarney-Clark Directive should be collected into two DP camps near Naples. By late June about a thousand 'Russians' had been assembled in camps at Bagnoli and Aversa. As over 42,000 Soviet citizens had been repatriated from the theatre since December 1944,[22] it was clearly the principle rather than the numbers that was at stake. As far as was known, these were the last Soviet citizens in Allied hands liable for return. With British adhesion to 'McNarney-Clark', events began to move swiftly. Exactly a month after the Cabinet decision had been made known to AFHQ, an elaborate plan was drawn up for the transfer of the prisoners to camps in North Italy, where they could be screened preparatory to being surrendered to the Soviets.

This plan bore the title of Operation 'Keelhaul'. 'Keelhauling' was a punishment formerly employed in the English navy,[23] whereby sailors were drawn by ropes under the hull of a man-of-war. Those who were fortunate emerged, half-drowned and torn by barnacles, on the other side, but many naturally did not survive. Operation 'Keelhaul' was the start of a like ordeal, from which only a proportion could hope to emerge alive. Generally these operational code names bore no intended association with the events planned,[24] but there were exceptions.[25] It seems likely that the name 'Keelhaul' could have been chosen for its cynical aptness or, alternatively, as a deliberate mark of disapproval. It is presumably a coincidence, though a curious one, that Russian prisoners in England had been held in a camp at Keele Hall in Staffordshire, now the site of a university.[26]

The prisoners at Bagnoli and Aversa had already been subjected to intensive screening. Now, on 14 August, Operation 'Keelhaul' swung into action. Elaborate precautions against suicide attempts were taken, and escorting troops carried supplies of small-arms, handcuffs and tear-gas grenades. Travelling via Rome, the two parties arrived at their new camps the next day; 498 from Bagnoli found themselves in a British camp at Riccione near Rimini, whilst a party of 432 from Aversa (mainly Turcomans) were taken to an American camp at Pisa. This arrangement resulted from 'the removal of Soviet [citizens] . . . being undertaken as a joint United States-British responsibility'. An immediate advantage deriving from this move was that AFHQ could now demand the withdrawal of the Soviet Repatriation Commission, as there was no longer any justification for its retention. As was noted in September: 'The Mission has given no abnormal trouble on repatriation matters for some months but their activities throughout Italy are an embarrassment from a security aspect.'[27]

British and American military authorities had long appreciated that espionage was one of the prime tasks of the Soviet Repatriation Missions. As their operations became increasingly flagrant, patience began to wear thin. In Austria a group of SMERSH agents were found disguised as American military police. General Mark Clark refused to readmit the

Mission unless certain conditions were stringently complied with.[28] AFHQ experienced similar incidents. In Greece the Soviet Mission had worked with the Communist ELAS in its attempts to take over the country by an armed coup. After British forces had suppressed the uprising, the Soviets stayed on. On 2 September 1945, Field-Marshal Alexander requested that the Repatriation Mission be withdrawn. As he pointed out, there were now no Soviet citizens left in Greece to repatriate. His request was refused by the Foreign Office: Thomas Brimelow had accepted a Soviet plea that two Soviet citizens might be hiding in Crete. By the end of the year the Foreign Office itself began to suspect the Mission's activities, suggesting they might be observed—though not actually stopped.[29]

Now that the remaining repatriables had been shepherded together, all that remained was for final screening to be conducted and the final handovers to take place. The Foreign Office notified AFHQ that categories of prisoners not covered by the McNarney-Clark Directive could well be included amongst those handed over by the British.[30] But this recommendation was ignored by those conducting screening operations.

In their new camps the prisoners were subjected to further screening examination. They had already undergone interrogation and selection by a Major Simcock at their original camp, but now a Russian-speaking officer was to repeat the process more rigorously. This was Denis Hills, already encountered in this book at the Cinecitta Camp outside Rome, and before that on his voyage to Odessa with the Turcomans from Taranto in March 1945. Since that experience, he no longer had any illusions about the fate awaiting repatriates, and was accordingly determined to let off the hook as many of the prisoners as he could. Screening was by no means a straightforward business, as there was rarely any means of corroborating a prisoner's testimony. Hills's approach was as follows. He had before him a copy of the McNarney-Clark Directive;[31] on the basis of this he started by sifting out all those who had definitely served in the German Army. Only these were liable for return, and he was careful not to include amongst them former members of the Todt labour force or other paramilitary organisations.[32] One or two test cases he submitted to GHQ, and gradually by trial and error evolved a system as fair as he could devise. None the less he clearly possessed considerable powers of discretion, and could without fear of repercussions label a man as a 'sheep' or a 'goat' quite arbitrarily. Representatives of the Soviet Repatriation Mission would present demands for particular prisoners, alleging war crimes or other justification for their reclamation. Captain Tom Gorringe was the officer who received these and passed on the requests to Denis Hills. The names of those demanded were written on scruffy pieces of paper, and the information on them was generally derived from informers whom the Soviet officers paid to hang around the camp and obtain material suitable for use in claims. Gorringe at once rejected any—the majority as it transpired—that contained the slightest inaccuracy. The value of Soviet allegations he learned at an early date when he was proffered a map on which the Curzon Line had mysteriously moved itself many miles to the west.

Soon Denis Hills realised that he was placed in a very delicate position. He had had delegated to him what in reality amounted to the power to sentence men to death or grant them a reprieve—a predicament brought sharply to his mind nearly thirty years later when he himself lay under sentence of death from a ferocious dictator. His sympathies lay strongly with the prisoners, and given a free choice he would have declared them all non-repatriable. But this, it was clear, was not possible. GHQ accepted all Hills's recommendations for reprieve, but it was an understood thing that a representative body must go back. The Foreign Office would insist on the return of a token number of hostages, and there existed limits to leniency beyond which AFHQ sensed it could not go.

In the end Hills suppressed his misgivings and exercised what he frankly admits was favouritism. As none of the men appeared to be guilty of war crimes in any real sense, he based his verdicts as much on the individual's capacity to survive in the slave labour camps as on anything else. One hundred Kabardines he set on one side in a body, learning years later that they had found a home in Damascus. The numbers were gradually reduced—there were some escapes—and Hills reached a point where he realized GHQ would accept no further reduction. As he ruefully told some of the survivors later, 'when the Soviet Union demands 400 men, I cannot send them 20.' This being so, he admits now that he included on occasion amongst those whom he registered as repatriable, men for whom he had taken a dislike. This was in the circumstances understandable, but added to the pangs of conscience that troubled him afterwards.

Great influence at Riccione was exerted over the Russians by their camp leader, a former Red Army officer, Major Pavel Petrovitch Ivanov. Ivanov believed, like the Cossacks in Austria, that co-operating loyally with the British camp authorities would go some way towards earning the inmates fair treatment. He discouraged escapes and—tragically—urged his fellows to be honest in their replies to Major Hills's questioning. Many in this way admitted their military status, thereby sentencing themselves to death.

Meanwhile preparations were being made for those registered as ex-Wehrmacht men to be delivered to the Soviets. GHQ was able to profit by previous experience and arrange elaborate precautions to prevent distasteful scenes of bloodshed such as had sullied previous operations of this nature. All the prisoners prepared at Pisa and Riccione were to be transferred in one swift operation. Rigorous measures were to be introduced to prevent escape or suicide, though at the same time guards were enjoined not to hesitate in shooting swiftly if occasion arose. The point of handover would be St. Valentin, near Linz in Austria, which had replaced Judenburg as the accepted reception point in July 1945.[33] On 2 April 1947 the operation received the ominous code name 'East Wind'.

Colonel Iakovlev, of the Soviet Mission in Rome, wrote to Major Simcock of the DP Division: 'Please send all the Soviet Citizens to Camp Nr. 300 at San Valentino (Austria). There it is everything reddy for them.'

Iakovlev had despatched one of his officers to Colonel Starov in Vienna to arrange matters. The officer travelling on this mission was none other than Major Shershun, last met with in this book when he was being abducted by NKVD men from a British ship in Norwegian waters. Like Sieyès, he had, however, survived and was still working in the same line of business. Orders on the Allied side provided 'for the use of handcuffs, tear-gas, straight-jackets and clubs first, with use of fire-arms to be reserved as a last resort'. Should anything unpleasant take place, however, Allied negotiators had arranged with Colonel Iakovlev that dead bodies would be accepted by the Soviets at destination. Once the preliminaries had been settled, it was arranged for all screened Russians held at Pisa and Riccione to be despatched northwards on 8 and 9 May. They had been held in the West for exactly two years.

The day the operation began there took place at the camp a curious ceremony. Twelve of the doomed men had wives and children. Segregated from their fellows, they were informed of what was intended for them. What followed is best described in a report drawn up by Denis Hills a week later.

> Prior to entraining, families whose men-folk were liable for repatriation were informed of the decision to hand them over to the Soviet authorities, and every precaution having been taken to prevent them mutilating themselves, they were given 24 hours in which to decide whether the males should travel alone or whether their dependents should accompany them.
>
> Very painful scenes of real agony ensued and were endured for 24 hours. When the final decision was made—and what other decision could possibly have been arrived at?—the husbands all refused to allow their dependents to accompany them. And further painful and unbearable scenes of parting were witnessed.
>
> The fact that not one husband consented to his wife and children accompanying him, whether the wife was willing or not, is sufficient proof of the terror with which they viewed the prospect of being handed over to

the Soviet authorities. The attitude of the men was summed up by one of them as follows. 'Please shoot me now—that I may die a merciful death and not end my days under torture.' These men were not heroes. They were, with one exception, very ordinary little men and it is very doubtful whether they have any crime on their conscience other than that of having turned their hand against a régime which to them is hateful.

It is impossible to exaggerate the painfulness of this aspect of Operation Eastwind. Breaking the news to these families that they were to be repatriated seemed equivalent to delivering a death sentence. The circumstances were made more macabre by the fact that wife and children were invited to share the fate of their men-folk if they wished. In retrospect, it is thought that it would have been more humane to have seized the men-folk for repatriation without offering them the choice of taking their dependents with them if they wished; for in the final event, the results were exactly the same.

Whilst this was going on the remaining body of 171 Russians was paraded in their cage. It was not yet dawn, and the men stood in ranks, trembling with cold and unpleasant anticipation. A column of lorries drove up at speed and halted outside the wire. A large body of British soldiers sprang out and ran to the gates. A party moved in and began hustling the prisoners outside. They were passed between a double rank of troops armed with sten-guns. Through this human passage were rushed the victims, and in groups of fifteen were placed in the trucks. Though legends grew up later amongst émigré Cossacks of wild scenes of violence, British Army preparations had in fact been so thorough that escape and resistance were impossible. The escort comprised 6 officers and 210 men of the Royal Sussex Regiment, commanded by Major Ben Dalton. Two jeeps, equipped with machine-guns, and armed motorcyclists guarded the convoy as it tore along deserted roads to Riccione.

The railway station had been completely taken over by troops. The entire area was temporarily enclosed by barbed wire and guarded by more than a company of the Sussex Regiment. Though a search of the prisoners had already taken place in their camp, another more thorough investigation was taken to check that none carried any object that could be used for a suicide attempt. In a siding stood an empty train with sealed doors and iron grilles covering the windows. There was no longer any doubt as to where they were going. Whilst the men were undergoing their search (several were found to have concealed penknives and razors about them), the camp leader, Pavel Ivanov, asked permission to speak to Denis Hills, who was standing nearby.

The selection of this man for return had in many ways been Hills's most agonising decision. He was an intelligent and likeable man, exceptionally co-operative and loyal in dealing with the affairs of the camp.

After much soul-searching, Hills decided that he was one of those physically and mentally resilient enough to face what awaited those sent back. Such were the criteria that had to be employed in effecting this last British offering to Stalin and Beria. Now Ivanov strode up to Hills; with a reproachful but not vindictive look he murmured: 'So you are sending us to our death after all. I believed in you. Democracy has let us down.'

Guards and prisoners boarded the train. With Major Dalton was a young British Intelligence officer, Alexander Wainman. A fluent Russian-speaker, it was his duty to act as interpreter. In this way he came to learn something of the feelings of these condemned men during this last journey into darkness.

It was now that my own particular task began, namely to explain to the men that they must not talk loudly, that they must remain seated and that, if they required to go to the lavatory, they were to raise their hand and be accompanied there by an armed guard.

The moment they heard me speak their language they turned to me as a man and asked where they were being taken. I replied with an evasive answer, but it was of no avail. They had already guessed what their fate was to be. 'Don't give us back to the Russians. Shoot us here if you want, but don't send us where we will be tortured.'

The faces of these men which had become almost expressionless as they climbed into the train now became animated. They began to talk among themselves. One young fellow of about twenty suddenly burst into tears. 'Not only we ourselves, but our families too will be shot.' This was the signal for the others, particularly for those of his own age. Within a few seconds half of the men in the carriage were sobbing. 'Doesn't this go against the conscience of the British Government and British people? How can you do a thing like this?'

I did not reply. Instead I tried to escape from my feelings by looking away from the men who were talking to me. My gaze fell upon some of our own troops, boys of the same age as those they saw suffering before their eyes. Their faces expressed bewilderment and compassion. 'It doesn't look as if they are too keen on the idea of going home,' said one of them in the typical English manner of under-statement. Another of the Russians turned to me—'All we want and ask is to be allowed to live as you yourself want to live, but if you can't help us, shoot us now and spare us the agony that lies ahead.'

It was too much for me. I could not answer. Instead I paused for a moment and then turned and ran quickly out of the carriage on to the gravel outside. I turned my face away from the train and my fellow countrymen. Tears were already running down my cheeks. I felt an inner satisfaction that the feeling of pity was not dead within me. Fortunately nobody came near me for the next few minutes. If I had had to speak at that moment I should have burst into sobs. For the next two hours the lorries went and returned each time with a new load of victims.

I had learnt my lesson the first time and in the other carriages I would call out the instructions rapidly and then disappear before the Russians had time to ask questions. [One man was persuaded to leave behind his dog, which a good-natured sergeant-major promised to adopt.] The man looked at me. 'I quite understand,' he said, 'I don't need the dog now'.

By about ten o'clock the train was loaded and stood in the hot sunshine until twelve-thirty, the hour scheduled for departure. The last man, who was brought in an ambulance, had been dragged from a sick-bed where he had spent the last 5½ months. He was suffering from a disease of the kidneys which the Medical Officer told me was incurable. He was quite fatalistic about the future. 'Life, in any case, had nothing in store for me. If I had stayed in Italy perhaps I should have dragged on for another two or three years at the most, so I feel it is better to hasten the end of my suffering.' He was given a berth in the medical coach which was attached to the train to deal with any cases of attempted suicide.

The journey took twenty-four hours from Riccione to St. Valentin in the Soviet Zone of Austria. I did not go near the prisoners again except to interpret for the MO on two occasions. I felt it was better not to talk to them. At night most of them lay on the floor and slept from sheer exhaustion. In every coach were half a dozen sentries, so that any attempt to escape would have been in vain. When morning came and we got near to the Russian Zone the prisoners gave their money and their watches to our soldiers. They tore their letters and family photographs to shreds and left them lying on the floor of the coaches. Several of them left copies of the New Testament behind them. As I watched the people in the stations coming and going about their business I realised what must be passing through the minds of these poor wretches. There, outside, was the world of freedom, but for them another fate was in store—torture, death or, at the best, ten years in a labour camp.

We came to the bridge over the river Enns which is the demarcation line between the American and Russian Zones. We saw the Russian sentries as the train passed over it. Now all hope had vanished. The train moved on for another five miles and stopped at St. Valentin where Col. Starov, Head of the PW and DP division of the Soviet Element of the Allied Commission for Austria, took over the prisoners . . . Carriage by carriage the men were unloaded but they were not the same men I had talked to twenty-four hours before. Then their faces had shown emotion, anxiety and a dread of the future, now they were like cattle so dead was the look on the face of each man. Yes! even the young boys who had sobbed their eyes out. They wore that expression which Westerners tend to think of as the Slavs' supreme indifference to death. I myself had once believed in this phrase. Now I knew how wrong I had been.

Out they marched as their names were called and squatted in groups in a clover field where sentries had been posted at a depth to prevent their escape. The list of names was badly compiled and it took an hour or more to make sure all the men were present. Besides Col. Starov, there were about a dozen more Soviet officers present. Some of them helped check names, others merely stood and watched. The only civilian was a fat villainous-looking man who had an air of the Gestapo about him. He told me he was the Tass [news agency] representative . . .

The train moved off on its return journey. In St. Valentin station I discovered from the Austrians that a train of cattle trucks had been ordered for that evening to take the men to Bruck an der Leitha, near the Hungarian frontier, where the Russians have a large camp. This was the last indication I had of their fate. It is mere conjecture to speculate as to what this will be. Some will no doubt be shot, others will serve five or ten years in a labour camp. One thing is certain, namely that every thinking English-man on that train was ashamed of the task he had been called upon to perform. A number of helpless human beings had been deliberately sacrificed as a political sop to appease the Soviet Government. I am still asking myself whether they will respect us any more as a result or whether they will merely smile to themselves at our naïveness.

Major Wainman's speculations about the prisoners' fate seem, alas, optimistic. Major Dalton noted in his subsequent report that Pavel Ivanov and the other officers and warrant officers were separated from the rank-and-file after having their names rigorously checked. 'I got the impression that they were going to be dealt with pretty summarily.' As for the minimum sentence likely to be imposed on the remainder, it was at this very time, in a successful bid to conciliate Western liberals, that Stalin officially abolished the death sentence—substituting for it the gentle alternative of *twenty-five years* in a penal camp.[34]

Next day another train left Riccione with nine of the married men who had spent the night deciding whether to take their wives and children with them to share their fate. Three of the original twelve had been excluded by Denis Hills on grounds of sickness and other pretexts. To escort the nine on their journey, ensuring that there were no suicides or other acts of indiscipline, an armed party of forty-four soldiers of the Royal Sussex Regiment travelled on board. They were commanded by Major John Stanton, who remembers the journey clearly. He explains that, probably as a result of deliberate policy, no rapport had time to develop between his men and the prisoners. His interpreter, however, was remarkably jittery—perhaps from motives similar to those of Alec Wainman. There were no serious incidents on the journey (except for a period when the nine had to be manacled), and next morning they duly arrived at St. Valentin. They were directed to draw up on an embankment amidst open fields. Below them stood a platoon of smart-looking Red Army soldiers; a moment later Colonel Starov and his staff entered Stanton's compartment.

When handed the list of nine prisoners, Starov was greatly taken aback. Suspiciously he accused Stanton of withholding a large number, and in particular he was very anxious to know where were the women and children. To all this Stanton could only repeat that he was merely the escort officer and had no control over who was or was not sent. At last Starov appeared to appreciate the force of this, but declared that he could not sign for the receipt of such a derisory number until he had consulted Moscow. Stanton concurred, and a staff officer jumped down from the train and disappeared. Resigned to a long wait, the Englishman offered Starov a drink. He discovered that all he had was neat Gordon's gin, but with this Starov appeared well satisfied.

They sat drinking and chatting amiably, when there was a flurry of activity outside. The same enormously fat civilian encountered by Dalton and Wainman the day before came scrambling up the steps. Though he was dressed in a light summer suit he was perspiring freely from his exertions. It was a lovely May day. All the Soviet officers present, from Starov down, displayed exceptional deference to this 'Tass correspondent'. The latter explained to Stanton, amicably enough, that he had got through to Moscow, permission being now granted to accept the nine prisoners and allow the British train to return. Stanton felt great relief—he suspected the Red Army unit of wishing to steal the engine (a favourite trick)—and was still happier when, some twenty minutes later, his train began shunting off on its journey back through Linz. At the same time he could not help remarking that the fat civilian's claim that he had contacted Moscow seemed remarkably thin: the track lay amidst open fields, and it was difficult to see how he could have made communication. As Stanton noted in his report: 'My personal opinion is that he was the highest authority present and that it was to him and not to Moscow that the Colonel applied for instructions.'

Up till the moment he left, John Stanton's prime consideration had been to carry out the operation efficiently. But now that he had time to reflect he began to feel increasingly uneasy. It had been impressed on him at his briefing that these men had fought against the British (this was almost certainly untrue),[35] but he found it hard not to feel deep compassion for the quiet and unresisting victims—allotted five British guards each, merely to prevent their cutting their own throats in desperate fear. They had impressed on him that they would all be killed after their delivery—a claim he felt might well be true. His contact with the Russians lasted a mere twenty-four hours, yet he says today: 'It was a horrid experience, it never left me.'

Others concerned felt similarly. Major-General James Lunt was at that time GSO II (Ops.) at GHQ. It was he who had drawn up the operational orders for Operation 'East Wind'. At the time he did so, he now frankly admits, he felt little sympathy for men he regarded as collaborators. But now, as he read reports by Hills, Dalton, Stanton and others, he began to feel sick at heart. Denis Hills's description of the agony of the bereaved wives struck a jarring chord, and he wondered whether they had not all been engaged in actions unworthy of a soldier. Punishment of the guilty was all very well, and the defeated in any war must expect at least some misfortune, but he knew he could not justify cruelties such as these reports described.

A contingent of Russian prisoners had also arrived at St. Valentin on 9 May from the American camp at Pisa. Its numbers showed once again the differing criteria employed by the two great Allies. The camps at Riccione and Pisa each initially contained roughly the same number of prisoners: rather more than 400. When Denis Hills reported that his screening had brought the number repatriable below the 200 mark, it was made abundantly clear to him that he could reduce it no further. Yet his American equivalent managed to get away with whittling *his* list down to a mere 75.[36]

Such was Operation 'East Wind', the last of the major forced repatriation operations of the post-war period of appeasement. Considerable public indignation was aroused in the West at the news that such an event had been allowed to take place when even liberal thinkers had become aware of Stalin's plans for world conquest. The indignation was accentuated by the fact that newspapers made much play with stories of numerous suicides and of savage violence employed by troops at the entrainments in Riccione and Pisa (the prisoners there travelled from Leghorn Station).[37] In London, a committee headed by the Duchess of Atholl and Mrs. Elma Dangerfield bombarded public figures with protests. A White Russian journalist, Anatol Baikalov, supplied them with voluminous evidence from refugees in the West.[38] On 21 May a Labour Member of Parliament, Richard Stokes (well known for his concern with humanitarian causes), rose in the House of Commons to enquire about the truth of disquieting reports concerning this last forced transfer of refugees to the Soviets. The Parliamentary Under-Secretary for Foreign Affairs, Christopher Mayhew, replied, defending the Government's interpretation of the Yalta Agreement, whilst at the same time repudiating reports of violence and attempted suicide acccompanying the operation.[39]

In fact there had been an attempted suicide on board the first train. A desperate prisoner had tried to slit his own throat, an attempt which Major Dalton's escorting party was only able to prevent after a sharp struggle. However, it would be unfair to accuse[40] Mayhew of suppressing evidence of this incident. Major Dalton had omitted all mention of it in his reports on the journey, relating that 'No physical violence was used during the journey' and that there were 'no incidents'. As Dalton himself explains, the violent incident 'was not incompatible with the report; I did not expect an uneventful journey and the precautions taken were anticipated and the event concluded as planned.'[41]

Unknown to the public, the Government was also receiving strong protests from influential quarters. General Burrows, former head of the Military Mission in Moscow, passed on to the War Office a plea for amnesty for Russians in Britain; it came from Count Bennigsen, holder of the MC and one-time liaison officer to Burrows at Archangel in 1919.[42] Major Wainman's report on Operation 'East Wind', quoted extensively above, had been drawn up at the request of George Young of MI 6. On receipt of this report at headquarters in Vienna, Young was appalled at the evident inhumanity of the continuation of so brutal a policy. He brought the damning evidence before Sir Henry Mack, British Political Adviser, who was equally disgusted. A strongly-worded protest was despatched to the Foreign Office; confirmation was received in reply that no further operations of this nature were contemplated.[43]

Forced repatriation had indeed drawn to a close. In June Denis Hills saved twelve Georgians from Lipari Island who were in danger of hand-over by the Italians. On the night of 8 July the Soviets kidnapped six old émigrés from a camp at Barletta; one committed suicide and the remainder were never seen again.[44] But appeasement was shifting into Cold War. Despite Soviet protests, the Ukrainian Galician Division was moved from Italy to Britain immediately after 'East Wind'.[45] Earlier in the year General McNarney had announced that 'for the first time a Soviet citizen could admit his citizenship and still legally remain in the United States zone of Germany'—a decision that resulted in the saving, inter alia, of thousands of Mennonite refugees from racial persecution in the USSR.[46] The Soviet reaction was predictable: a barrage of complaints burst about the ears of every Western government concerned. These were by now largely ignored, though it was not until March 1949 that the Soviet Repatriation Commission in Frankfurt was compelled to withdraw, which it did with exceedingly bad grace.[47]

Between 1943 and 1947 the Western democracies had returned to the USSR a recorded 2,272,000 Soviet citizens. About 35,000 Soviet citizens of the minority peoples of Russia (Ukrainians, Byelorussians, Kalmucks, etc.) were listed officially as being knowingly retained in the West.[48] In fact, a larger number than this managed to evade repatriation by forging DP papers awarding foreign national (Polish, Yugoslav) status, or by escaping in other ways. For obvious reasons no exact statistic of this grouping can be provided; estimates of between a quarter and half a million have been suggested.[49]

The majority of those returned went back in the early summer of 1945; after September there began a moratorium on forcible repatriation until the beginning of 1946. Between January 1946 and May 1947 only a few thousand were compelled to return, a small percentage of the whole. What disgusted many about these later operations was not their size, but the fact that they took place when it was clear to all but a deluded few that the country to which these people were being unwillingly delivered was a declared and ruthless enemy of the West.

Perhaps the most striking illustration of the paradox of British policy at this time is to consider a parallel operation. This was Operation 'Highland Fling', the purpose of which was to assist Soviet defectors in escaping from the Soviet Union to the West. It occurred simultaneously with Operation 'Keelhaul'. Thus many hundreds who wished to escape Marxist rule were helped out of Russia by British troops,[50] whilst others who had, for the most part, left Russia involuntarily five years earlier were sent back to have their throats cut.

16

National Contrasts: Repatriation Pressures in France, Sweden and Liechtenstein

So far only repatriations conducted under United States and British auspices have been described, but it would be wrong to imagine that it was only these two countries that were faced with the problem. A number of other governments had also to decide what must be done with Russians held by them, and each reacted in a distinctive way.

FRANCE

Only in France did the government face a problem in any way comparable to that which troubled the statesmen of Great Britain and the United States. Altogether, the 1st French Army and Resistance units captured some 15,000 Russian troops serving in the German Army, whilst another 20,456 voluntarily deserted to the French. Of the latter grouping, nearly half (8,000) joined the Free French and participated in the struggle on the Allied side.[1] In addition several thousand DPs were transferred by British and American forces to French control at the end of 1944. Serious disorders took place in their camps in January 1945, until SHAEF helped the hard-pressed French to provide adequate facilities.[2]

Two months after Eden had agreed to Stalin's demand for all Russians to be returned regardless of their wishes, General de Gaulle also visited Moscow and was induced to make a similar concession.[3] As a result a Soviet Repatriation Commission arrived in Paris, headed by General Dragun. One of his first acts on arrival was to assist in quelling the disturbances in DP camps by personally shooting ten men, chosen at random.[4] The Commission was composed entirely of NKVD officers, whose job it was to ensure the safe return home of all Russians on whom they could lay hands. In addition they were charged with distributing arms and money to the French Communist Party.[5]

As Russians in the camps all over France were chosen for repatriation, they were brought to the central assembly point at Reille Barracks in Paris. From there they travelled to selected transit camps, of which the most important was Camp Beauregard, just outside the city.[6] For some months security in the camp was lax, and the officials of Dragun's mission took pains to stress that a warm welcome and certain amnesty for all offences was awaiting all returning home. A prisoner who had previously been in the dreadful German camp on Alderney remembered reassuring visits and speeches from the Soviet Ambassador, Bogomolov. The effect of these was somewhat spoiled, however, by sinister menaces uttered by a senior NKVD officer in his cups. Drunkenness and plundering subsequently became prevalent amongst the dispirited inmates.[7]

An American official of the YMCA, Donald A. Lowrie, was greatly impressed by the Soviet officials when he called at the Embassy on 20 October 1944.

'All, regardless of their immediate past, will be returned to Soviet Russia,' said Ambassador Bogomolov. 'Some of these,' he added, 'are heroes, some of them may have been less strong-minded. No nation consists exclusively of heroes,' he remarked with a smile. 'But the Motherland would not be a mother if she did not love all her family, even the black sheep. Therefore, all of our citizens abroad will be received back home.'

Bogomolov went on to talk of the intolerable pressures imposed on many.

'If some could not withstand these pressures and joined the German forces or even served as police, guarding their fellow-prisoners in camps, in many cases this is understandable. Every man will be given a chance to redeem himself . . . All are accepted here, all return home, all are considered as sons of the Motherland.'

The Ambassador spoke warmly for a moment about the work of the YMCA. 'There are Christian young men all over Russia,' he reflected, 'only not organised.' Lowrie departed with the impression of a man who felt deeply for the tragedy of human beings caught up in events far beyond their understanding or control. He also thought Bogomolov possessed 'a good sense of humour'.[8]

Though Dragun's officials ranged widely in their search for scattered Russians, Camp Beauregard remained for several months administered by two of the prisoners themselves, named Ivanov and Titarenko. These had been formerly close collaborators with the Nazis, but were for the moment favoured by the NKVD. The transfer of loyalties was not a difficult one, as so many have found. But at the end of May 1945 security was suddenly tightened up. The camp was wired and the guards doubled. Numbers had sailed from the camp at Marseilles for Odessa in recent months, but now preparations were being made for the first overland repatriation convoy.[9]

A Ukrainian, who had decided that, despite the hazards, he wished to return has left a description of one of these journeys. He tells how he and his fellows were

> sent off well, with speeches, music, and banners, on trucks . . . They were driven to a collecting point near Leipzig and placed behind barbed wire. Instead of music, there were loaded machine guns. The welcoming speech was full of curses and threats. Then interrogations began: this was no longer the army, this was the NKVD. They asked an endless number of questions, and after each reply the interrogator would shout 'You liar!' The food was atrocious. Nor did the conversations among the men sound very comforting; there was talk of the horrible fate of the preceding parties.

Terrified by what he saw and heard, the narrator managed to escape by smuggling himself on board a returning American truck.[10]

Outside the camps, Dragun's NKVD operatives now began what many have described as a reign of terror. Unchecked by the French police—apparently on instructions from above—they unleashed in Paris a series of surveillances, spyings, kidnappings and murder.[11] In March 1946 a young Russian refugee, passing under the Polish pseudonym of Lapchinsky, disappeared from a Paris flat under mysterious and sinister circumstances. A former *Ostarbeiter* who had been liberated by the Americans, he arrived in the French capital in November 1944. There he was befriended by Count Ivan Tolstoy, a distant cousin of the present writer. One evening he arrived for dinner in an evident state of fear; in response to his host's enquiry, he replied that he was convinced he was being followed. His host and other guests were inclined to ridicule such fears, but nevertheless advised him to be cautious. Lapchinsky did not need this advice; those who knew him testified that he never opened his door to visitors; indeed, no visitors had called at all until a few days previously. The *concierge* remembered afterwards that three 'Poles' had come to call on the youth, but he had been out.

On the next occasion he was not. What precisely happened was never determined. Lapchinsky's room was discovered in a state of disarray; there were bloodstains everywhere, which bore signs of attempts at effacement. An eyewitness had seen a semi-conscious figure being dragged into a large black car, which then sped off to an unknown destination. Lapchinsky was never seen again, and the police were left with an apparently unsolved crime on their hands. But there seems no doubt—despite revelations by the Communist *L'Humanité* that it was all a Gestapo plot (in 1946!)—that the crime was the work of the NKVD.[12] Similar activities on their part had become widespread in that and the previous year, and the case was paralleled by the more celebrated kidnappings of the White Russian Generals Kutyepov and Miller in Paris in 1930 and 1937.[13]

Eventually, in May, the Minister of the Interior took the courageous step of protesting to the Soviet Ambassador concerning this series of crimes openly perpetrated on French soil. But the Coalition Government (which included Communist ministers), conscious of France's weakness and determined on appeasement, compelled his resignation.[14]

The French Army, unlike its Government, appears to have reacted to Soviet pressures with remarkable firmness. At Potsdam Novikov complained that in the zone of Germany occupied by the French 1st Army, propaganda by émigrés was being conducted amongst Soviet DPs, with a view to persuading them against return: 'In this case this activity is carried out with the active support on the part of the French military authorities of the "Sécurité-Militaire" '.[15] In the following month, NKVD General Vikhorev[16] began hunting for Russians in the French Zone of Austria. He discovered a camp containing possible prey at Felke, near the frontier of Liechtenstein, and was making ready to pounce, when an unsympathetic 'Lieut.-Colonel Fichelier, the officer in charge of camps in this zone, refused [his] request for admission to the above-mentioned camp, on the grounds that he had no instructions from Paris.'[17]

Considerations similar to those affecting Britain and the United States induced the French to bring the policy of forcible repatriation to a close in 1947. Virulent attacks were launched from Moscow in anticipation of this move, and the French were accused of concealing or preventing the return of Soviet citizens. These charges were firmly rejected by the French Foreign Ministry, who pointed out that most of the DPs whom the Soviets wished to seize were Ukrainians, Balts and other non-Soviet citizens. In a further statement, a French spokesman confirmed that Soviet officials exercised police power over Camp Beauregard, but claimed that the inmates were all volunteers for return. Sceptics 'observed that the barbed-wire barriers recently seen inside the camp's stone walls did not seem to confirm the voluntary presence of its inmates,'[18] but despite its apparent acquiescence in NKVD operations conducted on French soil, the Government was in fact moving towards taking a firmer line with the intruders.

A particularly flagrant case of kidnapping gave the French the sought-for pretext for closing the camp. The trickle of refugees passing through on their way back to the USSR had dwindled until it virtually came to a halt. Yet still the Soviet Embassy insisted on maintaining this huge settlement which, as outraged public opinion noted, was virtually a Soviet enclave on French territory. Over its portal were festooned red flags, surmounted by a colossal portrait of Stalin, brightly floodlit every night. There was every reason to suspect that Camp Beauregard had become a centre for Soviet espionage and subversion operations. The French Communist Party was known to be working towards a Soviet occupation of the country, just as it had supported Hitler's invasion during the Nazi-Soviet accord seven years earlier. In 1947 the prospect of an armed Communist *Putsch* in the interior, backed by Soviet arms and possibly troops, was by no means an improbable exigency. The Government at long last resolved to act.

A White Russian of French nationality, Dmitri Spechinsky, obtained a divorce from his Soviet-born wife. The three daughters of the marriage (who were, of course, French citizens by birth) had been consigned by a court at Nice to the father's custody. Not long afterwards mother and daughters disappeared, and the police, following a request from the father, managed to track them down to Camp Beauregard.[19] Spechinsky then applied to the police for recovery of his children. This request would earlier have been received with embarrassment and evasion. Now it was seized upon as affording the chance the Cabinet had required. (In May the Ramadier Government had expelled the Communists from their ministerial posts.)

If somewhat tardy, the action taken was prompt and effective. The mysterious camp, into which no French official had been admitted for over two years, was surrounded by a force of some 2,000 infantry, CRS police and plain-clothes detectives. In case of more serious trouble, two light tanks stood by. The Soviet Embassy was informed of the raid only twenty minutes before the first French soldiers came storming in under the giant picture of the Father of Peoples. Sure enough, the kidnapped Spechinsky children and their mother were found concealed in a barracks. A few days later, they would have been on a train bound for Moscow, and then Karaganda or Vorkuta. Maria, Zenobia and Olga were returned to their father; meanwhile the police ransacked the camp for evidence of further unwarranted activities.

In the entire compound were found only fifty-eight persons allegedly awaiting repatriation. But concealed in the clothing-store detectives came upon some odd items: 10 British sten guns, 2 Soviet submachine guns, 10 rifles, 1 shotgun, 52 cartridge magazines, 49 machine-gun ammunition drums, 5 boxes of cartridges, 10 grenades, and 7 revolvers. The Soviet Embassy explained that these toys were souvenirs retained by some of the Soviet citizens from their days of service in the Resistance. We may suspect a different purpose.[20]

Forcible repatriation thus came to an end in France some months later than the last Allied operation in Italy. In all some 102,481 Russians were returned. But in considering these numbers, and France's responsibility, some important factors should be remembered. Compared to the United States and Britain, France had emerged from the German occupation divided and weakened. Hundreds of thousands of French workmen, mainly from Alsace and Lorraine, had been seized by the Germans for forced labour and then liberated by the Red Army. It was not just that their number was infinitely greater than that of the British and American servicemen similarly released, whose fate so concerned Eden and Stettinius. As civilians they could have been much more readily detained by the Soviets than Allied servicemen. Britain and the United States had been at first inclined to arrange an agreement with the USSR for the mutual repatriation of liberated prisoners of war only, and it was only at Soviet insistence that it was agreed 'such an agreement should extend also to Soviet citizens and British subjects interned and forcibly deported by the Germans.'[21] As British officials noted at the time, there were virtually no such British subjects, whilst there existed several million deported Soviet citizens. It may be that a firm British approach could have excluded civilians from the agreement; we cannot know, since Foreign Office policy was based on a different approach. But for the French the boot was on the other foot: it was *they* who were anxious to retrieve deported civilians. Their negotiating position was infinitely weaker. Even at the time of the raid on Camp Beauregard, the Soviets were known to hold no less than 23,600 French civilian 'hostages'.[22]

The situation in France differed in another respect. It does not appear that French troops were called upon to batter unwilling repatriates into insensibility before flinging them on to trucks, or that French bayonets prodded small children into cattle-wagons for transmission to Siberia. NKVD agents themselves entered France to conduct operations. To some extent differing institutions of the state appear to have pursued virtually autonomous policies. Whilst Communist ministers in the Government extended their protection to kidnappers and murderers, the French Army in Germany and Austria obstructed the Soviet Repatriation Commission at every turn.

BELGIUM

Other countries faced their Russian problem on a smaller scale and with further permutations of policy. Belgium's 'Yalta Agreement' on repatriation was signed on 13 March 1945. Until the dissolution of SHAEF, camps containing Russians came under the control of HQ 21 Army Group's Civil Affairs branch. A British officer who administered one such camp at Termonde recalls that many of the inmates were reluctant to return home, but despite this they were placed on their train without incident.[23] The Soviet Repatriation Commission was headed by a Colonel Stemasov, who made regulation complaints about the prisoners' living conditions.

The British Ambassador noted 'that Soviet policy is to assemble if necessary by force all stray Russians in Belgium into collecting centres where they would be kept under strict control until an opportunity occurs of evacuating them to Soviet Union'.[24] In July the Belgian Government was assigned full responsibility for the activities of Soviet officials on Belgian soil, whilst Soviet citizens in former SHAEF camps were removed to Germany or repatriated direct to the USSR.[25] There were, however, still many Russians at large in Belgium and, before long, scenes similar to those enacted in Paris were taking place in Brussels.

> Difficulties are known to have developed when officers of the NKVD, acting for the Repatriation Commissar, resorted to kidnapping on at least one occasion in broad daylight in the streets of Brussels to achieve their ends. Soviet repatriation officers had on several occasions entered internment camps to 'persuade' Russian inmates to return. Such activities led the Belgian Minister of Justice on 28 December last to issue a circular to police and gendarmerie authorities instructing them to forbid repatriation officers to enter internment camps without express permission, and should they enter without authorisation to remove them by force. They were likewise to protect civilians from any act of violence.[26]

The Belgian Government was thus very much more forthright in its reaction to Soviet illegalities than the French or the British.

HOLLAND AND FINLAND

Of remaining Western European countries concerned, the Dutch followed a similar line to the Belgians.[27] Allied occupying and liberating forces were responsible for operations conducted in Norway, Denmark, Germany, Austria and Italy. Finland formed a special case. Soviet advances on the Eastern Front had compelled the Finns to accept terms dictated to them by the USSR, under the armistice agreement of 19 September 1944. An Allied Control Commission was established in Helsinki, which was, in the nature of things, largely the mouthpiece for Soviet threats and demands—demands the Finns were in no position to refuse. Several thousand Russian prisoners of war held in Finnish camps were ordered to be handed over, and the Finnish authorities had no alternative but to comply. Several hundred of the prisoners managed to escape when they learned of this. Rather than return home, these Russians preferred to live like wolves in the pine-forests, hunting down wild game and raiding isolated farmsteads. It was November in the Arctic Circle, but even this life was preferable to what awaited them at home.[28] This is particularly significant in view of the fact that all these men without exception were simple prisoners of war; they had had no contact with the Nazis or other Germans, had never been approached by Vlasov's officers, and had performed no work for the enemy war effort. This example alone should forestall any argument presuming that Russians in general were afraid to return home on account of guilty association with the Nazi cause; those who had no such connection took if anything even more desperate measures to avoid repatriation.

In addition the Soviets demanded and received a number of Russian émigrés, all of whom bore either Finnish passports or Nansen (stateless) certificates. As with the émigré Cossacks handed over by the British in Austria, the Soviet State was enabled to pay off grudges of a quarter-century's standing. A former Tsarist General, Severin Dobrovolsky, was executed in Moscow a few months after his arrival, whilst Stepan Petrisienko, who during the Kronstadt rebellion of 1921 was chairman of the counter-revolutionary sailors' council, died in a prison camp two years later.[29] Though the Soviet authorities were aided by quisling elements in Finland, it is scarcely possible to lay any blame on the people or government of that country, which was virtually in the position of an occupied state.

SWITZERLAND

In a very different situation was neutral Switzerland. A haven of refuge in Nazi-dominated Europe, escaping prisoners from all sides attempted to cross the frontier, either to escape again and continue the struggle, or to be interned in relatively comfortable conditions. Among these were many Russians. As early as March 1942 the British learned that a number had successfully entered the country, and the Foreign Office considered ways of sending them aid. Oddly, the Soviet Government did despatch funds for the care of their interned soldiers in Switzerland.[30] Possibly it was felt that a failure to do so would excite unfavourable comment in the West, as it would be possible for Allied and neutral observers to witness camp conditions. A further consideration may have been that the prisoners might well have to be lured out of Switzerland when the time came, as the Swiss tradition of neutrality and asylum would preclude any forcible surrender.

With the invasion of France and the consequent opening to the Allies of the Franco-Swiss frontier, a party of 804 of these Russians took the opportunity of crossing into France. They embarked at Marseilles for return to Russia via the Middle East route. A Soviet repatriation official from Paris, named Tcherniak,[31] had managed to persuade them of the good life to be enjoyed in the victorious Soviet Union. But another party of 500 remained suspicious and declined to go.[32]

Increasing chaos behind the German lines, coupled with the creation of the 'Vlasov' Divisions, enabled further parties of Russians to slip across the frontier into Switzerland during the last months of the war. An entire unit, comprising many émigrés and commanded by a Colonel Sobolev, is said to have marched over, to be disarmed and interned.[33] By the end of May 1945 there were some 9,000 Russians in Swiss territory. Following its usual softening-up practice, the Soviet Government issued a number of strident accusations: the Swiss were beating up innocent prisoners, returning them to the Gestapo, and so on. The incident on which all this was based appears to have been the discourteous treatment of some drunken Russians by Swiss sentries.[34]

Before long a full-blown Repatriation Commission was despatched by General Dragun to Switzerland. The usual measures of cajoling, bullying and threatening were employed, with varying success. In September an intelligent Russian from Fribourg sent an appeal to the British Legation in Berne. Ivan Klimenko explained that many Russians felt they could not return to their own country, but were being placed under increasing and frightening pressure by the Soviet Military Delegation to do so.

Klimenko ended with the fervent hope that the Swiss would continue to honour their ages-old tradition of political asylum, and that the Allies would employ their influence to sustain the high principles for which they had professedly fought the war.[35]

What happened next still awaits a full investigation. In fact most of the Russians did go home, though no physical force was employed by Swiss troops or police. But I am informed by a high authority that the Swiss indicated clearly to the recalcitrant remainder that, if they did not return voluntarily, force would be used against them. Whether this threat would really have been implemented we cannot tell. To the terrified Russians the threat was enough; they knew well what the British and Americans were doing in neighbouring Austria and Bavaria, and were also aware that fugitives forcibly returned could doubtless expect a worse fate than that accorded to 'volunteers'. The vast majority accordingly agreed to return.

SWEDEN

All in all, it seems just to assert that ordinary British and American people cannot fairly be charged with the stigma of supporting the agreements entered into at Moscow and Yalta. They knew nothing of the circumstances, and their governments estimated, doubtless correctly, that they would have recoiled at the measures effected by their rulers had they known the full story. As similar secrecy was the rule in France, Switzerland and other countries considered earlier in this chapter, we may perhaps entertain the same presumption in their cases.

However, in the case of two European countries, unconsidered so far, the question of forcible repatriation was discussed and resolved upon in the full glare of national publicity. Newspapers and radio debated the question at length, and the issue was set before the respective peoples over a period of months.

The two countries to be considered were Sweden and Liechtenstein. Though the Russian soldiers involved were not 'Victims of Yalta', the course of operations in both cases is well worth considering for two reasons.

The problem facing the Swedish Government concerned a party of 167 men: 7 Estonians, 11 Lithuanians and 149 Latvians, who arrived in early May 1945 on the islands of Gotland and Bornholm. They were for the most part soldiers of the 15th Latvian Division. By the closing weeks of the war the Division was in serious disarray, and with the final destruction of the German Army it began to fragment into a number of scattered and fleeing units. Of those who managed to escape across the Baltic, 126 had sailed from the mouth of the Vistula. They got away from Danzig on 27 March, the day the city fell to the Red Army, in three Latvian ships which had put into the port. Two days later they reached the German-occupied Danish island of Bornholm. There they stayed for a month, until Soviet air and naval craft began bombarding the port of Rønne. That was on 7 May, when the Baltic troops (they accompanied a larger body of civilians) sailed to the Swedish port of Ystad. Another party of forty-one landed on the island of Gotland the next morning. Caught amongst Wehrmacht troops trapped in the Courland pocket, they had made on board a tug, the *Gulbis*, sailing through a foggy summer night from the port of Ventspils.

The Balts on Gotland were interned by the Swedish authorities in a camp at Havdhem on the island. Their compatriots at Ystad spent a fortnight similarly interned at Bökerberg; soon afterwards, all 167 Balts were gathered together in one camp. It was at Ränneslätt, near Eksjö in southern Sweden. There they were housed in comfortable quarters, exchanged their German uniforms for Swedish, and settled down to a pleasant round of labour in the brisk warm air of a Swedish summer.[36]

These Balts formed a tiny section of the mass of refugees who had made their way into Sweden. There were in particular several thousand German soldiers. On 2 June 1945 the Soviet Ambassador in Stockholm, Madame Kollontay, enquired of the Ministry of Foreign Affairs what the Swedish Government intended to do about these interned troops. The Allies had inserted in the Armistice terms which required German units to surrender to the nearest Allied command. Thus all Germans on the Eastern Front should give themselves up to the Red Army. The Armistice naturally did not apply to Sweden, but would the Swedes nevertheless align their policy on that of the Allies? To this the Swedish Foreign Office replied, after a brief consideration, that it would do so. However, the matter had yet to be confirmed by the Government.

On 15 June the Cabinet met and approved the Foreign Office accord. Considerable discussion had taken place at the Advisory Council on Foreign Affairs on 11 June and subsequently in the Cabinet itself. Two separate but related issues were discussed: should Sweden come into line with the Allied Armistice provisions enforcing the surrender of German troops to the nation on whose front they had been fighting at the time of their surrender; and should Sweden consent to a Soviet demand for the extradition of some 36,000 *civilian* Baltic refugees? The second request was refused on humanitarian grounds. The first was accepted as reasonable, which would mean in practice that all Germans who could be shown to have escaped from the Eastern Front would be shipped to the USSR. At the Cabinet meeting, the Minister for Foreign Affairs, Christian Günther, concluded his argument in favour of extraditing the military refugees with a few brief but significant words: 'Among the Germans there are also a few other groups, those who enlisted but are not really Germans. There's a group of Balts, for instance. But we can't be expected to sit here making distinctions between them. They're all part of the German Army and I suppose should all be extradited.'

It was in this casual way that the decision on the Balts was taken: they were caught up amongst the Germans, and at this stage not considered as a separate problem. On the next day the Soviet Embassy was informed of the Swedish Government's decision. Sweden's compliance was the more remarkable in that it was in response to a Soviet *enquiry*, not a demand. But the matter was settled, and Swedish military authorities began talks about transport arrangements. Their opposite number was the Soviet Naval Attaché, Slepenkov; a naval officer who appeared to know oddly little about naval affairs.[37]

Thus the situation rested for several months. The Soviet authorities were arranging shipping in their usual dilatory fashion, whilst the Balts lived on in their camp unaware that the jaws of the trap had opened. Then, in November, the news of the planned extradition leaked out. The Coalition Prime Minister, Per Albin Hanson, managed to silence the press temporarily, but once a sniff of what was in the air reached opposition circles the hunt was up. In Britain, wartime censorship and press agreement to tread warily in the interests of the emergency situation had enabled the Government to keep people from learning anything about repatriation operations. But in neutral Sweden no such gag could be imposed, and shortly after the Prime Minister's 15 November plea to newspaper owners to preserve secrecy, the storm burst and the matter became thenceforward a public controversy. On 19 November a national newspaper published the Foreign Office decision, and from the next day the protests began to roll in.

Though hostile feeling was widespread and highly vociferous, it came largely from certain recognisable sections of the public. The Swedish Church and its congregations was in the van of the attack; as early as 20 November a group of church leaders called on the Foreign Minister to deliver a strong protest. The Minister, a Social Democrat named Osten Undén, gave them a freezing reception. 'I'm at a loss to understand this particular sentimentality in regard to the Balts,' he told Bishop Björkquist.

Undeterred, the Church set about raising funds, drawing up petitions, and exciting nationwide opposition to the proposed measure. This disgust for what was regarded as a betrayal of Swedish honour and flagrant disregard for human rights was shared by members of the small opposition Conservative parties. The Swedish soldiers guarding the camp at Rännelätt drew up a protest agreed upon by every single officer and NCO: 'Our loyalty to King and country is incorruptible and we shall unswervingly obey given orders. But our consciences and our honour as soldiers enjoin us to express in the strongest possible manner our sense of shame in having to assist in the imminent extradition.'[38]

But though the opposition was vociferous and influential, it was mainly confined to that minority of society whose views derived from a moral base independent of current thinking. From a Christian and humanitarian point of view the delivery of these innocent men—men, at least, whose guilt remained to be proved—into the hands of their enemies—enemies whose cruelty, it was believed, could only be paralleled by that of the vanished Nazis—was an act abhorrent in itself. Other considerations must be extraneous when weighed against factors central to moral teaching.

Meanwhile, the Balts themselves were not slow to size up the situation and exacerbate it. Prompted by shrewd sympathisers from outside, officers and men began a hunger strike on 22 November. So drastic was the regimen followed that within a week the entire contingent had to be transferred to hospitals in southern Sweden. Doctors became increasingly worried about their patients' condition; but worse had already taken place. On 28 November a Latvian officer named Oscars Lapa was found dead in his barrack room. Some time during the night he had committed suicide: the electric light was still burning when they found him in the morning. Late on the previous evening he had expressed fear of the NKVD. He had taken precautions to ensure that he never fell into their clutches.[39]

Another case was that of Edvard Alksnis, who had been a young officer in the Latvian army. Believing his fate to be sealed, and judging that it would be better to die in Sweden than in the frozen camps of GULAG, he stabbed himself with a pencil, piercing his right eye.

But Alksnis did not die. He was saved by a medical miracle. The pencil was nearly six inches long, and yet its base lay concealed beneath the blood streaming from his eye-socket. It had penetrated part of his brain and nearly reached the back of his skull. A Swedish surgeon succeeded in removing it and repairing the damaged brain.

Nearly a year passed by. Then one day he read in a newspaper that the Soviets were pressing for the return of remaining Latvian soldiers. All his old fears rose up again; he escaped and sailed with others in a tiny fishing smack through the Gulf of Bothnia and the Baltic. In spite of alarming gales they succeeded at last in putting in near Berwick-on-Tweed. Alksnis was taken to a nearby hospital, then to London. There, British surgeons completed the cure their Swedish confrères had begun, and indeed regarded the case as one of exceptional interest. Today, apart from one puckered and sightless eye, he appears physically little affected by his ordeal. Emotionally he is calm and reflective, and lives quietly with his family. He talks impassively of his night of horror, having no regrets. After all, his friends went back into permanent darkness, whilst he lives, as he says, in freedom.[40]

To return to Alksnis's fellow-Balts. The declaration of a hunger-strike, the suicide of Oscars Lapa and the attempted suicide of another, and the sufferings of the Latvians in hospital were all headline news. As already described, protests filled the air, and the Government became acutely embarrassed. The Cabinet decided to play for time, and on 26 November a postponement was announced. There was relief when Swedish officers informed the Balts, but the hunger strike continued, as no assurances had been given that they would not be handed over at a later date. Their suspicions were justified: on 4 December the Cabinet again met to consider the question, and came to the conclusion that the decision of 15 June still stood. Four days later the Advisory Council on Foreign Affairs met and confirmed the decision, only one (Conservative) member dissenting.[41]

The only gesture conceded to the objectors was to institute a last-minute screening, as a result of which a few Balts were reclassified as civilians and in consequence granted asylum. The hunger strike petered out, and the surviving Balts were collected into a camp at Gälltofta in southern Sweden. Now they were kept isolated from press and public. Their camp was heavily wired and guarded, whilst searchlights glared in on them throughout the night. Christmas passed, and it was the January of 1946. Gälltofta lay on a bare, snow-covered plain. Icy winds came shrieking from the east, shaking the icicles hanging from the barbed wire and driving flurries of snow around the Balts' wooden huts. It no longer required much imagination to picture similar camps far off beyond the icy Baltic.

On 18 January the Swedish Foreign Office learned that a Soviet ship, the *Beloostrov*, was approaching the port of Trelleborg. The date for the Balts' extradition was arranged for 23 January. A great body of plain-clothes police was being drafted in from all over southern Sweden. They were armed and prepared for strong resistance, but the Balts came quietly. They were taken in buses to Trelleborg, and it was not until they were moving through the streets of the port that any trouble started. A Latvian suddenly drove his fists through a window and began sawing his wrists against the broken glass. The Swedish police threw themselves on to him and dragged him out of the bus. He was patched up at a first-aid shelter and then taken, screaming, on board the *Beloostrov* in a stretcher.

In another bus, which contained twelve victims and nine policemen, one of the latter was observant enough to snatch a razor-blade from a prisoner as he took it from his pocket. But when the bus stopped by the quay in Trelleborg, it was found that another Latvian had been more successful. As everyone stood up to get out, a policeman noticed that a prisoner opposite was behaving strangely. He had half risen, and then slumped against the side of the bus. Blood was streaming from a hole in his neck. The policeman hurled himself at him, wrenching him down on to the seat, and tearing a dagger from weakening fingers. But Lieutenant Peteris Vabulis evaded his guards at the moment he was seized: his corpse was laid out on the quay, whilst his living comrades filed past and up the gangway.

Vabulis had written to a friend a week before, lamenting that he had not attempted escape the previous summer.

Despite my youth, [he continued] I've seen a lot, both in Latvia and on my travels through many foreign countries in Europe. I have seen countries where slavery prevails and countries which deliver slaves to them quite openly. As this is happening in our century it is not hard to die, for if such things are allowed to continue, the end of the world must be near. I feel sorry for my wife and my children who are to lose their breadwinner in such a harsh way, just when hope and the prospects of a reunion were greatest. But each one of us must bear his fate, and we ourselves cannot change it.

Peteris Vabulis was buried in Sweden, whilst his compatriots sailed to their new life. The *Beloostrov* slid silently out of the harbour and forward to the east. Before long the foggy night closed round her and Swedish onlookers turned back to their homes.[42]

The Baltic problem was closed, though controversy over the Swedish Government's decision has continued ever since. Even while the fate of the Balts hung in the balance, fierce debate on the subject divided the country. Those who favoured the granting of asylum were, broadly speaking, people holding religious or conservative political views. The Social Democrat governing party, the trade unions and the left-wing press unanimously supported extradition. As Foreign Minister Osten Unden declared, 'there was not the slightest reason to suspect the Soviet administration of injustice, and . . . it was tactless to regard the Soviet Union as anything but a state governed by law.'[43]

Alone among nations enforcing repatriation, the Swedes conducted a public opinion poll on the subject. Of the representative section polled, no less than 71% considered that at least part of the thousands (there were many civilians as well) of interned Balts should be despatched 'home'. Reasons given varied only in the degree of harshness and intolerance expressed. Furthermore, a social analysis was conducted among those who answered. It turned out that the highest proportion of those favouring extradition lay amongst the working classes and readers of Socialist newspapers.[44]

It has been persistently alleged that the decision to return the Balts was connected with the announcement, in the middle of the Ränneslätt hunger strike, that Soviet-occupied Poland might not after all be able to deliver 1,000,000 tons of coal urgently needed by Sweden. The charge that such an exchange was made was even alluded to in a taunting Moscow propaganda broadcast,[45] but what substance there is in it cannot yet be determined. The Swedish Foreign Ministry, unlike those of Britain and the United States, has not released to public scrutiny state papers of 1945.

During the war, three Soviet trawler crews were interned in Sweden for the duration. With the coming of peace in 1945, Ambassador Chernyshev urged them to return to the Motherland. Suspicious and fearful, they expressed initial reluctance, but most eventually agreed. An NKVD officer, who subsequently examined their files, discovered that the overwhelming majority had been sentenced for their 'crime' to between ten and fifteen years in labour camps. Of the remainder, few saw their families again, and all were penalised by being refused work.[46] It is improbable that their fellows who had actually fought against the USSR in the German Army would have been more leniently treated.

It is true that a Swedish author, preparing a book on the extradition of the Balts, was invited to the Soviet Union in 1967 to meet some of the survivors. They described at length the warm welcome they had received on return, a fatherly chat from an NKVD officer, and the release into civilian life soon after of 90% of those returned. A few really culpable ones were sent to camps, but none was sentenced to death. When being interviewed, one or two seemed to hint that they might have another story to tell. The author, however, saw no good reason to distrust testimony so freely given, and published it as evidence that the Balts' resistance in Sweden had been a fuss over nothing.[47]

It is instructive to compare this account with one by Solzhenitsyn. A Soviet destroyer had gone aground on the Swedish coast in 1941, and the crew was interned for the duration. In 1945 they returned to the USSR, when they were at once sentenced to terms in forced labour camps. But rumours of their fate eventually trickled back to Sweden and were published in the press. To counter this, the Soviet authorities invited selected Swedish journalists to come to Russia and interview the men. Meanwhile the prisoners were collected from their camps and taken to a gaol in Leningrad. There they were well fed for two months, allowed to grow their hair, and provided with decent clothing. The Swedish journalists arrived, interviewed the men, and learned that the rumours had been quite false. All were living happily at home, and expressed indignation at the bourgeois slanders spread about them. The Swedes were impressed by all they heard, and returned home to publish refutations of the earlier story. What they did not know, however, was that the sailors had received notice that if they did as they were told, they would be favoured by not having a second sentence imposed when their first expired. If they did not, they would receive a bullet in the skull.[48]

LIECHTENSTEIN

For Liechtenstein the drama opened in a much more abrupt manner. Late in the evening of 2 May 1945, the local commander of the Frontier Police was informed that a military column was on the point of crossing the frontier from Austria. Hastily summoning the handful of men he had under his command, he drove up the road from Schellenberg towards Feldkirch. Ahead, on either side of the highway, came files of armed infantrymen, whilst on the road itself a column of motorised vehicles drove slowly forwards under a haze of dust. The police officer's shouted command to halt was ignored or unheard; disregarding the disparity in numbers and equipment between his little band and that of the heavily-armed invaders, he ordered his men to fire warning shots. As the fusillade rang out and echoed in the mountains above, a staff car at the head of the motorcade skidded to a halt. An officer sprang out, shouting: 'Don't shoot! Don't shoot! There is a Russian General here!'

The General himself alighted and came forward, extending his hand in greeting. Short, dapper and intelligent-looking, he introduced himself as Major-General Boris Alexeievich Holmston-Smyslovsky, lately of His Imperial Majesty's Guards, and now Commander of the 1st Russian National Army. His men had come to a halt, awaiting orders. Above them floated the white, blue and red tricolour of Imperial Russia; in a car in their midst sat the Heir to the Throne of All the Russias, the Grand Duke Vladimir Cyrillovich, great-grandson of Tsar Alexander the Second. The puzzled frontier-policeman scratched his head, and retired to telephone his superior officer in Schaanwald.

The origins of this extraordinary unit were as follows. Boris Smyslovsky was born in Finland in 1897. He joined the Army, and rose to the rank of captain in the Imperial Guards. After the Civil War, in which he fought on the White side, he emigrated to Poland. Subsequently he moved to Germany, joining their Army and attending the *Kriegs-akademie*. Throughout, his view had been that Russia could only be freed with foreign assistance, and it was to this end he was working. When war broke out with the Soviet Union, Smyslovsky served on the Eastern Front, commanding what was at first a training battalion for Russians volunteering for the anti-Bolshevik struggle. Eventually this swelled to twelve fighting battalions, as well as large bodies of partisans operating behind Soviet lines, totalling some 20,000 men. The High Command of the Wehrmacht raised the body to Divisional strength at the beginning of 1943, under the title *Sonderdivision R*: 'Special Division, Russia'. Smyslovsky was the first Russian to command an anti-Bolshevik Russian unit in the war, and this body remained a regular formation of the Wehrmacht until the end. His officers were in part former subalterns in the Tsar's Army, and in part volunteer ex-Red Army officers. There were clashes of temperament and outlook at first, but eventually Reds and Whites harmonised perfectly; they were just Russians. To this day Smyslovsky maintains that, if the Germans had conducted themselves to all captured Russians in this way, there can be no question but that the concept of a national and civilised Russia would have achieved irresistible strength in the Motherland.

But already in 1943 he realised that Germany could not win the war. The defeat of Stalingrad and the failure of the Nazi leadership to pursue an intelligent anti-Communist policy were to Smyslovsky inevitable pointers to impending ruin. On a visit to Warsaw he sought out a Swiss journalist and asked his advice on where to seek asylum in Europe if things went wrong. What about Switzerland? The Swiss opposed this idea, pointing out that Switzerland might be subjected to intolerable pressures to surrender fugitives from the Axis forces. Try Liechtenstein, was his advice; it is the antechamber to Switzerland. It is a tiny country, linked to Switzerland in a customs union but quite independent. There one might be able to lie low till the storm lifted.

The war drew to its close, and on 10 March 1945, when Himmler and other Nazi leaders were making belated attempts through Vlasov and the Cossacks to create an independent Russian ally, Smyslovsky's force was raised to the status of the 'ist Russian National Army', with Smyslovsky himself promoted to Major-General. It was the time when Buniachenko led his ill-fated attack against the Red Army on the Oder and marched on Prague, and when Cossack and White Russian forces were conducting a fighting retreat from the Balkans. Disparate Russian and Ukrainian units converged on Austria as the tide rose round the shrinking area still held by Germany. A major part of his unit having dispersed, Smyslovsky set off westwards with his surviving body of men. With authorisation from his superiors, he intended to link up with the émigré *Russki Corpus* from Belgrade and Shapovalov's 3rd Division of the ROA.⁴⁹ But these schemes failed as everything around disintegrated with unexpected speed. To General Vlasov he spoke on the telephone (they had met twice before), informing him of his decision. The exchange was cordial, but Vlasov would not deviate from his planned course of seeking refuge in Bohemia. Smyslovsky reminded him of the fate of Admiral Kolchak—betrayed by the Czechs to the Bolsheviks in 1920—and bade the ROA leader farewell.

With a small remnant of his followers. Smyslovsky moved to Feldkirch, the easternmost town of Austria. It was there that he met the young Grand Duke, accompanied by his adviser, General Voitsekhovsky. (Ironically, it had been Voitsekhovsky who led the final White attempt to rescue Kolchak after his betrayal). Smyslovsky agreed that the Grand Duke and his party should accompany him in crossing the frontier. In this way the last of the Romanovs set off under the protection of the old Russian flag, and surrounded by Russian troops. Shortly before reaching the frontier his car broke down. General Smyslovsky remembers his misgivings, as he assembled a part of his men and requested their aid in dragging the Grand Ducal car onwards. They were young men whose formative years had passed under the teachings of Bolshevism. How would they react when told that in their midst was the heir of 'Nicholas the Bloody'? To his surprise and pleasure, the soldiers volunteered with enthusiasm, and for the last quarter-mile or so Vladimir Cyrillovich's car was dragged forward by former Red Army men. It was a bizarre moment, where two ages seemed to intermingle.

At 11 p.m. the cavalcade crossed into Liechtenstein. General Smyslovsky's men moved in military formation, but with the strictest orders not to open fire, whatever the provocation. It was an unpleasant moment when they first faced the levelled rifles of the Swiss frontier guards. With his 450 men the General could have forced a passage with little difficulty, but in doing so he would of course forfeit all chance of obtaining asylum. He calculated that the Swiss might perhaps kill ten and wound a further twenty at most, but when they found their fire was not returned they would be obliged to stop. The gamble worked: the only casualty was a bottle of Martell brandy in the General's staff car.[50]

On the night of their arrival the newcomers were disarmed, the weapons being removed to Vaduz (they were later dumped by the Swiss in the Bodensee, where they presumably still lie). Altogether the group consisted of 494 people: 462 men, 30 women and 2 children. Only the Grand Duke and his immediate staff were denied asylum, and returned to Austria next day. He was, however, in no danger of being handed over to his enemies. General Smyslovsky with his wife and staff was found quarters in the Hotel Waldeck in the village of Schellenberg, whilst the men settled down in two vacant schoolhouses. The women moved into another hotel. Soon afterwards they were found more permanent quarters, the General transferring to the Hotel Löwe in the capital (he occupied a room vacated by the former French Prime Minister, Pierre Laval). They were cared for by the Liechtenstein Red Cross, which had been founded in the same week, with the Princess of Liechtenstein as President and active helper.[51] There was at first considerable fear lest French Communists belonging to para-military maquis bands operating on the skirts of the 1st French Army might cross the frontier to kidnap some of the Russian officers, but this danger faded as the French High Command brought the bandits to heel.

But a much more menacing danger remained. On 10 May General Smyslovsky sent an appeal to Prince Franz Josef II of Liechtenstein, appealing to His Highness to extend the traditional humanitarian asylum to himself and his people. Two days later came news that many of

Vlasov's men had fallen into Red hands in Czechoslovakia, and at the end of the month they learned of the infinitely more disturbing events at Lienz and further east in Austria. In August the Americans carried out their brutal operation at Kempten; the Russians in Liechtenstein could feel the net closing. Then, a few days later, a Soviet mission arrived in Vaduz to arrange repatriation. On 16 August the entire Russian contingent gathered in the town-hall to hear the representatives of their country. By a curious chance, an internee instantly recognised one of the Soviet officers as an NKVD man he had encountered at home. Baron Edward von Falz-Fein, a Russian-speaker who acted as interpreter in all these encounters, told me that almost without exception the Soviet delegates gave every appearance of being drawn from the lowest element of the criminal classes. Numerous photographs indicate that, as far as external appearances go, his verdict errs if anything on the mild side.

The NKVD representatives issued their usual medley of cajolements and menaces, and in this and subsequent visits induced about 200 of the internees to agree to return. According to General Smyslovsky, their reasons were mixed and impossible to dissect satisfactorily. Many appeared hypnotised by the appearance of those who had until so recently exercised powers of life and death over them; others feared they might eventually in any case be delivered by force; some, again, believed in the Soviet officials' promise of an amnesty, whilst many more felt an overpowering *nostalgie de la boue*. In all, about two-thirds had, by the time the Soviet mission ended its last visit, volunteered for repatriation. These figures are of great interest, since very likely they provide a rough indication of overall percentages favouring exile and return amongst Russians in the West in 1945. They effectively disprove the extreme estimate of Professor Epstein, who considers that, given a choice, *no* Russians captured in German uniform would have opted for repatriation.[52] They show equally that, had the Allies too insisted on a voluntary basis for return, the Soviets would still have received a sizable number: enough, perhaps, not to lose face excessively. The overall percentage of volunteers for return would in that case very possibly have been reduced, as it was undoubtedly fear that they would one day in any case be extradited that led many of Smyslovsky's men to 'volunteer'. Nearby events at Lienz and Kempten had had their effect, and NKVD representatives at Vaduz were not backward with hints that the same might happen in Liechtenstein.[53]

The volunteers departed by train to the Soviet Zone of Austria. They promised to write to those remaining; some letters came from Vienna, and then silence. No word from that day to this was ever heard from the men after their return home. The remainder stayed on for over a year more in Liechtenstein. Finally, word was received that the Argentine was prepared to accept them as immigrants. In the autumn of 1947 about a hundred of the remaining men sailed to Buenos Aires to start their new life.[54] General Smyslovsky himself accompanied them with his wife. In Liechtenstein he had been visited by Allen Dulles, head of American Intelligence in Switzerland, and other Western military experts eager to prise secrets from this unrivalled source of information on the Soviet Union. For, quite apart from his own knowledge, Smyslovsky still maintained contact with anti-Soviet agents and resistance groups inside Russia. Later, what remained of this apparatus was handed over to General Gehlen's espionage organisation in the American Zone of Germany. General Smyslovsky was able to continue making use of his military expertise, however, becoming a lecturer and adviser to the Argentine Government on counter-terrorism.

Though some of his men who volunteered for repatriation did so becuase they felt that the government of Liechtenstein might at a later stage weaken and accept Soviet demands, there was in fact at no time any danger of this happening. The then Prime Minister (*Regierungschef*), Dr. Alexander Frick, made it clear to the author that his Government never contemplated this for a moment. 'Ours is a small country, but it is one governed by laws,' he stressed calmly. But what if the Soviets, the Allies or the Swiss had applied pressures Liechtenstein could not resist? Dr. Frick explained that he had been prepared for this. So long as Liechtenstein retained control over her internal affairs, no Russian should go back involuntarily. If, on the other hand, force was threatened which they could not resist, his Government would have resigned. He would have launched appeals to world opinion and the international press against the inhumanity of the proposed measure and the interference in the affairs of a sovereign state. No such pressures were exerted, as it happened. Both the Prince and Dr. Frick stressed to me that the entire population of Liechtenstein was at one on this issue; indeed, the Government received petitions from farmers and peasants, who begged that Christian charity and aid be given to these friendless wanderers.[55] A small, Catholic and traditional-minded people, they saw the human tragedy and were convinced that this aspect far outweighed considerations of political expediency or material advantage.

Indeed, as far as the latter qualification was concerned, the people of Liechtenstein displayed an indifference that would have appalled a Swedish Social Democrat. The entire population of Liechtenstein in 1945 totalled a mere 12,141 people, whose annual budget ran to two million Swiss francs. Yet the inhabitants of this purely agricultural country provided without a single complaint expenditure of 30,000

Swiss francs per month for the maintenance of the Russians during a period of over two years. On top of this they paid all the expenses for the emigration to Argentina, the total disbursed amounting to nearly half a million Swiss francs.[56] Three years later the West German Government accepted responsibility for this expenditure and repaid Liechtenstein, but that this should happen could not have been foreseen at the time.

It could of course be said that in the case of Liechtenstein the Soviet Union held no bargaining counters. The British, American and French governments had the swift return of liberated prisoners of war to consider, just as the Swedes had their load of Polish coal. It is true, indeed, that Liechtenstein itself coveted neither people nor possessions held up in the East. But a very material consideration remained. Liechtenstein is a constitutional principality, one in which the Prince enjoys immense prestige, both personal and political. But the sovereign state was until 1945 only a part, and a small part, of the Prince's territorial interests. Enormous holdings in Bohemia constituted the main source of the family's wealth, and indeed the present Prince Franz Josef II is the first actually to reside at Vaduz. In 1945 the restored Czech Government respected in principle the rights of property, though in fact Communist local committees had taken control of many of his assets in the country. The Prince took legal proceedings for their restitution, and a decision of the High Court was pending when the Communists seized control in 1948, thereby abolishing at one stroke the ownership of private property and the rule of law. The Prince might well have thought twice before offending those who were in a position to deny him his own. But he no more considered this factor than did the humblest of his subjects the payment of a heavy tax burden to maintain the castaways.

So it was that tiny Liechtenstein, a country with no army and a police force of eleven men, did what no other European country dared. The Soviet Repatriation Commission was informed firmly from the beginning that only those who wished to return to Russia would be permitted to go; no deviation from this policy was ever contemplated. When the Commission alleged, for example, that General Holmston-Smyslovsky was required for trial on war-crime charges, the Government politely but firmly requested proof. None was forthcoming, and the matter rested. No unpleasant repercussions occurred, and the Soviet Mission eventually departed, angry but resigned.

I asked the Prince if he had not had misgivings or fears as to the success of this policy at the time. He seemed quite surprised at my question.

'Oh no,' he explained, 'if you talk toughly with the Soviets they are quite happy. That, after all, is the language they understand.'[57]

17

Soviet Moves and Motives

NOT FAR FROM DZERZHINSKY SQUARE IN MOSCOW, IN FURKASOV LANE, lies the entrance to the archive building of the KGB. In its underground chambers are stored details of all important operations undertaken by this organisation and its predecessors. Off one of its darkened passages must lie cabinets containing SMERSH and NKVD files on the repatriation operations of 1943–7. Even when the Soviet régime is one day overthrown it is unlikely that these documents will ever see the light of day. For the archive storage is equipped with devices that can at once destroy the whole dark catalogue of crime, by the discharge of explosives or destructive acids.[1] Thus one half of the source material needed for the story unfolded in this book is inaccessible to scholars.

Despite this, enough evidence can be culled from elsewhere to build up a picture that must be substantially accurate. Alexander Solzhenitsyn spoke to many of the returned prisoners in Soviet camps, and devoted to the subject a chapter of *The Gulag Archipelago* entitled 'That Spring'. Other inmates of the camps of GULAG have filtered westwards over the years, bringing their own accounts. Officers from the NKGB and SMERSH have defected and told the story from the other side. Other assorted sources light up shadowy corners from unexpected angles, and I think it can be claimed that the resultant picture, though partial, is substantially correct.

The first and most important point to note is that the Soviet Government regarded all Soviet citizens who had passed even temporarily out of their control as traitors, irrespective of the circumstances which had led to their removal or of their conduct in exile. Mr. Gerald Reitlinger has attempted to excuse this attitude by suggesting that Red Army soldiers, driven beyond reason by their own and their country's sufferings, understandably ran wild on occasion and massacred recaptured Russians in German uniform.[2] Revulsion at Nazi crimes might make many tolerant of excesses committed in such circumstances, but in fact

Mr. Reitlinger's explanation is untenable. The returning prisoners did not come under the control of Red Army units and were in consequence rarely ill-treated by the regular forces.

In fact, we may reject out of hand the possibility that the Soviet Government's attitude towards its repatriated subjects was in any way governed by the behaviour of the hated Nazis. For the policy of treating all captured Soviet prisoners as traitors had been laid down long before the German invasion of Russia: indeed it was first put into effect when Soviet Russia and Nazi Germany were close allies. After the close of the Finnish War in March 1940, Russian prisoners captured by the Finns were released and returned home. In Leningrad they marched amidst general acclamations under a triumphal arch blazoned with the legend 'The Fatherland Greets Its Heroes'. The heroes were marched straight on to railway sidings, placed in Stolypin carriages, and whisked off to slave-labour camps.[3] It made absolutely no difference what their conduct had been during the conflict; they ranged from brave officers who had succumbed to the Finns' superior tactics (Captain Ivanov ended up in Ustvymlag[4]), to poor Katya from Leningrad who, after capture, had worked for the Finns as a waitress (she was packed off to a slave-gang at Potma[5]). Such prisoners had neither given aid and comfort to an invader, nor been influenced by an anti-social ideology; nor were either of these offences even suggested. It was the knowledge they had gained of the non-socialist world that constituted their 'crime'.

Russian prisoners who later fell into German hands were well aware that a sinister fate had overtaken those earlier captured by the Finns. In one large camp it was found that no one had ever come across a returned prisoner from Finland. The conclusion was that they had all been liquidated.[6]

There was nothing secretive about the Communist attitude to those of its citizens who fell into enemy hands. The notorious Article 58–1b of the Law of 1934 prescribed appropriate punishment for such people. During the war itself Stalin issued a number of 'Orders' (*Prikazy*) threatening draconian measures against 'deserters' and prisoners of war. Order No. 227, for example, was 'issued in 1942, not only issued but also actually read out to all troops of the Red Army . . . Such Orders were issued in 1943 and again in 1944, this time with some variations relating to current Soviet military tasks.'[7] A Russian doctor, captured in 1941, ignored the order that Soviet soldiers should commit suicide rather than surrender. 'What possible benefit, military or other, could arise from such action?' he asked himself.[8] At the very end of the war, a British prisoner released in the East reported that individual Red Army soldiers carried a copy of one of these minatory Orders of the Day.[9]

After their liberation from Nazi captivity, Russians in British and American custody drew attention to the Orders—irrefutable evidence that they had been prejudged in their absence.[10] Neither the prisoners nor the Western Allies could be ignorant of Soviet intentions.

It was enough for a Russian soldier to fall momentarily behind the German lines (no rare occurrence under the conditions of Stalin's 1941-2 strategy) and fight his way back, like poor Shukhov in *A Day in the Life of Ivan Denisovitch*, to receive instant punishment. Shukhov was luckier than some, with his ten-year sentence in the Socialist Way of Life Camp. Svetlana Stalin tells how Beria 'carried out the abominable liquidation of whole army units, at times very large ones' temporarily cut off by the Germans in 1941. This attitude persisted throughout the war: in February 1943 two private soldiers rescued by their own men were shot dead on the spot.[11] Elsewhere, Stalin's need for skilled men caused him to temper injustice with mercy. Two fighter pilots whose planes had crashed behind the German lines, and who had made their way back to their unit, were at once pounced upon by the regimental Commissar. Through the Divisional Special Section they were taken off at night to the far-off 'Re-education Camp for Airmen' in Alkino, near Ufa in the Urals. There they were flogged and starved until the corruption was considered to have been purged out of them. They were then released and returned to their unit, the Red Air Force being short of good pilots.[12]

But these were the lucky few. For those who had fallen into German hands and not managed to escape, the punishment was to be proportionately more severe. A Soviet general horrified Eisenhower by explaining that captured soldiers were useless soldiers, and should be abandoned.[13] Stalin could at least claim impartiality in this respect. Within a month of the German invasion, his son Yakov was captured north of Smolensk. German officers interrogating him found him to be an 'out-and-out Bolshevik'; he refused to accept the possibility of Germany's conquering Russia, but did express fears of a successful Russian uprising against the Party dictatorship. On 19 July he sent brief greeting to his father, whose only response was to despatch his son's wife Yulia to gaol. Several attempts were made by the Germans to exchange him, first for some Germans stranded in Iran, later for Field-Marshal von Paulus. Then Hitler himself, possessing family feelings denied to his fellow-dictator, proposed that Yakov should be exchanged for his (Hitler's) nephew, Leo Raubal, who had been captured after Stalingrad. Stalin refused, declaring stoutly that 'war is war'. In his camp Yakov learned of his father's repudiation and was quite crushed in spirit. Despite this, he never renounced his Bolshevik principles and is said to have met his subsequent death like a soldier. Walking in a garden one day, Stalin told

Zhukov of his secret affliction. The Germans had captured his son, but, said the father sternly and proudly, 'Yakov will prefer any kind of death to betrayal.' The Marshal was deeply moved at this display of emotion; he was not to know whose was the betrayal.[14]

No matter who he was, a man who had managed to glimpse life outside the Socialist Sixth of the World must necessarily be suspect. Red Air Force planes were despatched on special missions to bomb German prisoner-of-war camps containing Russians.[15] Nor was it only men who suffered; recaptured women were despatched at once to camps in the Arctic Circle and elsewhere.[16] It was thought inconceivable to Lenin's heirs that anyone could come in contact with non-socialist people and ideas and preserve their Marxist faith intact. A Red partisan leader fought for two years against the Germans behind their lines in the Ukraine. He had been decorated—and was then thrown into the Lubianka Gaol.[17] Perhaps the most remarkable case was that of a soldier named Lebedev. Captured by the Germans, he had been placed in Auschwitz. There he miraculously survived, despite the fact that he had been leader of the Russian section of the anti-Nazi resistance within the camp. When the Red Army liberated the few survivors in 1945, Lebedev was amongst those who were seized by the NKVD, packed into a cattle-wagon, and trundled off eastwards to work for a socialist future under the care of GULAG.[18] Roy Medvedev suggests that the most striking illustration of the nature of Soviet Communism is the fact that the wives both of the country's President (Kalinin) and of its Foreign Minister (Molotov) languished for a time in prison camps.[19] We may go further: it was a political system whose rulers genuinely feared that a man whose knowledge of the outside world was confined to two years' experience of Auschwitz must necessarily be in danger of abandoning his socialist principles. Fear lest good Communists should be unduly impressed by the flashy achievements of Western technology was on other occasions a major consideration; we may remember the old woman at Judenburg with her provocative Singer sewing-machine. But that could not have been the case with Comrade Lebedev. For once Marxist ingenuity had anticipated capitalist science: gas-chambers equivalent to those at Auschwitz had been in operation at Vorkuta as far back as 1938.[20]

One of the very few works published in the Soviet Union openly describing the fate of returned prisoners of war treats of a similar episode. In 1966, during the Khrushchev 'thaw', Yuri Pilyar's *Lyudi ostayutsya lyudmi* (*People remain human after all*) was published in Moscow. Pilyar had spent several years as a prisoner of the Germans in Mauthausen. On being 'liberated' by the Red Army, he was sent to a forced-labour camp in the Urals. There ex-Vlasov troops, Cossacks and genuine prisoners of war were mingled, no distinction being made between their 'crimes'.

Impressive too was Soviet organisation of the administrative arrangements for the homecoming. This had been in prospect from an early date. Alexander Foote, a Soviet spy reporting to his superiors in Moscow, put forward a flippant suggestion. 'Once I submitted the project of sending abroad a special commission to liquidate the traitors of the Soviet cause. With a sympathetic and understanding smile I was told, however: "Why rush, soon there will be no place on earth where the traitors could hide; they will simply and easily fall into our hands." '21 The official announcement of the appointment of a Repatriation Commission to bring this about came on 24 October 1944—significantly, a week after Eden had promised Molotov that he would see to it that all exiles were returned. The head ('Delegate') of the new Commission was to be Colonel-General Filip Golikov.22

The choice of Golikov was a curious one. It was, after all, the Soviet contention that ferocious punishment must be visited on all Russian soldiers captured by the Germans, since only incompetence or cowardice could have brought about their surrender. It might seem incongruous, therefore, that Stalin chose to select to head the repatriation operations an officer who was, by all accounts, one of the most cowardly and incompetent in the Soviet service. Worse than this, he was one of those bearing prime responsibility for Soviet unpreparedness for war in 1941— a deficiency which was the chief cause of most of the prisoners falling into German hands in the first place. From July 1940 he had been Chief of the Intelligence Directorate of the Red General Staff. As such, his role consisted of a series of unredeemed blunders. He ordered the arrest of most of his best counter-espionage agents operating abroad, and repressed efficient GRU (Military Intelligence) cadres. Despite this, he received ample warnings of the impending Operation 'Barbarossa'. Realising that Stalin was, however, terrified by awareness of Soviet unpreparedness for war (largely owing to the 1938 purge), he flattered his leader's susceptibilities by altering alarmist reports and in general playing down legitimate fears of German intentions. It was as a direct result of this deliberately-induced self-delusion that so many Russians became prisoners in 1941.23 Later, at the siege of Stalingrad, he was reported by Krushchev to have become almost mad with fear in face of German onslaughts; he had in consequence to be dismissed from his command.24

Golikov's deputy in the Repatriation Commission possessed a personality and record worthy of his superior. General K. D. Golubev was a physical giant—useful qualification in a society which had (as an embittered intellectual in a pre-war labour camp lamented) in many ways reverted to the values of the Tertiary Epoch.[25] But, as the American General Deane noted, 'unfortunately his mental stature did not conform to the size of his body.' He was in fact a greedy, bullying simpleton.[26] It comes as no surprise to learn that within two months of the outbreak of war he had been dismissed from his command 'for gross inefficiency'.[27] It is difficult to avoid concluding that Stalin had singled out these two Fred Karno veterans deliberately. In accordance with his notoriously sadistic sense of humour, he was enjoying the joke, at the expense either of the two blundering generals, or at that of the returning prisoners, arraigned for their supposed cowardice and guilt by two of the most cowardly and culpable officers in the army.

However, neither Golikov nor Golubev played any real part in the organisation of the Repatriation Commission. As regular officers, they formed respectable 'window-dressing' for the department. The real work was performed by the main administration of counter-intelligence (GUKR) of SMERSH and the NKGB (military counter-intelligence of the secret police). The NKGB operated against recaptured Soviet citizens within the Soviet Union, SMERSH against those abroad. From June 1941 the twin organisations had been concerned with keeping the subject Soviet population behind the lines in a proper state of terror, and arresting men (like Solzhenitsyn) who returned from German encirclement; later, as the tide began to turn after Stalingrad, they moved into liberated areas, massacring hundreds of thousands suspected of disloyalty.[28] Now, in 1945, they prepared to tackle the massive task of absorbing the millions of hostages returned by the West.

From General Golikov's Repatriation Commission missions were despatched all over Western Europe.[29] All the western officers coming in contact with the string of colonels and generals leading them had the same baffling experience. Whenever matters relating to military service were broached, the Soviet officers betrayed embarrassment and ignorance. As General Vikhorev in Paris blurted out: 'I was not in the Air Force during the war . . . I was in another branch of the service . . .'[30] The fact is, of course, as a former officer of SMERSH explains, 'the members of these missions were regular Chekist officers from Smersh.'[31] If Stalin derived amusement from the incongruity of men like Golikov being placed in a position to punish captured Russian soldiers, the rôle played by their subordinates should have provided him with even more delight. Golikov and Golubev were at least regular soldiers. But few if any SMERSH officers had ever engaged in any fighting. They could kick in the ribs of Ukrainian girls brought for interrogation, or shoot dead a small boy who stepped out of line to see his mother.[32] But to face head-on the tanks of Sepp Dietrich's 1st SS Armoured Corps would have been another matter. As Major Shershun explained shamefacedly to Czeslaw Jesman, his wartime task had been to escort machinery being evacuated eastwards.[33] Men with records like this were empowered to knock liberated war heroes into cattle-trucks,[34] yelling at them: 'Why did you let yourself be captured?' 'Why didn't you escape?' 'Why didn't you liquidate any Vlasov men?'[35]

As to this last jibe, SMERSH had undoubtedly killed infinitely more Red Army men than the whole ROA and Cossack Corps put together.[36]

Chekists in the Repatriation Missions were allowed extraordinary freedom in pursuing their varied tasks.[37] Where the writ of SMERSH did not run unimpeded, recourse was had to the infiltration of undercover agents, together with the use of blandishments, threats and blackmail. No extra powers were required for the seizure of identified Soviet citizens; these the British and Americans were willing to hand over in any case. But it was important to induce as many as possible to 'volunteer'. Firstly, widespread refusals could arouse dangerous revulsion amongst Allied soldiers detailed to arrange repatriation. Secondly, British politicians could more easily justify their policy by claiming that few Russian prisoners were seriously objecting. In addition, there were the Disputed Persons, whom the British and Americans would not return unless they volunteered.

SMERSH (or NKVD) agents operated in two capacities: openly, through their accredited representatives, and covertly, through undercover agents, infiltrated or recruited amongst the prisoners. Patrick Dean noted that a Russian woman in London had been 'brutally interviewed by a Soviet officer'.[38] This woman was resolute in refusing to return home; on other occasions slighter pressure was effective. In May 1945 one of the volunteers for repatriation was a certain Vladimir Olenicz.

> Later Olenicz, who was in tears, stated that the Russian officer who interrogated him was a member of the NKVD (Russian Secret Police), who reminded him that his family were living in Soviet territory. No threats were used and nothing out of place was said, but he knew what lay behind the Russian officer's words and was afraid of him and of what might happen to his family. He therefore agreed to return to Russia as a Soviet subject, and although concerned as to what the future might hold for him, was prepared to stand by his decision.

This man was in fact a Polish citizen; clearly he had little alternative but to return.[39] At the Foreign Office Christopher Warner had earlier expressed his confidence that NKVD pressures of this sort would do the trick.[40]

In the camps SMERSH speedily set up an 'inner ring' of agents and informers; 'commissars' headed groups amongst those held, ensuring that few dared refuse to return.[41] Informers were readily induced by methods such as those just described to assist in drawing up 'black lists', tracing fugitives still at large, and so on. At a camp outside Vienna one newly released prisoner of war shot another who had fallen under this suspicion. 'He's been making up lists for a long time to give to the NKVD if they come. A dog deserves a dog's death.'[42] Prisoners already returned were naturally interrogated, to find the names of Russians evading repatriation.[43] The ROA and Cossack units had inevitably been infiltrated by Soviet agents even before their surrender.[44] All in all, operations were conducted by SMERSH officers employing selected prisoners. In France, for example, sixty NKVD men worked under General Dragun's Mission; half were regular operatives from the USSR, the remainder ex-prisoners hoping to earn a reprieve.[45] They are unlikely to have succeeded.

Many of the Russians brought back to Britain from France in 1944 had to be placed at once in hospital, to recover from the cruelties perpetrated on them by the Germans. Professor S. Sarkisov, of the Russian Red Cross Mission, issued an appeal from his office at 65, Inverness Terrace, 'through the Press to the public and to the different organisations in this country who know the residence of these Russian sick citizens and to ask them to send the names and the addresses to the Mission in London'. The War Office and Home Office declined to assist the Professor in his humanitarian labours—an obstruction of 'Allied Representatives' which irritated John Galsworthy at the Foreign Office.[46] However, as is well known, the Soviet Red Cross in the time of Lenin formed largely a camouflaged branch of the Cheka. Later it played a major part in NKVD operations abroad (such as the murder of Trotsky). It flourishes today under KGB tutelage.[47]

Having segregated the prisoners and, with British and American help, transported them home, the next step facing the NKVD was the reception of the hostages in the Soviet Union itself. Great numbers proceeded no further than the rim of Soviet-occupied territory. In Berlin, *The Times* reported on 4 June 1945, 'Russian traitors in Vlasov's army were, almost without exception, dealt with summarily.' At the exchange point at Torgau: 'An entire wing of the prison was designated to death row. Those who were condemned to die, for the most part, had seen service with Vlasov's army. On standing now before their barred windows, they cried with passion, "We die for our fatherland, not for Stalin!"'[48] When the Cossacks were handed over in Austria, large numbers (including most of the officers) were shot within a few days: in the Judenburg steel-mill, in the collection centre at Graz, and on the road to Vienna.[49] The number so disposed of was undoubtedly considerable. As the suicides had anticipated, theirs was probably the more fortunate fate. Solzhenitzyn saw a Vlasov man being flogged mercilessly by a SMERSH sergeant; another captured near Bunzlau was tied to two bent birch trees and torn apart.[50] How many thus perished immediately on arrival cannot be known; the number clearly ran into thousands.[51]

The majority who were spared for the moment were passed through an elaborate screening process. As already described, at Judenburg and elsewhere all their possessions—even a proportion of their clothing— were confiscated and destroyed. Men, women and children were at once divided, preparatory to being despatched to separate camps.[52] On the banks of the Elbe an NKVD officer watched DPs being returned by the Americans in barges from Tangermünde. NKVD troops greeted them with kisses and hugs. Then, when the Americans were out of sight, all changed abruptly. 'Look sharp, now, you traitors. Put your belongings down and line up over there!' Ferocious dogs strained at their leashes as the astonished DPs sprang to obey. The same officer (he subsequently defected to the West and wrote his memoirs) caught a glimpse of the fate of the women. At a DP camp near Küstrin the NKVD commandant showed him a wired enclosure containing several thousand naked females of all ages. The commandant explained: 'If you feel like it . . . you can have any of these women for a couple of cigarettes or even for a glass of water. There is no running water in their barracks.'[53]

To receive this vast horde of homeless people the Soviet administration commandeered *Ostarbeiters'* camps and other improvised centres in which the prisoners could be gathered. These varied considerably: most were wired and guarded, but others had to receive so great an influx at one time that it was impossible to impose more than rough-and-ready security measures. In May 1945 Nikolai Komaroff was with a party of Cossacks at Sillian in Austria. He decided quite voluntarily to seek work in the Soviet Zone, and travelled to a reception camp at Kapfenberg. But there he was seized with misgivings and decided to return. It was a chance decision—one which meant that thirty years later he still lives in freedom.[54]

Another who travelled still further into the wolf's maw was Shalva Yashvili, whose adventures were recounted in Chapter One. In 1945 he was in Italy; the British despatched him with other Georgians to the huge Soviet camp at Taranto. There Yashvili accepted Major Gramasov's assurances of Soviet forgiveness, though he silently reflected that it was the Soviet Union that ought to be asking forgiveness of the prisoners, after the unjustifiable abandonment of its captured citizens. In August he travelled north by train with 250 of his comrades. They were under British guard, but here there was no question of forcible repatriation. It was not until they had descended at a railway station twenty miles inside the Soviet Zone of Austria that anyone realised that anything was wrong. Yashvili watched his Georgian major salute the Soviet colonel. The colonel, by his appearance a Buryat or Mongol, did not return the salute and uttered a few words inaudible to men in the ranks. The major returned, 'his face like ashes'. The party filed out of the railway station, to face a waiting circle of SMERSH men armed with submachine guns. Now they knew they were trapped.

The Georgians were shepherded to a nearby camp, where they stayed two nights. Yashvili at once decided to escape; he felt that natives of sunny Georgia would have little chance of surviving in Magadan. In Taranto he and some friends had formed a football team, which played in friendly matches with British and American troops. Now he and his team-mates engaged in urgent discussions as to the possibility of flight. An Austrian huntsman passing near the camp offered to take them by secret routes to the British Zone, but before plans could mature they were ordered to set off for the east.

There began a long, slow and disorderly march. Food was delivered occasionally by trucks, but several days went by without a meal. Once Yashvili and a couple of friends were nearly shot out of hand by a raging NKVD officer who caught them lagging behind to cook in a farmhouse. Finally they came to an enormous improvised camp by Wiener Neustadt: there were perhaps 60,000 returning refugees there. Guards patrolled the perimeter, but there was no wire fence, and the milling inhabitants were subjected to no controls within the camp. A roll-call would have been impossible. Brooding continually on escape, Yashvili noted that one side of the camp was bounded by a small river. Guards were stationed on the ground beyond, but with the general noise and bustle of the thronging thousands it did not seem impossible to find a means of slipping past them.

With three Georgian friends equally determined on flight, Yashvili studied the river scene. The guards opposite never seemed to relax their vigilance, but it was noticeable that much of their time was spent in studying and passing comments on the crowd of women washing clothes on the river bank. Young girls hitched up their skirts to wade in, laughing and shouting to each other. They were hot, lazy August days, the war was over, and one can scarcely blame the sentries if their attention was held more by the brown legs and arms of their pretty compatriots than by the four young men paddling about in rolled-up trousers in their midst. That these should clamber casually out on the far bank to dry in the sun was natural enough, and who could notice if a moment later the four had vanished?

They crouched in a thick clump of bushes, munching tinned pork and drinking from a flask of wine bartered for a Polish cap from a Red Army truck driver. Then, after nightfall, they made their way westwards to the hills. For days they tramped on, guided only by the position of the sun. They fed on potatoes grubbed from the fields, boiled in helmets conveniently littering the countryside. At length, after several narrow escapes, they won through to the American Zone. Today Yashvili lives contentedly in the West, rather more appreciative of civic freedoms than many of his casual hosts.

Yashvili's account may serve as a corrective to the idea that SMERSH conducted reception arrangements with universal efficiency. The fact is that the organisation was vastly overstrained by its massive task. As one SMERSH officer, stationed in Austria, explains:

> There were not enough people in our Baden administration for such an enormous operation. All the reserves from the town of Modling were drawn in, but even then we were shorthanded. GUKR Smersh urgently sent special groups of PFK [Vetting and Screening Commissions] staff to Austria, Germany and Hungary from their own reserves on Soviet territory, but even then there were nowhere near enough of them.
>
> At GUKR Smersh, Abakumov had to borrow people from other main administrations of the NKGB, such as the Secret Political Administration, the Industrial or Economic Administration, the Investigation Administration and even from the Operational Administration. I know from the documents which went through the Smersh Third Branch in which I worked that at the request of Merkulov, People's Commissar for State Security, Beria also helped out with personnel, and loaned us officers from the NKVD Police Administration, Investigation Administration and to some extent from the Third Administration of GULAG. Of course, when all these officers reached us they were already kitted out with army uniform.

The PFK screening units had the task of sorting out Soviet citizens into different categories. Roughly speaking, there were three basic groupings. The first consisted of those considered to be enemies of Soviet power, including of course all found in Vlasov or Cossack uniforms. The second group was classed as 'relatively clean', that is to say, nothing could be proved against them. And the third consisted of a minority held to have a 'clean' record of loyalty to the Soviet régime. Generally speaking, the first group was meant to be despatched to forced-labour camps, the second to perform forced labour tasks outside the camps, and the fortunate third to be 'directed' to labour on post-war reconstruction.[55] This was the outline plan, but in fact the magnitude of the task was overwhelming. Both the categories and the punishments were frequently blurred and intermingled.

The screening went on for years, during which time the prisoners were not idle. An ex-prisoner recalls that his cell-mates 'came from screening camps in the Donbas area, where they had been working underground rebuilding the coal-mines flooded by the Germans during the war. Others came from similar camps in central Russia.' This did not count as punishment, however; their sentences to terms of forced labour came later. Of the fortunate minority not considered as enemies of Socialism, many were at first allowed home. 'Later, however, they all ended up in prison.'[56] A colonel in charge of such a camp was obsessed with the possibility that most of his charges were spies for the Americans, and ensured that such dangerous people ended up in the camps. Even when freed, before or after sentence, to go home, the prisoners and their families were treated as outcasts. A commissar explained: 'For many years to come we shall have to keep a watchful eye on all who have been prisoners of war.'[57]

Even people whom the Germans moved by force were held to be tarnished with the same guilt. A 17-year-old Ukrainian girl was kidnapped by the Nazis and forced to work in the Krupp munitions factories in the Ruhr. There she developed tuberculosis, coughing and spitting blood incessantly. When the British liberated her and sent her home, she thought joyfully of the future. There were bound to be shortages, 'but people would certainly go to a little trouble about a girl whom the Nazis had made sick'. But for her there was no Ukraine. She was not even screened, but despatched straight to Kolyma in a sealed train.[58]

It did not even matter if ex-prisoners volunteered to return. One group, conscripted into the Todt Labour Force for work on the Atlantic Wall, heard General Golikov's appeal on Moscow Radio, and made their way enthusiastically to the frontier. Under the triumphal arch they passed, brushed the flowers from their shoulders, and travelled in the red cattle-trucks straight to the stomach of GULAG. A year later they were dying of dystrophy.[59]

The journey itself provided a foretaste of camp life. In July and August 1945 Poles living at Biecz in southern Poland heard a mysterious series of trains race through their railway station. They always travelled late in the evening, hurtling by at speed. Watchers caught a glimpse of wired and barred cattle-trucks, interspersed now and then with a machine-gun platform. One evening such a train halted briefly at Biecz. Guards sprang out, forming a protective circle, submachine guns at the ready. Through partially opened sliding doors bystanders could see tightly-packed groups of ragged men.

'Who are you?' shouted the Poles.

'Prisoners of war!' came a hollow cry.

'Where are you going?'
'To Siberia!'
The engine whistled, the guards sprang back in, and the darkened cargo moved onwards. The trains were using the Cracow-Lvov southern route, perhaps to avoid giving the inhabitants of Warsaw this preview of socialist benefits.[60]

As winter approached, the unheated trains began to develop a terrible casualty rate. Prison-trains arriving at northern camps regularly included two carriage-loads of corpses coupled behind. These were the men and women who had starved or frozen on the way. At other times the dead were not disturbed, and were only distinguished when they failed to descend on arrival.[61] For the living, the amazing artefacts of Western culture were plundered without mercy. Old denim jackets, socks, fountain-pens that worked—all were seized by NKVD guards and their criminal friends amongst the prisoners.[62]

A Latvian lady was travelling home in September 1945. She was in a goods-wagon, containing forty-five people and their luggage.

We stacked the sacks at both ends and in the middle in a single row. I was high up like a hen on a perch. Next to me there was a tiny window with a little nail and string where we hung a child's potty—at the other end another mother had the same. If anyone needed to use it while on the way, they simply asked to be handed 'the little rose'. You see in our wagon there was no lavatory . . . After a few days we arrived in Žitomira. We travelled with endless detours . . . In the wagon, not far from Žitomira an old sick lady died. Having stopped in Žitomira, we begged the railway guard to allow us to bury her. We were allowed to do so. We dug a little grave right beside the railway track—we laid out in a white sheet the dead Latvian mother; at the last moment a young Ukrainian woman rushed up to us with her dead baby that had died in another wagon—we put it next to the old lady—and buried both. We put on top a cross and flowers.

Also in their wagon was Professor Šubert, one of Latvia's most loved composers. He died on 11 October, still on the same journey. For seven more hours his dead body remained seated in the packed wagon as it jolted on its way. At Žlobin they stopped, and asked if they might bury him. Permission was refused; the passengers were told to leave him naked on the platform. He could be buried later with a couple of other corpses dropped off the train.

Nevertheless we dressed Prof. S. in his underwear, socks, wrapped a new sugar-bag cloth with a string around him and two youths from our wagon carried himrever ently out of the wagon and put him down on the platform.

We were left at that station until midday the next day in spite of all. In the evening and during the night there was a thunderstorm with downpours of rain. Towards evening we were moved to different rails. The next morning our two youths jumped out of the wagon to go and look if Prof. S. had already been buried. They returned pale with the news that Prof. S. was still lying there, totally robbed, soaked, in the mud . . . We did not tell Mrs. S.[63]

The overwhelming majority of returned prisoners ended up as slave labour of one sort or another. Most of the Cossacks surrendered in Austria were despatched to the complex of camps around Kemerovo, south of Tomsk in Central Siberia. The majority died under unbearably cruel treatment.[64] The Vlasov soldiers were everywhere. A Finn encountered numbers from Britain in the notorious Butyrki Gaol at Moscow.[65] Elsewhere, survivors met them in Karaganda, Krasnaya Presen, Marraspred, Vorkuta and numerous other Soviet versions of Maidanek and Auschwitz.[66]

At Vorkuta, Aino Kuusinen encountered the sheep restored to the fold.

Before long [in 1945] thousands more PoWs made their appearance, this time members of General Vlasov's army who had turned traitor and fought on the Nazi side. Many were in chains. These unfortunates were sent to dig coal in distant zones; I chanced to meet one, a colonel, who was seriously ill and was admitted to our hospital. Learning that I was a political prisoner, he said that he expected to be shot before long, but that his hatred for the régime would live on.[67]

Many were former army surgeons, now forbidden to practise.[68]

But the history of those repatriated Russians assigned to penal camps is the history of GULAG, and for our understanding of that it is superfluous to look beyond the pages of Solzhenitsyn's Gulag Archipelago. What we shall probably never know with any degree of accuracy is the number of repatriates absorbed into the twenty or twenty-five million slaves held in Soviet camps at that time. Any statistical breakdown of the figures must remain largely guesswork. According to an official Soviet account issued in 1945, 5,236,130 Soviet citizens had been liberated and repatriated. Of these, some 750,000 were still in transit. The remaining 4,491,403 had been settled in their homes or provided with employment elsewhere. The state set them up with grants of loans, foodstuffs and building materials. Particular care was taken to provide special facilities for the children.[69] A Western supporter of the Soviet régime, writing in a more critical milieu, concedes that perhaps 500,000 of those returned were sent to camps. Anyone, however, who could prove a legitimate reason for being captured could be sure of exemption, 'and officers, as a rule, were not punished'.[70]

A former officer of the NKVD, who had access to that organisation's files, provides what appears to be a more accurate estimate. Altogether, some five and a half million Russians were repatriated from formerly occupied areas in 1943–7. Of these

  20% received a death sentence or 25 years in the camps (a virtual death sentence—prolonged);
15–20% received sentences of 5 to 10 years;
  10% were exiled to frontier regions of Siberia for a period of not less than 6 years;
  15% were sent as work conscripts to Donbas, Kuzbas and other devastated areas. These were not allowed to return home after the expiration of their sentence;
15–20% were allowed to return home, but could rarely (as unregistered labour) find work.

These estimates, which must be very rough, do not add up to 100%. Possibly the missing 15–25% can be assigned to 'wastage': people who 'went to ground' in Russia, died in transit, or escaped.

The number that suffered is not restricted to those formerly in German captivity, however. All relatives of people momentarily out of Soviet control remained permanently suspect. In 1950, for example, a 14-year-old girl was persuaded by the NKVD to spy on her father, a former prisoner. The reverse could as easily happen, with the internal security forces blackmailing former prisoners to inform on friends and relatives. A cloud hung over all associated with such people: the brother of a man repatriated by the Americans was refused a job on these grounds.[71] A novel by the Soviet author Feodor Abramov, *Two Summers and Three Winters*, set in a postwar Russian village, had as a recognisable character an ex-prisoner permanently ostracised as a 'traitor'.[72] The network of GULAG was filled with male and female relatives of those who had fled from the Red Army to the West in 1945. Though the Soviet judiciary could have had recourse to the law of 1934, which attributed guilt by association, trumped-up charges were generally preferred, perhaps indicating a faint consciousness that all was not well with such a juridical concept.[73]

On 17 September 1955, the Khruschev Government issued an important amnesty for imprisoned repatriates. Numbers surviving were released, whilst those with longer sentences had them reduced.[74] But it is certain that, after ten years in Socialist corrective camps, the majority of prisoners had long since succumbed to the ravages of icy cold, starvation, sickness and savage ill-treatment. A few survived, amongst them a score or so of the old émigrés surrendered by the British in Austria. It was they who brought back to the West authentic accounts of GULAG camps.

18

Legal Factors and Reasons of State

So STRONG WAS THE EUROPEAN TRADITION OF GRANTING POLITICAL asylum that no nation before 1939 appears even to have contemplated compelling the return home of citizens whose lives or liberty might be thereby endangered.[1] In that year, however, occurred what seems to have been the first agreement made by two states in modern times to contain a provision compelling the repatriation of unwilling exiles. In 1939 Nazi Germany and Soviet Russia signed the famous Ribbentrop-Molotov Pact. Amongst the unpublished clauses of that agreement was one whereby political opponents of either régime who had sought refuge on the other's territory would be returned. At the railway-station of Brest-Litovsk, officers of the Gestapo and NKVD met in friendly fashion to exchange prisoners. Whilst the Germans handed over some anti-Communist Russians, the Soviets presented Himmler with a number of Marxist Jews and Germans to whom they had previously afforded asylum.[2]

Another such extradition agreement took place less than a year later. On 21 June 1940, at Compiègne, the victorious Germans, in the presence of Hitler himself, presented a delegation of the French Government with terms for an armistice. The French were in no position to bargain; their armies were defeated, and their ally was withdrawing her forces at Dunkirk. Despite this, General Weygand 'strenuously objected to many of the German demands. One of the most odious of them obligated the French to turn over to the Reich all anti-Nazi German refugees in France and in her territories. Weygand called this dishonourable in view of the French tradition of the right of asylum, but when it was discussed the next day the arrogant Keitel would not listen to its being deleted.'[3] The French were obliged to swallow this clause, and some time later the Nazi equivalent of Ratov's and Dragun's Repatriation Commissions appeared in France to hunt out the fugitive Germans.

Numbers were removed by the Gestapo, to unknown destinations; others were made to work in slave-gangs on the trans-Sahara railway (ironically, alongside Russians later handed over by the British to the Soviets). Against this, many volunteered under pressure to work for the Todt labour organisation, where they were actually paid. Certainly there is no evidence of wholesale massacres of these German refugees.[4]

But these were precedents hardly likely to commend themselves to Western statesmen. Russians in German service were clearly in an anomalous position. Could they claim the protection of the Geneva Convention to which their country did not belong; and if so, would that preclude their being handed back to the Soviet Government against their will?

It might be thought that the texts of the Conventions—the Hague Conventions of 1899 and 1907, the Geneva Convention of 1929—would settle the matter at once, but unfortunately they are not specific on the central point at issue. This point is: if the Russian prisoners were regarded as recaptured Soviet soldiers or civilians, then naturally there could be no objection to their returning home. Even if the Soviet Government were then to treat them with barbarity, it would be no *legal* concern of the British or German Governments. But what if Russians serving in the German Army, who wore German uniforms and had sworn an oath of allegiance to the Head of the German State, were to be claimed as *German* soldiers? Could such a claim be upheld; and, if so, would it inhibit the legality of their transfer to the Soviet Union? These are the questions we must now consider.

The three interested parties, Britain, Germany and the United States (all of whom were signatories of the Conventions), adopted differing standpoints on this issue. A Foreign Office legal adviser, Patrick Dean, set out Britain's viewpoint in a closely-reasoned argument in September 1944:

In spite of the provisions of the Geneva Convention it is not possible for a soldier who is captured by his own forces while he is serving with the enemy forces to claim *vis-à-vis* his own government and his own law the protection of the Convention. We should certainly not be prepared to grant such a right to a British subject captured while serving in the German forces. If such a man is captured by an Allied force the Allied government is entitled to hand him over unconditionally to his own government without rendering themselves liable for a breach of the Convention. Any other procedure would place us in an indefensible position *vis-à-vis* the Allied governments, who would claim that we were trying to protect possible traitors from the penalties attaching to them under their own law.[5]

Some months later it transpired that United States policy was still radically different from Britain's on this issue. The Foreign Office learned this in a message passed on by their Washington Ambassador (Lord Halifax) on 28 March.[6] The difference was pointed out by a British Embassy official in a letter to Bernard Gufler of the US Special War Problems Division. His comments were requested, in view of the fact that 'the Foreign Office consider that the terms of the agreement between His Majesty's Government and the Soviet Union bind them to return to the Soviet Union even Soviet citizens who demand that they be retained as German prisoners of war.'[7]

Patrick Dean (later himself ambassador in Washington) had commented on the American notification of policy that 'the US attitude is in my view wrong and irreconcilable with the Crimea Agreement . . .'[8] Later, he explained this view more fully:

'. . . though there is no definite obligation [in the Yalta text] upon HMG to repatriate to the Soviet Union Soviet citizens who do *not* want to go, the clear indication from the wording of our agreement is that such Soviet citizens are in fact to be handed over to the Soviet Authorities whatever their own wishes may be.'[9]

This apparent *non sequitur* did not impress Mr. Gufler. After setting out anew the reasons lying behind the American view, and noting that repatriation was not forced by the US on citizens of any state entitled to claim the protection afforded by a German uniform, he continued:

As I recollect from my period of service protecting British interests in Germany, our Embassy there under instructions from your Government informed the German authorities that the wearing of a British uniform carried with it the right to full protection as a British soldier under the Geneva Convention. I understand that your government has continued to maintain this position that a uniform covers the wearer regardless of nationality and has so informed the German Government in connection with the Belgian incident that formed the occasion of a German protest to both our Governments. I further understand that your Government is not compelling persons of nationality other than Soviet found among German prisoners of war held by you to return to the custody of their respective governments against their wills.

It is felt in our Department that our policy in this matter is consistent all the way through and that the policy of your Government involves an inconsistency which would be difficult to sustain in so far as concerns British treatment of Soviet nationals taken in German uniform. Since a reversal of our present policy towards Soviet nationals would in our opinion involve us in an inconsistency and in possible conflict with the spirit and provisions of the Geneva Prisoners of War Convention to which your Government is also a party, it would be greatly appreciated in the

Department of State if you could inform us on what basis your Government has reconciled this matter.[10]

The British Embassy referred to the Foreign Office for 'instructions as to the further pursuit of this discussion with the Department of State'. Before passing the matter over to the legal expert, John Galsworthy summed up his views in what seems to be a fair assessment of the Foreign Office argument:

As far as I know, the basis of our interpretation is one of expediency. We have enough trouble with the Russians over the categories of persons whom they claim as Soviet citizens and whom we do not regard as such [e.g. Poles and Balts], without adding to their number all those who, for personal or political reasons, do not wish to be regarded as Soviet citizens (though that is their status) but desire to be held as German prisoners of war. A number of the latter are, in addition, persons who have a guilty conscience for having *actively* collaborated with the Germans against the Russians, and it would seem incongruous to expose Anglo-Soviet relations to any further strain for the benefit of persons who have been active against our own 'Ally'. This is not, of course, the whole story: some of the people whom we are obliged to hand over are persons who have suffered under the Soviet régime for no fault of their own, have not fought against it, and are merely trying to escape it.[11]

Galsworthy probably had in mind the harrowing examples submitted by Brigadier Firebrace to the Foreign Office in the previous month.[12] Patrick Dean, to whom Galsworthy next passed Gufler's letter for a comment on the legal aspects, confined himself to the question of Russians in the Wehrmacht claiming the protection of German nationality. He started by asserting:

We have never taken the view that if a man for any reason adopts the uniform of the armed forces of a country which is at war with his own state he is thereby entitled to claim the protection of the P/W Convention against his own military authorities or those of his allies. If this view were tenable all traitors could evade responsibility and could claim to be treated as prisoners of war in accordance with the Convention by merely putting on enemy uniform and fighting actively against their country.

Dean concluded by conceding that, though there might be flaws in the British case, the Foreign Office was safe from criticism as it had refrained from admitting publicly its commitments.

'I agree with the State Department's argument that this strictly leads to an inconsistency when compared with what we have said about uniforms being paramount as regards prisoners of war, but as far as I know we have carefully avoided being driven into making a public statement on this point throughout the war.'

'In spite of the inconsistency,' Dean summed up, 'it seems to me that our view is correct . . .' But, he hastened to add, there was no need to submit his argument to the contentious Gufler. 'I do not think that it is really necessary to reply to the State Department unless the Department wish to do so.'[13]

The 'inconsistency' to which Gufler had alluded, and which Dean admitted, was the contrast between the Foreign Office attitude to the captured Russians, and the policy it had previously followed. When Eden arrived in the Crimea for the Yalta Conference, the Foreign Office telegraphed him to point out that: 'In regard to treatment of Prisoners of War, hitherto the principle has, with few exceptions, been respected as between the German Government and His Majesty's Government that the uniform and not the nationality of a prisoner governs his treatment.' This principle had been invoked to Britain's advantage when wishing to protect 'Czechs, Poles, Belgians and others serving in British uniform and who may now be liberated.' Accordingly, the Foreign Office recommended that the proposed agreement at Yalta should include a form of words stating that 'all persons who wear [British or American] uniforms . . . shall, irrespective of their nationality, be treated as members of those Forces for the purpose of this agreement.'[14] At about the same time an identical view was expressed by the Foreign Office representative, Walter Roberts, at a conference of the Directorate of Prisoners of War in London.[15] Following this meeting, Roberts proposed that Molotov be asked to confirm 'that for the purposes of the aforesaid Agreement any person who at the time of his capture by the enemy was serving in the forces of any of the contracting parties shall be regarded as a citizen or subject of that party'.[16]

Needless to say, Molotov had reasons for declining to accept this proposal. As Colonel Phillimore of the War Office noted: 'We were forced reluctantly to abandon the point about Allied nationals serving in British forces. The Soviet negotiators pointed out that this was raised at a late stage and that they required more time to consider it.'[17]

If the British had had their way, therefore, the Yalta Agreement itself would have contained the very stipulation Patrick Dean was concerned to deny existed. Dean appears to have tacitly conceded that Britain's unaltered practice had hitherto been not to 'look behind the uniform'. What he claimed was that the Russians came into a special category, as they had adopted 'the uniform of the armed forces of a country which is at war with [their] own state'. Patrick Dean's argument suggested that the captured Russians were not in fact German soldiers at all, but simply captured Russian traitors. The British had every right to return them to their own country, and the Soviets every right to punish their treachery. There is much that is appealing in this argument. Can one really expect that, in wartime, men who had donned the enemy's uniform and fought against their own country should expect to escape punishment by pleading membership of the enemy's forces? Surely this would be simply issuing a licence to treason? There would also follow the incongruity that any national who transferred his allegiance to an enemy power and worked for that power *as a civilian* would be liable to punishment as a traitor on his recapture. But if he went further, and actually fought against his own country in the enemy's armed forces, he would be protected from punishment by the Geneva Convention. This would appear quite illogical.

In practice, however, it is unlikely that any but a few such cases would arise in the event of conflict between normally governed states. Under Articles 44 of the 1899 Hague Convention and 23 of that of 1907, it is forbidden to compel the citizens of a hostile power to take part in any military operations against their own country. This would restrict to volunteers only the degree of 'permissible treason' under the Conventions. It is unlikely, under anything approaching normal civilised conditions, that large bodies of a nation's citizenry could be persuaded voluntarily to take up arms against their own people. Nor is it probable that the military would be enthusiastic over the idea of raising bodies of armed and disciplined nationals of the hostile state behind their own lines. Of course, this is just what did happen in the case under review, when the Germans recruited nearly a million Russians into their armed services. But it is precisely because the Soviet Union was not a civilised state in any acceptable meaning of the word that this anomalous situation had arisen. The Soviet Union had refused to adhere to the Hague and Geneva Conventions. This was a wholly exceptional case, where the unprecedented savagery of the government actually created 'traitors'. As George Orwell wrote of the German recruitment of Russians: 'Supposing that one can usefully employ prisoners in this way, and then trust them with weapons in their hands, why was this done to Russian prisoners and not to British or Americans?'[18]

We are concerned here, however, with the purely legal aspects of the matter. Were the Russians 'German' prisoners of war? Patrick Dean's expert opinion was 'no', and this opinion was accepted by his government throughout the major repatriation operations. It is an opinion we must now examine.

In Article 79 of the Geneva Convention it is laid down that a Central Agency 'shall be charged with the duty of collecting all information regarding prisoners . . . and the agency shall transmit the information as rapidly as possible to the prisoners' own country *or the Power in whose service they have been'* [Author's italics]. It is clear from this that a prisoner need not have been a national of the country in whose army he was serving, and equally that no distinction should be made on these grounds with regard to his treatment. The implication is also un-avoidable, from the context, that the choice of nationality rests with the prisoner, and not with the captor power.

The Hague and Geneva Conventions are not explicit on this point, unfortunately. But, apart from the British Government's attitude in the single instance under discussion, the signatory nations appear to have accepted from the beginning that it was wrong to look behind the uniform. The reason is clear. Once one belligerent power arrogates to itself the right to single out for harsh treatment some of the enemy soldiers held in captivity, it will not be long before retaliatory measures are imposed by the enemy. These would escalate on both sides, and the Conventions would soon be disregarded altogether. The British Government, as was shown earlier, did indeed fear that the Germans would retaliate on British prisoners if they discovered what was happening.

Only seven years after the signing of the Yalta Agreement, Britain and the United States were faced with a similar problem. Thousands of Chinese soldiers captured in Korea resolutely refused to return home. British and American diplomats argued cogently, and ultimately success-fully, that to compel their return was inhumane and contrary to inter-national law.[19]

Legal experts generally have concurred in rejecting Dean's argument. Susan Elman, in a discussion of the case of Chinese Malays captured by Malaya when serving in hostile Indonesian forces, cites numerous pre-cedents to prove that former nationality does not affect a soldier's status in the army in which he serves, and hence his status as a prisoner of war.[20] Other authorities likewise conclude that forcible repatriation is clearly contrary to the spirit of international law and the Geneva Convention.[21]

An American jurist cited, in support of the Russian prisoners in 1945, the remarkable parallel of Charles Lee. A British officer fighting in the American War of Independence, he deserted to the Americans and rose to the rank of major-general. In 1776 he was captured by the British and sentenced to death as a traitor. But General Washington himself inter-posed, claiming that 'Lee's status was that of a war prisoner and entitled to all the privileges and protection as such.' The British conceded the point, and Lee was paroled and exchanged.[22]

Many people must nevertheless find it difficult to see how Russians in 1944 and 1945, fighting in German uniform against their country or its allies, could claim treatment as ordinary prisoners of war when captured. But the Foreign Office had insisted from the outset of the war that such protection should be afforded to foreign nationals in British service. Many Frenchmen, for example, fought in British uniforms against the legally constituted government of their own country. To say that the Vichy Government was oppressive in character and acting contrary to the nation's best interests is but to make the parallel closer. Yet the Germans never contested British claims that such men when captured should be regarded as British prisoners.

Perhaps the weakness in Patrick Dean's reasoning may be best illustrated by picturing an analogous state of affairs. In 1944 the British War Cabinet authorised the raising of a purely Jewish military unit, the Jewish Brigade. The Brigade saw service towards the end of the Italian campaign, between March and May of 1945.[23] Let us suppose that Jews of German birth and former nationality serving in the Brigade had fallen into the hands of the enemy at this time and been subjected to maltreatment. The Foreign Office had been hitherto successfully insistent that Jewish prisoners be treated in the same way as other Commonwealth prisoners.[24] Had the German Government denied Jews of German nationality the protection of the Convention, would Patrick Dean have accepted this as just, on the grounds that the German authorities 'would claim that we were trying to protect possible traitors from the penalties attaching to them under their own law'?

The truth of the matter appears to be that the Foreign Office argument was not the real justification for its policy. The refusal to allow captured Russians the protection of the Geneva Convention was in opposition to previous and subsequent British interpretation. It was also unacceptable to the German[25] and American[26] Governments. The reality was, as John Galsworthy confessed, that 'the basis of our interpretation is one of expediency'. Dean's argument that the Russians were traitors, and so excluded from the provisions of the Convention was, it seems, intended for departmental consumption only. It was not transmitted to the American or German Governments. Indeed, the Foreign Office went to elaborate lengths to ensure that none of the interested parties learned of its novel interpretation of the Geneva Convention, so little confidence does it seem to have had in its argument.

British soldiers in the field at all levels continued, in all innocence, to accept the surrender of Vlasov units under the terms of the Convention. When the German Commander South-West, General von Vietinghoff, surrendered to Field-Marshal Alexander on 2 May 1945, the text of the terms included 'Vlasovskie and other military and para-military forces and organisations . . .' The surrender itself was referred to as a 'capitulation' under 'the Hague rules'.[27] The forces referred to included Domanov's Cossacks, Ghirey's Caucasians, and the Turcoman Division.

It is true that, after the final surrender of Germany a few days later, the Allies 'argued that, while enemy troops captured before the surrender should continue in their legal status as prisoners of war, the forces still in the field or in home garrisons at that time, should fall into a special category of 'surrendered enemy personnel' (known in brief as SEP, or SP), and, as such, would not be entitled to claim, as of right, the conditions and treatment laid down by the Geneva Convention for prisoners of war.'[28] Thus the 15th Cossack Cavalry Corps, which had come under German Command South-East, was refused (on instructions from General McCreery) surrender terms under the Geneva Convention.

But there was nothing sinister in this. As Colonel Gerald Draper, an international authority on questions relating to the legal position of prisoners of war, explains: 'The reason was simple. We had not the resources to feed and guard in PoW camps such enormous numbers of capitulated troops, and we did not want to be held to the GPW (1929) onerous obligations . . .'[29] It is, indeed, highly questionable whether such action was valid at all, since Article 96 of the Convention declares that a state wishing to repudiate the Convention must give a year's notice. But, as Professor Draper points out, the purpose was solely to evade the impossible responsibility of quartering and supplying the entire surrendered German Army on the relatively generous scale stipulated by the Geneva Convention. This certainly did not imply any intention of abrogating the humanitarian provisions of the Convention, which continued as the soldier's guide.

To the soldiers on the spot there was no question of any new evaluation of the standards of humanity required to be maintained. Field-Marshal Lord Harding, who frequently discussed the matter with Alexander, has told the author unequivocally: 'I look upon the Geneva Convention as the guideline when dealing with prisoners of war.' And at the very time of the surrenders of Cossack units in Austria, officers continued to apply the terms of the Convention to capitulating enemy units.

Colonel Sir Geoffrey Shakerley was then a major in the Rifle Corps. In early May he was ordered to proceed to a spot north of Grafenstein in Austria and persuade a German SS unit to surrender. He declares today that 'I am certain that my orders were to negotiate the surrender under the terms of the Geneva Convention and to stress also the fact that the surrender was to the British Army. The Adjutant of the German Force mentioned these conditions of surrender at least twice during our conversation.' After consulting with his CO, the Adjutant 'returned and asked if some Cossacks with them could surrender at the same time under the same terms—there were around 100 of them. I said yes.

Details were arranged and they surrendered to us the next morning.' These Cossacks were placed with others of the 1st Cavalry Division in the cage at Weitensfeld and later surrendered to the Soviets. Major Shakerley, who afterwards received reports of this, was deeply disturbed 'in view of the fact that I had in good faith given the terms of surrender as stated'.[30] The story had an unhappy ending, but the point is established that, for the Army at least, what Field-Marshal Harding terms 'the etiquette of war' had not been changed by the SEP ruling. This had only been introduced for purely administrative purposes.

When Patrick Dean argued that Russians falling into British hands were not entitled to the protection of the Geneva Convention, he had, in addition, apparently overlooked the fact that their status as prisoners of war—and consequent position in international law—had been accepted by responsible British authority from the outset. Three days after the D-day landings, Colonel Phillimore of the War Office wrote that 'these men will at present, despite their Russian nationality, be treated as German prisoners of war. Foreign Office agree to this . . .'[31] And, in case there be any ambiguity in the matter, we may note that on 9 August, 1944, the Combined Chiefs of Staff informed Eisenhower that 'Allied nationals captured when serving in a German para-military formation . . . will for the present be treated in all respects as prisoners of war in accordance with the Prisoners of War Convention.'[32]

It was swiftly realised that this raised a serious complication: 'If we treat any of them as prisoners of war they have under International Law to be registered as such and their names notified to the protecting power' (*i.e.*, Switzerland).[33] And, as the Deputy Adjutant-General, Lord Bridgman, pointed out, this could have embarrassing consequences.[34] For the Protecting Power was obliged to maintain the interests of the prisoners as defined in the Convention, and it was not difficult to see what that might lead to. As it was, the prisoners' rights were carefully concealed both from themselves and from the Protecting Power. On no recorded occasion, for example, was Article 84 of the Geneva Convention adhered to: 'The text of the present Convention . . . shall be posted, whenever possible, in the native language of the prisoners of war, in places where it may be consulted by all the prisoners.' Again, Article 26 would, if adhered to, have prevented the 'use of deception' operations conducted against the Cossacks and others: 'In the event of transfer, prisoners of war shall be officially informed in advance of their new destination . . .' Had the text of the Convention been posted in the camps, as required by Article 84, the prisoners would have learned that they had the right to transmit complaints to the Protecting Power (Article 42). We may envisage the use to which an intelligent prisoner could have put this right, and understand the fears of Bridgman and his colleagues.

The danger did not only come from the direction of the prisoners themselves. Brought up in a country which knew nothing of the Geneva Convention, they could not have guessed at the rights enjoyed by Western Europeans and by their own country before October 1917.[35] But the German Government, in whose service the prisoners had been, and the Swiss as Protecting Power, might well wish to enquire into the treatment accorded them. Britain was the captor power, and was responsible for their good treatment. It was decided to conceal what was being done from both Germany and Switzerland.

In December 1944 the German Government enquired, through the Swiss, about the treatment being accorded to captive Russians serving in the German Army. On 27 January 1945 Major W. L. James of the War Office wrote to Patrick Dean: 'We agree with your view that in reply to this enquiry it is important that we should avoid any statement which would give the Germans an opportunity for saying that we have disregarded the normal rule that a prisoner should be treated in accordance with the uniform which he was wearing when captured, irrespective of his nationality.' The day after the agreement was signed at Yalta an evasive reply was accordingly delivered to the Swiss.[36]

No sooner was this danger past than another arose. The International Red Cross Committee was charged with the duty of proposing to a belligerent power the establishment of a Central Agency, for the transmission to their own country of information concerning the prisoners (Article 79).

On 2 January, 1945, M. Haccius, of the London Delegation of the Red Cross, wrote to the Foreign Office. He informed them that his headquarters in Geneva had sent him a newspaper cutting referring to the presence of the Russian prisoners in Britain, and continued: 'In their covering letter Geneva ask us to let them know what status has been accorded to Russian PoW and whether they are given the protection of the Convention. I should be glad if you could enable me to reply.'

Patrick Dean, noting that 'we must be careful what reply is sent', proposed a draft couched in suitably non-committal terms. However, Colonel Phillimore at the War Office responded with a note of alarm: 'In view of the note we received from the Swiss Legation . . . dated 4th December . . . on the subject of non-German nationals captured by us we regard this as a dangerous enquiry. We suggest that the International Red Cross Committee might well remain unanswered for the present.'

Matters remained thus up to the last week of the war, when John

Galsworthy (for Geoffrey Wilson) took up the matter once again with Phillimore.

'The letter from Haccius has now been unanswered for nearly four months and we wondered whether you still saw any objection to our replying to it on the lines of the enclosed draft. It is, as you will see, very vague and does not answer the specific questions raised by the International Red Cross Committee, but you will appreciate that this is not accidental.'

The time of danger was now safely past, and Phillimore concurred. 'In view of the unconditional surrender of the German Forces, there is surely no longer any danger of repercussions in this matter.'

The way being now clear, Geoffrey Wilson replied briefly to M. Haccius. After an apology for the delay, he stated, despite the evidence, that all 'Soviet citizens who have fallen into our hands while wearing German uniforms have insisted that they had been conscripted into the German forces against their will, and they are therefore being treated as liberated Soviet citizens...'[37]

Ultimately, even the Foreign Office appears to have come to doubt the legality of its policy. It had always held, in every instance but that of the Russians in the Wehrmacht, 'that from the point of view of international law the status of such persons depends not upon their nationality, but upon their membership of the ... forces.'[38] It also admitted privately that 'this aspect of the Yalta Agreement ... is, of course, in opposition to our traditional attitude towards political refugees...'[39] Finally, as John Galsworthy minuted quietly on 23 July 1945, some 'Russians captured in German uniform (as opposed to Soviet displaced persons and prisoners of war), ... claim to be regarded as German prisoners of war and to be held under the Geneva Convention. The British authorities have now allowed the distinction.'[40]

These purely legal aspects of forced repatriation have been examined in part because of their intrinsic interest. To the British, the injustice of traitors escaping retribution through invocation of the Geneva Convention seemed flagrant. To the Americans such a consideration appeared slight compared with the risks of abrogating international agreements that had succeeded in materially alleviating some of the worst horrors of modern warfare. In general, the Germans, too, honoured this aspect of the Convention; it was fortunate for many Czechs, Poles, Norwegians and other Continental nationals in British uniform that they did so.

However, the plain truth is that the Foreign Office was influenced by important considerations of national policy, and the question of the Geneva Convention was only a peripheral issue amongst much greater ones.

What then were the real considerations that led Britain to disregard her commitments under international law in this way? The reasoning of Sir Anthony Eden, now Lord Avon, was set out in Chapter Two and, as no one has since suggested that there were any other important factors, we may take his argument as representative.

Probably his most persuasive point was that which concerned British and Commonwealth prisoners who had been liberated in Eastern Europe by the Red Army. At Yalta he estimated that they numbered about 50,983,[41] though in fact the true figure turned out to be less than half that: the Soviet General Golikov announced that by 1 September, 1945, Soviet repatriation authorities had despatched home 23,744 freed British prisoners.[42] It was not the numbers that were important, however, but the principle. Today Lord Avon writes that 'My dominant concern was for the return of our prisoners of war from East Prussia and Poland and I was not prepared to take any action which might jeopardise this.' The safe and speedy return of these men was indeed of prime importance. But what precisely was it that Eden feared?

He himself, despite frequent requests, declines to elaborate in any way beyond the words quoted above. It has, however, recently been alleged by others that Stalin had threatened that, unless the British sent back *all* Russians in their hands, he (Stalin) 'would keep British and American prisoners as hostages'.[43] This, at first glance, carries conviction. But let us examine it further. The Cambridge historian, Dr. John Guy, has pointed out that there is no evidence preserved anywhere in the British war archive to suggest that this reprisal was feared by the British, let alone intended by the Soviets.[44] But is there evidence, independent of Foreign Office records, that the Soviets contemplated at any time holding released Allied prisoners hostage for the return of their own liberated citizens in the West? It is, after all, true that Allied prisoners freed in Poland and Prussia were subjected to delays before being returned home, whilst the Soviets made vociferous claims for their own citizens alleged to be detained in the West.

At Luckenwalde, south of Berlin, Stalag IIIa prisoner-of-war camp was liberated by the Red Army on 6 April. Despite the proximity of the US 9th Army at Magdeburg, the Red Army refused to allow British and American prisoners to make their way across country westwards, despite American attempts to achieve their release. On one occasion a column of twenty US trucks arrived to ferry back Allied prisoners, but Soviet guards prevented this, even going to the lengths of firing shots above the convoy. The prisoners became increasingly dismayed, particularly when the local Red Army commander spoke of the possibility of their returning via Odessa. And when they heard a Russian broadcast on their camp radios, claiming that the Allies were unjustly attempting to retain 800 Russians captured in Normandy, many concluded that they were indeed being held hostage. For some this view was apparently confirmed when they were eventually handed over to the Americans. A month after the first Soviet armoured car had come storming up the *Lagerstrasse* of Stalag IIIa amidst the frenzied cheering of the prisoners, they were taken to a bridgehead on the Elbe where 'we were exchanged one for one with Russians who had been freed from the Germans by Allied Forces.'[45]

But though this sounds like a perfect example of the sort of blackmail that is now said to have been feared, that was not in fact the case. Shortly before the prisoners' release, SHAEF noted their presence at Luckenwalde and the measures being taken for their care by the Red Army, without expressing any misgivings as to the possibility of their being detained.[46] In fact, the reason for the delay was purely administrative: the Allies were in the midst of negotiating arrangements for overland exchange of prisoners.[47] As for the 800 detained Russians mentioned in the Soviet broadcast, this was a group alleged to have been transferred by the Americans from Britain to the United States.[48] This turned out to be an error; moreover the 800 cannot have been amongst those Russians exchanged on the Elbe, as they returned home by sea from Liverpool.[49]

There were, however, two instances when blackmail *was* threatened by an important Soviet official. General Ratov, unsavoury head of the Soviet Repatriation Mission in Britain, had been putting forward to Brigadier Firebrace claims for prisoners whom the British did not regard as Soviet citizens (Disputed Persons):

'After lunch in the camp, he attempted to return to the question and said that he thought if we acted in this way, they would have to retain fifty British ex-PoW in Odessa. He added "and how would you like that?" I told him that I would report his remarks to higher authority. This I think pulled him up and he made no further reminder.' For the rest of the day Ratov remained in a very chastened mood.[50]

In August Ratov had moved to Norway to supervise repatriation of Russians held there. Once he put forward energetic claims to a large number of Disputed Persons whom the British regarded as Poles. At a conference at Trondheim, he angrily informed Brigadier H. G. Smith that 'there were half-a-million British personnel (ex-PWs) in Russian hands and none of them was detained under spurious pretences. In his opinion they should have been kept as an object of barter and then the attitude of the British authorities with reference to the Soviet Citizens might have been different.'[51]

These two outbursts by General Ratov are very revealing. After his threat to Brigadier Firebrace he was clearly extremely worried lest the London Embassy or Moscow learn how far he had exceeded instructions. A brusque warning from Firebrace provided one of the rare occasions when Ratov was silenced outright. His similar grumble to Brigadier Smith was equally clearly an impromptu notion of his own. He had multiplied the number of British prisoners some twentyfold and, much more significantly, implied that his advocacy of tough bargaining on these lines was out of line with the views of his government. Moreover, in the first of these examples, what Eden states that he feared had actually taken place without ill effect. Firebrace declined to hand over prisoners whom Ratov and his government regarded as Soviet citizens; Ratov threatened reprisals, but had to climb down the moment he was taken seriously.

We can be justified in assuming that, if the possibility of retaining British hostages had ever been envisaged in exchanges between Ratov and his superiors, it had merely been to reject it. Nor is it at all likely that Stalin would have considered the confrontation suggested by Eden's present-day defenders. One of his prime motives in wanting the return of all his fugitive subjects was fear of the conclusions that might be drawn in the West from any widespread refusal to go back. To offend Western public opinion by deliberately retaining their released soldiers, and to declare openly that he was doing it in order to compel the return of hundreds of thousands of ordinary Russians who would contemplate suicide rather than return home—such a move on Stalin's part seems very improbable. As it was, after routine protests he accepted the defection of a million or more Disputed Persons and escaped Soviet citizens without taking wild retaliatory measures.

It is worth noting in this context that Soviet representatives were very careful, for obvious reasons, never to admit publicly or in writing that they were demanding that Britain and America compel those unwilling to do so to return. On one rare occasion, when a Soviet general in Italy demanded that force be used, the British invited him to put this specific request in writing. 'Major-General Suslaparov declined.'[52] The Soviets were indeed desperately anxious that the Western general public should not learn that such a provision existed, let alone was necessary. A Frenchman who saw too much was abducted to Siberia,[53] and Soviet escorting officers displayed great nervousness when their charges came in view of the English populace.[54] The Foreign Office was fully aware of the Soviet fear of publicity,[55] though it made no use of this knowledge.

The Foreign Office claim, not expressed until thirty years after the event, that Stalin might have contemplated holding liberated British prisoners hostage, must in any case be weighed against the infinitely more fearful risk which the policy of forced repatriation incurred. This was that Hitler might seize on the maltreatment in Russia of Wehrmacht prisoners as an excuse to massacre British prisoners (in 1945 under the control of the savage SS General Berger) in retaliation. It is well known that he was eagerly searching for just such a pretext,[56] and here the Foreign Office was taking an unequivocal gamble with the same British lives—one, too, which was recognised *at the time.*

Could the Foreign Office have therefore declined to return all or some of those reluctant to be returned? As they never tried or contemplated trying, we can only speculate. But there is abundant evidence to indicate the probable course of an alternative policy. It has been shown throughout this book that the Americans, faced with an exactly similar problem, reacted in a very different way. For a long time after the Foreign Office acceptance of Soviet demands in October 1944 they continued to reject the idea of forcible repatriation. For longer still they upheld the provisions of the Geneva Convention. When their first bloody incident took place at Kempten, they temporarily abandoned the use of force altogether, and when they resumed it in January 1946 it was applicable only to certain restricted categories. Officially they did not envisage the employment of force against civilians, still less against women and children. They were appalled at any suggestion that White Russian émigrés should be deceived or forced into returning. Yet on no recorded occasion did the Soviets attempt to discriminate against liberated Americans in their hands. No GI had his return from Odessa or at Torgau delayed by five minutes as a result of his government's policy.

All the indications show therefore that firmer negotiations in 1944–5 would have enjoyed a strong probability of success. Precisely what alternatives courses lay open must be a matter for debate. It might have been urged, for example, that the reciprocal agreement at Yalta should cover liberated prisoners of war only, thus excluding the vast horde of civilian Russians uncovered by the Allied armies.[57] Further repatriation voyages might have been halted after the first reports of atrocities at Odessa. The use of force could have been confined, from the beginning, to restricted categories of prisoners, as was ultimately laid down (without ill effect) in the McNarney–Clark directive. Certainly the Foreign Office could safely have declined to order operations involving brutality to women and children. There were numerous alternatives to complete acceptance of all Soviet demands.

By chance, a rather similar situation occurred around the same time in Hungary. It was discovered that the pro-Nazi Secretaries of State, Baky and Endre, were arranging the deportation of Hungarian Jews to German concentration camps. News of this, and of the terrible fate of those deported, reached the Regent, Admiral Horthy. In a towering rage, he at once ordered the cessation of these operations and dismissed the two secretaries, referring to them as 'filthy sadists'. Yet in declining to permit the sacrifice of these victims he risked a very great deal. For the armies of Hungary's powerful ally lay on her frontiers, and were quite capable of overthrowing the government, either directly or by supporting a *Putsch* of the Fascist Arrow-Cross Party.[58]

To suggestions of this sort Foreign Office officials would doubtless have replied by suggesting that any sign of firmness on the part of the British might have imperilled completion of the crucial agreement at Yalta. But what was that agreement worth? The plain fact is that the Soviets from the beginning regarded it as 'just another piece of paper'. Virtually every important provision was flouted by them. In July 1945 the Foreign Office compiled a bulky file, listing Soviet failures to comply with almost every measure to which they had agreed. These ranged from 'lack of facilities for British contact officers' to 'maltreatment' of British prisoners. The report summed up by stating 'that the Soviet authorities entirely failed to give effect to several of the most important provisions of the Yalta Agreement'.[59] The Americans detailed similar complaints, General Deane stating roundly that 'every agreement which was made regarding the treatment of American prisoners of war liberated by the Red Army was violated...'[60]

Perhaps the Foreign Office would have risked discomfort or inconvenience to liberated British prisoners had it taken a firmer line. But it is equally arguable that British prisoners still in German hands incurred the far more terrible risk of reprisals at the hands of the SS, as a result of the policy actually pursued. That the British were despatching Wehrmacht soldiers to be murdered and tortured in Russia could well have provided the pretext for terrible last-minute atrocities in a stricken Germany. In the event this did not happen, but the Foreign Office had no justification for being certain that such restraint would prevail. In no parallel case had an equivalent risk been taken.[61]

The speedy return of the British prisoners was a principal justification for the policy unswervingly supported by the Foreign Office for nearly three years. Yet it was only during the first months of forcible repatriation that this consideration existed. As early as 20 June 1945, Walter Roberts of the Foreign Office reported that not only was there 'no known case of reprisals against either our prisoners of war or their wives', but that also, as the overwhelming majority had been returned, there seemed little further danger in this direction.[62] In August a new factor temporarily arose with the last-minute Soviet intervention in the war against Japan. A few British and American prisoners were released by the Red Army in Manchuria, and the Western Allies secured Soviet agreement to the extension of the Yalta Agreement to cover prisoners freed in the Far East.[63] But by the beginning of September it was noted at the War Office that 'our interest in complying with Russian demands is now very much less strong than formerly. These discussions began when we were still concerned to recover large numbers of ex-prisoners of war in Russian hands, whereas now there are very few left. This removes one very serious reason against refusing to hand these unfortunate people over to the Russians.'[64] Accordingly, as we have seen, British and American military opinion hardened against the continuation of a policy that had always been inhumane and was now unnecessary.

Yet it was from this time on that Foreign Office officials redoubled, if anything, their efforts to ensure that not a single Russian escaped. True, the major part of those repatriable had already gone back. But the hounding that ensued of small parties of frightened men, women and children—even down, on occasion, to individuals—seemed only to transfer the chase to a level almost of personal vindictiveness. All this was detailed in Chapters Fourteen and Fifteen, and need not be recapitulated here. Enormous efforts were employed over a year to induce the Americans to abandon their more Christian standpoint. Indeed, it seems likely that American concessions to harshness, reluctant as they were, came about in large part as a result of British pressure.

Nor was the Foreign Office ignorant of what fate awaited the Russian prisoners. When Thomas Brimelow drew up his Christmas report on young Kalkany, he knew well what lay in store for him. Reports of massacres and murders at Odessa and Murmansk had been filed and commented on in Whitehall from an early date. Men and women petitioning against return or attempting to register as Disputed Persons were known to be certainly doomed. Of a Russian whom the Foreign Office wished to return, Patrick Dean wrote that 'undoubtedly he will be executed'.[65] In November 1945 the British Embassy in Moscow reported on Soviet ill-treatment of returning Russians, who were universally treated as suspect, deported in droves to the East, and 'roughly treated, worse in fact than the German prisoners'. John Galsworthy commented: 'The reports brought back by British officers who have accompanied Soviet repatriates on their way home, as well as incidental information from other sources, leave no room for doubt that the . . . repatriates . . . are received by the Motherland in a callous and often brutal manner: they are tainted by outside contacts and therefore highly suspect.'

Isaiah Berlin, at the Moscow Embassy, reported on a conversation with an unusually frank Red Army general, who admitted that 'our people look into every nook and cranny to extract our prisoners of war [in the West]—and they're treated pretty rough too when they *are* got hold of, segregated and all that.' 'The NKVD?' Berlin asked—all he got was a meaning look. This report was read by the Permanent Under-Secretary, Sir Alexander Cadogan. His equanimity was not disturbed.

Readers of *The Gulag Archipelago* may compare Sir Alexander's account of that historic institution: 'Unemployment presents no problem in Russia. The unemployed are rounded up and marched off to work—maybe hundreds of miles away—in the development of Russia's vast wealth which has been neglected for centuries.'[66] This was true enough. Of prisoners and DPs returned in 1945, together with deported nationalities (Estonians, Poles, Georgians, Chinese etc.), it is estimated that at least two and a half million were deployed in slave-labour gangs.[67] These in turn released manpower required to maintain Red Army forces at strength in occupied Eastern Europe.[68] Cadogan, in January 1945, minuted: 'It is difficult to be moved by their [Soviet] solicitude for these poor devils of whom they will probably shoot a considerable proportion on their return to Russia.'[69]

Foreign Office officials cannot have been happy about this aspect of the policy they were enforcing. They felt it to be a necessary sacrifice for the furtherance of vital diplomatic needs. Firstly there was the necessity of maintaining the alliance against Germany; when the war was over, close co-operation with the Soviet Union seemed the only way to establish a new international order on the ruins of the old. The fate even of several thousand Russian fugitives could not be allowed to obstruct this grand design.

This was no cynical policy of *Realpolitik*. Eden and his advisers were not postponing an inevitable confrontation; they sincerely believed in Stalin's goodwill. Eden himself felt for Stalin strong affection and admiration. These sentiments were shared by his permanent officials, who assisted him in drawing up two important reports for the Cabinet, on 14 June and 9 August 1944, on Soviet policy. The first stressed Soviet 'enthusiastic' desire for co-operation with Britain and America. The second expatiated at length on the Foreign Office's conviction that the Soviet Union after the war would be unlikely to wish to interfere in the affairs of neighbouring states. It was felt, for example, that 'Poland will be left with genuine independence and free from excessive Russian interference in her internal affairs.' All in all, it was concluded 'that the Soviet Government will try a policy of collaboration with ourselves and the United States (and China), whether within the framework of a World Organisation or without it, if it fails to materialise'. An analysis of political pressures within the Soviet Union was attempted, based on assessment by experts at the Moscow Embassy and the Northern Department: 'It may well be that there are still two schools of thought in the Soviet Union: one collaborationist [with the West], the other holding that the Soviet Union can and should trust nobody and must rely upon her own might and such use as she can make of her friends in foreign countries. Fortunately, from all evidence and appearances, it seems that Stalin is the protagonist of the first school and that it is in the ascendant.'[70]

Any attempt to rock the boat could only endanger the constructive collaboration here envisaged, possibly enabling Stalin's illiberal opponents in the Soviet Union to gain undue influence. Suggestions that the Soviet Union could represent a potential threat, however ably presented, were ridiculed by Northern Department experts like John Galsworthy and Christopher Warner.[71] General Martell, who until March 1944 had been head of the Military Mission in Moscow, believed that Foreign Office policy consisted largely of 'licking the Bolshies' boots till we were black in the face'. News that one holding such views was to address the Royal Central Asian Society on 'Operations in Russia' so worried Warner that 'I cannot help thinking that these activities should be stopped.' Martell had suggested that Britain might from time to time assert her position when negotiating with the Soviets.[72]

Eden was so convinced of the necessity of suppressing dissentient viewpoints that he managed to prevent the circulation even to the Cabinet of views on Soviet Russia different from his own. On 1 September 1944, Winston Churchill circularised a fascinating document amongst his Cabinet colleagues. This was a full account of 'Facts and Tendencies in Wartime, 1944', drawn up by Ronald Matthews, Moscow Correspondent of the *Daily Herald* from 1942 to 1944. He was a Socialist, married to a Russian wife. Though his movements in the Soviet Union had been severely restricted, he had succeeded in constructing an amazingly accurate picture of Soviet society and policy. Though thirty years of research into Soviet studies have since passed by, it would be hard to fault a line of Matthews' penetrating analysis. After describing Stalinist totalitarianism at home and the menace of what was likely to be Stalinist foreign policy in the future, he went on:

> It is of absolutely paramount importance that the Western Powers should be able to give Russia at the end of the war . . . a sense of security. Though I think it is just as important from all points of view that they should be able to do so without making concessions to her which they feel to be unjustified. Such concessions would only make for further rankling ill-feeling; nor do I think the Russians will ever really trust us till we show firmness as well as conciliation in our dealings with them. I may be wrong,

but I cannot help feeling that the effects of our giving in to them on points on which we feel we are right is doubly unfortunate. First, it loses us their respect (the Russians respect and respond to tough bargaining). And, secondly, it may well give them not confidence in us, but a sense that we are temporarily buying them off, just as the Germans and they bought each other off in August 1939.

Churchill was clearly impressed by this report, but the picture drawn by Matthews clashed too harshly with Foreign Office interpretations of the situation, as a covering note on the document explains: 'At the suggestion of the Foreign Secretary, the Prime Minister gave instructions for this paper to be withdrawn from circulation.'[73]

British and American attitudes to forced repatriation cannot be considered in isolation. They formed aspects of overall policy towards the Soviet Union, and were unavoidably secondary to the main issues. Foreign Office officials held that Stalin's intentions towards the West were beneficent, and that to work in co-operation with him was not only possible but also essential to British interests. The fate of the Russians whose return they enforced was an unfortunate but unavoidable sacrifice to the greater aim.

Postscript:
The Suppressed Evidence

Sir Herbert Butterfield once wrote an illuminating essay on the pitfalls facing historians conducting research into recent political history. One passage in particular seems relevant to the present study.

> There are two maxims for historians [he wrote], which so harmonise with what I know of history that I would like to claim them as my own, though they really belong to nineteenth-century historiography: first, that governments try to press upon the historians the key to all the drawers but one, and are very anxious to spread the belief that this single one contains no secret of importance; secondly, that if the historian can only find out the thing which government does not want him to know, he will lay his hand upon something that is likely to be significant.[1]

On 5 April 1954, an American scholar, Julius Epstein, visited the United States Government's Historical Records Branch in Alexandria, Virginia. Flicking through the catalogue, he came upon a card with the intriguing title: '383.7—14.1—Forcible Repatriation of Displaced Citizens—Operation Keelhaul.'

Epstein filled out a slip, and waited with that anticipatory exhilaration with which all scholars are familiar. Moments later the archivist returned ... to inform Epstein that this particular file was classified and not available. The index card, which seems to have been included in the catalogue by an oversight, was at once removed.

Professor Epstein now launched himself into a fifteen years' struggle to obtain the release of this secret file. For years he conducted a voluminous press campaign, composed of a veritable rain of articles, broadsheets and letters. He ranged widely in his treatment, frequently discussing cases of forced repatriation of nationalities other than Soviet, but returning again and again to his main topic. When was the United States going to allow historians access to the forbidden documents?

The United States has always been more liberal than the British Government in allowing the early publication of state archives, as the splendid series of *Foreign Relations of the United States* abundantly testifies. Then, in 1966, a Freedom of Information Act was signed by President Johnson, becoming law the following year. This law enabled a private citizen to take the Government to court in order to require it to release to public access a desired document. The Government was entitled to refuse only on the grounds that such release would endanger national defence and security. Epstein saw here the opportunity to claim release of the restricted 'Keelhaul' papers, and filed a law-suit against the Secretary of the Army in 1968. The judge, however, rejected his suit, finding 'that the circumstances are appropriate for the classification made by the Department of the Army in the interest of "the national defense or foreign policy".'

Both in court, and afterwards in print, Epstein ridiculed the idea that classification could be still applicable to this particular event, now twenty years in the past. The Congressman who had been originally responsible for the sponsoring of the Freedom of Information Act, John E. Moss, testified that this ruling flouted the clear intention of the Act.[2] Professor Epstein decided to appeal against the judgment. But despite a persuasive and credible brief, the appeal failed. The only result of all this effort was that the Adjutant General, who carefully re-examined the suppressed file, authorised the release of four of its component documents. These proved to be wholly innocuous papers relating to Operation 'Keelhaul', and merely stimulated curiosity as to what could be so sensitive about the remaining retained documents.[3]

With this material before him, the present author re-examined the evidence to see if any further leads could be obtained. One significant fact that had emerged during the legal proceedings was that the objection to declassifying the documents came, not from the United States Army, but from the British Government. By agreement, documents emanating from the joint British-American AFHQ could only be released by consent of both parties. This consent the British withheld. I wrote to check that this was indeed the case. On 13 December 1974, I heard from the General Services Administration of the National Archives and Records Service in Washington. The reply stated:

Allied Force Headquarters file 383.7—14.1, 'Forcible Repatriation of Displaced Soviet Citizens—Operation "Keelhaul", is still classified and thus restricted. There is no objection to declassification of the Operation "Keelhaul" records from the standpoint of the United States Government. However, as the records were created and are owned and controlled jointly by the British and United States Governments, British concurrence in declassification must be obtained. Since the British authorities have expressed their inability to agree to the declassification and release of the Operation "Keelhaul" files, we have no alternative but to respect the British decision on this matter.'

I next wrote to the Ministry of Defence in London to ask whether they still possessed the original copy of file 383.7—14.1 (the Americans have only a photocopy). The reply considerably surprised me. The Ministry had possessed the files, but 'All three volumes were physically destroyed in 1968 or 1969 as not being worthy of permanent preservation under the Public Records Act 1958. A record of the exact date of destruction was not kept.'

But if the documents were of so little value, why did the British Government continue to veto their release by the United States? And if they had been destroyed, how could the British continue to assess the dangers of revealing their contents, which must necessarily diminish with time? Was it a coincidence that they were destroyed in 1968 or 1969, at the very time the United States authorities requested and were refused permission to release them?

The Ministry of Defence explained further:

In the case of file 383.7—14.1 the American authorities communicated with the British Government in August 1974 through the offices of the British Army Staff, Washington, intimating that in view of certain press articles which had been recently published, and contrary to their understanding of the situation, they were in some doubt as to whether privileged access had been given to that particular file by the British. They asked for clarification on this point, and whether, if such access had been given and our position compromised, we would be prepared to release the file to the general public. In reply, we advised them that we continued to regard file 383.7— 14.1 as personally sensitive and therefore subject to a 75-year closure period, and that no privileged access had been or would be given.

'Personally sensitive' implies that some person or persons is represented in a manner that could be damaging to them if now revealed. It is, of course, impossible to speculate as to what sort of unpleasant revelation might be involved. It would surely be reasonable, however, to assume that some exceptionally discreditable or damaging issue is at stake. We have only to reflect on what *is* accessible amongst the papers referred to in compiling the present book to conclude that File 383.7— 14.1 holds some very remarkable secret indeed. It has not been lightly withheld. The Americans have asked for British consent to its release on at least two occasions, in 1968 and 1974. The file must have been carefully examined before refusals were given. By the latter date the Foreign Office and Defence Ministry had released a vast amount of material covering, apparently, every aspect of forced repatriation. Only one file remained sacrosanct.

Though I could not see the files, I wished to ascertain if possible to which aspect or period of the operations they applied; perhaps this might afford some clue. In response to my enquiry, the Ministry replied that 'records show that AFHQ file No. 383.7—14.1 was opened in June 1946 and contained correspondence to September 1947'. This increased the mystery. What could there be about the relatively minor and well-documented Operations 'Keelhaul' and 'East Wind' that must continue to be kept dark?

I discussed the matter with two men who, more than any others, should be familiar with operational planning at AFHQ during that period. Field-Marshal Lord Harding was then Commander-in-Chief in Italy, whilst General James Lunt drafted the plans for Operation 'East Wind'. Preserved documents would certainly have included correspondence between GHQ Central Mediterranean Force and the Combined Chiefs of Staff in Washington, as well as discussions at Staff level and with the US Commander and Political Adviser. General Lunt in particular remembers a full report he drew up for AFHQ, describing the operations. But, as for material so lurid as still to require classification, neither can recall anything remotely on these lines. I applied to the then American Political Adviser to AFHQ, Joseph N. Greene, Jr., but he too has no memories of hidden scandalous material.

Once again there came a fresh and unexpected twist in the story. The Ministry of Defence statement that file 383.7—14.1 covered the period only between June 1946 and September 1947 turned out to be incorrect. So far from being concerned only with the winding-up of operations, the documentation covers virtually the whole period of forcible repatriation in the Mediterranean theatre, from 1944–47. This came out when the Pentagon unobtrusively released a few score sheets from their photocopy.

These range from January 1944 to January 1947. With a few exceptions, they relate either to routine Soviet complaints made by their Military Mission in Italy in 1944, or to minor aspects of Operation 'Keelhaul' (provision of interpreters, etc.). All are wholly innocuous in character and, almost without exception, have duplicates accessible in the Public Record Office. This is scarcely surprising, since the documents were released with the prior consent of the British Defence Staff in Washington.[4]

The field is in this way opened enormously. Whatever it is the British Government is so anxious to conceal could have taken place anywhere in Italy or British-occupied Austria between 1944 and 1947.[5] Much does indeed remain obscure, particularly in connection with decisions such as that to hand over the émigré White Russians at Lienz in May 1945. It is to be hoped that the United States Government will review its decision to continue classification despite British objections. Many Americans mistakenly continue to believe that it is an American scandal that is being suppressed.[6] Surely after more than thirty years it is time for suspicions to be cleared and for the public to know the truth.

The timid, or selfish, policy of the Western Romans had abandoned the Eastern Empire to the Huns . . . The King of the Huns . . . concluded, and the conclusions of Attila were irrevocable laws, that the Huns, who had . . . deserted the standard of Attila, should be restored, without any promise, or stipulation, of pardon. In the execution of this cruel and ignominious treaty, the Imperial officers were forced to massacre several loyal and noble deserters, who refused to devote themselves to certain death; and the Romans forfeited all reasonable claims to friendship of any Scythian people, by this public confession, that they were destitute either of faith, or power, to protect the suppliants, who had embraced the throne of Theodosius . . . It would have been strange, indeed, if Theodosius had purchased, by the loss of honour, a secure and solid tranquillity; or if his tameness had not invited the repetition of injuries.

Edward Gibbon, *The Decline and Fall of the Roman Empire.*

Notes

1 A first-rate account of the surrender of the Cossack units in Austria had been published by the Pole Josef Mackiewicz, *Kontra* (Paris, 1957). (I am indebted to my friend Mr. Constantine Zelenko who, amongst much other help, presented me with a copy). In 1964 my friend Peter Huxley-Blythe issued a readable outline of the whole story, *The East Came West* (Caldwell, Idaho, 1964). Above all, there existed the two volumes of Cossack memoirs splendidly edited by General Vyacheslav Naumenko: *Великое Предательство: Выдача Казаков в Лиенце и Других Местах (1945—1947)* (New York, 1962–70), and the bibliographical work of M. Shatov, *Библиография Освободительного движения народов России в годы Второй Войны.* (New York, 1961). All these works drew largely on émigré Russian testimony. In Germany several important accounts of the Vlasov movement had appeared, following Jurgen Thorwald's indispensable *Wen sie verderben wollen: Bericht des grossen Verrats* (Stuttgart, 1952). More recently, further studies began to appear. Some of these drew on hitherto neglected or unavailable British and American evidence and began the important process of placing the tragic events in their correct perspective. The most notable of these were: Mark R. Elliott, 'The United States and Forced Repatriation of Soviet Citizens, 1944-47', *Political Science Quarterly* (1973), lxxxviii, pp. 253–75; Julius Epstein, *Operation Keelhaul: The Story of Forced Repatriation from 1944 to the Present* (Old Greenwich, Connecticut, 1973); Nicholas Bethell, *The Last Secret: Forcible Repatriation to Russia 1944-7* (London, 1974) (a useful review of all three works by Ralph T. Fisher Jr. appeared in *Slavic Review* (1975), xxxiv, pp. 823–5); Edgar M. Wenzel, *So gingen die Kosaken durch die Hölle* (Vienna, 1976).

2 BBC interview on 17 November, 1974 with Mr. Janis Sapiets, who kindly supplied me with a transcript.

3 'The Prevention of Literature', *Polemic* (January, 1946), ii, p. 7.

4 FO.371/47897, 5.

5 *Cf.* WO.32/11137, 186A, 225A, 257A, 263A, 298A.

6 FO. 371/47909, 181.

7 Ibid., 191

8 *Parliamentary Debates (Hansard) House of Lords Official Report* (1976), ccclxix, p. 313. Another former diplomat, Lord Campbell of Croy, made the same point (p. 320).

9 *East–West Digest* (1976), xii, pp. 719–20.

10 *The Gulag Archipelago* (London, 1974), i, pp. 240–1.

CHAPTER ONE

[1] Roy Medvedev provides, as one of the innumerable instances of the Soviet Union's unpreparedness for war, the fact that 'airfields had to be enlarged for new types of planes, so construction companies of the NKVD went to work on most military airfields all at once, putting them out of use until the late fall'. (Let History Judge: The Origins and Consequences of Stalinism (London, 1972), p. 449). Cf. John Erickson, The Road to Stalingrad (London, 1975), p. 70.

[2] For the Red Army's chronic shortage of transport for artillery ammunition at this time, cf. The Road to Stalingrad, p. 73.

[3] David Littlejohn, The Patriotic Traitors (London, 1972), p. 296; cf. further The Road to Stalingrad, pp. 82, 109. For a similar example of daring effrontery to that given by Yashvili, cf. E. H. Cookridge, Gehlen: Spy of the Century (London, 1971), pp. 87–8.

[4] Report of the International Committee of the Red Cross on its Activities during the Second World War (September 1, 1939–June 30, 1947) (Geneva, 1948), i, pp. 409–15, 417, 419–20.

[5] Ibid., pp. 420–1.

[6] Ibid., pp. 415–6, 418–19.

[7] Ibid., pp. 421–2; iii, pp. 56–60.

[8] Ibid., i, pp. 424–5.

[9] Gerald Reitlinger, The House Built on Sand (London, 1960), pp. 90, 100–1.

[10] H. Krausnick, H. Buchheim, M. Broszat and H-A. Jacobsen, Anatomy of the SS State (London, 1968), p. 515. Dr. Jacobsen objects that on 17 July 1941 the Soviet Union informed Germany (through the medium of the Swedish Government) that it would adhere to the Hague Convention of 1907; and that Germany chose deliberately to ignore this offer (ibid., pp. 527–8). But this 'offer' was patently a blind, as the Soviets were simultaneously refusing to implement the vital clauses 14 (exchange of lists of prisoners), 15 (Red Cross access to camps), and 16 (postal and parcel services) (cf. Les Conventions et Declarations de la Haye de 1899 et 1907 (New York, 1918), pp. 112–4). The USSR never again referred to the matter, despite repeated requests from the Red Cross, the Axis powers and the Western Allies that it should adhere to the Conventions. One may in any case refer to the authoritative passage in the Great Soviet Encyclopedia: 'In regard to the rules concerning prisoners of war the Government of the USSR does not consider itself bound by any international agreements what-soever . . . (quoted in David J. Dallin and Boris I. Nicolaevsky, Forced Labor in Soviet Russia (London, 1948), pp. 282–3; cf. Hermann Raschhofer, Political Assassination: The Legal Background of the Oberländer and Stashinsky Cases (Tübingen, 1964), p. 101).

[11] 'N.N.N.', На Фронте 1941 года и в плену (Buenos Aires, 1974), pp. 60–1.

[12] Marcel Junod, Warrior without Weapons (London, 1951), pp. 222–31.

[13] Rudolf Semmler, Goebbels—the Man next to Hitler (London, 1947), pp. 182–5; Alan Bullock, Hitler: a Study in Tyranny (London, 1952), p. 711. A similar incident had taken place in 1940 (Willi A. Boelcke (ed.), The Secret Conferences of Dr Goebbels (London, n.d.), p. 41. In 1945 it was SS General Berger who controlled PoW camps in the Reich (Heinz Höhne, The Order of the Death's Head (London, 1969), p. 540.).

[14] Lt.-Gen. N. N. Golovine, The Russian Army in the World War (Yale, 1931), pp. 78, 89; Daniel J. McCarthy, The Prisoner of War in Germany (London, 1918), pp. 14, 36–8, 64–5, 75, 126–8, 140, 187–8, 192–4, 216; cf. W. Dögen, Kriegsgefangene Völker (Berlin, 1919); The Gulag Archipelago, i, p. 242. Numbers of parcels were also received from Britain via Berne (FO. 371/37060).

[15] V. D. Nabokov (ed.), *Письма Императрицы Александры Федоровны къ Императору Николаю II* (Berlin, 1922), i, pp. 411, 433, 487, 488, 522, 541, 543, 572, 581, 585, 586, 591, 600, 612, 628–9; Paul P. Gronsky and Nicholas J. Astrov, *The War and the Russian Government* (Yale, 1929), pp. 258–9.

[16] *The Russian Army in the World War*, pp. 87–92, 102–3; cf. the statistical analysis on pp. 95–100.

[17] Alexander Dallin, *German Rule in Russia: 1941–1945* (London, 1957), p. 427.

[18] *The House Built on Sand*, pp. 98, 446.

[19] *The Prisoner of War in Germany*, pp. 130, 132.

[20] *The Russian Army in the World War*, pp. 92, 205.

[21] W. E. D. Allen, *The Ukraine: a History* (Cambridge, 1940), p. 273. The total number of Ukrainians amongst the Russian prisoners was between seven and eight hundred thousand.

[22] *The House Built on Sand*, p. 120; cf. *The Patriotic Traitors*, pp. 301–2.

[23] *The House Built on Sand*, pp. 257–84; cf. John A. Armstrong, *Ukrainian Nationalism: 1939–1945* (New York, 1955), pp. 123–5; Malcolm J. Proudfoot, *European Refugees* (London, 1957), pp. 78–93.

[24] *German Rule in Russia*, p. 427; *The House Built on Sand*, p. 446.

[25] Frank H. Epp. *Mennonite Exodus* (Altona, 1966), pp. 357–63. I am indebted to Dr. Epp for his kindness in presenting me with a copy of this scholarly work. Professor Proudfoot gives the number of ethnic Germans evacuated as 350,400 (*European Refugees*, p. 38).

[26] Cf. the account by a Kuban Cossack in *Великое Предательство*, i, pp. 63–4.

[27] Vladimir Petrov, *It happens in Russia: Seven Years Forced Labour in the Siberian Goldfields* (London, 1951). pp. 369–70. Cf. Jurgen Thorwald, *Wen Sie Verderben Wollen: Bericht des grossen Verrats* (Stuttgart, 1952), pp. 130–3. This book gives an invaluable account of German policy towards the Russian resistance movements in 1941–5, and like General Naumenko's (*v*. n. 26 supra) still awaits an English translation. 'Jurgen Thorwald' is the *nom-de-plume* of the writer Heinz Bongartz (*Spy of the Century*, p. 316).

[28] *It happens in Russia*, pp. 377–8.

[29] Konstantin Cherkassov, *Генерал Кононов: Ответ Перед Историей за Одну Попытку* (Melbourne, 1963), i, pp. 120–40; *Wen Sie Verderben Wollen*, pp. 70–80.

[30] Mikhail Koriakov, *I'll Never Go Back* (London, 1948), pp. 111–12.

CHAPTER TWO

[1] FO.371/43382, 6–9. Other reports note desperate resistance put up by Vlasovite troops on the Smolensk Front, and the presence of Armenian troops in the Département de Lozère.

[2] Alfred D. Chandler (ed.), *The Papers of Dwight David Eisenhower: The War Years* (Baltimore, 1970), iii, pp. 1870–1.

[3] FO.371/43382, 54.

[4] Molotov's original reply is in ibid. 55. Cf. John R. Deane, *The Strange Alliance* (London, 1947), pp. 186–7.

[5] FO.371/43382, 4–5, 7, 27, 31.

[6] *European Refugees*, p. 114.

[7] On 17 June the War Office received a summary of information derived from such interrogations (WO.32/11137, 3A).

[8] For a personal account of the sufferings of the Russians on Alderney, *v.* 'Voinov', *Outlaw: The Autobiography of a Soviet Waif* (London, 1955) pp. 222–4.

[9] Imperial War Museum, photograph B.6267. *Cf.* B.6266. The second of these Turkestanis is described as being an Uzbek from Namangan.

[10] S. Orwell and I. Angus (ed.), *The Collected Essays, Journalism and Letters of George Orwell* (London, 1968), iii, pp. 252–3.

[11] Joseph Scholmer, *Vorkuta* (London, 1954), p. 119.

[12] WO.32/11137, 19A.

[13] FO.371/43382, 59.

[14] Ibid., 75.

[15] *The House Built on Sand*, p. 350.

[16] WO.32/11137, 20B.

[17] Cf. WO.32/11119, 1A–8A, 13A–14C, 35A, 36A.

[18] *The Papers of Dwight David Eisenhower*, iii, p. 2031.

[19] Louis P. Lochner (ed.), *The Goebbels Diaries 1942–1943* (New York, 1948), p. 383; cf. Ronald Seth, *Jackals of the Reich: The Story of the British Free Corps* (London, 1972).

[20] Cf. Walter Bedell Smith, *Moscow Mission 1946–1949* (London, 1950), pp. 14, 115; *Foreign Relations of the United States . . . 1944*, iv, p. 1264. A similar fear lest the German invaders in 1941 uncover evidence of the slave-labour system resulted in the massacre or hasty evacuation by the NKVD of thousands of slaves (Vladimir and Evdokia Petrov, *Empire of Fear* (London, 1956), p. 98; Antoni Ekart, *Vanished without Trace: The Story of seven years in Soviet Russia* (London, 1954), p. 99; Victor Kravchenko, *I Chose Freedom* (London, 1947), p. 405; Joseph Scholmer, *Vorkuta* (London, 1954), p. 168; *It happens in Russia*, pp. 356–7; Joseph Czapski, *The Inhuman Land* (London, 1951), pp. 69–80). The repatriated prisoners in 1945 had in turn to be massacred or quarantined in camps lest they spread tales in Russia of Western freedom and prosperity (*Moscow Mission 1945–1949*, pp. 279–80; *The Gulag Archipelago*, i, pp. 32–3, 238; Ronald Hingley, *Joseph Stalin: Man and Legend* (London, 1974), pp. 370–1.)

[21] PREM.3.364/8, 296.

[22] WO.32/11137, 53B.

[23] Ibid., 53A.

[24] Photographs of freed Russian forced-labour workers, taken in May 1943 at Enfidaville in Tunisia, are in the Imperial War Museum (NA.2818–21). 120 were former members of the Spanish International Brigade, who had fled to France in 1939, and been interned in Algeria in 1941. For a full account, *vide European Refugees*, p. 94; FO.371/33042; WO.32/11137, 33A, 33C, 43A, 45A, 49B. In December 1943, four Russians with a machine-gun from an 'Anti-Bolshevik Legion' crossed into Spain; after prolonged negotiations they were repatriated a year later via Gibraltar and Naples (FO.371/43349). Col. E. P. L. Ryan, DDMI of Persia and Iraq command, testifies to the willingness with which many prisoners returned (*Sunday Telegraph*, 30 November 1975).

[25] *The Gulag Archipelago*, i, pp. 82–3.

[26] The Imperial War Museum possesses photographs of such prisoners, captured at the Anzio offensive (cf. NA.15317–8).

[27] WO.32/11137, 34A.

[28] Ibid., 9A, 12A–15A.

[29] Ibid., 29B.

[30] Ibid., 10A.

[31] Ibid., 46A, 56A.

[32] Ibid., 6A.

[33] Ibid.

[34] Ibid., 110.

[35] Ibid., 39A.

[36] Cf. a War Office criticism in ibid., 96.

[37] Presumably following Goebbels's order of 28 April 1942 that 'individual instances of bolshevik cannibalism and other atrocities are now to be put out on the greatest possible scale'. (*The Secret Conferences of Dr. Goebbels*, pp. 232–3.)

[38] I am grateful to the Earl of Selborne for kindly making available to me his grandfather's Cabinet Papers. These will eventually be deposited in the Bodleian Library.

[39] PREM.3.364/8, 293–5.

[40] FO.371/40444.

[41] Information from Mr. L. H. Manderstam, confirmed by documentary evidence. There was widespread resentment in the FO against the activities and even the very existence of SOE. This was described to me by the late Major-General Sir Colin Gubbins, former head of SOE.

[42] WO.32/11137, 56A.

[43] *Report of the . . . Red Cross*, i, pp. 423–5; iii, p. 55.

[44] FO.371/33000.

[45] FO.371/37060.

[46] *Political Science Quarterly*, lxxxviii, p. 258.

[47] FO.371/33000. Maclean had been recruited as a Communist agent in his Cambridge days (*Empire of Fear*, p. 271).

[48] *New York Times*, 24/7/45; *The Times*, 16/8/45; cf. *Foreign Relations of the United States: Diplomatic Papers 1945*, v, *Europe* (Washington, 1967), pp. 1066–7.

[49] WO.32/11137, 71B.

[50] WO.32 11683. A Russian ex-submarine commander who led one unit was decorated by the French Government (Alexander Foote, *Handbook for Spies* (London, 1964), p. 145). Cf. Alfred J. Rieber, *Stalin and the French Communist Party 1941–1947* (New York, 1962), p. 84. Those Russians who had under compulsion joined the German forces but wished to desert to the Allies were deprived of any reasonable incentive for doing so. Despite this, and a widespread knowledge of what did in fact happen to those who had already surrendered, large numbers of Russians took an early opportunity of working for the Western Allies. In September 1944 numerous Caucasians serving under German command in Yugoslavia killed their officers and deserted to pro-Allied partisans. (Julian Amery, *Approach March: a venture in autobiography* (London, 1973), pp. 376–83. Amery managed to save two of these men from forcible repatriation (pp. 404–5).) In Italy, 'I Bn 314 Regt, encouraged and guided by a Russian officer, brought out their prepared white flags and turned their arms on their German leaders.' (WO.170/4240 (2/4/45)). Two members of 'Popski's Private Army' were recruited from similarly deserting Russians (Lt.-Col. Vladimir Peniakoff, *Private Army* (London, 1950), pp. 367–8, 412), whilst a Turcoman named Tinio performed such excellent guerilla fighting in the Apennines that he received a certificate of honour from an American divisional commander (*Operation Keelhaul*, pp. 105–7). Photographs 20193 and 20365 in the Imperial War Museum portray escaped Russians fighting for the Allies in Italy and Crete in November 1944. In France, Allied Intelligence learned as early as 1943 that Armenian troops planned, 'when the time was ripe, they would turn their rifles against the German oppressor' (FO.371/43382, 26).

After the landings of June 1944 had taken place, a very high proportion of 'Russians' went over as soon as they could to Eisenhower's forces. On the Dutch island of Texel 700 Georgian soldiers were ordered on 6 April 1945 to prepare to resist an Allied landing. They rose against the Germans, holding out against a garrison of 4,000 for three hard-fought days before being compelled to surrender. As a Canadian Army report noted: 'This group had previously got in touch with the Dutch Underground Movement and worked closely with them, and on their instructions, removed mines from certain areas and this was invaluable at the time of the landing of Canadian forces subsequently' (FO.371/47902, 111-14; FO.371/47903; WO.32/11139, 340A. News of this uprising caused dismay at General Vlasov's headquarters (*Wen sie verderben wollen*, pp. 463-4).). From Egypt the British forcibly repatriated Alexander Rado, the man who had masterminded Soviet wartime espionage in Switzerland (David J. Dallin, *Soviet Espionage* (Yale, 1955), pp. 228-9; cf. FO.371/50606, 149-53). Rado's recently-published memoirs (Sandor Rado, *Codename Dora* (London, 1977)) significantly omit all reference to his treatment on return to Russia.

⁵¹ Letter of 26/5/49 to M. de Saint-Prix, from Monseigneur Soulas, Vicar-General of the Bishop of Valence (Drôme).

⁵² One source says the 'Mongols' bore 'Turkestan' and 'Azerbeidjan' on their sleeves (Jean Veyer, *Souvenirs sur la Résistance dioise 1941-1944* (Die (Drôme), 1973), p. 71).

⁵³ 'Voinov', (*Outlaw*, pp. 227-8) provides an account of Ivanov, whom M. de Saint-Prix encountered releasing his prisoners. For the Soviet use elsewhere of Nazi collaborators, cf. the accusations levelled against a Major Gruzdiev (FO.371/47904, 154). The foregoing account is based on information kindly supplied by MM. de Saint-Prix and Vistel, Resistance leaders in the Rhône Valley, both of whom cite the additional testimony of further eye-witnesses.

⁵⁴ FO.371/43382, 79-83.

⁵⁵ WO.32/11137, 101A (6B); FO.371/40444.

⁵⁶ WO.32/11137, 18A; ibid., 10A, 11A, 40A, 234A (2B). Later in his Cabinet Paper of 3 September, Eden conceded that those refusing to return had been retained. But, by suppressing the evidence submitted to him of NKVD pressures applied to the 'volunteers', he was able by implication to represent the number of unwilling repatriates as derisory.

⁵⁷ Robert E. Sherwood, *Roosevelt and Hopkins: An Intimate History* (New York, 1948), p. 717. Cf. Saul Friedländer, *Counterfeit Nazi* (London, 1969), pp. 150-4; 'Hungarian Offer to Allow Jews to Leave Hungary' (CAB.66/53, 167-9). Even in 1939 the Foreign Office had been concerned to prevent the emigration of Jews fleeing persecution in Germany, Poland and Roumania; officials feared the exodus might irritate Ibn Saud. (Dr. Martin Gilbert informs me he is preparing a book on this subject).

⁵⁸ PREM.3.364/8, 287-92.

CHAPTER THREE

¹ *Let History Judge*, p. 448.

² WO.32/11137, 101A (9A, 11A, 12A).

³ Ibid., 94A.

⁴ Ibid., 6A.

⁵ Ibid., 92A; cf. 67. Grigg omitted all reference to the subject in his autobiography *Prejudice and Judgment* (London, 1948).

[6] WO.32/11137, 98A–B.

[7] CAB.66. 54, 168–9.

[8] CAB.65. 43, 126.

[9] Selborne Papers.

[10] *The Parliamentary Debates* (*Hansard*) *House of Lords* (London, 1948), clvi, pp. 1152–82.

[11] *The House Built on Sand*, pp. 283–4. British Intelligence, which since 1942 had been engaged in a programme of subversion amongst Germany's foreign workers ('Operation Trojan Horse'), estimated on the eve of D-Day that there were 1,500,000 Russian workers and 700,000 PW and civilian internees: 'All over Germany. Employed especially in agriculture and armament industry'. Evidence was cited of the Nazis' fear of an uprising or general subversion (FO.898/340). For further evidence of this, cf. Hans Bernd Gisevius, *To the Bitter End* (London, 1948), p. 516. The German Resistance remained astonished that the slave labourers did not rise up until after the collapse. (ibid., p. 400).

[12] FO.371/43382, pp. 104–5.

[13] Ibid., 64–7. It has occasionally been suggested that Russians surrendered in response to Allied leaflets promising immunity from return to the USSR. However, the American document cited in support of this allegation by Professor Epstein (*Operation Keelhaul*, pp. 28–9; cf. *The Ukrainian Quarterly*, x, p. 360; Alan Brownfeld, 'Operation Keelhaul', *Human Events* (1971), p. 765; John Barrett, 'Operation Keelhaul': An Unknown Allied War Crime', *East–West Digest* (1972), viii, p. 195) is clearly addressed to *German* soldiers. In fact, US propaganda on occasion naïvely promised return to Russia as an *inducement* to surrender! Dr. Erhard Kroeger has described to me the amusement of General Vlasov on learning that the Americans had in this way prolonged the resistance of the Russian defenders of Brest (cf. also Wilfried Strik-Strikfeldt, *Against Stalin and Hitler* (London, 1970), pp. 200–1). The British had abandoned any idea of proffering amnesty at an early stage (FO.371/43382,51; cf. 32–49). Leaflets dropped over France in 1944 were printed in Russian and Armenian. They appealed to 'non-German soldiers in the Wehrmacht' to surrender, and the leaflet itself contained a safe-conduct to be honoured by the Allied troops. The only reference to the terms of such a surrender was an instruction to the captor forces that: 'Any soldier displaying this pass . . . should be treated according to International Law.' (FO.818/456); Armenian troops had been reported in the Lozère on 7 March 1944 (FO.371/43382,26). Copies of this leaflet were found on Russians brought to Britain, who complained that more had not been promised (ibid., 81). SOE had issued other leaflets (ibid., 105), and Mr. Manderstam tells me that some of these *did* offer asylum. One of these leaflets is preserved in FO.371/56715, and assures deserting Russians that the Anglo-Americans 'guarantee everyone a free and independent life.' 900 ROA men at Namur gave themselves up on the strength of this promise.

[14] Ibid., 80. An appeal to Eden (18 August) presumably met with no better response (Selborne Papers).

[15] H. A. R. Philby, *My Silent War* (London, 1968), p. 8.

[16] Cf. however, Churchill's comment on Soviet tactics, quoted in James F. Byrnes, *All in One Lifetime* (London, 1960), p. 383; also the quotation from Gogol on p. 386.

[17] FO.371/43382, 138–42. Mr. L. H. Manderstam has kindly supplemented these reports with his own memories.

[18] CAB.66.54, 7.

[19] WO.32/11137, 115

[20] Ibid., 109A.

[21] Ibid., 111A.
[22] Ibid., 110, 111, 113A.
[23] Ibid., 114, 116–17.
[24] *The Strange Alliance*, p. 183; CAB.66/60, 203.
[25] *The Strange Alliance*, pp. 183–4.
[26] WO.32/11137, 136A.
[27] Ibid., 137A.
[28] Ibid., 138–40.
[29] Ibid., 149A, 152–3, 160A, 163A, 165A, 174A.
[30] Ibid., 170A.
[31] Ibid., 181A.
[32] Ibid., 187A.
[33] Ibid., 183A.
[34] Ibid., 189A.
[35] The Earl of Avon, *The Eden Memoirs: The Reckoning* (London, 1965), pp. 479–81.
[36] WO.32/11137, 192A, 193A, 194A, 195, 196, 198A.
[37] PREM.3.364/8, 276–7. Cf. WO.32/11137, 198A.
[38] W. S. Churchill, *The Second World War* (London, 1954), vi, pp. 186–203; Sir Llewellyn Woodward, *British Foreign Policy in the Second World War* (London, 1962), pp. 307–8.
[39] The Earl of Avon, *The Eden Memoirs: Facing the Dictators* (London, 1962), p. 153. Eden's visit to Moscow occurred at the height of the Kirov purge.
[40] PREM.3.364/8, 269. Cf. *The Reckoning*, pp. 483–5.
[41] PREM.3.364/8, 270.
[42] WO.32/11137, 225A.
[43] PREM.3.364/8, 266–7; Attlee, as Deputy Prime Minister, was informed on 13 October (268); WO.32/11137, 226A.
[44] Ibid., 203C.
[45] Ibid., 204.
[46] PREM.3.434/4, 34–5, 63. Cf. ibid., 434/7, 47; WO.32/11137, 203D.
[47] WO.32/11137, 219A, 220A.
[48] PREM.3.434/2 (17 October).
[49] WO.32/11137, 222A.

CHAPTER FOUR

[1] *The Times*, 7/3/31. Churchill made a similar speech at Chingford soon afterwards (ibid. 23/4/31).
[2] *Forced Labor in Soviet Russia*, pp. 54, 84–7.
[3] PREM.3/51/1; 61–2. However, in the Far East it was an English ship, renamed the *Nikolai Yezhov*, which transported slave-workers to the Kolyma goldfields (*It happens in Russia*, p. 172).
[4] *Foreign Relations of the United States, Diplomatic Papers 1944* (Washington, 1966), iv, pp. 1241–4; *The Papers of Dwight David Eisenhower*, iii, p. 2031.
[5] CAB.88/30; 451.
[6] WO.32/11137; 19A, 51A.
[7] Ibid., 75B.
[8] Ibid., 58A; *Foreign Relations of the United States, 1944*, iv, p. 1244.
[9] Ibid., pp. 1245–6; *The Strange Alliance*, p. 185.

10 WO.32/11137,77A; *Foreign Relations of the United States, 1944*, iv, pp. 1245, 1246–7.

11 Ibid., pp. 1251–3, 1255, 1263; WO.32/11119, 268A. The British received identical complaints at the same time (WO.32/11137, 162A; WO.32/11119, 26B).

12 *Foreign Relations of the United States, 1944*, iv, pp. 1247–9.

13 For Kirk's high moral character and understanding of Soviet affairs, cf. Charles E. Bohlen, *Witness to History* (London, 1973), pp. 56–66.

14 *Foreign Relations of the United States, 1944*, iv, p. 1250; WO.32/11137, 164A–C, 166A. The American representative in the Mediterranean frequently learned of Allied policy from his British counterpart in this way (cf. Robert Murphy, *Diplomat Among Warriors* (London, 1964), p. 207).

15 WO.32/11137, 156B, 213A, 214A, 234A, 240A.

16 *Foreign Relations of the United States, 1944*, iv, pp. 1253–4.

17 WO.32/11137, 168A.

18 *Foreign Relations of the United States, 1944*, iv, pp. 1257–9.

19 Ibid., p. 1261.

20 Ibid., pp. 1267–70.

21 *Foreign Relations of the United States, 1944*, iv, pp. 1259–60.

22 CAB. 88/30, 451. The Mission had arrived from Britain in the previous month (WO.32/11119, 41A).

23 Ibid., 256A.

24 CAB.88/30, 449–50.

25 *Foreign Relations of the United States, 1944*, iv, pp. 1252–3.

26 Ibid., p. 1262.

27 Letter to the author, dated 20/5/74. Cf. *Witness to History*, p. 199.

28 WO.32/11137, 302A.

29 *Foreign Relations of the United States, 1944*, iv, p. 1264.

30 Ibid., pp. 1265–7; *The Strange Alliance*, p. 188.

31 Molotov's complaint was a repetition of the one made by the Soviet Ambassador to Stettinius on 2 November (*Foreign Relations of the United States, 1944*, iv, p. 1261). For good measure, the British received a stern dressing-down four days later (WO.32/11119, 138C).

32 *Foreign Relations of the United States, 1944*, iv, pp. 1270–1, 1272.

33 Ibid., pp. 1267–70. For the Soviet list of camps in which the prisoners had been held hitherto, *v.* p. 1260. On 2 November Admiral Leahy (President Roosevelt's Chief of Staff) had urged concurrence with British policy (p. 1262).

34 Ibid., pp. 1272–3.

35 *Foreign Relations of the United States: Diplomatic Papers 1945*, v, *Europe* (Washington, 1967), p. 1068. Cf. *The Last Secret*, p. 27.

36 Scholmer, *Vorkuta*, p. 172.

37 FO.371/43382, 136–7.

38 This account was kindly supplied to me by Colonel Frankau. For the voyage of the 2,000 Russians on board the *Franconia*, cf. CAB.88–30, 458; FO.371/47895.

39 *The Strange Alliance*, p. 184; *Foreign Relations of the United States, 1944*, iv, p. 1251.

40 Ibid., pp. 1270, 1272; *The Strange Alliance*, p. 188.

41 Ibid., pp. 188–9; WO.32/11681, 1A; *Foreign Relations of the United States, Diplomatic Papers: The Conferences at Malta and Yalta 1945* (Washington, 1955), pp. 416–8.

42 WO.32/11137, 322A, 327A.

43 Ibid., 380A–382A; WO.32/11681, 8A, 13, 21A.

44 CAB. 66/61, 111–2; CAB.65/49, 55.

45 WO.32/11681, 6A, 20A.

46 *Witness to History*, p. 166.

47 *The Conferences at Malta and Yalta*, p. 416.

48 Ibid., p. 418; Edward R. Stettinius, Jun., *Roosevelt and the Russians: The Yalta Conference* (London, 1950), pp. 37, 41.

49 PREM.3.51/6.

50 WO.32/11681, 168B. This is a copy of the document whose apparently continued classification by the US authorities is regretted by Professor Epstein (*Operation Keelhaul*, p. 44).

51 *Foreign Relations of the United States, 1945*, v, pp. 1067–72.

52 *The Strange Alliance*, pp. 191–2.

53 PREM.3.364/9, 435; *Roosevelt and the Russians*, p. 68; *The Reckoning*, pp. 510–11.

54 WO.32/11681, 52A.

55 PREM.3.51/3, 7, 27–31.

56 WO.32/11137, 252A; CAB.88–30, 460–2. The British held 18,496 (WO.32/11119, 218A).

57 *The Conferences at Malta and Yalta*, pp. 691–3.

58 Ibid., pp. 693–6.

59 Ibid., pp. 697, 756–7.

60 Ibid., pp. 754–6; CAB.88–30, 463. The draft text was discussed with a Soviet representative the next day. Only minor alterations were suggested (*The Conferences at Malta and Yalta*, pp. 863–6).

61 PREM.3.51, 9; PREM.3.364/9, 390, 392–5.

62 CAB.66/63, 109–10, 115. Nevertheless the *Daily Telegraph* was able to publish a full résumé and extracts from the text two days later (13/2/45).

63 Piers Dixon, *Double Diploma: The Life of Sir Pierson Dixon, Don and Diplomat* (London, 1968), pp. 146–7.

64 CAB.65/49, 76.

65 Robert Conquest, *The Nation Killers: The Soviet Deportation of Nationalities* (London, 1970), pp. 105–7.

66 G. A. Tokaev, *Comrade X* (London, 1956), p. 257.

67 H. R. Trevor-Roper (ed.), *Hitler's Table Talk 1941–1944* (London, 1953), pp. 548, 599; *The House Built on Sand*, pp. 185–6.

68 Ibid., p. 86.

69 FO.371/47900.

70 WO.32/11681, 99A.

71 *Witness to History*, p. 199.

72 W. Averell Harriman and Elie Abel, *Special Envoy to Churchill and Stalin* (New York, 1975), pp. 416–17.

73 Roosevelt's illness or vanity had led to both President and State Department arriving very ill-prepared at the conference (James F. Byrnes, *Speaking Frankly* (New York, 1947), p. 23. Cf. Eisenhower's remarks, *Crusade in Europe* (New York, 1948), p. 439).

74 *Foreign Relations of the United States, 1945*, v, pp. 1067–72, 1075–7. For some reason this essential volume was inaccessible to Professor Epstein (cf. *Operation Keelhaul*, pp. 41–6). The fact that it is now available has rendered many of his speculations unnecessary.

75 *Foreign Relations of the United States, 1945*, v, pp. 1083–4. Generals Eisenhower and McNarney were sent a full summary of this letter on 29 March (WO.204/897, 145A).

[76] *Foreign Relations of the United States, 1945*, v, pp. 1093-4. On the same day the Department of State issued a spirited defence of its policy towards Russian prisoners (WO.32/11119, 297A); this was in response to a Soviet broadcast of 30 April (ibid., 284A).

[77] FO.371/47899, 89.

[78] *Polemic* (Sept.-Oct. 1946), v, pp. 48-9.

[79] For British proposals, see WO.32/11681, 190A (9A-17A); WO.32/11139, 335A.

[80] *Foreign Relations of the United States, 1945*, v, p. 1092.

CHAPTER FIVE

[1] WO.32/11137, 51A, 182A.

[2] Ibid., 144A. Cf. WO.32/11119, 32A.

[3] The cynical implication of the proposed change in status was exemplified by General Vasiliev's confession that he wished the prisoners to remain within wired camps: it was just that they should not actually be called prisoners (ibid., 62A).

[4] *Foreign Relations of the United States, 1944*, iv, pp. 1254-5; cf. p. 1261.

[5] WO.11137, 128A, 129A, 145A, 147A; WO.32/11647, 1C.

[6] Ibid., 207A.

[7] Ibid., 215A; WO.32/11119, 62A.

[8] WO.32/11137, 179A.

[9] Ibid., 194A; PREM.3.364/8, 270.

[10] Professor Trevor-Roper advances these as the two considerations providing the British 'claim of necessity' (*The Last Secret*, p. xii).

[11] WO.32/11137, 225A.

[12] Ibid., 220A; PREM.3.434/4, 34-5, 63.

[13] PREM.3.364/8, 250-6.

[14] Cf. *Joseph Stalin: Man and Legend*, p. 270.

[15] WO.32/11137, 119A, 120A, 162A, 185A, 188A, 217A.

[16] Ibid., 301A. Soviet reports had earlier stated that 'terrorist methods are being used to recruit Soviet citizens for Foreign Legion' (*Foreign Relations of the United States, 1944*, iv, pp. 1263-4).

[17] 'Voinov', *Outlaw*, p. 241; FO.371/56719. In January 1946 the NKVD feared that the West was about to send a Russian émigré army to invade the USSR (*Outlaw*, p. 241).

[18] *Foreign Relations of the United States, 1944*, iv, pp. 1251-2.

[19] WO.32/11137, 263A.

[20] WO.32/11119, 105A-B. On 28/1/46 Brimelow expressed the same view (FO.371/57835).

[21] WO.32/11137, 379A.

[22] Ibid., 298A.

[23] Ibid., 303A, 310A, 311A. Eden had, however, carelessly used such a phrase to Molotov on 16 October 1944 (PREM. 3. 434, 34).

[24] WO.32/11137, 312A; cf. 313A. For Home Office comments on this suggestion, v. 320A.

[25] FO.371/37010.

[26] WO.32/11137, 321A, 322A.

[27] Ibid., 383A.

[28] WO.32/11681, 9A; cf. 11A; WO.32/11137, 327A.

[29] Ibid., 390A (text of the Agreement).

30 WO.32/11681, 144A; cf. FO.371/47895.

31 WO.32/11647, 11A; FO. 371/47897.

32 WO.32/11647, 10A, 11A.

33 Cf. CAB. 88/30, 452; WO.32/11137, 257A.

34 Ibid., 327A.

35 WO.32/11683, 107A.

36 'Civilian deserter': a curious concept perhaps unconsciously illustrative of the Foreign Office view of a political refugee.

37 FO.371/47908, 253–9; cf. FO.371/47907. Faschenko was born on 15/5/28 (WO.32/11119, 99D). Cf. ibid., 177A; FO.371/56711.

38 FO.371/47909, 191–4; cf. FO.371/47910. Krokhin himself surrendered later in the year under slightly odd circumstances, which suggested to the Foreign Office that he might have been a Soviet 'plant'. (FO.371/47910,222).

CHAPTER SIX

1 A photograph of such a group, with a naïve commentary, appeared in a British pro-Stalinist publication appropriately named *The Leader* (14/4/45, p. 6). Such press notice was rare.

2 FO.371/43382, 59.

3 Ibid., 80–1.

4 Ibid., 75.

5 Ibid., 79.

6 WO.32/11119, 14B–D, 17B.

7 Ibid., 13A; cf. 12A.

8 Ibid., 10A, 17A–B, 18A; WO.32/11137, 103A–105A.

9 Ibid., 107A.

10 WO.32/11119, 26A–B, 29A.

11 As will be shown, Soldatenkov was a renegade in Soviet pay, and was no doubt in this instance acting as a 'plant'.

12 *Великое Предательство*, ii, pp. 227–9; WO.32/11119, 42A–B; FO.371/56714. Geoffrey Wilson of the FO was impressed by the 'conspiracy' (WO.32/11119, 26A). In justification of the fears of the FO and the Soviet Embassy, it may be admitted that a vocal and active White Russian group in contact with the prisoners *could* have brought the widespread fears of the prisoners to public knowledge, which might in turn have encouraged mass escapes and protests, and as a likely result have shattered the pretence of the Allied Forces Act.

13 Ibid., 18A, 21A, 22A, 27A, 36B; WO.32/11137, 108A, 114A, 115; accounts by Brigadier Firebrace and Mr. Jesman. A few days later Soviet officers also visited the camp at Kempton Park, this time providing the prisoners with even more fulsome assurances (WO.32/11119, 38A–B).

14 Ibid., 24A, 25A, 39A–B.

15 Ibid., 52D.

16 Ibid., 65A; cf. 19A.

17 PREM.3/364, 277; cf. WO.32/11137, 226A.

18 PREM.3/364, 276.

19 Ibid., 270.

20 WO.32/11141, 11A.

21 Ibid., 21A, 5A.

22 WO.32/11119, 88A; WO.32/11141, 20A; cf. WO.32/11137, 218A.

²³ Lt.-Col. Tamplin, Mr. C. Jesman.

²⁴ C. Jesman.

²⁵ WO.32/11141, 2A.

²⁶ Ibid., 33A–35A, 48A, 49A; WO.32/11119, 96A. A further telegram ordered commandants not to use force on any prisoners refusing to leave camp; instead they would be punished and reported to the Soviet authorities (WO.32/11141, 38A).

²⁷ Ibid., 47B.

²⁸ Ibid., 51A.

²⁹ FO.371/43382, 174.

³⁰ WO.32/11119, 184A–B; FO.371/43382, 185–6. Major Cregeen's account was confirmed by another eyewitness, the U.S. Embassy Secretary John F. Melby (*Foreign Relations of the United States, 1944*, iv, p. 1264). Cf. *The Times*, 11/11/44. The able-bodied men were at once sent off to the North-Western Front, whilst invalids and old people were despatched to labour camps in Siberia (*Великое Предательство*, ii, pp. 231–2).

³¹ WO.32/11119, 145A.

³² PREM.3/364, 255.

³³ Ibid., 250. At the same time Sir Orme Sargent urged the Chiefs of Staff to expedite shipping arrangements for the remainder (WO.32/11137, 280A).

³⁴ Mr. H. Haley, a Russian-speaking naval officer, writes to tell me how he helped a desperate group of these men to obtain playing-cards in a Leeds shop. On their return to Russia the prisoners would have found the gambling mania endemic in the labour camps (H. Becker, *Devil on My Shoulder* (London, 1955), pp. 155–6).

³⁵ Cf. David Caute, *The Fellow-Travellers: A Postscript to the Enlightenment* (London, 1973), pp. 61–2. At Devizes in July 1944 an Intelligence report noted that a large number of PoWs had 'some education, a somewhat smaller group are illiterate' (FO.371/43382, 80).

³⁶ Stalin announced the restoration of epaulettes for Red Army Officers on 6 January 1943.

³⁷ The sources for the preceding account are WO.32/11119, 211A & B, 216A, 219A, 220A; FO.371/50606, 144–5, 214–19; and information kindly supplied by Mr. and Mrs. Backshall.

³⁸ WO.32/11683, 96A.

³⁹ The same scene was described to me by Lt.-Col. Tamplin.

⁴⁰ WO.32/11141, 64A, 71A, 80A, 118A.

⁴¹ Unto Parvilahti, *Beria's Gardens* (London, 1959), p. 57; cf. *Let History Judge*, p. 273; *Empire of Fear*, pp. 65–6; *It happens in Russia*, p. 193.

⁴² *The Gulag Archipelago*, i, p. 444.

⁴³ Cf. 'A. I. Romanov', *Nights are Longest There: Smersh from the Inside* (London, 1972), p. 46.

⁴⁴ *The Times*, 12/3/45. The Moscow correspondent of *The Times* was described by Ronald Matthews of the Socialist *Daily Herald* as an 'uncritical friend of the Soviet Union' (CAB.66/54, 125). On 31 December 1943 *The Times* had published an article exulting over the public hanging of German prisoners at Kharkov. Several passages convey the latent sadism that so often appears to have impelled Western admirers of the Soviet dictatorship (cf. Arthur Koestler, *The Yogi and the Commissar, and other Essays* (London, 1945), p. 152).

⁴⁵ WO.32/11141, 20A.

⁴⁶ To quote Tass (FO.371/43382, 174).

⁴⁷ WO.32/11119, 186A.

[48] WO.32/11141, 113B.

[49] Ibid., 104B.

[50] Letters of 29/4/74 and 24/7/74.

[51] Interview with Mrs. Josef Garlinski, 14/5/74.

[52] Prince Lieven and Mr. Jesman; Denis Hills noted the practice in Odessa in the spring of 1945.

[53] Cf. the account by Ronald Matthews (CAB.66/54, 127).

[54] Elinor Lipper, *Eleven Years in Soviet Prison Camps* (London, 1951), pp. 266–9; Robert Conquest, *The Great Terror* (London, 1968), pp. 353–5. Averell Harriman appears still to accept this tour at its face value (*Special Envoy to Churchill and Stalin* pp. 331–2).

[55] Milovan Djilas, *Conversations with Stalin* (London, 1962), p. 70.

[56] FO.371/409, N.7584.

[57] The sources for this account of the *Almanzora*'s voyage are information kindly supplied to the author by Mr. Jesman, and his contemporary report contained in WO.32/11119, 323C.

[58] WO.32/11137, 141A.

[59] WO.32/11119, 64A, 78A.

[60] Ibid., 112A.

[61] Ibid., 93A–B.

[62] Ibid., 230A, 231A.

[63] Ibid., 240A–B, 241A–F, 265A–D; WO.32/11683, 5B.

[64] FO.371/47897, 5–6.

[65] FO.371/43382, 75.

[66] FO.371/47897, 108–9.

[67] Ratov was wrong: hundreds did escape during the invasion (cf. *Forced Labor in Soviet Russia*, p. 107; Bernhard Roeder, *Katorga: An Aspect of Modern Slavery* (London, 1958), p. 21; *Against Stalin and Hitler*, pp. 26–7). Some joined the Vlasov movement; one is reminded of the Roman slaves who in A.D. 409 fled the city to join the invading army of Alaric (J. B. Bury, *History of the Later Roman Empire* (London 1923), i, p. 177).

[68] FO.371/47897, 111–3.

[69] Information kindly supplied by Mr. E. G. Henson, who was so informed by a British officer of the escort.

[70] WO.32/11119, 323B.

[71] Ibid., 323A.

[72] FO.371/47901, N.7586.

[73] FO.371/47908, 162. He goes on to argue that Eden's promise at the 'Tolstoy' conference and the consistent application so far of forcible repatriation provide respectable legality for the policy.

[74] See, for example, eyewitness accounts by Red Army officers (*I'll Never Go Back*, pp. 60–73; *Comrade X*, pp. 289–94).

[75] FO.371/47944, N.5856.

[76] *Eleven Years in Soviet Prison Camps*, pp. 278–9. A 21-year-old Polish girl contracted syphilis and gonorrhoea after being raped in a Magadan barrack by twenty criminals (pp. 156–7).

[77] FO.371/47901, 44.

[78] Ibid., 48.

[79] *The Dark Side of the Moon* (London, 1946) p. 99; cf. Anita Priess, *Verbannung nach Sibirien* (Manitoba, 1972), pp. 55–6. For photographs of starving children from GULAG camps, see Elma Dangerfield, *Beyond the Urals* (London, 1946).

80 *Verbannung nach Sibirien* p. 61.

81 *Eleven Years in Soviet Prison Camps*, p. 123. It is instructive to compare the very different treatment accorded to convicts' children in pre-Revolutionary times; cf. James Young Simpson, *Side-Lights on Siberia: Some Account of the Great Siberian Railroad, the Prisons and Exile System* (London, 1898), pp. 249–50, 295.

82 Some of his earlier activities in this field are indicated in FO.371/29515, N.4115. In the previous December we find Sabline exceedingly anxious to obtain information about émigré efforts in France to aid the newly-liberated Soviet citizens (FO.371/51130).

83 WO.32/11119, 26B.

84 FO.371/47895, 128–30. M. Sabline and the Russian House were of course long familiar to members of the London White Russian community.

85 FO.371/47910, 222.

86 WO.32/11647; information from Mrs. Child, my uncle the late Mr. Auguste Bergman (Minister at the Estonian Legation), and the Latvian Legation in London. As Brigadier Firebrace pointed out to me, the anticipated fate awaiting an unsuccessful attempt to get on the Disputed List led very many non-Soviet citizens to accept repatriation and trust to their luck.

87 FO.371/47904, 154–9.

88 WO.32/11647, 15A–16A.

89 WO.32/11683, 126A, 146A–B, 147A. An administrative error had delayed the repatriation of this party; they had been declared Soviet citizens in August (ibid., 166).

90 Ibid., 296A, 298A, 299A.

91 File at end of ibid., 12A.

92 After September they were held in camps on the Continent (WO.32/11137, 302A).

93 Batches of children are listed, for example, in WO.32/11119, 27A and WO.32/11141, 26A.

CHAPTER SEVEN

1 The Imperial War Museum possesses a number of photographs of such prisoners (Ref. Nos. N.A.15317–8, 7584, 16230–1, 16437, 19205).

2 Since the 1930s the Cossacks had been eagerly awaiting outside aid (*I'll Never Go Back*, p. 168).

3 *Великое Предательство*, i, pp. 63–4.

4 This is a necessarily very brief summary of the vicissitudes of the *Kazachi Stan*. Abundant documentation may be found in ibid., pp. 19–110, 256–8; *Kontra*, pp. 81–91. I also received useful supplementary information from Mrs. Tatiana Nikolaevna Danilievitch, who joined the Cossacks with her husband at Novogrudok, and accompanied them to Tolmezzo and later Lienz.

5 This similarly brief account is based on those of the Caucasian commander, Sultan Kelich Ghirey (WO.170/4461) and the Ossetian cavalry officer, G. Tuaev (*Великое Предательство*, ii, pp. 96–100). Mr. 'Yashvili' (whose history was related in Chapter I) was with the Georgian Committee in Berlin, when it was evacuated to N. Italy in February 1945. I have also been helped by Mr. Witalis Ugrechelidze, a Georgian who was temporarily in the Paluzzo settlement at this time.

6 So they informed Mr. Patrick Martin-Smith, then in a local SOE unit. For 'Cossack' crimes in the Carnia, cf. *The Sunday Telegraph*, 10/11/74, letter from Mr. Richard Darwall. If it be true that they were part of a deliberate German policy, then

this further exculpates the Cossacks. For they, unlike the Caucasians, had no German commanders. Amongst the Caucasians were men of the same races that committed the abominable crimes occurring at much the same time in southern France. A reliable Cossack source pins the blame firmly on the undisciplined Caucasians (Nikolai Krasnov, *The Hidden Russia* (New York, 1960), p. 10). Any excesses that were committed by Cossacks must be regarded as the more dishonourable in view of the chivalrous behaviour of Marshal Giovanni Messe's Corps in Russia (cf. Peter J. Huxley-Blythe, *The East Came West* (Caldwell, Idaho, 1964), pp. 37–42).

[7] WO.170/4988. Unfortunately War Diaries are not paginated, but the date generally provides a ready reference.

[8] The lesser Georgian princes, like those of early Ireland, received their rank from the number of cattle their sons herded.

[9] WO. 170/4461; WO.170/5022; FO.371/47955. About this time a Georgian girl, describing herself as Secretary of the Georgian Liberation Movement, arrived in Udine and contacted a local SOE unit. She had come to beg the Allies to liberate Georgia from the Soviet yoke, and had *hitchhiked* all the way from Georgia! (information from the late Mr. Edward Renton).

[10] *Великое Предательство*, i, p. 114; ii, p. 21–2.

[11] Ibid., ii, p. 100. These Germans first made a vain attempt to forbid the exodus (p. 171).

[12] *Kontra*, pp. 121–3; *Великое Предательство*, i, p. 258.

[13] Mauthen and Kötschach are two villages facing each other across the Gail, and may for convenience be regarded as one location.

[14] Cf. *Великое Предательство*, i, p. 115. A correspondent of *The Times* was reportedly in the area at this time (ibid., ii, pp. 23, 29–30). Nicholas Bethell thinks the Germans ordered the Cossacks to halt, but were unable to enforce the command (*The Last Secret*, pp. 78–9).

[15] *Великое Предательство*, i, p. 135. For accounts of the terrible journey from Tolmezzo to Lienz, v. ibid., pp. 112–9, 132–5, 258; ii, pp. 21–2; *The East Came West*, pp. 117–21; *Kontra*, pp. 125–33; T. Kubansky, *A Memento for the Free World* (Paterson, N. J., 1960), pp. 39–41.

[16] Cf. *The Hidden Russia*, p. 26.

[17] *Великое Предательство*, ii, pp. 20–8; *The Hidden Russia*, p. 11.

[18] Bethell thinks the meeting was held in the railway station (*The Last Secret*, p. 80); the rendezvous was in fact in the rather more comfortable *Hotel* Bahnhof!

[19] *Великое Предательство*, ii, pp. 28–30; WO.170/4461.

[20] *Великое Предательство*, ii, p. 23. Unfortunately the archives of neither *The Times* nor *The Daily Mail* preserves any record of these interviews; nor are the reporters who could have been present now alive. But the article 'Babel Round Trieste' in *The Times* for 15 May 1945 may have drawn upon this interview.

[21] WO.170/4461. In the Imperial War Museum is a series of photographs of the Cossack settlements around Lienz taken on 9–10 May by a Sgt. Levy (NA.24983–7). There is also a short film taken on 10 May (A924/12).

[22] WO.170/4461.

[23] *Великое Предательство*, i, pp. 139 ,142, 170. A roll had been taken in Gemona seven months previously (8 September 1944) (ibid., ii, pp. 95–6). As Domanov called for a list of officers on 27 May (ibid., pp. 211–2), it appears that his staff possessed no recent figure.

[24] Ibid., p. 101. On 26 May the Buffs held a census of the Caucasians (WO.170/4993), whereas Lt.-Col. Malcolm informs me that none was taken for the Cossacks.

This is borne out by the fact that only on 27 May did the Cossacks themselves draw up an up-to-date list of officers (*Великое Предательство*, i, p. 212).

25 Nicholas Bethell is mistaken in thinking that Musson ordered the Cossacks to proceed to the area west of Lienz (*The Last Secret*, p. 81); their advance parties had already arrived there, as Musson's order of 7 May shows (WO.170/4461).

26 WO.170/4993.

27 Brig. H. N. H. Williamson, *Farewell to the Don* (London, 1970), p. 148; S. A. Malsagoff, *An Island Hell: A Soviet Prison in the Far North* (London, 1926), p. 14; V. Naumenko (ed.), *Сборник мамериалов о Выдаче Казаков в Лиенце и Других Местах в 1945 году.* (Orangeburg, 1956), xiii, p. 10.

28 Information kindly supplied by Prince Azamat Guirey.

29 WO.170/4388; WO.170/4988.

30 WO.170/4389.

31 *Великое Предательство*, i, p. 140.

32 Peter Kenez, *Civil War in South Russia, 1918* (Berkeley, 1971), pp. 271–2. For the recruiting of Russian PoW in Germany, *v.* John Silverlight, *The Victors' Dilemma* (London, 1970), p. 321.

33 For General Krasnov's career in two world wars, cf. *The East Came West*, pp. 45–53; *Civil War in South Russia, 1918*, pp. 46, 140–9, 269–71; *The Victors' Dilemma*, p. 275.

34 WO.170/4396.

35 WO.170/4461; WO.170/4988; *Kontra*, pp. 148–9.

36 *Farewell to the Don*, pp. 68–9, 105–6; cf. pp. 20–1, 107; *Civil War in South Russia, 1918*, pp. 181–3.

37 Sven Steenberg, *Wlassow: Verräter oder Patriot?* (Köln, 1968), p. 128. His views on the role and organisation of the Cossacks appear to have been intelligent (ibid., p. 135), but are unlikely to have borne great weight.

38 It is gratifying to be able to report that this old lady was not handed over during the entrainment on 1 and 2 June, and Major Davies remembers her living in Peggetz some months later.

39 *Великое Предательство*, ii, pp. 48–9; *Kontra*, p. 146.

40 Ibid., p. 144; *Великое Предательство*, i, p. 140.

41 WO.170/4988.

42 *The East Came West*, p. 147; *Великое Предательство*, i, p. 140.

43 *Kontra*, p. 147; *Великое Предательство*, i, p. 140; ii, p. 37.

44 WO.170/4993; WO.170/4241.

45 *ВеликоеПредательство*, i, p. 122. In view of the following day's events, we may regard this version as all too probable. Cf. p. 140. Domanov's belief was that the British action resulted from excesses committed by the Caucasians (*The Hidden Russia*, p. 18; cf. pp. 15–16). The arms were in any case scanty (WO.170/4241—they are listed in WO.170/4988).

46 WO.170/4396. At the same time a comprehensive order was issued to all troops in the Drau Valley to stand on the alert, patrolling to prevent possible escape attempts or resistance to the disarming (ibid.).

47 'There is little doubt that the officers of both forces did all they could to ensure compliance with the disarmament orders issued to them by the British battalions concerned.' (WO.170/4461).

48 *The Hidden Russia*, pp. 18–19.

49 *Великое Предательство*, i, pp. 141, 273–4.

50 Ibid., p. 275; 'in Africa', as Alexander Shparengo speculated (p. 161).

[51] Ibid., pp. 244–50.

[52] Ibid., pp. 179–80.

[53] Ibid., pp. 153–4, 181.

[54] For Krasnov and Domanov's faith in the British, cf. *The Hidden Russia*, pp. 15, 17–18.

[55] *Великое Предательство*, i, pp. 158–9.

[56] Ibid., p. 142.

[57] WO.170/4461. For an interesting analysis of the statistics, cf. *Великое Предательство*, i, pp. 144–5.

[58] Ibid., pp. 150–2; ii, p. 196.

[59] Ibid., i, pp. 149–50.

[60] Ibid., pp. 159–65.

[61] Account kindly supplied by General Sir Geoffrey Musson. For the events of 28 May, cf. *Kontra*, pp. 152–8.

CHAPTER EIGHT

[1] This account, as with much else in this and the previous chapter, is based on information supplied by General Sir Geoffrey Musson, Lt.-Col. Alec Malcolm, and Major W. R. Davies.

[2] *Великое Предательство*, i, pp. 141, 148; ii, pp. 21, 41–2, 299.

[3] *The Last Secret*, p. 104. The charge that the *Kazachi Stan* had fought fiercely in the war is repeated on pp. 89, 134 and 164, and by Professor Trevor-Roper in his introduction (p. xii).

[4] WO.170/4461; cf. the Buffs' War Diary for 13 May (WO.170/4993).

[5] *The East Came West*, pp. 72, 206.

[6] He arrived at Tolmezzo from Berlin on 12 February (*Великое Предательство*, i, p. 99).

[7] Information from Mrs. Tatiana Danilievich. Fortunately she and her husband escaped the handover operations at Lienz.

[8] WO.170/4388; WO.170/4396.

[9] WO.170/5025.

[10] WO.170/4993; WO.170/4461; *Великое Предательство*, i, p. 106.

[11] Ibid., ii, p. 66.

[12] *The Last Secret*, p. 113.

[13] Ibid., p. 104; *The East Came West*, pp. 127, 138–9; *The Hidden Russia*, pp. 40–1. Domanov's ADC and interpreter, Butlerov, thought Domanov had had forebodings of ill, but in the absence of concrete evidence felt that any open speculations on his part would result in large-scale disorders that could only justify British repressive measures (ibid., pp. 17–18).

[14] Information supplied by Lt.-Col. Alec Malcolm.

[15] *Великое Предательство*, i, pp. 166, 178.

[16] Ibid., ii, pp. 278, 300; *The Hidden Russia*, p. 25; *The East Came West*, p. 206. The authors of the latter account mistakenly say the petitions were handed to Lt.-Col. Malcolm; it was of course Lt.-Col. Bryar who received them. The letter to Alexander again reminded him of their common service in the anti-Bolshevik cause (*Великое Предательство*, i, p. 269).

[17] Ibid., p. 176; ii, pp. 67–8.

[18] WO.170/5025.

[19] *Великое Предательство*, i, pp. 191–2, cf. pp. 194–5. It can be imagined that this

incident also fanned the flames of the absurd suspicion that the Cossacks were being betrayed by Domanov. One can only add that, if trusting the British were the mark of a traitor, then equal suspicion must light on General Krasnov, who likewise had faith in their honour (*The Hidden Russia*, p. 15).

[20] *Великое Предательство*, i, p. 166; ii, p. 300.

[21] Kelech Ghirey made a similar reply when requested to give commands to the Caucasians (ibid., i, p. 169).

[22] Ibid., i, p. 178.

[23] Ibid., pp. 167, 270; ii, pp. 278–9, 300–1.

[24] WO.170/5025. Cf. *The Hidden Russia*, pp. 27–9.

[25] BBC broadcast, 29 October 1974 (cf. *Radio Times*, 24/10/74, p. 13); *Великое Предательство*, i, pp. 166, 270. The attempted suicide was an officer named Sutulov, who was taken to the field hospital (ibid., ii, p. 300).

[26] Ibid., i, pp. 167–9.

[27] WO.170/4461; WO.170/5034. An officer is said to have escaped on the journey (*Великое Предательство*, i, pp. 169–70).

[28] Ibid., pp. 167, 269.

[29] Ibid., p. 301; WO.170/4461 (reports of Major Goode of 56 Recce Regt. and Sgt. Charters of the 2nd Lancashire Fusiliers); BBC Broadcast, 29 October 1974.

[30] WO.170/5025.

[31] Letter of 7/11/74; cf. also *The Sunday Express*, 25/8/74. For further accounts of the transfer of the Cossack officers from Lienz to Judenburg, cf. *Kontra*, pp. 181–6; *The East Came West*, pp. 132–42; *The Last Secret*, pp. 110–23; '*The Kensingtons': Princess Louise's Kensington Regiment* (London, 1952), pp. 225–7. For statistics of the officers, cf. *Великое Предательство*, i, pp. 144–6.

[32] Information from General A. Holmston-Smyslovsky, who knew Nikolai Krasnov in Buenos Aires. I am greatly indebted to the late Lt.-Col. Count Stepan Zamoyski for a prolonged loan of his copy of the English edition of Krasnov's memoir.

[33] *Великое Предательство*, i, p. 174; photographs of the bridge and steel-mill at Judenburg are to be found in vol. ii, between pp. 128–9. The murdered officer was named Kraus (*So Gingen die Kosaken durch die Hölle*, p. 54).

[34] *Nights are Longest There*, pp. 153–4; this description tallies even in passing details with Nikolai Krasnov's, providing striking confirmation of the accuracy of the latter's account. Shkuro was, however, awarded the CB, and not the KCMG.

[35] *The First Circle* closes with an ironical commentary on this subject; cf. also *The Gulag Archipelago*, i, p. 528, Such vans were also employed to remove corpses from the Lubianka Gaol. (Peter Deriabin and Frank Gibney, *The Secret World* (London, 1960), p. 138).

[36] *The Hidden Russia*, p. 72; cf. pp. 221–3.

[37] Cf. in particular *Nights are Longest There*, pp. 236–9.

[38] Z. Stypulkowski, *Invitation to Moscow* (London, 1951), pp. 266, 294.

[39] *The Hidden Russia*, p. 135.

[40] Quoted in *Великое Предательство*, ii, pp. 296–7.

[41] *The Hidden Russia*, p. 76; cf. p. 125. A few more details of the generals' stay in Lubianka have been recorded by a fellow-prisoner, a German radio commentator (Erich Kern, *General von Pannwitz und seine Kosaken* (Oldendorf, 1971), p. 196). The Museum display doubtless also includes the group photograph taken at Baden-bei-Wien.

[42] *The Hidden Russia*, pp. 77, 249, 325–26.

43 *Nights are Longest There*, pp. 151, 236, 248. Cf. the author's own fears (p. 240).
44 *Moscow Mission 1946-1949*, p. 115.
45 *All in One Lifetime*, pp. 378-9. The MVD set up the special 'EM' Department to watch the émigrés (*Empire of Fear*, pp. 257, 261-3, 287).
46 *The House Built on Sand*, p. 392.
47 Nikolai Krasnov's interrogators in Lefortovo were desperately anxious to induce him to confess to being 'a saboteur and terrorist' (*The Hidden Russia*, pp. 99-101).

CHAPTER NINE

1 *Великое Предательство*, i, p. 156.
2 Ibid., pp. 181-3.
3 Ibid., i, pp. 183-6. Where possible I have checked Olga Rotova's invaluable account with Major Davies. For Major Davies's denial on the morning of 29 May that he knew the officers would not return, cf. the account by another English-speaking Cossack woman (ibid., p. 123).
4 WO.170/4461.
5 *Великое Предательство*, i, pp. 124, 147, 199; ii, p. 60.
6 *Kontra*, p. 188; *Великое Предательство*, i, p. 124.
7 Ibid., pp. 124-5.
8 Ibid., p. 186; *Kontra*, p. 189.
9 WO.170/4461.
10 *Великое Предательство*, i, pp. 106-7; ii, pp. 171-3.
11 WO.170/4461.
12 Ibid.; WO.170/4993.
13 *I Chose Freedom*, p. 405. Viktor Kravchenko learned of this incident when working for the *Sovnarkom* in Moscow, the authority which controlled such plants.
14 WO.170/4993; WO.170/4461.
15 Cf. *Forced Labor in Soviet Russia*, p. 271.
16 *Великое Предательство*, ii, pp. 74-5. Cf. the touching account of an Astrakhan Cossack's farewell to his camel, in *The East Came West*, pp. 71-2.
17 *Великое Предательство*, i, p. 190.
18 Ibid., p. 259.
19 'Die Kosakische Tragödie', *National Zeitung* (30/5/75), p. 6.
20 WO.170/4461; *Великое Предательство*, i, pp. 225-6.
21 WO.170/4461; *Великое Предательство*, i, p. 229.
22 Ibid., pp. 200-3. Lord Bethell's apparent belief that soldiers were 'trying to push people off the bridge' (*The Last Secret*, p. 143) is incorrect. The Revd Kenneth Tyson tells me that what he saw was men of the Argylls trying 'to prevent them from getting onto the bridge and across it to "freedom".'
23 *Великое Предательство*, i, pp. 227-30.
24 Ibid., p. 209. Dr. Pinching does not recall this brief exchange, but thinks it consistent with his state of mind at the time. He himself saw the battalion's tough 2 i/c, Major Leask, weeping.
25 Ibid., i, pp. 205-6, 228-9; ii, p. 54.
26 WO.170/4461.
27 WO.170/4988.
28 *National Zeitung*, 6/6/75.
29 *Великое Предательство*, ii, pp. 110-2. For the incident with the dog, see also ibid., i, p. 233.

30 Ibid., i, pp. 134, 201, 233; ii, p. 54; *National Zeitung*, 30/5/75.

31 *Великое Предательство*, i, p. 210.

32 Ibid., p. 233. Dr. Pinching recalls a 'four- or five-storey hospital' in Lienz, but cannot confirm or refute the authenticity of this account. On 29 June 'a Medical Officer at NUISDORF Hospital informed the Coy Commander there, that most of the people intended to commit suicide.' (WO.170/5018).

33 Cossack sources, which give the names of the family, list only two children (*Великое Предательство*, i, p. 233; ii, p. 111).

34 Ibid., i, p. 234.

35 Ibid., p. 210.

36 Interviews in *National Zeitung*, 6/6/75, and *Kleine Zeitung* (Klagenfurt, 29/5/75). As the morning's events unfolded, outraged Austrians are said to have rung the church bells at Dölsach and elsewhere (*Великое Предательство*, i, p. 221). For further accounts of suicides, see *So Gingen die Kosaken durch die Hölle*, pp. 19–20, 26.

37 Cf. A. Petrovsky, *Unvergessener Verrat!* (Munich, 1965), p. 287.

38 WO.170/4396.

39 Bethell has unwittingly conflated the two episodes (*The Last Secret*, p. 132).

40 'At OBER DRAUBURG are the corpses of eight COSSACKS shot whilst trying to escape.' (WO.170/4389).

41 Cossack accounts allege the presence of armoured cars ('Tanketki') at Peggetz (*Великое Предательство*, i, p. 228). In fact, they were not, but at Oberdrauburg a squadron from 56 Recce Regiment assisted the West Kents (WO.170/4396). Again the two warning volleys did not take place at Peggetz (as alleged in *Великое Предательство*, i, pp. 200, 225) but at Oberdrauburg.

42 The account of operations near Oberdrauburg is taken from the War Diaries: WO.170/5022; WO.170/5018; WO.170/4461.

43 *Великое Предательство*, i, pp. 206–8.

44 Information from Major J. W. French, then 2 i/c of the battalion. 60 Cossack grooms were withheld to care for horses used in British Army point-to-points that summer (*Великое Предательство*, ii, pp. 81–5. For the history of these horses and of the beautiful mare Katinka, cf. Lt.-Col. A. D. Malcolm, *History of the Argyll and Sutherland 8th Battalion 1939–47* (London, 1949), pp. 252–8; Lt.-Col. G. I. Malcolm of Poltalloch, *Argyllshire Highlanders 1860–1960* (Glasgow, 1960), pp. 116–7).

45 Cf. *Великое Предательство*, pp. 55–6.

46 WO.170/4461. Elsewhere in the same file the much higher estimate of 'some 4,100' is given.

47 *Великое Предательство*, i, p. 191.

48 WO.170/4396; WO.170/4461.

49 For a vivid account of the hazards of one such successful crossing, *vide Великое Предательство*, i, pp. 201–3. Nikolai Krasnov's wife Lily stayed hidden in the mountains, returning to Peggetz when she learned of the amnesty belatedly extended to old émigrés. Her husband learned of this years later from a Cossack in the Kamyshlag forced labour camp complex near Omsk (*The Hidden Russia*, pp. 221, 332). And Mrs. Tatiana Danilievitch has described to me how she lay concealed in a Lienz cellar throughout the critical time.

50 WO.170/4396.

51 WO.170/4461; cf. *The Last Secret*, pp. 151–6.

52 WO.170/4461; information from Mr. Duncan Macmillan, officer i/c the convoy.

53 I am indebted to Mr. Reg Gray for a vivid account of his experiences; also for the genial hospitality dispensed at his excellent inn (The Ship, at Handbridge, Chester). Cf. *Cheshire Observer*, 2/11/73.

CHAPTER TEN

[1] *General von Pannwitz und seine Kosaken*, p. 161; *Unvergessener Verrat!*, pp. 145–6, 243–4.

[2] Ibid., p. 137; *General von Pannwitz und seine Kosaken*, pp. 20–1. Bethell is wrong in supposing von Pannwitz to have been 'a Russian-speaking Balt' (*The Last Secret*, p. 77).

[3] *The House Built on Sand*, pp. 343–7.

[4] *General von Pannwitz und seine Kosaken*, pp. 126–8. For the history of the Cossack Corps, cf. also Col. C. Wagner, 'Zur Geschichte des XV. Kosaken-Kavallerie-Korps', *Deutsches Soldatenjahrbach 1972* (München, 1972), pp. 117–27.

[5] *General von Pannitz und seine Kosaken*, pp. 159–61.

[6] Cf. *Великое Предательство*, ii, p. 320.

[7] Information kindly supplied by Col. Sir Andrew Horsbrugh-Porter, Bart.

[8] *The King's Royal Rifle Corps Chronicle, 1945* (Winchester, 1946), p. 55; WO.170/5026. Photographs of the disarmament are in the Imperial War Museum collection, 25020–2; and film A 927/2.

[9] Imperial War Museum photo 25019.

[10] Information from Mr. Garry Maufe.

[11] For the disposition of the surrendered 15th Cavalry Corps, *v.* WO.170/4184; *Великое Предательство*, ii, pp. 172–3, 321; *Unvergessener Verrat!*, pp. 147, 225.

[12] Communication to the author from Brigadier Hills. The account of Hills' antecedents in *The East Came West*, p. 97, is inaccurate, and appears to be based on a confusion of identities.

[13] Information from Mr. Jeremy Pemberton. Colonel von Renteln was handed over to the NKVD at Judenburg on 28 May. For a while he was held in a camp at Stalinsk, south of Novosibirsk, and is said to have died in prison later on (*Великое Предательство*, ii, p. 325). Field-Marshal Alexander subsequently maintained that his status as envoy had not been infringed, as he had not been granted a safe-conduct (*Wlassow: Verräter oder Patriot?*, p. 229).

[14] Information from the late Mr. Edward Renton.

[15] Information from Major Arthur Radley. Major Radley was a liaison officer at 8 Army HQ, and met the officer, Major Himmighoffen, near Klagenfurt.

[16] WO.204/7211; *Великое Предательство*, ii, p. 146.

[17] WO.170/4241.

[18] The transfer took place on 22 May (WO.170/4241; information from Brigadier Clive Usher, who confirms the reason for the transfer).

[19] WO.170/4352.

[20] WO.170/7211.

[21] WO.170/4352.

[22] Ibid.; WO.170/4241.

[23] *Великое Предательство*, ii, pp. 137–8, 141, 321.

[24] Ibid., pp. 137, 145.

[25] WO.170/4241. Several German officers escaped at this time. For a 'Wanted' notice issued by 46 Division, cf. WO.170/4353.

[26] Cf. *The Hidden Russia*, pp. 34, 55; *General von Pannwitz und seine Kosaken*, pp. 195–6. The Cossack account of von Pannwitz's moves after his arrival at Judenburg (*Великое Предательство*, ii, pp. 138–42) appears to be entirely mythical.

[27] WO.170/4352.

²⁸ Information supplied by Mr. M. A. C. Frewer.
²⁹ *Wlassow: Verräter oder Patriot?*, p. 217; information from Colonel Constantin Wagner. The latter categorises Cherkassov's biography of Kononov as an unreliable hagiography.
³⁰ WO.204/7211.
³¹ For first-hand Cossack accounts of this episode, cf. *Unvergessener Verrat!*, pp. 102–4, 267–73; *Великое Предательство*, ii, pp. 175–7.
³² Information supplied by Lt.-Col. Denys Worrall; cf. also WO.170/5000; Laurence E. Stringer, *The History of the 16th Battalion the Durham Light Infantry 1940-1946* (Graz, n.d.), pp. 63–4.
³³ *Unvergessener Verrat!*, p. 103. A breakdown of the total statistics is provided in WO.170/4353. Over 7,000 horses were returned at the same time. For a period at least after their surrender to the Soviets, these horses remained under the care of Cossack grooms. Major-General Sir John Winterton recalls seing columns of horses being led by Cossacks inside the Soviet Zone at that time.
³⁴ Information supplied by Major-General K. C. Cooper.
³⁵ *Katorga*, p. 47. It is just possible that we are dealing here with the party referred to on p. 163 (*infra*).
³⁶ Information from General Sir Horatius Murray and Lt.-Col. Robin Rose Price; WO.170/4337; WO.170/4982; WO.170/5026.
³⁷ Information from Brigadier Clive Usher, Brigadier James Hills and Colonel Constantin Wagner.
³⁸ Communication from Brigadier Hills.
³⁹ Information from Mr. Garry Maufe.
⁴⁰ WO.170/4631; cf. WO.170/4832.
⁴¹ The incident in the cage at Weitensfeld is based on the printed memoirs of the Cossack officers V. Ostrovsky, A. Sukalo (*Великое Предательство*, ii, pp. 143–71) and A. Protopopov (*Unvergessener Verrat!*, pp. 73–8); and on eye-witness accounts provided by Major George Druzhakin, Brigadier Clive Usher, Brigadier James Hills, Lt.-Col. Robin Rose Price, Lt.-Col. Henry Howard and the Revd T. M. H. Richards. Cf. also WO.170/5026. The Imperial War Museum possesses a film of the Welsh Guards parading at Klagenfurt on 21 May (A933/2).
⁴² Information from Revd T. M. H. Richards, who tells me that numerous photographs were taken at the time. Unfortunately these appear to have been dispersed or destroyed. The Regimental Adjutant of the Welsh Guards, Major D. R. P. Lewis, informs me that none is preserved in Regimental records.
⁴³ WO.170/4629; information from Colonel Sir Andrew Horsbrugh-Porter.
⁴⁴ *Великое Предательство*, ii, p. 152.
⁴⁵ Information from General Sir Horatius Murray, Brigadier Clive Usher, Brigadier James Hills and Lt.-Col. Henry Howard.

CHAPTER ELEVEN

¹ WO.32/11119, 230A.
² BM.3928/PW1, 298A.
³ WO.32/11119, 27A.
⁴ Ibid., 103A.
⁵ WO.32/11137, 6A.
⁶ Ibid., 51A.
⁷ FO.371/43382, 69; cf.FO.371/47903, 240.

8 WO.32/11119, 153A.

9 WO.204/2877.

10 FO.371/47895; FO.371/47896; FO.371/47901; FO.371/47902.

11 *Unvergessener Verrat!*, p. 104; *The East Came West*, p. 206.

12 *Великое Предательство*, ii, pp. 242, 246.

13 *Nights Are Longest There*, p. 154.

14 *Parliamentary Debates (Hansard) House of Lords Official Report* (London, 1976), ccclxix, col. 314. However, Lord Hankey was not with the Northern Department in 1945, and the evidence suggests that the Foreign Office played no direct part in the extradition of the old émigrés.

15 *The Last Secret*, p. 104.

16 *Kontra*, p. 185; Vasil Ivanic, *Стежками Життя* (New Ulm, Minnesota, 1962) pp. 294–5. Cf. the statistics provided in *Великое Предательство*, i, pp. 143–7, 270–1.

17 Ibid., ii, p. 103.

18 Ibid., p. 104.

19 Information from Major W. R. Davies. Cf. *Великое Предательство*, i, pp. 231, 261.

20 WO.170/4461. The fact that many of the Georgian officers came from Paris was also recorded.

21 Information from Major-General P. B. Gillett, Secretary to the Central Chancery of the Orders of Knighthood.

22 Cf. Robert Jackson, *At War with the Bolsheviks: The Allied Intervention into Russia 1917–1920* (London, 1972), p. 180; *The Victors' Dilemma*, p. 277.

23 Theoretically he commanded the training unit of the 15th Cossack Cavalry Corps, though in fact the effective commander at Döllersheim was a Lt.-Col. Stabenow (information from Col. Wagner). Shkuro held, as described earlier in this book, a roving commission. On 2 May 1945 he was not with his unit: the Ukrainian General Shandruk met him at Völkermarkt, quite drunk (Lt. Gen. Pavlo Shandruk, *Arms of Valor* (New York, 1959), p. 273).

24 WO.170/4241. The 'Ataman Group' refers in all probability not to Domanov and his staff (elsewhere referred to as 'HQ Cossack Army' (WO.170/4988)), but to a special parachute-saboteur unit known as as 'Ataman Group'. (*Великое Предательство*, i, p. 145). For General Shkuro's 'reserve units', cf. *General von Pannwitz und seine Kosaken*, p. 161; *Kontra*,p. 147.

25 *The Last Secret*, p. 98; cf. p. 117.

26 WO.170/4241.

27 WO.170/4388.

28 Information from Lt.-Col. Alec Malcolm.

29 Cf. Cyril Ray, *Algiers to Austria: A History of 78 Division in the Second World War* (London, 1952).

30 WO.170/4183, 460, 487.

31 For a Russian's account of such an operation at Ancona in mid-May 1945, see *Великое Предательство*, ii, p. 202; cf. pp. 220–1.

32 *Arms of Valor*, pp. 254–86.

33 For the history of the Ukrainian Division, cf. *The Patriotic Traitors*, pp. 327–9, 332. I have drawn also on a detailed account provided for me by a former soldier of the Division, Mr. Mykola Wolynskyj. For the Potsdam Conference and subsequent history of the Division until its release, cf. WO. 204/440; FO.371/9804; FO.371/47903; BM.3928/PW1; FO.371/57880.

34 The body of General Wrangel, at his dying behest, 'was buried in the little

Russian church at Belgrade, which he regarded as the last refuge of the White movement'. (*The Victors' Dilemma*, p. 359).

35 The history of the conduct of the *Schutzkorps* in World War II is recounted in D. P. Vertepov, *Русский Корпус на Балканах во Время II Великой Войны*; cf. also *Wen Sie Verderben Wollen*, pp. 251–2; George Fischer, *Soviet Opposition to Stalin* (Harvard, 1952), p. 97; *Kontra*, p. 160; *It happens in Russia*, pp. 412–6, 427–8. On 13 May 5 Corps held 'White Russians 4,433' (WO.170/4243), and it seems likely that this is a reference to the Corps, since there appear to have been no other screened bodies of White émigrés at that date in Austria. In August, however, a report states that there were only 2,700 at Klein St. Veit (FO.371/47903, 184); many may well have made off in the interval. Cf. ibid., 185. The latter moments of the Corps before surrender are described by Ara Deljanic (*Wolfsberg 375* (San Francisco, 1975)). Cf. FO.371/5789 5–6, FO.371/56711.

36 *Великое Предательство*, ii, 160. At Potsdam the Soviets handed the British a complaint that Rogozhin was heading an anti-Soviet force around Klagenfurt (FO.934/5(42), 92).

37 *It happens in Russia*, pp. 400–2.

38 *Великое Предательство*, i, pp. 250, 253, ii, pp. 157, 159, 160, 204, 338; *Kontra*, p. 166. The arbitrary nature of the classification is revealed by the case of Major Ostrovsky, He, in the 15th Cavalry Corps, was held to be liable for extradition, whilst his brother in the *Schutzkorps* was not! (*Великое Предательство*, ii, p. 160).

39 *Arms of Valor*, p. 291; *Foreign Relations of the United States: The Conference of Berlin*, i, p. 797. On 22 May the Vatican had issued a similar protest on behalf of other exiles (ibid.).

40 Information from Mr. Oleg Kravchenko. Despite extensive enquiries at the headquarters of the British Red Cross and elsewhere (I am greatly indebted for considerable assistance to the Archivist, Mrs. J. Fawcett), I have failed satisfactorily to identify this gallant officer. The account of 'Colonel Hills' in *The East Came West*, p. 97, seems to have confused the real Col. Hills (who never served in Russia) with the saviour of the *Schutzkorps*. Both officers were operating in the same district, but Brigadier Hills today has no recollection of the other. There do, however, seem to be strong reasons for inferring that the saviour of the *Schutzkorps* was the late Sir John Selby-Bigge. This is the opinion of Lady Falmouth (former Deputy Chairman of the British Red Cross Society), as she tells me; there is also the fact that on two occasions at least he is known to have confronted Gen. Keightley over similar incidents.

41 Information from Mr. Bruce Marshall.

42 This reconstruction of the events of 28 and 29 May is based on discussions with Brigadier Usher, Lt.-Cols. Howard and Rose Price, and Major Druzhakin; also WO.170/4982 and WO.170/5026.

43 Brigadier G. L. Verney had assumed that the first Cossack general he met on entering Austria must necessarily be a war criminal. Despite this, he joined the rest at Brigadier Usher's conference in opposing the transport of prisoners to what might well be death without trial (Typescript memoir of Major General G. L. Verney, DSO, MVO, p. 142, kindly loaned to me by his son, Major Peter Verney).

44 WO.170/4396.

45 WO.170/4988.

46 They were then out of Brigadier Musson's control, it should be noted.

47 WO.170/4461.

48 *The Hidden Russia*, p. 332; *Великое Предательство*, i, pp. 238–40.

49 Ibid., ii, pp. 56–7.

[50] Information from Major-General H. E. N. Bredin and Brigadier C. E. Tryon-Wilson. For the task assigned the London Irish Rifles, *vide* WO.170/5045. Bethell's account (*The Last Secret*, pp. 150–1) is confused; he apparently failed to understand the nature of Col. Bredin's appointment.

[51] WO.170/4461; WO.170/4396; *Великое Предательство*, i, pp. 138, 240–1.

[52] WO.170/4461; *Великое Предательство*, i, p. 208; ii, pp. 35–6.

[53] Extracts from a conversation with General Sir Horatius Murray.Cf. his letter to *The Times*, 7/12/74.

[54] 1,225 were registered as 'grooms' and later spirited away (information from General Murray and Brigadier Usher; the figure is supplied in WO.170/4982). Bethell cites an instance of the disappearance of some 1,700 others (*The Last Secret*, p. 133). Colonel Wagner thinks he had about 10,000 men with him; under 4,000 were sent to Judenburg on 29 and 30 May (WO.170/4982).

[55] For convenience in quotation, I cite the English version (*The Hidden Russia*, pp. 18–19). This, however, unaccountably substitutes the name 'Stone' for that of Major Davies (cf. N. N. Krasnov, *Незабываемое 1945–1956* (San Francisco, 1957), p. 27).

[56] *Великое Предательство*, i, p. 141; cf. pp. 139, 142; *Kontra*, p. 154.

[57] In 1958 Colonel Malcolm recalled the presence of Intelligence Officers from Divisional HQ in Lienz at this time (*The East Came West*, p. 212).

[58] *Великое Предательство*, i, p. 175.

[59] No copy or record of its reception is held at the Royal Library at Windsor (information from the Librarian, Sir Robert Mackworth-Young); in the Library at Lambeth Palace (information from the Librarian, Mr. E. G. W. Bill) or private papers of Archbishop Fisher (information from the Dean of Westminster); nor at the Headquarters of the Comité International de la Croix-Rouge (information from M. P. Vibert, Head of the Documentation Department).

[60] *The Hidden Russia*, p. 32; *Великое Предательство*, ii, p. 279. This account of the Soviet reception of Krasnov and Shkuro is also confirmed by the British officer present (*The Last Secret*, p. 119).

[61] WO.170/4461.

[62] *A Memento for the Free World*, p. 42.

[63] WO.170/4461.

[64] *Civil War in South Russia*, p. 182; *Farewell to the Don*, p. 20; WO.170/4461; *The Hidden Russia*, p. 25; *Великое Предательство*, i, pp. 169 (cf. 168), 172, ii, p. 104.

[65] Ibid., i, p. 169. These arms are to be seen in the photograph of Shkuro in vol. ii, between pp. 128–9.

[66] WO.170/4389. All Cossack and Caucasian officers had been required to surrender their swords on the morning of 27 May (*Великое Предательство*, i, p. 122). These were held separately from the remainder of the officers' kits, and Domanov's sword was ordered to be despatched to the Soviets at Judenburg (WO.170/4388). The British officer who handed it over noticed that the Soviet officer accepting it 'registered much disappointment' that it was a battle sword and not 'ceremonial variety'. (WO.170/5025). A weapon which was not handed over was a beautiful Cossack dagger (*kinjal*), presented to General Krasnov by Tsar Nicholas II. This was offered by Lydia Krasnov after her husband's departure to Major Davies, who politely refused it.

[67] WO.170/4993; *Великое Предательство*, i, p. 180; ii, p. 301; WO. 170/5025. The list was checked at SMERSH Headquarters at Baden-bei-Wien before being sent on to Moscow (*Nights are Longest There*, p. 154).

[68] FO.371/51227. The interview is dated 18/7/45, but Lady Limerick tells me that,

though she remembers the interview with Gen. Keightley, on consulting her diaries she finds she was not in Austria in July. The interview apparently took place in England, in which case perhaps Keightley flew over especially to counter Selby-Bigge's charges.

⁶⁹ He was Assistant Adjutant General of the Adjutant General's Sub Branch and Administrative Services Control Branch in Vienna, and subsequently P/A to prisoners of War and Displaced Person Division of the Allied Commission. (Information from Major P. H. Cordle, Headquarters Grenadier Guards.)

⁷⁰ 'Unconditional Surrender in Austria', *Journal of the Royal United Service Institution* (1954), xcix, p. 265.

⁷¹ WO.170/4241. A newsreel film of a visit paid by Gen. Keightley on 12 May 1945 to a Soviet general at Wolfsberg is held by the Imperial War Museum (A927/3).

⁷² Ministry of Defence file BM.3928, 2A, 31A.

⁷³ Ibid., 18D. Other captured Russians were being delivered to the Soviets in Austria at this time and the Soviets had been assured at the time of the German surrender in Italy that 'Vlasov' forces would be handed over as hitherto. (WO.204/1596.)

⁷⁴ PREM.3/364, 741–2.

⁷⁵ BM.3928, 4A.

⁷⁶ Ibid., 8A, 15A.

⁷⁷ Ibid., 7A, 24A, 26A, 40A; WO.32/11119, 325A, 326A; BM.3928, 37A.

⁷⁸ Ibid., 40B; cf. 18C, 19A.

⁷⁹ WO.170/4241.

⁸⁰ This is Bethell's view (*The Last Secret*, p. 74).

⁸¹ WO.214/4183; WO.214/359.

⁸² WO.170/4183, 487.

⁸³ Nigel Nicholson, *Alex* (London, 1973), pp. 47–66.

⁸⁴ PREM.3/364, 750; *The Second World War*, vi, p. 647. Cf. *The Patriotic Traitors*, p. 365. The War Office was asked the same day to supply the information (BM.3928, 9A–11A).

⁸⁵ PREM.3/364, 748.

⁸⁶ BM.3928, 18A, 22A.

⁸⁷ PREM.3/364, 254.

⁸⁸ CO.730/13; I am greatly indebted to Dr. Martin Gilbert for supplying me with this and the following quotation.

⁸⁹ 15 July 1921 (CO.730/3).

⁹⁰ Cf. Harold Macmillan, *The Blast of War: 1939–1945* (London, 1967), p. 609.

⁹¹ *Tides of Fortune: 1945–1955* (London, 1969), p. 17. The British prisoners were not 'obtained in exchange'; their transfer had been proceeding unimpeded for some weeks (cf. BM.3928, 18C, 19A).

⁹² Cf. WO.32/11137, 62C; 388A. Macmillan can hardly have been referring to Byelorussians, as there was no such grouping amongst the Cossacks.

CHAPTER TWELVE

¹ This account of the end of the ROA is based on Reitlinger, Thorwald, Dallin, Fischer and Steenberg's histories. Leading participants cited in the text enabled me to supplement and correct the published accounts. In addition I gained great help from a 283-page account of the Vlasov movement, drawn up by a very senior German officer, entitled *Die Behandlung des russischen Problems während der Zeit des ns Regimes in*

Deutschland. Professor John Erickson generously supplied me with a photocopy of the original typescript in his possession.

[2] *The Goebbels Diaries*, pp. 330, 347–8. For Vlasov's subsequent meeting with Goebbels, *v. Against Stalin and Hitler*, pp. 109–10.

[3] Ibid., pp. 194–9.

[4] What follows is based largely upon a first-hand account of events related to the author by Dr. Erhard Kroeger. Dr. Kroeger confirms that Reitlinger's statement that the meeting was arranged for 19 July (*The House Built on Sand*, p. 360) is incorrect, and hence his consequent deductions.

[5] *Against Stalin and Hitler*, pp. 196–8.

[6] Ibid., pp. 206–8. *The Times* noted this revolution in Himmler's attitude on 11/10/44.

[7] For a sympathetic account of Vlasov and his entourage at Dahlem, *v. It Happens in Russia*, pp. 435–9.

[8] 'Voinov', *Outlaw*, pp. 230–1.

[9] *The Hidden Russia*, p. 223; *Katorga: An Aspect of Modern Slavery*, p. 156. For accounts of the Prague meeting, cf. *The Patriotic Traitors*, pp. 309, 323–5; *Soviet Opposition to Stalin*, pp. 88–9, 194–200. *The Times* of 15/11/44 contained a brief notice of the Prague assembly. Later, on 8/4/45, *The Observer* published a long and well-researched article on Vlasov and his career.

[10] Armstrong, *Ukrainian Nationalism*, pp. 179–85.

[11] For the KONR and ROA levies, cf. *Soviet Opposition to Stalin*, pp. 94–104. *The Times* gave a report on 16/12/44.

[12] *Wlassow: Verräter oder Patriot?*, pp. 186–7; *The House Built on Sand*, pp. 376–7. Dr. Kroeger interviewed some of the deserters the day after their surrender.

[13] The Foreign Office received an account of this march from an escaped British PoW (FO.371/47955).

[14] I am indebted to Professor Oberländer for the account which follows. He was able to check names and dates from his diary. Both Reitlinger's (*The House Built on Sand*, p. 386) and Steenberg's (*Wlassow: Verräter oder Patriot?*, p. 227) versions of this episode contain inaccuracies now corrected.

[15] *Pravda*, 2/8/46. Epstein asserts that he attempted suicide before being surrendered (*Operation Keelhaul*, p. 72). Cf. *Wlassow: Verräter oder Patriot?*, p. 240.

[16] *The Last Secret*, p. xiv.

[17] *Wlassow: Verräter oder Patriot?*, pp. 194–5.

[18] *Against Stalin and Hitler*, pp. 228–36.

[19] The appeal was broadcast at 6.50 a.m. on 6 May (for details, see Rudolf Ströbinger, 'Wlassow auf der Seite der Tschechen', *Die Welt*, 26/2/74).

[20] This account of Buniachenko's actions in Prague is largely based on the reminiscences of Dr. Kroeger, as well as the written authorities already detailed.

[21] The description of Vlasov's last moves before his capture is based on Steenberg's full account (*Wlassow: Verräter oder Patriot?*, pp. 216–26). This draws on important eyewitness accounts, previously unavailable, and supersedes the earlier narratives of Fischer, Thorwald and Reitlinger.

[22] FO.371/47955.

[23] *Foreign Relations of the United States: Diplomatic Papers, 1945*, v, p. 1099.

[24] *New York Herald Tribune*, 2/6/46.

[25] *Nights Are Longest There*, p. 152.

[26] *Wlassow: Verräter oder Patriot?*, p. 240.

[27] Information from General A. Holmston-Smyslovsky.

²⁸ Though the KGB do not appear to have laid hands on the typescript until September of that year (cf. *Новое Русское Слово*, 7/9/73), it is not unlikely that they had prior knowledge of at least part of its contents. Certainly Solzhenitsyn's 'defence' of Vlasov aroused fury in Soviet official circles (George F. Kennan, 'Between Earth and Hell', the *New York Review* (21/3/74) p. 3).

²⁹ I quote from the summary and extracts issued by Radio Free Europe: 'General Vlasov's Last Hours', Radio Free Europe *Research*, 27/4/73.

³⁰ Cf. *The Road to Stalingrad*, pp. 352-3. Retired Red Army Colonel-General Ivan Korovnikov repeated the Soviet accusation in a letter to *The Times* of 26/2/74. A reply, by the present writer, defending Vlasov's character in general terms, was published on 1 March 1974, also in *The Times*.

³¹ This account flatly contradicts the text of the Soviet announcement of Vlasov's execution in 1946. There it was stated that he and his fellows were charged 'as agents of the German espionage service . . . All the accused admitted their guilt . . .'

CHAPTER THIRTEEN

¹ Cf. *The House Built on Sand*, pp. 305-7, 337, 346-7, 393-4.

² 'Shalva Yashvili' was an inmate of the camp at Taranto at this time, and informs me that many of the prisoners believed Major Gramasov's continual promises that Stalin had extended an amnesty to all returning Russians. For details of the voyage cf. FO.371/47895.

³ SHAEF HQ had for some time been pressing for repatriation along this route (CAB.88/30, 457, 460). For the camp at Marseilles, cf. *Outlaw*, p. 230.

⁴ *The Last Secret*, p. 197.

⁵ *The East Came West*, pp. 180-1.

⁶ *Wen Sie Verderben Wollen*, pp. 572-4.

⁷ *Katorga*, p. 173.

⁸ 'Arabs seek to aid Soviet Deserters', *New York Times*, 15/12/46.

⁹ WO.32/11139, 335A, 337A; cf. WO.32/11681, 190A (15A, 17A).

¹⁰ Text of the Halle Agreement and details in *European Refugees*, pp. 207-11.

¹¹ *I'll Never Go Back*, pp. 139-41.

¹² *European Refugees*, pp. 210-1; F. S. V. Donnison, *Civil Affairs and Military Government North-West Europe 1944-1946* (London, 1961), p. 350. Cf. Gen. Golikov's remarks reported by Tass (FO.371/47900).

¹³ Extracts from an account written by Major-General Wilson, and kindly supplied by his daughter, Mrs. Julian Wathen.

¹⁴ Jean E. Smith (ed.), *The Papers of General Lucius D. Clay: Germany 1945-1949* (Indiana, 1974), i, pp. 30-1.

¹⁵ Information kindly supplied by Mr. N. F. Chawner.

¹⁶ Information kindly supplied by Mr. Michael Bayley.

¹⁷ *Invitation to Moscow*, p. 285.

¹⁸ Letter of 22/10/72 to the Editor of *Sunday Oklahoman*, kindly loaned to me.

¹⁹ Information kindly supplied by Mr. Geoffrey Dunn. Many Russians died on the journey after drinking spirit distilled from potatoes. The continual need to seek spirituous oblivion seems to have extended across the spectrum of Soviet society, from the forced-labour camps of Kolyma to Stalin's select parties in the Kremlin (cf. *Eleven Years in Soviet Prison Camps*, pp. 213, 244-6; *Conversations with Stalin*, pp. 106-7).

²⁰ *European Refugees*, pp. 210-12.

[21] Communication from Mr. Michael Bayley.

[22] Communication from Major W. Thompson.

[23] Communication from Captain J. Pereira.

[24] A fugitive Red Army officer met in May 1945 many wandering Russians in Germany declaring a desire for return home (*I'll Never Go Back*, p. 202).

[25] Communication from Mr. Anthony Smith.

[26] *European Refugees*, pp. 211–12.

[27] *Scotsman*, 2/3/46.

[28] CAB.88/39, 84.

[29] Ibid., 89–91.

[30] Forrest C. Pogue, *The Supreme Command* (Washington, 1954), pp. 510–11.

[31] Extracts from Major I. A. Nicholls's contemporary diary, kindly loaned to the author. For Swedish harsh treatment of the Russians passing through, cf. Pev Olov Enquist, *The Legionnaires*, (London, 1974), p. 86.

[32] *The Times*, 12/6/45; *New York Times*, 12/6/45.

[33] General Thorne's instructions for the repatriation are to be found in FO.371/47904. SHAEF estimates of nos. and localities are in CAB.88/39, 87–8 (22/6/45).

[34] FO.371/47904, 80–2.

[35] Ibid., 149.

[36] The account of the voyage of the *Aba* is based on information kindly supplied by MM. Britniev and Jesman, and Lt.-Col. Lloyd-Williams's report (FO.371/47904, 150–3). Prince Leonid Lieven was in the companion vessel *Stella Polaris*, and confirmed details of these accounts.

[37] CAB.88/39, 85.

[38] FO.371/47904, 82–3. Cf. General Thorne's detailed account of the whole operation in FO.371/47903. The total repatriated is given as 83,580. On 8/8/45 a full report was sent to the new Foreign Secretary, Ernest Bevin (FO.371/47904).

[39] FO.934/5 (42), 108. They also (14/8/45) sent a detailed complaint that insufficient clothing had been supplied for those returned! (FO.371/47903, 170–2). Prince Lieven had seen the British-supplied clothing removed on the Murmansk quay.

[40] FO.934/5 (42), 103–4.

[41] Evidence is preserved in FO.371/47904 and FO.371/47905.

[42] See the fears expressed by the British Ambassador (FO.371/47904, 78–80).

[43] 7,800 were sent from Denmark (FO.371/47905), and account must be taken of those sent at this time from France, Belgium, Switzerland, Italy and Greece.

CHAPTER FOURTEEN

[1] *Foreign Relations of the United States, Diplomatic Papers: The Conference of Berlin* (*The Potsdam Conference*) *1945* (Washington, 1960), i, pp. 800–1.

[2] Text in *European Refugees*, pp. 460–2. Cf. Julius Epstein, 'Forced Repatriation: Some unanswered Questions', *Russian Review* (1970), xxix, pp. 209–10.

[3] Quoted in *Operation Keelhaul*, pp. 100–1.

[4] *Foreign Relations of the United States, Diplomatic Papers 1945*, v, pp. 1097–8.

[5] FO.371/47902, 26. As late as 8 July, US military authorities had been allowing Russians a choice (FO.371/47902, 27–8).

[6] WO.32/11137, 168A. It appears to have been a knowledgable German who enlightened his Russian fellow-prisoners (WO.204/897, 145A).

[7] WO.32/11119, 297A–B.

[8] *Foreign Relations of the United States, Diplomatic Papers 1945*, v, pp. 1094–5.

[9] Ibid., pp. 1905–6.

[10] Ibid., pp. 1069, 1084.

[11] Captured Russians had been held at Fort Dix since the previous October (*Foreign Relations of the United States . . . 1944*, iv, p. 1260), where numbers had already been sifted out as 'claimants to Soviet citizenship' (WO.204/897, 23A). The decision to repatriate the original 118 had been made by the JCS on 8 June (*Foreign Relations of the United States . . . 1945*, v, p. 1103).

[12] *New York Times*, 30/6/45; *New York Herald Tribune*, 30/6/45; FO.371/47905, 52–5.

[13] *New York Times*, 1/7/45; *New York Herald Tribune*, 1/7/45. Professor Epstein states that the men were actually placed on board the *Monticello*, but once there they broke loose and damaged the ship's engines, thus preventing their departure. But this would appear to be a duplication of an incident occurring earlier at Seattle (*Operation Keelhaul*, p. 103). It may have been the State Department that ordered the change of plan. Professor Epstein refers to a letter 'from Grew to me' which 'documents the fact that Grew, as Acting Secretary of State, had recalled a ship from the mid-Atlantic after he learned that some Russians being repatriated had committed suicide'. (Ibid., p. 46). Epstein refers to an appendix for the full text of this letter, but this is unaccountably omitted. Unfortunately he died shortly before I was able to make enquiries on this point.

[14] FO.371/47905, 52–5.

[15] *Foreign Relations of the United States . . . 1945*, v, pp. 1098–9.

[16] Ibid., pp. 1100–2.

[17] Ibid., pp. 1103–4.

[18] *Operation Keelhaul*, p. 104. For further details of incidents at Fort Dix, *v. The Last Secret*, pp. 166–70.

[19] FO.371/47900, 266–72.

[20] WO.32/11119, 317A–321A.

[21] WO.204/2877. For Cinecitta Camp, cf. C. R. S. Harris, *Allied Administration of Italy 1943–1945* (London, 1957), pp. 170, 442.

[22] WO.170/4461.

[23] *Великое Предательство*, i, pp. 240, 264; ii, pp. 56–9. I have checked these Cossack accounts with Major W. R. Davies and Captain Duncan Macmillan. From an entry in the Argyll's War Diary it seems these Cossacks were to have been handed over on 29 June (WO.170/4988). Presumably the operation was delayed on Alexander's instructions.

[24] FO.371/47903, 12–16, 238–41. Cf. FO.371/47955.

[25] FO.371/47906.

[26] FO.934/5(42), 79–84. In the previous month Churchill had required and received figures of the numbers of Russians captured and returned to the USSR (PREM.3.364, 746).

[27] FO.934/5(42), 85–9, 97–102; PREM.3/364, 710–6; *Foreign Relations of the United States, Diplomatic Papers: The Conference of Berlin (The Potsdam Conference) 1945* (Washington, 1960), ii, pp. 1162–4.

[28] A letter from one of these officers was published in *Sunday Times*, 13/1/74.

[29] Information kindly supplied by Mr. Tom Gorringe.

[30] On 11 July (WO.204/440).

[31] *Foreign Relations of the United States . . . (The Potsdam Conference)*, i, pp. 797, 801; FO.371/47902, 100–1.

[32] For these reasons I find it difficult to accept Don Cook's suggestion that 'had

Churchill not been out of office three weeks later, it seems almost certain that he eventually *would* have changed the course of the horrendous affair'. ('On revealing the "Last Secret"', *Encounter* (1975). xiv, p. 82).

[33] Cf. *Double Diploma*, p. 174.

[34] Herbert Feis appears to be mistaken in this respect (*From Trust to Terror: The Onset of the Cold War, 1945–1950* (New York, 1970), p. 57.

[35] *Foreign Relations of the United States* . . . (*The Potsdam Conference*), i, pp. 794–800; ii, pp. 1165–6; FO.934/5(42), 90–6, 103–6.

[36] Communication from Mr. Ian Bogaert.

[37] He did know (cf. WO.32/11119, 328A); cf. *The Legionnaires*, p. 233.

[38] Information kindly supplied to the author by Mr. Antonevics.

[39] So he recalls, but the document is perhaps more likely to have contained the usual definition of what constituted a Soviet citizen in British eyes.

[40] Information kindly supplied to the author by Mr. Shorland Ball.

[41] See p. 88.

[42] *Foreign Relations of the United States* . . . *1945*, v, pp. 1103–4.

[43] *Великое Предательство*, i, p. 8.

[44] Witnessed by Mr. A. C. Lord, a DP in Kempten at the time.

[45] For the Kempten incident I have drawn on a detailed eyewitness account by a survivor, at the time a 17-year old girl. She was interviewed by Miss Natalie R. Lukianova, who transmitted the story to Mr. Jack Taylor Jr. I am exceedingly grateful to him for providing me with a copy. Cf. *Baseler Nachrichten*, 2/10/45; *Великое Предательство*, ii, p. 378; *The Last Secret*, pp. 171–4. UNRRA was not officially intended to assist in forcible repatriation. But UNRRA's strong concern to see DPs returned to their country of origin, coupled with the largely unauthorized activities of Communist infiltrators, resulted on occasion in its lending aid to operations far from consonant with the humanitarian aims of its foundation (cf. *European Refugees*, pp. 292–3; *The Ukrainian Quarterly*, x, pp. 361–2; *Operation Keelhaul*, pp. 93–4, 195; *The East Came West*, pp. 186–9). Such activities were eventually ended by General Clay (*Arms of Valor*, p. 313).

[46] *Foreign Relations of the United States* . . . *1945*, v, pp. 1106–7.

[47] *Speaking Frankly*, p. 67.

[48] *Foreign Relations of the United States* . . . *1945*, v, pp. 1104–5. Murphy recalled this incident when faced with a parallel situation in Korea a few years later. That episode, however, had a happy ending (*Diplomat Among Warriors*, p. 437).

[49] WO.32/11681, 189A.

[50] FO.371/47903, 235–7.

[51] Ibid., 234.

[52] FO.371/47904.

[53] Ibid., 147–8.

[54] WO.204/440.

[55] WO.214/63A.

[56] WO.204/440; WO.204/359; WO.32/11119, 324A.

[57] Ibid., 327A. All these accusations were rebutted in a lengthy report despatched to the War Office by General Templer (ibid., 328A).

[58] *Sunday Times*, 13/1/74.

[59] Communication to the author from Col. Alec Wilkinson. This proposed hand-over of Soviet citizens resulted from an agreement made by British and Soviet officers on 13 August at Leoben (WO.170/4243). On 9 May 1975 I enjoyed the convivial hospitality of the Land Steiermark MG Association reunion dinner, and heard from

all sides confirmation of the truth of Col. Wilkinson's forthright account.

⁶⁰ Information kindly supplied by Lt.-Col. R. B. Longe. 21 Army Group misgivings about the application of the Geneva Convention had been dismissed by Galsworthy and Dean on 13 and 15 August (FO.371/47903, 116). Cf. also *European Refugees*, pp. 214–7.

⁶¹ The Flensburg incident requires better documentation. The C.O. was an officer named Willis (WO.32/11119, 328A), whom I have been unable to trace. For the murder of the Pole Hrebinka, *v.* the report in FO.371/47906. Possibly the two murders referred to are, in fact, accounts of the same incident.

⁶² Communication from Mr. Fred Ralph. The men may have comprised a unit of Col. Tereschenko's Ukrainian 'Free Cossacks' (cf. *Arms of Valor*, p. 254).

⁶³ Information kindly supplied by Lt.-Col. Shadwell, supplemented by his correspondence of the period.

⁶⁴ FO.371/47905, 167–72. Instructions to their Political Adviser in Germany (Christopher Steel) were despatched on 25 August (FO.371/47904).

⁶⁵ Text in *European Refugees*, pp. 216–7.

⁶⁶ Ibid., pp. 217–8. So much was this the case in Schleswig-Holstein, that Col. Shadwell thought that Bevin had totally ended forcible repatriation. A pathetic and moving appeal from a group of the menaced Russians was filed by the F.O. without comment (FO.371/47905, 30–1).

⁶⁷ WO.204/440. Alexander telegraphed the Combined Chiefs of Staff on 30 August to ask for instructions on the use of force, whilst at the same time expressing his own distaste for such a policy (FO.371/47904, 196–8).

⁶⁸ For the reasons behind this delay, *v.* FO.371/47906, 276.

⁶⁹ FO.371/47904, 162–7, 190; FO.371/47905, 25.

⁷⁰ WO.32/11119, 326A. Lord Bridgeman, whilst suggesting delaying tactics, was also resigned (ibid., 325A). A leader in *Manchester Guardian* (31/8/45) advocated a similar policy to that advanced in private by the War Office: no forced repatriation without proved war guilt.

⁷¹ FO.371/47905, 26–7; WO.204/440.

⁷² FO.371/47903, 242; FO.371/47905, 23; FO.371/47906, 98, 110–112. Molotov had asked for the speeding up of repatriation to be raised as a topic at the London conference (ibid., 90–7).

⁷³ FO.371/47906, 233, 240, 243, 248.

⁷⁴ Ibid., 234, 237–9, 250, 260; FO.371/47904, 206–7.

⁷⁵ FO.371/47906, 232, 254–9; FO0371/47907, 56–60.

⁷⁶ FO.371/47906, 251; *Foreign Relations of the United States . . . 1945*, v. pp. 1106–8.

⁷⁷ FO.371/47907, 62, 106–10, 125.

⁷⁸ FO.371/47906, 272–5, 279; FO.371/47907, 112.

⁷⁹ Ibid., 98–9.

⁸⁰ FO.371/47910, 15.

⁸¹ FO.371/47908, 242–3; FO.371/47910, 14–21.

⁸² John Barrow, *The Life and Correspondence of Admiral Sir William Sydney Smith*, G.C.B. (London, 1848), i, pp. 263–64; cf. M. H. Keen, *The Laws of War in the Later Middle Ages* (London, 1965), pp. 156–85.

⁸³ Letter to the author.

⁸⁴ *Moscow Mission 1946–1949*, pp. 12–14; *Operation Keelhaul*, p. 50. Patch had expressed sympathy with Vlasov's aide, Malyshkin, six months earlier (cf. p. 293).

⁸⁵ *European Refugees*, p. 212.

⁸⁶ Information kindly supplied by Lt.-Col. David B. Rooke, MC. Cf. David

Daniell, *The Royal Hampshire Regiment* (Aldershot, 1955), p. 265. This operation took place in November or December 1945, *i.e. after* F.-M. Montgomery's edict. As violence was not required, it was perhaps regarded as coming within the scope of the new ruling. Alternatively, it may have occurred as a result of the War Office's fresh notification of HMG policy to Montgomery on or about 11 December (FO.371/ 47910, 13, 20).

[87] Major Lloyd (FO.371/47907) and Mr. Hynd (FO.371/47909, 104–6). A petition by the Ukrainians themselves was ridiculed as 'very silly' by Thomas Brimelow (FO.371/47908, 290–1); he was similarly impatient with émigré Russians praising Eisenhower's stand (FO.371/47907, 119–20).

[88] FO.371/47908, 162–4; FO.371/47910, 117–8; *New York Herald Tribune*, 18/11/45.

[89] FO.371/47908, 156; FO.371/47909, 42–4, 50. There was some confusion as to what constituted the celebrated '55' (FO.371/47910, 34).

[90] Ibid., 13, 20.

[91] Ibid., 74–8, 81–2, 85–6.

CHAPTER FIFTEEN

[1] Georgi K. Zhukov, *The Memoirs of Marshal Zhukov* (London, 1971), pp. 665–6.

[2] *Moscow Mission 1946–1949*, pp. 12–14.

[3] *Foreign Relations of the United States* (*1945*), v, 1108–9.

[4] Their protest was issued on 24 December (ibid., ii, *General: Political and Economic Matters* (Washington, 1967), pp. 800–1; cf. p. 1161.

[5] FO.371/47910; cf. ibid., 164, 167–70; FO.371/56712; FO.371/56716.

[6] *Foreign Relations of the United States, 1945*, v, pp. 1110–11.

[7] Ibid., *Diplomatic Papers: The British Commonwealth; Western and Central Europe 1946* (Washington, 1969), v, pp. 133–4, 152; FO.371/47910, 74–5, 83–4, 87–8; BM.3928/PW1, 63A, 66A–68A.

[8] *Foreign Relations of the United States . . . 1946*, v, pp. 141–2; *New York Times*, 20/1/46; *Daily Mail*, 21/1/46; *Sunday Express*, 20/1/46; *The Last Secret*, pp. 189–91. A photograph of the stricken camp immediately after the operation was published recently in *National Zeitung*, 29/11/74.

[9] *Operation Keelhaul*, pp. 213–5; *New York Times*, 25/2/46; *The Times*, 27/2/46. Russian émigrés in America kept up a barrage of criticism of the new policy. Distinguished figures in this context were Prince Serge Belosselsky-Belozersky and Archbishop Vitaly (*Во Времия Россиǐ* (New York, 1965), pp. 31–41). A year later former Russian Prime Minister Kerensky issued a public appeal for the granting of asylum (*New York Times*, 24/1/47).

[10] Bethell thinks they were driven *west*, but he has evidently confused Munich the capital with a small town of the same name (München) in eastern Bavaria (*The Last Secret*, p. 193).

[11] *Wen sie verderben wollen*, pp. 577–8; Ernst von Salomon, *Der Fragebogen* (Hamburg, 1951), pp. 785–6, 791–2; *The Last Secret*, pp. 191–3; *Stars and Stripes*, 6/3/46; *The Times*, 26/2/46; *New York Times*, 26/2/46; *Зарубежье* (Munich, March–June 1976), pts 1–2, p. 27. The film is held by the National Archives and Records Service in Washington, no. AFCR-3M-2122, file card no. ADC 5824.

[12] *Yorkshire Post*, 14/5/46.

[13] *New York Times*, 15/2/47.

[14] *Foreign Relations of the United States, 1946*, v, pp. 154–6, 170.

[15] Cf. ibid., p. 171.

[16] BM.3928/PWI, 68A; WO.32/11119, 331A.

[17] Information from Lord Hankey; FO.371/56711.

[18] FO.371/56710.

[19] *History and Human Relations* (London, 1951), p. 203.

[20] CAB.129/10, 52-4. The Soviet Foreign Ministry was informed on 8 July (WO.32/11141, 185A; cf. 181A-184A). Cf. FO.371/56714; FO.371/56716; FO.371/56717; WO.32/11119, 330A, 331A.
cf. 181A-184A). Cf. FO.371/56714; FO.371/56716; FO.371/56717.

[21] *Foreign Relations of the United States, 1946,* v, pp. 193-4; WO.32/11141, 186A; BM.3928/PWI, 104A, 120A.

[22] Ibid., 298A.

[23] Apparently from a very early date. Cf. Austin Lane Poole, *From Domesday Book to Magna Carta* (Oxford, 1951), p. 438.

[24] *Crusade in Europe,* p. 518.

[25] Cf. Churchill's choice of 'Argonaut' for the Yalta Conference (Prem.3.51/1, 67). An American official referred to the Russians moved in Italy as having been 'keel-hauled' (WO.0100/12A/309).

[26] FO.371/47907, 30, 35.

[27] For Operation 'Keelhaul' see Великое Предательство, ii, pp. 192-3, 211; WO.204/1593; WO.0100/12A/308.

[28] *Foreign Relations of the United States . . . 1946,* v, pp. 197-8.

[29] FO.371/47905; cf. WO.214/63A for Alexander's comment. Mr. J. H. S. Ashworth has described to me his experiences in Trieste early in 1946. His posting was to accompany a Soviet Repatriation officer, Major Nosov, and obstruct his attempts to spy on British military installations. For the Repatriation Missions as espionage centres, cf. *Soviet Espionage,* pp. 331-2, 348; *Nights are Longest There,* p. 171.

[30] BM.3928/PWI, 232A-233A, 250A-251A.

[31] *e.g.* WO.0103/8571, 71A.

[32] At the Cabinet Meeting of 6 June 1946, Ernest Bevin had rejected a plea that former members of the Todt labour force be exempt from repatriation (WO.32/11119, 331A).

[33] WO.170/4241.

[34] *The Hidden Russia,* pp. 106-7, 240-1; *The Gulag Archipelago,* i, pp. 88-9.

[35] Over half the nine were Cossacks, and had therefore presumably *not* fought the British (Великое Предательство, ii, p. 222).

[36] The foregoing account is based on personal information kindly supplied by Mr. Tom Gorringe, Mr. Denis Hills, Major-General James Lunt, Lt.-Col. J. R. G. Stanton and Professor Alexander Wainman. Accounts by Russian prisoners are given in Великое Предательство, ii, pp. 192-218; I have been carefully through these with Mr. Hills, who confirms their accuracy, except in the apparently fictitious accounts of widespread casualties at the time of the entrainments on 8 and 9 May. 'Merten' refers to the Camp Commandant, Lt.-Col. Martin; whilst 'Captain Samit' was a Maltese named Zammit. Denis Hills's report is quoted from the cyclostyled reproduction circulated by Professor Epstein; an abbreviated version was published in the *Sunday Oklahoman,* 21/1/73. Orders and reports are preserved in files WO.0100/12A/308—9. The titles of a number of relevant files, still withheld under the thirty-year ruling, are provided in the *Index to Combined Chiefs of Staff Committee Memoranda 1942-1947* (E1.60). Cf. also *The Last Secret,* pp. 196-203. Col. Starov, who received the parties at St. Valentin, had been conducting repatriation operations since January 1945 (in Egypt) (WO.32/11139, 340A).

[37] Cf. *New York Times*, 6/7/47. British newspapers also covered the operation, apparently the first time they did so.

[38] *Великое Предательство*, ii, p. 221.

[39] *Parliamentary Debates (Hansard) House of Commons* (London, 1947), ccccxxxviii, cols. 2318–9.

[40] *The Last Secret*, p. 203.

[41] WO.0100/12A/309; communication from Colonel Dalton.

[42] WO.32/11683, 318A–322A. Bennigsen's plea was passed on to the Foreign Office, where it was arranged for him to see Thomas Brimelow.

[43] Information from Mr. G. K. Young. Wainman's report was also passed on to Sir Stewart Menzies, head of MI6.

[44] *Великое Предательство*, ii, pp. 221–2.

[45] WO.01303.8571, 80A; *The Times*, 24/5/47.

[46] *New York Times*, 15/2/47. For the purely racial motivation of Soviet measures against the Mennonites, cf. *Katorga*, pp. 141–2; *It happens in Russia*, pp. 296–7.

[47] *European Refugees*, pp. 417–8.

[48] Ibid., pp. 217–8.

[49] *Soviet Opposition to Stalin*, pp. 111–2; *The House Built on Sand*, p. 393; cf. p. 284; *Joseph Stalin: Man and Legend*, p. 371; *Political Science Quarterly*, lxxxviii, p. 255. A report in the *Scotsman* (2/3/46) estimated that 40% of all Russians in the West did not want to return home.

[50] Information from Major James Scott-Hopkins, M.P., who as a serving officer took part in *Operation Highland Fling*. He tells me that evidence indicated that his unit's activities were well known in resistance circles within the USSR.

CHAPTER SIXTEEN

[1] WO.32/11683.

[2] *Civil Affairs and Military Government North-West Europe 1944–1946*, pp. 346–7; WO.32/11137, 301A.

[3] *I'll Never Go Back*, p. 160. The author of this book, frequently quoted here, worked at the Soviet Embassy in Paris from May 1945 to March 1946. A regular, 'Yalta-style', agreement was entered into by both countries on 29 June 1945. Cf. FO.371/56714.

[4] *European Refugees*, pp. 129–30.

[5] *Forced Labor in Soviet Russia*, p. 293; *I'll Never Go Back*, pp. 160–3.

[6] Ibid., pp. 166–7.

[7] *Forced Labor in Soviet Russia*, pp. 293–4.

[8] WO.32/11119, 103A.

[9] *Outlaw*, pp. 226–34. For details of the Marseilles-Odessa convoys, cf. FO.371/47895.

[10] *Forced Labor in Soviet Russia*, pp. 294–5. For further disturbing accounts of repatriation from French camps, cf. *Великое Предательство*, ii, pp. 189–92.

[11] For two first-hand accounts, cf. *Outlaw*, pp. 236–43; *I'll Never Go Back*, pp. 197–8, 210–11.

[12] Ibid., p. 205; cf. the French newspaper accounts in *Le Populaire*, 8/3/46; *Combat*, 9/3/46; *L'Humanité*, 11/3/46.

[13] Geoffrey Bailey, *The Conspirators* (London, 1961), pp. 89–117, 227–267.

[14] *I'll Never Go Back*, p. 162; *Forced Labor in Soviet Russia*, p. 295.

[15] FO.371/47903.

[16] Cf. *I'll Never Go Back*, pp. 160–1.

[17] FO.371/47905, 242. A. I. Romanov's assertion that the French Government and Army 'hardly extradited anyone at all' (*Nights Are Longest There*, p. 236) is only true of the latter. Romanov's work in the Third Branch of KRU would very likely have given him opportunities of seeing reports from French military zones, from which he may have formed false assumptions concerning policy in metropolitan France. A Ukrainian friend of the author, Mr. Constantine Zelenko, who was in a DP camp in French-occupied Austria, has testified to the excellent reputation the French Army enjoyed amongst refugees for the strong stand it took towards the Soviet Repatriation Commission at Innsbruck.

[18] *New York Times*, 28/5/47, 5/6/47; *Le Monde*, 5/6/47.

[19] The Repatriation Commission had long been applying pressure to return on Soviet women married to Frenchmen (*I'll Never Go Back*, pp. 196–7).

[20] For the raid on Camp Beauregard, *vide Le Figaro*, 16–17/11/47; *Le Monde*, 16–17/11/47; *New York Herald Tribune*, 16/11/47; *The Sunday Times*, 16/11/47.

[21] WO.32/11681, 51A.

[22] *European Refugees*, p. 418.

[23] Information kindly supplied by Lt.-Col. L. S. Ford.

[24] WO.32/11137, 300A.

[25] FO.371/47902,106–8.

[26] *The Scotsman*, 2/3/46. Cf. further FO.371/56710; FO.371/56712; FO.371/56713.

[27] FO.371/56712.

[28] *Chicago Daily News*, 13/11/44.

[29] *Beria's Gardens*, pp. 21, 285.

[30] FO.371/32986; FO.371/33023. On 2 July 1942 3 Russians were drowned in an attempt to swim the Rhine (ibid.).

[31] WO.32/11119, 103A.

[32] FO.371/43364. For the journey of the 800 returners, *vide* pp. 89–90.

[33] *Combat*, 18/3/46.

[34] FO.371/47859; FO. 371/47893.

[35] FO.371/47859.

[36] O. Freivalds and E. Alksnis, *Latviešu Karavīru Traģēdija Zviedrijā* (Copenhagen, 1956), pp. 9–74. I am indebted to Mr. John Antonevics for a loan of this authoritative and well-illustrated account of the Baltic troops in Sweden.

[37] *The Legionnaires*, pp. 89–91, 96–9, 103–10.

[38] Ibid., pp. 174–6, 193–4, 217–26, 252–3, 256–7, 259–60.

[39] Ibid., pp. 179–85, 195–8, 280–2, 293–4, 311–20; *Latviešu Karavīru Traģēdija Zviedrijā*, pp. 139–58.

[40] Information supplied by Mr. Edvard Alksnis. I was generously provided with further first-hand accounts of the Balts' stay in Sweden by Mr. Eriks Zilinksnis, a Latvian who escaped repatriation by successfully claiming civilian status.

[41] *The Legionnaires*, pp. 226–7, 321–36.

[42] Ibid., pp. 376–400; *Latviešu Karavīru Traģēdija Zviedrijā*, pp. 191–218.

[43] *The Legionnaires*, p. 172.

[44] Ibid., pp. 273–4.

[45] Ibid., pp. 227–8, 235, 446.

[46] *Empire of Fear*, pp. 195–7.

[47] *The Legionnaires*, pp. 416–508. A film by Johan Bergenstrahle was made of this book. It was shown in Sweden under the title *Baltutlämningen*, and abroad (at the London National Film Theatre on 7 April 1975) as *A Baltic Tragedy*. Essential to an

understanding of the long-term moral effects of Social Democracy on the Swedish people is Roland Huntford's brilliant study, *The New Totalitarians* (New York, 1972).

[48] *The Gulag Archipelago*, i, p. 83. For a similar example of the hoodwinking of visiting Western experts, cf. Aino Kuusinen, *Before and After Stalin* (London, 1974), pp. 51-2.

[49] Yet another émigré 'army', under General Kramer, had withdrawn at this time into the mountains (*It Happens in Russia*, pp. 464-6).

[50] For the preceding account and what follows I have received the greatest help from General Holmston-Smyslovsky. His Imperial Highness the Grand Duke Vladimir also provided me with an account of his own experiences. Further details are given in: General B. A. Holmston-Smyslovsky, *Избранные Статьи и Речи* (Buenos Aires, 1953), pp. 11-39; Claus Grimm, 'Internierte Russen in Liechtenstein', *Jahrbuch des Historischen Vereins für das Fürstentum Liechtenstein*, lxxi, pp. 44-7, 59-66. This latter monograph is a model of scholarly research, and indeed represents the only fully satisfactory account of forcible repatriation to appear in print so far. An interesting though confused account of these events appeared in the French newspaper *Combat* (18/3/46).

[51] Dr. Emil Heinz Batliner, *25 Jahre Liechtensteinisches Rotes Kreuz: 1945-1970* (Vaduz, 1970), pp. 27-8.

[52] *Operation Keelhaul*, p. 34.

[53] A sinister threat to this effect was made by an officer of the Soviet Mission on 29/11/45 (*Jahrbuch des Historischen Vereins für das Fürstentums Liechtenstein*, lxxi, p. 89).

[54] Ibid., pp. 94-6; *Neue Zürcher Zeitung*, 12/9/47; *The Manchester Guardian*, 12/9/47.

[55] For specimens of these petitions, cf. *Jahrbuch des Historischen Vereins für das Fürstentums Liechtenstein*, lxxi, pp. 82, 84, 86, 92-4.

[56] Ibid., pp. 80, 96.

[57] I am greatly indebted to His Serene Highness for the considerable help afforded me during my stay in Liechtenstein; also to his *Kabinettsdirektor*, Dr. Robert Allgäuer, who rendered me great assistance over a long period. Further useful material to that already cited appeared in the *Liechtensteiner Volksblatt*, 7/5/75 and 10/5/75.

CHAPTER SEVENTEEN

[1] *Nights Are Longest There*, p. 136.

[2] *The House Built on Sand*, pp. 394-5.

[3] *Joseph Stalin: Man and Legend*, pp. 303-4; *I'll Never Go Back*, p. 113; *The Gulag Archipelago*, i, p. 77. For individual examples, cf. *Beria's Gardens*, p. 65; *Outlaw*, p. 195.

[4] *The Gulag Archipelago*, i, p. 243.

[5] *Before and After Stalin*, pp. 200-1.

[6] *На Фронте 1941 года и в плену* p. 75.

[7] Information supplied by Professor John Erickson, to whom I am greatly indebted for a full explanation of the nature of these *Prikazy*. Cf. *The Gulag Archipelago*, i, p. 81. Other 'Orders' referred to are Nos. 260 and 270 of 1942 (*Operation Keelhaul*, p. 149; *Forced Labor in Soviet Russia*, p. 283). Cf. also *Against Stalin and Hitler*, pp. 30, 34, 101.

[8] *На Фронте 1941 года и в плену*, p. 38.

[9] *Daily Mail*, 30/5/45.

[10] Russian prisoners in Egypt quoted Order No. 131 to the British (WO.32/11137, 45A, 56A); at Fort Dix in the USA Colonel Rogers passed on a similar report (*The Last Secret*, p. 168).

[11] *Only One Year*, p. 353; *The Secret World*, p. 49.

[12] *Why I Escaped*, pp. 154–7, 180. Still luckier were a divisional chief of staff and full colonel, who were merely harassed and spied upon on their return. But that was in the still critical days of early 1943 (*The Secret World*, p. 51). It was only privates who were completely expendable.

[13] *Crusade in Europe*, pp. 468–9.

[14] *Against Stalin and Hitler*, pp. 32–3; FO.371/47925; Svetlana Alleluyeva, *Twenty Letters to a Friend* (New York, 1964), pp. 160–3; *Only One Year* (London, 1969), pp. 193–4, 349; *Let History Judge*, p. 468; Werner Maser, *Hitler* (London, 1973), pp. 6–7; *The Memoirs of Marshal Zhukov*, p. 582.

[15] *Outlaw*, pp. 216–7.

[16] *The Hidden Russia*, pp. 202, 226; *Nights Are Longest There*, pp. 84–5.

[17] *Beria's Gardens*, p. 38.

[18] Information from Mr. Josef Garlinski (also a survivor of Auschwitz) and Herr Hermann Langbein, Secretary of the Comité International des Camps. The same fate was reserved for prisoners freed from Buchenwald (*The Gulag Archipelago*, i, p. 243). For a description of Buchenwald immediately after the liberation, cf. *I'll Never Go Back*, p. 145; and for other cases of PoW ending up in GULAG, Edward Buca, *Vorkuta* (London, 1976), pp. 18, 30, 54, 175.

[19] *Let History Judge*, p. 349.

[20] *Samizdat: Voices of the Soviet Opposition*, p. 171.

[21] *Soviet Espionage*, p. 231; Alexander Foote, *Handbook for Spies* (London, 1964), p. 155. The 'Director' had privileged access to Stalin (p. 153).

[22] *European Refugees*, p. 154.

[23] V. Petrov (ed.), '*June 22, 1941*,' *Soviet Historians and the German Invasion* (Columbia, 1968), pp. 180, 252–4, 257; *Let History Judge*, pp. 447, 452; *The Gulag Archipelago*, i, p. 240.

[24] *Khruschev Remembers*, pp. 194–5. For a photograph of the hero, *v.* Geoffrey Jukes, *Kursk: the clash of armour* (London, 1968), p. 8.

[25] Ivan Solonevich, *Russia in Chains* (London, 1938), pp. 302–3.

[26] *The Strange Alliance*, pp. 188–9.

[27] *The Road to Stalingrad*, p. 202.

[28] *Nights Are Longest There*, pp. 119–20, 169–70; *I Chose Freedom*, pp. 427–8; *Let History Judge*, pp. 466–7; *The Road to Stalingrad*, p. 176.

[29] Details of the missions, their organisation, membership, etc. are to be found in *European Refugees*, pp. 154, 157, 213–4, 290; WO.32/11119, 158A–160A, 228A; WO.32/11139, 7A, 83A, 216A–217A; WO.32/11647, 13A; etc.

[30] For a representative selection of such encounters, cf. *The Legionnaires*, p. 108 (in Sweden); *I'll Never Go Back*, pp. 160–1 (in Paris). Czeslaw Jesman testifies to the non-combatant experience of Vasiliev and Shershun in Britain and Denis Hills recalled the same of Colonel Iakovlev and his aides in Italy.

[31] *Nights Are Longest There*, p. 171.

[32] *Eleven Years in Soviet Prison Camps*, p. 74.

[33] This was also the job of 'A. I. Romanov' (*Nights Are Longest There*, p. 34). Beria had assumed control of this transportation in 1941 (*I Chose Freedom*, p. 404); it was conducted largely by slave labour.

[34] For examples of such soldiers, any one of whom had undergone hardships in war greater than the experience of all SMERSH, cf. *Let History Judge*, pp. 467–8.

[35] *Forced Labor in Soviet Russia*, p. 286.

[36] See the account of the massacre in *Nights are Longest There*, pp. 167–9.

[37] Cf. *European Refugees*, pp. 156–7, 271.

[38] FO.371/47901, 43.

[39] FO.371/47899.

[40] WO.32/11137, 101A (6B).

[41] Ibid., 45A, 46A, 56A (Alexandria); WO.32/11119, 14D (Butterwick Camp); FO.371/43382, 83 (Kempton Park). Numerous other examples will be found throughout the present work.

[42] It happens in Russia, pp. 452–3.

[43] WO.32/11683, 196A.

[44] Nights are Longest There, p. 127; Великое Предательство, i, p. 186.

[45] Outlaw, p. 241.

[46] WO.32/11119, 210A; FO.371/47896; FO.371/50606, 189–94.

[47] Antony G. Sutton, Wall Street and the Bolshevik Revolution (New Rochelle, 1974), p. 87; Soviet Espionage, pp. 122, 406–7; KGB, pp. 11–12.

[48] Verbannung nach Siberien, p. 24.

[49] Великое Предательство, i, pp. 146–7, ii, p. 355.

[50] The Gulag Archipelago, i, pp. 256–7; I'll Never Go Back, p. 116.

[51] It was allegedly said in England that half (5,000) the prisoners sent to Murmansk in 1944 were murdered (WO.32/11119, 240B). It is highly unlikely that the figure was anything like as high as this.

[52] Cf. Outlaw, p. 239; Великое Предательство, ii, p. 53.

[53] Anatoli Granovsky, All Pity Choked: The Memoirs of a Soviet Secret Agent (London, 1955), pp. 212–14.

[54] Information kindly supplied by Mr. Nikolai Borisovitch Komaroff.

[55] Nights are Longest There, pp. 172–5; Forced Labor in Soviet Russia, p. 284. Accounts of the initial reception of the Cossacks in Austria are to be found in Великое Предательство, i, pp. 173–5, ii, pp. 240–66, 277–96; Unvergessener Verrat!, pp. 249–50.

[56] Vanished without trace, pp. 302–3.

[57] Why I Escaped, pp. 223–8.

[58] Eleven Years in Soviet Prison Camps, pp. 281–2.

[59] Vanished without trace, pp. 236–7. A similar case is described by Edward Buca (Vorkuta, p. 184).

[60] My informant is obliged to remain anonymous, as he has relatives still living in Soviet-occupied Poland. Cf. the description by John Fischer, The Scared Men in the Kremlin (London, 1947), pp. 118–9.

[61] The Gulag Archipelago, i, p. 573.

[62] Ibid., p. 507.

[63] This eyewitness account by Mrs. Liepins was kindly supplied to me by her relative, Mrs. Jana Hale. Cf. European Refugees, pp. 218–9; Fischer described one of the staging-posts near Kharkov aerodrome (The Scared Men in the Kremlin, pp. 117–8).

[64] For full accounts, cf. Великое Предательство, ii, pp. 237–92, 297–317, 319–39; Unvergessener Verrat!, pp. 261–3, 336.

[65] Beria's Gardens, pp. 60–1.

[66] Cf. The Hidden Russia, pp. 115–16, 137–8, 164–5; Katorga, p. 7; Urszula Muskus, Dlugi Most: Moje Przezycia w Zwiazku Sowieckim 1939–1956 (London, 1975), pp. 124–5. I am grateful to Mr. Jan Pirozynski for presenting me with a copy of this moving work.

[67] Before and after Stalin, p. 177. In a prison at Lvov they were hurled naked into cells (Buca, Vorkuta, p. 11).

[68] Scholmer, Vorkuta, p. 141.

[69] International Labour Review (Montreal, 1945), lii, pp. 533–4. On 28 August Pravda published a long article describing the sufferings of Russians under German rule and measures being taken for the rehabilitation of the survivors. Great stress was

laid on the need for political reindoctrination of such people, 'for many hard and long years cut off from their country'. (FO.371/47905, 38–41).

[70] Alexander Werth, *Russia: The Post-War Years* (London, 1971), pp. 24–5; cf. p. 105. With this bald assertion, cf. *The Gulag Archipelago*, i, p. 248–51; also *I Chose Freedom*, pp. 427–8; *Only One Year*, pp. 254–5.

[71] *The Secret World*, pp. 77–8, 99, 101–2. For an example of one of the 15% allowed to return home, cf. the case of a cripple in *Why I Escaped*, pp. 104–5.

[72] *Russia: The Post-War Years*, p. 22. For further literary treatment of this subject, cf. Alexander Werth, *The Khruschchev Phase* (1961), pp. 163, 202–3, 205. Not until 1955, with Khruschev's amnesty, could a different portrayal be attempted (cf. Roman Kolkowicz, *The Soviet Military and the Communist Party* (New Jersey, 1967), p. 120).

[73] *Devil on my Shoulder*, p. 173; cf. *Twenty Letters to a Friend*, p. 185.

[74] The text is reprinted in *Великое Предательство*, ii, pp. 318–9.

CHAPTER EIGHTEEN

[1] Virtually all Soviet treaties signed after World War I specifically prohibited forced repatriation (Jan F. Triska and Robert M. Slusser, *The Theory, Law, and Policy of Soviet Treaties* (Stanford, 1962), p. 201; cf. *Operation Keelhaul*, pp. 14–15).

[2] Two of these victims, placed in Nazi concentration camps, have provided first-hand accounts of their experiences: Alex Weissberg, *Conspiracy of Silence* (London, 1952), pp. 493–7; Margarete Buber, *Under Two Dictators* (London, 1949), p. 167. Cf. R. J. Sontag and J. S. Beddie, *Nazi-Soviet Relations 1939–1941* (Washington, 1948), p. 138. The NKVD had deported a Jewish Marxist refugee to Germany as early as 1936 (*I Chose Freedom*, p. 210).

[3] *The Rise and Fall of the Third Reich*, p. 744.

[4] *The Yogi and the Commissar*, pp. 87–90.

[5] WO.32/11137, 164A–C.

[6] WO.32/11681, 168C.

[7] FO.371/47899, 93.

[8] FO.371/47896.

[9] FO.371/47908, 162.

[10] FO.371/47899, 94–6.

[11] Ibid., 89–90.

[12] FO.371/47897, 108–13. Cf. Chapter Six of this book, pp. 137–9.

[13] FO.371/47899, 90. Dean's views were forwarded to the Washington Embassy on 12 June (97–8).

[14] PREM.3.364/9, 433; cf. WO.32/11681, 60B.

[15] Ibid., 117A.

[16] Ibid., 120A–B.

[17] Ibid., 127D. Further efforts on these lines were proposed (WO.32/11119, 230A) but later abandoned.

[18] *Polemic*, v, p. 49.

[19] *Witness to History*, pp. 300, 349–52; *Diplomat Among Warriors*, pp. 436–9; Dean Acheson, *Sketches From Life of Men I Have Known* (New York, 1961), pp. 101–3; idem, *Present at the Creation* (London, 1970), pp. 652–3. Bohlen, Murphy and Acheson had all been closely concerned with the Russian repatriation problem in 1945.

[20] 'Prisoners of War under the Geneva Convention', *The International and Comparative Law Quarterly* (London, 1969), xviii, pp. 178–87.

[21] Myres S. McDougal & Florentine P. Feliciano, *Law and Minimum World Public Order* (Yale, 1961), pp. 88–9; cf. *Operation Keelhaul*, pp. 13–21.

[22] Letter of Herbert A. O'Brien, *New York Herald Tribune*, 2/12/45.

[23] *Encyclopaedia of Zionism and Israel* (London, 1971), pp. 618–9. I am indebted for this and the following reference to Mr. Jack Barnett, Director, Israel Information.

[24] C. C. Aronsfeld, 'The "Special Treatment" of Jewish Prisoners of War', *Wiener Library Bulletin* (1964), xviii, p. 23.

[25] WO.204/897, 145A.

[26] *Foreign Relations of the United States* ... *1945*, v, p. 1084. The United States, in the case of the Fort Dix prisoners, violated the stand it had adopted. But this was a single (if somewhat cynical) compromise; cf. *The Strange Alliance*, p. 187.

[27] WO.204/1596.

[28] *Journal of the Royal United Service Institution*, xcix, p. 262.

[29] Letter to the author. Proudfoot states in passing that 'Soviet soldiers, whether used as a part of the German labour force or not ... could hardly claim the usual rights of prisoners of war under the Geneva Conventions, since their own country had not signed them.' (*European Refugees*, p. 109) This is incorrect; Article 82 stipulates clearly that: 'In time of war, if one of the belligerents is not a party to the Convention, its provisions shall, nevertheless, remain binding as between the belligerents who are parties thereto.'

[30] Letter to the author.

[31] FO.371/43382, 33; cf. WO.32/11137, 14A.

[32] CAB.88/30, 438; WO.32/11137, 101A (6B), 187A.

[33] Ibid., 34A.

[34] Ibid., 105A.

[35] Cf. *Великое Предательство*, ii, pp. 146–7.

[36] FO.371/50606, 224–7.

[37] WO.32/11119, 198A, 200A, 280A, 282A, 302A; FO.371/50606, 15, 138–9.

[38] WO.32/11681, 164A.

[39] FO.371/47902, 100.

[40] Ibid., 106.

[41] PREM.3/364, 394.

[42] FO.371/47905, 190.

[43] Nicholas Bethell, 'A Brutal Exchange', *Sunday Times*, 6/1/74; letter from Lords Hankey and Coleraine (*Observer*, 7/12/75).

[44] *The Times*, 7/12/74.

[45] Information kindly supplied by Mr. Tom Slack and Mr. Neil Macdonald, RAF and South African Air Force officers liberated from Luckenwalde. My letter to *The Times* (30/11/74) drew what I now realize to be a false inference from the limited facts then at my disposal.

[46] WO.32/11139.

[47] *The Last Secret*, p. 65.

[48] WO.32/11139, 309A.

[49] On 28 March (cf. WO.204/897, 148A).

[50] FO.371/47897 (11 April, 1945).

[51] Conference of 16/8/45 at Zone HQ (transcript of minutes kindly loaned to me by Mr. V. Britniev, then of PWX).

[52] WO.204/2877.

[53] *The Gulag Archipelago*, i, p. 517.

[54] FO.371/47904, 154.

[55] FO.371 47901, 45.

[56] *Hitler's Table Talk*, pp. 696–7.

[57] This distinction was conceded by a Soviet negotiator at the *Tolstoy* conference (PREM.3/364, 256).

[58] C. A. Macartney, *October Fifteenth: A History of Modern Hungary 1929-1945* (Edinburgh, 1957), ii, pp. 301-9. Finland likewise refused to persecute her Jews; years later a Finn in a Soviet penal camp was thanked by a group of Jews for his country's honourable stand (*Beria's Gardens*, pp. 116-8).

[59] FO.371/47964; cf. WO.32/11139.

[60] *The Strange Alliance*, p. 34; cf. pp. 189-201, 293-4; *Foreign Relations of the US ... 1945*, v, p. 1101. Bethell's suggestion that 'it seemed in the summer of 1945 that Stalin was observing this agreement' (*The Last Secret*, p. 47) is wide of the mark: cf. the remark of Stettinius, US signatory to the Agreement (*Roosevelt and the Russians*, p. 274).

[61] WO.32/11137, 87, 100A.

[62] FO.371/47901, 45. By September it was reckoned they were all back (FO.371/47904).

[63] Ibid., 162-3; WO.32/11681, 189A; *Foreign Relations of the US ... 1945*, v, p. 1105.

[64] WO.32/11119, 325A.

[65] FO.371/47901, 43.

[66] FO.371/47858.

[67] S. Swianiewicz, *Forced Labour and Economic Development* (Oxford, 1965), pp. 23, 42-4; cf. *The Hidden Russia*, p. 70; *Beria's Gardens*, pp. 111-12; *The Gulag Archipelago*, i, pp. 271-2; *I Chose Freedom*, pp. 404-6; Scholmer, *Vorkuta*, p. 139-40, 212; *Vanished without Trace*, pp. 228, 254-5; *Forced Labor in Soviet Russia*, pp. 297-8.

[68] Cf. Scholmer, *Vorkuta*, p. 202.

[69] FO.371/50606, 185.

[70] CAB.66, 114, 173-9.

[71] Sir Thomas Preston, British Consul in Ekaterinburg at the time of the murder of the Imperial family, had submitted an able paper on the subject (FO.371/43336; cf. further FO.371/43335).

[72] FO.371/43361.

[73] CAB.66, 121-31. For Churchill on Foreign Office methods, cf. *Winston Churchill: The Struggle for Survival 1940-1945*, p. 201.

POSTSCRIPT

[1] *History and Human Relations*, p. 186.

[2] *Operation Keelhaul*, pp. 197-206.

[3] No. 24,275 in the United States Court of Appeals for the Ninth Circuit ... Brief of Amicus Curiae on Behalf of Appellant (San Francisco, 1969).

[4] I am greatly indebted to Mr. Jack H. Taylor, Jr., the distinguished American journalist, who supplied me with photocopies of these documents. He also transmitted to me over a long period much other valuable material, the result of his own researches.

[5] The title 'Operation Keelhaul' given to these files raises the question whether *all* the forced repatriation operations, at any rate in the Mediterranean theatre, did not come under this generic title. Lord Bethell's stricture (*The Last Secret*, p. 217) on Prof. Epstein is misplaced—as he would have realised had he read Mr. Taylor's article: 'Operation Keelhaul: America's Top Secret Shame', *Sunday Oklahoman*, 21/7/74.

[6] Even a scholar such as Mark Elliott appears unaware of the British veto (*Political Science Quarterly*, lxxxviii, p. 262).

ADDENDUM

The Ministry of Defence files referred to in the notes as WO.0100/12A/308, WO.0100/12A/309 and BM 3928/PWI are now accessible in the Public Record Office as WO.204/1593B and C.

Index

compiled by Robert Urwin